The Child Welfare Challenge

Modern Applications of Social Work
James K. Whittaker, Series Editor

Psychotherapeutic Change through the Group Process
Dorothy Stock Whitaker and Morton A. Lieberman

Integrated Ego Psychology (Second Edition)
Norman A. Polansky

Behavioral Methods in Social Welfare
Steven Paul Schinke, editor
With a foreword by James Whittaker and Scott Briar

Human Behavior Theory and Social Work Practice (Third Edition)
Roberta R. Greene

Social Work with the Aged and Their Families (Third Edition)
Roberta R. Greene

Social Treatment
An Approach to Interpersonal Helping
James K. Whittaker

Evaluation in Child and Family Services
Comparative Client and Program Perspectives
Tiziano Vecchiato, Anthony N. Maluccio, and Cinzia Canali, editors

Assessing Outcomes in Child and Family Services
Comparative Design and Policy Issues
Anthony N. Maluccio, Cinzia Canali, and Tiziano Vecchiato, editors

Building Community Capacity
Robert J. Chaskin, Prudence Brown, Sudhir Venkatesh, and Avis Vidal

HIV, AIDS, and the Law
Legal Issues for Social Work, Practice, and Policy
Donald T. Dickson

Family Group Conferencing
New Directions in Commmunity-Centered Child & Family Practice
Gale Burford and Joe Hudson

Human Behavior in the Social Environment (Fifth Edition)
A Social Systems Approach
Ralph Anderson, Irl Carter, and Gary Lowe

Solution-Based Casework
An Introduction to Clinical and Case Management Skills in Casework Practice
Dana Christensen, Jeffrey Todahl, and William C. Barrett

Effective Participatory Practice
Family Group Conferencing in Child Protection
Marie Connolly with Margaret McKenzie

Protecting Children and Supporting Families
Promising Programs and Organizational Realities
Gary Cameron and Jim Vanderwoerd

The Child Welfare Challenge

Policy, Practice, and Research
Third Edition – Revised and Expanded

Peter J. Pecora, James K. Whittaker, Anthony N. Maluccio, Richard P. Barth, and Diane DePanfilis, with Robert D. Plotnick

ALDINETRANSACTION
A Division of Transaction Publishers
New Brunswick (U.S.A.) and London (U.K.)

Library of Congress Catalog Number: 2009007968
ISBN: 978-0-202-36306-6 (cloth); 978-0-202-36314-1 (paper)
Printed in the United States of America

Library of Congress Cataloging-in-Publication Data

The child welfare challenge : policy, practice, and research /
    Peter J. Pecora—3rd ed. rev. and expanded.
        p. cm.
    Includes bibliographical references and index.
    ISBN 978-0-202-36306-6
        1. Child welfare—United States. I. Pecora, Peter J.

HV741.C512   2009
362.7—dc22   2009007968

Contents

Preface

Purpose

Within a historical and contemporary context, this book examines major policy, practice, and research issues as they jointly shape current child welfare practice and possible future directions. In addition to describing the major challenges facing the child welfare field, the book highlights some of the service innovations that have been developed and that are addressing these challenges. Program reforms are being implemented and agencies have never been better able to identify the challenges they face and concentrate the resources that they have in an informed manner.

Child welfare's focus is on families and children whose primary recourse to services has been through publicly funded child welfare agencies. In particular, we will consider those historical areas of service—foster care and adoptions, in-home family-centered services, child-protective services, and residential services—where social work has a legitimate, long standing, and important mission and role. We lay no claim to comprehensiveness, and many areas of practice such as day care, family support, and early intervention invite further exploration. Readers also should be conscious of the many other fields of practice in which child and family services are provided or that involve substantial numbers of social work programs, such as services to adolescent parents, child mental health, health, education, special education, and juvenile justice agencies.

Organization of Content

The book discusses the major policy, practice, and research issues as they jointly shape current child welfare practice and possible future directions. Each chapter describes how policy initiatives and research data can or should influence program design and implementation. In general, each chapter will follow a similar format, describing the central policy and program issues in the context of the major research findings in that area. Program challenges and future directions are discussed, along with suggested readings for further information. In each area, we hope to show how practice *has* changed in response to policy initiatives and empirical findings and what challenges lie ahead.

Child welfare practitioners and the families they serve are affected by the larger social contexts in which they interact. In America, this social context includes values that sometimes encourage parents to view children as property, without rights as individuals. In addition, family services and client self-improvements are often hindered by oppression in its various forms: institutional racism, sexism, and discrimination against individuals according to their religious beliefs, sexual orientation, and handicapping conditions. These have been discussed elsewhere (for example, see Bricker-Jenkins, Brissett-Chapman, & Issacs-Shockley, 1997; Hill, 2006; Mallon, 2007b) and will also be attended to in these pages because child welfare practitioners must be cognizant of these conditions and incorporate strategies for helping clients overcome discrimination into their case plans if long-term success is to be achieved. One of the requisites for developing such case plans is knowledge of the cultural issues related to each family, i.e., staff members must be "culturally and linguistically competent" (Hernandez, Nesman, Isaacs, Callejas, & Mowery, 2006). These practice competencies require specialized training and practice skills. How some of these contextual issues affect service delivery in various program areas is a theme of the book.

The mission, goals and key outcomes of child welfare are presented in Chapter 1. Each of these major components have been evolving over time and groundbreaking work is underway in certain counties and states. Key demographic trends, laws, and other policies that shape child welfare services are discussed in Chapter 2. While many barriers remain in fully operationalizing high quality frontline practice based on the philosophical principles discussed earlier, a number of important perspectives are being synthesized to move the field to a more effective service paradigm—"family-centered child welfare practice" that builds upon ecological, competence, developmental, and permanency planning perspectives. Discussed more fully in Chapter 3, this paradigm illustrates how children and families influence and are influenced by the multiple environments of family, neighborhood, school, and workplace—as well as society. These perspectives are part of an ever-evolving knowledge base where theory, research, and "practice wisdom" all inform program design and practice.

Child and family well-being are inextricably linked with family income. In Chapter 4, Robert Plotnick outlines the major economic security issues facing the United States today, and provides some contrasting data from other countries. This chapter also reviews key family income supplement strategies, including the Earned Income Tax Credit.

Readers will note the considerable amount of attention paid to child abuse and neglect (Chapters 5 and 6). Many social work professionals feel that child protective service issues have dominated the child welfare service delivery system at the cost of more preventive or rehabilitative services. While we agree with many of these concerns, we have included considerable material on child maltreatment for a number of reasons: (1) the seriousness of this enduring social problem and the consequent importance attached to it in the field (nowhere in child welfare is the fundamental tension between child protection and family preservation more clearly highlighted than in the area of child maltreatment); (2) the need for social workers—in a range of practice settings beyond public child welfare—to be knowledgeable about the phenomenon of child maltreatment and its consequences; and (3) the rapidly changing nature of our knowledge base regarding this phenomenon, and therefore the importance of addressing the latest policy, research, and practice issues.

We build on this content in Chapter 7 with a focus on child abuse prevention and family support services. A slow but steady increase in research and thoughtful conceptual reviews have enriched this area of policy and practice. There are many more summaries of key risk and protective factors at the community, family and individual levels, along with promising strategies.

In Chapters 8 and 9, we describe the policy, research findings, and program design issues for foster care, family reunification and kinship care services. Even though there is a large body of research about foster care, including issues related to placement and permanency planning, less is known about how timely reunification can be encouraged by strategic policies. Similarly, while the use of kinship care (foster care provided by relatives or American Indian clan members) has increased, state policy for supporting kinship care varies. Key policy and practice challenges remain to be addressed, despite the passage of P.L. 110-351, the Fostering Connections to Success and Increasing Adoptions Act.

Related to these issues of foster care and kinship care is how to prepare and support youth who are placed for transition back to their birth families or emancipation to the community. While some resources are invested in this area, policy and programs need more refinement—including the rigorous testing of life skills development approaches. These issues are discussed in Chapter 10. Adoption as a key form of permanency planning has grown tremendously, in part due to federal and state fiscal incentives, as well as a growing awareness of the benefits of adoption for children. Policy and program design issues for the various forms of adoption are presented in Chapter 11.

Many children will not thrive in their birth families, foster families or adoptive families unless they receive appropriate treatment for cognitive, emotional, behavioral, or substance abuse disorders. A broad range of mental health promotion and treatment strategies exist now (National Research Council and the Institute of Medicine, 2009). Chapter 12 considers a range of intensive treatment services such as Multi-Systemic Therapy, Multidimensional Treatment Foster Care, and residential treatment/group care. The book ends with a close look at what organizational requisites are necessary for effective services such as staffing, supervision, program quality improvement, and information technology. These are some of the necessary components for implementing any proactive model effectively.

We are in debt to many child welfare scholars who preceded us and on whose works we drew. Their many excellent texts and articles are ones that readers are referred to throughout this volume. Our goal is to convey some of the substantial contributions that social work has made to meeting the needs of families and children, articulate areas of practice and policy that have made progress since earlier editions, and detail the considerable work that remains.

Acknowledgments

A large number of academic and professional colleagues, students, and other collaborators have contributed to the development of this Third Edition. The world of child welfare services is growing around the globe and we are fortunate to be in regular contact with leading scholars, program managers, and policy makers in the US and other countries. We have benefited greatly from their example, their advice, their critiques of our work, and their encouragement. In many cases, we have known these colleagues for a substantial part of our careers—with others, they have added new voices to the work. The quality of this current edition is deeper because of what they have done and taught us. We, of course, take full responsibility for any errors or omissions contained within this volume.

Our students have also taught us much of what should be addressed in a child welfare course through their questions and reactions to earlier material and to draft versions of this edition. It is they who are the future of child welfare, and we hope this book will contribute to their preparation for excellence in the field. In addition, foster parents, foster care alumni, and staff members at many public and private child welfare agencies shared realities of the practice world with us.

We appreciate the dedication of Delia Armendariz and Justin Anderson for their patience and skill in formatting these chapters and preparing much of the references list. Mary Hodorowicz greatly aided the preparation of Chapter 11. Finally, we thank William Bell, Renee Kaplan, and Cari DeSantis of Casey Family Programs whose support helped make the completion of this Third Edition possible.

1

Purpose and Goals of Child Welfare

As we complete this third edition of *The Child Welfare Challenge*, child and family services are struggling to effectively serve families but large and small child welfare agencies are making progress and generating promising innovations (e.g., Lindsey & Schwartz, 2004). In this new edition, we have taken a more assertive stance regarding the reforms needed in child welfare, informed by the many collaborations underway with public and voluntary child welfare agencies. We firmly believe that major changes in approach are essential in certain areas, such as reforming Title IV-E funding to be more flexible and available for services; fuller implementation of community-based Alternative Response Systems, subsidized kinship care, subsidized guardianship, and the advancement of post-permanency services. We believe that these changes will improve the design, funding, and outcomes of child and family services in the United States and in many other countries.

Yet, child welfare services are a system of last response when more preventive and universal services fail. When educational programs are unable to engage children and families and high truancy rates persist, when public housing and job creation are not sufficient to make safe housing affordable, and when maternal and child health does not ensure that most mothers are ready and able to parent when they are called on to do so, child welfare services cannot be easily transformed. At the time of writing, more and more families are struggling just to get by. This checklist, developed by the National Center for Children in Poverty, identifies critical problems facing low- and moderate-income families that will have to be addressed if child welfare services are to fulfill their functions:

- *Child poverty remains unacceptably high and stagnant.* The child poverty rate has been stagnant since it began to rise in the early 2000s. Despite some indications of economic growth, child poverty has not returned to the levels seen in the late 1990s. Today, 18 percent of America's children live in families that are officially considered poor.
- *Full-time work is not always enough to provide for a family.* Research consistently shows that a full-time job at low wages is not enough to

support a family. In fact, on average, it takes an income of *twice the federal poverty level*—$40,000 a year for a family of four—to make ends meet. Nearly 30 million Americans work in jobs that pay poverty-level wages.

- *Many families do not have access to critical supports and services, such as childcare, paid sick leave, and mental health services.* Many families lack access to affordable, high-quality childcare. Nearly 76 percent of low-income workers do not have any paid sick leave to care for themselves or a sick family member or personal leave to attend events related to special needs of their children. And an astounding 75 percent to 80 percent of children and youth in need of mental health services do not receive them.
- *More children lack health insurance.* In 2005, for the first time in nearly a decade, the number of children who lack health insurance increased. Eleven percent of all American children are uninsured. Fully 20 percent of low-income children lack health insurance. Comprehensive health insurance coverage is critical to improving children's access to care as well as to ensuring good health.
- *Too few young children have access to quality early experiences.* Programs like Early Head Start can prepare young children for a productive life, but only 62,000 infants and toddlers are currently served. Low-income three- and four-year-olds are less likely to have access to preschool programs than their more well-off peers. (Source: Retrieved January 23, 2007 from http://nccp.org/rel_18.html)

The need for improving basic family supports is starkly evident in child welfare. In 2007 in the U.S.A., 5.8 million U.S. children were reported as abused and neglected, with 1,397,800 confirmed victims (U.S. Department of Health and Human Services, 2009, p. iii). (See http://www.acf.hhs.gov/programs/cb/pubs/cm07/summary.htm.) The United States federal government estimated that 496,000 children were placed in foster care in family and non-family settings as of September 30, 2007 (U.S. Department of Health and Human Services, 2008), with about 783,000 children served during the 2007 federal fiscal year.[1]

The numbers of children placed into out-of-home care, under Child Welfare Services (CWS) supervision, have risen substantially since 1980, but have been decreasing, nationally, at a steady slow pace since 2000. This decrease has occurred despite a slight increase in the number of children entering out-of-home care and is largely attributable to a growing number of children moving on to guardianship and adoption. (See http://www.acf.hhs.gov/programs/cb/stats_research/afcars/trends.htm.) There is remarkable variation in the rate of change in placements and exits as counties in the same state may have quite different foster care caseload dynamics (Wulczyn & Lery, 2007). African-American and Native American children are, however, more generally over-represented in foster care in many communities than would be expected by their sheer numbers in the population. Hispanic or Latino children are generally not overrepresented

Table 1.1
Children in America: Selected Facts and Figures

National Child Demographics	
Child population under age 18 in 2005 [1]	73,469,984
White children under 18 in 2005 [2]	58.3%
Nonwhite children under 18 in 2005 [3]	41.7%
Children and youth under 12 in 2005 [4]	61.8%
Children and youth age 12 and older in 2005 [5]	38.2%
Who Cared for America's Children in 2005?	
Both parents[6]	67.3%
Mother[6]	23.4%
Father[6]	4.8%
Grandparent[6]	2.2%
Other relative[6]	1.3%
Foster parent[6]	0.3%
Non-relative[6]	0.7%
Number of women with no husband present who were raising their own children under 18 years[7]	8,420,887
Our Most Vulnerable Children	
Children living in families with incomes below the poverty line in 2004[8]	12 million
Children living in extreme poverty in 2004[9]	5 million
Referrals for possible child abuse or neglect in 2006[10]	3.3 million
Children substantiated or indicated as abused or neglected in 2006[11]	905,000 victims
Children who died as a result of abuse or neglect in 2006[12]	1, 530
Children in foster care on September 30, 2006[13]	510,000
Children adopted from the public foster care system during the fiscal year ending September 30, 2006[14]	51,000
Children waiting to be adopted from the public foster care system as of September 30, 2006[15]	129,000

Sources: Child Welfare League of America (2004). A national fact sheet 2004 - Children 2004: vision, action, results. Washington, DC: Author, p.1; and statistics from the U.S. Department of Health and Human Services, Administration on Children, Youth and Families.

Table Notes

1. U.S. Bureau of the Census, Current Population Survey, Population Reference Bureau. (2006). Special tabulations of the supplementary survey. Washington, DC: Author.
2. Ibid.
3. Ibid.
4. U.S. Bureau of the Census, Population Estimates. (2005). State Single Year of Age and Sex Population Estimates: April 1, 2000 to July 1, 2005. Washington, DC: Author. Retrieved September 17, 2007 from http://www.census.gov/population/www/socdemo/hh-fam/cps2005.html
5. Ibid.
6. U.S. Bureau of the Census. (2005). Household Relationship and Living Arrangements of Children Under 18 Years, by Age, Sex, Race, Hispanic Origin: (Table C2). Washington, DC: Author. Retrieved September 17, 2007 from http://www.census.gov/population/www/socdemo/hh-fam/cps2005.html
7. U.S. Census Bureau, American Community Profile (2005). Table 1. General Demographic Characteristics. Washington, DC. Retrieved September 17, 2007 from http://factfinder.census.gov/servlet/ADPTable?_bm=y&-geo_id=01000US&-qr_name=ACS_2005_EST_G00_DP1&-ds_name=ACS_2005_EST_G00_&-_lang=en&-_caller=geoselect&-state=adp&-format=
8. National Center for Children in Poverty (NCCP), Columbia University. (2005). Who are America's Poor Children? New York: Author. Note that data for calendar years 2002, 2003 and 2004 were averaged because of small sample sizes in less populated states.
9. Ibid.
10. U.S. Department of Health and Human Services, Administration on Children, Youth and Families. Child Maltreatment 2006 (Washington, DC: U.S. Government Printing Office, 2008). p. iii. Retrieved May 18, 2008 from http://www.acf.hhs.gov/programs/cb/pubs/cm06/cm06.pdf
11. Ibid.
12. Ibid.
13. U.S. Department of Health and Human Services, Administration for Children and Families, Children's Bureau. (2006). The AFCARS report No. 13: Preliminary FY 2005 estimates as of September 2006. Washington DC: U.S. Department of Health and Human Services, 2005. Downloaded November 7, 2006 from http://www.acf.hhs.gov/programs/cb/stats_research/afcars/tar/report13.htm. Note that this number dropped to 496,000 in 2007. See http://www.acf.hhs.gov/programs/cb/stats_research/afcars/trends.htm
14. Ibid
15. Ibid.

---

according to their presence in the general population, although this does occur in some communities. The field is struggling to understand why this occurs and what, if any, relationship it has to the proportion of minority child welfare staff, the training of staff, or the configuration of other experiences and services that are associated with child welfare involvement like maternal arrest.

There are, however, new resources and ideas reshaping child welfare practices in many communities. Some agencies in Illinois, New York City, and other areas are making successful efforts to reduce the length of stay of children in out-of- home care, reducing the level of restrictiveness of child placements, and increasing the proportion of children placed with relatives (i.e., kinship care) in guardianship and adoption. In addition, the number of children being adopted or securing a form of permanence through guardianship has more than tripled over the last two decades, and the time to adoption has been decreased significantly in nearly every states (Avery, 1998; U.S. Department of Health and Human Services, 2003). These innovations may increase further with new initiatives underway such as child welfare demonstration waivers, expedited adoptive parent assessments, expedited approvals of subsidy applications, increases in judicial personnel, and heightened attention by the agencies and courts to the need for more timely permanency planning. For example, in New York City, the number of children in foster care has declined dramatically since the mid-1990s and thousands of children who were already placed in out-of-home care are being adopted (New York City Administration for Children's Services, 2004, p. 7). In addition, an improved information system now allows the city of New York to assess the performance of every private agency in terms of the time needed to achieve permanency for the children in their care. This approach is used to protect children from being placed in poorly performing agencies and rewarding those agencies that are accomplishing a great deal for children (New York Acts to Ease Process in Foster Care, http://www.nytimes.com/2007/03/22/nyregion/22foster.html?pagewanted=1&_r=1&fta=y, retrieved April 13, 2008).

Chapter Outline

In the subsequent sections of this chapter, we will review the mission, goals, and the philosophical underpinnings of child welfare services. Some of the most crucial challenges facing child welfare leaders today will also be presented.

Mission and Goals of Child Welfare Services

The mission of child welfare has long been to respond specifically to the needs of children reported to public child protection agencies as abused or neglected, or at risk of child maltreatment. Recently, there has been more emphasis on looking beyond public and private child welfare agencies to involve communities as a whole in the protection and nurturing of children, and to formulate collaborative community efforts to prevent and respond to child abuse and neglect. Our knowledge of the interplay of risk and protective factors at the child, parent, family, neighborhood and community levels has grown to underscore the need to look beyond the parent-child dyad. Although all children have highly individual needs and characteristics, they live in the context of their families; families live in the context of their cultures and communities;

and communities in the context of their social, economic, cultural and political environments (Child Welfare League of America, 2003).

When child welfare services fails to incorporate and draw upon the richness and strength embodied in this context of family life, it cannot effectively respond to the needs of vulnerable children and troubled families. While agency mission statements provide the overall context for service, it is essential that key goals or outcomes are specified to help guide such key functions as establishing agency strategic plans, policy formulation, funding decisions, and worker practice within a context of philosophical values and scientific practice (American Humane Association, et al., 1998; Wulczyn, Barth, Yuan, Harden, & Landsverk, 2005). System goals and expected outcomes are discussed in the next section.

Key Goals and Outcomes for Child Welfare Services

Child welfare services as a field is gaining more clarity and consensus about its primary mission. There is one primary goal and two secondary goals for child welfare services: The primary goal is to protect children from harm. The second goal is to preserve existing family units, which we understand to include both birth-family or relative families as appropriate. The third goal is to promote children's development into adults who can live independently and contribute to their community, which may require a variety of permanency planning alternatives such as family reunification, placement with relatives, different forms of guardianship (depending upon local law), and adoption—including in rare situations *planned* long-term foster care or kinship care with some kind of legal safeguards such as guardianship (US Department of Health and Human Services, 2003).

There is some debate in the field about placing child safety as a superior goal to family support—some organizations such as the CWLA (2003) argue that without an emphasis upon both child safety and family support, simultaneously, neither will happen in an equitable manner. Yet, the effectiveness of the system in achieving positive child development and *well-being* has also been rightly criticized (e.g., Berrick, Needell, Barth, & Jonson-Reid, 1998; Maluccio & Pecora, 2006). The key components of each of these major goals (also called "outcome domains") are summarized below.

Safety. The core goal for child welfare services, according to federal policy and most states, is keeping children safe from child abuse and neglect. This includes children living with their birth families, returned home to their families, and children placed in out-of-home care. In terms of concrete outcomes, citizens should be looking to child welfare services to *prevent children from being mal-treated* and to *keep families safely together* that are functioning at a minimum standard of parenting. Child welfare workers operate on the philosophical basis that all children have a right to live in a safe environment and receive protection from abuse and neglect. For example, the focus of child welfare services (CWS) should be to deliver services that are preventive and non-punitive and that are geared toward parent rehabilitation through identification and treatment of the factors which underlie the problem.

At the most general level there is a firm consensus regarding the mission of child welfare services: it is designed to protect children from child maltreatment committed by their parents or other caretakers. But in translating this broad mandate into policy guidelines and practice, the consensus breaks down in a variety of areas such as defining what is child abuse or neglect, establishing standards for agency intervention, and specifying what constitutes a minimum standard of parenting (popularized by the question "what is a good enough parent?"). It also is a policy and practice area that would benefit from increased attention to research findings emerging on risk, resilience, and protective factors as staff members assess family safety.

Standards used in case decision-making seriously affect provision of services. Historically, the standard used for CWS intervention has been based on the "best interests of the child." Such a broad and subjective standard skewed caseworkers' actions toward frequent removal of children. This approach to practice resulted in an emphasis (and a public expectation) that child welfare services should be used to improve all areas of family functioning. In addition, child placement was also justified because it was the "best" plan for the child. The public and certain community agencies might have expected that family functioning had to be improved from to an unrealistically high level before the case was closed.

That expectation is no longer feasible or ethical. It is not feasible because high caseloads and a shortage of services have forced agencies to target their services to clients most in need. From an ethical standpoint, laws protecting parent rights and family privacy prohibit forcing services upon families whose functioning does not fall below a certain minimum standard of parenting. These families are generally best voluntarily engaged and served by other community agencies. Knowing from research that most youth want to have ongoing contact with their families, whether they are at home or not (Chapman, Wall, & Barth, 2004), we assume that the development of more effective in-home services will be welcomed by youth and parents, alike.

Finally, we lack the research data that allow us to predict what is in the child's best interest, beyond protecting children in severe situations. While risk assessment and case decision-making approaches have improved, the social sciences are not yet able to predict outcomes for children in relation to determining whether child placement would be superior for many cases (Doyle, 2007; Stein & Rzepnicki, 1983). Child protective services and child welfare staff are instead focusing on *minimum standards of parenting,* with a requirement that involuntary CWS intervention proceed only if there is evidence that children have been harmed or will be at risk of maltreatment in the near future.

In most states, CWS workers are encouraged to focus on minimally adequate care and levels of risk to the child, rather than requiring that all parents provide some "optimal" level of nurturing. The types of services available to help parents meet a minimal standard of parenting heavily influence CWS decision making and the case plan to be implemented. No agency has a completely adequate range of services, but within most communities there should be a variety of resources to supplement and support what CWS staff can provide, such as crisis nurseries, treatment day care, home-based services and parenting support groups. Finally, perhaps one of the most pivotal determinants is client ability or willingness to use the services. Regardless of what a worker can do for or plan with a family, a successful outcome is dependent upon the ability of family members to benefit from the service and their willingness to work with child welfare staff and to engage with allied service providers required by the court.

Permanence.[2] When the state steps in to protect an abused or neglected child, it is not enough for the state to make the child safe; the state must also consider the child's needs for permanent and stable family ties. Besides protecting a child, the state should ensure that the children will be brought up by stable and legally secure permanent families, rather than in temporary foster care under the supervision of the state. This principle has been well established in federal law, first by the Adoption Assistance and Child Welfare Act of 1980, then by the Adoption and Safe Families Act of 1997, and then by the Adoption Promotion Act of 2003. While permanency alone does not guarantee a normal healthy childhood, it is a key factor in the successful upbringing of children for a number of reasons. First, many mental health experts have proposed that stable and continuous caregivers are important to normal child development. Children benefit from secure and uninterrupted positive emotional relationships with adults who are responsible for their care in order to learn how to form healthy relationships later on (Appleyard, Egeland, & Sroufe, 2007). They do not benefit from uninterrupted emotional relationships that traumatize them, result in elevated stress, and may diminish their capacity for learning and social relationships.

Second, children need parents who are fully committed to caring for them, and it is easier for parents (whether biological, foster, or adoptive) to maintain a strong commitment to the child when their role is secure. Children are likely to feel more secure under the care of parents than of child welfare agencies. In addition, fully committed parents are more likely to provide conscientiously for the child's needs.

Third, having a permanent family adds a critical element of predictability to a child's life, thereby promoting their sense of belonging. Being in foster care and never knowing when and where one might be moved can impose great stress on a child. With a permanent family, a child can form a more secure sense of the future and can better weather other difficulties and changes in childhood and adolescence (Casey Family Programs, 2003; Kerman, Maluccio, & Freundlich, 2008).

Fourth, autonomous families generally are more capable of raising children than is the state (Berrick, et al., 1998; Goldstein, Freud, & Solnit, 1973). Decision-making for children in state supervised foster care tends to be fragmented and diffuse because it is shared by child welfare workers (only some of whom have social work education), professional therapists and evaluators, foster parents, court personnel, and biological parents. Full-time permanent parents, who concentrate far more personal commitment and time on the child than any professional, are best able to make fully informed and timely decisions for a child.

In terms of concrete outcomes, citizens should be looking to child welfare services for a number of permanency-related outcomes, including *purposeful case plans* that explicitly address the child's legal status and need for permanency planning. If permanent placement is an important goal for abused and neglected children, it follows that service plans for such children should be designed, in part, for that purpose. Whether a service plan has been logically designed to achieve a safe and permanent home for the child is a key indicator by which to measure the appropriateness of the plan and, ultimately, to measure the plan's success and that of the child welfare agency (Casey Family Programs, 2003; Hardin, 1992).

Permanency planning is the systematic process of carrying out, within proscribed time frames, a set of goal-directed activities designed to help children live in safe families that offer them a sense of belonging and legal, lifetime family ties (Maluccio, Fein, & Olmstead, 1986). Permanency planning thus refers to the process of taking prompt, decisive action to maintain children in their own homes or place them in legally permanent families. Above all, it addresses a single—but crucial—question: What will be this child's family when he or she grows up? It embodies a family-focused paradigm for child welfare services, with emphasis on providing a permanent legal family and sensitivity to ensuring family continuity for children across the life span (McFadden & Downs, 1995).

The goal of permanency for each child is also reflected in federal legislation, namely, the Adoption Assistance and Child Welfare Act (AACWA) of 1980 (P.L. 96-272) and the Safe and Stable Families Act of 1997, which were enacted following decade of advocacy on behalf of children in out-of-home care and state reforms that suggested the efficacy of a range of strategies to achieve greater permanency. As summarized in Chapter 2, federal policy mandates the states to promote permanency planning for children and youths coming to their attention through such means as subsidized adoption, procedural reforms, time limits, and, above all, preventive and supportive services to families. Each state has enacted legislation or policies designed to implement these acts, resulting in major changes in service delivery and, apparently, changes in outcomes for children in foster care and their families (see Chapter 2; Anderson, Ryan, & Leashore, 1997; Barth, Wulczyn, & Crea, 2005; US DHHS, 2004).

As the meaning of permanency planning is considered, one should note that there are different options or routes to it (Kerman, et al., 2008; Thoburn, Murdoch, & O'Brien, 1986; US DHHS, 2007). These include maintaining the child in her or his own home; reunification of placed children with their biological families; adoption; and permanent or long-term foster family care in special situations, such as those of older children with ongoing relationships with their birth parents. This hierarchy of options is generally accepted in the field of child welfare. This does not mean, however, that any one of these options is inherently good or bad for every child, although the greatest preference is for maintaining or reuniting the child with the biological family. It does mean that in each case there should be careful assessment and extensive work to maintain children with their own families or to make other permanent plans when it has been demonstrated that the parents cannot care for the child. In short, permanency planning encompasses both prevention and rehabilitation and can serve as a framework for child welfare practice in general. It involves attention not only to children in care but also to those who are at risk of out-of-home placement (See Chapters 7, 8, and 9).

Other outcomes (framed in italics to help distinguish them from one another) include children being *placed in the least restrictive placement* possible, *with siblings* whenever possible, with *minimal placement moves or disruptions*, and with a *timely resolution of their legal status* so that they can be adopted by a caring adult if a birth parent is unable to care for them.

Child well-being. Achieving child well-being means foremost, that a child *is safe from child abuse or neglect.* This requires that a *child's basic needs are met* and the child has the *opportunity to grow and develop* in an environment that provides adequate nurture, support, and stimulation. In this outcome domain we include children's education, mental health, health, and social behavior (Wulczyn, et al., 2005). Although child welfare services is not singularly responsible for these, CWS should be expected to work with other parties to achieve these goals and, when children are under the guardianship of CWS should take the lead in coordinating efforts related to achieving these outcomes.

Family well-being. Family well-being is generally not viewed as an outcome of today's child welfare services but might be thought of as an outcome in a reformulated child and family services program that is concerned not only about the impact of services on children but on each family member. In this usage, family well-being means that a family has the capacity to care for its children and fulfill their basic developmental, health, educational, social, cultural, spiritual, and housing needs. It would imply that children's services workers have some responsibility for locating these essential services and supports for the sake of the family's well-being.

The federal outcome standards and child and family service reviews, summarized in Table 1.2, are based on the safety, permanency, and wellbeing concepts (Milner, Mitchell, & Hornsby, 2001; United States General Accounting Office, 2004). This framework reflects parts of the one we propose here—that CWS is responsible for achieving outcomes related to safety and permanency. The CWS is also responsible for engaging in activities that will result in the provision of education, health, and mental health services that will assist a child who needs them (these "system outcomes" are not shown in Table 1.2 but will be discussed in Chapters 3 and 7). The federal government does not have a comparable domain for "family well-being" although this is part of what we would consider to be the optimal practice framework that underlies work that is done to support, strengthen, and preserve families in order to achieve the safety and permanency goals.

Additional Philosophical Underpinnings of Child Welfare Services

Besides the focus on child safety, permanence, and other well-being areas, we believe that a core set of philosophical principles can be used to inform the selection of key outcomes for child welfare and the strategies for achieving them. The principles can also provide useful guideposts for agencies as they design performance-based contracts, implement managed care approaches to service delivery, or design staff development programs.

The following section draws material from a summary of philosophical principles and recommended performance indicators that was developed by the Pew Commission on Foster Care (2004), researchers (Wulczyn, et al., 2005) and a consortium of private foundations, national professional associations, researchers, agency administrators, foster care alumni, a state legislator, juvenile court judge, and a parent representative (American Humane Association, et al., 1998). This list is not intended to be exhaustive or definitive.

1. Community supports for families. Families raise children within communities. Family efforts are affected by the community's social and economic health. Communities, therefore, need to support families in providing a safe and nurturing child-rearing environment. Healthy communities offer both formal and informal supports to families which clearly help to prevent harm to children, prevention efforts are key component of the child welfare system.

Sound social, economic, and moral reasons compel equal attention and resources to preventive programs and to services that support child well-being and effective family functioning. Basic supports such as jobs, housing, and community economic development are needed so that child welfare services can stem the causes of child maltreatment, rather than simply responding after children have suffered abuse or neglect. Although CWS does not have a principal responsibility for the quality of community life, child welfare efforts can be implemented, often in concert with other government and civic organizations,

Table 1.2
Data Indicators for the Child and Family Services Review:
Ranges, Medians, and National Standards for the Child and Family Services
Review (CFSR) Data Indicators*

DATA INDICATORS	Range	Median**	National Standard**
DATA INDICATORS ASSOCIATED WITH CFSR SAFETY OUTCOME 1–CHILDREN ARE, FIRST AND FOREMOST, PROTECTED FROM ABUSE AND NEGLECT.			
Of all children who were victims of a substantiated or indicated maltreatment allegation during the first 6 months of FY 2004, what **percent** were not victims of another substantiated or indicated maltreatment allegation within the 6-months following that maltreatment incident? (45 States)	86.0 – 98.0	93.3	**94.6 or higher**
Of all children served in foster care in FY 2004, what **percent** were not victims of a substantiated or indicated maltreatment by a foster parent or facility staff member during the fiscal year? (37 States)	98.59 – 100	99.52	**99.68 or higher**
DATA INDICATORS ASSOCIATED WITH CFSR PERMANENCY OUTCOME 1 – CHILDREN HAVE PERMANENCY AND STABILITY IN THEIR LIVING SITUATIONS			
Permanency Composite 1: Timeliness and Permanency of Reunification (47 States)*	50 – 150	113.7	**122.6 or higher**
Component A: Timeliness of Reunification****			
Measure C1.1: Of all children discharged from foster care to reunification in FY 2004 who had been in foster care for 8 days or longer, what **percent** were reunified in less than 12 months from the date of the latest removal from home? (This includes the "trial home visit adjustment.") (51 States)	44.3 – 92.5	69.9	No Standard
Measure C1.2: Of all children who were discharged from foster care to reunification in FY 2004, and who had been in foster care for 8 days or	1.1 – 13.7	6.5	No Standard

longer, what was the median length of
stay **in months** from the date of the
latest removal from home until the date
of discharge to reunification? (This includes
the "trial home visit adjustment.") (51 States)

Measure C1.3: Of all children who   17.7 –68.9   39.4   No Standard
entered foster care for the first
ime in the 6-month period just
prior to FY 2004, and who
remained in foster care for 8 days or
longer, what percent were discharged
from foster care to reunification in
less than 12 months from the date of
latest removal from home?
(This includes the "trial home
visit adjustment.") (47 States)

Component B: Permanency of Reunification**
Measure C14: Of all children who   1.6 – 29.8   15.0   No Standard
were discharged from foster care to
reunification in the 12-month period
prior to FY 2004 (i..e., FY 2003),
what percent re-entered foster care
in less than 12 months from the
date of discharge? (47 States)

Table Notes

* The data shown are for the national standard target year of FY 2004. Each State will be evaluated against the standard on data relevant to its specific CFSR twelve-month target period. The national standards will remain the same throughout the second round of the CFSR.

**The medians and the national standards for the safety and composite data indicators are based on an adjustment to the distribution using the sampling error for each data indicator. The medians and national standards for the composite data indicators are from a dataset that excluded counties in a State that did not have data for all measures within a particular composite. The range and medians for each individual measure reflect the distribution of all counties that had data for that particular measure, even if that county was not included in the overall composite calculation.

*** A State was excluded from the calculation of the composite national standard if (1) it did not submit FIPS codes in its AFCARS submissions (1 State), or (2) with regard to composite 1 and 2, it did not provide unique identifiers that would permit tracking children across fiscal years (four states).

****Children are included in the count of reunifications if the reason for discharge reported to AFCARS was either "reunification" or "live with relative." They are not included in the count of "reunifications" if the reason for discharge reported to AFCARS was "guardianship," even if the guardian is a relative.

Source: Retrieved May 18, 2008 from http://www.acf.hhs.gov/programs/cb/cwmonitoring/data_indicators.htm.

DATA INDICATORS ASSOCIATED WITH CFSR PERMANENCY OUTCOME 1 – CHILDREN HAVE PERMANENCY AND STABILITY IN THEIR LIVING SITUATIONS*	Range	Median**	National Standard**
Permanency Composite 2: Timeliness of Adoptions (47 States)	**50 – 150**	**95.3**	**106.4 or higher**

Component A: Timeliness of adoptions of children discharged from foster care

Measure C2.1: Of all children who were discharged from foster care to a finalized adoption during FY 2004, what **percent** were discharged in less than 24 months from the date of the latest removal from home? (51 States)	6.4 – 74.9	26.8	No Standard
Measure C2.2: Of all children who were discharged from foster care to a finalized adoption during FY 2004, what was the median length of stay in foster care **in months** from the date of latest removal from home to the date of discharge to adoption? (51 States)	16.2 – 55.7	32.4	No Standard

Component B: Progress toward adoption for children in foster care for 17 months or longer

Measure C2.3: Of all children who were in foster care on the first day of FY 2004, and who were in foster care for 17 continuous months or longer, what percent were discharged from foster care to a finalized adoption by the last day of FY 2004? The denominator for this measure excludes children who, by the end of FY 2004, were discharged from foster care with a discharge reason of live with relative, reunification, or guardianship. (51 States)	2.4 – 26.2	20.2	No Standard

Measure C2.4: Of all children who were in foster care on the first day of FY 2004 for 17 continuous months or longer, and who were not legally free for adoption prior to that day, what percent became legally free for adoption during the first 6 months of FY 2004? (Legally free means that there was a parental rights termination date reported to AFCARS for both mother and father.) The denominator for this measure excludes children who, by the last day of the first 6 months of FY 2004, were not legally free, but had been discharged from foster care with a discharge reason of live with relative, reunification, or guardianship. (51 States)	0.1 – 17.8	8.8	No Standard

Component C: Progress toward adoption of children who are legally free for adoption

Measure C2.5: Of all children who became legally free for adoption during FY 2003 (i.e., there was a parental rights termination date reported to AFCARS for both mother and father), what percent were discharged from foster care to a finalized adoption in less than 12 months of becoming legally free? (47 States)	20.0 – 100	45.8	No Standard

Table Notes

*The data shown are for the national standard target year of FY 2004. Each State will be evaluated against the standard on data relevant to its specific CFSR twelve-month target period. The national standards will remain the same throughout the second round of the CFSR.

**The medians and the national standards for the safety and composite data indicators are based on an adjustment to the distribution using the sampling error for each data indicator. The medians and national standards for the composite data indicators are from a dataset that excluded counties in a State that did not have data for all measures within a particular composite. The range and medians for each individual measure reflect the distribution of all counties that had data for that particular measure, even if that county was not included in the overall composite calculation.

***A State was excluded from the calculation of this composite either because (1) it did not submit FIPS codes in its AFCARS submissions (1 State), or (2) with regard to composite 1 and 2, it did not provide unique identifiers that would permit tracking children across fiscal years (4 States).

DATA INDICATORS ASSOCIATED WITH CFSR PERMANENCY OUTCOME 1 – CHILDREN HAVE PERMANENCY AND STABILITY IN THEIR LIVING SITUATIONS*	Range	Median**	National Standard**
Permanency Composite 3: Achieving Permanency for Children in Foster Care for Long Periods of Time (51 States)*	**50 – 150**	**112.7**	**121.7 or higher**

Component A: Permanency for children in foster care for long periods of time

Measure C3.1: Of all children who were in foster care for 24 months or longer on the first day of FY 2004, what percent were discharged to a permanent home prior to their 18th birthday and by the end of the fiscal year? A child is considered discharged to a permanent home if the discharge reason is adoption, guardianship, reunification, or live with relative. (51 States)	8.1 – 35.3	25.0	No Standard
Measure C3.2: Of all children who were discharged from foster care in FY 2004 who were legally free for adoption at the time of discharge (i.e., there was a parental rights termination date reported to AFCARS for both mother and father), what percent were discharged to a permanent home prior to their 18th birthday? A child is considered discharged to a permanent home if the discharge reason is adoption, guardianship, reunification, or live with relative. (51 States)	84.9 – 100	96.8	No Standard

Component B: Children growing up in foster care

Measure C3.3: Of all children who either (1) were discharged from foster care in FY 2004 with a discharge reason of emancipation, or (2) reached their 18th birthday in FY 2004 while in foster care, what percent were in foster care for 3 years or longer? (51 States)	15.8 – 76.9	47.8	No Standard
Permanency Composite 4: Placement Stability (51 States)	**50 – 150**	**93.3**	**101.5 or higher**
Measure C4.1: Of all children who were served in foster care during FY 2004, and who were in foster care for at least 8 days but	55.0 – 99.6	83.3	No Standard

less than 12 months, what percent
had two or fewer placement
settings? (51 States)

Measure C4.2: Of all children who were served in foster care during FY 2004, and who were in foster care for at least 12 months but less than 24 months, what percent had two or fewer placement settings? (51 States)	27.0 – 99.8	59.9	No Standard
Measure C4.3: Of all children who were served in foster care during FY 2004, and who were in foster care for at least 24 months, what percent had two or fewer placement settings? (51 States)	13.7 – 98.9	33.9	No Standard

Table Notes

*The data shown are for the national standard target year of FY 2004. Each State will be evaluated against the standard on data relevant to its specific CFSR twelve-month target period. The national standards will remain the same throughout the second round of the CFSR.

**The medians and the national standards for the safety and composite data indicators are based on an adjustment to the distribution using the sampling error. The medians and national standards for the composite data indicators are from a dataset that excluded counties in a state that did not have data for all measures within a particular composite. The range and medians for each individual measure reflect the distribution of all counties that had data for that particular measure, even if that county was not included in the overall composite calculation.

***A state was excluded from the calculation of this composite because it did not submit FIPS codes in its AFCARS submissions.

to reduce the harms associated with undermining community characteristics and to increase the capacity of communities to support good parenting. So, cooperative housing, sober living programs, or family support agencies with extended childcare hours may help to provide community resources needed to help families under strain.

Preventive and family supportive services, such as school-based parent resource centers and crisis nurseries, that are easily accessible to all children and families in their own communities and integrated with other community support systems (such as housing, health care, education, and early child development) are critical underpinnings for a responsive child welfare system. No single model or system will fit all communities. (See, for example, DePanfilis & Salus, 2003; Schorr & Marchand, 2007; U.S. Department of Health and Human Services, 1999).

2. Family-centered services. Responsive child welfare approaches offer family-centered services that directly address the needs and interests of individual children and families (see Chapter 3). When families are actively involved in making key decisions about their children and designing services to meet their needs, it is more likely that the family's capacity to parent safely its children will be increased (Fraser, Pecora, & Haapala, 1991; Schorr & Marchand, 2007).

Effective child welfare agencies work to create an atmosphere in which families feel comfortable in speaking honestly and openly about their strengths and needs. In partnership with families, these agencies strive to construct service responses that support effective family functioning and allow children to remain safely with their families. Help is family-driven, and the availability of a particular funding stream should not be allowed to drive the provision of services that do not address the needs of a specific child and family.

Most families have the motivation and capacity to be actively involved in providing or creating provisions for their children's safety and well-being, as long as they are properly supported. Indeed, with about 2 million reports of maltreatment founded to be substantiated, but fewer than 250,000 children entering foster care—most of them to later return home—and fewer than 100,000 children going on to leave foster care to an exit other than the parents or relatives, CWS finds that the birth family is likely to be the continuous parent for at least 95 percent of abused children. Even when a child's parents cannot be her or his primary caregivers, family members and extended family are a vital part of the caring circle for children and can contribute to the child's growth and development.

When a child has been placed outside of his or her own home, agency workers should strive to maintain relationships of continuity for the child, ideally with birth parents and with kin or previous caregivers. If other out-of-home care is required, the least restrictive, most family-like setting possible, which is responsive to a child's special needs, is the preferred setting for this care (see for example, Melaville & Blank, 1993). It should be noted, however, that *routinely* making same race foster care or adoption placements is not allowable under the Multi-Ethnic Placement Act and IEPA, unless the child has unique cultural needs (e.g., speaks only Spanish).

3. Cultural competence. Children and parents of color represent the largest group served by child welfare. According to the U.S. Census Bureau, immigrant and refugee families represent the fastest growing portion of the U.S. population (see http://www.census.gov/ipc/www/usinterimproj/). A culturally competent child welfare system is one that develops behaviors, attitudes, and policies to promote effective cross-cultural work. By engaging in a cultural self-assessment process to help both the organization and individual workers to clarify their basic cultural values, agencies can address how agency and worker values may affect serving clients with different cultural orientations than those of the agency and its workers and improve the access, availability, acceptance, and quality of services to all cultural groups being served. Providing workers, and the agency or organization as a whole, with a flexible context for gaining and expanding cultural knowledge, understanding the dynamics arising from cultural differences, and promoting the successful adaptation of services to meet unique cultural needs in partnership with community members, is the most effective way for agencies to improve their cultural competence (See, for example, Harper, et al., 2006; The Business Council and The Conference Board Partnership for 21st Century Skills, 2006).

Many service reforms—detailed later in the book—are being developed with attention to cultural issues in their implementation. Such attention is critical to the development and use of effective services. Emerging evidence indicates that such interventions are more likely to be effective (Hernandez, Nesman, Isaacs, Callejas, & Mowery, 2006; Wells & Briggs, in press), although rigorous reviews of existing child and adult mental health interventions suggest that their success is robust across racial and ethnic groups (Huey & Polo, 2008; Lau, 2006; Miranda, Guillermo, Lau, Kohn, Wei-Chin & LaFromboise, 2005).

4. System accountability and timeliness. A well-organized service delivery system, accountable to specific performance standards and time frames for service provision, is essential to effectively protect children and strengthen families. The child welfare system's effectiveness is being measured in terms of its ability to produce defined and visible outcomes for children and families through a continuum of resources. Multiple perspectives on these outcomes are considered in the continuous process of improving services that can be shown to:

- prevent family problems from occurring in the first place;
- increase and maintain children's safety and families' emotional health and ability to care for their children during a stressful time or transition; and
- prevent re-victimization or another family problem, or slow progressively deteriorating conditions.

Effective services are those that are timely from a child's perspective, that is, services are provided quickly enough to respond to a child's or youth's developmental and emotional needs. Evidence is piling up that the most important years for intervention are the earliest—as assistance provided to children younger than five has a far greater impact on lifetime earnings and well-being than investments in adolescents and young adults (Heckman & Masterov, 2007). Nonetheless, there are critical periods for youth who are involved with CWS, including such critical times as children face when they are reaching the age of majority and must leave the custody and care of foster care. Service providers and the system as a whole can recognize the imperative of children's developmental time frames and critical developmental periods and ensure that services are organized to coincide with them. Service provision that is sensitive to a child's sense of time helps: (1) children to remain in or be placed in safe and permanent homes; (2) child welfare workers to more effectively perform their jobs; and (3) workers and the courts to make critical decisions with greater wisdom and competence (See Bernstein, 2000; Berrick, et al., 1998; Young, Gardner, Coley, Schorr, & Bruner, 1994)

5. *Coordination of system resources.* A cohesive system of family-centered, community-based, culturally competent, timely, and accountable services and supports for children and families is what we are striving for in child welfare. Organizing system resources to ensure consistent, reliable coordinated service delivery, along with the availability of informal supports for families in their own communities, will maximize the effectiveness of the child welfare system.

At the individual family level, formal efforts to coordinate services and supports are necessary among different providers serving the same family. The child welfare system and its workers have a responsibility to act as coordinators by ensuring that all family needs are identified, assessed, and met with a coordinated plan to provide resources that will achieve specific outcomes for children and their families.

At the systems level, formal cooperative agreements or protocols can increase the cohesiveness of related services provided by different agencies. Funding that is not limited to specific service categories or that allows for the provision of a combination of resources to meet individual child and family needs also strengthens a coordinated response to families. This approach to resource allocation may allow communities the flexibility to meet local needs and to provide a holistic array of services, resources, and informal supports for children and families (see, for example, Daro, Budde, Baker, Nesmith, & Harden, 2005; Kamerman & Kahn, 1989).

Evidence-Based Treatments and Child Welfare Services

Overview

One of the current areas of innovation in child welfare and related fields is the continued development and diffusion of child, parent, and family interventions that have a strong theory and evidence base (Stambaugh, Burns, Landsverk, & Reutz, 2007; Weisz, Jensen-Doss, & Hawley, 2006). While various national and regional associations or organizations may vary somewhat in terms of the criteria that must be met for an intervention to qualify as "evidence-based" or an EBP, these interventions must have research data from rigorous control group studies or multiple single case/single subject design studies that have been replicated by researchers independent of the model designers, and have a theory base where the mechanisms described in the logic model or theory of change have been supported by process and outcome data (Chadwick Center for Children and Families, 2004; Chambless & Hollon, 1998; Hoagwood, Burns, Kiser, Ringeisen, & Schoenwald, 2001; Jensen, Weersing, Hoagwood, & Goldman, 2005).

Some of the organizations that are reviewing and screening evidence-based interventions include the California Clearinghouse for Evidence-Based Practices, Child Welfare League of America (CWLA.org), Coalition for Evidence-Based Policy (http://www.excelgov.org/evidence), Promisingpractices.net; http://www.evidencebasedprograms.org/; Substance Abuse and Mental Health Services Administration: (SAMHSA.gov), and other related program areas: www.bris.ac.uk/Depts/CochraneBehav.

Examples of Evidence-Based Treatments

Examples include the following intervention models, and these and other EBPs will be featured in summary tables in Chapters 7, 9 and 12—as well as cited, where relevant, in other chapters:

- Functional Family Therapy (FFT)
- Homebuilders
- Multidimensional Treatment Foster Care (MDTFC)
- Multisystemic Therapy (MST)
- Nurturing Program
- Parent Management Training (PMT)
- Parent Child Interaction Therapy (ages 4-12) (PCIT)
- Parenting Wisely
- Project Safe Care
- The Incredible Years
- Triple P—Positive Parenting Program

Note that many of these interventions have been rated as "promising" (e.g., Homebuilders) as compared to "well-supported effective" (e.g., Triple P) (see http://www.cachildwelfareclearinghouse.org/scientific-rating-scale.php). We will generally highlight the interventions with the strongest evidence base—such as those used in the general population for successfully treating many conditions with interventions that are largely behavioral or cognitive-behavioral and that address symptoms, behavior, and functioning. Such interventions tend to be relatively brief and actively engage caregivers in parenting practices. In fact, dropping a child off at a clinic for individual therapy is of very limited value, particularly for externalizing disorders. At the present, however, effective behavioral or cognitive-behavioral interventions are not uniformly available across the country, especially through the Medicaid-funded providers by whom many youth in care are served.

Evidence-based interventions that have been identified to address the mental health needs of youth in foster care are delivered largely by the mental health system. In many jurisdictions, however, the mental health and child welfare systems are disconnected; consequently, the special needs of youth in foster care often go unmet. Youth in foster care could greatly benefit from the provision of specific mental health interventions within the child welfare system. At the very least, they would benefit from a targeted collaboration between the two systems to provide these much-needed services in community mental health systems in a way that incorporates the unique needs of youth in foster care. Youth in foster care must be able to rely on the public mental health system to provide them the medically necessary mental health services to which they are entitled. Integrating evidence-based practices into existing child welfare and child mental health services will require new paradigms for implementation research including careful analyses of the factors within the policy environment and the agency context, which enhance or impede the incorporation of "what works" for vulnerable children and their families (Weisz & Simpson-Gray, 2008). These and some of the other challenges of each grouping of child, parent and family EBPs will be discussed briefly in the chapters mentioned above.

Recommendations from National Child Welfare and Child Mental Health Experts

In 2005, Casey commissioned several experts to conduct a review of the research literature on the intersection of child welfare and child mental health. As part of their report, these experts outlined several key recommendations that would move evidence-based practice forward:

- Examine the evidence base for interventions to treat common clinical conditions and complex conditions experienced by youth in foster care.
- Assess the availability of evidence-based interventions at the local level and nationally to assure relevance and explore adaptations needed for youth in foster care. This includes (1) tracking the progress of dissemination studies of mental health interventions in foster care; and (2) testing clinical interventions relevant to the needs of children in foster care to determine readiness for large-scale adoption.
- Learn from the challenges of intervention, adoption, and dissemination efforts prior to making policy decisions (e.g., stakeholder buy-in, the importance of policy and organizational factors, and factors contributing to sustainability).
- Identify promising evidence-based interventions to meet mental health needs at the local level, including additional interventions that should be implemented within child welfare, in contrast to those typically provided in the mental health system.
- For evidence-based interventions that require the expertise and resources of the mental health system, develop a partnership between mental health and child welfare with clearly explicated roles of each

system, preferably with joint child welfare and mental health and/or Medicaid funding (Landsverk, Burns, Stambaugh, & Rolls-Reutz, 2006).

Conclusion

Current Status: Significant Costs and Complex Family Situations Constitute Crucial System Challenges

Advances and challenges in child welfare. Child welfare policy is slowly being shaped by advances in research and practice in risk, resiliency, and protective factors and a developmental perspective. Much of this work has begun with a growing attention to the needs of infants. Landmark books like "Neurons to Neighborhoods" (Shonkoff & Phillips, 2000), rigorous research reviews (Heckman & Masterov, 2007), and special research summaries (Center on the Developing Child at Harvard University, 2007) reinforced the importance of responding to the needs of very young children as a high priority in CWS. Although these principles have not yet been given much credence in child welfare policy, recent changes to the Child Abuse Prevention and Treatment Act have given more impetus to providing early intervention services to CWS-involved young children. A mechanism for carrying this work forward needs to be developed—perhaps linked to existing laws like CAPTA or Promoting Safe and Stable Families or the Abandoned Infants Assistance Act. Policy that addresses the needs of infants as a special population can be inspired by the remarkable series of state and federal legislative initiatives on independent living that have been generated since 2001 on behalf of adolescents ready to leave foster care.

Other advances in the response to child abuse and neglect have emphasized, in a modest way, how children with varied psychological makeup and differing amounts of social supports respond differently to various healing approaches (Kendall-Tackett & Giacomoni, 2003). Trauma-focused interventions have now been developed for children who have been sexually abused (Cohen, Mannarino, Zhitova, & Capone, 2003) and physically abused (Kolko & Swenson, 2005), respectively. In a broader way, the development of "alternative" or "differential" or "multiple" response systems are now allowing agencies to diversify the way that families are engaged by CWS, with many families no longer experiencing a forensic style of interviewing and data collection in order to establish whether victimization occurred and, instead, are being served voluntarily.

Over the past five decades, research studies (e.g., Fanshel & Shinn, 1978), ability to mine large state child welfare data sets to look at permanency outcomes (Barth, Courtney, Berrick, & Albert, 1994; Wulczyn, et al., 2005), program scandals (e.g., Barth, et al., 1994; Wooden, 1976), class action lawsuits regarding unmet mental health needs, multiple placements or other problems (National Center for Youth Law, 2007), surveys of former foster youth (Cook, 1994; Courtney, et al., 2007; Pecora, et al., 2006), studies of service outcomes (Jaudes, Bilaver, Goerge, Masterson, & Catania, 2004) and effective advocacy by adoptive parents (Project Craft) (Lauffer & Carlson, 1979) and others have contributed to a wide range of policy reforms. A few examples are listed below:

- Focused family-centered services to strengthen parenting;
- Child-centered early intervention and remedial services for children with substantiated abuse, based on increased understanding of importance of early brain and social development;
- Attempts to allow access to substance abuse treatment services as soon as parents go to court and to make the hours and local accessible as part of a "one-stop shopping" approach (Choi & Ryan, 2007);
- Linkages across service delivery systems such as mental health, education and juvenile justice;
- Use of least restrictive placement environments that facilitated the closure of some residential institutions; and
- Permanency planning for children to secure a stable family if their birth-parents are unable to care for them within a reasonable period of time.

Finance issues. The child welfare system is financed by a patchwork of federal, state, and local government budgets that total approximately $25.7 billion per year. In addition, private child welfare agencies draw on fund raising and endowments to provide substantial resources beyond what they receive from government funds (DeVoight, Allen, & Geen, 2008). At the same time, recent federal legislation (i.e., ASFA) has eroded states' abilities to draw down federal funds, with an increasing burden of child welfare funding shifting to the states (National Conference of State Legislators, 2006).

The majority of the funds paid for the provision of out-of-home care for children supervised in some way by public child welfare agencies. The amount spent on placement-oriented services—as compared to in-home services—is at least five times greater (Pew Foundation, 2008). This is, in great part, because the federal government will match expenditures for eligible children in out-of-home care—regardless of the cost of that care—but does not do the same for children who continue to live with their parents.

Children who are receiving ongoing child welfare services are more likely than the general population to be younger than six and older than fifteen; to experience high levels of health, mental health, and educational problems; and to have parents who also experience high levels of involvement with substance abuse, mental illness, and/or corrections (Berrick, et al., 1998; NSCAW, 2005). Consequently, child welfare agencies need a readily available array of supplemental services, well-trained and supervised staff members, and low staff turnover to be effective.

Even with this level of funding, the U.S. Government Accountability Office (2004), the Pew Commission (2004), and others have documented that the child welfare service programs are in crisis, that workers have excessive caseloads, and that poor salaries and working conditions lead to high staff turnover and uneven job performance. State-by-state and county-by-county analyses reveal a huge variation in placement rates, length of stay in foster care, and other key indicators (United States General Accounting Office, 2004; Wulczyn, Chen, & Hislop, 2007), which indicates that there are cities, counties, or other areas that are experiencing good to excellent system performance in key areas. So, good service delivery systems succeed despite (and in some cases *because of*) local community conditions.

We have listed what we view as some of the most crucial challenges in Table 1.3. The field is currently addressing some of these "child welfare challenges" successfully in some communities. For example, we have new evidence that foster care length of stay in many states is decreasing and the number of children in foster care has dropped, nationally, from a high of 567,000 to 496,000 in 2007 (AFCARS: http://www.acf.hhs.gov/programs/cb/stats_research/afcars/trends. htm, retrieved April 13, 2009). The field has developed more options for children (e.g., kinship care, treatment foster care, wrap around services, family-based support services, subsidized guardianship, and shared family care). Independent living programs are better funded than ever before and new states (e.g., Iowa) are now extending care from age eighteen to twenty-one. In addition, adoptions with public CWS have increased to a new high of 51,000 in 2006. Research (while still in need of improvement) is the most robust it has ever been and finally includes data collection that transcends electronic and paper case record reviews to obtain the views of parents and youth who have received child welfare services (Barth, et al., 2002). Federal Title IV-E programs are providing stipends to recruit and retain new workers and for staff to return to school for child welfare-focused graduate education to help professionalize the field.

Practice transformations. The field of child welfare has undergone continuous transformation in the past twenty years—a process that has reaffirmed the importance of strengthening families and providing services in the "least restrictive environment." The field, more than ever, struggles to fulfill its tripartite mandates: to protect the child while preserving the family and promoting the future well-being of children whenever possible. Thus, staff members are attempting to build upon family strengths and resources rather than focusing exclusively on individual deficits. Yet, helping families to provide adequate care for their children has been made more difficult because of continuing high rates of poverty, substance abuse, parental incarceration, parent mental health problems, and a lack of basic supports such as housing, medical care, and mental health services. When the provision of these and other services is insufficient and children must be placed, a growing emphasis has been to place the children with relatives, kinship members, or in a foster home arrangement as geographically near the family as possible to facilitate contact between the children and their families.

While child welfare agencies in some parts of the country continue to suffer from inconsistent political and child welfare program leadership and underfunding, there is also a growing realization that "business as usual" in many areas of child welfare is not adequate for strengthening families and protecting children. Consequently, a number of service reforms are being implemented.

Innovative service delivery models. The use of more community-based and neighborhood-based programs, school-based services, wraparound services, youth employment programs, certain managed-care techniques, and a variety of community-based initiatives is broadening the mix of service options. As important, these innovations are enabling child-welfare agencies to become more

Table 1.3
The Top Ten Child Welfare Challenges

1. Ensuring that child welfare services work collaboratively with community resources and allied agencies such mental health, employment, housing, public assistance, and education to strengthen families that without special supports would otherwise need child welfare services.

2. Ensuring that children do not become involved with child welfare services when income assistance, job training, and other preventive or remedial social service programs could have prevented caregiver abuse and neglect.

3. Ensuring that children and families receive services that result in high levels of child safety and child well being.

4. Ensuring that the safety needs of children and the rights and responsibilities of parents to care for their own children are balanced so that children are not removed unnecessarily from their parent(s) care when the children have been abused or neglected.

5. Ensuring that families of children placed in foster care are given the opportunity to experience timely and effective family reunification services so they do not remain in care an undue time nor return home prematurely.

6. Ensuring that children placed into foster care who cannot otherwise go home are able to develop a life-long connection to a caring adult, including adoption.

7. Ensuring that services are financed and organized so that higher-cost programs provide more benefit to children than lower cost programs and are focused on the children most in need of them.

8. Ensuring that child welfare services are delivered fairly and not based on the race, ethnicity, geographical location, or sexual orientation of the child or family.

9. Ensuring that child welfare services experience continuous improvement as a result of routine monitoring of the delivery of the services and the outcomes.

10. Ensuring that child welfare services allow scrutiny by researchers and the media in ways that maximize public understanding but minimize threats to the confidentiality of clients.

integrated into the community and better positioned to call upon the economic development, educational, mental health, housing, vocational education, and other community resources for assistance in achieving the shared outcomes they have for children and parents. Strides are also being made in developing new cost-effective treatment strategies.

System of care approaches. Arising from innovations in mental health services, Systems of Care approaches seek to operationalize a philosophy about the way in which services should be organized for children and their families, with three core values: (1) child and family-centered, (2) community-based, and (3) culturally competent. These service delivery systems, by implementing these core values, are attempting to reduce barriers to service, more extensively involve parents and children, and increase the coordination of services. More recently, these approaches are being reformulated to include better integration with child welfare services (Stroul, 2002; Stroul & Friedman, 1996).

Partnerships with public health and substance abuse treatment. A number of "home visiting" models of child abuse prevention and family support are being pilot-tested using public health nurses, social workers and/or other types of staffing designs (e.g., Marcenko & Staerkel, 2006; Olds & Kitzman, 1995). These programs hold promise of more extensive partnerships between child welfare and public health agencies, as well as the potential to strengthen universal and selective preventive services in non-stigmatizing ways (see Chapter 7).

Similarly, because of the association between substance abuse involved families and child placement, the need for prevention and treatment programs and partnerships between child welfare, drug court, early childhood, education, mental health, primary health care, and substance abuse treatment facilities are crucial (see, for example, Barth, Gibbons, & Guo, 2006; Office of Early Childhood, Substance Abuse and Mental Health Administration, 1998; Young & Gardner, 2002). Some discussion has begun about better integrating TANF and child welfare agencies, especially since the shrinkage of the TANF caseload by 60 percent in the first six years and since the rising awareness that such a high proportion of TANF clients are involved, or will be involved with CWS (e.g., see the *Wisconsin Works* reports).

Increased accountability. CWS is trying to achieve new levels of accountability with respect to service delivery process and outcomes. Administrators and practitioners are reexamining and then refining their intervention models to better achieve the short-term and intermediate results for which they should be held accountable. Federal and state child and family service reviews are capturing qualitative and quantitative indicators of service delivery and systemic outcomes. Funders such as the United Way, state and county governments are reinforcing this approach through a focus on achieving key results and performance-based contracts, or performance bonuses (See, for example, Center for the Study of Social Policy, 1994; Friedman, 1997; Wulczyn, Zeidman, & Svirsky, 1997).

Restructured funding mechanisms. The field has been hampered by federal and state funding policies that have rewarded the wrong program emphases such as completing child abuse investigations (rather than preventing the need for new ones) and keeping children in foster care (instead of securing a more permanent home for them). So agencies are now striving to align funding priorities and performance incentive mechanisms to support preventive services and more program flexibility. Witness the more recent Title IV-E waivers for pilot programs and recent proposals to reform federal legislation related to performance measurement, funding methods, and performance incentives (e.g., American Public Human Services Association, 2005; Pew Commission on Children in Foster Care, 2004). (See Table 1.4 for a newspaper editorial about this issue.) Several cities or states (NYC, OH, TN) have now ended funding of agencies based on a per diem system because that approach rewards agencies that keep children in care longer and does not give them any incentive to reduce lengths of stay. Instead, the approach involves risk-adjusting the problems that children face in leaving care and, then, rewarding agencies that can provide a planned exit from care that is earlier than predicted from the models of what is the expected duration.

Racial disproportionality is beginning to be addressed. Program leaders in a number of states and counties have recognized the need to expeditiously move children of all races and ages to a more permanent family situation (Berrick, et al., 1998; Center for the Study of Social Policy, 2006). In contrast, what has emerged more slowly is the realization that major forms of racial disproportionality exist in terms of services provision and achievement of permanency outcomes (Chibnall, et al., 2003; Hill, 2006; Hines, Lemon, Wyatt, & Merdinger, 2004). This disproportionality may closely reflect the disproportionately greater needs of African American children—as reflected by higher infant mortality and child homicide rates and more arrest and incarceration of their parents—and may reflect ways that agencies have failed to adequately respond to opportunities to help African American families. Almost certainly all of the disproportionality that exists is not simply a matter of need—but separating the amount of disproportionality attributable to the need and that portion attributable to bias is difficult to accomplish (Barth, 2005; Kohl, 2007).

Future Directions

The challenges discussed above paint a vivid picture of where child welfare services need to be improved in the years ahead, building on the accomplishments that have been made in recent years. This chapter is intended to estab-

Table 1.4
Newspaper Editorial Support for Federal Funding Reforms

Congress Needs to Change How Federal Foster-Care Funds Provided

It's been three years since the Pew Commission on Children in Foster Care came out with its recommendations on helping provide permanent families for kids whose lives have been filled with trauma and upheaval. The report also advocated for greater help and support for those children in foster care who reach age 18 and suddenly find themselves on their own with nowhere to turn.

This week on Capitol Hill, some of those young people testified about their lives going from one foster home to another, and their failure to find a permanent family. Others told of the fears they faced when they were no longer eligible for foster care and had to forge their own lives with little guidance and few resources.

Their testimony was part of a push by the Pew Commission and the North American Council on Adoptable Children to give states more flexibility in using federal funds for the best interest of the children involved. Too often, states don't get federal child welfare money until after a child is taken away from his or her family and put into state custody. That gives states a financial incentive to take children out of their homes, rather than working with parents to resolve issues and keep families together.

In cases where parents should not regain custody of their children, sometimes reliable relatives are able to take custody instead of the children being placed in foster care. Policies need to be shaped to encourage, rather than discourage, such arrangements.

With more than a half-million U.S. children in foster care—twice as many as 20 years ago—the Pew Commission was established to study ways to help improve their lives. Members sought ways restructure funding to help keep families intact or place children in permanent families sooner, instead of an ongoing series of foster homes.

At the time they issued their report in 2004, Pew Commission members acknowledged that the foster care system had helped remove many children from unsafe, unhealthy family environments, but it needed to do a better job of moving them into permanent homes.

In addition to placing children with permanent families, Congress also is being lobbied to increase funding for medical and therapeutic help for children adopted out of foster care, and to better prepare foster children who "age out" of the system and are left basically on their own at age 18.

We supported implementation of many of the commission's recommendations when they were issued three years. The need has not subsided since then. Reforms are needed urgently. While three years may not seem like a long time in the federal bureaucracy, we need to remember that for every year that goes by, another 24,000 children "graduate" from the foster care system and must face life by themselves. They need more support if they are to become successful adults.

We hope Congress agrees and acts soon.

Source: Battle Creek Enquirer (Michigan), March 14, 2007.
BYLINE: The Enquirer SECTION: OPINION; Pg. 6A.

lish a foundation for the chapters that follow. The emphasis upon achieving a number of key outcomes as the most important criterion upon which to judge the effectiveness of child welfare agencies is important for practice as well as policy. Key laws and other policies that shape child welfare services are discussed in Chapter 2.

Notes

1. These data are from the federal Adoption and Foster Care Analysis and Reporting System (AFCARS)—which used data from forty-five states and other jurisdictions, including Washington, DC and Puerto Rico, to derive these estimates. For total children served in 2007, see: http://www.acf.hhs.gov/programs/cb/stats_research/ afcars/trends.htm Note that AFCARS data are periodically updated, therefore, the data cited may not match the data on the current website
2. Adapted from Mark Hardin, Establishing a Core of Services for Families Subject to State Intervention, pp.11-12 (ABA, 1992).

For Further Information

Barth, R.P., Gibbons, C., & Guo, S. (2006). Substance abuse treatment and the recurrence of maltreatment among caregivers with children living at home: A propensity score analysis. *Journal of Substance Abuse Treatment, 30*(2), 93-104. This study showed that clients who received substance abuse treatment were nearly twice as likely to have another child abuse report within eighteen months. It explored reasons why participation in substance abuse treatment may result in greater involvement with CWS.

Conners, N.A., Bradley, R.H., Mansell, L.W., Liu, J.Y., Roberts, T.J., Burgdorf, K., et al. (2004). Children of mothers with serious substance abuse problems: An accumulation of risks. *American Journal of Drug and Alcohol Abuse, 30*(1), 85-100. Findings from this study suggest that children whose mothers abuse alcohol or other drugs confront a high level of risk and are at increased vulnerability for physical, academic, and social-emotional problems.

Center on the Developing Child at Harvard University (2007). *A Science-Based Framework for Early Childhood Policy: Using Evidence to Improve Outcomes in Learning, Behavior, and Health for Vulnerable Children.* http://www.developingchild.harvard. edu
Compelling summary of the benefits of early childhood supports.

Friedman, M. (1997). *A guide to developing and using performance measures in results-based budgeting.* Washington, D.C.: The Finance Project. Presents a conceptual framework for how to measure agency performance that emphasizes quality and results.

Wulczyn, F., Barth, R.P., Yuan, Y.Y., Jones-Harden, B. & Landsverk, J. (2005). *Beyond common sense: Child welfare, child well-being, and the evidence for policy reform.* New Brunswick, NJ: Transaction. Uses key child welfare data to outline promising policy directions.

Wulczyn, F.H. & Chen, l. (2007). *Foster Care Dynamics 2000-2005: A Report from the Multistate Foster Care Data Archive.* Chicago: University of Chicago, Chapin Hall Center for Children. Updated report of foster care placement trends using a large number of states.

2

Key Child Welfare Legislation and Other Policies

Major National Legislation that has Helped Shape Child Welfare Services

Chapter Overview

Child welfare services are, fundamentally, local services provided in with substantial variations in local district offices, county agencies, and states. States make policies about such fundamental issues as what is reportable for child abuse and neglect, what timeframes are required for investigation, and how much foster, adoptive, and group home providers will be reimbursed for their care. (The *Child Welfare Information Gateway* has a remarkable compendium of state child welfare policies on more than 30 topics, http://www.childwelfare. gov/systemwide/laws_policies/state/retrieved, April 14, 2008). States and localities also provide the vast majority of the funding for investigation and in home services as well as, increasingly, placements into out of home care. Overall states and localities provide a little over 50 percent of child welfare funding (DeVoight, Allen, & Geen, 2008) and the federal government provides much of the rest (private donors, foundations, and non-profit organizations also make a significant investment in child welfare services).

Using this fiscal leverage, federal policies set broad parameters around the state and local actions. Key federal policies that are most related to child welfare are summarized in the Appendix. This summary table covers legislation including adoption, child protection, income support, education, early intervention, family support foster care. The major federal child welfare policies are discussed in chronological order of first passage. Several of these policies have been amended many times—sometimes under new titles (e.g., there have been two predecessors of the Chafee Independent Living Act) but sometimes under the original title (as with the Child Abuse Prevention and Treatment Act).[1] Although we do not discuss Medicaid, TANF, or Title XX in this chapter we recognize that these federal policies have substantial impact on child welfare involvement and may provide far more support for in-home services than is provided by the legislation discussed below.

State and federal expenditures on child welfare services are substantial and continue to grow. In 2006, states spent $12.4 billion in federal dollars, $10.7 billion in state dollars, and $2.6 billion in local dollars. Between 2004 and 2006, federal spending increased by 3 percent, state spending by 14 percent, and local spending remained virtually unchanged. The Social Services Block Grant (SSBG) (including Temporary Assistance for Needy Families (TANF) funds transferred to SSBG) and Medicaid experienced the largest increases between 2004 and 2006 (16 percent and 19 precent, respectively), while modest increases occurred with Title IV-B (1 percent) and Title IVE (2 percent) (DeVoight, Allen, & Geen, 2008, pp. iv-v). These expenditures are complemented by county expenditures as well as those of non-profit agencies (e.g., local child abuse prevention programs) that raise substantial amounts of support from private citizens.

Child Abuse Prevention and Treatment Act of 1974 (P.L. 93-247)

This legislation was originally passed in response to public concern about the abuse of children—concern that was stimulated, in part, by the publicizing of "battered child syndrome" in the early 1960s based on the work of pediatric radiologists (see Chapter 5 in this text; Anderson, 1989). The purpose of the Act was to provide financial assistance for demonstration programs for the prevention, identification, and treatment of child abuse and neglect, and to establish a National Center on Child Abuse and Neglect (American Civil Liberties Union, 1977; Child Abuse Prevention and Treatment Act Report, as cited in Light, 1973, p. 238; Stein, 1984).

Not only did the Act provide a means of funding more programs in this area, it mandated that states must provide for the reporting of known or suspected instances of child abuse and neglect. CAPTA has never provided much funding for CWS but may have had the largest impact of any piece of child welfare legislation by greatly enlarging the pool of children coming to the attention of public authorities as potentially in need of care and protection, without providing dependable resources or guidance necessary to enable states to deal more effectively with this population (McGowan, 1990; Pew Foundation, 2008; Schorr & Marchand, 2007).

Thus, the implementation of the Child Abuse Prevention and Treatment Act has been a great stimulus to the development of child welfare services across the nation but has left the development of a practice framework and resources for investigation and in-home services largely to the states and localities. Some additional specificity has been added to the requirements of CAPTA in recent years. These provisions are most noteworthy. As of 2001, states must, now, adopt policies and procedures to address the needs of infants identified as being affected by illegal substance abuse or withdrawal symptoms resulting from prenatal drug exposure (alcohol exposure is not covered). More recent amendments now require that a "plan of safe care" be developed for infants affected by illegal substance abuse although the statute does not specify which agency or entity must develop this plan. As of 2004, states must now refer children younger than three who have been substantiated for abuse or neglect to IDEA Part C services so that they may receive a developmental assessment.

The Indian Child Welfare Act of 1978 (P.L. 95-608)

Traditional beliefs, customs, and values about child rearing and protection provided the infrastructure of traditional American Indian/Alaska Native child welfare. Through community values, shared responsibility for children, peer pressure, and other cultural practices enforced by extended families, a natural child welfare system existed. Unfortunately, this natural system of protection for children has been broken and distorted by historical events. Since the earliest contact by non-Indians, most attempts to "civilize" American Indian and Alaska Native people focused on children. Ongoing efforts were made to separate children from their families as a way to assimilate and acculturate Native people. For example, both the government and private institutions developed military-like boarding schools for American Indian/Alaska Native children where generations of children were reared. By 1900, tribes had been effectively stripped of their natural systems of child rearing and protection. Other federal policies resulted in the transition of thousands of American Indian/Alaska Natives away from reservations to urban areas. During the 1950s and early 1960s the practice of placing Native children with non-Indian adoptive families became widespread. At that time, the general belief was that assimilation was the only realistic alternative for American Indian/Alaska Native people because tribes were unable to protect their own children (see for example, Casey Family Programs, 2007; Cross, 2006; Cross, Earle, & Simmons, 2000; Halverson, Puig, & Byers, 2002).

In 1978 Congress enacted the Indian Child Welfare Act (ICWA), finding that "there is no resource more vital to the continued existence and integrity of the Indian Tribe than their children" and "an alarmingly high percentage of Indian families are broken up by the removal, often unwarranted, of their children...by non-tribal public and private agencies." The act creates procedural safeguards in matters pertaining to the custody and placement of Indian children. It was an important first step in strengthening federal and state policy toward Indian families. Briefly stated, the major provisions of the act are as follows:

Tribes are given exclusive jurisdiction over reservation Indian children. An exception is made for reservations in those states which have assumed jurisdiction over reservations under the authority of P.L. 83-280 (1953). Tribes in such states can petition the secretary of the interior to reassume their jurisdiction over child welfare matters. According to the Act, "full faith and credit" must be given to the judgments of tribal courts over child welfare cases.[2]

State jurisdiction over child custody hearings can be transferred to the tribe. Cases of Indian children not residing or domiciled on the reservation can be transferred to the tribal court at the request of the tribe, parents, or Indian custodian unless either of these parties objects or the court finds "good cause" to the contrary.

Both tribes and parents of Indian custodians have the right to be notified of and to intervene in state court proceedings. The party seeking custody of an Indian child is required to notify the parents and the tribe. All tribes that might be the Indian child's tribe should be notified. If either of these parties cannot be located, the secretary of the interior also must be notified. Emergency removals can be made without notification, but subsequent hearings must follow notification procedures.

Higher standards of evidence are applied to state custody proceedings involving Indian children. A foster care placement may be ordered only if it is proved by "clear and convincing" evidence, including the testimony of a qualified expert witness, that continued custody by the parent or custodian is likely to result in serious emotional or physical damage to the child. Termination of parental rights can only be ordered if evidence to this effect is "beyond a reasonable doubt," which is a more stringent level of evidence. Expert testimony is required here as well. In both cases, it must be shown that active efforts have been made to prevent family breakup. The Act also authorizes the secretary to pay for legal services to parents if not provided by the state.

The Act specifies placement preferences for states in placing Indian children in foster and adoptive homes. First preference is to be given the child's extended family, then to foster homes licensed or approved by the tribe, then to other Indian foster homes or appropriate Indian institutions. Tribal governments may legislate their own preferences and state courts ordinarily must follow them. Standards for the selection of Indian homes are to be the prevailing social and cultural standards of the Indian community.

Voluntary placements of Indian children for foster care or adoption must be well informed and are revocable in certain cases. Any parent of an Indian child must execute consent in writing before a judge who certifies that the consent was explained in a language that the parent understood. Consent cannot be given prior to ten days after the birth of a child. The parent may withdraw consent to a foster care placement at any time. He or she may withdraw consent to adoption up until the entry of the final decree of termination or adoption. If the parent can show that consent was obtained under duress, an adoption may be overturned up to two years after finalization.

Grants to Indian tribes and organizations to establish Indian child and family services are authorized. Many considered this the most important section of the Act, providing some mechanism for Indian-delivered preventive services.

Unfortunately, to date insufficient funds have been allocated to implement this section. Placements can be overturned if it can be shown that the aAct was not followed with respect to notification, rights to intervention and transfer, counsel for parents, standards of evidence and testimony, and consent procedures.

Those involved in the implementation of the Act have noted numerous inconsistencies in language and confusion in interpretation in several key areas, in major part stemming from the problems encountered in trying to pass the legislation (Gross, 1989). Among these inconsistencies are definition of "Indian child," especially Alaskan Native children, lack of clarity over notification procedures, and definitions of "expert witness" and "good cause." Although guidelines for state courts were published in the Federal Register, each state has developed court rules for its judges. Judges and child welfare agencies are responsible for following the act in the face of difficulties in interpretation and confusion over procedure. They must determine tribal affiliations in order to notify parents and tribes and be fully aware of court and service requirements. If the Act is not followed, it will be Indian children who suffer from the disruption of homes and placements.

While the Indian Child Welfare Act has improved services to many Native American families, serious problems remain. For example, the Act only applies to tribes recognized by the U.S. Bureau of Indian Affairs (National Center for Children in Poverty, 2005). Furthermore, in one study in four states, proactive efforts were documented in only 41 percent of the records of cases under state jurisdiction. A case record review in the four states revealed that 53 percent of the Native American children were placed in non-Indian homes (Plantz, Hubbell, Barrett, & Dobrec, 1989, p. 25):

> Factors that respondents believe deter or undermine implementation of the ICWA include unfamiliarity with or resistance to the Act; lack of public agency experience in working with tribes; staff turnover; lack of funding; concern about tribal accountability for providing services and caring for children; and absence of tribal courts with the authority to assume jurisdiction over proceedings involving tribe members. (p. 26)

What is helping to improve implementation of the law is the passage of more specific state, Indian child welfare laws that promote specific reforms and compliance mechanisms by state and local agencies. Although there is very little research on the implementation of ICWA and its influence on children, Hand (2006) has argued that growing employment and retention of more Native American staff appears to be improving services in some communities, along with more culturally appropriate practice frameworks and the training of existing staff members in the provisions of the federal and state laws. In other areas, helpful strategies include "state/tribal agreements that provide formal support for substitute care placements and for child welfare services; training and technical assistance to help develop tribal welfare services" (Plantz, et al.,

1989, p. 26). A recent major improvement was included in P.L. 110-351 which ensures that Indian tribes have direct access to IV-E funded programs, including the foster care and adoption program as well as the newly proposed Child and Family Services Program, Subsidized Guardianship Program, and Permanency Incentive Program. The bill also provides financial resources directly to Indian tribes to provide technical assistance and start up costs associated with implementation.

The Adoption Assistance and Child Welfare Act and the Adoption and Safe Families Act

Public Law 96-272, the Adoption Assistance and Child Welfare Act (AACWA) and its successor, the Adoption and Safe Families Act (ASFA) of 1997 are in many ways the most important pieces of child welfare legislation in the last twenty years. The Act recognized the major problems in the child welfare, service delivery system and attempts to promote a number of empirically validated practice approaches and service delivery guidelines. The Act amended Title IV-A and Title IV-B of the Social Security Act and created a new act, Title IV-E. Thus, P.L. 96-272 essentially established a two-tier funding framework, with additional procedural and practice requirements for higher levels of funding.

Through the funding regulations, the Act discouraged state use of long term custodial foster care. Instead, funding prompted pre-placement preventive services for families in crisis and permanency planning for children unable to remain with their own families. A new adoption subsidy program was created as well. Finally, the Act required the maintenance or institution of a number of "best practice" requirements by state child welfare programs.

The AACWA (P.L. 96-272) created Title IVE and, thereby, set up a two-tier system for funding child welfare services. Although there were some limitations on the ability of states to draw down federal foster care payments to match the payments they provided for each child who spent a day in foster care or group care, the creation of Title IVE provided a substantial incentive to states to use foster care.[3] Technically, Title IV-E funds can be transferred to the Title IV-B funding allocation, which allows more flexible use of funds not based on child-specific funding (this has, however, rarely been done).

During the first decade of AACWA the proportion of federal dollars spent on foster care, in contrast to in home care, grew from 2 to 1 in 1981 to 8 to 1 in 1992 (U.S. GAO, 1993). Thus much more funding was available after children were removed from homes than it was for helping families before removal or after children were returned home. In order to receive Title IVE monies, states had to institute or document a number of program or procedural reforms. Some of these reforms and other significant aspects of the act are presented below. To receive maximum federal financial participation in their child welfare programs, states were required to implement or use the following programs or procedural reforms:

- state inventory of children in care (requires a one-time listing of all children who have been in foster care for six months or more by case number, date of birth, date of initial and current placement, date of last administrative or judicial review, and other information);
- statewide information system (provides data so that the legal status, demographic characteristics, location, and goals for placement of every child currently receiving foster care services or who has been in foster care within the preceding twelve months are known);
- pre-placement preventive services (includes twenty-four-hour emergency caretaker and homemaker services, day care, crisis counseling, individual and family counseling, emergency shelters, access to emergency financial assistance, and temporary child care); agencies must demonstrate they have provided "reasonable efforts" in terms of their services to prevent child placement (this requirement was limited under ASFA);
- reunification or permanent planning services (a core of reunification services must be provided such as day care, homemaker or caretaker services, and family and individual counseling for parents and children; other services appropriate for reunification may also be provided such as respite care and parent education; further services to facilitate adoption or legal guardianship are included such as legal, adoptive services, staff training, and adoption follow-up);
- detailed case plan (must incorporate goals for reunification or other permanent placement, documentation of caseworker's actions);
- periodic case review (must occur and includes judicial or administrative review every six months and dispositional hearing by a court or court-appointed administrative body within eighteen months of the child's placement);
- standards for care (placement must be in the least restrictive setting available, with close proximity to parents and with relatives where possible);
- procedural safeguards regarding removal and placement agreements parents and child (if appropriate age and circumstance) must participate in the development and approval of case plans; child removal without judicial determination is only allowed in emergency situations; there must be an availability of fair hearings for child, parent, or foster parent who feel they have been aggrieved by a child welfare agency;
- standards for payment (federal payments are allowed for group care non-detention services where such facilities do not exceed a certain number in a state);
- Indian child welfare (tribes can be reimbursed directly for Title IV-B child welfare services);
- voluntary placement guidelines (federal reimbursement is available for the first 180 days if state meets above requirements);

- adoption subsidies for children with special needs (adoption subsidies for special-needs or low-income children).

One of the most important innovations in AACWA is making federal funds available for subsidized adoption for children who are classified as having special needs and who come from families that are income eligible. Children with special needs or those described as hard to place are generally children available for adoption who are over twelve years of age, are handicapped, belong to a minority group, or are part of a sibling group to be placed together. In order for children to receive subsidized adoption funds, they must be eligible for AFDC (a requirement which continued even after AFDC was replaced by TANF), or SSI. (The Fostering Connections to Success and Increasing Adoptions Act of 2008 was signed into law by President Bush [P.L. 110-351] in the last days of his administration and "de-links" a child's eligibility for federal adoption assistance payments from the AFDC income requirements and all other income eligibility requirements for children adopted from foster care.) Finally, a key provision of the Act stipulated that adoptive families do not have to pass a "means test" in order to receive subsidized adoption payments—this was to insure that families were not unduly financially disadvantaged by adopting children.

In summary, the Adoption Assistance and Child Welfare Act of 1980 (PL 96-272) was a landmark piece of legislation that provided a federal policy framework and set of fiscal incentives that were consistent with what current research then showed to be "best practice" standards and procedures. This law set several cornerstones upon which our current law rests.

In 1997, Congress passed the Adoption and Safe Families Act (ASFA). Some view this as revolutionary child welfare policy and others view it as largely tweaking the provisions of AACWA. In either case, ASFA's impact on child welfare service processes and outcomes will be expressed through its main tenets: (1) emphasizing that ensuring children's safety is the first priority of the law; (2) shortening the time to the termination of parental rights (TPR) hearing; (3) identifying instances where reunification efforts do not have to be made for families; (4) requiring termination of parental rights even when an adoption resource is not available; (5) requiring states to seek termination of parental rights when children have been in out of home care for fifteen of the previous twenty-two months; (6) mandating that states do concurrent planning, rather than planning only for reunification and then seek alternatives when such plans fail or are deemed inappropriate; and (7) directing agencies to adopt children across geographic boundaries.

Although ASFA prominently features "safety" in its title and language, relatively few provisions directly address safety. The main functional provision related to safety was that reasonable efforts are not required in all circumstances and that states must specify such reasonable efforts and reunification exceptions in their laws. Other more modest provisions intended to heighten safety require

criminal record checks for substitute caregivers and require the federal government to develop a system of evaluating the performance of states in providing
for the safety of the children they serve.

The greatest concern was focused on reducing "foster care drift" (Maas &
Engler, 1959) and expediting adoption. The re-emergence of concern about
placement instability was spurred by research showing that even infants were
experiencing multiple placements—30 percent had four or more placements—
during the first six years of life (Berrick, et al., 1998) Such research belied the
notion that young children who remained in long-term foster care experienced
a life that was stable or permanent (Digre, 1996). A stanchion of ASFA became
"Foster care is a temporary setting and not a place for children to grow up"
(Administration for Children and Families, 1998, p. 2).

The alternative to placement instability that was embraced by the ASFA
drafters was adoption. Many adoption provisions arose from ASFA. These provisions made the 1990s the decade of adoption by virtue of becoming the fourth
major adoption law or decree (accompanying the *MultiEthnic Placement Act*,
the *Interethnic Adoption Provisions*, and *President Clinton's Adoption 2002*,
which established adoption performance bonuses for states with the intention
of doubling adoptions within five years). There were also many state adoption
initiatives (e.g., New York's *Adoption 6000*) arising prior to the passage of
ASFA. In short, the revving of adoption activity preceded ASFA but has been
sustained by it.

ASFA was predicted, by some, to direct child welfare down the wrong path.
The predictions of ASFA's imminent harms were strident and abundant. ASFA
drew sharp criticism because of the belief that its passage tipped the scales from
a commitment to family reunification to a preference for adoption. One of the
key concerns was that ASFA rewards states for increasing adoptions, via the
reauthorization of the adoption bonus program started under Clinton's Adoption
2002 initiative, not reunification (Moye & Rinker, 2002). Stein (2003) argued
that this was a blatant attack against the poor and their lifestyles, part of a broader
pattern of social engineering, in an attempt to move children from primarily
one-parent households to two-parent households. Another major consternation
about ASFA—among the most widely and intensely cited—is that twelve months
is not long enough for effective services for families (Stein, 2003). In particular,
critics argues that substance abuse is the predominant reason for children's
placement into out of home care and that substance abuse treatment typically
needs to be lengthy so that addicted parents have a chance to overcome relapse
and achieve sobriety before a decision is made about their ultimate parental
fitness (Semidei, Radel, & Nolan, 2001). With such short timelines, there was
widespread concern that they are likely to lose their children permanently, even
when they are trying to recover (Moye & Rinker, 2002)

The nearly concurrent end of the AFDC entitlement and evolution of a time-
limited welfare program (i.e., TANF) caused grave concern that child welfare

would become even more dominated by families in poverty. Scholars had long argued that children often entered out of home care for "reasons of poverty alone," which led to several dire predictions that TANF would swell the child welfare services caseload (e.g., Courtney, 1998). This was, again, viewed as an attack by policy makers on the poor, as poor parents are particularly unable to reestablish employment, housing, and stability within twelve months, so they lose custody of their children (Wilhelm & Creedy, 2002).

Because of the impact this law is having on the delivery of child welfare services, an abridged summary from the Child Welfare League of America (1997) is provided below. According to their analysis ASFA:

ASFA reauthorized, expanded, and renamed the Family Preservation and Support Services Program. The set-asides in Promoting Safe and Stable Families were maintained for the Court Improvement Program, evaluation, research, training, technical assistance, and Indian tribes. State plans were required to contain assurances that in administering and conducting service programs, the safety of the children served will be of paramount concern. ASFA further clarified that for the purposes of the maintenance of effort requirement in the program, "non-federal funds" may be defined as either state or state and local funds. This change was made retroactive to the enactment of the Family Preservation and Support Services Program (P.L. 103-66) on August 10, 1993.

In addition to the funds to prevent child abuse and neglect and to assist families in crisis, the program's funds specifically included time-limited reunification services such as counseling, substance abuse treatment services, mental health services, assistance for domestic violence, temporary childcare and crisis nurseries, and transportation to and from these services. Adoption promotion and support services were also included—these were defined as pre- and post-adoptive services and activities designed to expedite the adoption process and support families.

AFSA continued eligibility for the Federal Title IV-E Adoption Assistance Subsidy to children whose adoption is disrupted. Any child who was receiving a federal adoption subsidy on or after October 1, 1997, now remains eligible for the subsidy if the adoption is disrupted or if the adoptive parents die.

ASFA authorized adoption incentive payments for states. The Act authorized $20 million for each of FY 1999-2003 for payments to eligible states which exceeded the average number of adoptions the state completed during the FY 1995-1997 baseline years, or in FY 1999 and subsequent years, in which adoptions of foster children are higher than in any previous fiscal year after FY 1996. The amount of the bonus was set, at that time, as $4,000 for each foster child adopted and $6,000 for each adoption of a child with special needs previously in foster care. To be eligible to receive these payments for FY 2001 or FY 2002,

ASFA required states to provide health insurance coverage to any special needs child for whom there is an adoption assistance agreement between the state and the child's adoptive parents. These provisions have now been strengthened by P.L. 110-351 (Fostering Connections to Success and Increasing Adoptions Act) that extends the state incentives for an additional five years, updates to FY 2007 the adoption baseline above which incentive payments are made, doubles the incentive payments for adoptions of children with special needs and older children adoptions, and gives states 24 months to use the adoption incentive payments.

ASFA required states to document efforts to adopt. States are required to make reasonable efforts and document child specific efforts to place a child for adoption, with a relative or guardian, or in another planned permanent living arrangement when adoption is the goal. The law also clarified that reasonable efforts to place a child for adoption or with a legal guardian may be made concurrently with reasonable efforts to reunify a child with his or her family.

ASFA addresses geographic barriers to adoption. States are now required to assure that the state will develop plans for the effective use of cross-jurisdictional resources to facilitate timely permanent placements for children awaiting adoption. The state's Title IV-E foster care and adoption assistance funding is conditioned on the state not denying or delaying a child's adoptive placement, when an approved family is available outside of the jurisdiction with responsibility for the child. ASFA conditions federal funding upon the state granting opportunities for fair hearings for allegations of violations of the requirements. The U.S. General Accounting Office was required to study and report to Congress on how to improve procedures and policies to facilitate timely adoptions across state and county lines.

ASFA establishes new time line and conditions for filing termination of parental rights. Prior federal law did not require states to initiate termination of parental rights proceedings based on a child's length of stay in foster care or, even, have a presumption that this should be done. Under ASFA, states must file a petition to terminate parental rights and concurrently, identify, recruit, process, and approve a qualified adoptive family on behalf of any child, regardless of age, that has been in foster care for *fifteen out of the most recent twenty-two months.* Since ASFA, a child is considered to have entered foster care on the earlier of either the date of the first judicial finding of abuse or neglect, or sixty days after the child is removed from the home.

This new requirement applies to children entering foster care in the future and to children already in care. For children already in care, states are required to phase in the filing of termination petitions beginning with children for whom the permanency plan is adoption or who have been in care the longest. One-third must be filed within six months of the end of the state's first legislative session following enactment of this law, two-thirds within twelve months, and all of them within eighteen months. A state must also file such a petition if a court has determined that an infant has been abandoned (as defined in state law) or if a court has determined that a parent of a child has assaulted the child, or killed or assaulted another one of their children. Exceptions can be made to these requirements if: (1) at the state's option, a child is being cared for by a relative; (2) the state agency documents in the case plan which is available for court review, a compelling reason why filing is not in the best interest of the child; or (3) the state agency has not provided to the child's family, consistent with the time period in the case plan, the services deemed necessary to return the child to a safe home.

ASFA sets new time frame for permanency hearings. Former federal law required a dispositional hearing within eighteen months of a child's placement into out-of-home care. ASFA established a permanency planning hearing for children in care that occurs within twelve months of a child's entry into care. The hearing requires a determination of whether and when a child will be returned home, placed for adoption and a termination of parental rights petition will be filed, referred for legal guardianship, or another planned permanent living arrangement if the other options are not appropriate.

ASFA modified reasonable efforts provisions in P.L. 96-272. States continue to be required to make reasonable efforts to preserve and reunify families, for most children and families but ASFA includes the requirement that states make some exceptions and the allowance for states to add additional exceptions. In making decisions about the removal of a child from, and the child's return to, his or her home, the child's health and safety shall be the paramount concern. The *reasonable efforts requirement does not apply in cases in which a court has found that*:

- the parent has subjected the child to "aggravated circumstances" as defined in state law (including but not limited to abandonment, torture, chronic abuse, and sexual abuse);
- the parent has committed murder or voluntary manslaughter or aided or abetted, attempted, conspired or solicited to commit such a murder or manslaughter of another child of the parent;
- the parent has committed a felony assault that results in serious bodily injury to the child or another one of their children; or
- the parental rights of the parent to a sibling have been involuntarily terminated.

In these cases, states would *not* be required to make reasonable efforts to preserve or reunify the family but are required to hold a permanency hearing within thirty days and to make reasonable efforts to place the child for adoption, with a legal guardian, or in another permanent placement.

ASFA required states to check prospective foster and adoptive parents for criminal backgrounds. For the first time, under ASFA, states became required to provide procedures for criminal record checks for any prospective foster or adoptive parents, before the parents are approved for placement of a child eligible for federal subsidies. When a criminal record check reveals a felony conviction for child abuse or neglect, spousal abuse, another crime against a child (including child pornography), rape, sexual assault, or homicide, final approval of foster or adoptive parent status shall not be granted. In a case of a felony conviction for physical assault, battery, or a drug-related offense that was committed in the past five years, approval could not be granted. States were allowed to opt out of this provision either through a written notice from the Governor to the U.S. Department of Health and Human Services (DHHS), or through state law enacted by the state legislature.

ASFA required notice of court reviews and opportunity to be heard to foster parents, pre-adoptive parents, and relatives. Although this had long been considered best practice in many jurisdictions, ASFA mandated that a foster parent, any pre-adoptive parent or relative caring for a child must be given notice of, and an opportunity to be heard in, any review or hearing involving the child. This provision does not require that any foster or pre-adoptive parent or relative be made a party to such a review or hearing.

ASFA required assessment of state performance in protecting children. In what is proving to be a very influential provision of ASFA, DHHS was required to develop--in consultation with governors, state legislatures, state and local public officials, and child welfare advocates--a set of outcome measures to be used to assess the performance of states in operating child protection and child welfare programs to ensure the safety of children and a system for rating the performance of states with respect to the outcome measures. This process has now become well established and is embodied in the Child and Family Services Review program.

ASFA expanded child welfare demonstration waivers. The new law authorized DHHS to conduct up to ten demonstration projects per year from FY 1998 through 2002. The basic idea of the waivers is that some procedural safeguards can be waived as long as the overall effect is no greater expenditure of funds and no worse child welfare outcomes (the hope is for better outcomes, of course). Specific types of demonstrations have been attempted, and a substantial proportion completed. These efforts include projects designed to identify and address reasons for delay in adoptive placements for foster children; projects designed to address parental substance abuse problems that endanger children and result in placement of a child in foster care; and projects designed to address kinship care. Eight states (CA, DE, IL, IN, MD, NC, OH, OR) received approval for these waivers, some of them (CA and IL) for more than one waiver. The waiver in Illinois allowed the state to pay relatives who were providing guardianship a payment like the foster care or adoption subsidy was very successful and showed increases in permanency and savings estimated in the hundreds of millions of dollars (Testa, in press). This experiment was largely responsible for Section 101 in P.L. 110-351 that gives states the option to use federal Title IV-E funds for kinship guardianship payments for children cared for by relative foster parents who are committed to caring for these children permanently when they leave foster care. During the latter years of the Bush administration, no new waivers were granted because the Bush administration sought to encourage states to go farther than these targeted waivers and agree to block grant all of Title IVE and Title IVB. The future of the waivers is unclear at the time of writing.

ASFA Outcomes

After more than a decade of implementation the impact of ASFA can begin to be detected. Beem (2007) believes that the Adoption and Safe Families Act (AFSA) and the Personal Responsibility and Work Opportunity Reconciliation Act (PRWORA), taken together, represent a fundamental philosophical shift. Like PRWORA, ASFA establishes standards for personal behavior, attenuates rights claims because of these standards, and sets comparatively severe and time sensitive consequences if those standards are not met. Both acts thus reinforce the idea that there are minimum civic responsibilities that obtain for all Americans. But these policies also endorse the claim that government has some reciprocal burden to help make sure citizens can meet these responsibilities. In the current political landscape, the notion of reciprocity offers the best argument for advancing the cause of child welfare, and poor families generally.

Noonan & Burke (2005) studied which children are at greatest risk for the termination of parental rights and responsibilities using 2003 AFCARS foster care data from New Jersey. They found that timing of reunification and of terminating parental rights are very different. While the likelihood of reunification increases over time, the likelihood of terminating parental rights decreases over time.

Second, adoptability appears to factor into the parental rights termination decision. They found that the characteristics of the child are very influential in determining how much time a child will spend in care before the parental rights are terminated. More specifically, African American children, children of Hispanic decent, children who experience multiple placements and older children will spend more time in care until the termination of parental rights. Furthermore,

African American children, children of Hispanic decent, and children with multiple placements are less likely to be reunited with their parents.

Since current federal and state data indicate that these children will spend significantly more time in the CWS supervised out of home care, policies should be established to improve the outcomes for these children. For example, there should be incentives in place for families who adopt children from the groups who are remaining in foster care the longest without a permanent placement. Social workers may be less inclined to terminate parental rights if adoptive parents have not been identified. Extensive counseling should be available for these children to assist them in overcoming any emotional problems in order to increase their chances of adoption. While this paper indicates a distinct difference between children who are discharged to their parents and the children whose parents have their rights and responsibilities terminated, it is just a beginning in analyzing the impact of the termination of parental rights (Noonan & Burke, 2005).

At the request of Congress, the Government Accounting Office (GAO) examined state implementation and impact of ASFA's reforms specific to: (1) the "15 of 22 months" provision to initiate termination of parental rights and (2) the provision to bypass reunification efforts ("fast track") in extraordinarily high-risk situations. The GAO analyzed national child welfare data, surveyed all fifty states and the District of Columbia, and conducted on site reviews with six states (Illinois, Maryland, Massachusetts, North Carolina, Oregon and Texas) to obtain information on implementation and outcomes. Because of design and data limitations, the outcomes that were noted could not be attributed exclusively to ASFA reforms. (This was, in part, because many states had adopted similar provisions prior to ASFA.) Nonetheless, the GAO report reveals two trends in improved outcomes for children in care: the number of adoptions post-ASFA and promising practices to surmount traditional barriers in moving children into permanent placement. Additionally, the states visited by the GAO acknowledged that ASFA plays an important role in their new focus on permanence for children within the first eighteen months that they enter foster care. More specifically, adoptions had increased 57 percent since passage of the Adoption and Safe Families Act. The GAO report also featured the major challenges impeding their ability to comply with ASFA timelines and the promising practices to resolve these challenges—all designed to expedite children into permanent placement (Spaccarotelli, 2003; U.S. General Accountability Office, 2005) (see Table 2.1).

In summary, the primary goal of ASFA was, and remains, to ensure safety and expedite permanency for children in the child welfare system. The evolution of ASFA and the changes in child welfare services and outcomes that follow ASFA are part of the story that unfolds through out this book. In general terms, the early concerns about the likelihood of ASFA unfairness were focused on the probability that a substantial number of parents would, more than ever, lose

Table 2.1
Challenges and Promising Practices of the Adoption and Safe Families Act
(P.L. 105-89)

Challenge	Promising Practices
Systemic Court Problems Delay Judicial Determinations	Permanency Mediation Program dispute resolution process in a non-adversarial setting between family members and potential adoptive parents. Avoids lengthy appeals to TPR.
	Multi-jurisdictional courts in rural communities addressing the lack of rural judges trained and experienced in child welfare issues. One state developed a cluster court system in which a judge trained in child welfare issues rotates among courts in a cluster of rural communities.
Finding Adoptive Families for Children with Special Needs	Listing children's profiles on state and local websites.
	Exploring adoption by adults significantly involved in the child's life.
	Featuring profiles of children on local television news, radio, and newspapers.
	Adoption celebrations.
	Facilitating a statewide exchange of information among social workers about children and awaiting parents.
	Targeting recruitment to local churches for special needs children, including minorities.
	Providing subsidies to relatives and foster parents who become legal guardians, utilizing IV-E waivers.
	Improving stability with better matches between adoptive families and children. Mental health assessments of the child's readiness to bond and the family's ability to meet the child's needs as well as providing training for families.
Placing Children Across Jurisdictions	Increasing staff to improve interstate compacts.
	Publicizing profiles of awaiting children on websites, media in other states.
	Collaborating with private agencies to recruit adoptive parents in other states.
	Contracting with private agencies for home studies in other states to Expedite ICPC (Interstate Compact on the Process of Children).

	Allowing social workers in other states to perform home studies.
Accessing Needed Services for Families	Professionals assess substance abuse problems of parents and engage them in treatment. Family group conferencing among parents, relatives, child welfare agency staff, CASA volunteers, and other professionals to develop plans addressing the child's need for safety and permanency and to assure that the family has access to services necessary in order to fulfill the permanency plan.

Sources: Spaccarotelli, C. (2003). *Adoption and Safe Families Act: Has It Made a Difference? Washington*, DC: Court Appointed Special Advocates Association. (Mimeograph). Retrieved September 18, 2007 from http://www.casanet.org/library/adoption/asfa-has-made-a-difference.htm. Government Accountability Office. (2002). *Foster care recent legislation helps states focus on finding permanent homes for children, but long-standing barriers remain.* (GAO Report -02-585) See www.gao.gov/new. items/d03397.pdf.

the right to parent—perhaps with no opportunity to demonstrate their fitness to parent during the receipt of reunification services. At this point, we have not seen a concurrent rise in the number of children going into out of home care although there has been a reduction in the likelihood that children will be reunified since ASFA (Barth, Wulczyn, & Crea, 2005). In the meantime, the adoption rate has increased markedly. This suggests that the long hoped for growth in adoption—which was to have come from the group of children who would otherwise have had long stays in foster care—may have been partially a result of competition between adoption and reunification. This was clearly not an intended consequence of ASFA.

Yet, even with some successes—especially in the area of greater information for accountability and a reduction in the numbers of children in foster care—the weaknesses in the underlying structure of AACWA and ASFA are increasingly apparent. The availability of federal funds for foster care maintenance payments has been falling steadily because states must prove that youth are eligible for federal payments based on a family's eligibility for AFDC (a program that ended in 1997). This has had a marked impact on what is called the "IV-E penetration rate." Now, many states are only able to recoup the federal share of foster care—on average, 50 percent of the cost—for fewer than 30 percent of their children. At the same time, the proportion of funds allocated for preventive and protective services in the Safe and Stable Families (IVB) program has only increased modestly. Secondly, states remain unable to transfer funds to prevention or family support services that are typically funded through Title IV-B, which has a much smaller allocation of federal funds. These concerns about the lack of flexibility in funding have been counterbalanced by concerns that a marked increase in flexibility in foster care funding might diminish the national commitment to developing proper training and administration of these services.

In 2004, the Pew Foundation created an independent expert panel to look at the state of child welfare policy and financing and they have made recommendations that are intended to balance the interest in greater flexibility to fund services to families and the concerns that funding remains available to support administration and training of a quality child welfare services system. The Pew Commission report recommended that federal adoption assistance and federal guardianship assistance be available to all children who leave foster care to live with a permanent, legal guardian (not just those who came from eligible families). The commission further suggested that the federal government join states in paying for foster care for every child who needs this protection regardless of family income (family income refers to the income of the family from which the child is removed), including children who are members of Indian tribes; and including children who live in the U.S. territories. The Pew Commission also recommended allowing states to "reinvest" federal dollars that would have been expended on foster care into other child welfare services if they safely reduce the use of foster care. States could use these funds for any service to keep children out of foster care or to leave foster care safely.

The Commission also recommended more flexible child welfare funding. They proposed an indexed Safe Children, Strong Families Grant that combines federal funding for Title IV-B, Title IV-E Administration, and Title IV-E Training into a flexible source of funding. With this approach, additional funding would be provided in the first year, and the grant would be indexed in future years. To determine this amount, each state's grant amount would be based on its historical spending of IVB and IVE funds. (Note, this might work well for states that have continued to have high rates of foster care expenditures but might penalize those who have dropped their IV-E spending, in recent years.) In addition, the total base funding level would be enhanced by $200 million in the first year of implementation. In subsequent years, each state's allocation would (a) grow by 2 percent plus the inflation rate, as measured by the Consumer Price Index; and (b) states would be required to match the federal grant funds, just as they currently are required to match federal IV-B and IV-E dollars (Pew Commission, 2004, pp. 16-17). These provisions are intended to (a) be sure that the value of this allocation is not lost to inflation, over time, and (b) to be sure that there is "maintenance of state level of effort" and states to not reduce their investment in CWS as the federal investment increases.

The end of the story of child welfare fiscal reform has not been written, and never will be, but at the time that this book went to press there remained a stalemate between those who feared giving up the IVE entitlement and those who sought more flexible funding that would be preserved and made available to families at home, if out of home care was reduced. Child welfare scholars and program managers are arrayed on both sides of this debate. They are looking for a compromise, and one compromise that is being forwarded by children's advocacy groups is to keep funding guaranteed but also make it more flexible and eliminate the adoption and foster care eligibility requirements so all children are eligible for IVE funding for foster care or adoption, respectively. This is unlikely to be seen as a fundable alternative given the consistent pressure on the federal treasury. The Pew Commission updated their work in 2006 and indicated that their recommendations on streamlining court processes were well under way to being achieved but that the needed financing reforms were not yet accepted.

Multi-Ethnic Placement Act of 1994 (P.L. 103-382) and Interethnic Adoption Provisions of 1997

Approximately one-third of the children placed in foster care will never return to their birth parents, leaving those children in need of permanent homes. And certain groups of children wait longer than others will to belong to a new family. For example, minority children—who made up over 60 percent of those in foster care nationwide in 1994—wait longer than other children (Hill, 2007; U.S. Government Accountability Office, 2007). Berrick, Needell, Barth, and Jonson-Reid (1998), and Barth (1997), have also documented delays in permanency planning for children of color. Although these delays have been reduced in the last decade, they remain in many jurisdictions.

In 1994, the Multi-ethnic Placement Act (MEPA) was signed into law by President Clinton eliminating policies that favor same-race placements. The law is intended to prevent discrimination in the placement of children in foster care and adoption on the basis of race, color, or national origin, to decrease the time children wait to be adopted, and to ensure agency recruitment of a pool of foster and adoptive parents who reflect the racial and ethnic diversity of the children available for adoption. MEPA prohibits states or any agencies that receive federal funds from delaying or denying the placement of any child solely based on race, color, or national origin. In 1996, MEPA was amended by the Inter-Ethnic Adoption Provisions Act. This revision removed language explicitly permitting the consideration of race and ethnicity as one of a number of factors used to determine the best interests of the child and adds penalties for states not in compliance with the law. Through this amendment, Congress intended to eliminate delays in placement that can be avoided because they are based on the requirement of racial matching. More specifically, race, culture, or ethnicity may not be used as the basis for denial of placement, nor may such factors be used as a reason to delay any foster or adoptive placement.

Any child welfare agency that receives federal funds is affected by the Inter-Ethnic Adoption Provisions Act of 1996 (IEAP). However, the law does not affect the Indian Child Welfare Act, or the responsibilities of the states to be in compliance with ICWA standards for eligible Indian children in their care. This is so, because the ICWA is based on tribal membership (basically, dual citizenship) of American Indian children who belong in tribes. Thus, tribes have protection under the law that is not afforded to other children or cultural communities who may believe that adoption within the community is best for the community or the children in it.

In the past, many children of color have experienced significant delays before being placed with a foster family or for adoption because of the reluctance of caseworkers to make trans-racial placements. According to the data, lower reunification with the biological family is a contributing factor of African-American children staying in the system for longer periods (Barth, 1997), although this is changing and reunification rates for African American children—although slower to develop—have caught up with white children (Wulczyn, 2004). One of the reasons for the large number of African-American children involved with child welfare and in foster care is the high incident of substance abuse among African-American children in the system is due to high incident of substance abuse among African-American parents (Courtney, 1998) and to higher rates of parental incarceration, which is associated with placement into foster care (Phillips, et al., 2004). Involvement with child welfare services is strongly correlated with higher rates of poverty because of discrimination and single motherhood. A lack of effective drug treatment and the lack of resources for the families may also be contributing to this trend. Some states and agencies had policies that discourage trans-racial placements or that allow lengthy searches for same race families before authorizing trans-racial placements. Whatever the reasons, there is no debate that there is a disproportionate, to the population, number of African American children in foster care. At the same time, some non-African American families continue to be informally discouraged from ever applying to adopt African American children, according to the Office of Civil Rights, which recently fined Hamilton County (Cincinnati) Ohio for failure to implement MEPA.

It is too early to determine the full effects of these changes in statute. While MEPA requires states to make diligent efforts to recruit families that reflect the ethnic and racial diversity of children needing homes, IEAP prohibits states and agencies from denying anyone the opportunity to adopt on the basis of race. The lack of federal funding may hinder diligent recruitment of families of color as most, state child welfare agencies may rush to process interracial adoption, rather than allocating enough money for recruitment of families of color. (See Chapter 11 for more information.)

Because of the large number of multi-ethnic children awaiting a more permanent home, major service reforms were needed and MEPA was one attempt to address these problems. Among the challenges in fully implementing this Act is the very real dilemma that ethnic minority administered and staffed child welfare agencies are rare; and that, where adequately funded and staffed, these agencies appear to be able to place children of color in same/similar race homes.

In terms of specific implementation barriers to adoption placement that fit the intent of these laws, the Government Accounting Office in a recent review of MEPA, identified the following three barriers: (1) translating legal principles into practical guidelines and strategies for caseworkers where much confusion exists about the Act; (2) changing long-standing casework beliefs and practices, such as placement of children in same-race homes is in the best interests of children; and (3) developing compliance monitoring systems (U.S. General Accounting Office, 1998). These two laws remain controversial: The Evan B. Donaldson Adoption Institute has recommended that the IEPA be repealed, leaving MEPA in place, http://www.adoptioninstitute.org/policy/20070921_testimony_federal_mepa.pdf

The John H. Chafee Foster Care Independence Program, the Foster Care Independence Act (H.R. 3443), and the Education Training Voucher

These pieces of legislation are the most important federal policies for helping youth placed in foster care in terms of preparing for living in the community. They are summarized below in the following sections. The six major purposes of the John H. Chafee Foster Care Independence Program are listed below:

1. To identify children who are likely to remain in foster care until eighteen years of age and to help these children make the transition to self-sufficiency by providing services such as assistance in obtaining a high school diploma, career exploration, vocational training, job placement and retention, training in daily living skills, training in budgeting and financial management skills, substance abuse prevention, and preventive health activities (including smoking avoidance, nutrition education, and pregnancy prevention);
2. To help children who are likely to remain in foster care until eighteen years of age receive the education, training, and services necessary to obtain employment;
3. To help children who are likely to remain in foster care until eighteen years of age prepare for and enter post-secondary training and education institutions;
4. To provide personal and emotional support to children aging out of foster care, through mentors and the promotion of interactions with dedicated adults;
5. To provide financial, housing, counseling, employment, education, and other appropriate support and services to former foster care recipients between eighteen and twenty-one years of age to complement their own efforts to achieve self-sufficiency and to assure that program participants recognize and accept their personal responsibility for preparing for and then making the transition from adolescence to adulthood; and

6. To make available vouchers for education and training, including post-sec-
    ondary training and education, to youths who have aged out of foster care
    (National Foster Care Awareness Project, 2005; The Foster Care Indepen-
    dence Act of 1999, P.L. 106-169).

"Chafee," as it has become known, also instituted a state educational and training voucher program under this law's section, even though it is, technically,
an amendment to the Social Security Act. Vouchers under the program may be
available to youths otherwise eligible for services under the state program under
this section. For purposes of the voucher program, youths adopted from foster
care after attaining age sixteen may be considered to be youth otherwise eligible
for services under the state program under this section. In addition, the state may
allow youth participating in the voucher program on the date they attain twenty-
one years of age to remain eligible until they attain twenty-three years of age,
as long as they are enrolled in a post secondary education or training program
and are making satisfactory progress toward completion of that program. The
voucher or vouchers provided for an individual under this section:

1. May be available for the cost of attendance at an institution of higher educa-
    tion as defined in section 102 of the Higher Education Act of 1965; and
2. Shall not exceed the lesser of $5,000 per year or the total cost of attendance,
    as defined in section 472 of that Act.

The amount of a voucher under this section shall be disregarded for the
purposes of determining the recipient's eligibility for, or the amount of, any
other federal or federally supported assistance, except that the total amount of
educational assistance to a youth under this section and under other federal and
federally supported programs shall not exceed the total cost of attendance, as
defined in section 472 of the Higher Education Act of 1965, and except that
the state agency shall take appropriate steps to prevent duplication of benefits
under this and other federal and federally supported programs. The program
must also be coordinated with other appropriate education and training programs
(National Foster Care Awareness Project, 2005; Title 2 of the Promoting Safe
and Stable Families Amendments of 2001).

"Chafee" made a major step forward in extending foster care beyond age
eighteen, although this was limited and at the discretion of states, which were
allowed to use up to 30 percent of these funds for room and board for youths
ages eighteen to twenty-one, transitioning from foster care. It also gave states
the option of to extend Medicaid to these older youths transitioning from foster
care. Additional provisions include:

*   Clarifying that independent living activities should not be seen as an
    alternative to adoption for children, and can occur concurrently with
    efforts to find adoptive families for these children;

- Adding adoptive parents to the groups to receive training with IV-E funds to help them understand and address the issues confronting adolescents preparing for independent living;
- Adding achievement of a high school diploma and incarceration to the list of outcomes to be developed by the Secretary of DHHS to assess the performance of states in operating independent living programs, and requiring the secretary to submit to Congress with its report on outcomes and data a plan for imposing penalties on states that do not report data; and
- Establishing a $500,000 minimum allotment for states under the John H. Chafee Foster Care Independence Program. (See http://thomas.loc. gov, www.childrensdefense.org, and www.cwla.org)

While many aspects of these related laws are positive, and the resources for this program are quite substantial compared to funding available for CAPTA or Title IVB, the funding levels for the basic Chafee independent living services are not fully adequate to meet the needs of the over twenty thousand youth who emancipate from foster care every year, and the many more youth who are placed in care as adolescents who need life skills training and employment experience to help them develop into healthy adults (see Chapter 10).

Fostering Connections to Success and Increasing Adoptions Act
(P.L. 110-351)

The Fostering Connections to Success and Increasing Adoptions Act promotes permanent families for children through relative guardianship and adoption and improving education and health care. In addition, the law provides, for the first time, many American Indian children access to important federal protections and support. The bill also provides additional supports to older youth who reach the age of majority without a permanent family by extending federal support for youth to age 21. the main provisions of this new law are listed in Appendix A and have been highlighted in other sections of this chapter.

Current Policy Challenges

Overview

There are a number of pressing policy challenges facing child welfare services, some of which are underscored by the mixed success the U.S. is having in meeting the basic needs of children, for ensuring their safety, health, relationships, and opportunities and supporting families as the foundation for positive child development. A cross-section of some of the most important policy challenges are listed in the sections that follow.

Using knowledge of risk, protection, and resiliency to achieve integration in child welfare-related policy. We have described the major policies that influence the well-being of children and families as they are served in child welfare. Funding fragmentation and the lack of services integration were noted, along with many of the policy developments that illustrate how some of the risk and protective factor research lessons are or can be applied. To implement these lessons, child welfare agencies need adequate funding for key programs, as well as new and more effective ways to tie funding to indicators of success.

Note that a number of writers have commented how child welfare agency policy and performance incentive mechanisms are not aligned with best practice (e.g., Wulczyn, Zeidman, & Svirsky, 1997), and that the child welfare service delivery system needs to be overhauled to better address societal and community factors (e.g., Adams & Nelson, 1995; Edna McConnell Clark Foundation, 2004; Lindsey, 2004; Pew Foundation, 2004, 2008). Yet there is not agreement about what would be risked by taking different approaches—e.g., providing greater flexibility in how Title IV-E funds are spent. The risk and protective factor literature has much to offer as child welfare policies and programs are refined.

Underfunding of Early Intervention Services and Inconsistent Federal Leadership

Early intervention services have long been recognized as important for helping families avoid involvement with the child welfare systems or placement of their children. Best practices for early intervention programs involve a range of family-centered services, which focus on meeting the needs of the child within the context of his or her family and larger environment. For example, in the course of early intervention, parents may be referred to job assistance or adult education, and may receive assistance in obtaining housing and health care. Child-centered early intervention programs have been linked with improved child development across multiple domains (Center on the Developing Child at Harvard University, 2007; Graham & Bryant, 1993). With better prevention strategies, we could also help families avoid having their children enter the child welfare system (see Chapter 7).

But more unified leadership with strategic policies to enhance family support is needed at the federal and state levels. For example, communities must invest public resources into evidence-based programs embedded in local communities that support parents and strengthen families (e.g., Communities that Care, FAST—Families and Schools Together). We must also raise the public profile of the importance of affordable childcare, and increase awareness among policymakers about the importance of *family economic security* in preventing children from entering child welfare system. This need is underscored by the large proportion of children entering child welfare due to parental neglect. As mentioned earlier, more effective mental health and substance abuse interventions for parents would also reduce youth entry into foster care.

The philosophy undergirding early intervention is becoming more grounded in the concepts of risk, resiliency, and protective factors. Ideally, early intervention services promote well-being and optimal development by providing comprehensive community-based support services to help improve child developmental outcomes. Yet these services are under-funded and, as discussed in more detail below, states lack flexibility to use federal funds for family support that are currently designated for placement services.

Family Support Services Policies Are Not Backed by
Coherent Funding Strategies

Family support services, which offer important protective factors for children, are often a lifeline for families and include services like a parent hotline, crisis nursery services, environmental adaptations, personal assistance, mental health, and crisis intervention. These supports allow families to care for their children at home rather than seeking expensive, and generally publicly financed out-of-home care (Bruns & Burchard, 2000).

The goals of family support services include enabling families to raise their child at home by reducing stress, and by strengthening and enhancing caregiving capacities (Walton, Sandau-Beckler, & Mannes, 2001). Utilization of formal support services by family caregivers plays a significant role in reducing the burdens and stress associated with caring for a child, and helping families obtain services for unmet needs. Family support services across the U.S. are usually jointly financed by the federal and state governments, often with Medicaid resources and are typically administered by state or county governments. Not surprisingly, given the vast differences among the states in the provision of social services, there is tremendous variability among the states in the level of funding allocated for family support and the types of available services. Consequently, these services are often not only underfunded, but are among the first programs to be cut in times of economic downturns.

Block-Granting of Key Child Welfare Funding Mechanisms Needs Careful
Thinking

A number of federal leaders have submitted proposals to Congress under which states would be allowed to use federal foster care funds not only to support children in out-of-home care, but also on child abuse prevention and post-adoption services. For example, several proposals were made to dramatically change the system for funding key child welfare programs, including foster care entitlement under Title IV-E of the Social Security Act.

This is an attempt to address the family support issue raised above. But the downside to these proposals is that the overall budget support for children's services funding would decrease if all the areas under that legislative area are considered. Families no longer would have an entitlement to funding in that particular area, such as would occur with block-granting Medicaid and food stamps (Finegold, Wherry, & Schardin, 2004, p. 5). But it is becoming increasingly clear that the current federal funding approach is not working well and is becoming worse over time. Policymakers and the public must be educated about the importance of adequate funding for child welfare programs, where the funds are tied to performance-based results (Casey Family Programs, 2004).

Policy and Funding to Treat Mental Health and Substance Abuse Problems Must be Redesigned

Fragmented funding streams and policies fail to encourage effective treatment of co-morbid (i.e., co-occurring conditions) that are much more common in the United States than commonly thought (Kessler & Magee, 1993). For example, substance abuse problems are present in about 50 to 60 percent of the families where children are placed in out-of-home care (Besinger, Garland, Litrownik, & Landsverk, 1999; Young & Gardner, 2002). Many agency administrators are "braiding" or cobbling together multiple funding streams when more coordination at the federal state levels is badly needed to maximize the effectiveness of scarce dollars (Johnson, Knitzer, & Kaufmann, 2003).

Differential Response Approaches to Child Protective Services Intake Need to be Further Tested

New intake approaches are attempting to divert low risk families to supportive programs other than child protective services. Initial research data indicate either no differences or that families in alternative response systems receive more services (U. S. Department of Health and Human Services, 2005; Zielewski, Macomber, Bess, & Murray, 2006). More recent reporting by child welfare administrations indicates that these strategies can help to divert families from more formal child welfare services involvement, (e.g., Marts, Lee, McRoy, & McCroskey, 2008) especially when the links to community-based support services are strong. These systems, however need continued evaluation because without additional research data, how will the field know for example, which families benefit most from these system designs, which children are most vulnerable and what different roles should be fulfilled by law enforcement, medical, legal, and voluntary social services personnel?

Kinship Care Funding, Licensing, and Practice Policies Need to be Aligned

Care of children by extended family members is quite common; more than 6.1 million children in the U.S. live in households headed by relatives other than their parents who provide full-time care, nurturing, and protection (U.S. Census Bureau, 2006). Most are cared for by their grandparents and the vast majority of these children live with kin as a result of voluntary arrangements made by their families. However, beginning in the 1980s, when federal reimbursement for out-of-home placement of children with kin was made comparable to reimbursement for non-kin placements, states began to use kinship foster care as a placement option for children in court-ordered out-of-home care (Hegar & Scannapieco, 1998). In 2005, kinship foster homes provided care for 124,153 (24 percent) of the children in out-of-home care, making kinship care the second most common placement (U.S. Department of Health and Human Services, 2006b).

Many of these grandparents have assumed this responsibility without a parent in the home. Kinship caregivers often lack the information and range of supports they need to fulfill their parenting role. In an effort to remedy this situation, a group of child and aging advocacy/research organizations has prepared Kinship Care Fact Sheets, which provide state-specific data and information for all the states directing kinship caregivers to support services that can help make their jobs easier (Children's Defense Fund, 2004). More important, P.L. 110-351 authorizes the funding of "Kinship Navigator" programs to help relatives connect the children with the services and supports they need. It also authorizes separate licensing standards to change non-safety licensing requirements that create barriers to children living with relatives in foster care on a case-by-case basis (e.g., square footage requirements and minimum numbers of bedrooms or bathrooms per person). But much more work needs to be done to help sort out the policy inconsistencies in licensing and support of these families (see Chapter 8).

Increase Tribal Access to Federal Child Welfare Services Funding and Improve Infrastructure

The passage of P.L. 110-351 in 2009 allowed American Indian tribes to access Federal Title IV-E funds directly (section 301). Many tribes have exercised their jurisdiction over Indian children but have underdeveloped services and need to build important infrastructure such as management information systems and quality improvement programs. The Act allows states and tribes to continue to operate or create Tribal/State agreements to administer the IV-E program. P.L. 110-351 also creates the option for tribes or tribal consortia to directly access and administer IV-E funds. This provision increases resources for Indian children and extends the IV-E protections to more Indian children. The Act also allows tribes to access a portion of the state's Chafee Foster Care Independence Program (CFCIP) funds and require the tribe to provide independent living services for tribal youth in the state.

Agency Policies Could Promote Better Assessment and Support of Gay, Lesbian, Bi-Sexual, and Transgendered Youth in Out-of-Home Care

Mallon (1999; 2007a, 2007b) and others have described how child welfare service delivery systems have not been designed with policies that would encourage staff members and foster parents to protect and nurture these youth who are already vulnerable to further victimization, depression, suicide, and placement disruption because of their sexual orientation.

Transition Policies and Support for Emancipating Youth Must Continue to be Strengthened

A shocking 3.8 million young people in the United States between the ages of 18 and 24 are neither employed nor in school—roughly 15 percent of all young adults (Nelson, 2004)—up from 13 percent in 2003 (see http://childtrendsdatabank.org). Too many alumni of the foster care system are part of that group: under-trained and underemployed. Many of these people are part of a large group of "marginalized youth."

The need is even more serious for youth served in foster care for long periods of time. Alumni of foster care vary widely in their level of preparation for emancipating from foster care and consequently are at risk of poor education and low wages (e.g., Cook, Fleishman, & Grimes, 1991; Courtney, et al., 2005; Goerge, et al., 2002; Pecora, et al., 2010). Society needs to promote investment in culturally relevant services, support, and opportunities so that every youth in foster care makes a safe, successful transition to adulthood. Independent living preparation must be re-designed to start at age ten and to use more wisely the available funds at the federal and state levels. A comprehensive transition development plan should be developed for every child that includes planning for supportive relationships, community connections, education, life skills assessment and development, identity formation, housing, employment, physical health, and mental health (Goodman, et al, 2001; Massinga & Pecora, 2004).

Employment training and experience should be increased for many youth while they are in care (which may require changes in some aspects of the Child Labor Act, which limits employment opportunities for youth). Policies and incentives should ensure that no young person leaves foster care without housing, access to health care, employability, and permanent connections to at least one adult (see Chapter 10).

All youth in high school should receive the tutoring and employment experience they need to show them that education and vocational training do matter when it comes to earning a living wage. Youth preparing to emancipate must have greater access to experiential life skills training (e.g., employment, driver's education), in addition to classroom-based training. Systems change is essential. The MacArthur Foundation transition scholars have documented how major American institutions have not kept pace with societal changes that require new ways of working to remove barriers to youth transition to adulthood (see Carnegie Council on Adolescent Development, 1989, and http://www.pop. upenn.edu/transad/index.htm for the reports from The Network on Transitions to Adulthood funded by the MacArthur Foundation).

Policies Should Provide Fiscal Incentives for Improving the Education and Workforce Preparation for Children and Youth in Foster Care

The Higher Education Act (HEA) gives virtually no consideration to the special needs of children and youth in foster care. But Congress recently made improvements to the HEA to provide greater opportunities for youth and young foster care alumni (Casey Family Programs, 2003b). Policy innovations are needed that strengthen elementary and secondary education, including special education.

Federal and state policies also must maintain the financial viability and array of services for the Medicaid and SCHIP programs for youth in foster care, and ensure that no young person leaves foster care without access to appropriate health care. Studies by a number of researchers have demonstrated the health care coverage gaps among foster care alumni (e.g., Cook, et al., 1991; Courtney, et al., 2007; Pecora, et al., 2005).

Child welfare policy needs to be refined so that more youth can achieve and maintain permanence in a reasonable time period through foster care, reunification, relative placement, guardianship, or adoption. This includes crafting policies to ensure that kinship care families have access to resources needed to raise healthy children in stable home environments. Adoption policy must address more thoroughly how to better respond to the legal concerns expressed through the MEPA and IEPA legislation summarized earlier and yet help ensure that children of color, whenever possible, are adopted by a caregiver of their same race.

Policymakers Need to Recognize Seriousness of Racial Disproportionality and Disparities in Access to Services

As exemplified by a recent GAO (2007) report, disproportional presence of African American and Native American children in foster care and the disparities in some outcomes for them is increasingly recognized as a major ethical, policy, and program design issue. First, we need to promote the investment of public resources into gathering critical data about African American, Native American, Asian, and Hispanic/Latino children receiving child welfare services. This includes understanding whether services are being provided that are commensurate—that is, not more intrusive or less intrusive—than indicated to meet the child's basic level of needs. The access for birth parents for children of color in the child welfare system to substance abuse and mental health services both prior to entering and during their contact with the system should be understood (Hill, 2001; Hines, et al., 2004), as should efforts to engage families to use those services (McKay & Bannon, 2004).

Second, through this information, we can enhance the national awareness of the disproportionate number of African American and American Indians/Alaskan Native children in foster care, the reasons for such disproportion, and possible solutions (note that Latino/Hispanic children may also be over-represented in foster care in certain communities, but not others [Hill, 2007]). Finally, communities can launch efforts to actually do something about these disparities.

Performance-Based Contracting Has Not Been Fully Implemented

State and county policies to promote evidence-based practice models and performance-based contracting have been hampered by a lack of knowledge of baseline conditions, sound target goals, infrastructure-funding gaps, and a lack of information about what practice models are currently evidence-based. Continuous quality improvement systems must be in place to enable agencies to steadily improve (Mordock, 2002; Pecora, Seelig, Zirps, & Davis, 1996).

Conclusion

Current Status

This chapter has focused on major policies that guide child welfare services in the United States, while discussing a wider range of policy and program challenges. It is a pivotal time, where states are passing legislation to address certain policy gaps or needs, such as instituting alternative response systems to support families, requiring stronger preparation for youth to transition from foster care, extending the length of time youth can remain in foster care beyond the age of eighteen, and enabling youth who exit foster care at the age of eighteen to receive health care services via Medicaid to the age of twenty-one, twenty-three, or twenty-five.

Future Directions

Federal CWS funding reform is likely to occur in the next few years now that policy refinements related to youth being allowed to remain in foster care beyond the age of eighteen and better support to kinship care parents was enacted through P. L. 110-351. The next chapter extends some of the concepts from chapters 1 and 2 as it outlines a family-centered approach to child welfare services.

Notes

1.   Special thanks to the public policy team of Casey Family Programs, and the legislative advocacy staff of the Child Welfare League of America for the policy briefs and

position statements that informed the legislative policy section of this chapter. In addition, foster care alumni, practitioners, and foster parents have taught us much about the real impacts of policy; we appreciate the time they have spent discussing research findings with us.

2. This description of the Indian Child Welfare Act is based on the following sources: Federal Register (1979), Hand, 2006; National Center for Children in Poverty, 2005; Unger (1978), and Wright (1980).

3. "Foster care maintenance" is defined as payments to cover cost of/or to provide food, clothing, shelter, daily supervision, school supplies, personal incidentals, liability insurance for child, and reasonable travel to the home for child visits. In the case of institutional care, the term includes reasonable costs of administration and operation of an institution.

For Further Information

Berrick, J. D., Needell, B. Barth. R. B. & Johnson-Reid, M. (1998). *The tender years: Toward developmentally sensitive child welfare services for very young children.* New York: Oxford University Press. One of the few books to link child development and child welfare perspectives.

Derezotes, D., Poertner, J. & Testa, M. (Eds.) (2005). *Race matters in child matters in chld welfare: The overrepresentation of African American children in the system.* Washington, D.C.: Child Welfare League of America. Examines dimensions of child welfare services for children and parents of color.

Wulczyn, F., Barth, R. P., Yuan, Y. Y., Jones Harden, B., & Landsverk, J. (2005). *Beyond common sense: Evidence for child welfare policy reform.* New York: Transaction De Gruyter. Provides recent data on children and family served in child welfare over time.

3

A Conceptual Framework for Child and Family-Centered Services

In recent years, there has been increasing emphasis on family-centered child welfare services in contrast with a more narrow focus on child safety. This is an approach that focuses on the family as the unit of attention. It is built on the premise that "human beings can be understood and helped only in the context of the intimate and powerful human systems of which they are a part," of which the family is one of the most important (Hartman & Laird, 1983, p. 4). How the family is defined has important implications for practice, including eligibility for service, distribution of resources, and helping approaches. By family we mean "two or more people in a committed relationship from which they derive a sense of identity as a family," thus including "nontraditional family forms that are outside the traditional legal perspective...families not related by blood, marriage, or adoption" (Nunnally, Chilman, & Cox, 1988, p. 11). As Gambrill (1997, p. 571) observes:

> Families may be defined by biological relatedness and/or living arrangements. There are many kinds of families including step-families, nuclear families, extended families, gay/lesbian families, single-parent families, families without children, families with grown children, and bicultural families.

In line with the above, "respect for diversity requires that *family* be defined openly and broadly so as to include whomever the family itself—with its unique culture, circumstances, and history—designates" (Allen & Petr, 1998, p. 8).

Chapter Outline

Family-centered child welfare services, of course, are consonant with the long-standing concern of social workers with families, especially in the field of child welfare. Accordingly, this chapter presents an integrative, child/family-centered conceptual framework for child welfare, along with selected implications for policy and practice (see Table 3.1). The framework builds on five major components: an ecological perspective, which offers a broad conceptual

Table 3.1
Common Risk Factors for Child Abuse and Neglect

Risk Factors
Child Risk Factors

- Premature birth, birth anomalies, low birth weight, exposure to toxins in utero
- Temperament: difficult or slow to warm up
- Physical/cognitive/emotional disability, Chronic or serious illness
- Childhood trauma
- Anti-social peer group
- Age
- Child aggression, behavior problems, attention deficits

Protective Factors
Child Protective Factors*

- Birth order—first born
- Health status—healthy during infancy and childhood
- Activity level—multiple interests and hobbies, participation and competence
- Disposition—good-natured, precocious, mature, inquisitive, willing to take risks, optimistic, hopeful, altruistic, personable, independent
- Developmental Milestones—meets or exceeds age-appropriate expectations
- Self-Concept—high self-esteem, internal locus of control, ability to give and receive love and affection
- Perceptive—quickly assesses dangerous situations and avoids harm
- Interpersonal Skills—able to create, develop, nurture and maintain supportive relationships with others, assertive, good social skills, ability to relate to both children and adults, articulate
- Cognitive Skills—able to focus on positive attributes and ignore negative
- Intellectual Abilities—high academic achievement

Parental/Family Risk Factors
- Personality Factors
- External locus of control
- Poor impulse control
- Depression/anxiety
- Low tolerance for frustration
- Feelings of insecurity
- Lack of trust
- Insecure attachment with own parents

Parental/Family Protective Factors**
- Structure—rules and household responsibilities for all members
- Family Relational Factors—coherence and attachment, open exchange and expression of feelings and emotions
- Parental Factors—supervision and monitoring of children, a strong bond to at least one parent figure, a warm

Table 3.1 (cont.)

Parental/Family Risk Factors (cont.)

- Childhood history of abuse
- High parental conflict, including domestic violence
- Family structure – single parent with lack of support, high number of children in household
- Social isolation, lack of support
- Parental psychopathology
- Substance abuse
- Separation/divorce, especially high conflict divorce
- Age
- High general stress level
- Poor parent-child interaction, negative attitudes and attributions about child's behavior
- Inaccurate knowledge and expectations about child development
- Mental health problems, including maternal depression
- Cultural "mis-match" (when a parent has a perception of normative development that is incongruent with that of the broader society and its service providers) (Coll & Magnuson, 2000, p. 102). For a discussion of the connection between social problems and child placement, see Berrick et al. (1998), Halpern (1990), Kamerman and Kahn (1990), and Pelton (1989 and 1994).

Community/Social/Environmental Risk Factors

- Low socioeconomic status of the neighborhood
- Stressful life events
- Lack of access to medical care, health insurance, adequate child care, and social services
- Parental unemployment; homelessness
- Social isolation/lack of social support
- Exposure to racism/discrimination

Parental/ Family Protective Factors (cont.)

and supportive relationship, abundant attention during the first year of life, parental agreement on family values and morals, emotional availability (parental accessibility and capacity for reading the emotional cues and meeting the emotional needs of the infant) (Osofsky & Thompson, 2000, p. 56).

- Reciprocity – mutually satisfying relationships are built between an infant/young child and a parent (Osofsky & Thompson, 2000, p. 55).
- Family Size—four or fewer children spaced at least two years apart
- Socioeconomic Status—middle to upper SES
- Extended Family—nurturing relationships with substitute caregivers such as aunts, uncles and grandparents
- Other positive social network support

Community/Social/Environmental Protective Factors***

- Positive peer relationships
- Extended family in close proximity
- Schools—academic and extracurricular participation and achievements, close relationship with a teacher(s)
- Reliance on informal network of family, friends and community leaders for advice

Sources:
Coll, C.G. & Magnuson, K. (2000). Cultural differences as sources of developmental vulnerabilities and resources. In J. P. Shonkoff & S. J. Meisels *Handbook of early childhood intervention. (Second Edition).* Cambridge: Cambridge University Press, 94-114. Hodges, V. Assessing for strengths and protective factors in child abuse and neglect: risk assessment with families of color. In Pecora. P.J. , & English, D. J. (1994). *Multi-cultural guidelines for assessing family strengths and risk factors in child protective services.* Seattle, WA: Washington State Department of Social Services and the School of Social Work, University of Washington. Osofsky, J.D. & Thompson, D. (2000). Adaptive and maladaptive parenting: Perspectives on risk and protective factors. In J. P. Shonkoff & S. J. Meisels *Handbook of early childhood intervention. (Second Edition).* Cambridge: Cambridge University Press, 54-75. U.S. Department of Health and Human Services Administration for Children and Families Children's Bureau, Administration for Children and Families, Office on Child Abuse and Neglect (2003). *EMERGING PRACTICES in the Prevention of Child Abuse and Neglect.* Washington, DC: Author. This report was prepared by Caliber Associates under contract number 282-98-0025 (Task Order 13) with the Children's Bureau's Office on Child Abuse and Neglect.

Table Notes

* Much of the research on the identification of protective factors has focused on individual traits. This category of protective factors refers to factors that are learned (self care and interpersonal attributes) as well as factors for which the individual has no control (birth order, gender). Individual attributes include (Garmezy, 1983, 1985; Rae-Grant, Thomas, Offord, & Boyle, 1989; Rutter, 1979, 1981, 1985, 1987; 1990; Werner, 1989).

** Family characteristics also act a protective factors (Garmezy, 1983, 1985; Rae-Grant, Thomas, Offord, & Boyle, 1989; Rutter, 1979, 1981, 1985, 1987; 1990; Werner, 1989).

*** Community characteristics include individuals and institutions, external to the family, that provide educational, emotional, and general supportive ties with the family unit as a whole or with individual family members. Community protective factors include (Garmezy, 1983, 1985; Rae-Grant, Thomas, Offord, & Boyle, 1989; Rutter, 1979, 1981, 1985, 1987; 1990; Werner, 1989).

---

lens for analyzing human behavior and social functioning within an environmental context; a risk and protective factors perspective, competence-centered perspective, which highlights practice methods and strategies that promote the effective functioning of children, parents, and families; a developmental perspective, which provides a frame of reference for understanding the growth and functioning of human beings in the context of their families and their families' transactions with their environments; and a permanency planning orientation to child welfare, which embodies a mandate to maintain children in their own homes or, if necessary, place them permanently with other families.

Theoretical Frameworks Underlying Child Welfare Policies and Programs and Family-Centered Practice[1]

Overview

While there is not universal agreement, a number of theoretical models appear to underpin some aspects of child welfare program design and policy: the ecological model, child development theories, social learning and social support theory, and models of risk and protective factors.

Ecological Developmental Models

Child characteristics interact with the experience of child maltreatment (risk) and foster care (protection) to produce outcomes. These characteristics include genetic factors, risk factors such as poverty, racism, and dangerous living environments, and family of origin characteristics and functioning (Cicchetti & Lynch, 1993; Fraser, 2004; Garbarino & Ganzel, 2000). In addition, family characteristics and functioning, other child/family supports, the quality and nature of services provided by various community agencies, and other factors interact with the experiences of child maltreatment to produce certain outcomes.

According to an ecological perspective delineated by Cicchetti & Lynch (1993, pp. 102-103), families (and foster families) can act as a powerful micro-system intervention that can have important protective and ameliorative functions for the youth. In terms of outcome areas, it is important to assess a range of domains, including mental and physical health, adaptive functioning, cognitive functioning, and social functioning. The ecological model espoused by Bronfenbrenner (2004) posits that individual development occurs and can only be understood within a larger family and social-environmental ecological context. In this model, the interplay of factors at the level of the individual, the family and the environment are all necessary to understand what appear to be individual behavior and individual outcomes. The ecological perspective draws from such fields as ecology, systems theory, anthropology, and organizational theory. In particular, it builds on ecology as a metaphor and thus on the study of the interactions between living organisms and their environments (Bronfenbrenner, 1979, 1986; Garbarino, 1992; Moen, Elder, & Luscher, 1995). This perspective requires identifying and analyzing risk and protective factors at the level of the child, the level of his or her family, and at the broader societal level. Children's development arises from the complex interplay of these interwoven elements.

Consider, as an example, the ecology of a family in the following situation of a young couple referred to an agency because of their neighbors' concern about possible maltreatment of their child:

This is the case of a young couple with a three-year-old son who is developmentally delayed. Both parents have unmet needs for affection, and they have not yet developed a sense of mutuality as a couple. In addition, it has been difficult for them to manage financially, as neither has had regular employment. The family has been moving from community to community in the past few years, in search of employment. (Adapted from Kirsh & Maidman, 1984, p. 11)

From this brief sketch, one can begin to see how and why the family is functioning poorly. There are numerous stresses in their environment. Their skills do not match the employment opportunities in their community; the couple has not been in one community long enough to develop adequate support systems; and they are not yet capable of giving each other much-needed support. At the same time, their son demands a great deal of attention. Under these circumstances, it is easy to see how the child might have become the target of his parents' frustrations and anger, especially in light of their own unmet needs.

As this example suggests, many personal, family, and environmental factors converge and interact with each other to influence the family. In other words, human behavior is not solely a function of the person or the environment, but of the complex interaction between them. As Kurt Lewin (1935) captured it decades ago, $B = f(P + E)$, that is, behavior is a function of person and environment in continuous interaction. When viewed from the perspective of ecology, the above case example suggests various principles useful in child welfare practice.

It is useful to conceptualize child welfare as a comprehensive continuum of services with a strong preventive component. Each child welfare service tries to prevent the use of a more intensive and intrusive service, and child welfare services in the aggregate endeavor to prevent the transition of children into more restrictive services like juvenile justice. The ecological perspective stimulates a marked shift from a narrow orientation of inadequate parenting to a broad view of child welfare that emphasizes a multifaceted practice approach to children and their families in the context of their life situation and environment (Germain & Gitterman, 1996; Pelton, 1991). Scholars from diverse disciplines have called attention to the impact of the environment on the child's development and functioning. Such authors as Kamerman and Kahn (1995) and Berrick, Needell, Barth, and Johnson-Reid (1998) have noted the importance of social policies that respond to the unique needs of young children and families. Finally, The Center for the Developing Child (2007) and Fraser (2004), among others, underscore the role of preventive services in ameliorating the effects of poverty and other stressful environmental factors.

Developmental Theory

Many theoretical approaches related to developmental theory are especially relevant to informing foster care practice. Three examples are briefly highlighted: First, attachment theory addresses relationships and traumas occurring prior to age two (Ainsworth, 1989; Weinfield, Ogawa, & Sroufe, 1997). Second, trauma theory, as researched by Briere & Scott (2006) Kendall-Tackett (2003) and others regarding the effects of abuse and neglect, offers explanations for variations in the types and impact of abuse and for the impact of immediate or delayed intervention. Third, Erikson's developmental theory is useful in understanding and predicting child adjustment sequelae, including for foster care (Downs & Pecora, 2004; Erikson, 1985).

Social Learning and Social Support Theory

Chamberlain (2003) and her colleagues (e.g., Fisher, Burraston, & Pears, 2005) have implemented one of the most promising evidence-based models of treatment foster care that is based on various theoretical perspectives, particularly social learning theory. The latter emphasizes the complex nature of social situations and holds that human behavior occurs within an interactive social context. Fisher and colleagues have also shown that changing the social environment can also change physiological functioning, as the young children in the Early Intervention Treatment Foster Care Program, for Pre-K children, results in marked improvements in the regulation of stress and attentiveness, as indicated by marked normalization of cortisol levels compared to children in a comparison group of children in conventional foster care (see http://www.mtfc.com).

Social support theory is just beginning to be recognized as important, as we document with even firmer data that placement disruptions and school dislocation result in poor adult outcomes (e.g., Pecora, et al., 2003; Ryan & Testa, 2004), in direct contrast to what we know about the buffering effects of a positive social support system (Maluccio, Pine, & Tracy, 2002). Such a perspective stresses the importance of providing consistent supports to children, birth parents, and foster families.

Risk and Protective Factors

Conceptually, risk and protective factors are those elements that respectively influence the chances of adverse outcomes and optimal development (Fraser, Kirby, & Smokowski, 2004). A number of important risk factors are associated with child maltreatment or behavioral problems that require child welfare agency involvement, including family poverty, parental substance abuse, parental mental illness, parental history of child maltreatment, social isolation, community lack of employment resources, and neighborhood gangs and crime (see Table 3.1).[2]

Research on protective factors associated with child maltreatment is more limited but is informed by the larger protective factor literature. Several studies have outlined general factors which differentiate resilient children from those who have serious adjustment problems. Protective factors appear to fall into three general categories: individual characteristics, family characteristics, and significant supportive others available through the community (Fraser, 2004; Garmezy, 1985; Rutter, 1990; Werner, 1989). Individual characteristics include attributes such as self-sufficiency, high self-esteem, realism, and altruism (Egeland, 2007). Family characteristics include supportive relationships with adult family members, harmonious family relationships, expressions of warmth between family members and mobilization of supports in times of stress. Finally, community supports refers to supportive relationships with people and/or organizations external to the family. These external supports provide positive and supportive feedback to the child and reinforce and reward the child's positive coping abilities (Fraser, 2004).

Similar to Parish & Whisnant (2006), the most important protective factors emerge from the family and community context—parental competence as nurturers and positive disciplinarians, carers and advocates for their children; having supportive parent social supports, peer networks, extended families and communities; inclusion in communities and activities of daily life, and available medical, educational, and financial resources to allow parents to provide appropriate care for their children.

There are compelling connections between poverty and child maltreatment. Low-income families are less likely to have access to adequate food, pre-natal and other medical care, and safe housing. They tend to have fewer social supports and experience more stress in child rearing—all of which can increase the risk of child maltreatment. Generally, poverty has a direct negative influence on maternal behavior, and subsequently on the quality of parenting children receive (Brooks-Gunn, Klebanov, & Liaw, 1995). For children, generally, living in poverty is associated with a host of negative consequences, including poor physical health, diminished cognitive abilities, emotional and behavioral problems, and reduced educational attainment (see Brooks-Gunn & Duncan, 1997; Leventhal & Brooks-Gunn, 2004). But the connection between poverty and foster care placement is complex and poverty is not so strongly associated with placement of children in foster care in nonurban areas as it is in urban areas (Barth, et al., 2006). In non-urban areas, children's behavior problems are very prevalent among children who are placed.

Risk and protective factor frameworks have descriptive utility for explaining resiliency in children and youths and for identifying predictors of adult outcomes. Protective factors can be personal (e.g., social competence) and environmental assets (e.g., supportive parents or other relatives) that buffer or suppress risk (Catalano & Hawkins, 1996; Fraser, 2004; Rutter, 1989).

Cultural Issues Related to Risk and Protection in Child Welfare

While the literature is sparse, the risk and protective factors present in many families and communities of color need to be recognized:

Assessing for risk of child abuse and neglect offers special challenges to practitioners who are unfamiliar with the diversity in culture of families of color. Families of color often have different family structures (Lynch & Hanson, 1992; Mindel, Habenstein, & Wright, 1988), child rearing practices (Lynch & Hanson, 1992; Mindel et al., 1988), gender and family roles (Lynch & Hanson, 1992; Mindel et al., 1988), and relationships to community (Lynch & Hanson, 1992; Mindel et al., 1988). Failing to accurately assess for these cultural differences might yield an incomplete assessment of the family especially as it relates to family strengths. Lack of resources related to poverty might also obscure a practitioner's ability to identify strengths. (Hodges, 1994, p. 1)

The preceding discussion offers a brief overview of the individual, family, and community protective factors that serve as a buffer to some children during stressful and or abusive situations. However, given the differences in family structure, child-rearing practices, and relationship to community, the degree to which the above factors apply to families of color is unclear. Certainly some of the characteristics are universal across ethnic and class background, middle- or upper-socioeconomic status and academic success for example. However, other factors may have a greater or lesser impact on families of color. In fact, some characteristics that apply specifically to families of color may not be represented in the above discussion. The following list of protective factors from Hodges (1994), while applicable to most families, may have special relevance to families of color:

- *Active Extended Family*: fictive or blood relatives that are active in the child life; provides material resources, childcare, supervision, parenting, emotional support to the child (Wilson, 1984).
- *Church or Religious Affiliation*: belongs to and actively participates in a group religious experience. Faith and prayer (Werner, 1989).
- *Strong Racial Identity*: exhibits racial pride, strongly identifies with ethnic group through clubs, organizations, political and social change movements.
- *Close Attachment to the Ethnic Community*: resides in the ethnic community, easy access to ethnic resources including social services, merchants, media (newspaper), demonstrates a commitment to the ethnic community.
- *Dispositional Attributes*: activity level, sociability, average intelligence, competence in communication (oral and written), internal locus of control (Werner, 1989).
- *Personal Attributes*: high self-esteem, academic achievement, assertiveness, quality of adjustment to single-parent household.
- *Supportive Family Milieu*: cohesiveness, extensive kinship network, non-conflictual relations.
- *External Support System*: involvement of absent fathers, male role models, supportive social environments of the African American community.

A modern and yet culturally traditional example of a strength-based and family-centered approach to caring for children and youth is the Te Aho Takitoru model of practice for caring for Māori children and teenagers. It is based on the Māori world view and key life principles; and was developed by a team of social workers from the Open Home Foundation in New Zealand (Te Whare Kaupapa Āwhina, http://www.ohf.org.nz/index.htm), a family services agency. Among the key concepts of the Tuapapa (the compass or backbone that guides their practice) are becoming, behaving, believing, and belonging. Major practice premises include:

- Whānau (birth and extended family) is the primary unit of care.
- Birth and extended family members are connected to hapu (sub-tribe), iwi (tribe) and waka (canoes).[3]
- Birth and extended family members desire wholeness and well-being that is measured in their own terms.
- Strong identity is fundamental to a sense of well-being.
- Birth and extended family members have strengths and capacities to find solutions.

Competence-Centered Perspective

Although its usefulness in clinical practice has been questioned (Wakefield, 1996a; 1996b), we believe that the ecological view is promising for the human services, since it heightens our awareness of the importance of an ecological person-environment perspective in understanding human beings and intervening in human problems. Also crucial is a related perspective about which there is a growing consensus in the human services, namely, a competence-centered or strength-oriented approach to practice that contrasts with the more traditional pathology or deficit model (Fontes, 2005; Maluccio, 1999; Rapp, 1998). While the metaphor of ecology provides a way of perceiving and understanding human beings and their functioning within the context of their environment, knowledge about competence development offers specific guidelines for professional practice and service delivery.

The competence perspective draws from ego psychology; psychodynamic psychology; and learning, developmental, and family systems theories. In social work as in other fields, competence is generally defined as the repertoire of skills that enable the person to function effectively. However, a distinction should be made between the notion of discrete competencies or skills and the broader, ecological, or transactional concept of competence. The latter may be defined as the outcome of the interplay among:

- a person's capacities, skills, potentialities, limitations, and other characteristics;
- a person's motivation—that is, her or his interests, hopes, beliefs, and aspirations; and

- the qualities of the person's impinging environment—such as social networks, environmental demands, and opportunities (Maluccio, 1981).

The ecological concept of competence leads to competence-centered social work practice, a perspective that explicitly holds that the promotion of competence in human beings is a central function of social work intervention (Maluccio, 1999). Competence-centered social work practice embodies a set of attitudes, principles, and strategies designed to promote effective functioning in human beings by focusing on their unique coping and adaptive patterns, mobilizing their actual or potential strengths, emphasizing the role of natural helping networks, building on their life experiences in a planned way, and using environmental resources as major instruments of help.

Developmental Perspective

By the developmental perspective, we mean a certain frame of reference for understanding the growth and functioning of human beings in the context of their families and their families' transactions with their environments. The developmental perspective is akin to the ecological perspective in that it views human behavior and social functioning within an environmental context. It goes beyond ecology, however, by bringing in other aspects such as the stages and tasks of the family's life cycle; the bio-psycho-social principles of individual growth and development; the goals and needs that are common to all human beings and families; and the particular aspirations, needs, and qualities of each person and each family in light of diversity in such areas as culture, ethnicity, race, class, and sexual orientation.

This highlighting of developmental theory should not be construed as minimizing the importance of attachment, trauma, social control, strain, and social learning theories. This includes such prominent aspects as the tasks and challenges associated with different individual and family developmental cycles; the repetition of the family life cycle in blended families; the role of family routines and rituals; the significance of cultural, ethnic, racial, and gender relativity; and the ways in which family functioning (cohesion, adaptability, communication, and role fulfillment) is in part dependent upon the developmental levels of individual family members. For purposes of this chapter, a number of themes flowing from the developmental perspective are highlighted:

- Family-centered services and practice need to take into account the concept of development, through explicitly considering this question: Which interventions are effective, with which specific child/family problems, in which environmental settings, and at what particular developmental stages? The stage of development seems to be increasingly important in the individual's as well as the family's ability to enter into and use help in the field of human services.

- Policies, services, and practice should reflect current knowledge about the development of women, minorities, and other special populations, rather than rely primarily on traditional models such as those derived from psychoanalysis.
- Individual as well as family development is multiply determined and always occurring (Freud, 1988; Kreilkamp, 1989). Indeed, implicit in the developmental perspective "is a thoroughgoing belief in the inevitability of change, in the dynamic tendencies inherent in human existence" (Kreilkamp, 1989, p. 89). At the same time, there may be some underlying individual characteristics that may be particularly difficult to change, especially in troubled families (Cadoret, et al, 1995).
- Peer groups play an important role in a child's development (Ryan, 2001).

Family-centered practice should be guided by an optimistic view of the capacity of children—and adults—to overcome early deprivation and other adverse early life experiences through nurturing and supportive experiences throughout the life cycle (see, for example, Fraser, 2004; Shonkoff & Phillips, 2000; and Weissbourd, 1996). In short, human development is a dynamic process that involves complex and interdependent connections among human beings, their families, and their social and physical environments (Germain, 1991). Human beings actively shape—and are also shaped by—their social/ecological contexts (Bronfenbrenner, 2004). In fact, a child- and family-centered perspective with these components seems applicable to many countries as well. This perspective has been further elaborated in the recent assessment framework adopted in 2008 by Scotland, which is designed to reflect a child's viewpoint (see Figure 3.1).

Permanency Planning Orientation

Another perspective that since the 1970s has influenced child welfare services and practice even more directly than either the ecological model or the competence orientation is that of *permanency planning*. As described in Chapter 1, since most children coming to the attention of the child welfare system are at risk of placement out of their homes, a comprehensive framework for child welfare practice must incorporate the values, goals, and principles of permanency planning.

Permanency planning embodies a number of key features:

- First, it is a *philosophy* highlighting the importance of the biological family and the value of rearing children in a family setting;
- Second, it is a *theoretical perspective* stressing that opportunities for stability and continuity of relationships should be thoroughly explored because they can promote a child's growth and functioning; [4]

Figure 3.1
Scottish My World Triangle

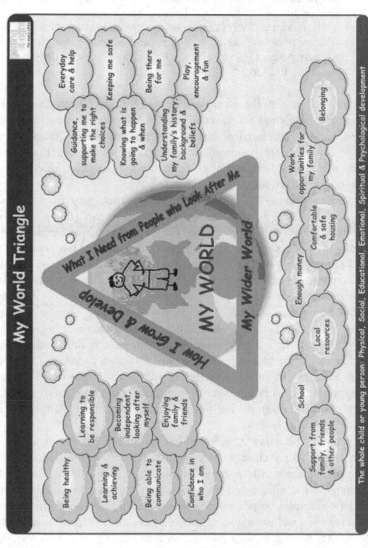

Source: Scottish Government. (2008). Scottish My World Triangle (version 3). Scotland: Author. Reprinted with Permission.

- Third, it is a *program* focusing on systematic planning within specified time frames for children who are in foster care or at risk of placement out of their home;
- Fourth, it is a *case management method* emphasizing practice strategies such as case reviews, contracting, and decision-making, along with participation of parents in the helping process; and
- Finally, it is an *active collaboration* among various community agencies, childcare personnel, lawyers, judges, and others working with children and their parents (Casey Family Programs, 2003; Maluccio, Fein, & Olmstead, 1986, pp. 5-15).

In conjunction with the other perspectives that have been described, permanency planning can be a powerful tool in our efforts to meet the needs of children, parents, and families through an approach that is consonant with a developmental rather than a remedial conception of services. Permanency planning has achieved a permanency of its own in the landscape of child welfare and has had a marked impact on service delivery.

Since the beginning of the 1990s, however, permanency planning has been questioned and perhaps seen as an outmoded response to a complex problem.[5] In our view, however, it is not outmoded. Indeed, it should endure, both as a philosophy and as a method or program, because it incorporates a basic value—namely, that every child is entitled to live in a family, preferably her or his own biological family, in order to have the maximum opportunity for growth and development. In today's context, it means serving children at risk of out-of-home care and their families through policies and programs that emphasize the safety of the child and balance concern regarding the parents' or children's problems with greater attention to the conditions that create or sustain family dysfunction. It gives serious attention to family preservation, through an array of services including intensive, home-based preventive and supportive services continuum; including providing after-care services to maintain the child in the biological or other permanent family following discharge from foster care.

Permanency planning requires collaboration among the various helping systems, particularly child welfare, courts, education, housing, health, and income maintenance. This includes strengthening the roles of mental health practitioners with children and youths in settings such as child guidance clinics, psychiatric programs, and the juvenile justice system. These systems can provide supports to child welfare workers, foster parents, and other childcare personnel and empower them to do their job—rather than burn out in an unrewarding and unsupportive work environment. Thus, a continuum of services is established from day care to residential treatment, as well as addressing juvenile court and other legal and procedural issues that inhibit the timely decision-making required in permanency planning.

Applying a Family-Centered Perspective

This chapter has thus far presented a comprehensive conceptual framework for child-focused and family-centered practice consisting of ecological, competence, and developmental perspectives along with a permanency planning orientation. The framework leads to a range of implications for policy and practice, which will be highlighted here and integrated in subsequent chapters.

Establishing a Continuum of Services

The ecological perspective ultimately requires a shift to a society-centered approach to child and family welfare that focuses especially on economics, employment, public health, and education. In the meantime, in response to the multiple needs of families in basic areas of living, there must also be comprehensive as well as intensive services. These include both "soft" services, such as counseling, and "hard" services, such as financial assistance. Various studies have shown that troubled families require a range of services to prevent out-of-home placement or to reunite children with their families (see, for example, Fein, Maluccio, & Kluger, 1990; Pew Foundation, 2008; Schorr & Marchand, 2007). As discussed further in Chapter 7, a continuum of services is often required to support families, including early intervention programs, concrete services such as housing and transportation, counseling, day care, and emergency foster care.

There should be emphasis upon a continuum of services providing both therapeutic help and environmental supports to the family before, during, and after the child's placement in care. Moreover, services should concentrate on strengthening the parents' coping and adaptive capacities. A family often may require services on an ongoing basis, even after the immediate crisis is resolved (Freundlich & Wright, 2003; Kagan & Schlosberg, 1989; Kaplan & Girard, 1994). In this regard, practitioners should challenge current state and federal policies that fund primarily programs providing time-limited help, with insufficient assessment of the need for follow-up services. What results is that families often fail when left unsupported after the time-limited service has ended. Through advocacy efforts, backed by research data, this trend must be reversed. Policymakers must acknowledge that many vulnerable families continue to need help, sometimes indefinitely, given their chronic problems and lack of supports in their environment. Society cannot expect such families to be "cured," even with intensive and excellent short-term help.

Emphasizing Neighborhood- or Community-Based Services

Research has also shown that services are most effective if they are not only comprehensive but also located at the neighborhood or community level. While the evidence base is mixed, neighborhood or community-based services appear to facilitate maximum responsiveness to the needs and qualities of each child or family (Daro, Budde, Baker, Nesmith, & Harden, 2005; Leon, 1999). The community orientation is seen in such practices as continuity between group care settings and community-based services, integrating services for "troubled" and "normal" youths, and expanding various types of family resource centers.

Community-based centers make a lot of sense, particularly since they provide help to families in their own natural surroundings and in non-stigmatizing or less stigmatizing ways. In addition to the continuum of services noted earlier, the community orientation requires flexible access, creation of new resources as gaps are identified, interagency and intra-agency collaboration, and monitoring of the delivery and effectiveness of services for particular families. Leon (1999) describes a "family support model" that reflects such a community orientation and that has been successfully implemented in Florida by means of Neighborhood Centers for Families. The model provides integrated services that incorporate the following features:

- neighborhood base;
- coordination with other community agencies;
- measurement of service effectiveness; and
- involvement of the community in collaborative efforts.

Restructuring the Family's Environment

Through the provision of comprehensive, community-based services, professionals have an opportunity to help families to restructure their environment, that is, to modify or enrich it so that it is more suited to their needs and qualities and more conducive to their positive functioning. Social workers have a major responsibility in this area, to help counteract the impact of the "sociocultural risks" noted earlier in this chapter. Although there is consensus about the need to improve a family's social and physical environment, it is often difficult to do so. But it does require, in addition, a major source of help often can be the family's own extended kinship system (Danzy & Jackson, 1997; Everett, Chipungu, & Leashore, 1991; Geen, 2003; Testa, 2001).

For example, family group conferences can be used to involve relatives and others significant persons in the family's environment to develop and implement permanency plans for a child. This innovative model of family decision-making in child welfare originated in New Zealand, based on indigenous decision-making practices. In that country, national law requires child welfare agencies to refer for family group conferences every substantiated case of child abuse and neglect. The conference, which is led by a court-appointed "care and protection coordinator," involves family members and kin, friends, professionals, and others who are in one way or another connected to the family. Its purpose is to help the extended family to reach a decision regarding care of the child in question, following extensive deliberations (see American Humane Association website: http://www.americanhumane.org/site/PageServer?pagename=pc_home; Burford & Pennell, 1995; Lupton, 1998).

The New Zealand model is increasingly being adopted in private and public child welfare agencies in the U.S., as a means of promoting involvement of the extended family in the care and protection of children at risk of child abuse and neglect and out-of-home placement. Merkel-Holguin & Wilmot (2004) provide a concise overview. Connolly and McKenzie (1999) delineate the application of family group conference concepts in the U.S., focusing on a model of decision-making that they call *Effective Participatory Practice*. Hardin (1996) and Crampton (2007) describe, in concrete terms, how family group conferences work; explain their advantages and pitfalls; and identify issues regarding their application in the U.S. We need continued and deeper evaluation of their effectiveness within the U.S. context.

Above all, restructuring the family's environment means that agencies and social workers must become involved in advocacy and social action, to help resolve the systemic or societal problems that lead to out-of-home care in the first place. There is ample evidence of a high correlation between entry into out-of-home care and social problems such as poverty, deprivation, and racism (e.g., Roberts, 2002). In particular, attention must be paid to establishing a living wage and decent employment opportunities for all families, with adequate income maintenance and day care services to support families struggling in the work force (see Chapter 4). From an ethical and practical standpoint, child welfare staff at times serve not only as clinical and administrative practitioners but as policy advocates.

The ecological perspective directs our attention to these larger social and economic forces and the environmental context in which families function. Permanency planning cannot substitute for preventive services; increased investment in our children and their families long before symptoms emerge is essential and in—the long run—more cost effective.

The emphasis on human strengths also leads to the view of parents as resources on their own behalf—as partners in the helping process—rather than as carriers of pathology. As we shift from a pathological view of parents to a competence orientation, we are more likely to identify strengths in parents themselves and involve them in growth-producing activities. As they are given adequate opportunities, parents and other family members are better able to mobilize their own potentialities and natural adaptive strivings. They are thus empowered to act on their behalf (Jensen & Hoagwood, 2008; Maluccio & Whittaker, 1988; Pinderhughes, 1995). For example, substance-abusing families and their consequent child neglect represent a huge current issue; empowering parents requires that we confront the lack of treatment facilities, housing, and employment training programs, among many needs.

To support the efforts of parents to be resources for themselves and their families, agencies need to stress educational approaches, such as teaching skills in social interaction, communication, advocacy, problem-solving, and parenting. Practitioners also need to emphasize the participation of parents and children in processes such as case contracting and decision-making. These principles are being implemented in the more effective child abuse treatment, family-based, and permanency planning programs.

Roles of Practitioners and Clients

From the family-centered perspective also flow various implications regarding the roles of social workers working with families, as well as the roles of biological parents and children, foster parents, and other childcare staff members. The primary role of the social worker is that of a catalyst or enabling agent—someone who actively and systematically helps the family to identify or create and use necessary resources. The worker uses flexible approaches and calls on a variety of resources to help provide the conditions necessary for parents to achieve their purposes, meet life's challenges, and engage in their developmental processes. Above all, practitioners should become experts in methods of environmental modification, use of existing community resources and natural helping networks, creation of new resources that may be needed by their clients, and mobilization of family members' own resources.

Roles of Biological and Foster Parents

In line with the emphasis on collaboration that is inherent in permanency planning, efforts should be made to have parents, foster parents, and other childcare personnel regard themselves as partners in a shared undertaking, with common goals and mutually supportive and complementary roles. This can lead to new helping systems that are ultimately more effective and rewarding for everyone concerned. For instance, as considered further in Chapter 8, foster parents can be involved as resources for parents through such means as role modeling or serving as parent aides (Kemp, et al., 2007; Warsh, et al., 1994).

As suggested by these authors, foster parents can become allies of biological parents and more actively involved in the treatment plan in behalf of each family, as long as their roles are clarified and they are provided with adequate supports and rewards. For example, ways can be found in at least some cases to enable a foster family or residential treatment center to become an extension of the biological family, rather than its substitute, as is now the case. Further, in many cases the foster family could become an integral part of the overall treatment program and help promote the adaptive functioning of the biological parents (see Chapter 12 and Kufeldt, 1994).

One emerging approach, known as *shared family care*, involves having parents with weak parenting skills live together with their children in foster or group care so they can observe and practice parenting in a protective environment (Barth, 1994; Barth & Price, 1999). The foster family becomes an "extended family" that can direct parents in crisis to community resources as well as offer emotional supports while the family reestablishes itself (Kemp, et al., 2007).

Roles of Children and Youths

Engaging children and adolescents is also important. Children and youths themselves can also be actively involved in the helping process, including reaching decisions regarding the best permanent plan for them. As practitioners become more comfortable in asking about their views, they find that children and youths have a lot to say that should be taken into account in planning services on their behalf (Chapman, Wall, & Barth, 2004). For example, some older children make it clear that they prefer to be in a long-term foster home with continuing contact with their parents rather than being adopted or placed in an institution (Barth & Berry, 1994). Yet, one young adult sibling of a sister who had been adopted—something that she had refused to allow—later said "why would anyone think I knew enough to be allowed to decide whether I wanted to be adopted—all I was thinking of was that having an adoptive family meant that I would have rules even after age 18" (personal communication from teen panel member, September 24, 2007). Other young people vividly express their views about their experiences in foster care through poems, essays, and stories (Desetta, 1996; Fay, 1989). Findings from a survey of youth in out of home care recently showed the complexity of the beliefs involved—these youth felt comfortable and cared for in foster care (less so in group care) but still wanted to go home; they began to shift away from the desire to go home as years went by (Chapman, et al., 2004).

Appreciating the young person's perspective of course is critical in child and family welfare services, as illustrated in the story in Table 3.2, which reflects a child's experiences in moving into foster care. In addition to understanding the child's perspective, we should consider that the contract or written agreement can be profitably used as a means of helping children to make decisions, assume responsibility for their behavior, and take some control over their lives. For example, with adolescents in foster care, agreements can be used to clarify the tasks to be performed by the young person, the foster parents, and the social worker so as to facilitate the process of preparation for emancipation and independent living (Casey Family Programs, 2003; Maluccio, Krieger, & Pine, 1990).

Table 3.2
A Foster Child's Story by Francisco Maltos (Francisco Maltos, M.S.W., was a foster care worker at the time this story was written.)

The following story of a child placed in family foster care is based on a true event, which is described with additional information from the experiences of other youths. It is intended to help readers imagine what it would be like to be a young person in this situation. The story reflects one child's lived experience and is presented here to underscore the importance of considering a child's background and perspectives in the provision of child welfare services. It should also be noted that foster care will continue to be a reality for many children despite the best efforts at prevention. When provided effectively, foster care can be a caring and culturally sensitive option for at least some children.

The Story

The time of year is early summer. You are ten years old. You live in a small house about ten miles from town. You are of Mexican descent. You have brown skin and black hair. You are healthy, and at this time in your life, you have no reason to have any fears. On the radio, Jose Alfredo is singing, a voice you are very familiar with.

Your mom calls for you to come and eat and says, "*Lavate sus manos y vengase a comer hijo*" (wash your hands and come to eat, son). Your mother was American born near the border, your father is a Mexican immigrant. You and your family have been living in Washington state now for eight years. Both of your parents are farm workers.

Your culture is Mexican. At home, your parents only speak Spanish. You speak English, but only at school. Your English is not as fluent as the other students and sometimes you are embarrassed by that because sometimes you are laughed at. At home, you watch mostly Spanish TV shows. You listen to Mexican music on the radio, and about the only American culture you are exposed to at home are the English TV shows you occasionally watch. On the walls of your home hangs a picture of the Virgin de Guadalupe and a brown Jesus Cristo (Jesus Christ). In the corner sits a colorful piñata that will be broken next week at a friend's birthday party.

Your mom calls you again to eat. Before you begin to eat, you bless yourself. Your plate is already served. You reach for a hot tortilla and use it to eat your food, which is *arroz*, picadillo, chopped papas (potatoes), and asparagus that your mom makes in a special sauce. You use silverware to eat some foods, but most of the time, you prefer using a tortilla. At the table, your parents are talking about El Cinco de Mayo festivities that are going on in town and you look forward to attending. Your father also talks about attending Spanish Mass where one of his *compadres* is going to baptize his newest born. Then after the baptism there will be a *barbacoa* (barbecue), where a goat will be killed and prepared to eat. Those are always fun because there is music, food, and kids your age.

Next month, your parents are invited to a Quincienera. There will be a big dance and a lot of children, and you always have a good time chasing one another on the dance floor, around and through the people as they are dancing. Besides the Quincieneras, you are familiar with the other traditions of breaking piñatas on birthdays, making *cascarones* for Easter, having tamales around Christmas, and *bunuelos* around New Year's.

Respect towards your parents is important. You risk being slapped if you are smart with them. No drinking or smoking is allowed in the home. You are forbidden to use bad words. You never raise your voice at your parents and you notice your parents don't do that with other people.

The only contact you have at home with Anglos is when they come to your home to sell things, or when they are looking for your parents to ask about the bills they owe. At school you hang around mostly Mexican kids. You have white friends too, but not as many. You feel content at home, and you have no reason to question who you are. Your identity as an individual is forming, and although you are still too young to conceptualize this into words, your identity as Mexican is important to you.

Then a traumatic event changes everything. Both of your parents have been arrested by federal agents as they are working that morning cutting asparagus. They are taken to the local jail and are charged with defrauding the government of food stamps and public assistance. Unknown to you, your parents have been engaged in this illegal activity for three years, and will now face an indefinite amount of time in jail or prison. Your parents fear what will happen to you.

That afternoon at school, you are called to the office to meet with a social worker from child protective services. The social worker is white. He talks to you, using words that you don't understand. There are no interpreters available to help. You have no other family or relatives that can take you, so the decision is made to place you in foster care.

When you arrive at the foster home in town, the home seems so big compared to yours. You ask the social worker how long you will be here and he says, "Not too long." A large, white woman answers the door. She smiles and walks you into the home. It smells strange; you don't like it. You hear English music, you see pictures of a white Jesus Christ. There is a dog in the home and you think that this is unclean. The odor of cigarettes is in the air, and it smells bad. You feel afraid — not just because you are not at home, but because you are in a strange home, you are in an Americano home. "Will they treat me bad because I am Mexican? What if I can't understand what they say? Will they make fun of me when I talk?" The foster mom tries to comfort you, but she frightens you because her voice is so loud, and you are not used to that. Some older boys and girls come in the home now and they look at you. "Are they staring at me because I'm not white, or are they just wondering who I am, like I am wondering who they are?"

That evening, you meet the foster father. He is loud too, and you think he must be angry. He shakes your hand and he grabs you tight. It hurts. You're not used to that either. After a while, you are called to eat. After the blessing, you look at your food and recognize nothing you eat at home except what looks like rice. You automatically reach for a tortilla that's not there. Instead, you grab a piece of bread and use that. You quickly hear: "Use your fork, not your hands." The other children stare. It's hard to swallow your food. You feel so out of place. When you try to answer their questions, they tell you, "Speak up, I can't hear you." You try to speak louder, but it's too hard because something inside of you says you're not supposed to.

After a few weeks go by, you are a little more comfortable. The other children have asked you to teach them Spanish. The foster mom hears you and tells you, "Stop that, speak English in this home." It hurts you to hear that. You want to tell her something but you don't. After awhile, you decide it's best to do as she says.

It's now been about three months and legal entanglements keep your parents in jail. In fact, they will both be sent to a federal prison in California for two more years.

At your foster home, you are becoming much more fluent in English and you like that. You have learned to like English music a lot, and you almost never listen to Mexican music. You never speak Spanish at home and you never eat any authentic Mexican food. Even the way you dress now is different. You like the baggy pants and T-shirts, as long as they have the brand names. You are starting to try some of the cuss words now, but you're not quite brave enough to use them in the house.

Months continue to go by, and the social worker has no luck locating any relatives, and there are no Hispanic families locally to take you.

Time passes, and now it has been about twelve months and, unnoticed by you, you are becoming quite acculturated. You only watch English TV shows, you never go to Mexican celebrations like Quincieneras or Cinco de Mayo, and English church is not quite the same as Spanish Mass. The only socializing you do is with the foster parent's friends and relatives, and it's very obvious to them that you are not a blood relative.

The social worker needs to decide on a permanent placement for you and because you have adjusted so well, he is going to recommend that you stay in the home under a guardianship approved by the juvenile court. The foster parents agree to this because they consider you to be like one of their own now.

It's been a quick year in foster care, and you don't even realize all that has happened to you. There is no telling how long you will be living in your new home.

Conclusion

Current Status

This chapter has presented a conceptual framework for family-centered child welfare practice based on the interrelated perspectives of ecology, competence, human development, and permanency planning. There are numerous examples of promising CWS innovations in these areas, discussed here and in the chapters that follow.

Future Directions

For such an integrative framework to become fully implemented in the reality of practice, a number of issues and challenges will have to be confronted in the years ahead. First, it will be necessary to adopt an institutional/preventive/developmental orientation to service delivery with children and families. This will involve, among other aspects, a shift away from the traditional remedial or "pick-up-the-pieces" approach; reallocation of more resources into community-focused early intervention activities; recycling of existing facilities from solely crisis services to a continuum of care; an explicit focus on policy issues and structural reform; willingness to change the substance as well as the form of services; and greater attention to issues of human diversity in service delivery.

Second, there will need to be much more in the way of (1) collaboration within the field of human services, especially linkages of child welfare with related systems such as education, income maintenance, juvenile justice, law, and mental health; (2) multidisciplinary collaboration, with clarification of respective contributions and working relationships; and (3) multiagency collaboration, with special attention to clarification of respective roles and purposes, issues of territoriality, competition for funds, fragmentation in service delivery, and a more effective public-private partnership (see Table 3.5).

Third, there will be a variety of challenges in the area of personnel, including meeting the need for highly skilled staff, offering a range of educational opportunities, providing rewards and career ladders, retraining existing personnel as programs and practices change, and clarifying the roles and functions of different kinds of personnel (see Chapter 13 for further discussion)

Last, but not least, it will be necessary, perhaps more than ever before, to avoid theoretical or ideological rigidities and provincialism. The future of child welfare demands that diverse disciplines, agencies, and professionals be

Figure 3.2
An integrative framework for family-centered child welfare practice.

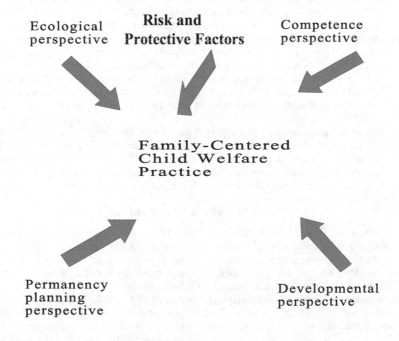

Source: Reprinted from Maluccio (1990)

ready to develop new theories, try new methods and approaches, and test their effectiveness in the provision of services to vulnerable families and children. The resulting integrative framework will thus be an open and evolving one, and the promise of a more effective continuum of services in child welfare will be more than an illusion.

Notes

1. Adapted from Pecora, Kessler, Williams, Downs, English, & White, 2010; and Maluccio & Pecora, 2006.
2. For a discussion of the connection between social problems and child placement, see Barth, Wildfire & Green (2006), Berrick, et al. (1998), and Pelton (1989).
3. Hapū is a Māori language word which refers to a social division of the *Māori* people of New Zealand, which is often translated as "subtribe." In general, a *hapū* is a division of a regional *Māori iwi* (tribe). Membership is determined by genealogical descent; a *hapū* is made up of a number of wh*ā*nau (extended family) groups. The literal meaning of the word is "pregnant," which is a metaphor of the genealogical connection that unites the members of the *hapū*. See http://en.wikipedia.org/wiki/Hapu.
4. It should also be noted that in some cases discontinuity can be beneficial. Maintaining continuous ties with families and communities may not, under many circumstances, have the advantages of discontinuity. Many parents, every year, make decisions to move their children to other schools in order to help them to improve educational attainment, even though it might involve disrupting children's friendships and possibly moving the entire household. In some child welfare cases, planned discontinuity can also benefit children. In one of the authors' cases, a judge seeking to maintain continuity between a mother incarcerated for murder and her three children (ages 2, 3, and 7) refused to free any of them for adoption because the older child had expressed interest in continuing relationships with the biological mother and younger children. By not having the option to discontinue their legal ties to their mother (while encouraging some continuous ongoing contact with her and each other), these children were exposed to long-term foster care, which is likely to have many placement moves and much discontinuity (Berrick, et al., 1998).
5. In a provocative essay, Gilligan (1997) proposes a shift from permanence to *resilience* as an organizing concept for child placement planning and practice. He defines resilience as "the capacity to transcend adversity" (p. 14). While continuing to embrace the positive aspects of the permanency planning perspective, he argues that it may be more helpful to strive to foster resilience in children.

For Further Information

Anderson, G.R., Ryan, A.S., & Leashore, B.R. (1997). *The challenge of permanency planning in a multicultural society.* New York: The Haworth Press. Thorough discussion of issues, concepts, and strategies in achieving permanency planning, particularly for African-American, Latino, and Native American children; gay and lesbian adolescents; and unaccompanied refugee minors.

Center on the Developing Child at Harvard University. (2007). *A Science-Based Framework for Early Childhood Policy: Using Evidence to Improve Outcomes in Learning, Behavior, and Health for Vulnerable Children.* Boston, MA: Author. Retrieved September 26, 2007 from: http://www.developingchild.harvard.edu. Summarizes recent brain science and child development research to make the case for supporting certain kinds of early childhood development programs.

Lynch, E.W. & Hanson, M.J. (1998). *Developing cross-cultural competence*. Second Edition. Baltimore, MD: Paul H. Brookes Publishing. Detailed guide for working with children and families from a range of ethnic, cultural, and racial groups.

Maluccio, A.N., Fein, E., & Olmstead, K.A. (1986). *Permanency planning for children: Concepts and methods*. London and New York: Routledge, Chapman, and Hall. Presents an integrative, in-depth discussion of the philosophy, theory, and practice of permanency planning for children and youths within a family-centered orientation.

Pew Foundation. (2008b). *Time for reform: investing in prevention: keeping children safe at home*. Philadelphia: Author. Retrieved January 28, 2008 from www.kidsarewaiting. org. Presents a rationale and research evidence for increasing CWS and community focus on family-centered services.

4

Economic Security for Families
with Children

Most of this text deals with child welfare and family services—the key programs, the important service delivery issues, the challenges facing such services, and the practice principles gleaned from careful research. Delivering and improving these services contribute to children's well-being and are central tasks of social workers. These services do not, by themselves, guarantee the well-being of children. For healthy growth and development, children need parents with adequate incomes to provide the material essentials of life—food, clothing, shelter, medical care, etc. If parental income is low or absent, children need to rely on income support programs for these resources.

This chapter examines child poverty in the United States, discusses its adverse effects on children, and describes current American antipoverty policies. It then evaluates these policies, compares the U.S. situation to that in other affluent countries, and discusses alternative strategies for reducing child poverty.

Income support programs and the low wage labor market are important parts of the social environment of many families who need child welfare services. The financial pressures faced by poor families, and financial emergencies that may arise if income support benefits are delayed or denied, put stress on those families and place their children at greater risk of maltreatment and placement in foster care. Social workers need to take account of these circumstances when planning services. Equally important, raising income may be an effective way to reduce families' needs for child welfare services and, thereby, ease the caseload burden on child welfare workers and reduce budgetary pressures on child welfare agencies. Improving children's lives calls for both an "incomes" strategy and the "services" strategy that social workers are more familiar with. This chapter's information about how labor market and income support policies affect families' economic security can help social workers develop a more integrated approach to child welfare policy issues and, more broadly, to improve children's lives.

The Economic Status of Families with Children

Trends in Incomes of Families with Children

Table 4.1 shows median family income for four selected years for all families with children under age eighteen, and separately for those with either one or two parents present.[1] All incomes are adjusted to the 2005 price level. With these "real" income figures, we can directly compare the purchasing power of incomes received in different years. Median family income was nearly stagnant between 1980 and 1990. During the prosperous 1990s, families with children fared well economically and the median rose 16 percent. But in the first 5 years of the new century, the median fell 4 percent. The trends are similar for white, black and Hispanic families, but the two minority groups have always had much lower median incomes than the whites.

When we compare married-couple to unmarried-parent families, important differences appear. Two parent families prospered between 1980 and 2000 as their median income rose 31 percent. The median fell slightly during the next 5 years but over the quarter century, it rose 30 percent. The median for families with a female parent and no husband increased 22 percent over the same period. In stark contrast, the median for families with a male parent and no wife fell 8 percent. The proportion of families with one parent grew from 19.6 percent of all families in 1980 to 31.1 percent in 2005. Families with a male parent and no wife have been the most rapidly growing family type and now account for more than 6 percent of all families with children. Since a growing proportion of children are likely to live in single parent families, widening income gaps between these families and married-couple families is a serious concern.

Poverty among Children

Measuring Poverty

Mollie Orshansky, an economist at the Social Security Administration, developed a definition of poverty in 1963. With a few changes, the federal government adopted it as the official definition of poverty in 1969, and has modified it in small ways since then. It provides a set of "poverty lines" that vary by household size, the age of the household head, and the number of children under eighteen. The lines are updated to match the change in the Consumer Price Index, so they represent the same purchasing power each year. For 2008 the poverty line ranged from $10,326 for a single person over age 65 to $47,915 for a family of 9 or more (U.S. Census Bureau 2007a). For a family of 4 with 2 children it was $21,834, or $420 per week. If a family's annual income falls below its poverty line, its members are counted as poor.

The official definition counts cash income from all public and private sources, except capital gains. It does not take into account public or private non-cash

Table 4.1
Median Real Income and Distribution of Family Types for Families with
Children; Selected Years, 1980-2005 (2005 dollars)

Median Income	1980	1990	2000	2005	Percent Change 1980-2005
All families with children	$47,941	$49,575	$57,470	$55,176	15.1
Married-couple families with children	$54,540	$59,757	$71,558	$70,853	29.9
Female-headed families, no husband present, with children	$18,992	$18,961	$24,842	$23,131	21.8
Male-headed families, no wife present, with children	$39,862	$36,515	$36,822	$36,568	- 8.3

Percentage of All Families with Children					Percentage Point Change, 1980-2005
Married-couple families with children	80.1%	73.6%	71.1%	68.9%	- 11.2
Female-headed families, no husband present, with children	18.1%	22.3%	23.1%	24.5%	6.4
Male-headed families, no wife present, with children*	1.8%	4.0%	5.9%	6.6%	4.8

Source: U.S. Census Bureau http://www.census.gov/hhes/www/income/histinc/f10ar.
html, accessed 6 April 2007.
*Figure is for 1978.

benefits such as food stamps, Medicaid, or employer-provided health insurance, nor does it subtract taxes. Yet both non-cash benefits and taxes affect a family's standard of living.

The official measure has been criticized on a number of grounds (Citro & Michael 1995). Some critics think the lines are too low. Some argue for different methods of adjusting the lines over time, for family size, or for the local cost of living. Some want to include non-cash benefits, subtract taxes, make other adjustments to income, or examine families' consumption rather than income. Despite these debates, the official measure remains an important social indicator and draws attention to the plight of the country's poorest residents.

Trends in Poverty among Children

In 2007, 18.0 percent of American children, or 13.3 million, were poor according to the official definition. Among children under age 6 the poverty rate was higher: 20.8 percent. If we use a poverty line 25 percent higher than the official one, which many would argue is a more realistic contemporary standard, the child poverty rate in 2007 was 23.8 percent. Children are by far the poorest age group in the United States. In 2007 the poverty rate among adults age 18 to 64 was 10.9 percent; among adults age 65 or more it was 9.7 percent.

Child poverty fell throughout the 1960s, gradually increased during the 1970s, and, as shown in Figure 4.1, sharply increased from 1980 to 1983. During the next decade it fell and then rose in line with the economic cycle. Since 1993 child poverty has trended down, interrupted by the recession in 2001-2003. Yet in 2007 the poverty rate among children of 18.0 percent was 1.8 percentage points *higher* than in 1976—30 years earlier—and 4.0 percentage points *higher* than in 1969, the year when child poverty was lowest.

Material Hardship among Children

Indicators of "material hardship" identify persons whose consumption falls short of socially accepted minimum levels (Beverly, 2001). Examples include not having enough to eat and going without needed medical care. Such indicators supplement the official, income-based poverty measure and increase our knowledge of the extent and nature of economic deprivation. Poor families with children face material hardships more often than their counterparts with higher incomes (Ouellette, et al., 2004). Yet most poor families do not experience each specific hardship, while some non-poor persons do. For example, in 1996, 6.0 percent of poor families lost gas or electric service (so 94 percent did not), compared to 3.2 percent of families between 100 and 200 percent of the poverty line and 1 percent of families more than 200 percent above the line. Corresponding figures for food insecurity were 32, 19.5, and 5.4 percent. Because there is no widely accepted measure of material hardship and data on it have not been regularly collected, it is difficult to compare studies and examine time trends.

Child Poverty, Race, Ethnicity, and Type of Family

Children's chances of being poor strongly depend on their race and ethnicity. Child poverty among blacks and Hispanics has always exceeded that for non-Hispanic whites and Asians and Pacific Islanders (Figure 4.1). From 1993 to 2001 poverty trended downward for all groups then remained flat or, for blacks, increased several percentage points. In 2006 the rates for blacks (33.4 percent) and Hispanics (26.9 percent) remained well above those for non-Hispanic whites

(10 percent) and Asians and Pacific Islanders (12.2 percent). In contrast, though child poverty among Asians and Pacific Islanders was much higher than among whites in the late 1980s, the gap has disappeared in recent years. Child poverty among Native Americans in 1999, the most recent year with data, was 31.6 percent—about the same as for blacks and Hispanics that year.[2]

Family structure is also a key determinant of poverty status. In 2006, 36.5 percent of families with children, a female parent, and no husband present were poor. Married-couple families with children had a poverty rate of only 6.4 percent. Families with children, an adult male, and no wife present had a rate of 17.9 percent. Since the early 1980s, poverty slowly trended downwards for female parent and married-couple families until 2000, then slightly rose or remained fairly steady. Poverty among male-parent families, in contrast, is currently higher than in the 1970s.

In 2006 non-Hispanic white children comprised 32 percent of all poor children. Non-Hispanic blacks accounted for 31 percent, and Hispanics (who may be of any race) accounted for 34 percent, and Asians accounted for 3 percent. Two-parent families accounted for 30 percent of all poor families with children. Families with a female parent and no husband present accounted for 62 percent, and families with a male parent and no wife present contained 8 percent. Though child poverty is concentrated in families with minority and female heads, we must recognize that poor children come from all types of families.[3]

Time Spent in Poverty

The longer children live in poverty, the more likely they are to suffer its negative consequences. Time in poverty is very unequally shared among children. Data from the 1980s and 1990s shows that half of all American children were never poor while growing up. Of the half that did experience poverty, 44 percent were poor for no more than 3 years of their childhood. Another 21 percent were poor 4 to 6 years, and a full 35 percent were poor 7 years or more (Rainwater & Smeeding 2003, p. 58).

International Comparisons

UNICEF (2007) measures child poverty in 24 middle and high-income countries in 2000. The study defines poverty as living in a household with cash income, adjusted for needs, less than 50 percent of median household adjusted income. This "relative" approach indicates the share of a society's children that is being left behind as the economy grows.[4] Figure 4.2 shows that the U.S. child poverty rate of 21.7 percent was by far the highest. The United Kingdom was next highest at 16.2 percent, followed closely by Italy, Ireland, Spain, and Portugal. Nine countries had child poverty rates less than 10 percent. The Scandinavian countries' rates were all less than 4 percent. The United States ranks seventeenth on a simple measure of material hardship available for twenty-one countries.[5]

Causes of Continuing High Levels of Child Poverty

Three main reasons explain why child poverty has remained high. First, during the past twenty-five years an increasing proportion of families have been unable to earn enough to stay out of poverty. Real earnings and wage rates among men with twelve or fewer years of schooling have fallen over the past twenty-five years. Low-skill women did better—real wages increased 5 percent for high school dropouts and 17 percent for those with 12 years of schooling (Blank & Shierholz 2006). Many workers with some post-secondary schooling have also had problems earning more than the poverty line in the 1980s, 1990s, and 2000s.

Though a full understanding of the why earnings lagged among low-skill workers eludes researchers, major factors likely include technological change and increasing international competition, both of which reduced demand for less skilled workers, and heavy immigration flows that increased the domestic supply of less skilled workers (Danziger & Gottschalk 1995). These market forces placed downward pressure on low skill workers' wages. Erosion of the real value of the minimum wage and the rapid decline since 1975 in trade unionization depressed the wages of less-skilled workers. Less-skilled men also have increasingly been likely to stop working or settle for part-time work.

Figure 4.1
Child Poverty by Race and Ethnicity, 1976-2006

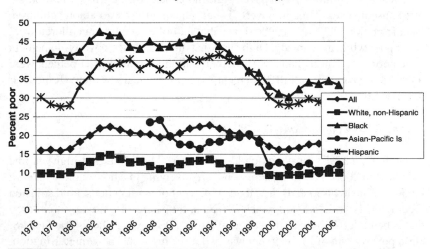

Source: http://www.census.gov/hhes/www/poverty/histpov/hstpov3.html, accessed August 29, 2007. Persons of Hispanic origin may be of any race. 1987 is the first year with data on Asian-Pacific Islanders.

These developments reinforced their declining real wages to produce substantial declines in real earnings.

Second, because of increases in divorce and non-marital childbearing, a larger fraction of children live with one parent. Mother-only families are much more likely to be poor than two-parent families because single mothers' earning power tends to be low, absent fathers often fail to pay child support, and public assistance benefits are low. Even when the single parent is the father, having one earner instead of two makes poverty more likely. This shift towards single parent families is a major reason why child poverty has remained high (Cancian & Reed, 2001). Because poverty among immigrants is more prevalent than among the native born, the rapid influx of immigrants that began in the 1980s is sometimes thought to be another demographic change that pushed poverty higher. However, unlike the changes in family structure, the increase in immigrants has had a negligible effect on poverty.[6]

Third, government income support benefits for families with children declined from the early 1970s to the early 1980s. Though they have increased significantly since then, they remain insufficient to pull millions of needy families over the poverty line.

Other social changes counteracted these poverty-increasing forces (Cancian & Reed, 2001). The average number of children per family declined. Since smaller families have lower poverty lines, this made it more likely that a given level of earnings would keep a family out of poverty. Increases in parents' educational levels and in the proportion of mothers in the paid workforce improved the earnings opportunities of families with children. These positive developments were too weak to overcome the adverse factors.

Child Maltreatment and Other Consequences of Poverty

Poor children are more likely to be hungry, threadbare, cold, crowded into poor housing, and without adequate medical care. Poor neighborhoods tend to be dangerous places to live and receive sub-par public services. Poor children are more likely to attend worse schools, do worse on tests of cognitive ability and educational achievement, have behavioral problems, complete less schooling, develop a criminal record, and earn less as adults (Duncan, et al., 1998; Wagmiller, et al., 2006). Children born to low income women have higher chances of infant and child mortality, poor health, and developmental disabilities (Starfield & Budetti, 1985). Besides all these adverse consequences of poverty, children in poor families are more likely to suffer maltreatment (Berger 2004; Paxson & Waldfogel, 2002) and be placed in foster care. Chapters 5 and 6 discuss the many factors, including poverty, associated with child maltreatment. No one of them completely explains this behavior. Child maltreatment occurs among all economic classes and most poor parents do not maltreat their children.

How should we interpret the association between low income and maltreatment? One explanation is that low income creates family stress that leads to a higher chance of abuse or neglect. A second is that poor parents may, despite the best intentions, be unable to provide adequate physical care to their children. To the extent these explanations are correct, reducing the number of families with low incomes would reduce child abuse and neglect.

Another possibility is that some parents' characteristics make them more likely to be both poor and abusive. For example, poor interpersonal skills, a short temper, or a drinking problem may cause an adult to lose jobs and have low earnings and make it more likely that he or she will be abusive. In families where poverty and abuse are jointly caused by some third factor, that factor must be directly addressed to curtail the abuse. Higher income will not eliminate the root cause of abusive behavior (the temper, heavy drinking, etc.). Such individuals may benefit from the service interventions discussed in chapters 7 through 9.

In some cases parents both suffer from the stresses caused by inadequate incomes and have characteristics that make them more likely to maltreat their children. For them, income and service strategies would both be in order.

A fourth possibility is that poverty raise a family's risk of being reported to a child protective agency. Poor families have more contact with persons required to report possible cases of maltreatment (e.g., in welfare offices, public health clinics, emergency rooms). If this is the main reason for the association between poverty and maltreatment, reducing poverty might reduce reported cases of maltreatment, but might not affect the actual level of maltreatment.

There is probably some truth in each interpretation. With the current level of knowledge researchers do not know how much of the association between poverty and child maltreatment is due to each. Still, reducing poverty will in no way increase child maltreatment; it will mean fewer children suffering from lack of basic material necessities and will improve children's life chances. If the first interpretation is most applicable, policies to reduce poverty have real potential to reduce the physical and emotional damages from child maltreatment.

Policies to Prevent and Reduce Child Poverty

Public policies that deal with child poverty have two broad goals. One is to *prevent* families from being poor by helping parents with low market skills earn their way above the poverty line and achieve self-reliance, which is so highly valued in the U.S. Policies to raise the earnings of poor parents are a subset of more general policies to improve the earnings of all low wage workers, most of whom either are now parents or will be.

The second is to ensure that a minimum level of resources is available to meet children's needs for food, shelter, health care, and other necessities if parents cannot adequately provide them out of earnings. To *reduce* poverty below what the labor market produces requires supplementing low private incomes with public cash transfers, tax credits, non-cash public benefits such as food stamps, and child support from absent parents.[7]

Policies for Increasing Market Incomes to Prevent Poverty

Increasing the demand for low wageworkers and, hence, their earnings can, in principle, be achieved by subsidizing firms to hire them. U.S. antipoverty policy has given little emphasis to this strategy.[8] The Work Opportunity Tax Credit provides tax savings to firms that hire low wage workers from families receiving Temporary Assistance for Needy Families (TANF) and food stamps, as well as other specified disadvantaged groups.[9] The Welfare-to-Work Tax Credit offers tax savings for hiring long-term recipients of TANF.

There is no evidence on either credit's effectiveness. The Targeted Jobs Tax Credit, a similar policy in force during 1979-1994, had a limited impact that mainly helped disadvantaged youth rather than adults with children (Katz, 1998). Many firms eligible for the credit did not claim it. Most credits went to firms that would have hired the targeted workers anyway. This suggests that the two current tax credits also have limited effects. Since they differ in some important ways from the earlier one, we should regard this inference as tentative (Bartik, 2001).

Federal "empowerment zones," "enterprise communities," and "renewal communities" offer tax breaks to firms that locate in and hire workers from economically distressed neighborhoods. Federal support for such efforts began in 1993. Most evaluations find no evidence that these programs generate new jobs. If there is an impact, the cost per new job is high—about $50,000. State and local enterprise zone programs, which are not usually targeted at poor neighborhoods, also have little effect on earnings of low-wage workers (Bartik, 2001).

Improving job readiness and occupational skills of low wageworkers to help them get better paying jobs has been the mainstay of efforts to prevent market income poverty. The primacy that Americans accord to work and their support of efforts to help persons become self-supporting ensure continued attention to these types of policies (Heclo, 1994) and may be why the U.S. has spent so much more on them than on demand side policies. Outlays for these "supply side" policies, though, are a small fraction of spending on income supplements.

The federal government pursues this "human capital" approach with two sets of activities. First are welfare-to-work grants to states and communities, which Congress enacted as part of welfare reform in 1996 and 1997. They aim to move welfare recipients into regular employment. Second are voluntary job training programs for dislocated workers and other persons facing labor market disadvantages. Currently the Workforce Investment Act (WIA) of 1998, which consolidated many programs and seeks to coordinate them better with other social services using "one-stop" delivery systems, guides most federal job-training policy.

Federal guidelines following enactment of TANF in 1996 allow states broad latitude in designing welfare-to-work programs. Most states have adopted "work first" programs that try to get TANF recipients into jobs as soon as possible. Participation in work or work-related activities is mandatory. Failure to do so risks a cut in benefits ("sanctions"). The programs help recipients prepare for jobs (interviewing skills, getting along on the job, organizing child care) and offer job search assistance. These are inexpensive services that focus on short term payoffs. Programs spend relatively little on longer-term classroom education and on-the-job training. Subsidized child care and help with transportation are available to facilitate participants' search and work efforts. TANF is discussed further in the income support section.

Mandatory welfare-to-work programs implemented before TANF usually increased work and earnings, led to less welfare use, and produced savings to public agencies that exceeded the costs of operation. The disappointing news is that most programs only increased earnings by $200 to $600 per year (Blank, 2002). Such small gains have a negligible effect on poverty among families with children. These findings underscore the challenges facing welfare-to-work programs if they are to achieve reductions in and poverty. The welfare-to-work programs instituted under TANF have not yet been carefully evaluated.

Along with welfare-to-work programs are employment and training programs that serve adults and youth in general. Participants may receive classroom instruction, job search assistance, and subsidized on-the-job training. Low-income persons have priority for these services, but are not entitled to them. Rigorous evaluations of programs implemented before WIA report earnings increases of about $850 per year (in 2005 dollars) for adult women. For adult men, some programs produced similar increases; others had no effect. In practical terms, gains of $850 are too small to have much impact on poverty. For disadvantaged youth most programs did not increase earnings. However, Job Corps, which offers a comprehensive set of services and has by far the highest cost per participant, tends to have larger impacts on youths' earnings and also reduces criminal activity (LaLonde, 2003).

Human capital programs can improve parents' and youths' (i.e., future parents) labor market performance and be productive investments in terms of returns per dollar spent. Since most programs invest much less per enrollee than the cost of a year of formal schooling, it is not surprising that they deliver, at best, modest increases in earnings. Improving the labor market prospects of low-skill, disadvantaged workers is a costly, slow process. Larger gains will require commensurably larger public investments.

Increasing the minimum wage. In 2007 Congress raised the federal minimum wage rate to $5.85 from $5.15, where it had remained for 10 years. The minimum will further increase to $7.25 in 2009. A full-time minimum-wage worker in 2009 will earn $4,200 more than in 2006. The higher earnings will trigger additional Earned Income Tax and Child Tax credits (discussed below), but a partial loss of a family's food stamp benefits. On net, in 2009 a family of 4 with 1 full-time minimum wageworker would be 5 percent above the poverty line, instead of 11 percent below, as it would be with a $5.15 minimum (Center on Budget and Policy Priorities, 2007a). Workers earning slightly above $7.25 will also gain as employers feel pressure to restore most or all of the gap between their wages and the minimum.

Concern that a higher minimum discourages job creation and leads to layoffs or fewer work hours among low-wage workers carries little weight, especially if our main interest is helping poor parents. Job losses among adults due to the minimum wage are negligible (Card & Krueger, 1995). Even if some jobs or work hours are lost, the higher wage per hour of remaining employment far offsets such losses and increases total earnings among low-skill parents affected by a rise in the minimum wage.

A more serious limitation of using the minimum wage to fight poverty is that relatively few poor families benefit much from an increase. Wage rates of most workers in poor families already exceed the minimum. Their poverty results from working too few hours because of family responsibilities, illness, or the difficulty of finding jobs. A higher minimum does little for them and their children, nor does it help families where no one works or the parents are self-employed. Though it seems counterintuitive, most minimum-wage workers live in families with incomes more than double the poverty line because they are teens whose parents earn good wages or adults living with other workers. Poor families receive less than 20 percent of the earnings gains generated by raising the minimum wage (Burkhauser & Sabia, 2007).

Other employment-related policies can play valuable supporting roles in helping poor families earn more. Tax credits and government spending for child care have grown rapidly since 1996. Additional spending to improve the accessibility, affordability, and quality of child care will further facilitate work and job retention by caregivers in poor families with young children (Blau, 2003). Improved routing of public transit systems, changes in the location of low-income housing, and stronger enforcement of fair housing laws can increase inner city parents' access to jobs and break down spatial barriers to employment created by housing segregation (Ferguson, 2001; Yinger, 2001). Better enforcement of policies to prevent employment discrimination will expand job opportunities for poor minority parents (Holzer, 1994). The effect on child poverty of these kinds of interventions will depend on their size and specific design.

The success of programs to increase earnings critically depends on having a healthy economy. Such programs will be largely ineffective in a recession, when employers will be reluctant to expand hiring even with tax incentives, and low-wage workers who upgrade their skills will find it hard to improve their earnings as job openings and promotion opportunities shrink. Unfortunately, economic knowledge about how to prevent recessions is incomplete and political circumstances sometimes prevent action that would minimize economic downturns.

Policies to affect family structure. A highly contentious approach to preventing poverty is grounded in the observation that increased non-marital childbearing and single parenthood are important reasons why child poverty has remained high. The Bush Presidency sought to reduce teenage non-marital childbearing via sex education that strongly emphasized abstinence. While abstinence-only programs have not proved effective, rigorous evaluations have identified other program models that do reduce teen pregnancies and births and are cost effective (Isaacs, 2007). Offering these programs on a voluntary basis to all teenagers might, over the longer term, reduce the number of children born to young women who are likely to be poor. Providing more family planning services to low-income women would also contribute to this goal.

The Bush Presidency also developed programs to foster "healthy marriages." Modest federal funds (about $150 million per year) were spent on media campaigns to inform young adults and the public about the benefits of marriage, programs to prevent divorce, programs that help couples who choose to marry develop the skills and knowledge to sustain a strong marriage, and evaluations of relationship-skills training. We do not yet know whether these efforts increase marriage and reduce divorce. If they do, child poverty rates may fall. On the other hand, marriage may have little effect on parenting quality, so except for the higher income, children may not benefit much from these policies (McLanahan, 2004).

Marriage promotion policy generates passionate advocates and opponents. It is too soon to know if the current approach, or alternative ones, will muster political support after President Bush leaves office. Supporters of marriage promotion policy need to recognize that a comprehensive strategy would go beyond relationship skills training to address other impediments to stable marriage such as the poor financial prospects of low-skill men, substance abuse, and domestic violence. Reforms that reduce economic disincentives to marry that are unintentionally present in some tax and income support policies would also be in order.

Supplementing Market Incomes to Reduce Child Poverty

Economic downturns are inevitable. Powerful long-term forces have been eroding job opportunities for the less skilled. We lack evidence that human capital programs can produce the large increases in earnings needed to substantially reduce market poverty. Moreover, labor market policies do not deal with families' short-term income needs produced by temporary unemployment or illness even when the economy is doing well, nor can they help children in families where the adults cannot be expected to work. It follows that efforts to reduce market poverty must be accompanied by income support policies that supplement market earnings.

The U.S. uses three approaches to supplement the market incomes of poor families with children: government income support programs, tax policy, and child support payments from the absent parent to the custodial parent. This section describes the main elements of these approaches, discusses important recent developments and controversies surrounding them, and reports on the extent to which they reduce child poverty.

In 2004 federal, state and local governments spent $1.34 trillion on cash and non-cash income support programs, or about 38 percent of all government spending (U.S. Census Bureau 2007b, tables 420, 460, 526). These programs are of two types: "social insurance" and "income assistance." Social insurance programs are financed by special taxes on workers, employers, or both. Contributors and their dependents have a right to receive benefits if earnings are reduced or eliminated by events such as unemployment, retirement, or death. The size of the benefit depends upon the amount of prior "covered" earnings, but not on the family's current income or assets. So an unemployed husband can collect benefits even if his wife is earning $90,000 a year. The major social insurance programs are Social Security (which insures against old age, death of a worker, and long-term disability), Medicare, unemployment insurance, and workers compensation for job related injury. Social insurance accounts for about 65 percent of government spending on income support.

Income assistance programs are financed by general tax revenues. Eligibility depends on having a low current income; few assets; and, usually, meeting another condition such as being blind or having children. Benefits decline as other sources of income increase and are independent of the amount of past earnings or taxes paid. Other labels for "income assistance" include "means tested assistance," "public assistance," and "welfare."

Income Support Programs for Children

The major cash income support programs for families with children are Survivors Insurance, TANF, the EITC, and SSI for disabled children.[10] The major non-cash programs for such families are food stamps, the child nutrition programs, Medicaid, and the State Children's Health Insurance Plan. TANF ("welfare") accounted for only 4 percent of all income assistance in 2004. Spending on the EITC is more than double that on TANF and provides the most cash income to needy families with children. About 75 percent of income assistance is provided in-kind rather than as cash, most of it through Medicaid.

Survivors Insurance

Survivors Insurance (SI) supports dependents of deceased workers who paid Social Security taxes. Children under age eighteen are entitled to benefits based on the deceased parent's earnings, as is the surviving parent until the youngest child is sixteen. Benefits grow with the rate of inflation. In 2005, 1.3 million children received benefits that averaged $644 per month.[11]

In accord with social insurance principles, benefits are higher for survivors of workers with higher earnings. Because the "replacement rate"—benefits as a percent of the worker's earnings—is larger for survivors of workers with low earnings than for survivors of high earners, the former suffer a smaller fall in their standard of living.

Temporary Assistance for Needy Families (TANF)

SI was enacted when most single mothers were widows to provide them and their children with financial support without going on welfare. Congress expected that the need for Aid to Families with Dependent Children (AFDC), established in 1935, would decline as more and more one parent families qualified for SI. Times changed. Most one-parent families now arise via divorce or non-marital births and do not qualify for SI. If their market incomes are low, they may receive income support from AFDC's successor, TANF.

AFDC was an entitlement—all eligible applicants received aid. It provided benefits without expecting recipients to make much effort to become self-sufficient, and did little to help those who wanted to work. Political support for this approach broke down by the 1980s. Emphasis shifted to viewing welfare as a reciprocal obligation: receiving a check and help with child care and other work-related services carries with it the expectation that a recipient look for and accept a job or participate in education, training, or other work-related activities. The new emphasis responded to conservatives who believed non-working single mothers relying on public support made poor role models for their children. Under this "welfare-to-work" strategy conservatives agreed to expand funding for work-related support services, while liberals gave up the policy that welfare mothers had a right not to work.

The controversial Personal Responsibility and Work Opportunity Reconciliation Act (PRWORA) became law in 1996. PRWORA fundamentally changed the structure of public assistance. It replaced AFDC with TANF and made important changes in SSI, food stamps, child care, and child support enforcement. TANF ended entitlement to welfare, let each state decide whether to aid all qualifying families and gave states more control over other elements of their welfare programs. TANF also aimed to reduce non-marital childbearing by requiring unmarried parents under age eighteen to live with an adult and stay in school to qualify for benefits and by giving states incentives to reduce non-marital births[12]

TANF combines labor market and income support approaches for fighting poverty. Like AFDC, it provides small monthly cash benefits. TANF's major focus is on promoting work and reducing reliance on public assistance. Perhaps the most dramatic difference from AFDC was setting time limits. Any family with a member who has received TANF as an adult for sixty months can receive no more federal TANF funds. A state may exempt up to 20 percent of its cases from this limit, but may impose tighter limits.

States quickly responded to the flexibility allowed by TANF. Some set shorter time limits; others planned to use state funds to support families after sixty months. They implemented a diverse array of welfare-to-work activities, work supports such as child care and transportation, and "diversion programs" that provide short term cash aid and work support to help families who applied for TANF from coming on the rolls. In a variety of ways states changed eligibility rules, increased the earnings recipients can keep and still receive TANF to help "make work pay," and established sanction policies (penalties for violating TANF rules).

Assigning states the major responsibility to provide aid, and under what conditions, represented a major change in the philosophy underlying the safety net. Advocates of devolution argued that state and local offices can better identify the needy, the type of aid that makes most sense, and the most effective way to deliver it. Others, concerned about differences in the willingness and fiscal ability of states to help the poor and assure fair administrative processes, hold the central government primarily responsible for income assistance, as it had been during the sixty years of AFDC. The debate about which level of government can best provide income support is an enduring one in our federal system.

State benefit levels vary widely under TANF, as they did under AFDC. In 2005 the maximum monthly benefit for a family of three ranged from $170 in Mississippi to $923 in Alaska. The median was $379, or 29 percent of the poverty line. Since 1970, the median inflation-adjusted benefit has fallen more than 50 percent (Committee on Ways and Means 2004, table 7-13). In mid 2007 TANF served 3.9 million persons in 1.7 million families in an average month, or about 30 percent of all poor families with children (U.S. Department of Health and Human Services 2007). The caseload was 33 percent of its level in 1994, the peak year. TANF cash assistance totaled $12.0 billion in 2004. The average benefit per family was $506. TANF also spends substantial sums on "non-assistance" (child care, transportation, counseling, job search assistance, and other forms of benefits), typically *more* than on cash assistance (U.S. Census Bureau 2007b, tables 551, 552, 553; and 2007c).

To date, welfare reform has been neither as successful as its advocates predicted nor the disaster its critics expected. Because of the healthy economy in the late 1990s and TANF's work-oriented approach, many women who formerly would have collected welfare instead worked, while most women who did go on TANF moved rapidly into jobs and off assistance. The welfare caseload fell to levels not seen in more than forty years. TANF appears responsible for about four-tenths of this decline. Yet TANF only moderately increased income and reduced poverty among low-income women, many of whom ended up with unstable jobs and inadequate childcare. At the same time, critics' predictions of lack of jobs, more severe poverty, and greater homelessness for women and children proved wrong. TANF may have helped reduce teenage childbearing but claims that it would strengthen marriage and reduce non-marital childbearing by older women have not been verified. TANF appears to have small positive cognitive effects for preschoolers and K-6 students, and small negative behavioral and educational effects for adolescents.[13]

A complete assessment of welfare reform needs several crucial questions answered over a longer time period (Blank, 2007). Will TANF be adequate in a major economic downturn? To what extent will persons who leave TANF be able to stay off? Time limits and sanctions affected few families in TANF's early years. What will happen when many cases approach their time limits or face sanctions? What is happening to the growing number of single mothers who neither work nor receive TANF and their children? Many of these "disconnected" women have multiple barriers to work. How well does TANF serve them? How will reform affect low-income children's schooling, work, and family formation choices?

Supplemental Security Income

Supplemental Security Income (SSI) provides monthly cash payments to needy aged, blind, and disabled persons. Children are eligible if they are blind or have a disability similar to one that would prevent an adult from working. Children also benefit indirectly if another family member receives SSI. Unlike TANF, the federal government establishes eligibility rules and provides a uniform benefit. States may supplement the federal benefit and almost all do so. Prior to 1990 eligibility was based on whether a child had one of a list of severe medical impairments. In 1990 the Supreme Court ruled that eligibility must be determined by assessing a child's "functional limitations." As a result the number of child SSI recipients rose from 309,000 in 1990 to 955,000 in 1996. The PRWORA did away with the functional limitation assessment and restricted eligibility in other ways. Mainly because of these changes, the caseload fell to 847,000 by 2000. Since then the caseload has risen. In 2005, 1 million children received an average monthly SSI benefit of $523 (Social Security Administration, 2006).

Nutrition Assistance and Health Care Programs

Most TANF recipients as well as low-income families not eligible for TANF qualify for food stamps. Food stamps are federally funded with uniform benefits across all states. A family's food stamps are reduced as its cash income, including TANF, increases. Since families in high-TANF states receive fewer food stamps than those in low-TANF states, food stamps reduce state disparities in benefit levels. In 2003 the income of a family of three that received the maximum combined food stamp and AFDC benefit was still below the poverty line in every state. In the median state, the combined monthly AFDC and food stamp benefit of $683 equaled 55 percent of the poverty line (Committee on Ways and Means, 2004, table 7-12).

In addition to food stamps, federal food assistance has concentrated on improving child nutrition. Through the school lunch and breakfast programs children in families receiving TANF or food stamps, or with incomes at or below 130 percent of the poverty line, may receive free meals. Children from other near-poor families receive smaller subsidies. In 2008, at a federal cost of $8.3 billion, 31 million children received subsidized lunches each school day, of which 15.4 million were free. The smaller breakfast program cost $2.4 billion and assisted 10.6 million children a day, of which 7.5 million received a free breakfast.

The Special Supplemental Food Program for Women, Infants and Children (WIC) provides food assistance to low income pregnant and postpartum women, their infants, and low income children up to age five. Participants must have incomes at or below 185 percent of the poverty line and be nutritionally at risk. WIC cost the federal government $6.2 billion in 2008 and served a monthly average of 8.7 million persons, 75 percent of them children.[14]

TANF families qualify for Medicaid, which covers many health care expenses. Medicaid is an entitlement jointly financed by federal and state funds and administered by states within federal guidelines. Many low-income children and pregnant women ineligible for TANF receive Medicaid because they meet other eligibility conditions. Congress created the State Children's Health Insurance Program (SCHIP) in 1997 to help states provide health care to uninsured low-income children not eligible for Medicaid. Those children typically live in families with incomes between 100 and 200 percent of the poverty line. Some states use SCHIP to cover low-income parents or pregnant women. A state may administer SCHIP as an expansion of Medicaid, as a separate child health program, or as a combination of the two. Like Medicaid, SCHIP is jointly financed by federal and state funds and administered by states. But SCHIP is not an entitlement—states are not obliged to provide coverage once their federal allotment is spent.[15] The share of low-income children without health insurance has fallen by more than one-third since SCHIP started. Growth in Medicaid and SCHIP enrollment of low-income children more than offset the decline in employer sponsored health coverage between 1997 and 2005. In 2004 Medicaid spent an average of $2,601 per enrolled low-income child and non-elderly, non-disabled adult (Kaiser Commission, 2006). In 2006 SCHIP spent an average of $1,830 on each of its 7.3 million enrollees, of whom 91 percent were children. While it is hard to argue that a dollar of health care assistance is just like a dollar of cash or food aid, Medicaid and SCHIP clearly provide critical assistance to low-income families with children.

Tax Policies and Poor Children

Taxes reduce the income available to poor families and, hence, their living standards. One welcome change in antipoverty policy since the mid-1980s has been the sharp decline in federal taxes on poor families. In 1984, a four-person family with earnings equal to the poverty line paid 10.1 percent of its income in federal income and payroll taxes. By 2000, federal tax reform and expansion of the EITC (see below) lowered the tax rate to *minus* 8.9 percent, which provided a tax refund of $1,547. By 2005 the rate had further fallen to minus 18 percent, where it will remain at least through 2010 (Committee on Ways and Means, 2004, pp. 13-73, 74). The steady expansion of the EITC, enacted in 1975, is the major reason why the tax burden declined. A low-income family with children receives credit against its federal income tax. The size of the credit depends on its earnings.[16] If the credit exceeds its income tax, it gets the difference as a refund. In 2006 the federal EITC provided $44.4 billion to 23.3 million low-income households (U.S. Internal Revenue Service, 2009). The EITC has become by far the largest cash assistance program for families with children.

The EITC is the U.S.'s core strategy to "make work pay" for persons with low earnings. In 2007 families with two or more children received an EITC of 40 cents per dollar earned up to $11,750. For example, instead of having $4,000 for working 400 hours at $10 per hour, the worker receives $5,600 (4,000*1.4). The maximum benefit was $4,716, or 22 percent of the poverty line for a four-person family. Families with one child received 34 cents per dollar earned up to $8,350, for a maximum EITC of $2,853. Families remained eligible for the maximum until income reached $15,400 ($17,450 for married couples). The EITC phased out gradually as income rose above $15,400 ($17,450). Single parent families with one child (two or more children) stayed eligible until income exceeded $33,200 ($37,750). For married couples the maximum eligibility levels were $2000 higher. The phase-out restricts benefits to poor and near-poor families. Income thresholds (and, thus, the credit) are adjusted for inflation each year. By 2008, twenty-four states and Washington, D.C. had enacted their own EITCs (Okwuje & Johnson, 2006). State EITCs add 4.9 to 43 percent to a family's federal EITC. They reduce the burden of state income taxes on low-income families and partly offset the regressive aspects of other state and local taxes. Most but not all state EITCs are refundable.

A low- or middle-income family with children under age seventeen can also benefit from the Child Tax Credit (CTC). In 2008 the CTC equaled 15 percent of the amount by which a family's earnings exceeded $8,500, up to $1,000 per eligible child. For example, a 4-person family with earnings equal to the poverty line in 2008 ($10,917) could have claimed a CTC of $363 (.15*[10,917 − 8,500]) (Center on Budget and Policy Priorities, 2009). Like the EITC the CTC is refundable. Unlike the EITC the CTC does not help families with earnings below $8,500.

Antipoverty Impacts of Government Income Support Programs and Taxes

Though child poverty remains high despite existing income support programs, the situation would be far worse without them. Row 1 of Table 4.2 shows
the percentage of children in families whose incomes from private sources
fall below the poverty line. Many, but not all of these families receive income
support. Row 2 shows child poverty after including all cash income support
in family incomes. This is the official poverty rate. Comparing rows 1 and 2
gauges the antipoverty impact of cash benefits. Row 4 shows the poverty rate
after we also include food, housing and medical benefits, taxes, and tax credits
in family incomes. Comparing rows 1 and 4 gauges the antipoverty impact of
a wider array of income support and tax policies. We see that in 1979, 20.1
percent of all children were poor based on market income. After counting cash
transfers the poverty rate was 16.4 percent so, as shown in Row 3, cash transfers
lifted 18.4 percent of market income poor children over the poverty line. (This
is the percentage difference between 20.1 and 16.4 percent.) When non-cash
benefits, taxes, and tax credits are counted in incomes, the poverty rate shrinks
to 13.6 percent and the antipoverty impact increases to 32.3 percent (Row 5).
Ten years later, after cuts in some means-tested benefits, public programs pulled
only 21.1 percent of market income poor children out of poverty. By 1999, the
antipoverty impact had rebounded to 31.8 percent due to restoration of some
program cuts and, more importantly, the expansion of the EITC in 1993. By
2005 the antipoverty impact had risen sharply to 40.1 percent, substantially
higher than in 1979.

Table 4.2 assumes that transfers and taxes do not affect market incomes. Since
such policies may affect work and other behaviors that increase market income
poverty, the exhibit probably overstates the antipoverty impact of government
programs. It captures the trend in antipoverty impact reasonably well.

Behavioral Side Effects of Income Support Programs

Ever since public welfare began, people have worried that it provides incentives for socially undesirable behaviors. Because many income-tested programs
provide benefits if a parent does not work and offset part of any earnings with a
cut in benefits, they tend to discourage work. Programs that provide significantly
different benefits to couples who marry, cohabit, or live apart may create incentives
to become an unmarried mother, divorce, delay remarriage, and make other choices
that result in more poor, single-parent families. There is little concern about work
disincentives from Social Security paid to survivors or disabled workers, or from
SSI for children since these recipients are not expected to work and tend to be
viewed as more "deserving" than recipients of income tested benefits.

The tradeoff between income support's beneficial impacts on poverty and
their possible undesired behavioral side effects poses a clear dilemma. Most

Table 4.2
Impact on Child Poverty of Government Cash, Food, Housing and Medical Transfers, and Taxes, 1979-2005

	1979	1989	1999	2005
1. Market income poverty rate	20.1%	22.8%	23.6%	20.2%
2. Post cash transfer rate (Official rate)	16.4%	20.1%	20.5%	17.6%
3. Percentage reduction in poverty due to cash transfers	18.4%	11.8%	12.1%	12.9%
4. Post-transfer, post-tax poverty rate	13.6%	18.0%	16.1%	12.1%
5. Percentage reduction in poverty due to all transfers and taxes	32.3%	21.1%	31.8%	40.1%

Source: For 1979, 1989, and 1999 http://www.gpoaccess.gov/wmprints/green/2004.
html. pp. H-39, 40, accessed April 30, 2007. For 2005: http://pubdb3.census.gov/
macro/032006/rdcall/2_001.htm accessed April 30, 2007.

Note: Market income is measured as all cash income from private sources, excluding capital gains. Post-cash transfer income is market income plus all cash government transfers. Post-transfer, post-tax income is post cash transfer income minus social security taxes and federal and state income taxes, plus Earned Income Tax Credits, food stamp benefits, and the estimated value of Medicare, Medicaid, school lunch, and housing benefits.

people want to help poor *children*, who can hardly be held responsible for their poverty, but do not want assistance to induce the *parents* to act irresponsibly. Yet, rules which curtail irresponsible behavior or at least curtail public subsidies to such behavior risk hurting the children by undercutting the basic missions of income support programs: providing a minimally decent standard of living, cushioning unexpected income losses and helping families obtain essentials such as food, housing, and medical care. People may strongly differ on how much weight to give these competing concerns. The tradeoff strikes at strongly held American values.

Empirical evidence shows that AFDC as well as non-cash assistance such as food stamps, Medicaid, and public housing tend to reduce work. The size of the reduction is hard to pin down. TANF appears to have increased employment and earnings compared to their levels under AFDC. The EITC appears to have induced a substantial increase in labor force activity by single parent families, even as it transfers substantial income to them. In two-parent families, it has had a small negative effect on work effort.[17]

Higher AFDC benefits for single parents were associated with greater rates of female headship and divorce, lower rates of remarriage, and a greater likelihood that a single mother lived independently rather than with her parents. While these behavioral responses tended to increase the number of low-income, mother-only families, the estimated effects were small. Higher AFDC benefits were also associated with small increases in the likelihood of becoming an unwed mother, but only among whites. PRWORA appears to have had little effect on marriage and overall fertility, but it may have helped reduce teenage childbearing. Research has failed to find a relationship between the EITC and marriage.

The weight of current evidence implies that demographic responses to AFDC accounted for only a small portion of the increases in female headship and nonmarital childbearing between the 1960s and 1996, and that PRWORA is also having minor effects. The main reasons for the increases almost certainly lie outside the income support system and probably reflect the growing social acceptability of single parenthood and cohabitation, declining stigma of unwed motherhood, improvements in women's earnings power, and declines in men's.

The Child Support System for Single-Parent Families

The child support system provides an important source of income to single-parent families. The family court system administered by each state may order the noncustodial parent to contribute monthly payments to help finance his or her children's material needs. To ensure that caretakers receive the payments, the state's child support enforcement agency now automatically withholds them from the noncustodial parent's earnings and sends them to the custodial parent. In 2005, 84 percent of noncustodial parents were the fathers (U.S. Census Bureau 2007, Table 2).[18]

Congress has passed major laws to help custodial parents secure and collect child support awards, and to enforce absent parents' financial obligations to their children. Title IV-D of the Social Security Act, enacted in 1974, established the federal Office of Child Support Enforcement to oversee state enforcement. It left basic responsibility for administering child support programs to the states, where it remains. The Child Support Enforcement Amendments of 1984 and provisions in the Family Support Act of 1988, the PRWORA of 1996, and the Deadbeat Dads Punishment Act of 1998 built on this foundation. To increase the percentage of single parents with child support awards, the laws mandate that states establish paternity for children born out-of-wedlock, operate programs to locate absent parents and cooperate to track them across state lines. TANF recipients must generally cooperate with state agencies to establish paternity and collect support payments. States must standardize child support awards by adopting uniform guidelines and review individual awards every three years and the guidelines every four years. These rules reduce unequal treatment of absent parents in similar economic circumstances and help awards keep pace with inflation. Other means of collecting payments and imposing penalties on absent parents who do not pay support have expanded. Absent parents may be required to pay for their children's health care expenses. These reforms are consistent with the strongly held value that parents should provide for their children, whether they live together or not.

States established paternity for 29 percent of out-of-wedlock births in 1987, for 46 percent in 1994, and for 85 percent in 2004. Support collected through government funded child support services rose 538 percent in real terms between 1982 and 2002. Thus, reforms have brought some progress. Yet in 2005 only 57 percent of all custodial parents had child support agreements, a scant increase from 57 percent in 1993. Of those entitled to payments in 2005, 47 percent received full payment, 31 percent received partial payment, and 23 percent received nothing. During the past two decades, the share receiving full payment has risen substantially, but the percentage receiving nothing has not appreciably changed. The average annual amount for families who do receive payments is low (about $5,300 in 2005).[19]

The difficulty of tracking absent parents and reluctance of some mothers to cooperate with public agencies for fear of alienating the fathers hamper enforcement. Excessive support orders for low-wage fathers (sometimes more than half their income) and their struggles to earn adequate, steady incomes hamper enforcement, too. While the system's performance has gotten better, further improvements could increase child support payments by billions of dollars.

Lessons from Abroad for Child Antipoverty Policy

A recent study of eight rich nations finds that, of all children in single-parent families who were poor based on market incomes, American policies took only 15 percent out of poverty.[20] Other countries' reductions ranged from 27 to 82 percent. For children in two-parent families, the U.S.'s reduction was merely 6 percent, compared to between 20 and 79 percent for the other countries (Smeeding, 2006). The small antipoverty impact of the U.S.'s income support policies is the reason why its post-transfer, post-tax child poverty rate was highest (see Figure 4.2) even though its market income poverty rate was not.

Several features of American social welfare policy explain this low antipoverty impact. The U.S. has consistently devoted a smaller portion of its economy to public social welfare spending than other western societies. Public commitment is tepid for providing income support to low-income families with both working and non-working parents. The EITC, pioneered by the U.S., is an important exception but, tellingly, only helps working families. The U.S. is one of the few countries without a child allowance that guarantees modest support for all children regardless of family income. Nor, in contrast to several European nations, does it guarantee child support for families with absent parents. Americans place high value on families earning their way out of poverty. Despite this, reluctance to expand the welfare state has meant that the U.S. also lags in providing work-related benefits—it provides relatively small subsidies for child care and is unique in not requiring paid family leave.

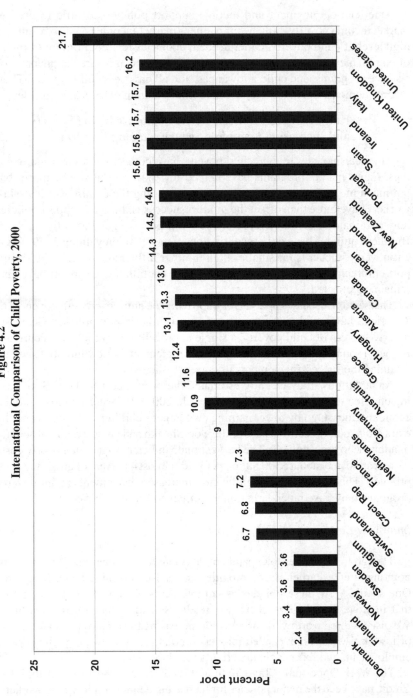

Figure 4.2
International Comparison of Child Poverty, 2000

American employment and income support policies do little to prevent market income poverty, little to supplement market incomes, and so result in a high level of child poverty. Other affluent countries rely on different of mixes of employment programs, work-related benefits, social insurance, income assistance programs, and child allowances, and all have less child poverty. Their records demonstrate that more effective mixes than the U.S.'s are feasible.

Program Challenge: Doing a Better Job of Reducing Poverty and Increasing Economic Security among Children

America's policies to fight child poverty have both successes and shortcomings. Labor market programs have helped low-skill workers earn more, but not much more. Powerful economic forces eroding the earnings of low-skill workers have more than offset the modest successes. Income support policies now eliminate about 40 percent of the child poverty generated by markets. But these policies have only recently done better than they did in 1979. Their antipoverty impact is far smaller than in other affluent countries. Child support enforcement has become more effective, but billions of support payments remain uncollected.

This section discusses options for improving the anti-poverty effectiveness of America's labor market, income support, and child support policies. Given the diverse sources of child poverty, a single approach is unlikely to be a cure-all. Rather, a sound strategy would combine complementary new initiatives, while retaining the successful elements of current policies.

An ambitious study recently estimated the overall cost to the U.S. of having children raised in poverty (Holzer, et al., 2007). It focused on losses to the economy (measured by lower earnings when poor children are adults) and the extra costs society bears because of the worse health and greater criminal activity of adults who grew up poor. The best estimate indicates that child poverty costs American society about $500 billion per year (almost 4 percent of gross domestic product). This suggests that significantly increased investments in antipoverty programs may have much larger payoffs than currently believed.[21]

Improving Earnings of Low-Skill Workers

Though U.S. policies to expand employment have sometimes shown disappointing effects, earlier efforts provide lessons for designing better programs. One should view these policies as complements to human capital programs that improve low-wage workers' job readiness and skills, not as substitutes. We discuss three worthwhile options for increasing the employment and wages of low skill workers: expanded jobs tax credits for employers, public service employment, and refundable tax credits for child care.

The Work Opportunity Tax Credit and its precursor, the Targeted Jobs Tax Credit, have been the major policies for increasing demand for low-skill workers.

A better alternative may be an expanded version of the New Jobs Tax Credit, which was tried in 1977-1978 and created jobs for low-skill workers (Bartik, 2001). A new version could provide a tax credit of, for example, 25 percent of the first $10,000 paid to each worker hired beyond 102 percent of a firm's (or non-profit organization's) previous year's employment. Providing a subsidy only up to $10,000 per worker, this program would tilt incentives towards hiring low-wage workers. Unlike current policies, new hires would not have to come from specific categories (e.g., on TANF) so they would not be stigmatized. To target spending most effectively, the credit would be available only in local labor markets with high unemployment. Public agencies would need to work closely with private employers to make sure they know about the credit and to help identify suitable job candidates. The subsidy rate, earnings limit and required increase over last year's employment can be varied depending on how enticing a program one wants.

Public service employment (PSE) programs fund government agencies to hire disadvantaged workers, usually for a temporary period. Public service jobs can provide experience that helps workers get private sector jobs and, combined with the EITC, can raise families with a full-time worker over the poverty line. The U.S. has tried a variety of PSE programs, but none currently operate. PSE can provide a solution when the economy weakens but policy makers still want to hold TANF recipients to strong work requirements. Extending PSE funding to non-profit organizations is an option as well.

PSE programs must contend with criticisms that they provide poor jobs that either are "make work" or largely substitute for jobs that otherwise would exist and thereby displace traditional public employees. For poorly designed and implemented programs, these criticisms are valid. But when done carefully, PSE seems to increase employment, creates modest displacement, produces valuable services, and may raise the long-run earnings of persons hired into PSE jobs. Any new PSE program will face two key tradeoffs: (1) jobs that are more likely to raise long term earnings tend to cost more and are harder to administer, and (2) the more PSE jobs resemble "real" jobs, the greater the value of their output but the higher the chances that they displace public employees (Ellwood & Welty, 2000).

Job tax credits may be the more promising option. They appear to have modest success at creating jobs. In combination with job search assistance and skills training programs, and bolstered by the EITC, they help raise incomes of low-skill adults. Compared to PSE their implementation has not been strongly criticized and they face fewer political obstacles.

Government assistance with child care helps poor parents combine work and family responsibilities. The Dependent Care Tax Credit lowers the net cost of child care but, because it is not refundable, it does not help poor families who pay no income taxes. Making it refundable, like the EITC and CTC, is the third option that would improve matters.

Improving Non-Welfare Income Support

Income support delivered outside the welfare system has important advantages. It does not stigmatize recipients nor involve them in a complex system with many requirements the way TANF does. Because non-welfare benefits do not decline as earnings increase, they promote self-reliance and do not discourage work. Two options along this line are improving the child support system and making the tax system more pro-poor.

Improving child support. Most states reduce TANF benefits by one dollar for each dollar of child support paid to a recipient. As a result, poor absent parents with children on TANF have little incentive to comply with support orders— most or all of their payments save the state money rather than increase their children's standard of living. Providing partial or total "pass through" of child support benefits for TANF families would both increase their income and encourage absent parents to more fully comply.

Two options focus on helping absent fathers comply with support orders (Sorenson and Oliver, 2002). If an absent father does not appear in court to establish his earnings capacity, states often impose default orders that are unrealistic for men with weak earnings prospects. States may backdate support orders to the child's birth date and many do. Both practices lead to large arrears that most poor fathers will never be able to pay. Some states have set up limited amnesty programs that cancel the arrears as long as an absent father pays his current order and participates in work activities. Congress could support more of these initiatives.

Option two addresses barriers to work that challenge many fathers of children on TANF. These barriers resemble those facing many poor custodial mothers, such as low education, limited work experience, poor health, and substance abuse. Public policy expects TANF recipients to work and, in return, provides welfare-to-work activities and work support subsidies. Public policy also expects absent fathers to work and pay support, but has largely failed to offer similar assistance. It is time to recognize the importance of helping both parents become more financially secure and expand employment services and other work supports for absent fathers.

A more pro-poor tax system. Three reforms would raise the EITC's antipoverty impact. The EITC provides more assistance to families with two or more children than to families with one child. Congress could establish a higher third tier of benefits for families with three or more children, while leaving in place the current benefit schedules for one and two child families. Second, federal law could provide fiscal incentives for states to expand their own EITCs or, for those without an EITC, to set one up. States could also expand their EITCs or enact them without such incentives. Third, since eligible families must file an income tax return to claim their EITC, federal and state agencies could improve outreach to increase tax filing.[22]

The federal income tax can also be made more pro-poor. The tax code reduces taxable income by $3,500 per child (as of 2008). This "exemption" lowers each family's taxes by $3,500 times its marginal tax rate. It is worth $350 per child for families in the 10 percent tax bracket and $980 for more affluent families in the 28 percent bracket. If Congress instead enacted a uniform credit that cost the same as the current exemption in terms of foregone taxes, poorer families would gain and richer ones lose.

Many countries provide small "child allowances." Since all children qualify for the same benefit regardless of family income, no one views them as welfare. A uniform income tax credit in combination with the refundable Child Tax Credit described earlier would approximate a child allowance, but only for families with at least $8,500 of earnings. To assist all families with children, we could instead replace the current exemption and the CTC with a child allowance.

Asset Building Policies

While cash and non-cash benefits raise incomes and pull some families over the poverty line, they do not provide a middle-class lifestyle or meaningful financial security. Asset building has emerged in recent years as an innovative idea to help low-income persons invest in their future, build private wealth that can cushion income losses and provide greater economic security, and reach the American dream of home ownership and a middle-class lifestyle. Asset accumulation may also give low-income parents and children more hope for the future, greater future orientation, and a larger stake in political participation (Schreiner & Sherraden, 2007).

One popular asset-building program is the Individual Development Account (IDA). It matches poor families' savings with public funds if the savings are placed in accounts restricted to investments in education, homeownership, and small business. IDAs usually provide financial education as well. Many states included IDAs in their welfare reform plans. Foundations, non-profit organizations, and governments are actively testing and evaluating a variety of small scale asset building programs and seeking to expand funding for them.

Asset building enjoys broad political support. Before settling on a specific program, we need answers to important questions. How would different asset building programs affect savings, home ownership, educational attainment, residential stability, child well-being, and other outcomes? How fully would the poorest of the poor use the new savings opportunities? What is the best way to implement and manage these kinds of programs? How much will a national program cost? Will major funding for asset building policies put downward pressure on spending for the traditional safety net programs and, if so, is this an acceptable tradeoff?

Conclusion

The information in this chapter can help social workers more effectively provide child welfare services. Labor market, income support and child support programs are important parts of the social environment of many families who need child welfare services. The financial pressures faced by poor families, and financial emergencies that may arise if income support and child support benefits are delayed or denied, put stress on families and place children at greater risk. Participating in a training program and taking a job are likely to affect family dynamics and child well-being. Social workers need to consider how to take account of these circumstances when planning intervention services.

Current Status

Currently, approximately one in six American children lives in a poor family. They are poor because their parents earn too little and their families receive inadequate income support benefits. To reduce poverty among children, public policy must help families earn more in the labor market and improve income support programs and child support enforcement.

Future Directions

Social workers are well positioned to observe and document the links between poverty and problems that bring families to the attention of child welfare agencies. They also should recognize that a minimally adequate standard of living is essential for promoting effective parenting and healthy child development. Attempts to teach parenting, coping, and mastery skills may be undermined by the financial pressure and psychological stress generated by low and unstable income. To improve the effectiveness of child welfare services, social workers have a professional responsibility to advocate for more effective antipoverty policies.

Notes

1. In this chapter, a "child" is any person under age eighteen.
2. Because of sample limitations, poverty among Native Americans is not measured annually, but instead is obtained from the decennial Census.
3. All figures are from the sources cited in figures 1 and 2.
4. International comparisons often use a relative measure. Since it differs from the procedure for setting the official U.S. poverty lines, we cannot compare U.S. statistics in Figure 3 to those elsewhere in the chapter.
5. Poor American children also spend substantially more years in poverty than poor German children, the only available comparison (Rainwater & Smeeding, 2003).
6. This conclusion assumes that large numbers of immigrants have had no effect on natives' wages and employment. Evidence on such effects is mixed (Hoynes, Page & Stevens, 2006).

7. A third important goal is to shield children from poverty's adverse effects on their physical, cognitive, and emotional development. Head Start, which strives to improve poor children's school readiness and health, is the best known of these programs. Child welfare and related social services help, in part, meet this goal. Space limits preclude discussion of these kinds of programs. See Isaacs (2007) for discussion of promising approaches. It is worth noting that income supplement programs serve the shielding goal, too.

8. Bartik (2001) has extensive discussion of demand side policies and how to make them more effective.

9. A "tax credit" reduces a company's taxes by all or part of the money it spends for a particular purpose, such as hiring low wage workers. Families may receive federal (and state) income tax credits for spending on designated purposes, such as child care.

10. Unemployment insurance, veterans benefits and workers compensation also help families with children. Since gains to children are largely incidental to these programs' main purposes, we do not discuss them.

11. If a minor child's parents receive Old Age or Disability Insurance benefits, the child is also entitled to benefits. About 1.8 million children received such benefits in 2005. The average monthly benefit of $301 was much less than that paid under Survivors Insurance (Social Security Administration, 2007, Table 5.f4).

12. PRWORA disqualified poor immigrants who arrived on or before August 22, 1996 (the day PRWORA passed) from most assistance, unless states chose to make them eligible, and limited benefits for immigrants who arrived later. Over time, Congress has softened restrictions on legal immigrants.

13. These conclusions, based on Blank (2002, 2007), Moffitt (2003) and Grogger & Karoly (2005) are tentative for several reasons. It is difficult to separate the effects of reform from the effects of the economic boom and of changes in other major social policies when TANF was being implemented. The diversity and complexity of state programs after 1996 makes it hard to characterize states' welfare policies and, hence, to identify effects of those policies. The available data have limitations for assessing the impact of welfare reform. And well done studies can yield different findings because they use different data or adopt different methodologies.

14. Data in this and preceding paragraph are from U.S. Department of Agriculture, Food and Nutrition Service, http://www.fns.usda.gov/pd/slsummar.htm, http://www.fns. usda.gov/pd/06slcash.htm, http://www.fns.usda.gov/pd/sbsummar.htm, http://www. fns.usda.gov/pd/10sbcash.htm, http://www.fns.usda.gov/pd/wisummary.htm, all accessed May 9, 2007.

15. For further information on Medicaid and SCHIP, see Committee on Ways and Means (2004), Ku, Lin, & Broaddus (2007), and Congressional Budget Office (2007).

16. Since 1993 childless workers are eligible but for much smaller benefits than families with children. For detailed discussion of the EITC, see Committee on Ways and Means (2004) and Holt (2006).

17. Evidence summarized in this and the next paragraph is from Blank (2002), Grogger & Karoly (2005), Hotz & Scholz (2003), and Moffitt (2003).

18. Lerman & Sorenson (2003) and Committee on Ways and Means (2004) offer detailed discussions of child support programs and policies.

19. Figures in this paragraph are from Committee on Ways and Means (1998), pp. 549, 605, 608, 650, 651; Committee on Ways and Means (2004), p. 8-6, 8-103, U.S.; Office of Child Support Enforcement (2005); and U.S. Census Bureau (2006) p. 3.

20. As explained in note 4, we cannot compare this antipoverty impact to those in Table 4.2.

21. This estimate relies on several key assumptions and should be viewed as tentative and uncertain.
22. Holt (2006) discusses other reform ideas.

For Further Information

Center on Budget and Policy Priorities. A major think tank focusing on public policies that affect low- and moderate-income people. Highly regarded source of information, analysis, policy ideas, strategies, and assistance for organizations working to reduce poverty. www.cbpp.org

Currie, J. (2006) *The invisible safety net: Protecting the nation's poor children and families*. Princeton, NJ: Princeton University Press. Highlights the importance of the safety net for families with children, discusses current challenges it faces and options for improving it.

National Center for Children in Poverty. A research organization dedicated to promoting the well-being of America's low-income families and children. Uses research to inform policy and practice. Has excellent data on child poverty and relevant public policies. www.nccp.org

5

Child Maltreatment Types, Rates, and Reporting Procedures

Introduction

Child maltreatment represents one of the primary reasons that children and their families are referred or reported to child welfare services (CWS) agencies for services. In 2006 in the U.S.A., 3.3 million referrals, involving the alleged maltreatment of approximately 6 million children were made to CWS (U.S. Department of Health and Human Services, 2008). Of those, approximately 905,000 children were confirmed as victims. Based on data drawn from a variety of sources, the estimated annual cost of child abuse and neglect is $103.8 billion in 2007 value (Wang & Holton, 2008, p. 2) (see Table 5.1).

The term, child maltreatment encompasses four major types of child abuse and neglect: (1) physical abuse; (2) neglect; (3) sexual abuse; and (4) psychological maltreatment. Many other threats to the health and safety of children are subsumed under these four types, including: prenatal drug exposure, chronic truancy, exposure to domestic violence, and untreated chronic health conditions. Commonly used definitions of child maltreatment are partially derived in federal law although they now diverge widely by state. Originally, passed in 1974 by the U.S. Congress, the Federal Child Abuse Prevention and Treatment Act (CAPTA) (42 U.S.C.A. §5106g) as amended by the Keeping Children and Families Safe Act of 2003, SP.L. 93-247, provides a foundation for national definitions of child abuse and neglect.

CAPTA provides minimum standards for defining physical child abuse, child neglect, and sexual abuse that States must incorporate in their statutory definitions in order to receive federal funds. Under CAPTA, child abuse and neglect means: (1) Any recent act or failure to act on the part of a parent or caretaker which results in death, serious physical or emotional harm, sexual abuse or exploitation; or (2) An act or failure to act, which presents an imminent risk of serious harm.

Table 5.1
Total Annual Direct and Indirect Cost of Child Abuse and Neglect
in the United States

I. INDIRECT COSTS

Indirect Costs	**Estimated Annual Cost (in 2007 dollars)**

Special Education $2,410,306,242
Rationale: 1,553,800 children experienced some form
of maltreatment in 19939. 22% of maltreated children
have learning disorders requiring special education.
The additional expenditure attributable to special
education services for students with disabilities was
$5,918 per pupil in 2000.
Calculation: 1,553,800 x 0.22 x $5,918 = $2,022,985,448

Juvenile Delinquency $7,174,814,134
Rationale: 1,553,800 children experienced some form
of maltreatment in 19939. 27% of children who are
abused or neglected become delinquents, compared to
17% of children in the general population, for a difference
of 10%. The annual cost of caring for a juvenile offender
in a residential facility was $30,450 in 1989.
Calculation: 1,553,800 x 0.10 x $30,450 = $4,731,321,000

Mental Health and Health Care $67,863,457
Rationale: 1,553,800 children experienced some form
of maltreatment in 19939. 30% of maltreated children
suffer chronic health problems.1 Increased mental health
and health care costs for women with a history of
childhood abuse and neglect, compared to women
without childhood maltreatment histories, were estimated
to be $8,175,816 for a population of 163,844 women, of
whom 42.8% experienced childhood abuse and neglect.
This is equivalent to $117 [$8,175,816 / (163,844 x 0 .428)]
additional health care costs associated with child
maltreatment per woman per year. Assume that the
additional health care costs attributable to childhood
maltreatment are similar for men who experienced
maltreatment as a child.
Calculation: 1,553,800 x 0.30 x $117 = $54,346,699

Adult Criminal Justice System $27,979,811,982

Rationale: The direct expenditure for operating the
nation's criminal justice system (including police
protection, judicial and legal services, and corrections)
was $204,136,015,000 in 2005. According to the
National Institute of Justice, 13% of all violence
can be linked to earlier child maltreatment.[12]
Calculations: $204,136,015,000 x 0.13 = $26,537,681,950

Lost Productivity to Society $33,019,919,544

Rationale: The median annual earning for a full-time
worker was $33,634 in 2006 . Assume that only
children who suffer serious injuries due to maltreatment
(565,0009) experience losses in potential lifetime earnings
and that such impairments are limited to 5% of the child's
total potential earnings.10 The average length of participation
in the labor force is 39.1 years for men and 29.3 years for
women ; the overall average 34 years is used.
Calculation: $33,634 x 565,000 x 0.05 x 34 = $32,305,457,000

Total Indirect Costs $70,652,715,359
TOTAL COST $ 103,754,017,492

II. DIRECT COSTS

Direct Costs   **Estimated Annual Cost**
                                                             (in 2007 dollars)

Hospitalization   **$6,625,959,263**

Rationale: 565,000 maltreated children suffered serious
injuries in 1993. Assume that 50% of seriously injured
victims require hospitalization. The average cost of
treating one hospitalized victim of abuse and neglect
was $19,266 in 1999.
Calculation: 565,000 x 0.50 x $19,266 = $5,442,645,000

Mental Health Care System $1,080,706,049

Rationale: 25% to 50% of child maltreatment victims
need some form of mental health treatment. For a
conservative estimate, 25% is used. Mental health care
cost per victim by type of maltreatment is: physical
abuse ($2,700); sexual abuse ($5,800); emotional abuse
($2,700) and educational neglect ($910)12 Cross-
referenced against NIS-3 statistics on number of each
incident occurring in 19939.

Calculations: Physical Abuse – 381,700 x 0.25 x $2,700 =
$257,647,500; Sexual Abuse – 217,700 x 0.25 x $5,800 =
$315,665,000; Emotional Abuse – 204,500 x 0.25 x
$2,700 = $138,037,500; and Educational Neglect –
397,300 x 0.25 x $910 = $90,385,750; Total = $801,735,750.

Child Welfare Services System   **$25,361,329,051**
Rationale: The Urban Institute conducted a study
estimating the child welfare expenditures associated
with child abuse and neglect by state and local public
child welfare agencies to be $23.3 billion in 2004.

Law Enforcement   **$33,307,770**
Rationale: The National Institute of Justice estimated
the following costs of police services for each of
the following interventions: physical abuse ($20);
sexual abuse ($56); emotional abuse ($20) and
educational neglect ($2).12 Cross-referenced against
NIS-3 statistics on number of each incident occurring in 1993.9
Calculations: Physical Abuse – 381,700 x $20 = $7,634,000;
Sexual Abuse – 217,700 x $56 = $12,191,200;
Emotional Abuse – 204,500 x $20 = $4,090,000; and
Educational Neglect – 397,300 x $2 = $794,600;
Total = $24,709,800

Total Direct Costs   **$33,101,302,133**

Source: Wang, C., & Holton, J. (2007). Total estimated costs of child abuse and neglect
in the United States. Chicago: Prevent Child Abuse America. Retrieved February 22,
2008 from http://www.preventchildabuse.org/about_us/media_releases/pcaa_pew_
economic_impact_study_final.pdf

    While federal legislation sets minimum definitional standards, each state is
responsible for providing its own definitions of child abuse and neglect within
civil and criminal laws. Definitions of child abuse and neglect are located primarily in three places within each state's statutory code:

- Mandatory child maltreatment reporting statutes (civil laws) provide
  definitions of child maltreatment to guide those individuals mandated
  to identify and report suspected child abuse. These reports activate the
  child protection process.
- Criminal statutes define the forms of child maltreatment that are criminally punishable. In most jurisdictions, child maltreatment is criminally
  punishable when one or more of the following statutory crimes have

been committed: homicide, murder, manslaughter, false imprison-
ment, assault, battery, criminal neglect and abandonment, emotional
and physical abuse, pornography, child prostitution, computer crimes,
rape, deviant sexual assault, indecent exposure, child endangerment,
and reckless endangerment.

- Juvenile or Family court jurisdiction statutes provide definitions of the
circumstances necessary for the court to have jurisdiction over a child
alleged to have been abused or neglected. When the child's safety cannot
be ensured in the home, these statutes allow the court to take custody of
a child and to order specific intervention and treatment services for the
parents, child, and family; recent statutes also allow agencies to forego
the provision of services to some families based on the type and severity
of maltreatment.

Together, these legal definitions of child maltreatment determine the
minimum standards of care and protection for children and serve as important
guidelines for professionals who are required both to report and respond to
reports of child abuse and neglect. This chapter defines the four major types of
child maltreatment, identifies procedures for reporting suspected incidents of
child maltreatment, and discusses the nature and extent of child maltreatment in
the U.S. In the next chapter, the child welfare agency response to this problem
through child protective services is addressed.

Types of Child Maltreatment

Child Physical Abuse

Child physical abuse may be defined as "physical acts that caused or could
have caused physical injury to a child" (U.S. Department of Health and Human
Services, 2008, p. 113). The public child welfare system becomes involved in
cases of child physical abuse when the act has been inflicted by a parent or
other person responsible for the child's care. The types of acts that may result
in injury or a serious risk of harm include: punching, beating, kicking, biting,
shaking, throwing, stabbing, burning, choking, or hitting with a hand, stick,
strap, or other object (Goldman & Salus, 2003).

It is important to distinguish between corporal punishment and physical
abuse. While many oppose the practice of spanking children, corporal punishment is still commonly practiced and is not against the law in any state. In general, hitting for the purpose of punishment or discipline is not usually considered
abuse unless more than a temporary redness results. Infants are an exception
and any hitting of an infant may be construed as abuse (Dubowitz, 2000b).

In addition, some cultural practices that may hurt children (e.g., circumci-
sion) are not defined as abuse. And, while many state laws suggest the need to
consider culture in the investigations of abuse reports, definitions of physical

abuse in each state law provide the actual guidance of when an act on the part of a parent or other caregiver that has resulted in harm to child, is actually considered to be abuse.

Child Sexual Abuse

Child sexual abuse is usually defined as nonconsensual sexual acts, sexually motivated behaviors involving children, or sexual exploitation of children (Berliner, 2000). Child sexual abuse includes a range of behaviors between an adult and a child, such as: oral, anal, or genital penile penetration; anal or genital digital or other penetration; genital contact with no intrusion; fondling of a child's breast or buttocks; indecent exposure; inadequate or inappropriate supervision of a child's voluntary sexual activities; and use of a child in prostitution, pornography, internet crimes, or other sexually exploitative activities (Goldman & Salus, 2003).

Child welfare agencies are usually only involved in cases of child sexual abuse within the family (i.e., biological, foster, adoptive, and stepfamilies). Sexual abuse within the family is most often committed by adults in a father relationship to the child, however, it is also committed by other relatives or caregivers, such as mothers, aunts or uncles, grandparents, cousins, or the boyfriend or girlfriend of a parent.

Psychological Maltreatment

Psychological maltreatment, also described as emotional abuse and neglect, include caregiver's *actions* (abuse) or *omissions* (neglect) that convey to children that they are worthless, flawed, unloved unwanted, endangered, or only of value in meeting another's needs (American Professional Society on the Abuse of Children, 1995; Brassard, & Hart, 2000).

Types of psychological or emotional *abuse* include:

- *Spurning (hostile rejecting and degrading):* verbal and nonverbal acts toward a child including belittling, degrading, shaming or ridiculing a child for showing normal emotions, public humiliation, consistently singling out a child to criticize or punish a child (American Professional Society on the Abuse of Children, 1995; Brassard and Hart, 2000).
- *Terrorizing:* caregiver behavior that threatens to hurt, kill, abandon, or place the child or child's loved ones or objects in dangerous situations (American Professional Society on the Abuse of Children, 1995; Brassard and Hart, 2000).
- *Exploiting or corrupting:* encouraging or modeling for the child to develop antisocial behavior such as participation in criminal activities (American Professional Society on the Abuse of Children, 1995; Brassard and Hart, 2000).

Types of psychological or emotional *neglect* include:

- *Delay in obtaining needed mental health care:* a child is not provided needed treatment for an emotional or behavioral impairment (Magura & Moses, 1986; Trocme, 1996; U.S. Department of Health and Human Services, 1996; Zuravin & DePanfilis, 1996).
- *Inadequate nurturance or affection:* marked inattention to the child's needs for affection, emotional support, attention, or competence; being detached or uninvolved, interacting only when absolutely necessary, failing to express affection, caring, and love for the child. This includes cases of nonorganic failure to thrive as well as other instances of passive emotional rejection of a child or apparent lack of concern for a child's emotional well-being or development. (American Professional Society on the Abuse of Children, 1995; Magura & Moses, 1986; U.S. Department of Health and Human Services, 1996).
- *Isolating:* the child is consistently denied opportunities to meet needs for interacting/communicating with peers or adults inside or outside the home; markedly overprotective restrictions that foster immaturity or emotional over dependency; chronically applying expectations clearly inappropriate in relation to the child's age or level of development; inattention to the child's developmental/emotional needs (Adapted from American Professional Society on the Abuse of Children, 1995; U.S. Department of Health and Human Services, 1996).
- *Permitting alcohol or drug use:* encouraging or permitting of drug or alcohol use by a child. At the seriously inadequate level, there is a pattern of this condition and the child has suffered physical or emotional consequences (U.S. Department of Health and Human Services, 1996).
- *Permitting other maladaptive behavior:* encouraging or permitting of other maladaptive behavior (e.g., severe assaultiveness, chronic delinquency) under circumstances where the caregiver had reason to be aware of the existence and seriousness of the problem but did not attempt to intervene. At the seriously inadequate level, the child has suffered physical or emotional consequences (U.S. Department of Health and Human Services, 1996).
- *Witnessing violence:* a child witnesses violence in the home, (e.g., partner abuse or violence between other persons who visit the home on a regular basis). At the seriously inadequate level, the level of violence is escalating and negatively affecting the child (U.S. Department of Health and Human Services, 1996).

Child Neglect

Child neglect is the most common and the least understood form of child maltreatment. In general, neglect refers to (1) acts of omission of care to meet a child's basic needs that (2) result in harm or a threat of harm to children (Dubowitz, 2000; DePanfilis, 2006). In the National Child Abuse and Neglect

Data System (NCCANDS), the annual national study of child abuse and neglect reports, the definition of neglect takes into consideration that conditions should not be classified by neglect if they are solely influenced by poverty. In that study (U.S. Department of Health and Human Services, 2008), neglect is referred to as a "type of maltreatment that refers to the failure by the caregiver to provide needed, age-appropriate care although financially able to do so or offered financial or other means to do so" (p. 112). How neglect is defined shapes the types of situations that professionals may report to Child Protective Services (CPS), a program within the larger umbrella of child welfare services (CWS), and also defines the CPS response to neglect. Because the goal of defining neglect is to protect children and to support families to meet the basic needs of their children, definitions help determine if an incident or pattern of behaviors or conditions qualify as neglect and therefore should prompt a child welfare response.

In their efforts to understand the ways a child's basic needs may be unmet, researchers have used case record classification systems (Barnett, Manly, & Cicchetti, 1993; Trocme, 1996; Zuravin & DePanfilis, 1996) or self-report measures with children and/or parents (Kaufman, Jones, Stiglitz, Vitulano, & Mannarino, 1994; Harrington, Zuravin, DePanfilis, Ting, & Dubowitz, 2002; Straus, Kinnard, & Williams, 1995). While the field is far from reaching a consensus on the best way to classify the various ways in which a child's basic needs are unmet, for the purposes of this chapter, types of child neglect are generally classified by the failure to meet a child's physical, supervision, cognitive –educational, or emotional needs. (Failure to meet a child's emotional needs has already been described in the section on psychological maltreatment.)

Types of physical neglect include:

- *Drug exposed newborn:* a newborn infant has been exposed to drugs because the mother has used one or more illegal substances during her pregnancy. Exposure may have resulted in negative physical consequences to the infant's health. At the seriously inadequate level, the caregivers are unable or unwilling to meet the special needs of the infant at birth (National Council of Juvenile and Family Court Judges, 1992).
- *Inadequate clothing:* chronic inappropriate clothing for the weather or conditions. At the seriously inadequate level, a child has suffered consequences such as illness or threat of illness (Magura & Moses, 1986).
- *Inadequate/delayed health care:* failure of a child to receive needed care for physical injury, acute illnesses, physical disabilities, or chronic condition or impairment that if left untreated could result in negative consequences for the child (Magura & Moses, 1986; U.S. Department of Health and Human Services, 1996; Zuravin & DePanfilis, 1996).
- *Inadequate nutrition:* failure to provide a child with regular and ample meals that meet *basic* nutritional requirements or when a caregiver fails

to provide the necessary rehabilitative diet to a child with particular types of physical health problems. At the seriously inadequate level, caregivers may intentionally withhold food or water from children and/or children are observed as malnourished or dehydrated (Magura & Moses, 1986; Trocme, 1996; Zuravin & DePanfilis, 1996).

- *Insufficient household furnishings:* Family lacks essential household and furniture or functions, e.g., no working sink, no beds for sleeping, no table for child(ren). Examples include leaking gas from stove or heating unit, peeling lead-based paint, dangerous substances or objects in unlocked lower shelves or cabinets; no guards on open windows; broken or missing windows; needles and other drug paraphernalia available to child(ren). At the seriously inadequate level, there are multiple household hazards that have resulted in physical injury to a child (Magura & Moses, 1986; Zuravin & DePanfilis, 1996).
- *Unsanitary household conditions:* presence of obvious hazardous unsanitary conditions in the home. Examples include heavy rodent infestation; rotting food and garbage left out for days; urine soaked mattresses; feces and other excrement rotting within household; home smells overwhelmingly of urine/feces/spoilage. At the severely inadequate level, a child is physically ill as a result of unsanitary conditions (Magura & Moses, 1986; Zuravin & DePanfilis, 1996).
- *Unstable living conditions:* moves of residence due to eviction or lack of planning at least three times within a six-month period or homelessness due to the lack of available, affordable housing or the caregiver's inability to manage finances. At the seriously inadequate level, a child has suffered negative consequences (Zuravin & DePanfilis, 1996).

Types of Supervisory Neglect include:

- *Abandonment:* desertion of a child without arranging for reasonable care and supervision in situations when children are not claimed within two days and when children are left by caregivers who give no (or false) information about their whereabouts. At the seriously inadequate level, a child has suffered negative consequences (U.S. Department of Health and Human Services, 1996).
- *Expulsion:* blatant refusals of custody without adequate arrangements for care by others or refusal to accept custody of a returned runaway. At the seriously inadequate level, a child has suffered negative consequences (U.S. Department of Health and Human Services, 1996).
- *Inadequate supervision*: child left unsupervised or inadequately supervised for extended periods of time or allowed to remain away from home overnight without the caregiver knowing the child's whereabouts. At the seriously inadequate level, the lack of supervision includes exposing the child to dangerous conditions, which may have resulted in negative consequences (Trocme, 1996; U.S. Department of Health and Human Services, 1996).

- *Inappropriate substitute caregiver*: failure to arrange for safe and appropriate substitute child care when the caregiver leaves child with an inappropriate caregiver. At the seriously inadequate level, the child may experience other forms of maltreatment as a result of being left with an inappropriate caregiver (Magura & Moses, 1986; Zuravin & DePanfilis, 1996).
- *Shuttling and Lack of Continuity of Parenting*: the child is repeatedly left at one household or another due to apparent unwillingness to maintain custody, or chronically and repeatedly leaving a child with others for days/weeks at a time. At the seriously inadequate level, a child has suffered negative consequences (Magura & Moses, 1986; U.S. Department of Health and Human Services, 1996; Zuravin & DePanfilis, 1996).

Types of Cognitive-Educational Neglect include:

- *Chronic truancy*: habitual truancy (minimum of twenty days) without a legitimate reason. At the seriously inadequate level, the child has experienced negative consequences that could have long-standing effects (U.S. Department of Health and Human Services, 1996; Zuravin & DePanfilis, 1996).
- *Failure to enroll/other truancy*: a child (age six) is not enrolled in school or a pattern of keeping a school-age child home for no legitimate reasons (e.g., to work, to care for siblings, etc.) an average of at least three days a month (U.S. Department of Health and Human Services, 1996).
- *Inadequate parental teaching/stimulating*: children have few if any games, toys, or play materials; parents may ignore children or think children a bother, children may have no place to do their homework, may not be assisted with their homework, and may not be exposed to natural opportunities to learn within the home. Consequences may include poor academic school performance problems or acting out or participating in status offences or more serious criminal behavior as the child gets older (Magura & Moses, 1986; Straus, Kinnard, & Williams, 1995).
- *Unmet special education needs*: a child fails to receive recommended remedial educational services, or treatment for a child's diagnosed learning disorder or other special educational needs or problems of the child (American Professional Society on the Abuse of Children, 1995; U.S. Department of Health and Human Services, 1996).

Identifying and Reporting Child Maltreatment

All states, the District of Columbia, the Commonwealth of Puerto Rico, and the U.S. territories of American Samoa, Guam, the Northern Mariana Islands, and the Virgin Islands have statutes identifying mandatory reporters of child maltreatment. A mandatory reporter is a person who is required by law to make a report of child maltreatment under specific circumstances. Individuals typically designated as mandatory reporters have frequent contact with children. Such individuals may include social workers, school personnel, health care workers, mental health professionals, childcare providers, medical examiners or coroners, and law enforcement officers (Child Welfare Information Gateway, 2005). Other professions that may be mandated in some states include commercial film or photograph processors, substance abuse counselors, probation or parole officers, and domestic violence workers on the list of mandated reporters. Members of the clergy are now required to report in approximately half of the states.

Approximately eighteen states and Puerto Rico require all citizens to report suspected abuse or neglect, regardless of their role or profession. In all other states, territories, and the District of Columbia, any person is *permitted* to report suspected incidents of child abuse and neglect. These voluntary reporters of child maltreatment are often referred to as "permissive reporters" (Child Welfare Information Gateway, 2005).

In all jurisdictions, the initial report of child abuse or neglect may be made orally to either the CPS program within the child welfare agency or to a law enforcement agency. As discussed earlier in this chapter, reporting laws provide definitions of child abuse and neglect to guide the reporter in knowing what circumstances should be officially reported to the CWS agency. Guidelines to define the circumstances a mandatory reporter should consider when making a report vary from state to state.

Typically, a report must be made when the reporter, in his or her official capacity, suspects or has reasons to believe that a child has been abused or neglected. Another standard frequently used is when the reporter has knowledge of, or observes a child being subjected to, conditions that would reasonably result in harm to the child. Permissive reporters follow the same standards when electing to make a report. (Child Welfare Information Gateway, 2005, p. 3)

Extent of Child Maltreatment

The scope of child maltreatment impacts the resources needed to respond to the problem. There are three basic approaches to estimating the scope of the problem. The first is to estimate the prevalence or incidence of child abuse or neglect through a "sentinel study" that surveys people who are designated as the official reporters of child abuse or neglect—social services, educational, medical, daycare, law enforcement, and other mandated or thought to be the most suitable reporters. Based on precise definitions of child abuse or neglect, this method attempts to estimate the actual number of children who are known by the sentinels to have experienced child abuse or neglect, whether or not a report was made to a Child Welfare Services (CWS) agency.

A second approach is to survey a general population of adults and/or youth directly to determine if they have been maltreated. The advantage of this approach is that it collects data directly from those who might have experienced the problem and, depending upon any response bias or hesitancy to identify themselves as victims, may provide the most accurate data. However, these studies are often compromised because of low response rates and because it is difficult to derive an estimate that generalizes to the nation as a whole unless sophisticated sampling procedures have been implemented.

The third way to understand the scope of the problem is to examine the extent of *reported* incidents of child abuse or neglect, with a focus on suspected and substantiated/confirmed/founded/indicated reports. Some drawbacks with this approach are that definitions vary across jurisdictions about what these determinations mean, and most importantly, this approach does not include all of the incidents of child abuse or neglect that actually may have occurred but were never officially reported—a substantial number according to the findings of the other two methods. However, the advantage of examining reporting is that these are the children and families reported to the public child welfare agency from which a formal societal response can result.

National Incidence Study of Child Abuse and Neglect

The National Incidence Study (NIS) of child abuse and neglect is a congressionally mandated, periodic research effort to assess the incidence of child abuse and neglect in the United States (Sedlak, 2001). The National Incidence Studies have been conducted approximately once each decade, beginning in 1974, in response to requirements of the Child Abuse Prevention and Treatment Act (CAPTA). Although the USDHHS Children's Bureau collects annual state-level administrative data on official reports of child maltreatment, the NIS studies are designed to estimate more broadly the incidence of child maltreatment in the United States by including both cases that are reported to the authorities as well as those that are not. A unique contribution of the NIS has been the use of a common definitional framework for classifying children according to types of maltreatment as well as the severity of maltreatment. The NIS gathers information from multiple sources to estimate the number of children who are abused or neglected and to provide information about the nature and severity of the maltreatment; the characteristics of the children, perpetrators, and families; and the extent of changes in the incidence or distribution of child maltreatment since the time of the last national incidence study. Because key demographic characteristics of maltreated children and their families are collected, NIS results provide information about which children are most at risk for child maltreatment.

The NIS design assumes that the maltreated children who are investigated by child protective services (CPS) represent only the "tip of the iceberg," so although NIS estimates include children investigated by CPS; they also include maltreated children who are identified by professionals in a wide range of agencies in representative communities. These professionals, called "sentinels," are asked to remain on the lookout for children they believe are maltreated during the study period. Children identified by sentinels and those whose alleged maltreatment is investigated by CPS during the same period are evaluated against standardized definitions of abuse and neglect. The data are unduplicated so a given child is counted only once in the study estimates.

Three national incidence studies have been implemented to date and the fourth NIS is currently in the data analysis stage (US Department of Health & Human Services, undated). The first NIS (NIS-1), mandated under Public Law (P.L.) 93-247 (1974), was conducted in 1979 and 1980 and published in 1981. The second NIS (NIS-2), mandated under P.L. 98-457 (1984), was conducted in 1986 and 1987, and published in 1988. The third NIS (NIS-3) was mandated under the Child Abuse Prevention, Adoption, and Family Services Act of 1988 (P.L. 100-294) and the Child Abuse, Domestic Violence, Adoption and Family Services Act of 1992 (P.L. 102-295), conducted between 1993 and 1995, and published in 1996 (Sedlak, 2001). Work on NIS-4 began in April 2004 with the sampling of 122 counties selected to represent the U.S. and within those counties, the selection of agencies, cases, and sentinels; recruitment occurred between 2004 and 2006; data collection proceeded through June 2007; and the reports are expected to be published by the end of 2008 (U.S. Department of Health and Human Services, undated-A).

Using an elaborate sampling methodology, the NIS selects nationally representative sample of counties to represent the U.S. population and weights the estimates based on this multi-tiered sampling methodology. Consistent with findings from the first two incidence studies, the NIS-3 indicates that the actual incidence of child maltreatment is much greater than the number of cases cited in published studies of "official" reports of child abuse and neglect. The nature of reporting skews estimates of the incidence of maltreatment because allied professionals, on average, report less than half of the cases of suspected maltreatment that they are aware of. The findings from national incidence studies over time have contributed to the conclusion that reports of child maltreatment are only the tip of the iceberg.

In examining the incidence of child maltreatment, different levels of official recognition or public awareness must be delineated. The methodology used for the National Incidence Studies (NIS 1, 2, and 3) was based on a model that used five levels of official recognition or public awareness of abuse or neglect. These levels are described below and illustrated in Figure 5.1.

Level 1. Those children reported to CPS where the allegation of abuse and neglect is either substantiated (i.e., indicated or founded) or unsubstantiated after an investigation.

Level 2. Those children who are not known to CPS but who are known to other "investigatory" agencies, such as police, courts, or public health departments. These agencies may have overlapping or even conflicting responsibilities concerning certain situations, such as felonious assault, homicide, delinquency, dependency, domestic disputes, "children in need of control," or nutrition and hygiene problems. Although Level 2 children are, in some sense, "officially known," they are not necessarily regarded by the community as abused or neglected in the same sense as Level 1 children are, and they do not necessarily receive assistance that specifically targets the abuse or neglect problems.

Level 3. Abused and neglected children who are not known to CPS or to any Level 2 agency, but who are known to professionals in other major community institutions, such as school, hospitals, daycare centers, and social services and mental health agencies. Children may remain at this level for any number of reasons. One reason may be definitional ambiguities as to what types of cases should be reported to CPS (or to other investigatory agencies). Other reasons related to the attitudes and assumptions of the professionals who are aware of these situations. For example, they may feel that they are in the best position to help, may not trust CPS to handle the problem appropriately, or may have apprehensions about becoming involved in an official investigation.

Level 4. Abused and neglected children who are recognized by someone outside the purview of the first three levels, such as a neighbor, another member of the family, or by one or both of the involved parties—the perpetrator and the child. However, none of the individuals recognizing the maltreatment at this level has made it known to persons at levels 1 through 3.

Figure 5.1
Levels of Recognition of Child Abuse and Neglect

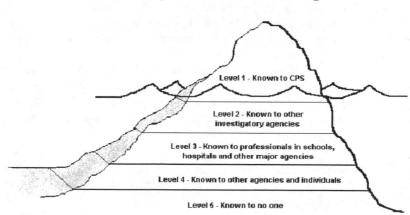

Source: NCCAN (1988). *Study findings: Study of national incidence and prevalence of child abuse and neglect—1988.* (p. 2.2). Washington, DC: U.S. Department of Health and Human Services.

Level 5. Children who have not been recognized as abused or neglected by anyone. These are the cases where the individuals involved do not regard their behaviors or experiences as child maltreatment and where the situations have not yet come to the attention of outside observers who would recognize them as such (NCCAN, 1988, pp. x-xi).

Findings from the National Incidence Study

Findings from NIS-3 (Sedlak & Broadhurst, 1996) are based on a nationally representative sample of over 5,600 professionals in 842 agencies serving 42 counties in the U.S. Due to sophisticated weighting of the data, results can be interpreted to represent the U.S. population at the time these data were collected. However, it is important to emphasize that results from the NIS-3 study are based on data collected about maltreated children identified through levels 1 through 3. Although a study methodology for conducting a national population based survey that would attempt to reach deeper into the iceberg was designed, in the final stages of contract negotiation for NIS-3, the federal government decided to not implement that study component (Sedlak, 2001). The NIS study uses two sets of standardized definitions of child abuse and neglect. Under the Harm Standard, children identified to the study were considered to be maltreated only if they had already experienced harm from abuse or neglect. Under the Endangerment Standard, children who experienced abuse or neglect that put them "at risk of harm" were included in the set of those considered to be maltreated, together with the already-harmed children.

Findings from NIS-3 suggest a steady increase over time in the numbers of children who met the definitions of child abuse or neglect in this study however only 28 percent of these children were investigated by CPS programs. Children who experienced poverty and resided in single parent households were at higher risk of child maltreatment but children of all racial and ethnic backgrounds were of equal risk of maltreatment. Further highlights from this study are outlined in Table 5.2.

Surveys of the Incidence of Child Maltreatment

In 1985, Straus and Gelles (1986) estimated that a minimum of one million children ages three to seventeen (residing in two-parent families) were subjected to serious physical abuse. If children maltreated in single-parent homes were added, this figure would be increased significantly, given the greater prevalence of child maltreatment in single-parent homes.

In a more recent nationally representative sample of children and youth ages two to seventeen years (Finkelhor, Ormrod, Thurner, & Hamby, 2005), child maltreatment was estimated to occur to a little more than one in seven of the

Table 5.2
Key Findings from NIS-3

Incidence

- There have been substantial and significant increases in the incidence of child abuse and neglect since NIS-2 was conducted in 1986.
- Under the Harm Standard definitions, the total number of abused and neglected children was two-thirds higher in the NIS-3 than in the NIS-2. This means that a child's risk of experiencing harm-causing abuse or neglect in 1993 was one and one-half times the child's risk in 1986.
- Under the Endangerment Standard, the number of abused and neglected children nearly doubled from 1986 to 1993. Physical abuse nearly doubled, sexual abuse more than doubled, and emotional abuse, physical neglect, and emotional neglect were all more than two and one-half times their NIS-2 levels.
- The total number of children seriously injured and the total number endangered both quadrupled during this time.

Child Characteristics

- Girls were sexually abused three times more often than boys
- Boys had a greater risk of emotional neglect and of serious injury than girls.
- Children are consistently vulnerable to sexual abuse from age three on.
- There were no significant race differences in the incidence of maltreatment or maltreatment-related injuries uncovered in either the NIS-2 or the NIS-3.

Family Characteristics

- Children of single parents had a 77 percent greater risk of being harmed by physical abuse, an 87 percent greater risk of being harmed by physical neglect, and an 80 percent greater risk of suffering serious injury or harm from abuse or neglect than children living with both parents.
- Children in the largest families were physically neglected at nearly three times the rate of those who came from single-child families.
- Children from families with annual incomes below $15,000 as compared to children from families with annual incomes above $30,000 per year were over 22 times more likely to experience some form of maltreatment that fit the Harm Standard and over 25 times more likely to suffer some form of maltreatment as defined by the Endangerment Standard.
- Children from the lowest income families were 18 times more likely to be sexually abused, almost 56 times more likely to be educationally neglected, and over 22 times more likely to be seriously injured from maltreatment as defined under the Harm Standard than children from the higher income families.

Table 5.2 (cont.)

Child Protective Services (CPS) Investigation

- CPS investigated only 28 percent of the recognized children who met the Harm Standard. This was a significant decrease from the 44 percent investigated in 1986.
- Although the percentage of children whose abuse or neglect was investigated declined, the actual number of children investigated remained constant.
- CPS investigated less than one-half of all Harm Standard children recognized by any source and less than one-half of all Endangerment Standard children recognized by any source except police and sheriffs' departments (52%).
- Schools recognized the largest number of children maltreated under the Harm Standard, but only 16 percent of these children were investigated by CPS.
- CPS investigated only 26 percent of the seriously injured and 26 percent of the moderately injured children.

Source: Sedlak & Broadhurst (1996)

child and youth population (138 per 1,000). The survey instrument measured five maltreatment types (physical abuse, sexual abuse, emotional abuse, neglect, and family abduction or custodial interference) and specifically excluded episodes of conventional corporal punishment. Of these types, emotional abuse (name calling or denigration by an adult) was the most frequent. Applying a standard of actual harm from abuse or neglect, the physical abuse rate was calculated at 15 per 1,000, the neglect rate to 11 per 1,000, and the overall child maltreatment rate to 124 to 1000 children. In this study, boys and girls experienced similar rates of maltreatment with the exception of sexual abuse, which was more frequently cited by girls. Physical abuse was highest among adolescents, whereas neglect was equally common across all age groups. Family adults were identified as the most common perpetrators although emotional abuse had a somewhat higher proportion of non-family perpetrators.

A similar survey of a population-based sample in North and South Carolina focused on the number of children at risk for specific sub-types of physical neglect: the provision of food, parental supervision, and access to medical care (Theodore, Runyan, & Chang, 2007). Results from this study indicated that 19 per 1,000 mothers reported that they were unable to provide enough food for their child on 1 or more occasions in the past month, 2 in 1000 children ages 0 to 6 were reportedly left home alone for more than 1 hour without adult supervision, and approximately 8.4 percent of mothers reported that, at least once in the past year, they were unable to obtain medical care for their child when they felt that it was needed.

Extent of Reported Child Abuse and Neglect

Each year, the U.S. Department of Health and Human Services releases a report from a national study of official reports of child abuse and neglect, the National Child Abuse and Neglect Data System (NCANDS). This national report is usually released in April during Child Abuse Prevention Month and summarizes information based on data submitted from state CWS agencies. To permit sufficient time for data submission and analysis, there is an approximate 1.5-year lag time between the year when reports of child abuse and neglect were made to CWS agencies and the publication date of the NCCANDS report. Information from these reports may be accessed online through the Child Welfare Information Gateway (undated). In 2006, approximately 3.3 million referrals for child abuse and neglect involving 6 million children were received by Child Protective Services programs within CWS agencies (U.S. Department of Health and Human Services, 2008). Of these referrals, CPS programs screened in 61.7 percent of referrals and screened out 38.3 percent for an investigation or assessment. The number of referrals received and the percentage of referrals that resulted in an investigation or assessment have remained relatively constant over the last five years.

David Finklehor and colleagues have studied the apparent decline of child abuse and neglect reporting since the 1990s and are convinced that this decline is not just an artifact of reporting systems (Finkelhor & Jones, 2006). They contend that at the same time that various forms of child maltreatment and child victimization (e.g., sexual abuse, physical abuse, sexual assault, homicide, aggravated assault, robbery, and larceny) have declined as much as 40 to 70 percent from 1993 to 2004 that other child welfare indicators have also improved during the same period (e.g., teen pregnancy, teen suicide, and children living in poverty). Using data from the National Study of Child Abuse and Neglect Data System between 1990 and 2004, they demonstrate significant declines in sexual abuse and physical abuse while at the same time rates of child neglect have stayed at relatively the same rates.

Types of Reported Child Maltreatment

In 2006, child neglect continued to represent the largest category of child maltreatment confirmed by CPS programs. During 2006, 64.1 percent of maltreated children experienced neglect, 16 percent were physically abused, 8.8 percent were sexually abused, 6.6 percent were psychologically maltreated, and 2.2 percent were medically neglected (U.S. Department of Health and Human Services, 2008).

Gender and Ages of Maltreated Children

For 2006, 48.2 percent of child victims were boys, and 51.5 percent of the victims were girls. The youngest children (ages birth to three years) had the highest rate of victimization (14.2 per 1,000 children) and the rate decreased as the ages of the children increased. Nearly three-quarters of child victims (72.2 percent) ages birth to three years were neglected compared with 55 percent of victims who were sixteen years and older.

A special analysis of infant child abuse and neglect (CDC, 2008) identified 91,278 infant victims under the age of 1 in 2006, most of who were classified as neglected (68.5 percent). And, a large percentage of infant victims were less than one month old (38.8 percent) and of these, most (84.3 percent) were less than one week old. Understanding the ages at which infants are most at risk of child abuse or neglect is very important for targeting prevention efforts.

Race and Ethnicity of Victims

In 2006, African-American children, American Indian, or Alaska Native children, and children of multiple races had the highest rates of reported child maltreatment victimization at 19.8, 15.9, and 15.4 per 1,000 children of the same race or ethnicity, respectively (U.S. Department of Health and Human Services, 2008). White children and Hispanic children had rates of approximately 10.7 and 10.8 per 1,000 children of the same race or ethnicity, respectively. Asian children had the lowest rate of 2.5 per 1,000 children of the same race or ethnicity. One-half of all victims were White (48.8 percent); one-quarter (22.8 percent) were African-American; and 18.4 percent were Hispanic. For all racial categories, except Native Hawaiian and Pacific Islander, the largest percentage of victims suffered from neglect.

Data from the National Survey of Child and Adolescent Well-Being (NSCAW), the only national longitudinal study related to children and families involved with public child welfare services, suggest that about half (51 percent) of all children known to CWS agencies are White/non-Hispanic, with African American/non-Hispanic children making up over one-quarter (34 percent), and Hispanic children—whether black or white—being less than one-fifth of this population (17 percent). This means that African American/Non-Hispanic children are overrepresented among children who are investigated by CWS agencies (as compared with children in the general American population) (US DHHS, 2005).

In older research in some jurisdictions, child maltreatment was also more likely to be indicated when families were African American or Hispanic than when they were Caucasian, and this over-reporting was not corrected during the investigative process. Consequently, disproportionality appeared to continue from reporting to substantiation (Hill, 2006; Sedlak & Schultz, 2001). More recent research (HS DHHS, 2005), in a broader nationally representative cross-section of counties, finds no such relationship however. The decision to substantiate cases, following investigation, and the placement of children into foster care was not related to the race of children—it was, instead, determined by the child and family characteristics and the type of maltreatment.

Perpetrators of Maltreatment

In 2006, nearly 83 percent (82.4 percent) of maltreated children were abused by a parent acting alone or with another person (USDHHS, 2008). Approximately, forty percent (39.9 percent) of children were maltreated by their mothers acting alone; another 17.6 percent were maltreated by their fathers acting alone; and 17.8 percent were maltreated by both parents (U.S. Department of Health and Human Services, 2008). Children maltreated by non-parental perpetrators accounted for 10 percent of all victims. The report also presents data for victims of specific maltreatment types in relation to perpetrator status. Of the children who were determined to be neglected, 86.7 percent were neglected by a parent. Of the children who were sexually abused, 26.2 percent were abused by a parent and 29.1 percent were abused by a relative other than a parent.

Maltreatment in Foster Care

Through the Child and Family Services Review (CFSR) (see Chapter 1), the U.S DHHS, Children's Bureau established a national standard for the incidence of child abuse or neglect in foster care as 99.68 percent free from abuse and neglect, defined as: *Absence of Maltreatment in Foster Care. Of all children in foster care during the reporting period, what percent were not victims of a substantiated or indicated maltreatment by foster parents or facility staff members?* The number of states in compliance has increased from sixteen states that met this standard in 2004 to nineteen states in 2006 (U.S. Department of Health and Human Services, 2008). During 2006, five states were unable to provide the data needed to compute this measure. This is understandable as accurate data about the abuse of children in foster care is difficult data to obtain. There are many reports that occur while a child is in foster care that are not the result of abuse by the foster parent or facility staff members—instead, these are reports that are processed and that refer to biological family members (DePanfilis & Girvin, 2005; US DHHS, 2005).

Child Fatalities Due to Abuse and Neglect

During 2006, an estimated 1,530 children (compared to 1,460 children in 2005) died from abuse or neglect—at a rate of 2.04 deaths per 100,000 children (U.S. Department of Health and Human Services, 2008). The national estimate was based on data from state child welfare information systems, as well as other data sources available to the states. While most fatality data were obtained from state child welfare agencies, many of these agencies also received data from additional sources. For 2006, nearly one-fifth (17.6 percent) of fatalities were reported by health departments and fatality review boards. The coordination of data collection with other agencies contributes to a fuller understanding of the size of the phenomenon, as well as to better estimation.

In 2006, more than three-quarters (78 percent) of children who died due to child maltreatment were younger than four years of age, 11.9 percent were four to seven years of age, 4.8 percent were eight to eleven years of age, and 5.4 percent were twelve to seventeen years of age (U.S. Department of Health and Human Services, 2008). Differences in the numbers of child maltreatment related fatalities over the years may be partly because of differences in the number of states that report these data as well as other factors in the compilation of data across states. For example, analysis of child fatality data in California shows the inconsistency between data that is identified as child fatality data by child welfare services, health department vital statistics data, and homicide data from the Department of Justice (Grimm, 2007).

Variations in Reporting Trends due to CPS Alternative Response Systems

An increasing number of states have implemented child welfare reforms that involve responding differentially to reports of child abuse and neglect. Described as Alternative, Differential, or Multiple Response systems, states have changed their practices to accept certain referrals of child abuse and neglect without formally logging the referral as a CPS report (US DHHS, 2003a). These practices (discussed in more detail in Chapter 6) have affected child abuse and neglect reporting and substantiation rates. In an effort to explore the relative impact that these child welfare reforms may have on child abuse and neglect reporting trends, the US DHHS contracted for a set of special analyses using case level NCANDS data (Shusterman, Hollinshead, Fluke, & Yuan, 2005).

A review of prior research (Shusterman, et al., 2005) suggested wide variations in the percentage of reports diverted to alternative response systems (e.g., from 42 percent to 71 percent) and in the impact that these systems have had on substantiation rates. Based on the NCANDS analysis of data from 2002, Figure 5.2 shows children who were the subject of a report by the type of response that their report received in each of the six states represented in the data set. The number of children who were included in a maltreatment report, as well as the proportion of children who received an alternative response, varied across these states. Kentucky, Missouri, New Jersey, and Oklahoma all had large number of children who were subjects of a maltreatment report (between 60,000 and 80,000), but in Kentucky and Oklahoma, only 27 and 20 percent, respectively, were referred to alternative response, while in Missouri and New Jersey, 64 and 71 percent, respectively were referred to alternative response. Minnesota (26,344) and Wyoming (4,355) had much smaller number of children who were subjects of a report. In Minnesota, 20 percent were

Figure 5.2
Comparisons of Types of Responses among Five States

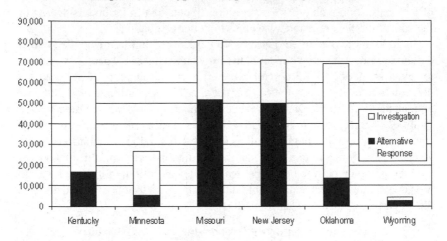

Source: Shusterman, Hollinshead, Fluke, & Yuan, 2005

referred to alternative response, while in Wyoming, 58 percent were (Shusterman, et al., 2005).

Findings from the NCANDS special analysis also found that alternative responses were more likely to be used for cases with less immediate safety concerns and that the investigative response was much more likely in cases of child sexual abuse (Shusterman, et al., 2005). This indicates that the programs may be operating as intended. Also supportive of the designed operation—no differences in types of responses were differentiated by race or ethnicity.

Recurrence of Child Abuse and Neglect

The recurrence of child maltreatment following a report to CPS is one index of the effectiveness of the public child welfare system. Experts have expressed concern that CPS programs across the country are faced with problems of such magnitude that their ability to protect children and prevent recurrences is severely compromised (Waldfogel, 1998a, 1998b). The movement to adopt risk assessment and safety evaluation systems to assess the likelihood of recurrence, to evaluate the potential safety of maltreated children, and to guide decision-making in child welfare (see Chapter 6) is an example of a policy movement that has evolved from this concern. For many victims who have experienced repeat maltreatment, the efforts of the CWS system have not been successful in preventing subsequent victimization. Through the Child and Family Services Reviews (CFSR) (see Chapter 1), the Children's Bureau has established the current national standard for recurrence of child maltreatment as 94.6 percent, defined as: *"Absence of Maltreatment Recurrence. Of all children who were victims of substantiated or indicated abuse or neglect during the first 6 months of the reporting year, what percent did not experience another incident of substantiated or indicated abuse or neglect within a 6-month period?"* The number of states in compliance increased from seventeen states in 2004 to twenty-three states in 2006. During 2006, five states were unable to provide the data to NCCANDS in order to compute this measure (DHHS, 2008). The national average percent of children without a new substantiated incident of child maltreatment increased from 91.9 during 2004 to 92.2 in 2006 with ranges from 87.3 to 98.4 percent. Although the increase of states in compliance suggests progress, the average rate of children without recurrences is very similar to averages reported in 2004 when the average percentage of children without maltreatment recurrences ranged from 86 to 98 percent with a median rate of 93 percent (US DHHS, undated-B).

Risk and Protective Factors Related to Child Maltreatment

Child maltreatment does not occur in a vacuum. There is a general consensus that factors that increase or decrease risk of child maltreatment should be conceptualized on multiple levels: Individual (ontogenetic development), Family (microsystem), Community environment (exosystem) and Culture [or society] (macrosystem). For example, individual factors could be those characteristics in a child (e.g., colicky, unresponsive to caregiver nurturing) or adult (e.g., low self-esteem, low impulse control) that influence their behavior and may contribute to child maltreatment. Familial factors may include low income, an intergenerational pattern of abuse or neglect, poor communication, and a lack of household routine with respect to meals and bedtime, among others (Belsky, 1980; Panel on Child Abuse and Neglect, National Research Council, 1993, pp. 110, 126-136). Ecological models further suggest that "when stressors (of a variety of kinds: parent, child, social conditions) outweigh supports (also of a variety of kinds), or when potentiating factors are not balanced by compensatory ones, the probability of child maltreatment increases" (Belsky, 1992, pp. 1-2).

To understand the nature of child maltreatment, the concepts of risk factors (transient/situational, enduring, underlying) (Kirby and Fraser, 1997; Masten & Wright, 1998; Thomlison, 2004) and compensatory and protective factors (transient/situational, enduring, underlying) and resilience of children (Masten & Wright, 1998) must be understood. What are risk factors? Thomlison (2004) suggests that *risk factors are those characteristics or conditions that, if present for a given child, make it more likely that this child, rather than another child selected from the general population, will experience child maltreatment* (pp. 94-95). Examples of risk factors may include factors such as parental drug addiction or serious mental illness, punitive parental attitudes, or the presence of domestic violence in the family. In contrast, a compensatory factor may be defined as a correlate of successful adaptation or development under both favorable and unfavorable conditions that may directly offset or counterbalance the negative effects of risk or adversity (Masten & Wright, 1998, p. 10). For example, having someone to turn to for concrete and emotional support in times of financial stress could compensate for the negative influence of the risk factor (financial stress). Similarly, a protective factor has been described as a correlate of resilience that may reflect preventive or ameliorative influences and as a positive moderator of risk or adversity (Masten & Wright, 1998). An example could be having strong, positive relationships within the family so that family members stick together through thick or thin and this reduces the negative impact that could result from living in a high-risk dangerous neighborhood (risk factor). Resilience is defined as successful adaptation or development during or following adverse conditions that challenge or threaten adaptive functioning or healthy development (Masten & Wright, 1998, p. 10). An example could be positive academic achievement of a child in the family, despite the fact that this child receives little cognitive stimulation from his/her parents. This phenomenon is why each child needs to be assessed individually as some children are more resilient than others in the face of child maltreatment.

It is important to understand these concepts as a foundation for conducting assessments that guide safety and service planning with children and families (see Chapter 6). While including a comprehensive review of risk and protective factors is not feasible for this text, a brief summary of risk factors that may increase the likelihood of child maltreatment is provided.

Connection to Alcohol and Other Drugs

Studies of child maltreatment and substance abuse have documented a connection both for parents and children/youth. (Information about the characteristics of children involved in child welfare is described below.) Alcohol and drug abuse or addiction can result in short- and long-term effects on individual users, their children, and entire family systems. Since the late 1990s, national attention has focused upon the interrelationship of familial substance abuse and the problems and needs of children who enter the child welfare system (US DHHS, 1999). Studies of the overlap between substance abuse and child maltreatment have generally found high rates of substance abuse ranging from about 19 to 79 percent (Besinger, Garland, Litrownik, & Landsverk 1999; Dore, Doris, & Wright, 1995; Pierce, 1991; US DHHS, 1999; Young & Grella, 1998). Evidence from NSCAW indicates that the proportion of all families involved with substance abuse problems in child welfare is likely to be about 20 percent—the proportion is significantly higher (about 42 percent) for children who enter foster care (US DHHS, 2005).

Compared to parents who do not use substances, parents who are known to have alcohol or other drug problems have been found with lower scores on measures of parenting knowledge and behavior (Velez, Janson, Montoya, Schweitzer, Golden, and Svikis, 2004), report higher levels of personal and environmental stress (Nair, Schuler, Black, Kettinger, & Harrington, 2003) and are significantly more likely to abuse and neglect their children over time, even after controlling for significant social and demographic risk factors (Chaffin, Kelleher, & Hollenberg, 1996). In particular, substance abuse was identified as a contributor to the growth in reports of child maltreatment during the 1990s.

Estimates of the number of families in the child welfare system affected by substance abuse vary depending upon the part of the system (Wang, 1998) and the geographic area studied with the highest rates found for court-involved samples (Besinger, et al., 1999). Nevertheless, it is well documented that problems associated with substance abuse have hindered the ability of the child welfare system to protect children and serve families (Tracy, 1994; U.S. General Accounting Office, 1997) and that that children whose parents abuse alcohol or other drugs are almost three times more likely to be abused, up to four times more likely to be neglected than children of parents who are not substance abusers (Besinger, et al, 1999; Dunn, et al., 2002; Kelleher, Chaffin, Hollinberg, & Fischer, 1994; Ondersma, 2002) and are more likely to experience placement of their children (Kelleher, et al.; Zuravin & DePanfilis, 1997) compared to families who maltreat their children but are not known to have substance abuse problems; and are found to stay in care longer than other children (Vanderploeg, Connell, Caron, Saunders, Katz, & Tebes, 2007). While parental substance abuse or addiction may increase risk of all types of child maltreatment, some studies have reported that substance abuse is more likely to be a factor in reported neglect than in reported physical abuse, sexual abuse, or emotional maltreatment (Herskowitz, Seck, & Fogg, 1989; USDHHS, 1993).

Of particular concern in recent years has been the increasing prevalence of methamphetamine manufacture, use, and addiction problems in the U.S. and among mothers in particular (National Institute on Drug Abuse [NIDA], 2005). Despite efforts to curb domestic production, methamphetamine use continues in previously affected parts of the country and new areas of the south and east coast are increasingly affected (United States Department of Justice [USDOJ], 2006). The use of methamphetamine by parents of young children is of particular concern to child welfare professionals. When parents use methamphetamine or are involved in manufacture, child safety and well-being may be compromised. Methamphetamine use and abuse pose risks to children and families because: (a) methamphetamine can be manufactured in homes where children live, introducing the risk of exposure to toxins; (b) use is associated with promiscuous sexual behavior, which may put users at risk for disease; (c) withdrawal can be characterized by long periods of sleep, leading to lack of supervision of children and other forms of child neglect; (d) the drug is associated with violent and paranoid behavioral side effects, which may increase the risk for physical abuse and raise concerns for child safety; and (e) methamphetamine use may damage the brain, resulting in memory and attention loss, depression, anxiety, and aggression, symptoms that may further impact parental capacity to adequately care for children and complicate the selection of appropriate intervention and treatment. These issues may present new challenges to service providers, even those accustomed to working with substance abusing parents (DePanfilis & Hayward, 2006).

Despite the overall high rates of substance abuse or addiction among parents involved in child maltreatment of their children, very few of these parents report receiving substance abuse treatment. Results from the National Survey of Child and Adolescent Well-Being (NSCAW) (US DHHS, 2005) suggest that only 2 percent of the in-home caregivers received drug or alcohol services, with those receiving child welfare services significantly more likely to report current or lifetime use. However, only one in ten parents reported the use of drug or alcohol services in their lifetime. Of the parents who were not receiving substance abuse treatment at the time of their NSCAW interview, only two of every one hundred caregivers reported that they "currently had a need for it" (US DHHS, 2005).

Parental Mental Health Problems

Children of parents or other caregivers with a history of psychiatric disorders are two to three times more likely to experience maltreatment than those without a parental history of mental health problems (Walsh, MacMillan, & Jamieson, 2002). This relationship may differ somewhat by type of mental illness and type of child maltreatment. Nevertheless, parental depression in particular has repeatedly been shown to be associated with problems in parenting (Lovejoy, Graczyk, O'Hare, & Neumann, 2000) and has been found to increase risk for all types of child maltreatment. For example, a review of five studies that compared parents who demonstrated depressive symptoms with those without symptoms suggested an increased risk of child physical abuse among those with depressive symptoms (Black, Haymen, & Slep, 2001). This relationship was also confirmed in relation to child neglect based on interviews with a community sample of respondents. In this study, individuals who self-identified as neglectful were significantly more likely to receive a diagnosis of depressive disorders (Chaffin, et al., 1996). Among in-home caregivers interviewed in the NSCAW CPS sample, 23 percent report experiencing major depression in the past twelve months (USDHHS, 2005). A history of parental depression also seems to increase the risk of child maltreatment recurrences (Baird, 1988; Baird, Wagner, and Neuenfeldt, 1993).

Exposure to Violence in the Home

Estimates of violence against women suggest that nearly 2 million women are physically assaulted annually and approximately one in five women is assaulted by a current or former partner during her lifetime (Gelles & Straus, 1988; Tjaden & Thoennes, 2000). Intimate partner violence between parents or other caregivers generates a negative environment in which all members of the household, particularly children, are directly and indirectly harmed (Carlson, 1996; Fantuzzo & Lindquist, 1989; Jaffe, Wolfe, & Wilson, 1990; Jaffe, Wolfe, Wilson, & Zak, 1986; O'Keefe, 1995). In particular, research has documented an overlap between child maltreatment and intimate partner violence (Appel & Holden, 1998; Edleson, 1999), although the specific overlap varies depending on the sample and definitions of intimate partner violence and child maltreatment. Among the 3,612 female caregivers interviewed as part of the NSCAW baseline interview, almost 32 percent reported a history of physical intimate partner violence during the previous twelve months, prior to the report of child abuse and neglect to a child welfare agency (Connelly, et al., 2006). When asked about domestic violence during their lifetimes, almost half (45 percent) of caregivers reported that they had experienced either minor or severe abuse, a rate of about twice as high as found in the general population (USDHHS, 2005).

In this same study (USDHHS, 2005), children ages five and over also reported on their exposure to violence in their homes. Over their lifetimes, these children reported that they witnessed high rates of violence. About one-third reported having seen adults shove, slap, or throw things at each other; over one-fifth of the children reported that they had seen an adult beat another adult; and more than one-tenth of the children reported that they have seen an adult point a gun at others. Whether witnessing intimate partner violence warrants a response by CWS agencies if children have not also been physically harmed has been vigorously debated since the 1990s (Edleson, 1999, 2004; Friend, Lambert, & Shlonsky, in press). Whatever the resolution of this debate, the findings are now clear that the CWS actions in these cases are not very invasive and cases involved with domestic violence have substantially lower likelihoods of resulting in placements of children into foster care than other cases (Kohl, Edleson, English, & Barth, 2005).

Characteristics of Children Involved with CPS Programs

Prospective longitudinal studies have documented that maltreated children are at risk for a range of problems in childhood, adolescence, and adulthood, including aggression, delinquency, and violent crime, depression, anxiety, and substance use problems (Horowitz, Widom, McLaughlin, & White, 2001; Lansford, et al., 2002; Widom & Maxfield, 2001). Understanding the specific consequences to children is important for arriving at the best possible professional response by the CWS agency (see Chapter 6). NSCAW provides a comprehensive picture of how these children involved in child welfare agencies are faring as described in the following sections (USDHHS, 2005).

Infants and Preschool Children

Infants and preschool children in this study were assessed with serious developmental delays (USDHHS, 2005). Fifty-three percent of all children aged three to twenty-four months were assessed on the Bayley Infant Neruodevelopmental Screener (BINS) as high risk for developmental delay or neurological impairment. Using the Battelle Developmental Inventory (BDI) with children aged 3 years and younger, suggested that these children whose families were investigated for maltreatment were close to one standard deviation under the normed mean, and 31 percent of these children had a T score on the total cognitive domain of the BDI that was lower than 2 standard deviations below the normed mean. It appears that these children are also at risk for impaired language skills. Based on assessments of 5-year-old children and younger in the CPS sample with the Preschool Language Scale-3 (PLS-3), children whose families were investigated for maltreated were below the normed mean but within one standard deviation, but 14 percent of all children aged 5 and younger had total scores on the PLS-3 that were lower than two standard deviations below the mean.

Children Aged Four and Older

The children in NSCAW (USDHHS, 2005), were assessed with respect to cognitive and achievement tests, social functioning, psychosocial well-being, delinquency, and sexual behavior. Cognitive and achievement test scores for children ages four and older generally fell within the lower end of the normal range. However 5 percent scored at least 2 standard deviations below the mean on the Kaufman Brief Intelligence Test. Children ages 6 and older tended to be slightly below the mean on reading and math scores but 5 percent had reading scores and 12 percent had match scores at least 2 standard deviations below the mean.

Some children involved with CWS agencies because of a report of child abuse or neglect also suggest the need for concern regarding their social functioning (USDHHS, 2005). In the NSCAW CPS sample, about 30 percent of children had low or moderately low scores for daily living skills and 38 percent were classified as having "fewer" social skills—twice the rate for the normative sample.

Children in the CPS—NSCAW sample (USDHHS, 2005) were five times more likely than the normative sample to have problem behaviors, as indicated by reports from caregivers, teachers, or the young people themselves. Depressive symptoms were also more common for children involved with CWS agencies compared to children in the general population (i.e., 15 versus 9 percent, respectively).

Consistent with prior research (Widom, 1989; Widom & Maxfield, 2001), some maltreated children display behavioral problems and engage in delinquent behaviors as a consequence of their early maltreatment experiences. In the NSCAW sample, caregivers classified about one-fourth of children ages six to fifteen as having delinquent behaviors—five times greater than the general population. One-fifth of the young people ages 11 and older who were interviewed admitted that they had engaged in at least 1 violent act within the previous 6 months, and 10 percent said they had been arrested during that episode. With respect to sexual behavior, about one-fourth of children between the ages of eleven and fifteen reported they had been involved in sexual intercourse.

Resilience among Maltreated Children

Despite the serious consequences of child maltreatment for some children, not all maltreated children experience these difficulties. Research has demonstrated that resilient children achieve positive developmental outcomes despite having faced significant adversities (Luthar, Cicchetti, & Becker, 2000; Masten and Coatsworth, 1995). Results from data analyzed from the Environmental Risk Longitudinal Study which describes a nationally representative sample of 1,116 twin pairs and their families suggested that resilient children were those who engaged in normative levels of antisocial behavior despite having been maltreated (Jafee, Caspi, Moffitt, Polo-Tomas, & Taylor, 2007). In this study, boys (but not girls) who had above-average intelligence and whose parents had relatively few symptoms of antisocial personality were more likely to be resilient versus non-resilient to maltreatment. In contrast, children who lived in neighborhoods with high crime and had parents with substance use problems and were low on social cohesion and informal social control were less likely to be resilient versus non-resilient to maltreatment.

Conclusion

Current Status

This chapter documents the incidence of child abuse and neglect, defines the various forms of child maltreatment, and describes the characteristics of families and children who are likely to be reported to CPS programs. Despite the high costs of child maltreatment to society and to the children and families themselves, some children are more resilient than others and are able to successfully transition to adulthood. Federal data for 2006 reveal little change in child maltreatment referral rates but a slight increase in substantiation rates.

Future Directions

Among the most urgent needs for reform is improving the consistency of definition and policy with respect to definition of child maltreatment and community responses to this major social problem. In the next chapter, the response of the CPS program to reports of child maltreatment is described.

Notes

1. Hammerle, N. (1992). *Private choices, social costs, and public policy: An economic analysis of public health issues.* Westport, CT: Greenwood, Praeger.
2. Chambers, J.G., Parrish, T.B., & Harr, J.J. (2004). *What are we spending on special education services in the United States, 1999-2000?* Palo Alto, CA: American Institutes for Research. Retrieved August 28, 2007 from http://www.csef-air.org/publications/seep/national/AdvRpt1.PDF
3. Widom, C.S., & Maxfield, M.G. (2001). *An update on the "cycle of violence."* U.S. Department of Justice, the National Institute of Justice. Retrieved August 27, 2007 from http://www.ncjrs.gov/pdffiles1/nij/184894.pdf
4. U.S. Bureau of the Census (1993). *Statistical abstract of the United States, 1993* (113th edition). Washington, DC: Government Printing Office. Retrieved September 6, 2007 from http://www2.census.gov/prod2/statcomp/documents/1993-03.pdf
5. Walker, E.A., Unutzer, J., Rutter, C. Gelfand, A., Saunders, K., VonKorff, M., Koss, M., & Katon, W. (1999). Costs of health care use by women HMO members with a history of childhood abuse and neglect. *Archives of General Psychiatry, 56,* 609-613. Retrieved August 22, 2007 from http://archpsyc.ama-assn.org/cgi/reprint/56/7/609?ck=nck
6. U.S. Deaprtment of Justice. (2007). *Key facts at a glance: Direct expenditures by criminal justice function, 1982-2005.* Bureau of Justice Statistics. Retrieved September 5, 2007 from http://www.ojp.usdoj.gov/bjs/glance/tables/exptyptab.htm
7. U.S. Department of Labor. (2007). *National compensation survey: Occupational wages in the United States, June 2006.* U.S. Bureau of Labor Statistics. Retrieved September 4, 2007 from http://www.bls.gov/ncs/ocs/sp/ncbl0910.pdf
8. Smith, S.J. (1985). Revised worklife tables reflect 1979-80 experience. *Monthly Labor Review,* August 1985, 23-30. Retrieved September 4, 2007 from http://www.bls.gov/opub/mlr/1985/08/art3full.pdf
9. Sedlak, A.J, & Broadhurst, D.D. (1996). *The third national incidence study of child abuse and neglect (NIS-3).* U.S. Department of Health and Human Services. Washington, DC.
10. Daro, D. (1988). *Confronting child abuse: Research for effective program design.* New York: Free Press.
11. Rovi, S., Chen, P.H., & Johnson, M.S. (2004). The economic burden of hospitalizations associated with child abuse and neglect. *American Journal of Public Health, 94,* 586-590. Retrieved September 7, 2007 from http://www.ajph.org/cgi/reprint/94/4/586?ck=nck
12. Miller, T.R., Cohen, M.A., & Wiersema, B. (1996). *Victim costs and consequences: A new look.* The National Institute of Justice. Retrieved August 27, 2007 from http://www.ncjrs.gov/pdffiles/victcost.pdf
13. Scarcella, C.A., Bess, R., Zielewski, E.H., & Geen, R. (2006). *The cost of protecting vulnerable children V: Understanding state variation in child welfare financing.* The Urban Institute. Retrieved August 27, 2007 from http://www.urban.org/UploadedPDF/311314_vulnerable_children.pdf

6

Child Protective Services

As discussed in Chapter 1, the passage of the Adoption and Safe Families Act of 1997 (ASFA) affirmed that child welfare agencies have a primary responsibility for assuring that children are safe from abuse and neglect (USDHHS, 2000). In this chapter we focus on the Child Protective Services Program, which is the first program that children and families typically encounter when they become involved with child welfare service (CWS) agencies.

The Child Protective Services (CPS) program, a core program in all child welfare agencies, leads efforts to ensure child safety in collaboration with community agencies. CPS follows core civil laws (highlighted in Chapter 5), through support from a combination of federal, state, and local funding mechanisms, to implement practices that constitute the government's response to reports of child abuse and neglect (Waldfogel, 1998a). Child welfare workers in CPS programs have the responsibility to respond to reports or referrals of child abuse and neglect and to implement service responses that will keep children safe from abuse and neglect (i.e., prevent the likelihood of future child maltreatment) and address the effects of child maltreatment on the child (e.g., behavioral or school problems) (DePanfilis and Salus, 2003). Thus, while the primary focus is on increasing child safety, it is also important that CPS programs work to enhance child well-being.

According to the National Association of Public Child Welfare Administrators (NAPCWA), (1999), the mission of the child protective services (CPS) program is to: (1) assess the safety of children; (2) intervene to protect children from harm; (3) strengthen the ability of families to protect their children; or (4) provide an alternative safe family for the child. The Child Welfare League of America (CWLA) also affirms this mission by suggesting that the CPS program assesses the risk to, and safety of, children; and provides or arranges for services to achieve safe, permanent families for children who have been abused or neglected or who are at risk of abuse or neglect. The CPS program also facilitates community collaborations and engages formal and informal community partners to support families and protect children from abuse and neglect (Child

Welfare League of America, 1999). The purposes of this chapter are to trace the path of child abuse and neglect reports from the point of referral through the process of providing ongoing services to children and families involved in the child protection system and to conclude by a brief review of research about the effectiveness of the CPS response. These purposes are addressed after first describing the philosophy for CPS programs.

Philosophy of Child Protective Services Programs

CPS programs operate based on a set of philosophical beliefs that drive the way in which they operate. Sometimes these principles are imbedded in laws and policies, other times they are built into education and training programs to guide service delivery. While the articulation of these beliefs may vary somewhat between state and local CPS programs, the themes among these principles are common service systems (DePanfilis and Salus, 2003).

- *A safe and permanent home is the best place for children to grow up.* Every child has a right to adequate care and supervision and to be free from abuse, neglect, and exploitation. It is the responsibility of parents to see that the physical, mental, emotional, educational, and medical needs of their children are met adequately. CPS should intervene only when parents request assistance or fail, by their acts or omissions, to adequately meet their children's basic needs and keep them safe.
- *Most parents want to be good parents and have the strength and capacity, when adequately supported, to care for their children and keep them safe.* Underlying CPS intervention is the belief that people have the strength and potential to change behaviors or conditions that may jeopardize a child's safety. Professionals must search for and identify the strengths in families that provide the foundation for change.
- *Families who need assistance from CPS programs are diverse in terms of family structure, culture, race, religion, economic status, beliefs, values, and lifestyles.* CPS agencies and practitioners must be responsive to, and demonstrably respectful of, these differences.
- *CPS efforts are most likely to succeed when clients are involved and actively participate as partners in the process.* CPS workers need to work in ways that encourage clients to fully participate in assessment, service planning, and other critical decisions in the CPS process.
- *Services must be individualized and tailored.* While people may have similar problems, there are elements that will vary from family to family. In addition, each family's strengths and resources are different. The community's response, therefore, must be customized to reflect the particular circumstances, strengths, and needs of each family.
- *CPS approaches should be family centered.* Parents, children, their extended families, and support networks (e.g., the faith community, teachers, health care providers, and substitute caregivers) should be actively involved as partners in developing and implementing appropriate plans and services to keep children safe and reduce the risk of maltreatment.

Tapping into the strengths and resources of a family's natural support network is fundamental to enhancing family functioning and keeping children safe.

Stages of the Child Protective Services Program Process

The Child Protective Services (CPS) Program, a core program in all child welfare agencies, leads efforts to ensure child safety in collaboration with community agencies. The CPS program follows core civil laws (highlighted in Chapter 5), implemented with support from a combination of federal, state, and local funding mechanisms (but mostly state and local), respond to reports of child abuse and neglect (Waldfogel, 1998a). The implementation of these laws is by child welfare workers who have the responsibility of being first responders to reports or referrals of child abuse and neglect. Following the receipt of these calls, child welfare workers select from a wide array of possible service responses that may forever change a child's life. The most fundamental intent of these actions is to keep children safe from abuse and neglect (i.e., prevent the likelihood of future child maltreatment) (DePanfilis and Salus, 2003).

CPS receives reports of suspected child maltreatment; assesses the safety of children; and provides or arranges for services to increase safety and well being of children who have been abused or neglected or who are at risk of abuse or neglect. Each situation proceeds through one or more of a series of CPS process stages: (1) Intake; (2) Initial Assessment/Investigation; (3) Family Assessment; (4) Service Planning; (5) Service Provision; (6) Evaluation of Case Progress; and (7) Case Closure. Key decisions vary at each of these process stages (DePanfilis and Salus, 2003). In recent years, some states have developed practices and policies to differentiate how particular types of cases are handled following a report of child abuse and neglect (U.S. Government Accounting Office, 1997). Referred to as alternative response, differential response, or dual track systems, these efforts promote new practices that affect how certain reports of maltreatment are handled (USDHHS, 2003a, 2003b). The responsibility of the CPS Program at each stage of the process remains essentially the same, whether or not an alternative response approach is implemented. (Further information about these CPS reforms is provided later in this chapter.)

Intake

The CPS Program is responsible for receiving and responding to reports or referrals of suspected child abuse and neglect. In some states, there is a statewide hotline for making reports. In other states, reports are made to the local CPS agency. CPS intake workers interview the person calling with a concern to assess whether the report or referral should be accepted for further investigation or assessment. Key decisions at this stage are: (1) to determine if the reported information meets the statutory and agency guidelines for child maltreatment and should therefore result in a face to face contact with the child and family and if so, to (2) determine the urgency with which the agency must respond to the report or referral by making direct contact with the child and family. In states with an alternative response system in place, the CPS Program Intake worker may also interview the reporter to understand whether the referral could be handled by a community agency, instead of the CWS agency. In those situations, the worker uses established criteria to assure an appropriate agency or community response. Overall, intake decisions are dependent on workers implementing consistent protocols for screening information and having accurate and sufficient information to improve the quality of decision-making (Wells, 2000). The intake process may include the mandatory review of all decisions by a supervisor in order to assure a consistent application of laws and policies.

Making the "wrong decision" at intake can result in both over inclusion and under inclusion of children in the child welfare system (Waldfogel, 1998a). Over inclusion occurs when inappropriate CPS reports are accepted for investigation and assessment and when these reports lead to unnecessary intrusion into family life. The burden on the system also increases making it difficult to respond to children who are truly at risk of maltreatment and/or harm. Under inclusion occurs when children and families who could benefit from services to keep their children safe, are screened out inappropriately possibly resulting in repeated reports to CPS before the system formally responds. Nationally, in 2005 out of 3.3 million referrals involving approximately 6 million children, 62.1 percent of referrals were screened in compared to 37.9 percent that were screened out (USDHHS, 2007).

Research on screening decision-making has suggested that varied factors affect the decision to accept or not accept the referral as a report of child abuse or neglect for an investigation or assessment. In a comprehensive study of the screening decisions in twelve local agencies from five states (Wells, Fluke, & Brown, 1995), when the researchers controlled for injury, maltreatment type, child age, referral source, presence of the perpetrator in the home, and completeness of information, they found that the office receiving the referral was the strongest predictor in the decision to investigate. This suggests widespread differences within and across states in the decision to respond to a referral of child maltreatment. Research has further suggested that organizational factors such as policies, procedures, customs, norms, and the workers' interpretations of these also predict whether or not a referral will be accepted for investigation or assessment (Wells, 1997; Wells, et al., 2004). The screening decision may also depend on the process of screening (e.g., depending on a worker to make the decision or requiring supervisory or team involvement) and unofficial interpretations of screening criteria, depending on the number of referrals and available resources at the time of the report (Tumlin & Geen, 2000). A source of wide variation in how child welfare reports are handled has to do with policy and practice related to helping families who have children with mental health problems—some communities receive many such reports for pre-teen and adolescent youth and assist them, and their families through CWS. Other communities are much less likely to do so (Barth, Wildfire, & Green, 2006)

Initial Assessment

After accepting a child maltreatment referral or report, an initial assessment/investigation must be completed by the CPS worker alone, the CPS worker and law enforcement as a team, a community service provider (if an alternative response system is in place), or the CPS worker in conjunction with another service provider. The initial assessment includes interviews with the child, siblings, parents or other caregivers, and others who may have information concerning the alleged maltreatment and the family. Two key assessments that are conducted at this stage include an assessment of the safety of the child (i.e., whether there is imminent risk of severe harm) and an assessment of the risk of maltreatment (i.e., the likelihood of future child maltreatment). These assessments while overlapping in purposes focus on distinctly different aspects of the problem. Hollingshead and Fluke (2000) illustrate the connection between the two assessments in a proposed model depicted in Figure 6.1. In this model, if children are considered to be at high risk of immediate severe maltreatment, they are considered to be unsafe. And if they are considered to be at risk of a lower severity of maltreatment at some longer time in the future, they may be considered safe but still at risk of future maltreatment. For example, in cases of chronic neglect (see definitions in Chapter 5), an assessment of the family might suggest that there is a reasonable likelihood that school age children will be left alone in the future but the likelihood of this event occurring is not predicted to occur in the short term, and if it occurs, it is not expected to result in severe consequences to a child.

Key decisions during the initial assessment/investigation stage are to determine: (1) if child maltreatment occurred as defined by state law; (2) if the child's immediate safety is a concern and, if it is, the interventions that will ensure the child's protection; (3) if there is a risk of future maltreatment and the level of that risk; and (4) if continuing agency services are needed to help the family keep the child safe, reduce the risks of future maltreatment, and address any effects of child maltreatment. In some states, the decision to offer continuing services is based on a determination or substantiation of a report of child abuse and neglect. In most states, the determination of whether child maltreatment occurred is referred to as finding of child maltreatment or may also be referred to as substantiated or indicated report. In states that have alternative response systems, instead of a finding of maltreatment, a decision may be made about whether services should be offered to the family because of a risk of child maltreatment. Some cases are closed at this stage if there is no basis to provide services to the child and family. Because children and families are not entitled to these in-home services, as they would be to placement into foster care, the

Figure 6.1
A Conceptual Model of Safety and Risk

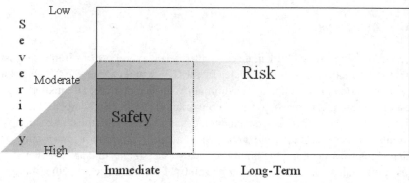

Source: Hollingshead, D., & Fluke, J. (2000). What works in safety and risk assessment for child protective services. In M. P. Kluger, G. Alexander, & P. A. Curtis (Eds.). *What works in child welfare.* (pp. 67-74). Washington, DC: CWLA Press.

availability of resources is also likely to enter into decision making about the service plan, although the impact of the availability of funds on service decisions has been little studied.

Assessment of Safety. CPS workers must make difficult decisions about the safety of maltreated children. Decision-making models for helping CPS workers balance the dual goals for child protection and family preservation have been around since the 1970s (DePanfilis & Scannapieco, 1994) but have been more widely implemented following the enactment of ASFA, which identifies child safety as one of the three national outcomes for which the US Department of Health and Human Services will hold state child welfare service agencies accountable (US-DHHS, 2000). An early review of ten safety decision-making models (DePanfilis & Scannapieco, 1994) suggested that although some criteria overlapped in these models, there were also wide differences in definitions, purposes, and the level of research support for the criteria used to guide decision-making.

More recent conceptualizations of child safety suggest that workers should consider three categories of factors in their safety assessments: (1) factors that when present suggest the potential of serious harm to a child; (2) factors that indicate that the family has protective capacities to manage these serious threats to harm; and (3) factors that indicate child vulnerability (Morton & Salovitz, 2006). For example, despite the fact that some children have been maltreated, an assessment of safety could suggest that there are no immediate threats of serious harm to the child because the family has protective capacities to keep a child safe and/or because even if a child could be maltreated in the future (risk of recurrence), the child's age and other capacities suggest that the potential consequence of the maltreatment would not result in serious harm. This proposed conceptualization is consistent with the view depicted in Figure 6.1 by Hollingshead & Fluke (2000). Contributing factors that could indicate serious threats of harm might include co-occurring problems in social functioning such as substance abuse, mental illness, and intimate partner violence (discussed in Chapter 5). Examples of protective capacities would include having an adult in the household with protective parenting abilities and/or having extended family members whose presence could control the impact of negative contributing factors. Child vulnerability factors include child characteristics that may make a child more susceptible to experiencing serious harm due to the actions or omissions of a caregiver. This could include characteristics like age, medical conditions, and physical handicaps that suggest a more negative consequence. It also could include the presence of child behavior or temperament that might serve as a stimulus for inappropriate reactions on the part of a parent or caregiver.

After CPS workers have evaluated the safety of children, they are responsible to implement safety plans to directly address the safety threats that may jeopardize a child's safety. In the safety plan, the worker targets the factors affecting the safety of the child and identifies, with the family, the interventions that will control the safety factors and assure the child's protection (DePanfilis & Salus, 2003). When possible, safety plans are developed to keep children safe in their homes. When that is not possible, safety plans involve placing children in out-of-home care settings (see Chapter 8).

Assessment of risk. Distinct from the responsibility to evaluate safety of children, CPS workers are charged with assessing the risk of maltreatment (i.e., the likelihood of future maltreatment) in order to develop service plans that will help families manage and reduce the risk of maltreatment over time. While safety assessments focus on the potential of immediate and serious harm and therefore the response to safety concerns involve the development of safety plans to control the conditions that threaten safety, risk assessments and broader family assessments (see below) and service plans that result from these assessments involve implementing change oriented services that will reduce risk of maltreatment over time. The process of assessing risk includes implementing protocols for interviewing all children, parents, and other family members associated with an abuse and neglect report to the CPS Program; gathering other information about the child and family, and then interpreting information. The process of assessing risk of maltreatment has been part of the responsibility of the CPS worker for a long time. For the last twenty-five years however, most CPS agencies in North America have adopted risk assessment models to guide the assessment of and management of risk (Mitchell, et al., 2005; Rycus & Hughes, 2003).

Risk assessment models are designed to help guide the collection of data, the organization of information, and the analysis and interpretation of information during the initial assessment of a CPS report and may also be used to measure the reduction of risk over time (Rycus & Hughes, 2003). Initially risk assessment instruments were developed to guide assessments by focusing workers on looking for and analyzing information about factors that had been found to predict child maltreatment in prior research. Sometimes referred to as consensus based risk assessment models, these models were structured as assessment outlines or matrices, sometimes with the ability to rate the factors that were of most concern based on anchors or descriptions of information that may indicate risk (Doueck, English, DePanfilis, & Moote, 1993).

A second category of risk assessment instruments are models described as actuarial models (Baumann, Law, Sheets, Reid, & Graham, 2005). These models use statistical procedures to identify and weigh factors that predict future maltreatment, are constructed from case record data, and are usually jurisdiction specific. Risk factors are selected after analysis of variables shown to be associated with new reports of child abuse or neglect or new substantiated reports of child abuse or neglect in the specific state or jurisdiction. These models are often the most concise as they are specifically designed to predict the risk of maltreatment in the future. However, some of the risk factors in these models may predict future maltreatment but may not be helpful for determining how to work with a family to reduce the risk of maltreatment. For example, a criminal record might predict future maltreatment but is not something that can be changed in the future. However, in general there is sufficient research to support the conclusion that actuarial risk assessment instruments have the greatest potential to reliably and accurately estimate the recurrence of child maltreatment (Shlonsky & Wagner, 2005). More recent conceptualizations suggest the need to integrate predictive models within the context of broader clinical assessment process. This approach, referred to as structured decision-making (SDM) guides workers to understanding the likelihood of future maltreatment but also to assess the strengths and needs of families (Shlonsky & Wagner, 2005).

Family Assessment

Which families receive continuing services varies from state to state and from county to county. In 2005, states reported that across the entire US, 60 percent of substantiated child maltreatment reports led to the provision of continuing services, 16 percent led to a referral to court to determine temporary custody of the child, guardianship of the child, or disposition of state dependency petitions; and another 27 percent of children and their families were provided services without a substantiated report (US DHHS, 2007). The variation is remarkable.

Continuing services were reportedly provided to 95 percent of cases (or higher) in AZ, AK, DC, KY, NV, NH, PR, and UT whereas fewer than one-third of children reportedly received ongoing services in CT, IL, ME, MD, OH, TN, and WI (US DHHS, 2007). Wulczyn and colleagues (2006) have shown that the amount of variation across states is not uncommonly replicated across counties within a state. Thus, there is remarkable variation in the way that CWS agencies respond to children and families; hopefully the majority of this variation is not based on errors in responding and, instead, results from the thoughtful differential response to the needs of children and families and the availability of a range of services—whether available through the CWS agency or community partners—that are most appropriate.

For families that are provided continuing services, the responsibility for working with the family is often transferred to a continuing service CPS worker who will begin to engage the family by conducting a comprehensive family assessment. If an alternative response system is in place, the worker responsible for conducting a family assessment could be a CPS worker or another worker in a community agency.

The family assessment is a comprehensive process for identifying, considering, and weighing factors that affect the child's safety, permanency, and well-being (Schene, 2005). During this stage, the CPS worker engages family members in a process to understand their strengths, risks, and service needs. The family assessment is framed to build on the two previous assessments (safety and risk) and given the emphasis on timeliness built into ASFA, the assessment of the family's strengths and needs should be considered in the context of the length of time it will take the family to provide a safe and stable home environment (USDHHS, 2000). Findings from the first fifty-two Child and Family Services Reviews identified a connection between the completion of comprehensive family assessments and positive outcomes for children and families (US DHHS, 2007). Because only one state among the initial fifty-two reviews performed adequately in this area, most states were asked to undertake renewed efforts in their Performance Improvement Plans (PIPs) to assure that their assessments went beyond the initial assessments of risk and safety to also consider the strengths and needs of family members in a comprehensive family assessment process.

To guide the assessment of factors and to increase practice accountability, CPS workers and other providers who have roles to conduct family assessments should consider the use of validated instruments that support the assessment of family strengths and needs. Both standardized self-report and observational measures are increasingly used in CWS agencies in an effort to focus services on specific outcomes that can be measured over time to indicate success of the intervention process (DePanfilis & Salus, 2000). Two instruments in particular that have been used in CWS agencies to target services and measure outcomes over time are the Family Assessment Form (Children's Bureau of Southern California, 1997) and the North Carolina Family Assessment Form (Reed-Ashcraft, Kirk, & Fraser, 2001). Examples of other family assessment measures can be found via searches on the internet, measurement databases, and reviews of measures (e.g., Fisher & Corcoran, 2007; Johnson, et al., 2006).

Key decisions during the Family Assessment stage are to determine: (1) which of the risk factors previously identified during the initial assessment (e.g., domestic violence, substance abuse, mental health problems) are the most important focus for intervention and services; (2) what protective factors or strengths exist that may be strengthened through supportive services; (3) what effects of maltreatment are observed in the child and/or other family members (e.g., child mental health or behavioral problems) and therefore should be the focus of services; and (4) the level of motivation or readiness of family members to participate in intervention that will reduce risk and address the effects of maltreatment.

Service planning. To be effective in keeping children safe, the right mix of services and supports must be tailored to the specific needs of each child and family. The selection of the right services should evolve from the family assessment. US DHHS Family Assessment Guidelines (Schene, 2005) suggest the need to develop service plans that specifically target the risk factors that create the most concern for the child and at the same time to use protective factors as points of leverage for the necessary changes in the family.

Key decisions at the service case planning stage are to determine: (1) the case outcomes, which will be the target of intervention (e.g., enhanced family functioning; behavioral control of emotions; enhanced parent-child interaction); (2) the case goals that will help family members achieve these outcomes; (3) the interventions and services that will best support the achievement of these goals and outcomes; (4) who will be the best provider of these interventions; and (5) the timeframes for evaluation of progress (DePanfilis & Salus, 2003).

Service provision. This is the stage during which the service plan is implemented. It is the role of the ongoing CWS worker to arrange for, provide, and/or coordinate the delivery of services to maltreated children, their parents or other caregivers, and to the family. These services may be provided by a child welfare worker in a continuing CPS program or may be provided by a child welfare worker in another continuing family-based services program within the CWS agency. The services that are selected to help families achieve outcomes and goals are based on an appropriate match of services to goals, use of best practice principles, and the degree of evidence of effectiveness among the service options.

Despite the responsibility of CWS to provide or arrange for services, there are very few studies that describe the exact array of services provided to children and their caregivers through continuing CWS. Interviews with in-home caregivers in the National Survey of Child and Adolescent Well-Being (NSCAW, 2005) explored parents own reports of the receipt of mental health, alcohol abuse, and drug abuse services. Since these problems are frequently identified as significant risk factors for child maltreatment (see Chapter 5), one would expect a high level of service utilization for these problems. At the time of the caregiver interviews, only 8 percent of families reported receiving mental health services and only 2 percent of caregivers reported receiving drug or alcohol services. However, in this same study, workers indicated that in general, 93 percent of caregivers had some type of service provided or recommended to them, that 50 percent of care-givers were referred to mental health treatment, and that 30 percent of caregivers were referred to parenting services. Even these numbers are low, however, since the purpose of opening an ongoing in-home CWS case is to provide services to reduce the risk of future maltreatment. Part of the explanation for this finding may be that parents reported that the child welfare workers were generally well regarded but that the services they referred the parents to were decidedly not highly rated (Chapman, Barth, & McCrae, 2003). Child welfare services have gener-ally lagged behind other fields in efforts to engage families in ongoing services, perhaps thinking that a court order or other intrinsic motivation is enough to get them to accept the use of offered services (cf., McKay et al., 2004).

Since part of the responsibility of continuing CWS services should also be to provide services to deal with the effects of child maltreatment, it is important to explore the degree to which children are provided with specific treatment services. Data from the CPS NSCAW (2005) found that overall, slightly more than 9 percent of children in their homes were receiving outpatient mental health services for emotional, behavior, learning, attention, or substance abuse problems. Children aged eleven years and older were more likely than younger children to receive these services. However, when service use was linked to scores on the Child Behavior Checklist (CBCL), approximately 40 percent of children in this sample scored in the borderline/clinical range, which suggests a higher service need.

Looked at from the other direction, among children who were involved with CWS and in the clinical range, only 40 percent received specialty mental health services (Burns, et al., 2004). Among youth with strong evidence of clinical need, only one-fourth had received any mental health care. There were also some differences in who received specialty mental health service receipt that depended on race and some that depended on age. For latency-age youths, be-ing of African-American race significantly reduced the likelihood of receiving specialty mental health care. In contrast, for adolescents who lived at home, the likelihood of receiving specialty mental health care was lower than for other children regardless of race.

The emphasis on evidenced-based practice, defined as the conscientious, explicit, and judicious use of current best evidence in making decisions about the care of clients (Gibbs & Gambrill, 2002) is slowly making its way into CPS practice and policy (Wells, 2007). States have contracted for services to help them integrate research into the selection of services and interventions. In

Kansas, for example, the state has contracted for a web-based evidence based practice tool that guides the user to find the latest research about strategies to achieve core child welfare outcomes, including the prevention of child maltreatment recurrences (University of Kansas, 2007). In 2007 in the state of Washington, the Washington State Institute for Public Policy was charged by their state legislature to study programs and policies that show evidence of reduced involvement in the child welfare system and to construct reliable estimates of the costs and benefits of evidence-based prevention and intervention programs (Lee, 2008). One of the outcomes examined in this program review is related to child safety (i.e., effectiveness of interventions at reducing the reported or substantiated incidence of child abuse and neglect). Yet, much of what goes on in child welfare is related to decision making, referral, and case coordination rather than changing behavior. Considerably less has been done in the development of evidence-based practices for decision-making and case coordination than in the area of treatment (Barth, 2007).

In California, there are multiple efforts to encourage the use of evidence-based practice as well as evidence-supported practices (i.e., practices with some evidence of effectiveness). The California Evidence-Based Clearinghouse for Child Welfare was established as an online resource to provide up-to-date information on evidence-based child welfare practices. The site may be searched by the key child welfare outcomes to identify programs with varying levels of research to support their effectiveness. A search by child safety (for example), identifies and classifies the level of evidence for practices related to decreasing the risk of child maltreatment and also rates the degree of relevance as a child welfare service. At the time of writing, there was only one evidence supported practice that had the highest ranking on scientific merit and child welfare relevance: Trauma Focused Cognitive Behavior Therapy (TF-CBT: Deblinger, Stauffer, & Steer, 2001).

On a local level, the California Bay Area Social Services Consortium (BASSC) Research Response Team was developed to respond to the emerging needs of county agencies for rapid information about their changing environments. Small-scale applied research projects are undertaken in close collaboration with agency administrators and line staff. The team has undertaken several projects to support CPS practice and policy (Bay Area Social Services Consortium, 2002).

Other chapters in this volume provide examples of the types of services and treatment that might be employed by CPS workers to help reduce the risk of child maltreatment and/or to help a child or other family members manage the effects of maltreatment. Key decisions at this stage include: (1) identification of the specific services that will be delivered, at what intensity, and for what duration; (2) determining who is best positioned to deliver these services; (3) determining appropriate intervals for evaluating family progress; and (4) specifying mechanisms for coordinating among service providers (e.g., developing and sharing information, schedule of team meetings, etc.).

Evaluation of progress. Assessment is an ongoing process that begins with the first client contact and continues throughout the life of the case. Progress toward achievement of outcomes and goals should be formally evaluated at least every three months (DePanfilis & Salus, 2003). Key decisions that must be made during this stage of the process include: (1) an assessment of the current safety of the child; (2) level of achievement of family-level outcomes; (3) level of achievement of goals and tasks in the service plan; (4) assessment of changes in the risk and protective factors previously identified; and (5) the level of success in addressing any of the effects of maltreatment on the child and other family members.

Case closure. The process of ending the relationship between the child welfare worker and the family involves a mutual review of progress and includes a review of the beginning, middle, and end of the helping relationship. Optimally, cases are closed when families have achieved their outcomes and goals, children are safe because the risk of harm and maltreatment has been reduced or eliminated, and because the specific effects of child maltreatment have been addressed. CWS cases are sometimes closed, however, when families still need assistance if community agencies are available to provide needed supportive services to the family. When needs are still apparent that go outside the scope of CWS, every effort should be made to help the family receive services through appropriate community agencies. However, some case closings occur because the client discontinues services and the agency does not have a sufficient basis to refer the situation to Juvenile or Family Court. When this happens, the CWS worker should carefully document what risks may still be present so that this information is available should the family be referred to the agency at a later time.

Child Welfare Service Reforms

Alternative Response Programs

Many child welfare service (CWS) agencies face a large volume of abuse and neglect reports, increasingly complex cases, and strained resources. Moreover, there is a growing recognition that many children and families do not require a traditional investigative response. Thus, many states have developed practices and policies to differentiate how particular types of cases are handled (U.S. Government Accounting Office, 1997). Referred to as alternative response, differential response, dual track, or family assessments, these efforts at system reform promote new practices that affect how certain reports of maltreatment are handled. Generally, investigation responses involve a forensic approach and include processes for determining if a child is at risk of child maltreatment or if child maltreatment occurred. Alternative responses are characterized by an emphasis on an assessment of the needs of families and children with less emphasis on determining if the maltreatment occurred (U.S. Department of Health and Human Services, 2003a).

Currently, at least twenty-nine states use alternative response systems, but the structure and processes of these systems differ by state. Several studies have profiled how alternative response systems are operating, and some have looked across states to describe characteristics of these systems, the types of clients the systems intend to serve, and the basic framework for how the system is set up. When an agency receives a report of child abuse or neglect, that report is assigned a track or path that designates the type of response it will receive. Findings from these studies indicate that the number of track options across states differs from two to five. Response tracks may be limited to alternative response or investigation, or they may include other, narrower tracks, such as resource linkage, law enforcement, and Family in Need of Services Assessment (U.S. Department of Health and Human Services [HHS], 2003). Additionally, a case can be officially tracked at the initial acceptance of a report of abuse or neglect, at the end of an introductory investigative period, or at another time by a external community agency with expertise relevant to the report at hand (Schene, 2001; Ziewlieski, Macomber, Bess & Murray, 2006, p. 1).

For example, Alameda County is the pilot site of California's first differential response program, Another Road to Safety (ARS). The ARS program uses a differential response model to screen risk at the county child maltreatment ho-tline and to offer services to families who meet the following criteria: screened out of traditional investigation; child age zero to five or a pregnant mother in the home; and residence in certain designated neighborhoods. The program is currently undergoing expansion to serve families with children over the age of five. ARS clients receive up to nine months of intensive home visiting and case management; some concrete services are provided and referrals are made to local service providers. The ultimate goal of ARS is to promote family safety and stability and to ensure positive child development.

There is relatively little research available on this promising approach. Some studies have examined the relationships between alternative response systems and incidence of child maltreatment—the main outcome of interest. Other studies have measured family safety, family engagement, and future interaction with the child welfare agency. For example, a study of the multiple response system in North Carolina found "...that its implementation appeared to have no harmful effects in safety, response time, or case decision-making, and families responded positively to the approach (Center for Child and Family Policy 2004). A review of Minnesota's alternative response system found similar results, concluding that the alternative response approach created more responsive and engaged families....[The] National Child Abuse and Neglect Data System (NCANDS) discovered that services are more frequently provided to alternative response families than families that have a traditional investigation, possibly because some investigated cases are not substantiated. The study also determined that families served through the alternative response are not necessarily at a greater risk for subsequent reports of child victimization than families that were investigated (HHS 2005)." (Ziewlieski, Macomber, Bess & Murray, 2006, pp. 1-2)

One area that has received scant attention is how families connect to services in such a system. One recent study explored this issue in two states, Kentucky and Oklahoma. The researchers found that connecting families to services in an alternative response system involves a complex set of steps with many factors at work. The process can be thought of as occurring in steps: conducting an assessment, providing referrals, connecting the family to services, and following up to ensure the family received them:

> At each step, many factors might affect whether a family connects to services. For example, whether a family is given the name of a provider to call themselves or taken by the child welfare worker to the provider may affect whether the family actually receives the service. How the family connects with the provider is in turn affected by availability and accessibility of services, along with the financial structure to support the services. It was not apparent from our interviews that public child welfare agencies and community providers were aware of or had addressed some of these complexities. Much thought was given to the approach that would be used during the assessment stage, but fewer guidelines are provided in policy or done in practice with regard to those parts of the process that occur after the assessment, such as when referrals are made, families are connected, and follow-up occurs. (Zielewski, et al., 2006, p. 13)

Effectiveness of Child Welfare Services

One marker of CWS effectiveness is the rate at which new reports of child abuse and neglect occur for families previously served by CWS agencies. As suggested in Chapter 5, the Children's bureau has established the current national standard for no recurrence of child maltreatment as 94.6 percent, defined as: *"Absence of Maltreatment Recurrence. Of all children who were victims of substantiated or indicated abuse or neglect during the first 6 months of the reporting year, what percent did not experience another incident of substantiated or indicated abuse or neglect within a 6-month period?" Between 2001 and 2004, after the first round of Child and Family Service Reviews, only six states were in compliance with this indicator (USDHHS, undated). By 2005, the number of* states in compliance with this indicator increased to nineteen states (USDHHS, 2007). However, while it is important to track the degree to which new reports are made to the CWS agency, this is a very rough indicator about whether children and families are any better off as a result of CWS intervention.

Very few studies have been conducted to evaluate the effectiveness of child protective services. Given the unevenness of services provided while families are involved with CWS agencies (see results from NSCAW study and from *Child Maltreatment 2005* above), the overall poor performance of CPS programs in reducing the recurrence of child maltreatment should not be a surprise. One study that followed families served by a CWS agency over five years found that after controlling for case characteristics and exploring the impact of nine CWS service related variables, the only service variable that predicted future substantiated reports was attendance at services. Families who were noted to attend the services identified in their service plans were 33 percent less likely to experience a recurrence of child maltreatment while their case was still active in the CPS program compared to families who were not noted to actually attend services (DePanfilis & Zuravin, 2002).

Efforts to explore the impact of client participation or engagement with child welfare services on service outcome (Littell, Alexander, & Reynolds, 2001; Littell & Tajima, 2000) have suggested that these concepts are multi-dimensional and that relatively simple models of client motivation employed in substance abuse treatment for example (e.g., Miller & Rollnick, 1991; Prochaska, DeClemente, & Norcross, 1992), may not perfectly apply with families served by CPS programs. A recent area of inquiry involves constructing methods for assessing the capacity of parents to change behaviors and conditions that increase the risk of continued maltreatment. Assuming that certain family characteristics may indicate a greater capacity to benefit from intervention, assessment procedures are being tested to explore their capacity to predict which families have the greatest potential to achieve a minimal level of parenting through intervention (Harnett, 2007).

Listening to parents themselves may provide further information about the quality of the CWS response, however, a review of methods for obtaining client feedback point out the complexity of obtaining reliable and valid views from consumers (Baker, 2007). Interviews with in-home caregivers in the NSCAW in-home services sample (US DHHS, 2005) explored a series of questions about service adequacy. Items addressed the extent to which they agreed that their worker offered them necessary help, had given them enough time to make changes, and offered them enough services. Overall, caregivers reported a low level of satisfaction with service adequacy (Chapman, et al., 2003). One recent qualitative study with consumers of CPS agencies involved the implementation of semi-structured interviews with mothers about their experiences with CWS (Palmer, Maiter, & Manji, 2006). Findings indicated that parents valued good referrals, concrete help, and emotional support. Their most negative experiences included having their initial requests for help turned down; being accepted for service, but not receiving much help; perceiving that they had been unfairly treated or harassed; and reporting being traumatized by the sudden, police-like removal of their children.

In general, there is evidence that clients who have a positive helping alliance with their workers are much more likely to complete assigned services (Girvin, DePanfilis, & Daining 2007; Weiss, 1993) suggesting that taking the time to truly engage family members as partners may increase retention in services, and ultimately positively impact service outcomes. Interviews with in-home caregivers in the NSCAW (2005) in-home CPS sample attempted to understand the degree to which caregivers perceived having a helping relationship with their worker. Interviewers asked caregivers how often their child welfare worker(s) (1) listened to their concerns, (2) understood their situation, (3) treated them with respect, (4) treated them fairly, (5) explained treatment and service options to them, and (6) met with them to develop an action plan to address their needs and concerns. Results suggested that recentness of worker-client contact, a lower number of workers involved with the family, and an investigation outcome that was neither substantiated nor indicated were significantly associated with higher perceived relationship quality. Caregivers reported the highest satisfaction, on average, with the following aspects of their worker relationship: feeling listened to, feeling respected, and feeling as though they were treated fairly.

One of the reasons that we are unable to completely understand whether families and children are any better off as a result of CWS intervention is that because this is a mandated service, it would be very difficult to implement a randomized controlled study design that would have a no intervention control group. A relatively new method, called propensity score matching, which uses complicated algorithms with existing data, may be what is needed in future studies when randomly assigning children and families to services versus no services is not feasible. A recent study used propensity score matching strategies to evaluate child welfare clients in relation to re-reports and developmental well-being for children of substance abuse treatment service recipients and non-recipients (Barth, Gibbons, & Guo, 2006). Findings of this study suggested that children whose caregivers used substance abuse services were more likely to have a re-report of child maltreatment than those whose caregivers did not use the services (presumably because they did not need them). The full explanation for this is not available, but the authors surmise that these reports may have been the result of closer drug testing and surveillance of treatment-involved mothers and that this may have resulted in early interventions (and related reports) when drug use resumed.

In another study, propensity score matching was used to evaluate the impact of parenting services among mothers involved with CPS (Casanueva, Martin, Runyan, Barth, & Bradley, 2008). The study found some modest benefits in maternal responsiveness and total parenting scores for mothers of three- to five-year-old children when these mothers received parenting services, as compared with mothers that did not receive parenting services. While these propensity score matching techniques are just beginning to be used to examine the effectiveness of CPS related interventions, use of these methods in the future could lead to greater understanding about what happens to children and their families following the receipt of CPS intervention.

Many states conduct periodic program evaluations of their CWS but results of these evaluations rarely make it into the published literature. Sometimes, these evaluations are mandated by state legislatures (e.g., Texas Health and Human Services Commission, 2005); sometimes they are conducted by child advocacy organizations (e.g., Richart & Brooks, 2006); and sometimes these studies are conducted externally by researchers under contract with the state CWS agency (e.g., Courtney, McMurtry, Bost, Maldre, & Power, 2002; Kinnevy, Huang, Dichter, & Gelles, 2005). While the purposes and evaluation designs make it difficult to compare, in general, results of these evaluations portray an overburdened system in need of significant system reform. Reforms of child protective services systems have been called for, for at least twenty years (e.g., Monro, 2005; USDHHS, 1993; U.S. General Accounting Office, 1997; Waldfogel, 1998a). These calls to action have been responded to by some child welfare service reforms (USDHHS, 2003a; USDDHS, 2003b). A review of reforms has identified changes in how states screen and triage reports of child abuse and neglect; how reports are investigated or assessed (including collaborations between CWS and law enforcement), and how CWS collaborates with community agencies (e.g., alternative response systems described above). It is too early to trace whether these reforms will lead to better outcomes but carefully tracking these new strategies in relation to child and family outcomes is definitely needed.

Conclusions

Current Status

Most children are referred to child welfare services because of concern related to child maltreatment or the risk of child maltreatment. The largest percentage of children served by the child welfare agency are served in their own homes through ongoing child protective services or family preservation services, yet, much more attention in federal and state policies and practice reforms has been placed on other parts of the child welfare system. A comprehensive picture of how well children and families are doing as a result of their ongoing involvement with the CWS system is lacking. Results of Child and Family Services Reviews have pointed to opportunities for improving the child protection service response by placing more emphasis on family assessments and tailored service responses.

Future Directions

Since most states are making this shift in their federal Performance Improvement Plans, there is an opportunity to professionalize the service response so that more families receive opportunities for participating in services that have the greatest chance of helping them address the effects of maltreatment and changing conditions and behaviors that increase the risk of future maltreatment and jeopardize their children's safety.

7

Family-Based Services

Family support programs address a wide range of family types and problems including the prevention of child abuse and neglect and placement into foster care. The establishment of a family support program such as "Healthy Start" (e.g., Breakey & Pratt, 1991; Roebuck, 2007) or a family-based treatment service like Homebuilders (see http://www.institutefamily.org/) reflects a philosophical stance that *a society should be willing to invest as many or more resources in prevention of problems in parenting as it would spend treating those problems or placing children in out of home care.* Implementing these programs also rests on the assumption that they can actually achieve their noble goals (the evidence base for these programs will be discussed later). The distinguishing feature of many of these programs is the provision of a wide variety of selective or indicated preventive interventions to children and families in the home and community setting. (Both of these programs will be described in the next section.)

Within the broad framework of Family Support or FBS programs there is wide variation across the nation in the kind of interventions, duration of services, size of caseloads, and components of service that characterize these programs. Even the goals are not always the same as some are specifically aimed at preventing child abuse (e.g., Healthy Families America) and others support broader health and developmental outcomes, with child abuse prevention a hoped for byproduct (e.g., Nurse Family Partnership). Perhaps this is one of the reasons why research findings on family support and family-based service programs have appeared inconsistent—despite some common purposes, there is considerable variation in the service characteristics of these programs. This chapter endeavors to explore that variation.

The programs themselves are often described using more specific terms such as community support, family support, family preservation, family-based, family-centered, home-based, and placement prevention services. The term family support has been used as an umbrella under which clusters a broad range of family-based services programs. The number of family resource centers (modern day settlement houses) have been growing steadily. Many of these are free standing but a sizable number are housed within schools such as Communities in Schools that helps low-income youth complete high school with diplomas (Milliken, 2007).

Program Types

A two-part typology of community support and family-based programs is presented next. One potential value of the typology is to help identify whether families have access to the variation in types of programming that these services offer.

1. Community support programs and family resource, support, and education services. Broad community-based interventions designed to bolster the infrastructure and support networks in a community in terms of education, housing, employment, medical care, transportation, child care, mental health services, and other key resources for families (Deborah Daro, Budde, Nesmith, & Harden, 2005; Spielberger, Lyons, Gouvea, Haywood, & Winje, 2007).

California, New York, and Colorado are just a few states with major state funded programs to support family resource centers. Foundations have also been strong supporters of FRCs. Colorado provides state funding to Family Resource Centers but also has support from many agencies that partner with them and such private sources as Carmelo Anthony, the Denver Nugget All-Star. "I came from an area where I saw poverty and hardship, and family resource centers make a big impact helping people in those situations," remarked Carmelo Anthony at a fall 2003 press conference announcing his selection of Family Resource Centers (FRC) as his community charity partner…" (http://www.familyresourcecenters. info/; retrieved February 16, 2008).

These community-based services assist and support adults in their role as parents. Services are available to all families with children and do not impose criteria for participation that might separate or stigmatize certain parents (Child Welfare League of America, 1989, p. 13). We will refer to these as "Family Support Services." Examples are the school- or community-based family resource centers being implemented in states such as Connecticut, Maryland, Kentucky, Minnesota, and Missouri (Farrow, 1991; Milliken, 2007; Schorr, 1997, pp. 285-296). Another example is the targeted community interventions in Florida that were underway in 2007. These programs included a network of health and social services providing support and intervention services, including universal risk screening and targeted home visitation, to high-risk pregnant women and new mothers; child care and early education programs, provide services for children with developmental delays, and improve children's school readiness; school-based intervention to improve children's adjustment to school and enhance their school success by identifying social-emotional and other developmental problems and providing referrals and intervention services to respond to these problems; and finally, a network of after-school programs for elementary and middle-school youth (Spielberger, et al., 2007).

2. *Family-Based Services* are specific manualized interventions that encompass a range of activities such as case management, counseling/therapy, education, skill-building, advocacy, and/or provision of concrete services for families with problems that threaten their stability. Examples include Homebuilders in Washington state, and Multisystemic Family Therapy, which is in operation in many states and several countries. These programs endeavor to achieve family strengthening and placement prevention goals in child welfare and mental health services and to help achieve reunification and placement stability goals in foster care and adoption (see, e.g., Walton, 1998). FBS programs also operating in juvenile justice and developmental disability services (e.g., Henggeler, Pickrel, & Brondino, 1999).

Some programs straddle the definitions presented here and provide both family support and family based services. For example, as described later in this chapter, the "Healthy Start" program, originated in Hawaii, initially provides services to all newborns and their families, irrespective of risk, and then provides a comprehensive array of health care, counseling, and concrete services to families judged to be at moderate to high risk of child maltreatment (Duggan, et al., 1999). For this reason, we generally categorize this program as a family support program.

One particular form of family-based services has been termed *Intensive Family Preservation Services (IFPS) or Intensive In-home Services* (Barth, et al., 2007). This grouping of services might be distinguished by the combination of case management with intensive therapeutic and other services. Some of these services are designed for families "in crisis," at a time when removal of a child is perceived as imminent, or the return of a child from out-of-home care is being considered. Yet, the reality is that this service model is also being applied to some long-term child maltreatment situations as a way to re-engage families with service providers, which do not involve crisis. These programs are delivered with more intensity (including shorter time frame and smaller caseloads), so they are often referred to as intensive family preservation service or IFPS programs. Caseloads generally vary between two to six families per worker. Families are typically seen between six and ten hours per week, and the time period of intervention is generally between four and twelve weeks. The most prominent example is the *Homebuilders* of Washington state, the original model developer, with variations of this model in use in other states, such as Michigan and North Carolina.

Community Support Interventions: Family Resource, Support, and Education Services

Overview

Prevention can involve efforts at the "universal," "selected," and "indicated" model of prevention levels (Mrazek & Haggerty, 1994; National Research Council and the Institute of Medicine, 2009) (see Figure 7.1). A variety of approaches have been developed to prevent further child maltreatment in families through various forms of family education and other supports. As discussed earlier, the term *family support* has been used as a generic category that often encompasses a broad range of family-centered or family-strengthening programs. In virtually all family-centered services, the family is not seen as entirely deficient but also containing strengths and resources to draw on in addressing their challenges (Spoth, Kavanaugh, & Dishion, 2002). To paraphrase Heather Weiss at Harvard, family support program staff do not view parents as "empty vessels" waiting to be filled up with professionally-derived child development knowledge, but as active partners in a search for the formal and informal supports necessary to carry out the difficult tasks of parenting. While family-based services and intensive family preservation services have both been cited as family support programs, these treatment programs are distinct from family support because family support services more appropriately fit the prevention categories of selective or indicated prevention.

Family resource, support, and education services, as community-based services, assist and support adults in their role as parents. Conceptually, at least,

Figure 7.1
The Spectrum for Preventing and Treating Mental,
Emotional and Behavioral Disorders

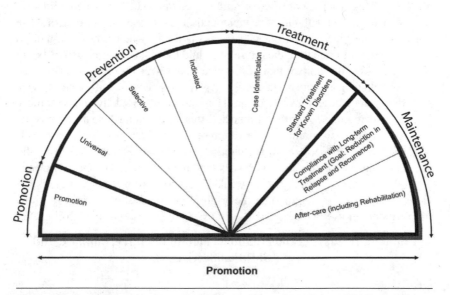

Source: National Research Council and the Institute of Medicine. (2009). *Preventing mental, emotional and behavioral disorders among young people: Progress and possibilities.* Washington, D.C.: National Research Council and the Institute of Medicine of the National Academies. http://www.nap.edu/catalog.php?record_id=12480

services are available to all families with children and there are no eligibility requirements that families or children must meet to participate certain parents. Yet, in practice, these services are just emerging and the new programs are typically situated in communities that have been identified as having a high need for the service. In practice, then, these services are *not* available to all parents—they are almost always situated in communities of substantial need.

A Closer Look at Defining Family Support and Other Prevention Services

This section will present a more detailed typology of family support services to help lay a foundation for highlighting some promising family support programs appropriate for the children and parents served by child welfare services. The relationship between parent and professional is defined as essentially collegial. The following list of value statements from the Family Resource Coalition is illustrative (Family Resource Coalition, 1983):

- Parenting is not instinctive; it is a tough and demanding job.
- Parents desire and try to do the best for their children.
- Parents want and need support, information, and reinforcement in the parenting role.
- Parents are also people with their own needs as adults.
- Programs should focus on and work with family strengths, not deficits.
- Programs should empower families, not create dependence on professionals.

Opinions range about how to achieve more "family support"—from arguments for provision of more entitlements and greater access to support services, to arguments for a *de-emphasis* of formal programs and professional involvement in support of natural helping networks.

As described by Cameron and Vanderwoerd (1997), Kagan and Weissbourd (1994), and Schorr & Marchand (2007), in recent years family support policy and program components have begun to be more clearly delineated, as these principles and strategies have been embraced by established agencies and institutions. Moreover, a growing body of knowledge is available to inform program decisions in settings such as schools, child health care, social services, and juvenile delinquency. However the following challenges identified by Spoth, et al. (2002) remain: (1) how to expand the set of rigorously evaluated, theory-driven interventions that have potential to reach large numbers of children, youth, and families; (2) identification of effective strategies for family recruitment and retention; (3) ensuring the cultural sensitivity of interventions; (4) applying a developmental life course perspective; (5) generating new strategies for linking higher-risk population subgroups with potentially beneficial services; (6) improved diffusion mechanisms for sustained, quality delivery; and (7) creating policies informed by research, including economic analysis.

A Promising Typology for Categorizing Family Support Programs

While a number of authors have attempted to categorize family support programs (e.g., Kagan & Weissbourd, 1994; United States General Accounting Office, 1995), a typology developed by Manalo & Meezan (2000) illustrated in Table 7.1 is the most appealing one that we have found because of its clarity and practical use in helping program administrators to be aware of the program design choices they may be making.

Perinatal and Maternal Health Derived Programs:
Home Visiting Programs

Part of the theoretical underpinning for nursing and public health-based family support services is research demonstrating that successful mother-infant relationships may be highly important for preventing future parenting problems. Parents are helped to deal with the inevitable stresses that a new infant brings to a family and are helped to feel comfortable in caring for that child. Thus, a promising approach to child abuse prevention efforts has been the voluntary use of home visitors for families with newborns and young children at-risk. Not until the late 1970s, when David Olds conducted the now landmark Elmira nurse home visitation study (Olds, et al., 1986), did these programs gain traction in the US. Since then, evidence of effectiveness has begun to emerge through rigorously conducted research. Mostly funded by states and foundations, in 2008, the federal government made its first significant investment in funding home visitation programs (Olds, Sadler & Kittzman, 2007).

Healthy Start in Hawaii

Some of the recent preventive efforts that have been developed are able to address not just physical abuse, but other forms of child maltreatment as well. The state of Hawaii developed a multi-dimensional approach to supporting and educating families to improve family coping skills and functioning, promote positive parenting skills and parent-child interaction, and to promote optimal child development: "Healthy Start." Note that there is another set of programs that have grown substantially over the past decade that are part of the National Healthy Start Association (NHSA). These programs promote the development of community-based maternal and child health programs, particularly those addressing the issues of infant mortality, low birth weight, and racial disparities in perinatal outcomes. These Healthy Start programs are rooted in the community and actively involve community residents in their design and implementation (Roebuck, 2007).

Hawaii's Healthy Start (HHS) program began as a demonstration child abuse prevention project. HHS was started in July 1985, in Oahu, and is a para-professional service model that was developed to support at-risk families

Table 7.1
A Typology of Selected Family Support Programs Based on the Primary Recipient of Service

Service Recipient	Service Provided	Description of Selected Potential Services
Infant/Toddler	Developmental Pre-School	School Readiness; Socialization; Recreation; Remedial Skills Training
	Health Services	Developmental Screening; Health Screening
	Resources	Toy Lending
Children	After School Programs	Social, Recreational, Educational, Therapeutic
	Human Skills Training	Problem solving, Assertiveness Training, Conflict Resolution
	Mentoring	Use of Adult Volunteers for Educational and Social Enhancements
	Services for Special Needs	Developmental Screening; Educational Screening;
	Children	Educational Enhancement; Advocacy for Services; Transportation
	Education	Remedial; Enhancement; Arts
	Counseling	Individual; Group
Youth / Adolescents	After School Programs	Recreation; Arts; Support Groups around Topical Issues; Leadership Programs; Vocational Readiness.
	Human Skills Training	Problem solving, Assertiveness Training, Conflict Resolution
	Educational	Remedial; Enhancement; Arts; GED Preparation
	Counseling	Individual; Group
	Employment Services	Job Training; Job Placement; Work-Study; Vocational Counseling
	Mentoring Programs	Use of adult volunteers for educational and social enhancements
	Prevention Programs	Substance Abuse; Teen Pregnancy
	Health Programs	Health Promotion and Prevention

Table 7.1 (cont.)

Adults	Counseling	Individual, group, couples
	Crisis Intervention	Personal, Interpersonal Physical Needs
	Emergency Services	Psychological Assessments; Shelter, Clothing, Housing, Food
	Drop-In Programs	Socialization and Recreation, Respite, Networking and Information Sharing; Parent Discussion Groups; Child Development Programs
	Employment Services	Job Training; Job Placement; Vocational Counseling
	Life Skills Training	Communication; Self-Esteem; Stress Reduction; Home Management; Child-Teaching Skills; Consumer Education; Health and Nutrition; Anger Management
	Mentoring Programs	Matches Adult Parents with New Parents
	Newsletters	Child Rearing Tips; Child Abuse Prevention
	Substance Abuse Prevention	Treatment Services, Relapse Prevention, Support Groups, Information and Referral, Counseling and Therapy
	Program Involvement	Peer Facilitation, Group Leadership, Paraprofessional Training, Program Planning
	Transportation	Facilitation for Service Linkage
Families	Advocacy	Advocating in other Service Systems; Work Benefits and Employment Opportunities
	Counseling	Family Counseling
	Emergency Services	Food, Clothing, Medical Care, Energy Assistance, Housing
	Thrift Shop	Provision at low prices of needed goods
	Health Services	Health Screening; Primary Health Care; Health Education; Well-Baby Care; Immunizations; Health and Nutrition Counseling; Occupational, Physical and Speech Therapy

Table 7.1 (cont.)

	Home-Based Services	Support, Education, Counseling, Child Abuse Prevention; Case Management
	Housing Assistance	Weatherization, payment assistance, housing repair and rehabilitation, home financing
Parent-Child	Services for Young Parents	Parenting Classes; Peer Support Groups; Crisis Intervention; Information and Referral; Advocacy; Case Management; Medical Services; Pre and Post-partum Home Visiting; Hotlines
	Health Services	Maternal-Child Health Programs; Pre-natal Care; Pre and Post-partum Home Visiting; WIC program
	Parent-Child Activities	Recreational Playgroups; Infant Stimulation; Parent-Child Interaction Training; Role Modeling
	Services for Families with	Counseling and Support; Parenting Skills; Advocacy in Other
	Special Needs Children	Systems including Education and Health; Transportation
Agency	Training	Workshops, Seminars, In-service Training on Child Development, Primary Prevention, Enhancement of Social Support, Program Planning and Development, Resource Development, Agency Administration, Evaluation, Interprofessional Training
Community	Advocacy	Public Awareness, Coalition Building, Community Education
	Training	Leadership Development for Community Members; Institutes and Workshops for the Community

Source: Manalo, V. & Meezan, W. (2000). Toward building a typology for the evaluation of family support services. *Child Welfare, 79(4),* 420-422. Reprinted with permission.

with newborns through home visits. Preliminary findings and the design of the program captured the nation's imagination and the program began to be replicated around the country. In Hawaii, the program was expanded to a statewide program in the fall of 2001 in order to identify and intervene with eligible environmentally at-risk families, as part of the expanded definition of special needs governed by Part C of the federal Individuals with Disabilities Education Act, the forerunner of No Child Left Behind.

With this program, home visitation services are offered to families of all newborns deemed at-risk via screenings performed in all hospitals in the state at the child's birth. Services are voluntary and intended to continue until the child reaches three years of age (or five years of age, if there is a younger sibling) and include linkage with a pediatric provider. Healthy Start has two major components. The first is Early Identification (EID) for statewide, universal population-based screening/assessment/referral. Eligible families screened and assessed positive are offered home visiting services. The second component, Home Visiting (HV) fosters family functioning, promotes child health/development, and enhances positive parenting skills for families engaged/retained in service in order to reduce the risk of child maltreatment by addressing the malleable environmental risk factors via information, support, and linkages to needed community resources (Hawaii State Department of Health, 1992). This approach is illustrated in Figure 7.2.

HHS endeavors to decrease the likelihood of child maltreatment by reducing parental/environmental stressors, (including establishment and utilization of a medical home), linkages with community resources such as health and mental health services, early childhood education, childcare, family literacy, employment, social services, developmental screening and appropriate child development education/interventions, service coordination and advocacy for families, and providing parents with knowledge of child development, child health, and positive parenting skills and problem-solving techniques (Breakey & Pratt, 1991, pp. 16-19).

Preliminary national evaluation results for the Healthy Start program are positive in some areas, but not overall. Positives include indicators of a favorable process including: linking families with pediatric medical care, improving maternal parenting efficacy, decreasing maternal parenting stress, promoting the use of nonviolent discipline, and decreasing injury due to partner violence in the home. No overall positive program impact emerged in the areas of: adequacy of well-child health care; maternal life skills, mental health, social support, or substance use; child development; the child's home learning environment or parent-child interaction; pediatric health care use for illness or injury; or child maltreatment. However, there were signs of the possibility of unmeasured benefits that might later accrue to families receive HFA including improved parent-child interaction, child development, maternal confidence in adult relationships, and reduced partner violence (Duggan, et al., 1999).

Figure 7.2
The Healthy Start Program Model

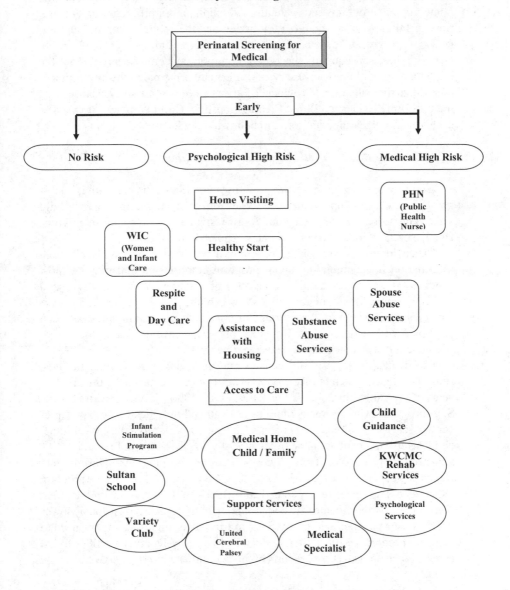

Source: Breakey, G., & Pratt, B. (1991). Healthy growth for Hawaii's "Healthy Start": Toward a systematic statewide approach to prevention of child abuse and neglect. *Zero to Three.* (Hoge & Idalski), p. 18. Reprinted with permission.

Significant differences were found in program implementation across the three agencies included in the national evaluation. The authors conclude that home-visiting programs and evaluations should monitor program implementation for faithfulness to the program model, and they should employ randomized control groups to determine program impact (Duggan, et al., 1999, p. 66). This has, subsequently, become a common concern observed about the implementation of innovative services and a core principle in the development of systems for evaluating the evidence base of child welfare services (see, e.g., the California Evidenced Based Clearinghouse for Child Welfare: http://www.cachildwelfareclearinghouse.org/; Schoenwald & Hoagwood, 2001).

What Does the Research Tells Us about Home Visiting?

While some of the home-visiting findings are mixed, the program model is being clarified; and improvements in some areas of parenting, increases in child safety and reductions in emergency room visits have been found (e.g., Olds, Henderson, & Kitzman, 1994; Sweet & Applebaum, 2004).

The outcomes of home-visiting programs have varied, considerably, although information is accumulating about program components that may be most beneficial. Parents feel that their relationships with the home visitor is crucial to the program (Krysik, LeCroy, & Ashford, 2008; Olds, et al., 1994; Sweet & Applebaum, 2004). With the shortage of nurses, use of parent aides has been attempted with varied results. But some programs have decreased the rate of subsequent occurrence of child abuse and neglect.

Treatment duration and/or intensity may indeed be key factors. In Olds' study, on average, each family received twenty-three visits during the first two years of their first-born child's life (Olds, et al., 1986). In the Hawaii Healthy Start program, which screens families at birth and provides home-based preventive services to almost 50 percent of the state's high-risk families (until the child is 3 to 5 years of age), the frequency of visits is weekly at first and then is adjusted according to the family's needs (Breakey & Pratt, 1991; Hawaii State Department of Health, 1992). MacLeod & Nelson (2000) found that the program effectiveness (as measured by statistical "effect size") varied with higher effect sizes for the thirteen to thirty-two visits and over fifty visits but curiously lower in effect for a program with thirty-three to fifty visits, underscoring the need to compare programs with similar models. DePanfilis & Dubowitz (2005) found no difference between CWS reports of those families served for six versus nine months.

Thus, the evidence for the effectiveness of this approach with families at risk of child maltreatment remains promising but mixed as researchers attempt to determine an optimum service composition, length and other additional factors. Marcenko & Staerkel, 2006 (p. 89) noted that because home visiting is only one part of a system of supports, and as such may not be effective without other pieces in place, the efficacy of the network of available community based services should be evaluated instead of testing one individual program.

While there is not yet consensus in the literature, prevention of abuse and neglect through home visiting appears to require these essential components.

1. Services should begin early, preferably during the prenatal period or shortly after birth, and should extend through the first few years of a child's life (Center on the Developing Child, 2007).
2. Home-based services need to occur frequently enough so that the home visitor gets to know the family, and the family gets to trust the person entering the home.
3. The primary goal of the home visitor should be to develop a therapeutic relationship with the parents (Institute for Family Development, 2008; Miller & Rollnick, 2002).
4. The home visitor, believing that maltreatment can occur in families and knowing the early signs of abuse and neglect, can provide a watchful eye in the home (Leventhal, 1996).
5. The home visitor should be able to model effective parenting.
6. The home visitor should not lose sight of the child's needs.
7. The home visitor needs to be able to provide concrete services to the family (Lewis, Walton, & Fraser, 1995).
8. If home visiting is going to have any impact on the occurrence of serious physical abuse, strategies will need to be developed to include fathers (or boyfriends) as well as mothers (Bergman, Larsen, & Mueller, 1986; Coakley, 2007; Starling, Holden, & Jenny, 1995).
9. Home visiting should not be provided in a "one size fits all" approach, but rather should be tailored to the family's needs (Leventhal, 1996; Walton, Sandau-Beckler, & Mannes, 2001).

Daro (2005), as well as Marcenko and Staerkel (2006, pp. 648-650) are also cautiously optimistic about the benefits of home-visiting programs and outline several ways to improve them. For example, first focus on key parenting skill assets and deficits. Hebbeler and Gerlack-Downie (2002) concluded the one program under examination was operating from a flawed theory of change. Home visitors, working from the assumption that all parents desire to be good parents, saw the goal of the intervention as helping parents feel good about themselves as people and as parents. Little attention was given to parent-child interaction, which could have been a behavioral indicator of parenting knowledge and skill gaps and a point of intervention (Hebbeler & Gerlach-Downie, 2002). The findings regarding the content of home visits and the potential negative impacts of past trauma on current parenting, suggest that greater attention to parent-child interaction may be a productive focus of home visits for some families. Supportive interventions with the intent of increased self-esteem for mothers may be inadequate to overcome the painful effects of early trauma awakened in the context of the present parenting relationship. It may be time to consider the purposeful pairing of home visiting programs with "parent mentor" models where parents who have had experience with child welfare services go on to coach parents newly reported to CWS (Cohen & Canan, 2006), community-based substance abuse treatment services, and other key interventions.

Other Promising Family Support Programs

While space does not permit a comprehensive review, specially designed school-based and other quality child care programs (McCartney, Dearing, Taylor, & Bub, 2007) have been found to have value in teaching parents positive parenting approaches such as the use of mirroring, commentary on the child's behavior, praise, and more positive family interactions (e.g., Kosterman, Hawkins, Spath, Haggerty, & Zhu, 1997; Nash & Fraser, 1998).

Recently broad, community-based interventions have been designed to bolster the infrastructure and support networks in a community in terms of education, housing, employment, medical care, transportation, child care, mental health services, and other key resources for families (Deborah Daro, et al., 2005). The best known of these is probably the Harlem Children's Zone, which starts with prenatal care, Baby College, enriched pre-school, and charter school education (www.hcz.org). The evaluation is not rigorous but the findings are promising. Another such example now operates in Florida and is designed to support children at different stages of their development (Speilberger, et al., 2007). This infrastructure of services is made up of the four primary programs and systems, as follows:

- The Healthy Beginnings service system, formerly known as the Maternal and Child Health Partnership, is a network of health and social services providing support and intervention services, including universal risk screening and targeted home visitation, to high-risk pregnant women and new mothers.
- The Early Care and Education system comprises several initiatives intended to improve the quality of child care and early education programs, provide services for children with developmental delays, and improve children's school readiness.
- The Children's Behavioral Health Initiative (CBHI) is a school-based intervention to improve children's adjustment to school and enhance their school success by identifying social-emotional and other developmental problems and providing referrals and intervention services to respond to these problems.
- A network of after-school programs for elementary and middle school youth is supported by Prime Time, an intermediary working to develop the quality of after-school activities in school-based and community programs (Spielberger, et al., 2007, p. 1).

While only in the early stages of implementation, the evaluators found that more of the 444 mothers worked in Year 2 (44 percent) than in Year 1 (14 percent). This marked change may be one reason for the aggregate Year 2 improvement in the mothers' well-being reflected in their household income and living conditions. Although mothers' estimates of their household income for the preceding year continued to be quite low, a smaller percentage in Year 2 than in Year 1 reported incomes of less than $20,000 (52 vs. 64 percent). There was some indication of improvement in their living conditions. A larger percentage in Year 2 (26 percent) than in Year 1 (20 percent) lived in a home that was owner-occupied rather than rented, and the mean score on the negative living conditions index was smaller in Year 2 (1.2) than Year 1 (1.4) (Spielberger, et al., 2007, pp. 4-5).

The evaluators praise the Palm Beach County initiative for how these leaders have implemented family support services in these four target communities but worry that not enough families are using the services or continue to use them. The evaluators note the following challenges, which appear common to many other community-based interventions, to be overcome:

- Keeping families involved in services over time;
- Making location and timing of services convenient for families;
- Providing continuity of services during periods of instability;
- Improving channels of communication for service information;
- Strengthening relationships with community organizations and other service systems;
- Engaging harder-to-reach families. (Spielberger, et al., 2007, pp. 9-11)

Children's Trust Fund Programs. Some prevention programs are being supported by surcharges on marriage licenses, birth certificates, and other taxing mechanisms in states—nearly every state now has a Children's Trust Fund and together they spend more than $100 million a year on prevention programming (National Alliance of Children's Trust and Prevention Funds, http://www.msu.edu/~millsda/about.htm, retrieved, March 22, 2008). The programs funded by some of the trust funds vary widely in terms of the coherence of their conceptual model for prevention and the rigor with which they are being evaluated. In contrast, other programs have been supported by state-wide legislation and are trying to take a more comprehensive approach. For example, see the West Virginia program (http://www.wvctf.org/), or the SCAN (Supportive Child Abuse Network), which uses a community-based approach that uses lay therapists and self-help groups as part of an effort to mobilize public awareness and support (Grazio, 1981). In other cities, like Richmond, Virginia, the networks increase accessibility to available family resources by providing free help lines or a 211 directory of services. As community leaders make this shift to focus on parent education and support, the challenge of linking families with available resources arises (see http://www.grscan.com/docs/ScanItFall06.pdf).

Center for family life's "Preventive Services Program" model. The Sunset Park, New York Center for Family Life's "Preventive Services Program" has a mission to help the families of Sunset Park, Brooklyn, remain intact. All families living in Sunset Park with a child under the age of eighteen are eligible for the center's services, which are accessible twenty-four hours a day. Funded through numerous public and private sources, all center services are free to family members. A non-experimental program evaluation found some evidence of effectiveness. At the conclusion of the study's data collection phase (30 months), almost all (98. 6 percent) of the 423 study sample children remained with their families. All five families in which a child had been placed continued to receive center services either in the preventive program, the neighborhood foster care program, or other center programs. In addition, 87.9 percent of the families' service needs had been addressed. Statistically significant positive effects were found on five of the eight child-centered problem/behavior factors in the ninety-two closed cases (Hess, McGowan, & Botsko, 1997).

The authors found three key program elements that differentiate the center's preventive program approach from other family preservation programs. These include: (1) broad accessibility to non-categorical services through multiple routes, including self-referral; (2) the comprehensive nature of the available within-center, community-based services provided through the preventive program; and (3) flexibility in service duration, including continuing access to preventive program services over time. As previously noted, these particular program characteristics are more typically found in family support programs (Kagan & Weissbourd, 1994; L. Schorr & Schorr, 1988; Zigler & Black, 1989). This program model provides one prototype for delivering comprehensive, integrated, and individualized services required by families with complex and varying sets of needs and problems (Hess, et al., 1997; Walton, et al., 2001).

Family-Based Services Programs

Family-based services encompass a range of activities such as case management, counseling/therapy, education, skill building, advocacy, and/or provision of concrete services for families with problems that threaten their stability. The philosophy of these programs differs from the more traditional child welfare services in the role of parents, use of concrete and clinical services, and other areas (Child Welfare League of America, 1989, p. 29).

Intensive Family Preservation Services (IFPS) are a special kind of FBS. This grouping of services might be distinguished by the combination of case management with intensive therapeutic and other services. Some of these services are designed for families "in crisis," at a time when removal of a child is perceived as imminent, or the return of a child from out-of-home care is being considered. Yet, the reality is that this service model is also being applied to chronic family situations, involving child neglect or abuse, which do not involve crisis. These programs often share the same philosophical orientation and characteristics as family-based services, but are delivered with more intensity (including shorter time frame and smaller caseloads), so they are often referred to as intensive family preservation service or IFPS programs. Caseloads generally vary between two to six families per worker. Families are typically seen between six and ten hours per week, and the time period of intervention is generally between four and twelve weeks.

Core Components of Family-Based Services

Based on the early writings of the FBS pioneers, The National Resource Center on Family-Based Services and Permanency Planning (2007, p. E1) considers the following to be the four essential components of family-based services or family-centered practice in child welfare:

1. *The family unit is the focus of attention:* Family-centered practice works with the family as a collective unit, insuring the safety and well-being of family members.
2. *Strengthening the capacity of families to function effectively is emphasized:* The primary purpose of family-centered practice is to strengthen the family's potential for carrying out their responsibilities.
3. *Families are engaged in designing all aspects of the policies, services, and program evaluation:* Family-centered practitioners partner with families to use their expert knowledge throughout the decision- and goal-making processes and provide individualized, culturally-responsive, and relevant services for each family.
4. *Families are linked with more comprehensive, diverse, and community-based networks of supports and services*: Family-centered interventions assist in mobilizing resources to maximize communication, shared planning, and collaboration among the several community and/or neighborhood systems that are directly involved in the family.

"Family preservation," as a distinct child-welfare intervention, targets families who are at relatively high risk of removal of the child or children (or at families who need support for reunification with a child removed already). Child maltreatment has been identified in these families and the goal is to prevent its re-occurrence (a form of "selected or indicated" prevention). Case management, counseling/therapy, education, skill building, advocacy, and/or provision of concrete services are provided. Most programs are currently found in child welfare agencies but derivative forms of services have developed and are also being provided in mental health centers (Henggeler & Sheidow, 2003), juvenile justice (Henggeler & Sheidow, 2003), and family reunification programs (Comer & Fraser, 1998; Timmons-Mitchell, Bender, Kishna, & Mitchell, 2006; Walton, et al., 2001).

Target Populations for Family-Based Services and Intensive Family Preservation Services

The target populations for FBS and IFPS programs vary greatly. For example, while the target population for both programs is generally families in serious trouble, including families no longer able to cope with problems that threaten family stability, families in which a decision has been made by an authorized public social service agency (or by the family) that there is substantial reason to place a child outside the home and families whose children are in temporary out-of-home care. Although a "crisis orientation" may be emphasized by some programs, these services may be appropriate for families seen by the child welfare, juvenile justice, or mental health systems, but not as a short-term intervention for adoptive or foster families facing potential disruption. The distinction between the various program categories is not definitive, but the taxonomy does help to clarify some distinguishing features of these types of programs and to suggest some of the program design questions facing practitioners and administrators in the field. Throughout the remainder of this chapter, when reviewing the general literature on family support, family-based or family-preservation services, we will use the term *Family-Based Services* (FBS). When referring specifically to programs that deliver both concrete and clinical services primarily in the home on an intensive basis (one to four months), we will use the term *Intensive Family Preservation Services* (IFPS). If we are referring to non-child welfare treatment programs (like Multi-Systemic Family Therapy) we will describe it as *Intensive In-Home Therapy*.

Current Status of FBS Programs

As described in Chapter 5, in many states only a small percentage of the children reported to CWS are ever placed in some form of substitute care. Some researchers argue that there are few "unnecessary" placements, and yet a proportion of those families experiencing the removal of their children could have been provided with FBS at an earlier time. In contrast, some jurisdictions have seen a decrease in child placement rates; how they achieved those reductions is worth a close examination

To address these problems, a number of policy and program innovations were instituted by federal, state, and local authorities. P.L. 96-272's requirement that every state provide "reasonable efforts" to preserve the family has led to renewed use of traditional programs to support families, including homemaker, emergency day care, parent aide, and crisis nursery services. These services have also been supplemented by FBS, which are designed to help families to remain together safely. Thus, a large variety of FBS programs have been developed by both private and public child welfare agencies. These programs are serving clients from child welfare, mental health, developmental disabilities, juvenile corrections, and other major service areas. A variety of staffing and treatment models were being employed, including those related to supporting families whose children are returning from foster care or residential treatment

While a complete description of the various states and agencies that have begun or funded FBS programs is beyond the scope of this chapter, the diversity of these programs is extensive. For example, in 1989 a form of FBS was designed and began operation by the well-recognized Boys Town in Omaha, Nebraska. Their model of family preservation services is strengths-based, builds on some of the well-recognized intervention techniques of their group care programs, but extends that work further in how their "Family Consultants" are trained and supervised (Peterson, Kohrt, Shadoin, & Authier, 1995). In New York City, a special FBS demonstration project resulted in accelerated parent-child reunifications using capitated prospective payments, greater flexibility in services and lower worker caseloads (Wulczyn, Zeidman, & Svirsky, 1997). Some of the agencies were unclear about how to use the additional funds that were offered, whereas others came up with innovative ways of transporting, housing, and serving families.

In Portland, Oregon, a IFPS program designed for and by African Americans to meet the needs of neglectful families showed early signs of success (Ciliberti, 1998; Nelson & Nash, 2008). Specially designed FBS programs are being implemented for other ethnic groups as well, such as Asian-Americans (Fong, 2001) and Native Americans (Mannes, 1990 (Red Horse, et al., 2000). Finally, one of the most well researched models of IFPS is Multi-Systemic Family Preservation Services (MST), which uses an ecological-based intervention approach with specific treatment protocols to enable the worker and family to address individual, family, school, and community factors rather than child maltreatment issues (Rowland, et al., 2005).

The field has therefore experienced a shift from a few small-scale and isolated demonstration projects to the use of FBS programs on a more extensive basis in a number of states, such as Florida, Illinois, Maryland, Michigan, Minnesota, North Carolina, and Tennessee. The implementation of these programs represents a commitment on the part of state and local governments to operationalize the principle stated earlier that society should be willing to invest as many resources in preserving families as might be spent for substitute family care (Lloyd, Bryce, & Schultze, 1980, p. 3). Thus, these services were developed to provide alternatives to out-of-home placement by improving family functioning and linking families to sustaining services and sources of support

Furthermore, some states have continued to fund previously developed placement prevention efforts such as homemaker, emergency day care, parent aide, and crisis nursery services. It is important to note that FBS programs will not replace the need for other types of child welfare services. Some families will always be in need of one or more of the other services in the child welfare continuum of service, such as family foster care, day treatment, or residential treatment. But FBS, like some of the other family support programs, represents a significant departure from the more legalistic and narrowly "person-centered" perspective—giving little attention to addressing the family's needs in a holistic manner (Farrow, 1991; Walton, et al., 2001)—that may have become the standard in many CWS agencies. FBS offers alternative conceptions of human services toward:

1. Establishing a service continuum—from preclusive prevention to secure treatment—with expanded capacity for individualized case planning through flexible funding and service eligibility;
2. Promoting competence and meeting basic developmental needs of children and families in "normalized" settings by teaching practical life skills and by providing environmental supports as opposed to uncovering and treating underlying pathology. Evidence for this trend is apparent in the explosion of educational or life-skills approaches (Danish, D'Angell, & Hauer, 1980); the move away from presumptive labeling and toward more developmentally focused, competence-oriented assessment; and by the move in many fields toward "normalization" of both the location and focus of treatment (Wolfensberger, 1972);
3. Considering services as family supportive and family strengthening, not as "child saving." The rapid expansion of crisis-oriented family-support services (Zigler & Black, 1989) and the renewed emphasis on family involvement in child-placement services (Jenson & Whittaker, 1987) all offer partial evidence of the strength of this idea;
4. Re-establishing a person-in-environment perspective in theory, empirical research, and clinical practice as a foundation for intervention design.

Program Limitations and Policy Pitfalls Need to Be Recognized

There are promising programs that do help families avoid foster care placement or shorten children's stays in care (Green, Rockhill, & Furrer, 2007). While family-based services represent a significant step in the evolution of social services, much of the more rigorous evaluation data was disappointing (Nelson, Walters, Schweitzer, Blythe, & Pecora, 2008). As mentioned earlier, while a number of case situations can be addressed by FBS programs alone, some families will always be in need of one or more other child welfare services such as day treatment, family foster care, residential treatment or adoption; and most will need other preventive or supportive services such as income support, child care, parent education, substance abuse treatment, or job training. Additionally, studies of FBS and other programs have repeatedly shown that many families need assistance with housing, food, medical care, employment, and basic financial support. Most of the families served by public systems live in communities with few resources to help parents or support healthy child development.

In addition, many families experience other problems, such as ineffective communication among family members, poor self-esteem, serious mental illness, lack of social support, and pronounced deficits in parenting or basic social skills. Many of these have long been understood to derive from larger societal problems and/or significant psychological or social impairments (Polansky, Ammons, & Weathersby, 1983; Polansky, Gaudin, & Kilpatrick, 1992; Schorr & Marchand, 2007). Thus, while significant foster care and residential treatment program savings may be realized for some children, FBS programs are just one of an array of services that must be available to support families throughout the life cycle. Without a broader network of family supports readily available, families may not be able to maintain the gains made during FBS, leaving children vulnerable. Furthermore, some families need services on a long-term basis and are not well served by a short period of intensive work. Other families need high quality foster care to help them through a difficult period or until an older child reaches adulthood (Kessler, et al., 2008). The children who may be least likely to benefit from placement into foster care are those who are older and had less severe abuse and problems prior to placement (Doyle, 2007); they may, conversely, be those who would best benefit from FBS.

It is incumbent upon evaluators and program staff to locate FBS programs within the larger network of services, and to emphasize to policy makers that both the short- and long-term success of these programs is dependent upon the family's ability to access a range of community services and other societal supports (Kohl, 2007). More immediately, an evaluator must consider how the availability of these services will affect the success of the program. While some families may need just FBS, attaining or sustaining family gains will require the availability of continuing evidence-based FBSs or other community services. In the next section, we address the evidence base for IFPS.

Selected Program Implementation Challenges in Family-Based and Intensive Family Preservation Services

Empirical Data Regarding Effectiveness Remains Mixed

Some FBS programs appear to provide a viable alternative to out-of-home placement for some children and help to improve family functioning in specific areas (Nelson, et al., 2008). The program evaluation results, while promising, do not show dramatic differences between control and treatment groups, and are far from conclusive (see, for example, Fraser, Nelson, & Rivard, 1997; Meezan & McCroskey, 1997; Schuerman, Rzepnicki, & Littell, 1994; Yuan, et al., 1990). As family-based services and the more intensive family preservation services have become more widely implemented, controversy over their effectiveness and suitability for protecting children in some family situations has grown. But one review of IFPS programs found that programs focusing on older youth with more oppositional behavior problems, youth where delinquency is a major problem, and families with a child with schizophrenia or other severe mental illnesses are successful (Fraser, et al., 1997; Nelson, et al., 2009). When IFPS programs with greater treatment fidelity are examined, the more positive findings are found successful (Fraser, et al., 1997; Nelson, et al., 2009).

So policymakers and program administrators should not abandon new initiatives in this area. A number of authors (e.g., Kirk, Reed-Ashcraft, & Pecora, 2003; Meezan & McCroskey, 1996) have cautioned that more research is needed where the FBS or FPS intervention is well specified and implemented consistently. In examining more closely sub-groups of consumers, or special outcomes such as reducing the number of moves that a child has (Wells & Whittington, 1993), we may find that different forms of FBS or FPS programs are needed (e.g., Bath & Haapala, 1994).

Studies have been confounded by a number of administrative and evaluation problems, however. Problems in administration include referral, staff training, and community resources. Evaluation problems include the use of non-experimental designs, small samples, poor case targeting, under use of qualitative designs, and inappropriate assessment measures (Nelson, et al., 2009). Recent meta-analyses of laboratory and clinic-based studies of psychotherapy have also found a lack of dramatic differences between control and experimental groups (Weisz, Weiss, & Donenberg, 1992). Across many different fields, evaluation studies appear to suggest that we cannot expect single services to produce dramatic changes in complex social problems.

Implementing Theory-Based Interventions

Despite the work of a number of program developers and researchers (e.g., Barth, 1990; Bryce & Lloyd, 1981; Henggeler, Schoenwald, Borduin, Rowland, & Cunningham, 1998; Jones, 1985; Kinney, Haapala, Booth, & Leavitt, 1991; Lindblad-Goldberg, Dore, & Stern, 1998), documentation of theories to guide FBS remains to be fully accomplished. Perhaps, this is where various qualitative approaches can make significant contributions (Wells, 1994). And yet, ideally, high quality evaluations use theory as a way of guiding the choice of dependent and independent variables, as well as the research design and measures. For example, in 1996 Fraser, et al. noted that family based-services were not likely to be an appropriate intervention for problems related to aggressive children, such as school failure, gang violence, etc., because they lack an intervention to strengthen information processing skills essential to a child's peer relations.

Case Targeting

Targeting services to cases at imminent risk of placement remains a serious challenge, assuming placement prevention is the purpose of FBS programs. Many of the largest FBS and IFPS studies with placement prevention objectives were unable to target services to children truly at risk of imminent placement, as evidenced by the fact that few children were placed within thirty days of referral to these studies.

Serious efforts are needed in programs with this target population to refine placement criteria, implement interdepartmental screening committees, involve juvenile court personnel, better manage the politics of implementation, and address staff concerns about child safety in order to improve case targeting and screening. Otherwise, we will continue to find only small differences in placement rates between treatment and comparison groups.

Being Clear about What is Being Used as Criteria for Success

In balancing a focus on outcomes and process, process objectives often are emphasized rather than results. Sorting out these issues is also complicated by differing policy emphases. Littel, et al. (1993) noted that workers will often indicate a case was successful because process requirements were met (e.g., meeting certain time constraints, providing services) and not because the family situation actually improved. Additionally, workers often emphasize "helping families" more than reaching aggregate measures of success, which indicates differences between program policy goals and individualized treatment goals.

Program Implementation

Another serious issue that has been inadequately addressed by many FBS initiatives is the need to achieve program consistency and rigor with respect to model specification, staff selection, staff training, program funding, quality control, staff turnover, and maintaining *planned* program refinement in contrast to model "drift" (Kirk, et al., 2003; Pecora, 1991). For example, during the third year of implementation, when control groups were being formed, a major California FBS evaluation encountered staff turnover and decreased state administrative support. Other recent statewide evaluation studies have also faced considerable methodological and implementation challenges.

Illustrated in Illinois (and other studies in California, Iowa, New Jersey, North Carolina, Utah, and Washington) the program implementation process, worker training, variation in services, and other implementation factors are critical in interpreting study findings and in developing effective research designs. Program consistency and quality must be at adequate levels prior to formal evaluations studies and replication of the model in other jurisdictions (e.g., Kirk, Griffith, & Gogan, 2004). This was documented in a replication study of MST, an intensive in-home therapy program that is derivative from the original Homebuilders, but is directed to non-child welfare applications (Henggeler, et al., 1999). One of the immediate challenges for FBS is to better address the fundamentals of program implementation that will lead to more accurate evaluation studies:

- *Be careful and rigorous about how we specify the treatment model.* For example, program leaders need to be able to specify the theory base underlying the program, the major intervention methods, caseload size, intensity, and approach to the provision of concrete services (if applicable). We often do not take the time to consider what it will really take to make a meaningful difference for consumers. And yet, in medicine, we often do not give someone half the prescription needed. So, program administrators need to be able to specify what it will take to make a difference in the lives of these families. Therefore, the field needs to have the data to say to legislators, for example, for high-risk families where neglect of young children is the issue, we need an average of twelve months of fairly intensive efforts, that are likely to be followed by some less intensive community services with occasional booster sessions to help get these children raised safely in a healthy manner. (Or if the parents are not showing substantial improvement and interest in the welfare of the children, termination of parental rights may need to be pursued.)
- *Staffing can clearly make a difference.* Selection criteria, training, performance standards, use of para-professional staff are all important to address.
- *Provide supervision and clinical consultation to staff to minimize treatment model drift.*
- *Establish an organizational and community climate supportive of continuing program innovation and ongoing quality assurance.*
- *Collect benefit-cost data.* In times of continuing funding scarcity, we need to be able to tie key outcomes to service costs. And if a service will be insufficient in power or intensity to have a major effect, then maybe we should invest in an intervention model that is more cost-effective or its effects in terms of fiscal benefits outweigh program costs (Kirk, et al., 2003).

These represent some of the major administrative and research challenges that the FBS and IFPS administrators and evaluators need to overcome. To date the field lacks conclusive evidence that FBS, or its more intensive derivative IFPS, prevents child placement. Also lacking is information about which types of FBS programs are most effective with different client sub-populations including those involved in physical abuse, neglect, parent-child conflict, or other areas. Additionally, there is a need for increased understanding of effectiveness with different age groups of children and of program components that contribute to success with different families (e.g., in-home services, active listening, client goal setting, concrete services). Studies are beginning to look at sub-populations and to estimate the value of different intervention components. These are all important evaluation goals, along with the fundamental need for FBS programs to assess effectiveness, to refine interventions, and to be accountable to funding agencies. Although it is premature to draw any conclusions about the effectiveness of any particular type of service for any particular clientele, as mentioned earlier, there are a number of promising intervention models with supportive research data that can be used as a foundation for program refinement in this field of practice in child welfare.

Need for Integrated Primary Health Care, Child Welfare, Mental Health, Substance Abuse Treatment and Other Services

As mentioned in Chapter 1, with the consistently high numbers of substance abusing parents involved in child welfare, the need for prevention and treatment programs becomes critical and partnerships between child welfare, early childhood, education, mental health, primary health care, and substance abuse treatment facilities are essential (see, for example, Iida, et al., 2005; Office of Early Childhood, 1998).

Community-Based Approaches are Essential

Schuerman, et al., (1994, p. xiii) have commented that "Family Preservation Services are often expected to solve major social problems one case at a time." Halpern (1990), Pew Foundation (2008), and Shonkoff (2004) underscore the need to recognize that child and family well-being is affected immensely by not only public policies and service programs, but by funding strategies, local community conditions, and neighborhood supports. This recognition is stimulating a range of neighborhood and community-based initiatives, as exemplified by the child protective service initiatives reviewed in Chapter 6 and other programs.

Promising community-focused programs have been described by Cameron & Vanderwoerd (1997), Kagan & Weissbourd (1994), Schorr & Marchand (2007), and Wynn, Merry, & Berg (1995). On a more child-focused level, Greenberg, Domitrovich, and Bumbarger (1999) and Kumpfer, Molgaard, and Spoth (1996) have found promising programs for preventing mental disorders in school-age children. These are the youth who may end up in child welfare or juvenile justice placements without early intervention services.

Conclusion

Current Status

The benefits to the families served by some family support programs parallel some of the other child welfare programs that use in-home teaching and other types of supportive interventions. But too few evaluation studies using rigorous experimental designs have been conducted, especially those including both self-report and archival data on key outcome measures for randomly selected intervention and control groups (Gomby, Culross, & Behrman, 1999). In addition, evaluation results have been less positive for some of these programs which have served lower risk children (Karoly, et al., 1998) and those that have targeted child abuse prevention as a key outcome, particularly for those programs of short duration, with a less tightly specified parenting curriculum, and those focusing on families who have already been referred to child protective services (Barth, 1991).

Home visitation has been cited as the "single most critical element in a comprehensive approach to preventing child maltreatment" (U.S. Advisory Board on Child Abuse and Neglect, 1991; Daro, 1993, p. 1). Substantial debate, however, continues regarding various prevention services regarding length of services, intervention methods, provider training, and what combination of services are best for certain ethnic groups by problem area (Daro, 2005). Furthermore, there is the question of whether to continue to provide periodic bursts of services to vulnerable families with older children, given findings that older children are also underserved by the CWS delivery system (Burns, et al., 2004) and at risk of child maltreatment (Jonson-Reid & Barth, 2000, USDHHS, 2008a). Finally, experts emphasize that prevention efforts must be multi-faceted in design to meet the unique needs of the client population. However, it has been observed that "the most useful systems will be ones that address the multiple causal factors associated with various types of maltreatment, target services to both the potential perpetrator and the potential victim, and build on the experiences of others in designing specific prevention services" (Berliner, 1993; Daro, 1988, p. 128).

Well-designed family support or other types of child abuse prevention efforts have the potential to be cost-effective in terms of the health care, special education, legal and other costs incurred by society in dealing with the social problem, not to mention the most important (and difficult to measure) costs of emotional harm to children. However, as discussed earlier, the evidence base, while growing, is inconclusive. And recently, some program experts have been concerned not only about program fidelity, but also about the difficulty in certain areas of connecting family support programs with child welfare programs. That is, they don't really serve the same clientele in many cases. A Rand analysis of early childhood programs noted concerns pertinent to FBS, particularly that we do not know the following:

- Whether there are optimal program designs;
- How early interventions can best be targeted to those who would benefit most;
- Whether the model programs evaluated to date will generate the same benefits and savings when implemented on a large scale;
- What the full range of benefits is;
- What the implications of the changing social safety net are (Karoly, et al., 1998, pp. XX-XXI).

Finally, we must identify the most important areas to be focused upon rather than on secondary risk factors. For example, is it a lack of a parent's social network, employment skills, practical knowledge of child development, sense of self-esteem and/or social skills that should be addressed? We need to avoid "single-variable" interventions in a complex area such as child maltreatment (Olds & Henderson, 1989). This is being shown to be particularly true as more community-based family support efforts are initiated and evaluated (see, for example, Schorr, 1997, pp. 301-379; Wynn, Costello, Halpern, & Richman, 1994). A move to theory-based interventions will help the field.

Future Directions

In conclusion, there remains some enthusiasm in the field for family support, FBS, and IFPS programs, but with the caution that FBS should not be expected to "address major social problems one family at a time" as so aptly put by the FBS researchers at Chapin Hall. There is growing attention to program and model refinements, but unfortunately, there have been few rigorous evaluations with experimental designs. These efforts are being complemented by the articulation of a variety of practice strategies available to families with diverse needs and characteristics. Regularly collected evaluation data and the careful gathering of feedback from children and parents can help guide these kinds of service refinement efforts. As our ultimate "stakeholders," they have valuable information to share.

For Further Information

Institute for the Advancement of Social Work Research. (2002). *Annotated Bibliography with Commentary on Family-Centered Practice*. Washington, DC: Author. Retrieved October 15, 2007 from: http://www.charityadvantage.com/iaswr/FCPBibliographyRev71202.pdf A review of selected references and citations in the area of family-centered practice.

National Resource Center for Family-Centered Practice and Permanency. This website and a twice-yearly newsletter showcase many resources and publish timely discussions of key concepts: http://www.hunter.cuny.edu/socwork/nrcfcpp/newsletters. html#pptoday

Pew Foundation. (2008a). *Life chances: the case for early investment in our kids.* Available at www.pewtrusts.org/uploadedFiles/American_Prospect_1207_EarlyEd-SpecialRep Articulates a rationale with examples for why early childhood supports is essential.

Pew Foundation. (2008b). *Time for reform: investing in prevention: keeping children safe at home.* Philadelphia: Author. Retrieved January 28, 2008 from www.kidsarewaiting. org. A timely review of key issues and concise summaries of promising programs in family support and child welfare.

Schorr, E., & Marchand, V. (2007). *Pathways to Prevention of Child Abuse and Neglect*: California Department of Social Services, Children and Family Services Division Office of Child Abuse Prevention. Outlines a comprehensive framework for preventing child maltreatment with examples across each strategy.

U.S. Department of Health and Human Services. (2004). *Child neglect demonstration projects: Synthesis of lessons learned.* Washington, DC: Child Welfare Information Gateway. Concise review of promising programs for addressing child neglect.

8

Family Foster Care

Family foster care, a phenomenon with ancient origins, continues to affect the lives of millions of children, youths, and their families. Following a review of its evolution, this chapter examines contemporary foster care in the United States within the context of the family-centered orientation to child welfare practice presented in Chapter 3. The major areas to be covered in this chapter are (1) evolution, definition, and direction of family foster care; (2) children and youths in family foster care; (3) professionalization of foster parents; and (4) effectiveness of services. The chapter will conclude with consideration of the current status of family foster care. Content pertaining to family reunification and kinship care will be covered in the next chapter and residential treatment will be discussed in Chapter 12 (Intensive Treatment Services).

Evolution of Family Foster Care

Early History

Family foster care in one form or another has a long history (cf.,Chambers, 1963; Hacsi, 1995; Kadushin & Martin, 1988). Kinship care, probably the most common precursor to family foster care, may have origins "under ancient Jewish laws and customs, children lacking parental care became members of the household of other relatives, if such there were, who reared them for adult life" (Slingerland, 1919, p. 27). Children from every culture continue to be raised by their kin when parents are unwilling or unable to fulfill the parental role.

In modern times in the United States, family foster care has been marked by a number of developmental milestones and federal laws. Family foster care began as an effort to "rescue" children who were "dependent"—or whose parents were "inadequate" and relying on charity; the movement was substantially stimulated by the Rev. Charles Loring Brace and the Placing Out System of the New York Children's Aid Society. Brace and his associates planned and promoted the transfer by train of tens of thousands of children from the streets of New York to the west or south, where they were placed with farming families in which they would work and grow up (Brace, 1872). While many children were orphans, others had one or both parents living. Most came from recently arrived immigrant families from southern Europe.

The transfer of those children eventually created much controversy, including opposition of the Catholic Church to placement of Catholic children with Protestant families, as well as resistance from child welfare professionals who were concerned about uprooting so many young people. As a result of these and other developments in child welfare services, such an approach eventually declined and Children's Aid Societies were established to provide and administer foster care programs within each state. These changes presage the current movement to provide children's care close to home.

By the 1950s, a range of out-of-home care options had emerged, including:

- receiving or shelter homes—in which children were cared for on an emergency, time-limited basis;
- wage (or free) homes—particularly for older children who contributed some work in return for receiving care;
- boarding homes—for which the agency or parents paid a board rate to the foster parents;
- group homes—for small groups of unrelated children; and
- larger residential homes (large campuses with many children).

In each of the above options, the emphasis was on providing a family setting for every child. Indeed, as early as 1909, the first White House Conference on Children proclaimed:

> Home life...is the highest and finest product of civilization. It is the great molding force of mind and character. Children should not be deprived of it except for urgent and compelling reasons. (Bremner, 1971, p. 352)

In the efforts to achieve the goal of a "secure and loving home," following the 1909 conference a complex child welfare services evolved encompassing both governmental and voluntary agencies. Gradually, family foster care, which had emerged in the latter part of the nineteenth century as a means of rescuing children from their "inadequate" parents, came to be considered a temporary service whose purpose was to reunite children with their families or place them, if necessary, in another family in which they could grow up. The evolution of foster care as a temporary service, however, often occurred more at the policy and philosophical levels than in practice. Many children remained in foster care for lengthy periods of time up through the end of the twentieth century. Especially since the 1950s, it became apparent that the goal of a "secure and loving home" was not being realized for many children, despite the proliferation of new agencies and additional resources.

Foster Care and Permanency Planning

Practice experiences; research findings from landmark studies such as those of Fanshel and Shinn (1978), Maas and Engler (1959), and Shyne and Schroeder (1978); and critiques of foster care in the 1950s and 1960s underscored a number of points:

- Despite its temporary purpose, foster care placement had become a permanent status for many children entering the services.
- Many children were drifting in foster care—going from one placement to another, with little sense of stability or continuity in their living arrangements.
- Children were often inappropriately moved out of their homes—with little effort to help the parents to care for them.
- Most of the children came from poor families—often families that were barely managing to survive on limited income from public welfare.
- Although some children were effectively helped through placement in foster care, for others the experience of separation from their families had adverse aspects, including losing track of siblings and other disrupted relationships.

As a result of these and other findings, as well as the rapid increase in the numbers of children going into foster care, questions were raised about the effectiveness of child welfare services. At the same time, there were other pertinent developments, such as the growth of the civil rights movement, which led to the child advocacy movement and to growing concern about the rights of children and parents. As discussed in Chapter 5, there was also the discovery (or rediscovery) of physical abuse of children by their parents or other family members—which led to a tremendous expansion of child protection services and, inevitably, an increase in the numbers of children going into out-of-home care.

Additionally, there was the rediscovery of the family, or rather, the family became respectable again as a social unit to be supported rather than blamed (Lasch, 1977). For example, irrespective of the actual success of various family policy initiatives, the family was a major theme of the Carter Administration in the 1970s. There also emerged conviction at the federal and state levels that needy people—including children—should be cared for in the least restrictive environment.

Legal and Policy Framework

Foster care practice and programs are governed by an intricate—and not necessarily coherent—set of policies and laws at the federal, state, and local levels. These are described in Chapter 2, and considered throughout this book.

For example at the federal level, policies that directly affect foster family care are embedded primarily in seven major laws enacted by the U.S. Congress during the last three decades.

Perhaps the most controversial, as well as sensitive, issue is that of balancing the rights of parents with those of children, especially children placed in foster care because of parental abuse or neglect (Pew Commission on Children in Foster Care, 2004). Despite the proliferation of statutes, policies, and legal procedures, decision-making in this area is heavily influenced by a number of idiosyncratic factors. These include, among others, availability of prevention and placement resources; values and biases of service providers; presence of strong advocates for the parents or children; attitudes of juvenile court judges toward placement; rigor of the screening process; ambiguities in definition of abuse, neglect, and child protection; and imprecise nature of information about human behavior and impossibility of predicting the future. The consequences of such an idiosyncratic approach to decision-making can be negative, as seen, for example, in some cases in which termination of parental rights is accomplished legally, but the child is then left to drift in foster care without any family connection or other permanent plan. Yet, discretion and flexibility can also be used for the greater good. For this reason, as suggested in Chapter 3, sound decision-making in foster care, as in child welfare in general, requires not only partnership between the family and service providers but also active collaboration among community agencies, child welfare workers, judges, attorneys, and others working with children and their parents.

Definition and Purpose of Family Foster Care

Foster care is generally used as a term encompassing not only family foster care, but also placement of children and youths in group homes and residential settings—a topic covered later in this chapter. Family foster care, the focus of this chapter, has been defined as:

> the provision of planned, time-limited, substitute family care for children who cannot be adequately maintained at home, and the simultaneous provision of social services to these children and their families to help resolve the problems that led to the need for placement. (Blumenthal, 1983, p. 296)

The above definition reflects various principles that are well accepted in the field of child welfare, as exemplified by the "CWLA Standards of Excellence for Family Foster Care" (Child Welfare League of America, 1995), although not fully realized in policy or practice. First, family foster care is conceptualized as a comprehensive family support service, and the family is regarded as the central focus of attention, as discussed in Chapter 3. Second, family foster care is carefully planned to be short term and to provide access to time-limited services and opportunities that can help families to become rehabilitated and children to grow up and develop.

The major functions of family foster care include emergency protection, crisis intervention, assessment and case planning, reunification, preparation for adoption, and preparation for independent living. To implement such functions, diverse forms of foster care are required, including emergency foster care, kinship foster care, placement with unrelated foster families, treatment foster care, foster care for medically fragile children, shared family foster care, and small family group home care. Also, long-term family foster care is an option for a small number of youths for whom family reunification, kinship care, or adoption are not viable permanency planning options.

In addition, there are indications that family foster care is responding to the substantial behavioral health needs of the children in care and becoming more treatment oriented. Specialized family foster care programs—particularly treatment foster care— for children and youths with special needs in such areas as emotional disturbance, behavioral problems, and educational underachievement, are gaining significant use (e.g., Chamberlain, 2003). Family foster care is, now, sometimes provided as a multi-faceted service, including specialized or therapeutic services for some children, temporary placements for children in "emergency" homes, and supports to relatives raising children through kinship care (Maluccio, Pine, & Tracy, 2002). (While there is little descriptive data on services to children in foster care, we believe that much of foster care is delivered without significant services for children other than referral to mental health agencies for treatment.)

Treatment Foster Care as a Specialized Form of Out-of-Home Care

There is a form of foster care that has emerged over the past twenty years that is more of a treatment-oriented service. It involves systematic evaluation and selection of prospective foster parents, more adequate compensation, greater foster parent training and supervision, lower caseloads for the workers, substantial participation of foster parents as members of the agency's service team, and more frequent involvement of foster parents in helping biological parents. The above characteristics, along with others, are described reports and in the "Program Standards for Treatment Foster Care" promulgated by the Foster Family-based Treatment Association (see http://www.ffta.org/). These standards provide a guide to quality programming and include a "Standard Review Instrument" that agencies can use to conduct a self-assessment.

Despite its growing acceptance at the philosophical level, treatment foster care is not well implemented in some communities and not all treatment foster parents are professionalized. However, there are many exemplary programs, such as Pressley Ridge School's PRYDE program in Pennsylvania, Multi-Dimensional Treatment Foster Care, and West Virginia, and Boys Town treatment foster care (Meadowcroft & Trout, 1990). There are a growing number of interventions that have a strong evidence-base that can be provided, such as

Parent Child Intervention Therapy (PCIT) (Timmer, et al., 2006), Trauma-Focused Cognitive-Behavioral Treatment (Cohen & Mannarino, 2004), and others.

Children and Youths in Family Foster Care and Their Families

Numbers in Care

Planning and delivery of foster family care should be informed by information that helps us to answer the following question: *What qualities of foster families and what mix of services do children and families need in order to promote the success of families in resuming their parenting and the development of children's behavioral and educational success?*

In response to the above question, we should first understand the situations of children and families coming to attention of child welfare services, especially in regard to their numbers, reasons for placement, age distribution, and race and ethnicity. In the 1990s there was a steady increase in children in foster care, including children in family foster care or group care. The United States federal government estimated that 496,000 children were placed in foster care in family and non-family settings in 2007. For further details on numbers of children in care, see the U.S. Children's Bureau website for state and national AFCARS data: www.acf.dhhs.gov/programs/cb/stats/afcars) (Gradually we are obtaining better data regarding children in out-of-home care nationally, even with some state gaps in reporting. In addition, available statistics tend to focus on children placed in out-of-home care through child welfare services and neglect those placed through mental health and juvenile justice services as well as those in informal foster care. For example, some parents may allow the transfer of custody of their child to the state agency because they cannot afford the level of care necessary to treat a child who is severely emotionally disturbed. While the federal government is now collecting data from most states through the Adoption and Foster Care Analysis and Reporting System (AFCARS), not all states are reporting on all items. For these reasons, we have reasonable but not precise estimates of the numbers of children in family foster care or in out-of-home placement in general. These certainly under-represent the total number of children living away from their parents because of concerns about their well-being. For the latest national and state AFCARS data, see http://www. afc.dhhs.gov/programs/CB/stats.

Reasons for Placement

Although precise data are not available, reports from the field document the changes in the kinds of children entering placement. Most children still enter foster care because of the consequences of parent-related problems, largely child abuse or neglect (Berrick, et al., 1998; U.S. Department of Health and

Human Services, 2007a). But a considerable number of children (especially adolescents) enter care because of behavioral problems (Barth, Wildfire, & Green, 2006). Some examples of child placements follow:

- Gloria, three-month-old daughter of a sixteen-year-old developmentally disabled girl without any family supports, has been placed in an emergency foster home since birth.
- Tyrone, age two, was placed in a pre-adoptive foster home following the mother's death due to HIV-AIDS—no known relatives or family friends could be located who could care for him.
- Bobby and Gerry, ages eight and two, were removed from their family due to physical abuse of both boys by their father, who visits them occasionally in the foster home.
- Lucy, age ten, and her family have been referred to the child protection unit of a county welfare department following a teacher's complaint that Lucy was neglected at home and an investigation showing that she was sexually abused by her mother's boyfriend.
- Steve, age twelve, has been in a treatment foster home following seven days of intensive psychiatric assessment and stabilization ever since his widowed father was hospitalized over a year ago for a psychiatric disturbance; the father had severely beaten Steve on at least two occasions for "misbehaving."

In addition, there is indication of increasing proportions of children entering care—and remaining there—from these groups: children with special health or developmental needs, children living in families with severe domestic violence, drug-exposed infants, children from multi-problem families and severely dysfunctional families, children from substance-abusing families, and adolescents with serious behavioral and/or emotional problems.[1] Furthermore, now as in the past, most children in foster care come from poor families—families with multiple problems in such areas as housing, employment, health, and education (Barth, Wildfire & Green, 2006; Fernandez, 1996). Research has also shown that large proportions of children in foster care have major learning problems in school (Blome, 1997; Courtney, Piliavin, & Grogan-Kaylor, 1995) and multiple health problems (Clausen, et al., 1998; Rubin, et al., 2005; Simms & Halfon, 1994; United States General Accounting Office, 1995). Also, children entering foster care have a history of difficult birth circumstances: exceptionally high rates of low birth weight, birth abnormality, no prenatal care, and families with three or more children (National Survey of Child and Adolescent Well-Being, 2005; Needell & Barth, 1998).

Age Distribution

We should also note the changing age distribution of children in out-of-home care and the consequent impact on service delivery. The proportion of adolescents in care, in particular, increased rapidly in the 1980s, as the permanency planning movement initially resulted in keeping younger children out of care, reuniting them with their biological families following placement, or placing them in adoption or other permanent plans (Maluccio, et al., 1990, p. 6). Adolescents still constitute a major group in the foster care population and they represent three different groups: those who were placed at an early age and have remained in the same foster home; those who were placed at an early age and have been moving from one placement to another; and those who were placed for the first time as teenagers, usually because of their behavioral or relationship problems.

Many youth enter foster care as adolescents—only a small fraction grow up in foster care any more (Wulczyn & Brunner-Hislop, 2001). In recent years, the greatest growth in foster care has resulted from an influx of very young children. Children from birth to one are the single largest group of children entering foster care—in some jurisdictions representing as much as 25 percent of all children who enter foster care (Wulczyn, Barth, Yuan, Harden, & Landsverk, 2005). In fact, 23 percent of all children admitted to foster care were 1 year of age or younger in 2006 (U.S. DHHS, 2008; Wulczyn, Harden, & Goerge, 1997). As Berrick, Needell, Barth, and Jonson-Reid (1998) explain in their extensive analysis of data from a range of studies, child welfare services, policies and laws have historically paid limited attention to the unique developmental needs and characteristics of pre-school children, especially infants; the emphasis has been on school age children and on undifferentiated services and programs. This pattern has been reflected in federal and state laws, notably the Adoption Assistance and Child Welfare Act of 1980 (Public Law 96-272). For example, this pioneering federal legislation set a maximum of 18 months for making a permanent plan for a child coming to the attention of the child welfare services, thus overlooking the potentially destructive impact of temporary foster care placement on infants and other young children. (Conversely, the tighter time limits in the more recently enacted ASFA may not adequately address the needs of older children and youths who enter foster care.)

When the above legislation was enacted nearly two decades ago, the greatest concern was about the plight of older children who had traditionally been placed in unstable, unplanned, long-term foster care that failed to promote their development. Understandably, the emphasis then was on the need of many of these youths for stability and permanence. In recent years, as mentioned above, there has also been a dramatic increase in the number of very young children coming to the attention of the child welfare services, including infants placed in foster care, as a result of such societal problems as poverty, homelessness, family violence, child abuse and neglect, and substance abuse.

Such an increase has served to underscore the inadequacy of existing laws, policies, and services. As a result, researchers, practitioners, administrators, and policy-makers have been challenged to serve young children in a more discriminating and responsive fashion and in accordance with their developmental needs. In particular, there has been further attention to the following question, which Wald raised over three decades ago: "How can we build in *developmental knowledge* to make the laws more sophisticated and more likely to serve the best interests of children" (Wald, 1975, p. 678). In this connection, Silver, et al. (1999) offer a comprehensive guide for professionals working with and on behalf of young children in foster care. In addition, Berrick, et al. (1998) formulate ways of improving child welfare services by explicitly building a developmental perspective into child welfare research, policy, and practice; effectively using knowledge about child development to propose laws and policies pertaining to child protection; and leading the way toward redesigning child welfare services for very young children by taking into account their unique needs and qualities and developmental processes.

Some of this emphasis is slowing bearing policy fruit, as the Child Abuse Prevention and Treatment Act reforms of 2001 called for the referral of children who experience substantiated maltreatment to be referred to early intervention (a.k.a. IDEA Part C) services so that they could receive developmental screening and intervention.

Gay and Lesbian Children and Youths

Nearly two decades ago, a special committee of the Child Welfare League of America called attention to the needs of gay and lesbian children and youths in the foster care services:

> Because of negative societal portrayals, many gay and lesbian youths live a life of isolation, alienation, depression and fear. As a result, they are beset by recurring crises disproportionate to their numbers in the child welfare services (Child welfare League of America, 1991, p. 2).

Although there is beginning attention to their situations and needs, gay and lesbian children and youths continue to be poorly understood and underserved. Ongoing challenges for practitioners include appreciating the uniqueness of gay and lesbian adolescent development; helping the adolescents to negotiate life within a hostile environment; helping them to confront the consequences of breakdown of the family services and the lack of family support; and understanding the rights of lesbian and gay parents in regard to child custody and visitation (Mallon, 1997, 1999; Stein, 1996; Wilber, Ryan, & Marksamer, 2006; Wornoff & Mallon, 2006).

Others have noted that many of these young people have a remarkable capacity for resilience (Savin-Williams, 1995). In an in-depth study of fifty-four gay and lesbian young people placed in out-of-home care in Los Angeles, New York, and Toronto, Mallon (1998) found that most were marginalized and struggling to function in society. On the basis of this study as well as other investigations, Mallon (1999) offers a number of recommendations for meeting the needs of these young people, including family foster care with gay and lesbian adults as foster parents and group homes designed for gay and lesbian adolescents for whom existing group home programs are not adequate.

Licensing lesbians or gay men as foster parents remains a controversial topic in child welfare in many states (Ricketts, 1991; Ricketts & Achtenberg, 1989). The Child Welfare League of America also recommends ongoing education and training for foster parents, child welfare workers, and often professionals (Wilber, et al., 2006). Mallon (2007) notes that these and other groups need to have a good understanding of the impact of societal stigmatization of gay and lesbian individuals and their families and to develop basic competence for preserving and supporting families and for the establishment of appropriate gay/lesbian-affirming child welfare services.

Children and Families of Color: Racial Disparity, Disproportionality, and Other Practice Issues in Foster Care

The Color of Foster Care

On September 30, 2006, approximately 3 in 5 of the 510,000 children living in foster care placements were children of color, although children of color represented only 42 percent of the child population in the United States. [2] This topic has become a central concern of child welfare programs and related advocates and funders because of the possibility that the disproportionality of some ethnic groups might indicate that the CWS policies, decision making, or service provision related to placement into out of home care are biased and unfair. Further, the hope is that by identifying patterns of ethnic and racial involvement in out-of-home care, additional strategies for providing more culturally competent services will be found so that children of all races and ethnicities will have equal access to family-sensitive, safe, and permanent service. This includes studying the different kinds of dynamics found at key decision-making stages (Dunbar & Barth, 2007), such as decision to place, reunify, or adopt a child (Hill, 2006, 2007; Kohl, 2007; Wulczyn, Zeidman, & Svirsky, 1997).

In this section, we discuss the basic rates of disproportionality of placement into out-of-home care for five major ethnic/racial groups in relation to their representation in the general population and find that African American and Native American children are over represented and white non-Hispanic and Asian children are underrepresented. Hispanic children when viewed nationally are represented in out of home care at about the rate of their representation in the general population, but in certain states and communities are over-represented in foster care. [3]

- Thirty-three percent (166,482) of the children in foster care were *African American* although African American children make up only 15 percent of the U.S. child population. African Americans were disproportionately represented in the child welfare services at a rate of 2.21:1 (33.21/15).

- Two percent (10,617) of the children in foster care were *American Indian or Alaskan Native*, but American Indian and Alaska Native children make up only 1 percent of the U.S. child population. American Indians and Alaska Natives were disproportionately over represented in the child welfare services at a rate of 2.12:1 (2.12/1).
- Nineteen percent (93,996) of the children in foster care were *Hispanic/ Latino*, but Latinos make up 20 percent of the U.S. child population. Latinos were disproportionately underrepresented in the child welfare services at a rate of 0.94:1 (18.75/20). Note, however, that in some states and communities, the proportion of Hispanic/Latino children in care is much higher than their proportion in the general population in that community.
- Forty-two percent (208,537) of the children in foster care were *non-Hispanic white*, while white children make up 58 percent of the U.S. child population. Whites were disproportionately underrepresented in the child welfare services at a rate of 0.72:1 (41.61/58).
- One percent (2,973) of the children in foster care were *non-Hispanic Asian*, while Asian children represented 4 percent of the U.S. child population. Asians were disproportionately underrepresented in the child welfare services at a rate of 0.15:1 (0.59/4). [4]

Maltreatment Rates: Reporting, Screening, and Investigation

Underlying rates of child abuse are very difficult to determine, which creates substantial difficulties for understanding whether children from different racial ethnic groups really need to be placed into out-of-home care or whether they may have been placed inappropriately. There are no statistically significant differences in overall maltreatment rates between black and white families, according to three national incidence studies (Hill, 2006). African American communities actually may have lower rates of child maltreatment than Caucasian communities, after controlling for differences in education, employment, and urbanicity (Ards, 1992; Korbin, Coulton, Chard, Platt-Houston, & Su, 1998). At the same time, African American children are between 1.8 and 3 times as likely to die from homicide or to experience a fatal injury—which very often is perpetrated by a family member (Bernard, Paulozzi, & Wallace, 2007). Also, African American mothers, involved with child welfare services, report that they use much more severe parenting methods and self-report much higher rates of maltreatment than parents of other races/ethnicities involved with child welfare services (Kohl, 2007).

Some research studies have found race to be an important factor in making reports to child protective services hotlines. Additionally, many public and private hospitals have over reported abuse and neglect among African Americans while they underreport maltreatment among Caucasians. Some earlier research studies suggest that race alone, or in interaction with other factors, is strongly related to the decision to investigate a call made to the child protective services hotline (Sedlak & Schultz, 2001). In contrast, more recent analyses from the NSCAW study have found little evidence of race effects because there are enough data to control for background effects, such as measures of family functioning and problems. So additional studies are needed that control for a variety of factors such as family structure, employment, urbanicity, and income level as a recent study found that disparity rates differed according to many of these factors (Wulczyn & Lery, 2007).

What Causes Disproportional Representation of Different Racial and Ethnic Groups?

What are the reasons for disproportional representation of children of color in the child welfare services? What is the "most appropriate" representation of any group of children in the child welfare services? Theories about causation can be classified into three types: parent and family risk factors, community risk factors, and organizational and systemic factors (McCrory, Ayers-Lopez, & Green, 2006; National Association of Public Child Welfare Administrators, 2006; U.S. Administration for Children and Families, 2003). The next sections describe each major reason, but it is important to note that risk factors, community factors, organizational factors, and services factors are often interrelated and do not operate in isolation.

According to theories about *parent and family risk factors*, children of color are overrepresented in the child welfare services because they have disproportionate needs. They are more likely to have risk factors, such as unemployment, teen parenthood, poverty, substance abuse, incarceration, domestic violence, mental illness, etc., that result in high levels of child maltreatment.[5]

Proponents of *community factors* assert that overrepresentation has less to do with race or class and more with residing in neighborhoods and communities that have many risk factors, such as high levels of poverty, welfare assistance, unemployment, homelessness, single-parent families, and crime and street violence that make residents more visible to surveillance from public authorities.[6] In contrast, theories about *organizational and systemic factors* contend that racial overrepresentation results from: the decision-making processes of CPS agencies, cultural insensitivity, and biases of workers, governmental policies, and institutional or structural racism.[7]

Summary

Much more needs to be accomplished, however, in the field of child welfare in response to the needs and qualities of Native Americans and other ethnic-minority children and families. For instance, greater attention must be paid to use of flexible program funds to address housing and other environmental needs that prevent family reunification or provide a reason for child removal. Agencies also need to take a closer look at their cultural or ethnic competency, both as organizational cultures and in terms of staff recruitment and training (Anderson, Ryan, & Leashore, 1997; Nash, 1999; Pinderhughes, 1997; and Stovall & Krieger, 1990). In this regard, the Child Welfare League of America has developed a guide to assist agencies in their move toward cultural competence (Nash, 1999). There can also be more extensive use of certain forms of other family-based services that are showing promise for meeting the special needs of ethnic-minority and other families through the provision of clinical and concrete services in the home setting (Fong, 1994; Kirk & Griffith, 2008; Kirk, Griffith, & Gogan, 2004).

In the face of expanding need, recruitment as well as retention of foster parents is becoming increasingly difficult (See, for example, Barbell & Freundlich, 2001; Pasztor & Wynne, 1995; Rindfleisch, Bean, & Denby, 1998; and Rykus & Hughes, 1998). The continuing shortage of foster families results from many factors, including the aging of current foster parents and the growing dropout rate of foster families, many of which are typically dissatisfied with the child welfare services. The "volunteer" labor pool, of which foster parenting is part, has been decreasing because of the increase in single-parent families and the movement of women out of the home and into the paid work force. In addition, the demands on foster families have increased substantially, because they are called upon to deal with youngsters with special problems and needs; moreover, foster parents increasingly experience a lack of supports and rewards in the face of the difficult job that they carry out. When projects have provided additional support, foster parent retention has improved (personal communication with Patti Chamberlain regarding Project Keep, described in Chamberlain, et al., 2006).

Noteworthy in this connection is the periodic publicity about abuse of foster children by foster parents—a phenomenon that creates considerable controversy—but about which little is known. Allegations of maltreatment involving foster families are of continuing concern, due to the need to protect already vulnerable children from mistreatment; agency and worker concern regarding legal liability; perceived problems of recruitment and retention of foster homes; and perceived harm to foster children, foster parents, and other foster family members owing in large part to how maltreatment allegations are handled. However, this subject has received relatively little attention from researchers, even though it has been identified as an emerging problem since at least the mid-1980s by foster parent organizations and others (DePanfilis & Girvin, 2005; Poertner, Bussey, & Fluke, 1999).

A study of an urban foster care population echoes earlier findings: reports of maltreatment in foster homes comprise a minuscule portion—1.1 percent—of all maltreatment reports; foster homes are at much higher risk of report than the general population; stricter definitions of maltreatment in foster care may influence report and substantiation rates; and foster homes have a lower substantiation rate—20 percent versus 35 percent—than the general public (Benedict, Zuravin, Brandt, & Abbey, 1994). The National Survey of Child and Adolescent Well-Being finds that children in foster care have substantiated abuse report rates that are about 9 percent during an 18 month period, but that the abuse was rarely by the foster parent or in the foster home, per se (it was more often by a parent during a pre-reunification visit or by another adult away from the foster home). Substantiated maltreatment by foster parents occurred in .75 percent of cases (Kohl, Gibbons, & The NSCAW Research Group, 2005). In light of the limited information and controversial nature of maltreatment of children in foster care, it is clear that further research is needed on its nature, extent, and impact. There is, in particular, a need to support the well-being of foster children and their foster families when abuse is alleged. Otherwise, seasoned foster parents will give up their career choice because of frustration with the agency response to them following an allegation against them by a youth in foster care.

Additional demonstration projects are needed to disseminate knowledge about foster parenting in the context of the contemporary crisis in child welfare. Much more remains to be done to recognize explicitly the central roles of foster parents in achieving the goals of foster care. Foster parents must be involved more fully as an integral part of the services team, as partners with agencies and social workers. And society must be more willing to provide them with the supports and services they need to do the job. It is a national tragedy that we spend more per day to house our pets in kennels than we allocate to caring for our next generation of citizens.

Training of Social Workers and Foster Parents

Another issue concerns the education and training of social workers and foster parents. By now it is widely recognized in the child welfare field that foster parents and social workers, as well as other service providers, need specialized training for practice in case situations involving family foster care. In most agencies, however, training tends to be fragmented and irregular. Extensive discussion of the purposes, content, and methods of necessary training is beyond the scope of this book. We would, however, like to stress several themes:

First, social workers, as well as foster parents, can best be helped to enhance their skills through a competency-based or performance-based approach to education and training (Hughes & Rykus, 1989). Such an approach stresses the development of practice-based competencies in the design, delivery, and evaluation of training in a specialized area of practice. There is considerable attention to selection of appropriate instructional methods, which typically include self-instructional materials, coaching, use of learning contracts, experiential exercises, and small-group interactions. Curriculum development is organized around what practitioners need to know and is based on a thorough analysis of the knowledge, skills, and attributes required of staff members (Warsh, et al., 1994, p. 6). Moreover, training is developed concerning areas identified as having highest priority for effective practice.[8]

Second, training opportunities need to be offered within a supportive agency environment—an environment that encourages professional development; treats "trainees" as adult learners and involves them in assessment of their training needs and selection of appropriate learning opportunities; and offers incentives and rewards such as career ladders, certification, and salary increments corresponding with increased knowledge and skills.

Third, foster care practice requires that social workers and foster parents have knowledge and competencies in a range of areas, including:

- child development;
- philosophy and practice of permanency planning;
- impact of separation and placement on children and their families;
- behavior management;
- appreciation of human diversity and sensitivity to issues of ethnicity, race, gender, sexual orientation, and socio-cultural aspects; and
- involvement of children and their biological parents in decision-making and goal planning.

Fourth, as practice in family foster care has evolved during the last decade, training programs have had to address a range of newer practice strategies and principles, in such areas as ecologically oriented assessment; goal planning that emphasizes contracting with clients and service providers; use of behaviorally specific, time-limited case plans; and case management. In addition, training materials are increasingly available in relation to practice with children and parents having special needs in such areas as HIV/AIDS, substance abuse, and family violence. (See, for example, NSCAW [2005] and training materials for domestic violence from the National Conference of Juvenile and Family Court Judges [2006].)

Placement Disruption and Other Forms of Placement Change

Prevalence

Some foster care researchers have focused on the phenomenon of disruption of foster home placement, that is, the need to replace a child, which is the child welfare literature is commonly (but we think erroneously) described as *breakdown*. Research in this area is limited but has grown in the past ten years. As Usher, Randolph, and Gogan (1999, p. 34) note:

> Further research concerning placement disruption should give greater consideration to the representativeness of study samples and move beyond simply counting the number of placements children experience.

In a review of related research from Australia, the United States, and the United Kingdom, Berridge and Cleaver (1987) indicated that breakdown rates have been reported as high as 50 percent of placements. In their own study, Berridge and Cleaver found breakdown rates in different agencies ranging from 6 to 20 percent within 1 year and from 20 to 48 percent within 5 years. In a study in the United States, Fein, et al. (1983) found that 50 percent of the cases of children placed in permanent foster care disrupted within 1.5 years. However, this was a small sample of fourteen children, most of whom were teenagers. In the comprehensive study of the Casey Family Programs mentioned earlier, which involved nearly six hundred children, (24.6 percent) of the placements had apparently failed, as the children ran away or were returned to the courts (Fanshel, et al., 1990).

In a California study, it was found that nearly half of all children who entered non-kinship foster care prior to age six and stayed for at least four years had three or more foster care placements during their stay (Needell, Webster, Barth, Armijo, and Fox, 1998). That means nearly one placement per year! This rate is lower (30 percent) for young children in kinship care but is 75 percent for children in specialized foster care and 85 percent for young children in group homes. (It should be recognized that some children in higher levels of foster care started off in lower levels of care and accumulated some of their placement count in those settings.) For example, Wilson (2000) found that 63 percent of youth in Washington state foster care had 1 or 2 placements, while 77 percent of the youth in James's (2004) California study had 3 or more placements. These variations illustrate the need to account for the amount of time spent in care when comparing the number of placements across samples.

Similarly, the number of placements varies widely across alumni and across agency sub-samples. Furthermore, in one study of three child welfare agencies (two states and one voluntary agency), about one-third (31.9 percent) of the alumni experienced three or fewer placements, but an equal percentage (32.3 percent) experienced eight or more placements throughout their child welfare career (see Pecora, et al., 2005). While over one-half of the sample had five or fewer placements (including one-fifth with only one or two placements), slightly more than one-fifth had ten or more placements. The cumulative percent line in Figure 8.1 indicates that approximately 95 percent of the sample had 15 or fewer placements, while the remaining 5 percent had as many as 31 placements (Pecora, Kessler, Williams, et al., 2010).[9] Clearly, *stable* or *permanent* are not words we would use to describe long-term foster care.

Although we cannot believe that all of these placements are necessary, it is difficult to know what these findings mean, because some placements are useful for such reasons as reuniting children with their siblings, finding potential adoptive homes, and attaining a better fit between children and families. Indeed, how should we view the breakdown of a placement? Also, even unplanned changes may not always be an experience with drastic and negative consequences, as generally assumed. Aldgate and Hawley (1986) contend that foster home breakdown should be redefined as a disruption in the placement and constructively exploited in the process of arriving at a long-term plan for the child. For example, according to these authors, workers can help the child, birth parents, and foster parents learn more about themselves as well as learn new skills through the experience of disruption.

However, there is growing evidence that we should minimize placement change for at least these five reasons, as presented by Pecora (2007). First, it *can minimize child pain and trauma.* Children entering out-of-home care undergo enormous changes. Apart from being separated from their family, many of these children are not able to maintain relationships with friends and community members (Johnson, Yoken, & Voss, 1995). Changing homes because of placement disruption compounds the immeasurable sense of loss these children must face by leaving behind relationships again and again. Festinger's (1983) landmark study of 277 alumni of care, entitled *No One Ever Asked Us,* revealed that most alumni experienced placement changes as unsettling and confusing. When rating their perception of foster care, the alumni's satisfaction was inversely correlated with the number of placements they had experienced. More research is needed that builds on the personal perspectives of the youth in care (Unrau, 2007).

Second, *placement stability increases child attachment and lessens behavior and mental health disorders.* Wulczyn and Cogan (2002, p. 2) cited an important child development-related reason: "Multiple placements are thought to have a pernicious impact on the development of attachment to primary caregivers, an early developmental milestone thought to be essential for the achievement of later developmental tasks (e.g. Lieberman, 1987; Provence, 1989; Fahlberg, 1991)." While the concept of child and adolescent attachment to adults is not an exact science and we have much to learn about helping children build new positive attachments, many youth and foster care alumni have commented on how important it is to minimize placement change and to be placed with siblings as a placement stabilizing strategy (James, Monn, Palinkas, & Leslie, 2008; Leathers, 2005, Herrick & Piccus, 2005).

In addition, various researchers have found that multiple placements may lead to child behavior problems (Newton, Litrownik & Landsverk, 2000) and mental health problems (Hussey & Guo, 2005; Rutter & Sroufe, 2000).[10] Indeed, Ryan & Testa (2004) found that these changes were linked with decreased school performance and delinquent behavior of males, and Pecora, Williams, Kessler, et al. (2003) found that lower placement change was associated with foster care alumni success, including high school completion, in a sample of twenty- to fifty-one-year-old alumni.

Third, *placement stability decreases school mobility and increases academic achievement.* While many child welfare staff and some new state laws try to minimize school change when a placement changes, in too many situations the child is forced to change schools. School mobility has been implicated as a clear risk factor for dropout (Rumberger & Larson, 1998; Rumberger, 2003). David Kerbow's (1996) longitudinal study of school mobility in Chicago found that it acted as both an individual and school level risk factor for low achievement. Highly mobile students fell almost a year behind in achievement by sixth grade. Non-mobile students in schools with high mobility rates were half a year behind by sixth grade. While the highest mobility rates (31 percent) were among children of single parent families, it is notable that the second highest rate (25 percent) was observed for children in households with no biological parent present (Stone, 2007). But the relationship among these variables is complex.

Given the deleterious impacts of school mobility, many have questioned to what extent this may be a particular problem with foster children (Conger & Finkelstein, 2003). The relationship between placement transfers and several academic outcomes has been discussed above. Two recent studies control for both placement and school transfers on selected academic outcomes. Conger and Rebeck's (2001) study actually found increases in attendance after school transfers. School transfers were unrelated to reading achievement but had a small negative effect on mathematics achievement. A stronger predictor of school achievement was school attendance. Burley and Halpern (2001) found that school transfers were negatively related to test scores for third and sixth grade students, but not ninth graders (not controlling for prior school performance and attendance) and high school completion. These results suggest that nature and quality of school transfers matters—that school transfers may have different relationships with different academic outcomes and, not surprisingly, that attendance loss may at least partially explain negative effects of school transfers among foster youth (Stone, 2007, p. 154).

Fourth, placement stability *maximizes continuity in services, decreases foster parent stress, and lowers program costs.* Placement changes disrupt services provision, stress foster parents (thereby lowering retention rates), take up precious worker time, and create administrative-related disruptions. Because we know so little about what causes placement change, the field is less able to predict and therefore prevent them. And yet the dynamics of these changes are important for other reasons. For example, adolescents who were placed alone after a history of joint sibling placements were at greater risk for placement disruption than those who were placed with a consistent number of siblings while in foster care. This association was mediated by a weaker sense of integration and belonging in the foster home among youth placed alone with a history of sibling placements (Leathers, 2005).

Fifth, *placement stability increases the likelihood that a child will establish an enduring positive relationship with a caring adult.* Clearly, the more stability a child has, the more likely it is that the child will be able to establish a stronger and more varied network of social support and enduring relationships with

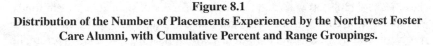

Figure 8.1
Distribution of the Number of Placements Experienced by the Northwest Foster Care Alumni, with Cumulative Percent and Range Groupings.

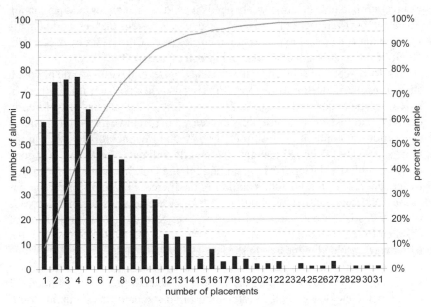

Source: Williams, J., Herrick, M., Pecora, P. J., & O'Brien, K. (2009). Working paper No. 4: Placement history and foster care experience. Retrieved July 6, 2009 from www.casey.org.

adults who care about him or her (Pecora, 2007, pp. 3-5). Much more research is needed about the cause and preventative mechanisms for placement change (Barth, Lloyd, Green, James, Leslie, & Landsverk, 2007).

Conclusion

Current Status of Family Foster Care

As discussed in Chapter 3, as a result of these and other related developments, by the 1970s there was much pressure to reform child welfare services, in large measure as a result of the landmark Oregon Project, which contributed greatly to the promotion of *permanency planning* as a large-scale national movement (Pike, 1976), a movement that has continued to evolve with attention to reunification (Pine, 1986) and close examination of the path to impermanence and a broad range of alternatives (Kerman, Maluccio, & Freundlich, 2008).

Despite the enactment of public policies such as the federal permanency planning law of 1980 (P.L. 96-272) and the Adoption and Safe Families Act of

1997 (P.L. 105-89) as well as the infusion of federal, state, and private funds, the number of children in foster care and the extent and complexity of the problems faced by them and their families continue to grow. It is, therefore, no exaggeration to note that foster care needs new ideas, resources, and personnel. Some authors even speak of a crisis in foster care—a crisis that is reported in the mass media and argued in professional circles (e.g., Curtis, Grady, & Kendall, 1999; Pew Commission on Children in Foster Care, 2004).

Yet, foster care must be understood as having several parts—some of which show positive indicators of a more family-focused approach to services. In several of the major states (e.g., California, Illinois) the number of children in conventional foster care has actually decreased in recent years, with increasing proportions of children in kinship foster care and treatment foster care. In the large states, the likelihood that any given child will enter foster care has gone up only modestly during the 1990s, although the likelihood of a child leaving foster care has decreased, too, resulting in the increase in the foster care population (Wulczyn, Harden, & Goerge, 1997). However, most of that decrease in exit rates is attributable to kinship care, suggesting that the proportion of children living with family is growing. Fortunately, the massive growth in the foster care caseload witnessed in the late 1980s that led the Select Committee on Children, Youth and Families (1989) to predict that the foster care census would now be 850,000 (by the year 2000) has abated. In New York state, for example, the incidence of all children entering foster care was six in one thousand in 1989, but in the late 1990s was less than three in one thousand (Wulczyn, Harden, & Goerge, 1997). In California, the foster care census topped out above 108,000 in 1998 but was down to 76,000 as of October, 2007 (http://cssr.berkeley.edu/cwscmsreports/Pointintime/fostercare/childwel/CWresponse.asp?data=frequencies%2Fdata&county=s&date=jul1998&demo=P0; retrieved October 1, 2007).

This does not mean that there are not massive challenges ahead for providers of out-of-home care for children. Recruiting and retaining quality foster parents is a necessity for effective child welfare services; having well-trained child welfare workers who understand the importance of permanency for children and options for achieving it is essential; flexibility in funding and approach is central to responding to so many diverse child and family needs is critical; and so is having adequate resources to help families and to accommodate a rapidly changing work environment for child welfare workers.

The challenges are evidenced in such areas as the typical pattern of dealing mostly with emergencies while the situations of other children and families deteriorate; the attrition rates of child welfare personnel, including foster parents; the substantial number of children who are further abused by the very foster care services in which they were placed because of abuse and neglect in their own homes; and the call for returning to a previously discontinued orphanage care (McKenzie, 1998; Pew Commission on Children in Foster Care, 2004).

At a time that work with birth families and relatives is being reemphasized, some foster care workers and foster parents are too overwhelmed to respond. One tragic indicator of this crisis is the high proportion of children in placement whose unmet cognitive, affective, and physical needs are interfering with their ability to learn and develop in a positive manner, as indicated earlier in this chapter.

Foster care services have improved in many ways in recent years, yielding more family-focused care, shorter lengths of stay, higher adoption rates, and practical approaches to working in a more preventive capacity with children in care and permanency planning are being developed (e.g., the *3-5-7* model summarized by Henry, [2005]; treating maltreated preschool aged children: Fisher, Gunnar, Chamberlain & Reid, [2000]). Yet, the problems embedded in child welfare services are evident in many places throughout the country, consistent with what Kamerman and Kahn (1990) argued from their national study of social services to children, youths, and families. While noting that there are some exemplary programs and practices, these authors found that the efforts of social services remain largely inadequate throughout the country:

> Available delivery systems, interventive methods, and line staffs are not equal to the legitimate and appropriate tasks which lie ahead for the social services. There is a need—on the basis of adequate resource commitments—for innovation and testing, for sharing and exchange, and for ongoing efforts to respecify mission and infrastructure. (p. 147)

Future Directions

In reflecting about the evolution and status of family foster care, readers may find themselves wishing for a set of more straightforward responses and solutions. Realities, such as resource limitations and the complexities of human behavior, make such solutions less viable. But high quality family foster care is still a dream worth pursuing. A body of knowledge and clinical insights exists and can be applied so that the services may serve vulnerable children and families more effectively than at present, especially as we listen to—and learn from—parents and children themselves.

Some state and voluntary agencies are striving to address these concerns with innovative strategies such as family based services and special reunification programs that are supported by a mix of public and private funding. But a more concerted effort at the legislative, policy, and programmatic levels must be made to maximize the quality of family foster care. Can we, as a society, rise to the challenge? As we reform our services, it is important that we listen to the perspectives of birth families and their kin, as discussed in the next chapter on family reunification and kinship care.

To do so, however, family foster care must become an integral part of a comprehensive network of services. These must include extensive family supports, especially concrete services such as housing, employment opportunities, health care, schooling, income assistance, and recreational services, along with substance abuse counseling, mental health services, and education for parenting must also be part of the network. As addressed in Chapters 7 and 12, such services would complement a more variegated, flexible network of out-of-home programs that can support families for varying periods of time by providing respite and a safe haven for children. If we are committed to the principle that no child's future is expendable, we have no choice but to be part of the efforts to improve family foster care services.

In addition, foster care must attract, support, and encourage adequately trained, supervised, and rewarded personnel, especially foster parents—our front line of help for many children and families. The major goal of child development within a family setting must be articulated and reinforced through program, policy, and supervision. And organizational supports must be maintained, particularly by providing family-centered services, placing emphasis on services to clients while reducing paperwork and other bureaucratic constraints, and advocating for flexible and sufficient funding at the federal and state levels.

Notes

1. For information on children with special needs and/or from multi-problem families, see Anderson, et al. (1998); Berrick et al. (1998); Dore (1999); Kupsinel & Dubski (1999); NSCAW (2005).
2. This section is, principally, adapted from the Casey Disproportionality fact sheet that was developed by Peter Pecora, Anne Havalchak, and Dennette Derezotes. See www. casey.org. Statistics drawn from U.S. Department of Health and Human Services (DHHS) (September 2006). *The AFCARS (Adoption and Foster Care Reporting System) Report.* Retrieved January 19, 2007 from http://www.acf.hhs.gov/programs/cb/stats_research/afcars/tar/report13.htm; The Annie E. Casey Foundation (2005). KIDS COUNT State level Data On-line. Retrieved May 19, 2008 from http://www.aecf.org/kidscount/sld/profile_results.jsp?r=1&d=1&c=9&p=5&x=146&y=5.
3. The data for Hispanic/Latino youth are more sparse (Derezotes, Poertner, & Testa, 2004) but there is some evidence which indicate that Latinos are overrepresented in selected states and counties at various stages of CPS decision-making:
    1. Hill (2005) compiled data showing that Latinos are overrepresented (i.e., have disproportionality rates that exceed 1.00) in ten states (see Table 4 in Hill, 2005).
    2. Hill's recent analysis of NCANDS/AFCARS state-level data shows Latinos are overrepresented in the State of Minnesota at both the investigation (1.33) and substantiation (1.33) stages, but not at the foster care placement stage (1.00). See Tables 6B, 6C and 6D in that report (Hill, 2007).
    3. County-level NCANDS/AFCARS data show Latinos are: (a) overrepresented in Ramsey County, MN at the investigation (1.13) and substantiation (1.25) stages; (b) overrepresented in King County, WA at the investigation (1.56) and substantiation (1.56) stages; and (c) overrepresented in Bexar County, TX (San Antonio) at all three stages: investigation (1.13), substantiation (1.13) and placement in foster care (1.13). See Tables 16, 17 and 20 in Hill (2007).

4. The Relative Disparity Rate or Relative Rate Index compares the likelihood of one group experiencing an event to the likelihood of another group experiencing the same event. Source: Barbara Needell, *"Race/Ethnic Disproportionality and Disparity in Child Welfare: New Views, New Measures"* power point presentation available at http://cssr.berkeley.edu/CWSCMSreports/presentations/.

5. Barth (2005); Chaffin, Kelleher & Hollenberg (1996); Walker, Zangrillo & Smith (1994); Wells & Tracy (1996).

6. Coulton & Pandey (1992); Drake & Pandey (1990); Garbarino & Sherman (1980).

7. Bent-Goodley (2003); Everett, Chipungu & Leashore (1991); McRoy (2004); Morton (1999); Roberts (2002).

8. See, for example, Zlotnik, Rome, and DePanfilis (1998) for discussion of education for child welfare practice in general; Anderson et al. (1997) for training child welfare workers for practice with children and families of color; Rykus and Hughes (1998), for consideration of training programs for foster parents and social workers; and Warsh, Maluccio, and Pine (1994) for suggestions on training social workers for family reunification practice.

9. Because Casey alumni spent more time in foster care, they had significantly more placements than the state alumni (an average of seven for Casey versus six for the state). Some placements for the Casey alumni occurred while in state care, as the time between the first out-of-home placement and entry into Casey averaged 3.5 years (median = 2.3 years). Almost one-third of Casey alumni (32.9 percent) were in placement for 4 years or more before entering Casey. Over the child's entire time in foster care, youth in the Casey services had more stability as measured by placements per year. Alumni averaged 1.2 placements per year, with the Casey alumni having a rate one-third lower than that of the state alumni. Accordingly, when placement change rate was trichotomized, a smaller percentage of Casey alumni were in the group with a high rate (defined here as 1.23 or more placement changes per year). This means that, within a services designed to provide stability, nearly half of the State sample and one-quarter of the Casey sample experienced an average of nearly five placements every four years (Pecora, Kessler, Williams, et al., 2009).

10. Barber and Defrabbrio (2004) in a study in Australia found that most children in foster care display improvements in their psychological adjustment while in care. Surprisingly, these improvements can occur despite frequent placement disruption during the first eight months in care. Beyond the eight-month point, however, placement disruption is associated with psychological deterioration. The basic explanation for this finding concerns change in the *reasons* for placement move up to and beyond the eight-month point. Many children change placement in the first eight months for positive reasons, such as to get closer to their families or to go to a better school. Beyond the eight-month point, however, those children who continue moving tend to do so because their foster placements break down. In other words, the concentration of difficult or distressed children is greater among those who move around for more than eight months than among those who move around for eight months or less (Knott, & Barber, 2004).

For Further Information

Child Welfare League of America. (2007). *Best practice guidelines for services to LGBT youth in out-of-home care*. Washington, DC: Author. This book contains the first-ever set of comprehensive guidelines for effectively serving LGBT youth in state care. These guidelines can be used to develop policies and practices governing the care of LGBT youth, create training materials for providers, or strategic plans for improving services to LGBT youth services-wide. CWLA web site: http://www. cwla.org/pubs/pubdetails.asp?PUBID=10951.

Courtney, M.E., Dworsky, A., Ruth, G., Keller, T., Havlicek, J. & Bost, N. (2005). *Midwest Evaluation of Adult Functioning of Former Foster Youth: Outcomes at Age 19.* Chicago, IL: University of Chicago, Chapin Hall Center for Children.

Derezotes, D., Poertner, J. & Testa, M. (Eds.). (2005). *Race matters in child welfare. The overrepresentation of African American children in the services.* Washington, DC: Child Welfare League of America. A series of articles on research, policies, and programs affecting African-American families and children coming to the attention of the child welfare services.

Haskins, R. Wulczyn, F. & Webb, M (Eds.). (2007). *Child protection research from the National Survey of Child and Adolescent Well-Being.* Washington, DC: Brookings. One of the most current national sources of demographic and outcome data available.

Kerman, B., Maluccio, A.N., & Freundlich, M. (2008). *Achieving permanence for older children and youth in foster care.* New York: Columbia University Press. Integrative discussion of the philosophy, theory, practice issues, and research of permanency planning for children and youth.

Mallon, G. P. (2006). *Toolbox No. 3: Facilitating Permanency for Youth.* Washington DC: Child Welfare League of America. Practical strategies, case review prototypes, and other resources for helping youth achieve permanency.

Palmer, S.E. (1995). *Maintaining family ties - Inclusive practice in foster care.* Washington, DC: Child Welfare League of America. Building on an intensive study of social workers in two Canadian child protection agencies, the author delineates practice principles for helping children in foster care and their parents maintain their "connections" and cope with the impact of separation.

Roberts, D. (2002). *Shattered Bonds: The Color of Child Welfare. New York City:* Basic Books. An incisive discussion of the issues of racial disparity in child welfare.

9

Family Reunification and Kinship Care

Family reunification is often viewed as the most desired outcome of out-of-home placement of children and youths. Successful family reunification, however, requires a full range of efforts that are supported by well-grounded theory and that respond carefully to the needs of children and their families. This chapter offers a definition of reunification; outlines program design principles; reviews evaluative research; and examines the increasing use of formal and informal kinship care.

An Expanded Definition of Family Reunification

The theory, policy, and practice of family reunification have traditionally been based on the premise that children and youth in out-of-home care need to be either returned to their families of origin or placed in another permanent setting. We challenge that premise, here, even though this either-or orientation is supported by the legal framework of federal laws that have been reviewed in previous chapters. In particular, termination of parental rights is expected to be sought when families have been unable to care for children in their own homes, even though there may be a potentially beneficial relationship between parents and children and even when no other permanent family has been, or was likely to be, found.

There are, however, many parents who love their children and want a relationship to them, but are unable to be full-time caregivers. The children may also want a relationship with their biological parents even though they cannot live safely with them (Chapman, Wall, & Barth, 2004), The child welfare services response to these parents has often been to test them beyond their limits by returning their children home without significant after care services or to terminate their parental rights and forever sever their family bonds. Such an either-or orientation is too simplistic and not always in the best interests of the child or the families involved in foster care. In its place, a family reunification orientation is needed that embodies a time-limited but flexible approach to working with children in out-of-home care and their families—an approach that recognizes and meets children's and families' individual needs. This re-thinking of family reunification has led to the development of the following expanded definition:

> Family reunification is the planned process of safely reconnecting children in out-of-home care with their families by means of a variety of services and supports to the children, their families, and their foster parents or other service providers. *It aims to help each child and family to achieve and maintain, at any given time, their optimal level of reconnection—from full reentry of the child into the family system to other forms of contact, such as visiting, calling, or corresponding, that affirm the child's membership in the family, and to contact with the family even following termination of parental rights and responsibilities.* (Modified from Maluccio, Warsh, & Pine, 1993)

Such a view of family reunification suggests that a flexible approach to preserving family bonds by responding to each child's and family's individual qualities and needs. In particular, it calls for fully respecting human diversity, especially culture, race, and ethnicity, and involving the family and its kin through such approaches as family group decision making and provision of "wrap around" services, as considered in later chapters.

It should, of course, be acknowledged that there are situations in which children must be protected through temporary, or even permanent, separation from their parents and that families that adopt or assume guardianship also must have say about the circumstances under which the children in their families have contact with biological family members. Guidelines have been developed for identifying such situations, including those where a child has previously died due to abuse or neglect; cases involving sexual abuse when the abuser continues to reside in the child's home; and situations in which parents refuse to recognize the need for services, such as substance abuse treatment, despite repeated efforts on the part of agencies. Even in these extreme cases, however, attention paid to preserving as much of the child's family as possible may help support the child's well-being. In short, reunification can occur in a variety of ways—and differing degrees—beyond physical reconnection.

Underlying Principles and Guidelines

Practice Principles

Redefining family reunification leads to a number of principles and guidelines for family reunification policies, programs, practices, and training, as discussed below, drawing from Warsh, Maluccio, and Pine (1994, pp. 3-4). As a form of preserving families, reunification embodies (1) conviction about the role of the biological family as the preferred child-rearing unit, if at all possible; (2) recognition of the potential of most families to care for their children, if properly assisted; (3) awareness of the impact of separation and loss on children and parents; and (4) involvement, as appropriate, of any and all members of the child's family, including members of the extended family or others who, while not legally related, are considered by the child and themselves to be "family." As considered in Chapter 3, *family group conferences* can be used to promote involvement of the extended family in the care and protection of "at risk" children. Reunification practice is guided by an ecologically oriented, competence-centered perspective that emphasizes promoting family empowerment, engaging in advocacy and social action so as to achieve societal conditions and structures that enhance family functioning, reaching for—and building on—the strengths and potentialities of parents and other family members, involving parents as partners in the helping process, and providing needed services and supports. Children in care, biological families, foster families, and other caregivers, social workers, court-appointed special advocates, attorneys, parent aides, and other service providers constitute an ongoing partnership promoted by effective teamwork. The differential roles of all parties should be clearly spelled out and understood.

A commitment to early and consistent contact between the child and family is an essential ingredient in preparing for and maintaining a successful reunification. Child-family contact can serve as a laboratory in which both parties work on the problems that may have contributed to the need for placement and learn new ways to be together again. Finally, family reunification services should be offered for as long as they are needed to maintain the reconnection of a child with the family. For many families, intensive family reunification services may need to be followed by less intensive services. For a few families, some level of service may be necessary until the child is ready for independent living.

The reunification of children and their families is more likely to be successful when an agency articulates its mission through a comprehensive framework of policies, in line with the principles and guidelines delineated above. In addition, effective reunification programs involve the commitment of agency administrators to hiring social workers with a range of family reunification competencies, empowering them through appropriate decision-making authority and opportunities to further develop their skills, facilitating all aspects of service delivery, and continually seeking new directions and pursuing program improvements.

An agency context that supports family reunification practice needs to address numerous aspects in relation to agency policy, direct practice with children and families, collaboration with other systems, and staff development. As considered in detail elsewhere (Kerman, Maluccio, & Freundlich, 2008; Pine, Spath, & Gosteli, 2005; Warsh, Pine, & Maluccio, 1996, pp. 71-180), such a supportive context includes agency policies that, among other aspects, provide adequate resources for supporting practitioners in their outreach to children and families; promote collaboration with other community systems, including other child and family agencies, judicial and legal personnel, state and local legislators, and schools of social work; and offer ongoing staff development programs focusing on family reunification and directed not only to its workers but also to other service providers and community representatives. We need to consider, in particular, how to provide effective services for vulnerable families such as those coming to the attention of child welfare agencies, including parents battling comorbid conditions such as substance abuse and poverty or housing difficulties and mental health problems (Choi & Ryan, 2007).

Concurrent Planning

A continuing innovation in child and family welfare is concurrent planning, that is, working "towards family reunification while, at the same time, developing an alternative permanent plan" (Katz, 1999, p. 72). The concurrent planning model, pioneered in Washington state in the early 1980s, was specifically designed for very young children who were drifting in foster care due to their family's chronic pathology. As explained by Katz (1999, p. 72), one of its originators, the model "addresses this difficult-to-treat family constellation by combining vigorous family outreach, expedited timelines, and potentially permanent family foster care placements to improve the odds of timely permanency for very young children."

At its best, concurrent planning represents team decision-making involving professionals, as well as the child, the child's caregivers, birth parents, and extended family members. Its central purpose is accomplished through comprehensive assessment of the parent-child relationship, parental functioning and support systems; front loading of services in such areas as financial assistance, parenting skills, health and mental health, substance abuse, and domestic violence; and frequent staffing, including child, family, caregivers, and service providers. Katz (1999) delineates strategies for implementing this model, particularly by completing an early assessment of the family's likelihood of being reunited; establishing with the family clear timelines for timely permanency; vigorously promoting frequent parental visiting; and using written agreements. Katz also calls attention to a number of pitfalls in implementation, including failing to consider cultural differences; equating concurrent planning with adoption while minimizing reunification efforts; designing case plans that are not family centered; providing insufficient training to social workers, foster parents, and family members; and not collaborating adequately with other community agencies. Recently, there have been calls for research to better assess the results, and unintended consequences of this casework approach (D'Andrade, Frame, & Duerr-Berrick, 2006). Handling conflicting loyalties in children, increased tensions between workers and birth parents, scarcity of foster-adoption homes, and other challenges must be addressed if concurrent planning is to achieve its goals (D'Andrade, et al., 2006).

Dynamics of Family Reunification Services

In recent years, there has been increasing research on the processes and effectiveness of family reunification services. One of the most basic ways to gauge success is the number of youth who exit foster care by being reunified with family—53 percent (or 154,103) of the nation's children who left child welfare supervised out of home care for any reason in 2006, left care in order to return home (US DHHS, 2008). This does not mean that 53 percent of the children who enter foster care are reunified—in some age groups this is substantially higher and in some it is less, but this can only be determined by following children from entrance into care until their exit and requires the use of an "entry cohort." Recent analyses based on the Chapin Hall Multi-State Archive entry cohort data provide some significant insights about entrances, exits, reunifications, and reentries into out-of-home care.[1] For example, reunifications have been declining during the time from 1990 to 2005 (Barth, Wulczyn, & Crea, 2005). This may be attributable to less effort and time to reunify or it may be that more difficult children are now entering care—the others being served at home—which could reduce reunification rates. Of all children entering care between 2000 and 2005, 40 percent were reunified with their own families and another 14 percent were discharged to the homes of relatives outside of the child welfare system (i.e., not in kinship foster care). Over 9 percent were adopted in this time period. The remainder was divided between those who "aged-out" of care, those who ran away, and those who exited for "other" reasons. The proportion of children who are reunified with their parents ranged, across states, from 31 to 51 percent, and the proportion of children adopted ranged from 3 to 13 percent. Of all the discharge destinations, family reunification account for the highest proportion of children from each age group. Infants are much less likely to be reunified with families than children of any other age groups. Children who enter as infants (age zero) are far more likely to be adopted than any of the other children.

The archive data helps us understand the changing dynamics of placement in a number of key states. Other recent studies have documented how too many children, particularly older adolescents, spend time in group homes and residential treatment centers instead of finding a permanent home (Freundlich & Avery, 2005). The findings of studies on the results of family reunification in other jurisdictions and with special program efforts, however, are inconsistent.[2] For example, a recent study was carried out to evaluate a private-public partnership with local public child welfare agencies in Hartford, Connecticut and Portland, Maine. The data show that families involved in the Family Reunification Program (FRP) are being reunified. A total of 254 children in 135 families received services from FRP staff. A total of 122 children (48 percent) of the 254 were reunified with their birth parents or the major caretaker from whom they had been removed. For this special reunification program group, the time to reunification was only 39.1 weeks (Pine, Spath, Maguda, Werrbach, & Jenson, 2007).

The findings that emerge from studies on family reunification can be applied with insight—albeit with caution—to policy and practice planning. For example, child welfare workers have long recognized the need to address the traumatic impact of separation and placement on children and their parents and other family members as a means of helping them move toward reunification (Kadushin & Martin, 1988). Engaging children and parents actively in the helping process, by providing not only therapeutic services such as Trauma-Focused Cognitive Behavioral Treatment (Cohen, Mannarino, Zhitova, & Capone, 2003) but also concrete assistance with their everyday needs, is critically important (Staff & Fein, 1994). Traditionally, the emphasis in child welfare practice has been on services to the children, in response to their immediate need for care and protection. While this is appropriate, parents also need special attention; help to them should be provided on an intensive basis to enhance their rehabilitation and increase the likelihood that they will be able to take their children back home, keep them there, and function as competent parents.

In this regard, successful outcomes depend on treating parents as individuals with problems and needs of their own, rather than solely as caregivers with responsibility for their children. In addition, parents and other family members need to be involved as partners in the change process and as active agents in preparing for reunification, including having an understanding of the reasons for placement, participating in developing goals, sharing in determining visiting plans and purposes, and evaluating their own progress (Warsh, Pine, & Maluccio, (1996), p. 125; also see, Kemp, Marcenko, Vesneski, & Hoagwood, [2007]).

Reentry of Children into Foster Care

Reentry of children back into foster care following reunification is a central dynamic of child welfare services. A recent analysis of cohort data from a group of major states revealed that about a quarter of the children who stay in care for less than one month reenter care within one year of exit. Children who stay in foster care longer have a smaller reentry rate than those with shorter duration. While only 16 to18 percent of children who stay in care between 6 to 12 months reenter, only 11 to 13 percent of those children with 12 to 23 months duration reenter care within 1 year. The reentry pattern for children with various spell lengths are similar for different entry cohorts. Of the 2000-2002 entry cohorts who were eventually discharged, 16 percent reentered within one year of discharge (Wulczyn, et al., 2007).

The cohort study also found the following key findings about who re-enters foster care:

- As expected, children who ran away from placement showed highest reentry percentage (58 percent). The reported figure may seem low, but it is partially explained by the fact that many runaways who did not reenter had reached the age of eighteen and were not eligible to return to foster care.
- About 16 percent of children who are reunified with families and 20 percent who are discharged to relatives return to foster care within 1 year of discharge.
- For children who join their families or live with relatives, the reentry rates are higher whenever foster care spells are shorter. Only among runaways and "other" exits was this not uniformly the case.
- The children in congregate care arrangements experienced the highest discharge level (95 percent), the highest reentry level given discharge (25 percent), and hence the highest overall reentry rate (24 percent).
- The children in non-relative foster care had moderate discharge levels (91 percent), moderate rates of reentry given discharge (15 percent), and hence moderate reentry levels (14 percent).
- Children in kinship foster care had lower discharge levels (88 percent) than both congregate care and non-relative foster care. Its reentry rate given discharge and the overall reentry rate are also the lowest at 9 and 8 percent respectively.
- The general pattern of longer spell duration corresponding to lower reentry rate applies to children in each primary care arrangement with the exception of children in congregate care of less than one month (Wulczyn, et al., 2007).

Other work on foster care caseload flows indicates that about 20 percent of children who leave foster care will return to care within a three-year time frame (Berrick, Needell, Barth, & Jonson-Reid, 1998; Wulczyn, Harden, & Goerge, 1997). Reentry appears to be most likely when foster care stays were short. About 25 to 30 percent of children who leave foster care before they have stayed 6 months will return to foster care. Children are also more likely to reenter during the first two years after they go home. A more recent study, McDonald, Bryson & Poertner (2006), may have illuminated an important distinction, finding lower reentry rates for very brief placements of thirty days or less, but higher rates for placements between thirty-one days to three months.

Children who exit care as infants have particularly high reentry rates—in one large urban county in California, this rate approximated 40 percent (Berrick, et al., 1998). In addition, there also appears to be a higher rate of reentry among minority adolescents (Fein, Maluccio, & Kluger, 1990; Wulczyn, Harden, et al., 1997).

While these data do support the case of some critics of the child welfare system (e.g., Pelton, 1989) that there is a revolving door with children repeatedly going home and returning to care, determining the ideal reentry rate is not a simple matter. While every discharge from care should be expected to be successful, a reunification program might not be giving any families the benefit of the doubt and only sending children home when there is evidence beyond a reasonable doubt that the reunification will succeed. Such a standard would prevent many children who could be successfully reunified from going home. Low reentries into foster care following reunification might also show that there are insufficient follow-up services to detect the need for reentry and could mean that children who went home were remaining there unsafely. The ideal reunification program has the resources to provide ongoing support to families that have a reasonable chance at reentry and, coincidentally, provides the vigilance necessary to see that post-reunification harms are rapidly observed and addressed. If child welfare information systems captured the distinction between children who came back into care in a planned way, following a monitored reunification failure and could contrast those situations from those in which a child was re-abused, we would have more useful information for improving reunification.

In a descriptive study conducted in New York City, Festinger (1996) investigated recidivism in a sample of 210 children from 20 agencies returning to their families from foster homes and group care settings. The study explored whether there were any differences between children who reentered care within two years of discharge and those who did not reenter, taking into account the characteristics of the children, their caregivers, and their social situations. The strongest predictors of reentry into foster care within one year of discharge were lower ratings of parenting skills by social workers and few social supports available to the families. The strongest predictors of reentry within two years were the number and the severity of problems experienced by the biological parents or substitute caregivers.

A reunification that does not result in entry back into foster care is not the sole goal of the foster care program. Foster care and reunification are tools to be used to protect the safety and well-being of children. There is evidence that stays in foster care may have beneficial effects and that reunification can result in risks far greater than reentry to foster care. In two studies in California using different samples and methods, investigators found that children of color who were reunified from foster care had higher mortality rates (Barth & Blackwell, 1998) and higher likelihood of transitioning to juvenile justice programs (Jonson-Reid & Barth, 2000) than children who remained in foster care. Taussig, et al. (2001) followed 149 youths in San Diego over a 6-year period. She found that children who are reunified with families after a brief stay in foster care were more likely to abuse drugs, get arrested, drop out of school, and have lower grades than those who stayed in foster care. Although these studies do not present a reason to abandon the current emphasis on family reunification or other forms of permanent living arrangements, we must be vigilant to monitor signs that programs need to be modified.

In order to sharply accelerate reunifications, we would first need to be sure that funding mechanisms are there to support post-reunification services, that service models are in place to adequately assist families, and that monitoring is sufficient to look after the safety needs of children following foster care. This has been one of the strongest reasons for arguing that the current funding mechanism, which only provides federal support under Title IVE when a child is in foster care and does not help pay for services after the child returns home, should be reformed.

There are three CFSR standards related to reunification and one focused on reentry. As of 2008, reunification is measured by the percentage of all reunifications that were accomplished within 12 months (this was the original CFSR standard and about 70 percent of cases that were reunified were reunified within the year), the median time to reunification, and the percentage of all children who are reunified within 12 months (http://www.acf.hhs.gov/programs/cb/cw-monitoring/data_indicators.htm, retrieved, April 23, 2008). These indicators are also wrapped into a composite.

The second standard is the Permanency of Reunification: Of all children who were discharged from foster care to reunification in the twelve-month period prior to FY 2004 (i..e., FY 2003), what percent re-entered foster care in less than twelve months from the date of discharge? (http://www.acf.hhs.gov/programs/cb/cwmonitoring/data_indicators.htm, retrieved, April 23, 2008). This standard had been that no more than 8 percent of children who were reunified in the first half of the fiscal year returned in the second half. A summary of 2001-2004 CFSR state reviews found that 8.6 percent or fewer children reentered foster care within 12 months of a prior foster care episode (US DHHS 2005).

The caseloads for both new entrants and reentrants have been declining as shown by the negative net changes in most monthly periods during 2000 to 2005 (Wulczyn, et al., 2007).The number of reentrants has been stable for each period between 2000 to 2005, ranged from 1,100 to 1,600. As with first entries, the shrinking caseload of reentrants is mostly induced by the larger number of discharges than reentries for most periods. This indicates that these states have not made much progress in helping some children to avoid coming back into foster care.

After Care Services

The value of providing supportive services to parents and children following reunification has been recently reemphasized (Freundlich & Wright, 2003) and is demonstrated in a number of studies. For example, Fraser, Walton, Lewis, Pecora, & Walton (1996) completed one of the few experimental evaluations of a state program established to reunify children in foster care with their biological families. These researchers randomly assigned the cases of foster children to: (1) a control group of fifty-three children whose families received routine agency services as a component of an overall foster care plan and (2) an experimental group of fifty-seven children whose families received intensive reunification services, with the goal of family preservation. The experimental group receiving intensive services were most likely to be reunited successfully with their families than those in the control group receiving routine services. These differences proved to be statistically significant at the conclusion of treatment as well as during the follow-up period. In particular, relatively brief but intensive, in-home, family-based services positively affected reunification rates and outcomes. Such services involved building strong worker alliances with family members, providing skills training to parents, and meeting the concrete needs of the children and other family members. The findings suggested that reunification is promoted through in-vivo family strengthening. After six years, the experimental group required less supervision time, lived at home longer, and were in less-restrictive placements than those in the control group (Walton, 1998).

A series of descriptive follow-up studies of children and adolescents discharged from foster care was also conducted in Great Britain, with emphasis on reunification issues (Biehal & Wade, 1996; Farmer, 1996). Despite certain methodological limitations, these investigations are quite informative in regard to the after care period. Farmer (1996) found that there were two distinctly different groups of children: the "disaffected" adolescents who had been removed due to juvenile offenses or truancy and the "protected" younger children who had been removed for abuse, neglect, or family breakdown. The most successful reunifications in both groups were first attempts; later reunifications had higher failure rates.

Biehal and Wade (1996), on the other hand, conducted a longitudinal study of adolescents leaving care in several public child welfare agencies. Their project involved both an initial survey of 183 youths during their first 3 to 9 months of independent living and semi-structured interviews with 74 of the adolescents, conducted soon after leaving care and on two later occasions during a 2-year period. In addition, the young people's social workers were interviewed on each occasion. In each phase, the researchers focused on the varied patterns of family contact and the quality of the children's and youths' relationships with their families.

Despite some methodological limitations and questions regarding the extent to which one can generalize to other populations, these studies are useful for policy and practice, because they shed light on the supports required by children and adolescents as well as their families. As various studies indicate, the services provided to children and their families in the post-reunification phase can be critical in helping to keep them together. Most notable are providing brief, time-limited but intensive services (Pierce & Geremia, 1999; Walton, 1998); connection to family members; sense of belonging to a family unit; offering a range of social supports to the families, including concrete services in areas such as health, housing, and income, as well as counseling services in areas such as parent-child conflicts and the challenges presented by the children's behavioral difficulties (Festinger, 1996; Fraser, et al., 1996); and facilitating ongoing supports to children and youths in regard to special education, treatment of emotional/behavioral and developmental/learning problems, and other special needs (Biehal & Wade, 1996; Landsverk, Davis, Ganger, Newton, & Johnson, 1996).

While most child welfare agencies offer post-reunification services that are, at first, intensive, but then taper off to a less frequent contact; some families may need some level of services indefinitely to maintain their children at home. These may now be more obtainable than ever because of a stipulation in Title IV-B, Part II (The Adoption and Safe Families Act –P.L. 105-89) that requires that some of these funds be spent on family reunification.

Parent Education and Training

As suggested by several studies cited in the preceding section, parent education and training should occupy a central position in work with parents and family members of children in out-of-home care, along with more traditional services. A sizable proportion of parents who are involved with ongoing child welfare services (CWS) recipients, at least 400,000 a year (US DHHS, 2005), will participate in voluntary or mandated parent training. In addition, among the nearly two-thirds of cases of families whose CWS cases were closed following investigation, approximately 28 percent (or about 448,000) will have parenting classes provided, referred to, or arranged by the child welfare agency. Parent-training programs are clearly a linchpin of governmental responsibility, first codified in 1980, to provide reasonable efforts to preserve, maintain, or reunify families who become involved with CWS (Barth, et al., 2005, p. 1).

According to Barth, et al. (2005), parent training has (or should have), essentially, four components: (1) parenting problems are assessed, (2) parents are taught new skills, (3) parents have a chance to apply the skills with their children, and (4) parents receive feedback about that application. Some of the interventions have broader goals and activities and include elements that transcend parent training (e.g., *Multisystemic Therapy*: Buchard, Bruns, & Buchard, 2002; Henggeler, et al., 2003), whereas other programs do not include all primary components. Although parent training is also a component of services to foster parents as well as biological parents (Chamberlain, 2003) and an important part of reunification services (Maluccio, Fein, & Davis, 1994; Walton & Dodini, 1999).

Parent education and training can be effective, especially when implemented with sensitivity into the qualities, needs, and expectations of parents from diverse racial, ethnic, and cultural groups (Banks, Hicks Marlowe, Reid, Patterson, & Weinrott, 1991). A study of the effectiveness of parent education and training programs that compared problem solving versus behavioral training approaches reports that the behavioral training groups produced the best results (Magen & Rose, 1994). A review by Landsverk and colleagues found reasonable research support for only a small group of parent training approaches. See Table 9.1 for a summary of parent training and other treatment approaches with strong research evidence—although not expressly for family reunification.

The added value of a group-based parenting program is that it allows parents and family members to meet other parents in a similar position. Importantly, when this takes place parents see that they are not alone and that other families have difficulties. Through discussions that arise naturally in these situations, parents experience a sense of community and support (Ainsworth, Maluccio, & Small, 1996; Kemp, et al., 2007).

An interesting example of this approach from a residential treatment center in California provides a key as to how such a program may need to be constructed (Carlo, 1993). This agency provides an education/support group, jointly led by

Table 9.1
Well-Established and Probably Efficacious Interventions
for Parenting Difficulties

Target Age	Intervention
Preschool	• Parent Management Training • The Incredible Years • Parent Child Interaction Therapy (ages 4-5) • Time Out plus Signal Set
School Age	• Anger Coping • The Incredible Years • Nurturing Program • Parent Child Interaction Therapy (ages 6-12) • Parenting Wisely • Project Safe Care • Problem Solving Skills Training • Triple P—Positive Parenting Program
Adolescent	• Anger Control Training with Stress Inoculation • Assertiveness Training • Multisystemic Therapy • Nurturing Program • Project Safe Care • Rational Emotive Therapy

Source: Landsverk, J., Burns, B., Stambaugh, L., & Rolls Reutz, J. (2006). *Mental health care for children and adolescents in foster care: Review of research literature.* Seattle, WA: Casey Family Programs. www.casey.org

a social worker and a child care worker, for parents of children placed in the group care program. The group:

> ...is used to didactically provide information about child management and to intro-
> duce parents to a range of behavior shaping and relationship building techniques.
> The parents are then provided with experiential opportunities through participating
> in daily life events, meal preparation, birthday parties, games and sports in the living
> unit in which the child resides. Here, they observe how child care workers manage
> children and have the opportunity to practice what they have heard talked about in
> the parent education/support group.

In two studies conducted to measure the effectiveness of the above approach, the data collected revealed that separately applied, neither the didactic (cognitive) nor an experiential only approach is "as powerful as both conditions conjoined...The two components have complementary value, and the effects of each is enhanced when they are together" (Carlo, 1993, p. 110). These studies suggest the need for practitioners to use experiential but formally constructed parent education, training, and support programs as part of the reunification process or children in foster care.

Parental Visiting

During the placement period, it is also crucial to sustain and enhance connections between children and their families, particularly parents or other caregivers. While not without certain critics (e.g., Delfabbro, Barber, & Cooper, 2002), parent-child visiting in foster care has been described as a crucial determinant of the outcome of foster care services (Burry & Wright, 2006; Hess & Proch, 1993; Mapp & Steinberg, 2007) and as the "heart of family reunification" (Warsh, et al., 1994, p. 49). In an extensive follow-up investigation of permanency planning for children in foster care, Davis et al. (1996) examined the relationship between parental visiting and reunification. The majority of children who had visited with their parents at the level recommended by the courts were reunified with their families. However, there was no significant relationship between parent-child visiting and whether the child remained in the biological home at a follow-up point a year after the reunification.

The findings of the above study suggest that explicit policies and practices should be instituted to facilitate parent-child visiting throughout the placement process and to use visiting deliberately as a therapeutic vehicle in preparation for reunification. Visiting helps maintain family ties and provides opportunities for family members to learn and practice new behaviors and patterns of communicating with each other, with the assistance of social workers and foster parents. Yet, visiting continues to be an under developed aspect of practice in foster care, with at best ambivalent attitudes by foster parents toward birth parents (cf. Erera, 1997). Moreover, in many cases parent-child visiting is infrequent and irregular or non-existent (Fernandez, 1996).

Such authors as Hess and Proch (1988); Kemp, et al. (2007); and Warsh, et al. (1994; 1996) offer guidelines for employing parent-child visiting as a strategy for reuniting children in out-of-home care with their families of origin. These authors emphasize that visiting should be carefully planned and implemented, with attention to its different purposes during each phase of the foster care placement. These purpose include: providing reassurance to the child and the family that the agency is concerned with reuniting them, if at all possible; assessing the children's and parents' capacity for reunification; offering opportunities for staff members to help parents and children to reconnect with each other and learn or relearn skills for being together; and documenting the progress of children and parents in becoming reunited. As Warsh, et al. (1996, p. 133) note, "Whether or not children are able to return home, visiting maintains family ties which may contribute to a child's healthy development." The natural bonds between children in foster care and their parents continue to be prominent for parents as well as children long after they are physically separated.

Researchers have identified a number of pertinent strategies for facilitating visitation and promoting connectedness between children in placement and their families (Altman, 2005; Dawson & Berry, 2002; Haight, et al., 2002; Haight, Kagle, & Black, 2003; Hess & Proch, 1988; Warsh, et al., 1996):

- placing children near their parents and other significant kin;
- placing siblings together, unless otherwise indicated (also see Leathers, 2002);
- encouraging foster parents to allow family visits in the foster home, unless contraindicated;
- requiring written visiting plans that specify such aspects as the purposes, frequency, length, and location of each visit;
- selecting visiting activities that provide children and parents with opportunities to learn more effective patterns of interaction; and
- preparing children, families, and foster parents for visits and giving them opportunities to work through their reactions before and after each visit.

Child Psychosocial Functioning as a Factor Affecting Reunification Success

A recurring question in the field of child welfare concerns the potential impact of the child's psychosocial functioning on the outcome of her or his placement in out-of-home care. Landsverk, et al. (1996) explored this theme in a descriptive, longitudinal study of 669 children who had been removed from their families and placed in either foster care or kinship care at a large county agency in California. The findings indicated that children with behavioral or emotional difficulties were half as likely to be reunified with their families as children without problems, regardless of their type of maltreatment, family circumstances, and other background characteristics. A more recent study in San Diego had similar findings—improvements in behavior resulted in a decrease in placement moves and an increase in reunifications (Chamberlain, et al., 2006).

The findings of the above study are consistent with the results of an earlier demonstration project that examined the efficacy of intensive, individualized services in improving the functioning of foster children with emotional and behavioral problems (Clark, Prange, Lee, Boyd, et al., 1994). The latter study involved a controlled experiment, with children assigned randomly to an experimental group receiving specialized services and a control group of children receiving standard agency services. The outcomes, in terms of the children's adjustment and the stability of permanency plans, were significantly more positive for subjects in the experimental group than those in the control group. In light of the findings, these researchers emphasized the importance of providing intensive services and supports as well as individualized permanency plans for children with, or at risk of, emotional and behavioral disorders.

Kinship Care

History

Kinship care is an ancient phenomenon. In many cultures, the practice whereby grandparents, older siblings, aunts and uncles, or other adults or elders assume responsibility for children unable to live with their parents is a time-honored tradition (Child Welfare League of America, 1994; Scannapieco & Hegar, 1999) (see Table 9.2). Kinship care for children who must be separated from their biological parents is attractive for many reasons, as it:

- enables children to live with persons whom they know and trust;
- reduces the trauma children may experience when they are placed with persons who are initially unknown to them;
- reinforces children's sense of identity and self esteem, which flows from their family history and culture;
- facilitates children's connections to their siblings; and
- strengthens the ability of families to give children the support they need (Wilson & Chipungu, 1996, p. 387).

Although it is not a new phenomenon, kinship care may be viewed as a new child placement paradigm due to "its recent embrace by the child welfare field, social work, and public policy" as a "model governing thought and practice" (Scannapieco & Hegar, 1999, p. 225). In recent years, it has become the first choice—rather than the last resort—in the continuum of services for children requiring out-of-home care (Ingram, 1996).

Table 9.2
A Child's Yearning for Placement with Her Grandmother

Decision making and planning in child welfare cases require listening to the voices of children. The poem that follows reflects children's yearnings for security in their lives, and especially for connections with their kin and with their familiar environments.

Grandma's House
By Chiemi T. Davis*
I'm scared...yesterday they came and got me.
I'm scared...my mom's using again and nobody's home.
I'm scared...where they going to put me?
I'm scared...who's going to take care of me?

I want to go to Grandma's house
Where I know the smells.
She'll cook my food and do up my hair.
She'll sing my songs, I can sleep in her bed,
She'll hold and rock me all night long.

I want to go to Grandma's house
Where I can go to my store.
Ms. Robinson, she'll be there
She'll yell and tell me to "git"
but first she'll give me a free soda and some "sugar" to go.

I want to go to Grandma's house
Cause my mom will know where I am.
She'll say "sorry baby" and kiss my hand.
Grandma will tell her "enough is enough"
She'll know she can't smoke here
She'll get straight and do what's right.

I'm scared...and I want to go to Grandma's house.

Note: Chiemi T. Davis is Managing Director, Systems Improvement Technical Assistance, Casey Family Programs.

Definition and Scope of Kinship Care

The Child Welfare League of America's Kinship Care Policy and Practice Committee defined kinship care as: "the full-time nurturing and protection of children who must be separated from their parents by relatives, members of their tribes or clans, godparents, stepparents, or other adults who have a kinship bond with a child" (Child Welfare League of America, 1994, p. 2).

Scannapieco and Hegar (1999, p. 3) further explain that there are different perspectives on what constitutes kinship care, a phrase that was originally inspired by Carol Stack (1974) in her work on extended kinship networks in the African American community. In particular, they note that kinship care includes both care entered into by private family arrangement and care provided through auspices of a public child welfare agency with legal custody of a child.

According to Nisivoccia (1996, p. 1), kinship foster care can be regarded as "a form of extended family preservation that offers continuity of family ties and maintains culture and ethnic identity while cushioning the trauma of foster care placement for children." Whether provided through informal or formal arrangements, it can be a culturally sensitive response that respects the child's and family's origins (Crumbley & Little, 1997, pp. 65-71).

Kinship Care under ASFA

Kinship care was a relatively unobserved part of child welfare services when the first major child welfare reform law was passed in 1980 (P.L. 96-272). By 1997, however, when the Adoption and Safe Families Act (ASFA) was passed, almost as many children were in kinship care as any other kind of care. Whereas Congress decided not to become involved in a major analysis of kinship care at the time ASFA was debated, ASFA does include language about kinship care that is crucial to understand.

ASFA requires that states file or join a petition to terminate parental rights and responsibilities when a child has been abandoned (in foster care for fifteen of the most recent twenty-two months), or the parent has been convicted of a very serious crime against his or her own child. Yet, there are three exceptions and the first one mentioned is that the child is placed with a relative (at the option of the state) (U.S. Department of Health and Human Services, 1998). This is an acknowledgment that being in the care of kin may provide a permanent plan with many desirable features.

At the same time, state and county agencies are reexamining their use of long-term kinship foster care because children who enter kinship care have such long stays and are dominating their caseloads. In a few places (e.g., New York City, Illinois, and Los Angeles County) renewed efforts are being made to explain the options of legal guardianship and adoption to kin in order to encourage them to follow those paths to permanency if appropriate. Several states (e.g., Illinois and California) are also using the flexibility provided by IV-E waivers to allow children to "exit" from the formal reunification or permanency planning program by giving the foster family a payment that is higher than the TANF payment but lower than a full foster care payment and will help kinship caregivers to care for the child but not requiring that they continue to have a child welfare worker or go to court on behalf of their child. We can expect to see considerably more innovation regarding reunification and kinship care in the years ahead.

Increase in Kinship Care

Although kinship care has long been used on an informal basis, there are an increasing number of children placed with relatives who become their permanent or long-term primary caregivers. More than 6.7 million children in the US live in households headed by relatives other than their parents who provide full-time care, nurturing, and protection. The number of children who are being raised in grandparent or other relative headed households has increased by more than 222,000 in just the past 5 years (U.S. Census: *2005 American Community Survey*). Most are cared for by their grandparents (Anderson, Ryan, & Leashore, 1997; Burnette, 1997; Goldberg-Glen, Sands, Cole, & Cristofalo, 1998). By conservative estimates, these caregivers are saving taxpayers more than $6.5 billion per year in federal foster care costs (US House of Representatives, 2000). (The figure is determined using the federal share of the average foster care payment times a hypothetical number of one million children. So, if one million children were to enter care they would cost the federal government $6.5 billion).

Nearly 1 in 4 youth in out-of-home care in the United States, (24 percent or 124,571) children were served in kinship (relative) foster homes versus 46 percent (236,911) were placed in a non-relative home as of September 30, 2006. As Crumbley and Little (1997, p. xiii) indicate, "This increase...has been attributed to parallel increases in divorce, marital separation, alcohol and other drug abuse, parental incarceration, child abuse, and AIDS-related parental incapacity or mortality."

In Illinois, for example, formal kinship care increased sevenfold between 1986 and 1995 (Testa, 1997), resulting in a policy change which limits the amount of foster care payments to relatives. A larger analysis conducted in 1993 of the policies of thirty-two states in regard to kinship care also indicated that this is the fastest growing type of placement (Gleeson & Craig, 1994). In San Francisco, nearly 55 percent of all children in care are with relatives (http://cssr. berkeley.edu/ucb_childwelfare/PIT.aspx; retrieved October 2, 2007).

The positive aspect of the trend toward greater use of kinship care is that it may indicate that child welfare agencies are becoming more sensitive to family, racial, ethnic, and cultural factors and the importance of family continuity in child development. Given that out-of-home care, whether family foster care, kinship care, or group care, needs to be both "child centered and family affirming" rather than solely child focused—this may represent an improvement in the quality and efficacy of these services (Ainsworth & Small, 1994). Less positively, the trend may be a response to the increasing difficulty in recruiting and retaining foster families. This long-standing difficulty and the rise in the number of children entering care, especially adolescents, indicate that without a growth in kinship care the child welfare system, in recent years, would have experienced a major placement finding crisis.

Kinship Care Policy and Practice Standard Issues

Policy Issues

Conway and Hutson (2007) discuss some powerful myths surrounding kinship care that may have an impact on policies or programs. For example, *"The apple doesn't fall far from the tree."* In fact, research shows that children living with relatives are no more likely—and are perhaps less likely—than children living with non-kin foster parents to experience abuse or neglect after being removed from their homes. A 1997 study found that non-kin foster parents were twice as likely as licensed kinship foster parents to have a confirmed report of maltreatment (Zuravin, et al., 1997). Furthermore, Illinois found that children in kinship foster care are at lower risk for maltreatment than are children in either specialized or non-relative foster care (The Children and Family Research Center, 1999).

A second myth is, *"It's your moral responsibility as a relative to care for these children."* By the very fact that they are providing this care, kinship caregivers agree with this statement. "They take the responsibility of raising their grandchildren, nieces, and nephews when the children's parents, for a variety of reasons, cannot. These caregivers lack neither morals nor a sense of responsibility; they do, however, lack resources. They may be living on a fixed income or be retired; whatever the reason, it is highly unlikely that they planned financially for raising a relative's child" (Conway & Hutson, 2007, p. 3).

Furthermore, the United States Department of Agriculture estimates that it costs at least $7,000 per year to raise a child. This calculation is based on the cost of raising the younger of two children in a single-parent, two-child household with a before-tax income of less than $41,700 (Lino, 2005). The vast majority of children living with relative caregivers are eligible for the Temporary Assistance for Needy Families (TANF) child-only grant. However, 70 percent of relative caregivers do not access TANF or any other public financial assistance. Even when caregivers access TANF child-only grants, this assistance amounts to, on average, just over $4,000 per year—or about 57 percent of the anticipated cost of raising a child (Office of Family Assistance, 2006).

As discussed above, kinship caregivers often lack the information and range of supports they need to fulfill their parenting role. In an effort to remedy this situation (Children's Defense Fund, 2004) a two-fold legislation was recently introduced by Senator Hilary Clinton to provide special tax breaks for these once-again-parents and, perhaps more importantly, to establish "kinship navigators" to advise these parents. However, more work needs to be done to help resolve the policy inconsistencies in licensing and support of these families. And much remains to be learned about the best ways to help ensure the success of kinship care placements for children (Burnette, 1997; Geen, 2003; Hegar & Scannapieco, 1998; Whitley, White, Kelley, & Yorke, 1999).

Kinship care, as previously noted, has traditionally provided for children separated from parents due to family impoverishment, neglect, abuse, or abandonment. A reemphasis on kinship care is of course in line with the emergence of the political rhetoric associated with conservative family values. This rhetoric is also associated with efforts to reduce the influence and cost of governmental services. Kinship care appears to fit this political paradigm, as it may be cheaper than non-relative foster care, especially if support services, including financial payments to kinship families, are less than those provided to non-relative foster parents. This may be so even though the pattern of service to kinship carers by comparison to non-relative foster carers indicates that kinship caregivers often receive low levels of service (Berrick, Barth, & Needell, 1994). Yet children in care with relatives—especially if the latter are paid the same as foster parents—stay much longer than other children, which means that kinship care is becoming more costly in many places (Berrick, et al., 1998). As a result, some states have moved to substantially curtail the use of kinship care and, instead, try to move children in kinship care to non-foster care status or to guardianship (which maintains the reimbursements to the kin, but reduces the court and case management costs).

A recent precise analysis of the entire range of foster parent costs—including, for example, higher costs for wear and tear on the home—was completed by a team of social workers and economists and clarifies the minimum adequate care rate, adjusted for state costs of living. This report shows that nearly every state is failing to adequately reimburse foster parents even while struggling to recruit enough foster parents to serve the children in their care (DePanfilis, Daining, Frick, Farber, & Levinthal, 2007).

The combination of a decline in the availability of non-relative foster care placements and a reemergence of conservative family values is not a good omen for children who need out-of-home care. Kinship carers, at least in the US, appear to be older and less well off financially and to have more health and mental health problems than non-relative foster parents. In a California study of twenty-nine kinship parents and thirty-three non-relative foster care parents designed to assess the quality of care, non-relative placements were rated on a number of measures as more physically safe than kinship placements (Berrick, 1997). This study also reported drugs and alcohol use and violence were more likely to occur in kinship care than non-relative foster care situations. Yet, despite these conditions, analyses from the NSCAW study find few differences between children in kinship and non-kinship care, with regard to their developmental outcomes (Barth, Guo, Green, & McCrae, 2007).

The role that "the state should play in support and supervision of relatives as caregivers is also controversial" (Hornby, Zeller, & Karraker, 1996, p. 410). For instance, should support be primarily financial or also service-related? Should relatives be required to receive counseling or other services if they simply request financial assistance? Should relatives be formally assessed, as with unrelated foster parent applicants?

Practice Standards

Although the use of kinship care has greatly increased, there are no established protocols to guide decisions about placing children with kinship carers. The Kinship Care Policy and Practice Committee of the Child Welfare League of America (1994) did, however, develop a series of recommendations, as outlined below.

- *Assess:* "the willingness and ability of kin to provide a safe, stable, nurturing home and meet the child's developmental needs" (p. 44).
- *Approval/licensing of kinship homes*: approval and licensing are necessary to ensure "a basic level of care for children in the custody of the state" (p. 47).
- *Services for children*: "kinship services must meet the range of needs of children cared for by kin" (p. 51).
- *Services for parents*: "Child welfare agencies should provide the services that parents need for support, rehabilitation, and enhancement of their functioning as parents" (p. 53).
- *Services to kinship families*: "Child welfare agencies should provide kin with the supports and services they need to meet the child's needs, assist the child's parents, and meet their own needs as caregivers" (p. 54).
- *Financial supports*: Financial supports for children in kinship care should be provided "at a level appropriate to meet the children's physical, mental health, and developmental needs" (p. 56).
- *Monitoring and supervision*: there should be "regular and frequent contacts between the agency social worker and the child and kinship parent to continually address the health, safety, and well-being of the child and the service needs of the kinship family" (p. 62).
- *Permanency planning*: The "child welfare agency should arrange the most appropriate permanent plan for the child—that is, reunification with parent, adoption by relatives, subsidized guardianship by kin, long-term kinship care, or nonrelative adoption" (pp. 63-71).

Outcomes of Kinship Care

Why Place Children with Relatives? Research Evidence

Besides cost savings, there are many other benefits of placing children, whenever possible, with relatives. First, *it helps keep families together.* Placing children with grandparents helps to maintain healthy connections to the family and its traditions. In many cases, kinship care giving enables sibling groups to remain intact. Children that are cared for by kin are able, to a greater extent, to maintain relationships with their birth parents and other family members (Annie E. Casey Foundation, 2005). Children who reunify with their birth parent(s) after kinship care are less likely to reenter foster care than those who had been in non-relative foster placements or in group care facilities (Courtney & Needell, 1997).

In addition, kinship caregivers provide stability to children and youth with incarcerated parents. According to a 2000 report from the Bureau of Justice Statistics, over 75 percent of mothers and about 18 percent of fathers incarcerated in state prisons in 1997 reported that their children were being cared for by a grandparent or other relatives (Mumola, 2000). Not only are some of these children not placed in foster care, the incarceration of a parent is often traumatic on a variety of levels for children, and living with family members can provide some measure of stability (Conway & Hutson, 2007).

Second, kinship care placements are more stable living situations. Children in kinship care have more stability in their living situation than they have in a non-kin foster care placement. Children placed with kin by the child welfare system are less likely to experience multiple placements, which has been linked by recent research to less involvement with the juvenile justice systems Ryan & Testa (2005), and more positive adult mental health, financial and other outcomes (Pecora, et al., 2005). (It bears repeating, however, that studies of children placed into kinship care indicate that they have fewer problems to start with than children placed into non-kinship care.)

Third, children in kinship care report more positive perceptions of their placements and have fewer behavioral problems. Compared to children in non-relative foster care and those in group care, children in kinship care are:

- More likely to report liking those with whom they live (93 percent versus 79 percent [non-relative foster care] and 51 percent [group care]) (NSCAW, 2005);
- More likely to report wanting their current placement to be their permanent home (61 percent versus 27 percent and 2 percent) (NSCAW, 2005);
- Less likely to report having tried to leave or run away (6 percent versus 16 percent and 35 percent) (NSCAW, 2005); and
- More likely to report that they "always felt loved" (94 percent versus 82 percent [non-relative foster care]) (Wilson & Chipungu, 1996).

Yet, it is important to understand that, in terms of scores in physical, cognitive, emotional, and skill-based domains, children in kinship care have scores, at their entry into care, that are much more like those of children who are able to remain at home following a child abuse and neglect investigation than do children in foster or group care, who have more extreme scores (NSCAW, 2005). The problems of children who enter kinship care are also much less than those who go into non-relative foster care.

Fourth, kinship families utilize and preserve cultural values. Historically, families of color, especially African American, Native American, and Hawaiian

families, have offered care to children in the extended family, providing culturally specific care that maintains the child's connection to the cultural norms and
practices that inform his or her identity.

Finally, kinship care may bolster states' ability to comply with federal
requirements by providing children with stability and permanency (Conway
& Hutson, 2007), although this is difficult to say because children who enter
kinship care have fewer problems at the time of placement and even the best
analyses have difficulty controlling for these differences (Rubin, O'Reilly,
Luan, & Localio, 2007).

Conclusion

Current Status

In reexamining the area of family reunification, it is necessary to take into
account recurring issues and dilemmas in child welfare. In family reunification practice, social workers, attorneys, judges, and others face a major challenge—deciding whether children, who have already been deemed to have
been at a risk significant enough so as to necessitate their placement, *can* return
home, and *when*.

This challenge raises a number of issues that must be taken into account in
the development of policy, program, and practice in family reunification, although the Adoption and Safe Families Act of 1997 provides some guidelines.
For example, these include:

- What evidence can help us assess the risk of returning children to their
  families versus the risk of prolonging their stay in out-of-home care?
- What is the minimum level of care and parenting that is adequate for
  family reunification? What constitutes "good enough" parenting?
- How can we assess the risks of returning children to their families versus
  the risk of prolonging their stay in out-of-home care?
- How can we maintain or restore optimism and a belief in the potential of
  even the most challenging families to do what is best for their children,
  while also accepting that some parents cannot care for their children?

To answer these and other related questions, *practitioners* as well as researchers need to be involved in the evaluation, thus contributing to the dynamic
interaction of research and practice for the purpose of enhancing services to
children and families. See Warsh, Pine, and Maluccio's (1996) and Bamba
and Haight's (2007) self-study guides and other materials to strengthen family
reunification services. These materials are designed to help administrators,
practitioners, and community representatives in the efforts to examine their
agency's family reunification policies, programs, and services; assess their
strengths and limitations; and plan for required changes. These materials can
be used directly by agencies in the regular course of providing services, so as

to contribute to knowledge building as well as program enhancement in the area of family reunification.

Family reunification of children from kinship and non-kinship care must occur in a way that protects children's safety and well-being. Increasing the number of children in foster care who are reunited with their families of origin or with relatives will often safely promote their growth and development. The studies reviewed in this chapter highlight a number of implications for policy and practice that can contribute to these purposes, especially through serving children and parents during the out-of-home placement episode, maintaining connections between children and their parents, and providing supports following reunification or placement in kinship care.

Future Directions

Our understanding of the perils of short foster care episodes combined with short post-reunification services calls for a longer vision of services. Besharov (1994) argues that brief services are not sufficient for many child welfare families and that we must think long-term. He concludes that the greatest barrier to that is not budgetary, but conceptual. New York, among other municipalities, encourages reunification and allows agencies to provide necessary aftercare services without incurring new costs by paying a fixed rate per case (Wulczyn, Zeidman, & Svirsky, 1997).

Even if the use of a capitated rate is not feasible, local funds, along with new funds available under the Family Preservation and Support Program could be used to provide post-reunification services. We should aim to establish a minimum length of combined out-of-home and in-home aftercare. However, since, each year in the U.S. as many as 25,000 children are reunified from foster care after stays of less than six months, IV-B funds would not be sufficient to extend post-placement services for these families unless funds were available to supplant nearly all other uses of IV-B (i.e., placement preservation). Clearly, IV-E funds must also be brought to bear if we are to routinely provide in-home post reunification services. Support for these very needed services could be enabled by allowing title IV-E funds to pay for case management for up to one year after reunification of children younger than five at the time of exit from care. Failing that, states may want to experiment with extended post-placement services under the new IV-E waiver provisions available to ten states.

Programs that guarantee extended periods of case management have been developed in lean fiscal times and have been shown to be cost-effective. In general, a dose-response relationship does exist for services and longer services are better (Barth, 1993). The current clientele in child welfare is younger and more vulnerable than ever before. Their child protection needs are extensive and so must be the services they receive.

As reflected in this chapter as well as throughout the book, attention to family reunification and kinship care is but one expression of the emphasis in child welfare and related fields on preserving families while also protecting children and maintaining their safety. The unique challenges of preserving families that have been separated through placement, however, require new thinking, informed policy changes, supportive programs, revised practice strategies, systematic attention to developing the competence of family reunification practitioners, collaboration among service providers, and emphasis on hope and compassion.

Notes

1. Overall, there are now fourteen states participating in the archive. Specifically, Arizona, Connecticut, Georgia, Illinois, Michigan, Missouri, New Jersey, New York, and Tennessee provided data on children who were already in care at the beginning of the time period shown for each state, as well as information on those children who entered care for the first time during that time period. Alabama, Iowa, Maryland, North Carolina, and Ohio provided only entry-cohort data, which consists of information on children who entered care for the first time during the time periods shown for each state (Wulczyn, Chen, & Hislop, 2007).
2. For British studies on the outcome of reunification services, see Bullock, Gooch, and Little (1998), Hill and Aldgate (1996), and Pinkerton (1994).

For Further Information

Bamba, S., & Haight, W. L. (2007). Helping maltreated children find their Ibasho: Japanese perspectives on supporting the well-being of children in state care. *Children & Youth Services Review, 29* (4), 405-427. A fascinating discussion of how the Japanese try to support child development for youth in foster care.

Bonecutter, F.J. & Gleeson, J.P. (1997). *Achieving permanency for children in kinship foster care: A training manual.* Chicago: University of Illinois at Chicago, Jane Addams College of Social Work. A series of training manuals and videotapes designed for child welfare caseworkers. The manual is comprised of six units covering formal and informal kinship care; its socio-cultural contexts; the impact of substance abuse on family systems; convening the kinship network; decision-making and empowering families; and supporting permanent plans. The tapes portray casework interviews with a family.

Geen, R. (Ed.) (2003). *Kinship care: Making the most of a valuable resource*, Washington, D.C.: Urban Institute Press. A data-based examination of kinship care policy, program design, and practice issues.

Hegar, R.L. & Scannapieco, M. (Eds.). (1999). *Kinship foster care—Policy, practice, and research.* New York: Oxford University Press. A comprehensive analysis of kinship care, by researchers, policy advocates, and practitioners from child welfare and related fields. Especially informative is a section with reports of research on kinship care. In addition, the editors thoughtfully define kinship care and place it in context "as the most recent of the paradigm shifts in child placement practice that have been necessitated by societal and demographic trends, as well as directed by changing professional beliefs and norms" (p. 11).

Kerman, B., Maluccio, A. N., & Freundlich, M. (2009). *Achieving permanence for older children and youth in foster care.* New York: Columbia University Press. Excellent compendium of essays regarding the research related to permanency planning for youth in foster care.

Testa, M. F., & Shook-Slack, K. (2002). The gift of kinship foster care. *Children & Youth Services Review. 24(1-2), 79-108.* Compelling article about the significance of kinship care.

Warsh, R., Maluccio, A.N., & Pine, B.A. (1994). *Family reunification—A sourcebook.* Washington, DC: Child Welfare League of America. Contains curriculum modules, handouts, and a bibliography aimed at training social workers, foster parents, and other providers working with families and children toward reunification from foster care. Major topics include a conceptual framework for reunification practice; family reunification competencies for social workers; differing perspectives on family reunification; developing policies and programs; and parent-child visiting.

Warsh, R., Pine, B.A., & Maluccio, A.N. (1996). *Reconnecting families—A guide to strengthening family reunification services.* Washington, DC: CWLA Press. A step-by-step guide showing administrators how to set up work teams of staff members from all levels of their agency so as to carry out a comprehensive self-assessment of their family reunification policies, programs, and resources.

10

Transition and Independent Living Services

Preparation for Adult Living is a National Challenge[1]

With significant numbers of workers retiring over the next ten years, many employers and youth development experts in the United States are concerned that not enough youth are developing the kinds of knowledge, skills, and personal discipline necessary for success in an increasingly complex, knowledge and technology-based, global economy. America's place among the group of nations with a highly innovative and competitive workforce will not be sustained if the next generations of youth do not have these opportunities for development (The Business Council and The Conference Board Partnership for 21st-Century Skills, 2006, p. 12). For example, between 2000 and 2015, about 85 percent of newly created U.S. jobs will require education beyond high school (Gunderson, Jones, & Scanland, 2005).

This research is not alone in pointing out some of the key life skills that youth need to develop into healthy adults. A recent review commissioned by the Gates Foundation (Benson, Scales, Hawkins, Oesterle, & Hill, 2004) included educational attainment, constructive engagement in school, employment, or homemaking, and civic engagement among its key dimensions of young adult success. Furthermore, a recent America's Promise Alliance Issue Brief underscored this concern:

> It is no secret that, as a nation, we have inadequately prepared millions of America's young people to participate in the workforce of the 21st century....The growing attention on test scores and graduation rates, however, often leads policymakers and practitioners to overlook other, equally significant ways in which we are short-changing America's young people. Specifically, a large percentage of the children and youth who will enter the workforce over the next two decades are lacking enough of the "soft" or applied skills—such as teamwork, decision-making, and communication—that will help them become effective employees and managers.... In fact, both federal and international commissions have concluded that these skills are essential prerequisites for high school graduates to enter the workforce successfully. (Deseco, 2005; US Department of Labor, 1991; Merrifield, 2000)[2] (America's Promise Alliance, 2007, pp. 1-2)

Adolescents Comprise a Large Proportion of Youth in Out-of-Home Care

So how do the facts and concerns presented above relate to youth in foster care? As noted in Chapter 8, the proportion of adolescents in care, in particular, increased rapidly in the 1980s, as the permanency planning movement initially resulted in keeping younger children out of care, reuniting them with their biological families following placement, or placing them in adoption or other permanent plans. Trend data shows that the overall rate of children in child welfare supervised out-of-home care has been slowly decreasing. But many youth are not in "foster care"—they are in group care. The proportion of youth in foster care who are adolescents has been rising consistently. Of the 303,000 children who entered foster care in 2006, 113,473 (37 percent) were aged 11 to 18; while the proportion of the youth aged 11 to 18 exiting care that year (2,942) was 43 percent (U.S. DHHS, 2006). Those youth ages 11 to 17 (youth age 18 are not included in the AFCARS statistics) also accounted for 33 percent (43,394) of the children who were waiting to be adopted in 2006. Of the 51,000 children who were adopted in that year, 19 percent were adolescents. Thus, even though nearly one in two youth in foster care are adolescents, about only one in five youth adopted from foster care was an adolescent at the time of adoption (U.S. DHHS, 2006).

Adolescents represent three different groups in out-of-home care: (1) those who were placed at an early age and have remained in the same foster home; (2) those placed at an early age and who have been moving from one placement to another; and (3) those who were placed for the first time as teenagers, usually because of their behavioral or relationship problems. Each of these groups has different careers in placement and after placement. As such, they require different approaches, resources, and plans.

Over 26,000 youth exited/"emancipated" from foster care without finding a more permanent living situation such as reunification, guardianship, or adoption—with another 2 percent (n=5,049) leaving care as runaways (U.S. DHHS, 2007). Youth who emancipate from out-of-home care have typically had relatively short stays there; Wulczyn estimates, from an analysis of children who entered foster care that less than 5 percent of children will really grow up in foster care (Wulczyn & Brunner-Hislop, 2001). The greatest proportion have entered care as adolescents but, nonetheless, have been unable to achieve an official CWS-approved reunification with their biological family.

Much can be done to better serve older children while they are in care and to provide them with better opportunities as they transition out of the system. Programs that draw on community resources, promote a system of care, link children to mentors, and teach them life skills hold promise for improving the lives of these children. This chapter reviews the purpose of these kinds of policies, provides example of promising programs and highlights policy and service challenges.

Developmental Needs of Older Youths in Foster Care

Youth development is a life-long process. According to the U.S. Department of Health and Human Services (DHHS), positive youth development means that adolescents receive the services and opportunities necessary to develop "a sense of competence, usefulness, belonging, and empowerment." For older youths in care (and especially for children who have survived abuse and neglect), needed supports include stable living situations; healthy friendships with peers their own age; stable connections to school; educational skills remediation; dental, medical, and vision care; mental health services; consistent, positive adults in their lives; and networks of social support. Life-skills preparation is also very important, covering such areas as daily living tasks, self-care, social development, career development, study skills, money management, self-determination, self-advocacy, and housing and community resources (U. S. Department of Health and Human Services, 2003).

Independent or Interdependent Living?

The growing proportion of adolescents in family foster care in the 1980s, coupled with the greater sensitivity to their needs, has led to expansion of programs addressed to adolescents. Stimulated in part by federal enactment of the Independent Living Initiative of 1986 (P.L. 99-272) and the subsequent infusion of federal funds, agencies have been developing services focusing on the preparation of young people in care for "emancipation" or "independent living" (Kerman, Maluccio, & Freundlich, 2008; Massinga & Pecora, 2004; Mech & Rycraft, 1995). The weak empirical foundation for independent living programs and the concept of independent living, however, has been criticized as having various negative connotations or consequences, such as creating unrealistic and unfair expectations of adolescents, foster parents, and practitioners; regarding the need of adolescents for connectedness with other human beings as a sign of weakness; and placing the burden for preparation for adulthood largely on adolescents themselves (Courtney, 2002; Maluccio, Krieger, & Pine, 1990; Montgomery, Donkoh, & Underhill, 2006).

As a consequence, we endorse a mindset of *interdependent living* in work with young people in foster care. This concept is based on the assumption that human beings are interdependent in their functioning and relationships with others and with community systems and resources. Such a concept is useful for practice with adolescents in foster care for various reasons:

> It is much more realistic than independent living; it is fair; and it is more consonant with real life and with the ideal concept of a community in which all people are mutually and constructively dependent. It also helps to dispel the myth of total autonomy of individuals, families, and nations. It is consistent with the growth of the self-help

movement, which stresses the value of learning to rely on one another, to serve as resources or each other. (Maluccio, et al., 1990, p. 11)

Helping adolescents in family foster care prepare for interdependent living and competent adulthood requires a range of services, strategies, and skills. The central thrust of practice should be to help adolescents develop qualities such as the following, through the combined efforts of foster parents, biological parents, social workers, and other service providers:

- competence and mastery of a range of tangible and intangible skills;
- satisfying and mutually gratifying relationships with friends and kin;
- ability to nurture their own children;
- responsibility for their sexuality;
- contribution to, and participation in, the community;
- making essential connections with others; and
- positive sense of self (Cook, 1997; Mech & Rycraft, 1995).

Yet, personal qualities alone are not sufficient—supportive services are also needed. New initiatives at the state and local levels are generating tutoring, scholarships, transitional supervised living, housing preference in county and local governments, and advocacy organizations for former foster youths, to name a few.

In fact, siblings and relatives become a very crucial resource for older youth in foster care—especially if kinship care (or guardianship with relatives) is heavily used as a mode of care giving.[3] Transitioning out of kinship foster care is different than from a non-relative foster home. For example, in most cases there is more of a shared sense of obligation inherent (but not guaranteed) in the involvement of relatives. Youth who left foster care in Barth's (1990) sample were asked if they could count on their non-kin foster parents for a small loan or staying with them in an emergency—the largest group said that they did not know because they had never talked about it. Kin might also not discuss these topics but we expect that there would be a greater understanding that kin will maintain a lifetime involvement. It is important to differentiate between these two groups to better ascertain which children need different types of support in the transition to adulthood. More specifically, those living with a non-relative foster family are more likely to need support to locate, initiate, or maintain relationships with their biological families or other relatives, and building *enduring* support networks, as well as more formal services like housing and income assistance.

Studies of Adolescents Leaving Foster Care and Foster Care Alumni

Until recently, little consensus existed about how and when to measure the adults who were served in foster care (alumni) functioning. These results have been sobering reminders of the agency's need to do more regarding preparation for independent living skills, employment training, relationship formation, and mental health counseling. More studies using multiple time points and longer-term follow-ups are needed. As described in Pecora & Wiggins (2009), some key large-scale follow-up studies have been conducted to measure the post-discharge functioning of youth who had been placed in foster care.

Most adolescents in family foster care are discharged to another plan, typically some form of independent living, upon reaching the "majority" age. Until P. L. 110-351 was passed in 2008, federal law defines this age as eighteen for these purposes—as children were not entitled to reimbursement for their foster care after age eighteen (unless they are finishing their high school diploma, in which case they can stay until age nineteen or unless they are covered by Chafee Act services). Although it is unrealistic in our society to expect people to be independent at age eighteen, readiness to function independently is another criterion that has been used in studies of the effectiveness of foster family care. The results have largely been negative, in contrast to the more positive findings of studies cited in the preceding section that compared the functioning of foster care graduates with that of their peers in the general population.

Under pressure from private and public agencies, juvenile court judges, class action lawsuits, physicians, and various other stakeholder groups, foster care systems are beginning to be held accountable for the effects of their services (United States General Accounting Office, 1999). As a result, although data are sparse, foster care service delivery systems have begun tracking a core set of outcomes encompassing the developmental needs of older youth outlined above (see Table 1.2 in Chapter 1). Very few programs, however, track other crucial elements such as employment experience while in foster care, decision-making skills, cultural identity, and social networking. The category of services designed to prepare youth to live as productive, stable adults following their stay in foster care is called independent living services. Even with the development of this service category, there are still serious concerns about the level of readiness and preparation for adults living among this population (United States General Accounting Office, 2004).

A recent study that shows that youth who live in Illinois, a state that entitles youth to stay in foster care until age twenty-one, had much better outcomes following foster care than those who made most children leave care at age eighteen (Courtney, et al., 2005). As a result, more than fifteen states (e.g., Iowa) have recently changed their laws to cover youth until age twenty-one, and federal legislation was passed in 2008 to require all states to provide Medicaid coverage to all former foster youth until age twenty-one and to extend the federal entitlement to age twenty-one (P. L. 110-351). In the meantime, though, most children in the U.S. who leave foster care will do so at age eighteen and have an uncertain likelihood of having any ongoing housing, health care, or income assistance.

Foster parents and social workers have consistently reported that most adolescents approaching emancipation are unprepared for independent living (cf. Biehal & Wade, 1996; Hill & Aldgate, 1996; McMillen & Tucker, 1999). For example, follow-up studies of young persons who grew up in out-of-home placement have also pointed to their lack of preparation for life after foster care. Former foster youths have consistently highlighted their needs in the following areas: interpersonal and social skills, money management, planning a budget, job training, finding a job, finding housing, maintaining a household, learning to shop, and maintaining family ties (Barth, 1990; Cook, 1997; Mech & Rycraft, 1995; Nollan, 1996). Also, in a longitudinal study that recently completed the first three waves of data collection, Courtney, Piliavin, Grogan-Kaylor, and Nesmith (1998) and Courtney, et al. (2005) found that children leaving care at age eighteen face a difficult future, as they suffer from emotional problems, are without financial help from relatives, and become vulnerable to homelessness and other problems.

Furthermore, it has been found that a high number of homeless persons have a history of foster care placement. For instance, 38 percent of the homeless in Minneapolis (Piliavin, Sosin, & Westerfelt, 1987) and 23 percent of those in New York (Susser, Struening, & Conover, 1987) reported a history of foster care placement during their childhood and/or adolescence. Perhaps most concerning, in a study of the homeless in Alameda County, CA, those who had formerly been foster children were the least likely to have an expectation of ever achieving permanent housing (Park, Metraux, & Culhane, 2005; Piliavin, Wright, Mare, & Westerfelt, 1996). A decade later, on the other side of the country, Park and colleagues (2005) confirmed these findings. They determined the prevalence of childhood experiences with child welfare supervision and placement among 11,401 young, sheltered homeless adults in New York City. Overall, 29 percent had a childhood child welfare history. Nearly three-of-four homeless adults with a child welfare history had been placed in out of home care. Childhood out-of-home placement was associated with an increased number of days spent in shelters among family shelter users and with an increased likelihood of experiencing repeated shelter stays. Clearly not having a permanent family diminishes the chances of leaving shelter.

In another study of the relationship between homelessness and foster care, Roman and Wolfe (1997) found that persons with a history of foster care placement are over represented in the homeless population. These authors also clarify the long-term implications of not providing permanent placements for children or adequate independent living programs for adolescents. Among those residents in homeless shelters who had children, the residents who had previously been in foster care were far more likely to have their current children in foster care than other residents (who typically know that their own children were living with relatives). So, a heightened vulnerability to homelessness is a concern for former foster children and for their future children.

The available research indicates that youth transitioning from foster care are likely to experience a number of negative outcomes. For example, studies have found that a higher proportion of these youth, than youth in the general population, are involved in the criminal justice system,[4] and that they are at higher risk of teen pregnancy and parenting (Nollan, Pecora, et al., 2000). Because most youth in foster care have changed schools multiple times, many have lower reading and math skills, as well as lower high school graduation rates.[5] In addition, youth transitioning from foster care are more likely to experience homelessness (Cook, et al., 1991; Courtney, et al., 2001, 2005). In fact, two studies found that one in eight foster care alumni who were never before homeless in their lives, did not have a place to call home for at least a week sometime after age eighteen (Pecora, Williams, et al., 2003; 2006). Other studies show that foster care alumni tend to have higher rates of alcohol and other drug abuse (Courtney, et al., 2005; Pecora, et al., 2005; Robins, 1966) and higher rates of unemployment and likelihood of dependence on public assistance.[6]

Readers should recall that the problems of children who enter foster care, and the family resources they have to rely on when they are in trouble, are not the same as those of youth in the general population—so these findings do not indicate that foster care makes youth worse off than they would have been. Indeed, many of them have indicated that they are grateful to have escaped a life of degradation and desperation (Barth, 1990; Courtney, et al., 1998). In fact, a recent study of older foster care alumni ages twenty to thirty-three years old (Pecora, et al., 2005) found the following examples of successful functioning:

1. Mental Health
   - 45.6 percent have no 12-month mental health diagnosis
   - 50.6 percent have SF-12 mental health score of 50 or above
2. Education
   - 84.8 percent had completed high school via a diploma or GED (Graduate Equivalency Diploma)
   - 20.6 percent had received any degree or certificate past high school
4. Employment/Finances
   - 67 percent have health insurance
   - 21.3 percent have household income at least three times the poverty level
   - 83.2 percent do not currently receive cash public assistance
   - 74 percent are working now or in school

However, a recent examination of youth employment in three states suggests a more complex picture, with many youth aging out of foster care being underemployed, large variation in patterns of employment by state, and a greater likelihood of employment when youth begin work before age eighteen. In all three states, youth were more likely to earn income for the first time during the four quarters prior to and the quarter of their eighteenth birthday than in the two years following (Goerge, et al., 2002). Follow-up alumni studies using state public assistance databases are much less expensive and have more complete data by avoiding non-participation rates (see Dworskey, & Courtney, 2000; The Urban Institute, 2008).

There are enough methodological concerns with past research (such as a lack of adequate comparison groups and low study response rates) that the results noted above need to be viewed with caution. Furthermore, several studies have found more mixed results, with some youth doing very well, while others struggle to complete classes and learn the skills necessary to succeed as young adults living more independently. For example, some studies show youth placed in foster care tend to have disproportionately high rates of physical, developmental, and mental health problems, but at least two large alumni studies have found that their average physical health and some areas of mental health functioning are on par with the general population (with alumni having more chronic physical health disorders) (Courtney, et al., 2005; Pecora, et al., 2005; 2010).

In summarizing what we know about the outcomes for older youth in care and foster care alumni, caution needs to be exercised. Not only do the study methods vary in type and rigor, but youth outcomes are affected by variables outside the control of those providing services, including characteristics of the child, the birth family, other relatives, and foster parents; ecological factors before services were begun (such as schooling, neighborhood environment); and the child's degree of resiliency.[7] In addition, because of the lack of "strengths-oriented" research and the media preoccupation with negative effects, the many success stories of older youth in foster care often are not publicized (Bernstein, 2000; Fisher, 2002; Pelzer, 2000). Stereotypes of poor foster care conditions abound, even though conditions are not deplorable and youth who are interviewed about their circumstances often report liking the foster family in which they live and feeling close to their foster parents (Chapman, Wall, & Barth, 2004), (at the same time, they very often report wanting to go home).

Further research on youth outcomes is needed to identify the nature and extent of supports required, the types of skill-building different groups of youth need, and the most promising strategies for delivering those services. Of equal importance is the need to link good outcomes to the cost to achieve them. Until the cost data are more available, including transparent reporting of appropriately co-mingled funding streams, child welfare organizations are not adequately accountable for the "real" costs of obtaining good results and are, therefore, less likely to make a winning case for the additional resources from either public or private funders (Massinga & Pecora, 2004).

Summary of Independent Living Challenges

The challenges in regard to preparation for independent living include preparing youths earlier in their placement, obtaining flexible funding for work study programs, offering better vocational assessment and training, providing adequate health care, and maintaining supports to these young people as they move into adulthood (Cook, 1997; Maluccio, et al., 1990; Mech & Rycraft, 1995). Such panoply of services is required because adolescents in foster care generally have limited supports in their families and social networks and are often emotionally, intellectually, and physically delayed from a developmental perspective.

Reviews of programs show a high degree of focus on clinical and rehabilitation services, while more universal or normative activities—school, recreation, making and keeping social contacts with peers, work skills, and job experience—are not emphasized strongly enough. A more balanced approach is necessary, particularly for placement of older children, who have a much shorter time to learn to be responsible for themselves. Being problem free does not equate to being fully prepared (Pittman, 2002). Witness the testimony of Terry (foster care alumnus): "Aging out of foster care shouldn't mean being totally on your own. The end of foster care cannot mean the end of a community's caring" (Hormuth, 2001, p. 30).

Despite the plethora of policies and programs, older foster children continue to experience substantial challenges, and foster care agencies struggle to keep older children in a stable foster home, to teach them life skills as early as possible, and to assist them to think seriously about life after foster care. In general, it is impossible to know how well the programs are working because most lack rigorously collected evaluation data (Collins, 2001; Courtney, et al., 2001; Wulczyn & Brunner-Hislop, 2001). Moreover, one of the challenges of providing a sufficient "dosage" of service is that many youth do not stay for a long time in foster care; in such cases, ensuring a child's safety may be the only realistic outcome to be measured (Berrick, Needell, Barth, & Jonson-Reid, 1998). Yet, of the 289,000 children leaving out-of-home care in 2006, 28 percent—including many older youth—had been in care for more than 2 years or more, enough time to have derived some possible benefit from a social service program (U.S. DHHS, 2008b).

Key Federal Policies and Promising Programs Related to Transition Services

A variety of policies and programs have been developed that address the needs of older youth in placement, either directly or indirectly.[8] For example, the Adoption and Safe Families Act attempts to improve the safety of children, to promote adoption and other permanent homes for children who need them, and to support families. The Independent Living Initiative and, subsequently, the Foster Care Independence Act of 1999 provide funding for services to prepare adolescents in foster care for independent living (see Table 10.1 and Chapter 2).

Other policies that can provide services for homeless and emancipating youth include the U.S. Department of Housing and Urban Development's Fam-

Table 10.1
The Foster Care Independence Act of 1999

On December 14, 1999, Congress enacted the Foster Care Independence Act to expand services for youth transitioning from foster care. Although an earlier Independent Living Initiative had been authorized in 1985, many service providers, youth advocates, and researchers expressed the opinion that a broader effort was necessary if these youth were to make a successful transition from foster care to independent living. To meet this need, the act created the Chafee Foster Care Independence Program (named in honor of Senator John H. Chafee as a testimonial to his longstanding leadership for children in foster care) and made several important changes in the provision of transitional services for youth in foster care, including:

- Extended eligibility for transition assistance to former foster care children up to age 21, three years longer than previously;
- Doubled the funding for independent living services to $140 million, and established a $500,000 minimum allotment for states;
- Permitted states to use federal funds to support a variety of financial, housing, counseling, employment, education, and other appropriate supports and independent living services for all children who are likely to remain in foster care until 18 years of age and to help these children make the transition to self-sufficiency;
- Clarified that independent living activities should not be seen as an alternative to adoption for children and can occur concurrently with efforts to find adoptive families for these children;
- Allowed states to use up to 30 percent of the funds for room and board for youths ages 18 to 21 transitioning from foster care;
- Gave states the option to extend Medicaid to older youths transitioning from foster care;
- Added adoptive parents to the groups to receive training with federal foster care funds to help them understand and address the issues confronting adolescents preparing for independent living;
- Mandated that states make benefits and services available to Native American children in each state on the same basis as other children;
- Required child welfare agencies to document the effectiveness of their efforts to help their former charges become self-sufficient;
- Added achievement of a high school diploma and incarceration to the list of outcomes to be developed by the Secretary of the U.S. Department of Health and Human Services to assess the performance of states in operating independent living programs; and
- Required the secretary to develop a plan for imposing penalties on states that do not report data, as required.

Although states have a great deal of flexibility in deciding how to use their CFCIP funds, the legislation suggests services that include assistance in obtaining a high school diploma; career exploration; vocational training; job placement and retention; training

Table 10.1 (cont.)

in daily living skills; training in budgeting and financial management skills; substance abuse prevention; and preventive health activities such as smoking avoidance, nutrition education, and pregnancy prevention. The Chafee legislation also specifies that funding may be used to provide personal and emotional support to children aging out of foster care, through mentors and the promotion of interactions with dedicated adults.

Despite the importance of independent living services to help youth transitioning from foster care to become self-sufficient, many states either have not drawn down the funds or are not using the funds as effectively as they could be. Advocates believe states will need to use these funds more "boldly, creatively, and effectively" to substantially improve outcomes for youth leaving foster care.*

Note: Adapted from Jim Casey Youth Opportunity Initiative. *Opportunity passports for youth in transition from foster care—A vision statement.* St. Louis, MO: JCYOI, April 2002, available online at http://www.jimcaseyyouth.org/docs/passport.pdf. U. S. Children's Bureau web site at http://www.acf.hhs.gov/programs/cb/programs/; Child Welfare League of America. (1997). *Summary of the Adoption and Safe Families Act of 1997.* Washington, DC: Author.

ily Unification and Youthbuild programs, and the DHHS' Transitional Living Program for Homeless Youth, Survivor's Insurance, and welfare programs, such as Temporary Assistance for Needy Families.[9] The Chafee Education and Training Vouchers (ETVs) are available to help college students from foster care pay for the cost of attending an approved postsecondary education or training program. They provide up to $5000 per student per year for former foster youth participating in a post-secondary education and training program. Federal ETV funds are allocated annually to each state based on the state's percentage of youth in foster care nationally. ETV funds can pay for expenses used to compute the total cost of postsecondary attendance. Examples of eligible expenses include tuition, application fees, books and supplies, room and board, dependent child care, transportation, and health insurance.

Recent amendments to Title IV-E of the Social Security Act attempted to support improvements for this population by increasing the amount of funds available to states for services and by compelling states to better address the needs of youth who are designated for independent living (Leathers & Testa, 2006). For example, youth age sixteen to twenty-one otherwise eligible for services under a state's Chafee Foster Care Independence Program are eligible to receive an ETV. Youth adopted from foster care after age sixteen are also eligible. Students may be eligible to age twenty-three if they received an ETV by age twenty-one. Individual states may further restrict eligibility for ETV services (see www.natl-fostercare.org).

Finally, in 2007, Congress reauthorized Higher Education Act and this legislation calls for TRIO programs to serve youth from foster care. TRIO Student Support Services and Talent Search Programs is a group of federal educational outreach programs to help underrepresented students prepare for and succeed in college. Students are low-income, disadvantaged, first-generation college students and students with disabilities from middle school through college age—depending on the TRIO program. Federal TRIO programs are designed to motivate and support students through the academic pipeline. Programs begin working with youth in middle school and continue development opportunities through post baccalaureate programs. The federal TRIO programs include: Upward Bound, Upward Bound Math-Science, Talent Search, Student Support Services, Educational Opportunity Centers, and The Ronald E. McNair Post-baccalaureate Achievement Program. Evaluations for TRIO Upward Bound, Talent Search, and Student Support Services programs can be found at the federal TRIO programs home page under "Program Evaluations" (www.ed.gov/about/offices/list/ope/trio/index.html). Recent evaluation findings and project performance data for the Talent Search and Student Support Services programs indicate that they have positive effects.[10]

On September 27, 2007, President Bush signed the College Cost Reduction and Access Act (HR 2669), which includes the Fostering Adoption to Further Student Achievement Act amendment—legislation that makes it possible for adolescents in foster care to be adopted without losing access to the aforementioned college financial aid and other benefits. Under the new law, youth who are adopted after their thirteenth birthday will not have to include their parents' income when determining their eligibility for financial aid. This keeps foster youth, and potential adoptive families, from having to make the difficult choice between having a permanent family and pursuing a college education. As a teenager, Sheila lived in foster care with her aunt. She knew that if she remained in foster care, she would receive enough financial assistance to enable her to go to college. "If my aunt adopted me," Sheila explained, "I would lose my benefits. I mean adoption is great and everything, but you sacrifice a lot" (NACAC, http://www.nacac.org/policy/news.html; retrieved October 3, 2007). Furthermore, an analysis of states' transition service-related policies indicates that the scope and quality of services provided to current and former foster youth, and the eligibility requirements for these services, varies widely.[11] In general, states provide minimal and varied assistance with education, employment, and housing, while even fewer states provide needed health and mental health services or assistance in developing support networks. For example, less than one-third of states have expanded Medicaid coverage to youth ages eighteen to twenty-one, but more states provide daily living skills instruction and financial assistance. While most states provide mentoring services, they generally do not utilize other methods of enhancing the support networks of youth.

Thus, although the range of independent living services offered has increased compared with a few years ago (Kerman, et al., 2002; Zwiebel & Strnad, 2002), much more could be done to improve these programs. Key barriers that states have identified include staff turnover, transportation problems, lack of coordination among the various services, limited involvement of foster parents, lack of youth employment opportunities, scarcity of housing and supervised living arrangements, lack of affordable education services, and shortage of mentors/volunteers (Kerman, et al., 2002; U.S. Department of Health and Human Services, 1999; United States General Accounting Office, 1999). The Fostering Connections to Success and Increasing Adoptions Act (P.L. 110-351) promotes permanent families for children through relative guardianship and adoption, and improving education and health care. The law also provides additional supports to older youth who reach the age of majority without a permanent family by extending federal support for youth to age twenty-one. (The main provisions of this new law are listed in the Appendix.) Two key transition services needing further emphasis to help youth transition successfully from foster care—mentoring and life skills development—are discussed in the following sections.

Mentoring

Mentors can be an important resource for youth transitioning from foster care. A 1995 study of pregnant and parenting African American teen girls defined natural mentoring relationships as "powerful, supportive emotional ties between older and younger persons in which the older member is trusted, loving and experienced in the guidance of others" (Klaw & Rhodes, 1995). The study found that youth who had natural mentors reported lower levels of depression than those who did not have such relationships, despite comparable levels of stressors and resources across both groups. Young mothers with natural mentors were more optimistic about life and the opportunities educational achievement could provide and were more likely to participation in career-related activities.

Other reports on adolescent development indicate that for youths with multiple risks in their lives, having a caring relationship with at least one adult (regardless of whether that adult is the youth's parent) is one of the most important protective factors (Carnegie Council on Adolescent Development, 1989; Melaville & Blank, 1993; Rhodes & DuBois, 2006; Wynn, Costello, Halpern, & Richman, 1994). Having a positive relationship with an adult is associated with better social skills overall due to the development of trust, compassion, and self-esteem that accompany such relationships. In a research brief, Child Trends (2002) reported that youth participating in mentoring programs exhibited better school attendance, greater likelihood of pursuing higher education, and better attitudes toward school than similar youth who did not participate in mentoring programs. Further, youth in mentoring programs were less likely than their non-mentored peers to engage in such problem behaviors as hitting someone or committing misdemeanor or felony offenses.

The evidence was somewhat mixed, however, with respect to drug use, and no differences were identified with respect to other problem behaviors such as stealing or damaging property, getting into fights, cheating, or using tobacco.[12] Nevertheless, overall, the non-foster care research suggests that mentors could help provide needed connections and supports for older children in foster care if the enduring relationships are close, consistent, and enduring and the programs are well-structured (e.g., Herrera, Grossman, Kauh, Feldman, McMaken, & Jucovy, 2007; Rhodes & DuBois, 2006).

Life Skills Development

Overview

As discussed above, youth who spend time in the child welfare system are more likely to have weaker support systems, lower levels of preparedness for independent living, and to leave home at younger ages than their counterparts in the general population. In addition, adults who formerly lived in out-of-home care may experience lower educational achievement, less stable work histories, greater reliance on public assistance, more incidences of homelessness, and many other challenging life outcomes.[13]

However, life skills development strategies and programs can better prepare youth for interdependent living. This section describes four promising strategies: (1) youth and caregiver involvement, (2) systematic skills assessment and planning, (3) life skills training, and (4) developing connections with foster and birth family members and with the greater community (CWLA Standards for Independent Living, 1989; Muskie School of Public Service, 1998; Sheehy, et al., 2002).[14]

Youth and Caregiver Involvement

Youth and caregivers are more invested in the life skills learning process when they are involved in all aspects of it, which is the first effective strategy for preparing youth to live on their own (Nollan, Horn, Downs, & Pecora, 2002). Involving youth as integral players in the development and implementation of their Independent Living Plans can have far-reaching effects. It encourages youth to take responsibility for their lives and demonstrates that youth in foster care can make good decisions for themselves. Agencies should integrate positive youth development philosophy in their programs. The literature on self-determination, positive youth development, and person-centered planning supports the importance of helping youth lead their own emancipation planning process (Clark, 2004; Festinger, 1983). (Also see http://www.youthcomm.org/Publications/FCYU.htm for a youth in foster care constituent organization. For person-centered planning, see: http://www.ilr.cornell.edu/edi/pcp/ or http://challengingbehavior.fmhi.usf.edu/personcentered.htm.)

Similarly, it is important to involve the child's caregivers in life skills assessment, transition plan development, and implementation of the transition plan. Using caregivers as the primary life skills teachers provides a several advantages (Mech & Fung, 1999). For example, caregivers can coach and model appropriate behaviors in real life situations; skills can be taught incrementally and can be tailored to the youth's unique strengths and needs; skills can be practiced in a safe environment; and progress can be regularly reinforced (Ryan, et al., 1988). Involving both youth and caregivers can also strengthen their relationship and ensure that both have a realistic understanding of what the youth needs to learn before leaving care (Nollan, Wolf, et al., 2000; Taber & Proch, 1987). A caregiver or other significant adult in the youth's life can offer life skills training formally (e.g., as part of an independent living group or program) and informally, utilizing strategies like "teachable moments" (Wolf, Copeland, & Nollan, 1998).

The Foster Care Independence Act of 1999 (P.L. 106-169) requires states to use Title IV-E training funds to train adoptive and foster parents to be effective teachers of life skills. Training increases awareness of the range of life skills that promote independence and helps caregivers assess their youth's needs for life skills development (Wolf, et al., 1998).

Systematic Skills Assessment and Planning

Systematic skills assessment is critical to the development of a transition plan based on the individual's strengths and deficits (Loman & Siegel, 2000). Assessment and planning should start when youth are young (e.g., ages six to eight) and involve youth, foster parents, and birth parents (if possible). It is recommended that a developmental, comprehensive assessment with known psychometric properties be used. One promising developmental assessment (for ages eight and older) is the Ansell-Casey Life Skills Assessment (ACLSA; see Nollan, et al., 2002 and www.caseylifeskills.org). With versions available for both youth self-report and caregiver report, the ACSLA has good psychometric properties and is useful for both practice and research.

Assessment is the first step in preparing youth for independent living. Assessment results can inform an overall transition plan, including goal setting and instruction. Planning is followed by learning and skill application. Measurement of progress completes the cycle.

Independent Living Skills Training

The third strategy in preparing youth for life on their own is focused skills training, which occurs after assessment and planning. Life skills training is positively related to job maintenance, high school completion, adequate health care, economic independence, and general satisfaction with life (Cook, 1994;

English, Kouidou-Giles, & Plocke, 1994; Kerman, et al., 2002; McMillen & Tucker, 1999; Pecora, Williams, et al., 2003; Scannapieco, Schagrin, & Scannapieco, 1995). As with assessment and planning, skills training needs to begin when youth are young (e.g., around ages six to eight). The most effective training experiences build on existing knowledge and provide real-world practice and experience. It is helpful to have tutors or mentors to reinforce these skills (Mech, Pryde, & Rycraft, 1995).

There are a variety of areas on which to focus life skills training. They include the broad categories of career planning, communication, daily living, housing, money management, self-care, social relationships, and work and study skills. As an example, consider GEAR UP—which is based on successful models for increasing the college enrollment rate of at-risk students, especially low income and first generation college students. GEAR UP programs serve a cohort of students beginning the seventh grade and follow the cohort through high school. This program employs partnerships committed to serving and accelerating the academic achievement of cohorts of students through their high school graduation. Initial program results suggest that GEAR UP programs have been successful in increasing the percentage of students taking a more challenging course load, better preparing these students for future college enrollment.[15]

Developing Connections

Developing connections with foster and birth family members and with the greater community is the fourth strategy. Social support networks for youth are often disrupted by placement (and events leading to placement) and need to be rebuilt. One way to promote connections is to consider a range of permanency options like guardianship, a birth family placement, adoption (even for older youth), and maintaining connections with foster and birth families.

While in care, it is important to promote strong foster family, birth family, and social support networks to buffer stress and provide support for finishing education, obtaining housing, finding employment, and receiving financial and other advice. Having a positive, strong relationship with an adult in and after care is related to positive adult outcomes (Cook, 1994; Mallon, 1998; Pecora & Wiggins, 2008; Sheehy, et al., 2002; Werner, 1989). Caregivers can be a vital part of a young person's support network because many youth stay in contact with their foster parents after leaving care (Courtney, et al., 2001; English, et al., 1994). Relationships with foster parents also ease the transition to independent living (McMillen, et al., 1997). Yet, there may need to be a specific discussion about the ways that foster families can support foster youth when they leave—because foster parent licensing may prohibit some activities (e.g., returning home for the weekend) and foster care resources may prohibit others.

In addition, relationships with the birth family are important, as at least one-third of youth tend to return to live with their birth families for support once they leave care (Courtney, et al., 2001). Others will rely on their birth families in this or other ways (Fein, Maluccio, & Kluger, 1990; Sheehy, et al., 2002). Thus, it is important to re-establish, guide, and support these relationships prior to discharge. Further, the development of other community connections (such as with a mentor) can help youth in foster care as they secure and retain jobs, obtain housing, manage their money, and live on their own (Mech, et al., 1995). Community connections also help replace the youth's reliance on the agency and can help youth address and resolve feelings of grief, loss, and rejection (Ryan, et al., 1988; Sheehy, et al., 2002).

One recent breakthrough receiving much attention is a set of techniques developed to locate relatives of in-care foster youth. Family Finders is an intensive relative search model with the ultimate goals of achieving permanency and supporting enduring family connections for children in the foster care system. Family Finders was conceived by Kevin Campbell in 1999 and is modeled after family-tracing techniques used by agencies such as the Red Cross to reunite families separated by international conflicts and natural catastrophes. Through the Family Finders program, foster care workers are trained to use various search tools including genealogical archives and commercial Internet-based services to find family members of children placed in out-of-home care settings. Since Mr. Campbell began training foster care workers in 2000, this model has spread throughout the country and is nationally recognized as a promising approach for finding permanent homes and family connections for many youth in the foster care system for who traditional attempts at finding permanent placements had failed.

The Family Finding model is comprised of six stages including: (1) "discovery" of at least forty family members for the child or youth; (2) "engagement" of those individuals who know the child best, including family members and others important to the child, to provide information about the child; (3) "planning" for the successful future of the child with the participation of family members and others important to the child; (4) "decision-making" for the future of the child (including a legal and emotional permanency plan) while taking into account the safety and well-being of the child; (5) "evaluation" of the permanency plan for the child; and (6) "follow-up supports" to ensure that the child and their family can access and receive informal and formal supports essential to maintaining permanency for the child.

Data collected through non-experimental evaluations, as well as anecdotal information, have provided evidence that the Family Finders model is successful in making family connections and finding permanent placements for children in the foster care system. Fourtunately, a rigorous evaluation using an experimental design of Family Finders was launched in 2008. Given the initial success of this program and the extent to which the model is currently being replicated on a national scale, experimental studies are essential for determining the efficacy and effectiveness of the model (Personal Communication, Kevin Campbell, October 10, 2007. Also, see http://www.nysccc.org/Conferences/2006Conf/

Hndout2006.htm).

Examples of Transition Programs

Life Skills Development

As mentioned earlier there is a dearth of rigorous research concerning transition programs for youth in or leaving foster care. One promising program is *Youth Emancipation Services* (YES) in San Diego, CA. YES serves youths ages fourteen to twenty-two, in or out of schools, who are currently or were formerly in foster care. The staff integrates structured programming with individualized services and supports, including basic education, life-skills training, mentorships, technology training, tutoring, and paid internships. Results include increased employment, education, and life skills. Treatment youths at post-test had more mature work and study habits, were more optimistic about the future, and had more independent living skills than the comparison group. Three months post program completion, 95 percent were in school, working, or both (Jones, 2001, http://www.casey.org/sandiego).

Employment

Two employment programs are highlighted.[16] First, Job Corps is a no-cost education and vocational training program administered by the U.S. Department of Labor that helps young people ages sixteen through twenty-four get a better job, make more money, and take control of their lives. There are over 120 Job Corps campuses across the nation. At Job Corps, students enroll to learn a trade, earn a high school diploma or GED, and get help finding a good job. Students are paid a monthly allowance, which increases over time. Job Corps provides career counseling and transition support to its students for up to twelve months after they graduate from the program. Evaluations of the Job Corps program has included random assignment studies (Schochet, Burghardt, & Glazerman, 2001; Wonacott, 2003), and these studies suggest that Job Corps has a positive return on investment. These evaluations cite improved educational attainment, increased earnings, and reduced recidivism after participation in Job Corps. (See http://jobcorps.doleta.gov/.)

Second, The US Department of Labor funds services to American Indians and Alaska Natives through the Division of Indian and Native American Programs (DINAP). DINAP-funded programs serve Native American communities that not only meet regulatory requirements, but also are administered in ways that are consistent with the traditional cultural values and beliefs of the people they are designed to serve (www.doleta.gov/dinap/). In an evaluation of tribal services conducted by Mathmatica, Hershey (1998) found that DINAP grantees provide a range of transportation, childcare, and alcohol and drug treatment support in addition to education, employment, and training services. This holistic approach, combined with other tribal services, such as Welfare-to-Work or Tribal Employment Rights Office services, appears to recognize the unique cultural needs of American Indian and Alaska Native communities served by DINAP grantees.

Housing Programs

One promising program that has been in operation for many years is Lighthouse Youth Services' Independent Living Program, in Cincinnati, OH.[17] They use the following strategies: Lighthouse's Housing Continuum includes several housing options for youth: Scattered-Site Apartments, Supervised Apartments, Shared Homes (four to five youth), Host Homes, and Boarding Homes. Youth can move from more structured living arrangements to less-restrictive living arrangements, depending on the level of support and services needed. Before entering the program, each applicant completes a thirteen-unit life skills training curriculum. Once youth move into apartments, Lighthouse pays the security deposit, rent, utilities, phone bills, and furnishings, along with a $60 per month living allowance. Lighthouse also provides counseling (at least weekly) and help finding jobs, earning GEDs, applying for college, and meeting other needs. The program, which is funded with county taxes, serves fifty to fifty-five young people, who stay an average of eleven months.[18] In terms of Lighthouse results, youth retain affordable housing at discharge, often taking over the lease of the apartment or accessing low-income housing. Youth experience living independently in their own apartment and learn budgeting, money management, and self-sufficiency skills. Youth make connections with caring adults and adult community resources.

Another housing innovation is the Chelsea Foyer program, which serves young people "aging out" of foster and residential care, homeless youth, and other young adults who lack the independent living and employment skills necessary to obtain affordable housing in New York City. Based on a successful European model and the first of its kind in the United States, the Chelsea Foyer is an innovative, supported, housing-based, job-training program for forty young adults in their late teens and early twenties. Participants live in a congregate setting and participate in an eighteen to twenty-four month personalized program, receiving onsite case management services and linkages to rigorous job training and placement, educational, and life-skills development resources.

The Chelsea Foyer is a collaboration between Common Ground Community and Good Shepherd Services. Good Shepherd has overall responsibility for the program including provision of intake, case management, youth development, mentoring, and other services. Common Ground provides facility management and building-wide security, as well as linkages to employment training. A third-party study of the Foyer's inaugural year indicates that the majority of residents were making progress in achieving their educational, employment, and independent living goals.[19] The San Pasqual Academy has also piloted a new approach to using a large institutional setting to help older adolescents with housing and life skills preparation (Jones & Landsverk, 2006).

Summary

Several strategies are recommended to effectively prepare youth for independent living. First, youth need to be involved and empowered to set their own goals as they prepare for independent living. Caregiver involvement is likewise critical to success. Second are systematic skills assessment and life skills planning involving both the youth and the caregiver. Third, once the plan is in place, life skills training and learning need to occur. Using a complementary set of competencies and activities compatible with assessment results is effective in achieving goals. Assessing progress after training is important for future planning and program evaluation. Fourth, relationships with foster family, birth family, as well as others in the community need to be nurtured so youth have viable support systems when they leave care. Federal and state sanctioned assessment, planning and teaching of life skills is relatively new (within the past twenty years). Thus, it is important for programs to carefully document assessment results, goals, and life skill programs and activities, as well as to rigorously evaluate their cost-effectiveness (Nollan, 2006).

Conclusion

Current Status

Transition policies and support for emancipating youth must be overhauled. Too many graduates of the foster care system are under-trained and underemployed (Courtney, et al., 2007; Pecora, et al., 2006). Society needs to promote investment in culturally relevant services, support, and opportunities to ensure that every youth in foster care makes a safe, successful transition to adulthood. Independent living preparation must be redesigned to start a very early age ten, not at age seventeen. A comprehensive transition plan should be developed for every child. It should include planning for supportive relationships, community connections, education, life skills assessment and development, identity formation, housing, employment, physical health, and mental health (Goodman, et al, 2001). Employment training and experience should be expanded for many youth while they are in care. Extending the age limit to allow youth to remain in foster care appears to be a promising approach (Courtney, et al., 2005) and seems to have growing momentum at the state and federal levels.

Future Directions

Policies and incentives should ensure that no young person leaves foster care without housing, access to health care, employment skills, and permanent connections to at least one adult. Systems change is essential. The MacArthur Foundation transition scholars have documented how major American institutions have not kept pace with societal changes that require new ways of working to remove barriers to youth as they transition to adulthood (Carnegie Council on Adolescent Development, 1989).

Notes

1. This section is adapted from Pecora, Plotnick, Kessler, O'Brien, Sepulveda, Williams, English, & White (forthcoming).
2. The federal commission reports: U.S. Department of Labor. The Secretary's Commission on Achieving Necessary Skills. (1991). *What Work Requires of Schools: A SCANS Report for America 2000*. Washington, DC: Author. (EDRS No. ED 332054); Merrifield, J. (2000). *Equipped for the Future Research Report: Building the Framework, 1993-1997*. Washington, DC: National Institute for Literacy. The primary international commission was the Organization for Economic Cooperation and Development's project, Definition and Selection of Competencies (DeSeCo); DeSeCo. (2005). *Definition and Selection of Key Competencies: Executive Summary* (30-Jun-2005). Retrieved August 9, 2007 from http://www.oecd.org/dataoecd/47/61/35070367.pdf
3. Boston has been working to increase the number of siblings placed together, as well as bolster foster parent recruitment and retention. A chronicle has been written by Joanne Edgar that documents the process and some of the outcomes of this collaborative. This is available online at http://www.caseyfamilyprograms.org/cnc/recruitment/turning_a_vision.htm
4. Jones & Moses, (1984). Courtney, Piliavin, Grogan-Kaylor, & Nesmith, (2001); McDonald, Allen, Westerfelt, & Piliavin, (1996). These comparisons must be viewed with caution as maltreated children and children from families in poverty would be more appropriate comparison groups.
5. See, for example, Blome (1997), Cook, Fleishman, & Grimes (1991); Festinger, T. (1983); Merdinger, Hines, Osterling, & Wyatt (2005).
6. See Alexander, G. & Huberty, T. J. (1993); Cook, et al. (1991); Courtney, et al. (2001); Zimmerman, (1982).
7. See, for example, Ainsworth, Maluccio, & Thoburn (2001); Kerman, Wildfire, & Barth (2002); Jones-Harden (2004), and Chipungu & Bent-Goodley (2004).
8. This section is adapted from Child Welfare League of America (1997).
9. Under the Family Unification Program (FUP), youth ages eighteen to twenty-one who left foster at age sixteen or older are eligible for housing assistance under the (FUP). Youth referred to the program receive housing vouchers funded through FUP. The vouchers are time-limited so that a youth can only have the voucher for eighteen months. The agency referring a young person to the program provides aftercare to each youth when they enter housing using a voucher. An array of services is available to youth in housing to promote successful transition to adulthood. See http://aspe.os.dhhs.gov/progsys/homeless/Programs.htm. The Youthbuild Program, funded under the U.S. Department of Housing and Urban Development, provides competitive grant awards to local agencies to provide job training, education, counseling, and leadership development opportunities to unemployed and out-of-school young adults, ages sixteen to twenty-four. Program participants participate in the construction and rehabilitation of affordable housing in their own communities. Many

graduates go on to construction-related jobs or college. Alumni receive post-program counseling. The program does not, however, provide housing to the youth participants themselves. See http://www.youthbuild.org/nofa/. Also, see the U.S. Department of Health and Human Services web site at http://www.acf.dhhs.gov/news/facts/youth. htm. Survivors Insurance, established in 1939, provides benefits to surviving dependents of a deceased worker who has paid Social Security taxes. Children under age eighteen are entitled to benefits based on the deceased parent's earnings record, as is the surviving parent until the youngest child reaches age sixteen.

10. See http://www.whitehouse.gov/omb/expectmore/. Enter TRIO in the "Name" or "Keyword" search box, http://www.ed.gov/about/offices/list/ope/trio/index.html.

11. Based on information provided by thirty-one states in their state plans to the U.S. Department of Health and Human Services to qualify for federal independent living funds. This analysis was commissioned by the Jim Casey Youth Opportunities Initiative, April 2002.

12. For example, youth in one mentoring program (Big Brothers Big Sisters) were 46 percent less likely to initiate drug use and 27 percent less likely to initiate alcohol use during the mentoring program than their non-mentored peers. In two other mentoring program studies that also examined substance abuse, mentored youth were less likely to initiate drug use over the long term (but not the short-term) than their peers not in the program. See Child Trends (2002).

13. This section was contributed by Dr. Kimberly A. Nollan.

14. A system that incorporates the first three strategies is available online for free at www.caseylifeskills.org. The skills learned in this system will help in forming social support networks. For a more complete discussion of these strategies, please see Nollan (2006).

15. ExpectMore.gov, retrieved March 12, 2006 (http://www.whitehouse.gov/omb/expectmore/). Enter GEAR UP in the "Name" or "Keyword "search box.

16. Special thanks to Eric Steiner of Casey Family Programs for summarization of these key programs.

17. Special thanks to Jan Waggoner of Casey Family Programs for identifying these key programs.

18. For more information about Lighthouse housing and other transition services see: www.lys.org, and http://www.aecf.org/publications/advocasey/fall2001/whoelse. htm and Kroner, (1988).

19. Adapted from http://www.goodshepherds.org/sub-programs_services/ps-residential_services.html Also see GSS Comprehensive Brochure, page 15. Downloaded 3/16/06 from www.goodshepherds.org/sub-publications_press/images/gss_brochure.pdf

For Further Reading

Child Trends. (2002). *Helping teens develop healthy social skills and relationships: What the research shows about navigating adolescence.* Washington, DC: Child Trends, (July issue). Concise summary of recent developmental research findings in this area.

Clark, H. & Davis, M. (2000). *Transition to Adulthood: A Resource for Assisting Young People with Emotional or Behavioral Difficulties.* Baltimore, MD: Paul H. Brookes Publishing Co. Addresses key challenges for youth with emotional and behavioral problems who are leaving various social care arrangements.

Joint Center Health Policy Institute. (2008). *Aging Out of the Foster Care System to Adulthood: Findings, Challenges, and Recommendation.* Washington, DC: Author. Retrieved March 17, 2008 from http://www.jointcenter.org/. Utilizes surveys and interviews with social workers and other stakeholders in the foster care system to begin to provide a portrait of youth transitioning from foster care. Report includes demographic information on youth who have aged out of foster care, state profiles on what services are available for youth upon leaving foster care, and information on youth transitions into school and/or the workforce.

National Foster Care Awareness Project (NFCAP). (2000). *Frequently asked questions II: about the foster care independence act of 1999 and the John H. Chafee Foster Care Independence Program.* Seattle, WA: Casey Family Programs. www.casey. org. Practical review of the major federal legislation and the programs supported by those laws.

Nollan, K. & Downs, A. (2001). *Preparing Youth for Long-Term Success: Proceedings from the Casey Family Program National Independent Living Forum.* Washington, DC: CWLA Press. These proceedings of a national forum on independent living include reports on research, the special needs of GLBTQ youth, as well as summaries of a selected cross-section of programs.

Osgood, D., Foster, E., Flanagan, C., Ruth, G. (Eds.). (2005). *On Your Own without a Net: The Transition to Adulthood for Vulnerable Populations.* Chicago: University of Chicago Press. Examines policy and program challenges facing various vulnerable populations such as youth placed in juvenile justice and foster care programs, only one of which is foster youth.

Sheehy, A. M., Oldham, E., Zanghi, M., Ansell, D., Correia, P. and Copeland, R. (2002). *Promising Practices: Supporting Transition of Youth Served by the Foster Care System.* Baltimore, MD: National Foster Care Awareness Project. Practical review of key practices for life skills development using existing programs as examples.

Shirk, M. & Stangler, F. (2004). *On their Own: What Happens to Kids When They Age Out of The Foster Care System.* Cambridge, MA: Basic Books. Eight personal stories of foster care alumni describe some of the challenges they faced during their transition. A collection of video stories of some of the youth was produced as well.

U.S. General Accounting Office. (1999). *Foster care: Effectiveness of independent living services unknown.* (GAO/HEHS-00-13) Washington, DC: USGAO. Landmark federal review of independent living programs.

11

Adoption and Adoption Services

Children deserve willing and able families to love and protect their safety and basic developmental capacities. Services described earlier in this volume are needed to help parents to accomplish this fundamental goal of family and community life. When that is not possible, American child welfare policy increasingly calls for temporary placement into the impermanence of foster care and then, failing reunification, the rapid placement of children into adoption. This is an approach that we share with almost no other country (Canada and Great Britain come the closest). Although national and international adoption statistics are imprecise, American's almost certainly adopt more children than all other countries combined. Since the early part of this century, the largest group of children adopted in the U.S. have come from foster care.

Adoption is widely accepted in the United States and has lost much of the stigma that once shadowed it. For the first time in 2000, the U.S. Census asked if the child was an adopted or a natural-born son/daughter—about 2.1 million children in U.S. households are adopted, about 8 percent of all the sons and daughters of householders in 2000 (Kreider, 2003). Though the percentage of children under age 18 who are adopted is 2.5 percent, this varies considerably at the local, county level from less than 1.9 percent to as high as 15.7 percent. Nearly two-thirds of Americans have a personal connection to adoption through a family member (Evan B Donadlson Adoption Institute, 1997, http://www.adoptioninstitute.org/FactOverview, retrieved November 17, 2007).

Adoption creates a legal family for children when the birth family is unable or unwilling to parent. Yet, adoption is not only a program for children. Adoption creates new families, expands existing families, and engages adoptive parents in the priceless costs and benefits of parenting. Birth parents who voluntarily place their child with adoptive parents may also benefit from adoption because it frees them from the parenting role, which they judge themselves unready to assume. Those who involuntarily relinquish children may experience relief and loss (Fessler, 2006). Adoption also offers birth parents the hope for a better life for their child. At its best, adoption meets the hopes of the child, the adoptive

269

parents, and the birth parents. American adoption law and practice have developed to address the needs of this adoption triangle. (See Table 11.1.)

Communities also have an interest in the policies and practices of adoption. The future of our communities and society depends on our children, and their future requires an adequate family life. Many communities within our society, especially Native American tribes, ethnic communities, and other self-defined communities such as foster parents and gay men and lesbians are asserting their right to adopt or to have first claim on children available for adoption. Because adoption occurs at the intersection of love and law, it evokes a powerful response from these communities. Adoption is a social and legal institution that reflects the status, interests, and moral views of nearly every social entity.

History of American Adoption

Early in U.S. history; children were more likely to be indentured than to be adopted. The end of indentured servitude was followed by the growth of orphanages and individual states first began to legislate and regulate adoption practices at that time (Whitmore, 1876). Regulations emerged to protect birth parents' rights to give or withhold permission for the child's adoption, adopting parents' rights not to have their child reclaimed and children's rights to be cared for by suitable adopting parents. By 1929, every state had adoption statutes. Statutes varied on several accounts, but all reflected concern that adoption promote the welfare of the child. The first regulations required social investigations of prospective adoptive parents and trial placement periods in prospective adoptive homes (Heisterman, 1935). A few states also required home visits by agents of the state child welfare department, the precursor to today's home study, although the rationale for the visits was rarely clarified (a legacy with influence today in the home approval process).

The nation's involvement in adoption in the middle part of this century was primarily through placement of infants by young unmarried women who were often not so voluntarily having their newborns placed with decidedly middle class married couples. Adoption was firmly controlled by private and, then, public agencies that made the arrangements and screened and chose the parents. The dominance of this form of adoption began to wane with the passage of Roe v. Wade in 1974, although infant adoptions of a typically more open and voluntary form continue. Adoption of older children began to reemerge after World War II. In 1949 the Children's Home Society began a "new type of child care program in North Carolina to provide ways and means of placing older children in institutions, in family homes for adoption" (Weeks, 1953, p. i). This effort was partly in response to waiting lists to place children in orphanages. Today, all American orphanages are closed or converted to residential care, and foster care is the typical setting for older children awaiting adoption.

Table 11.1
The Path to Older Child Adoption

Steps	Adoptive parent(s)	Child	Birth parent(s)
1	Parent contacts agency requesting information or home study	Child enters child welfare system via abuse, abandonment, or relinquishment	Parent is determined to be neglecting or abusing child
2	Group or individual home study begins	Child is determined unsafe at home and enters foster care	Parent should receive all reasonable efforts to prevent placement
3	Parents and agency identify type of child most suited to family	Child begins to be involved in counseling to address the possibility that child will be adopted. Older children have their rights to influence this decision explained.	Parent is determined to be likely to continue to endanger child or child is removed to enable correction of health or behavior
4	Agency completes home study and approves family		Parents should be offered to participate in reunification services, e.g., dug treatment, public housing provision, parent training
5	Parents review possible children for adoption		
6	Available children presented by social worker		
7	Visits with child begin	Child is determined unlikely to return home and enters foster/ adoption home	
8	Parents may be linked to adoption support group (developed during home study or after)	Child is determined to be unable to return home	Parent's progress in rehabilitating home and self is reviewed and found inadequate with no allowance for additional time
9		Child is transferred to the adoption program	Birth parent's rights are terminated by law
10		Adoption placement begins with supervision	
11		Adoption is legalized	Birth parents may be offered opportunity for open adoption or provided with post-TPR services

Types of Adoption

Adoption occurs through a variety of means involving different types of agencies and auspices, each with unique procedures and requirements. Taken together, approximately 119,000 children were adopted in 1990 (Flango & Flango, 1993). This number grew slightly to 127,000 children in 2000 and 2001 (Flango & Caskey, 2005), although the types of adoption placements have changed considerably. Generally, adoptions are grouped into four categories: stepparent, independent, relinquishment or agency, and intercountry.

Stepparent Adoptions

Stepparent adoptions refer to the adoption of children by the spouse of a parent. Stepparent adoptions differ from other adoptions because the adoption involves a child who is already legally in the family. In most states, stepparent adoptions are about twice as common as nonstepparent adoptions. Stepparent adoptions are typically administered separately from nonstepparent adoptions and, because of their impact on the distribution of family property, are often overseen in superior court or probate court. Approximately half a million children are adopted by step-parents at the current time (Flango & Caskey, 2005).

Independent Adoptions

Independent adoptions occur when parents place children directly with adoptive families of their choice without an agency serving as an intermediary. Intermediaries are most often counselors or attorneys. In the 1950s, agency adoptions and independent adoptions were about equal in number and primarily involved infants. Independent adoptions held steady at about 20 percent of all adoptions in the 1960s and 1970s (Meezan, Katz, & Russo, 1978) but have increased recently to nearly one-third (National Committee for Adoption, 1989). As of 2006, only four states (CO, CT, DE and MA) outlawed independent adoptions (McDermott, 2007). Nationally; between 15,000 and 17,000 children were adopted independent of agencies in 1992 (Stolley, 1993; Placek, 1999) and this number may have dropped since then, to about 13,000 in 1996 (Placek, 1999), but no statistics on independent adoptions are available for more recent years, consistent with the lack of federal involvement in independent adoption practice or policy.

Agency or Relinquishment Adoptions

Agency or relinquishment adoptions are those that follow the voluntary or involuntary legal severance of parental rights to the child and are overseen by a public or private agency providing foster care and adoption. The intent of

Table 11.2
Adoptions of Children with Public Child Welfare Agency Involvement by State,
Federal Fiscal Years 1995-2005: Percentage Increase over State Average
1995-1997 Baseline through 2005

States	Baseline (1995-98 Average)	1999	2001	2003	2005	Highest # Adoptions Completed	Increase Over Baseline
Alabama	133	153	238	329	336	336	153%
Alaska	105	137	278	208	204	278	94%
Arizona	357	761	938	839	1012	1012	183%
Arkansas	168	318	362	385	316	385	88%
California	3570	6416	9156	7473	7549	9156	111%
Colorado	458	719	749	1037	967	1037	111%
Connecticut	234	403	444	342	740	740	216%
Delaware	45	33	117	101	78	117	73%
Dist. of Columbia	118	166	231	242	310	310	163%
Florida	1127	1355	1508	2786	3020	3020	168%
Georgia	551	1143	1001	1097	1152	1152	109%
Hawaii	139	281	260	318	452	452	225%
Idaho	48	107	132	138	149	149	210%
Illinois	2814	7028	4106	2706	1838	7028	-35%
Indiana	571	764	901	766	976	976	71%
Iowa	394	764	661	1130	947	1130	140%
Kansas	366	566	428	546	649	649	77%
Kentucky	211	360	548	612	876	876	515%
Louisiana	309	356	470	497	469	497	40%
Maine	113	202	367	287	318	367	181%
Maryland	377	594	815	742	620	815	64%
Massachusetts	1112	922	778	733	832	922	-25%
Michigan	1993	2446	2980	2622	2884	2980	45%
Minnesota	301	633	567	644	732	732	143%
Mississippi	128	237	266	183	244	266	91%
Missouri	578	849	1101	1405	1309	1309	126%
Montana	124	187	275	224	244	244	97%
Nebraska	185	279	316	281	356	356	92%
Nevada	149	123	244	289	434	434	191%
New Hampshire	46	62	95	131	124	131	170%
New Jersey	670	732	1030	953	1380	1380	106%
New Mexico	160	258	369	220	289	369	81%

Table 11.2 (cont.)

New York	4742	4864	3935	3870	3422	3935	-28%
North Carolina	571	949	1327	1296	1203	1327	111%
North Dakota	63	143	145	120	152	152	141%
Ohio	1219	1868	2230	2420	2044	2420	68%
Oklahoma	380	830	959	1152	1015	1152	167%
Oregon	500	765	1071	849	1030	1071	106%
Pennsylvania	1297	1454	1564	1946	2065	2065	59%
Rhode Island	251	292	267	264	217	292	-14%
South Carolina	309	456	384	281	412	456	33%
South Dakota	56	84	97	144	113	144	102%
Tennessee	330	382	646	954	1114	1114	238%
Texas	1061	2056	2325	2504	3181	3181	200%
Utah	253	369	349	311	350	369	38%
Vermont	86	139	116	167	166	166	93%
Virginia	282	326	495	487	510	510	81%
Washington	675	1047	1204	1315	1306	1315	93%
West Virginia	190	312	362	322	368	368	94%
Wisconsin	511	642	754	1187	910	1187	78%
Wyoming	20	45	46	56	61	61	205%
TOTAL	30450	46377	50007	49911	51445		69%

Note: Indicates a baseline average from the years 1995-1997, as data was not available for these states in the year 1998 (source, AFCARS). Puerto Rico is not included in this chart because data prior to 1998 are not available.

the Adoption Assistance and Child Welfare Act of 1980 and of the Adoption and Safe Families Act of 1997 was to increase the number of relinquishment adoptions. This has occurred. Although good national data has only recently emerged, data from AFCARS shows a doubling of the number of children adopted from foster care from about approximately 25,693 in 1995 to a high of 51,691 in 2005. The growth in adoptions of children from foster care has been dramatic. The increase from the baseline years of 1995-1998 to 2005 was 69 percent (See Table 11.1). This growth appears to have been leveling off since about 2002. At the same time, the number of parental right terminations has risen to about 70,000 per year and is also, now, leveling off, as fewer children enter foster care, more remain with relatives, and more states begin to support kinship guardianships in addition to adoption. This may be an important respite for adoption services, as it will allow adoption agencies to focus on the quality of adoptions done and allow for a greater focus on the needs of the more than 350,000 children who have been adopted, in recent years, and are still being raised by their adoptive parents.

The federal government is clearly not done promoting adoption, however, as shown by P.L. 110-351 (see Chapter 2). De-linking of adoption subsidies from an income eligibility standard, described in Chapter 2, is one such effort. Eligibility for SSI now qualifies children for subsidies regardless of the SSI income requirements. The Act also ensures that there will be no disincentive to adopting children sixteen and older by given them full eligibility for federal independent living services (which had already included education and training vouchers). The Act also requires that states do a better job of informing potential adoptive parents that they are eligible for a tax credit that is not dependent on their adoption expenditures. P.L. 110-351 also requires that every child who is getting and adoption assistance payment be enrolled as a full time elementary or secondary school student, until they have completed school.

Little information is available to compare independent and agency adoptions. Evidence comparing independent and agency adoptions of infants found few differences in outcomes between them (Meezan et al., 1978). Parent satisfaction is high for both (Berry, Barth, & Needell, 1996). Efforts to make the infant home-study process more intensive, to screen adoptive families more rigorously, or to require extensive agency review of placements have not been founded on evidence that independent adoptions are less satisfactory than agency adoptions. Although fingerprint checks for felonious criminal behavior and assessments of the safety of the household are undoubtedly warranted to screen adoption applicants, adoption policies must be circumspect about using additional criteria to screen out families seeking to adopt children. These additional criteria add barriers to the recruitment, approval, and retention of adoptive families and may prevent adoptions. Adoption agencies are especially helpful when they focus on assisting applicants to determine the best kind of adoption for them and provide necessary pre-placement training and post-placement support for adoptive parents caring for children with special needs (Emery, 1993). Recent innovations in home studies—including SAFE (Structured Analysis Family Evaluation)—are endeavoring to standardize the home study format so that it can be used for foster care and adoptive placements across agencies and jurisdictions (Crea, Barth, Chintapalli, & Buchanan, 2009).

Adoptions can also be classified across types as either infant or older child adoptions. Infant adoptions (whether private, independent, or inter-country) are popular but somewhat controversial programs because they are sometimes perceived as principally for parents rather than for children and often provide well-to-do parents with the babies of disadvantaged mothers. Infant adoptions are perceived of as requiring little social commitment on the part of parents; yet adoptive parents do provide a vital service to newborns and their parents by freeing them from a situation viewed as untenable.

In contrast, older children adoptions—of abused, neglected, or abandoned children who cannot go home—are considered children's programs because the decision to place a child with a family is to address the child's welfare most and because parents' needs are secondary. The Child Welfare League of America's *Standards for Adoption Services* (CWLA, 1998) asserts that adoption is a means of finding families for children, not finding children for families. Yet, this dualistic appraisal of adoptions is somewhat unfortunate and makes it too easy to ignore the needs of the child or infant or independent adoptions, the needs of the parents in older child or agency adoptions, and the needs of consenting parents or abandoned children residing in a range of countries and communities. The future of improved adoption services rests on renewed attention to each program's ability to meet the needs of all parties to the adoption.

Regardless of the type, adoptions follow some general guidelines based on the premises that every child has a right to a family and that the child's needs are paramount. Arising from this fundamental right are other agency principles: that finality of adoption be made as soon as possible (after a sufficient trial of the placement's viability); that every party have options and assistance in weighing these options; that confidentiality be ensured as far as possible; and that agency services be available before and after placement.

Intercountry Adoptions

Intercountry adoptions involve the adoption of foreign-born children by adoptive families. In the United States, intercountry adoptions are a small but significant proportion of adoptions. Federal law requires a satisfactory home study. Private adoption agencies assist families by conducting family assessments for Latin American, Pacific Rim, or Eastern European adoptions. Also, children who are adopted must clearly be orphans. These adoptions raise a number of policy issues such as proper safeguarding of birth parent rights, cultural genocide, and resolving citizenship for the child. The nature and use of international adoptions merit careful review and analysis. More than 9,000 foreign-born children were adopted in the United States in 1991 (Immigration and Naturalization Service, 1991) growing to nearly 18,000 in 2000, increasing from roughly 5 percent of all adoptive placements to 15 percent (Flango and Caskey, 2005). The percentage of adoptions from foreign countries has increased from 5 percent in 1992 to 15 percent in 2001 (p. 40). Recent trends include new restrictions on Korean adoptions and an expansion in the number of countries from which children are being adopted, including Eastern European countries and, especially, China, which now accounts for more about one-third of all U.S. international adoptions (U.S. State Department, 2007). The expansion of adoptions from Russia and China may be sun setting, at the time of writing, as there are growing concerns about the safety of children adopted into the US and growing rejection of the notion that these countries are unable to care for their own children.

Special Needs Adoptions

Federal law describes special-needs adoption as indicating that a child in foster care cannot or should not be returned to the home of his or her birth parents and that the child has a specific factor or condition (such as ethnic background; age; membership in a minority or sibling group; or the presence of factors such as medical conditions or physical, mental, or emotional handicaps) that make it reasonable to conclude that the child cannot be placed with adoptive parents without providing adoption assistance or medical assistance. In addition, the state must find that a reasonable but unsuccessful effort has been made to place a child with appropriate adoptive parents without providing adoption or medical assistance. This latter requirement can be, and often is, waived if it would be against the best interests of the child. State regulations vary widely in their interpretations of the Adoption and Safe Families Act but generally identify special-needs adoptions as involving the adoption of children age three or older, ethnic children, handicapped children, emotionally or intellectually impaired children, or sibling groups of three or more. Almost all (88 percent) of the children adopted from foster care are judged to be special needs—the proportion of these children ranged from 16 percent (CT) to 100 percent (SC) in FY 2001 (Dalberth, Gibbs, & Berkman, 2005).

Between 1982 and 1986, the number of special-needs adoptions showed little or no growth (National Committee for Adoption, 1989), but the foster care population grew by 7 percent (Tatara, 1994). In contrast, by 2000, the growth of the foster care population was flat and adoptions were growing. Special-needs adoption of foster children accounted for about 10 percent of all exits from foster care in the early to mid-1980s (Barth & Berry; 1988). Between 1995 and 2004, about 19 percent of exits from foster care were by adoption (U.S. DHHS, 2007).

Major Adoption Legislation

Indian Child Welfare Act

For the first two hundred years, American adoption was legislated locally. The first major piece of national legislation influencing adoption was the Indian Child Welfare Act (ICWA) of 1978. The legislation provides legal guidelines to promote the stability and security of Native American tribes and families and to prevent the unwarranted removal of Native American children from their homes. The passage of ICWA was fueled by the recognition that as many as 30 percent of Native American children were not living in their homes but were residing in boarding schools, foster homes, or adoptive homes. Founders of the act asserted that the viability of Native American tribes was dissipating in the face of the removal of its children. The Act emphasizes protecting tribal communities and institutions (about half of Native Americans are members of tribes).

Within this broad Act are protections specific to adoption. Most notably, termination of a Native American's parental rights requires the highest standard of proof. Child welfare authorities must show beyond a reasonable doubt that the continued custody of the child by the parent or Native American custodian is likely to result in serious emotional or physical damage to the child. Thus, the court must find with virtual certainty that the child will be seriously harmed in the future before he or she is freed for adoption. This high standard protects tribal rights but leaves little latitude for overseeing the child's right to be safe.

Section 1915 of the Act legislates the adoptive placements of Native American children after termination of parental rights. Preference is given to placement with a member of the child's extended family, other members of the child's tribe, or other Native American families. The act places the rights of the tribe above those of the birth parent. For example, Native American parents who are tribal members cannot place their children for adoption with non-Native American families off the reservation; placement of tribal children is governed by the tribe.

As a result of these stringent provisions, ICWA has never been without controversy. Fischler (1980) argued that the greater sovereignty for Native American adults places Native American children in jeopardy. Further, by regarding children as the property of parents, families, and tribes, ICWA does not protect children adequately. Defenders of ICWA argue that a child's right to a lifelong cultural affiliation deserves at least as much protection as the right to household permanency (Blanchard & Barsh, 1980). They propose that the choice to protect culture is what tribal child welfare professionals have made explicit in their support of ICWA.

The impact of the Act has undergone little evaluation. The only assessment of ICWA implementation indicates that, as envisioned by the framers of the act, an increasing proportion of Native American children are being placed in foster and adoptive homes with Native American parents. Yet, Native American children in care are less likely than other children to have a case plan goal of adoption (Plantz, Hubbell, Barrett, & Dobrec, 1989). When they are adopted, this is very often by aunts and uncles or other relatives (Barth, Webster, & Lee, 2002). State and federal courts have yet to achieve a consistent balance between the interests of tribal survival, child welfare, and parental authority. The conflict is especially vexing when the parents of a Native American child want to place the child in a non-Native American family, or a tribe seeks to place a child on an unfamiliar reservation in which the child has no close family (Hollinger, 1989). These cases continue to be contested (Cross, 2006). The relationship between ICWA—which contains a very high standard for termination of parental rights—and subsequent child welfare legislation that requires time limits on foster care placements and termination of parental rights when those time limits are exceeded is just now being explored.

*Adoption Assistance and Child Welfare Act and Adoption and
Safe Families Act*

The Adoption Assistance and Child Welfare Act (AACWA) was passed in
1980, followed by the Adoption and Safe Families Act in 1997. The broad
mandates in the AACWA that child welfare agencies implement pre-placement
preventive services, programs to reunify placed *children* with their biological
families, subsidized adoption, and periodic case reviews of children in care.
Perhaps most importantly, AACWA instituted a time line of eighteen-months for
reunification or a decision to free a child for adoption. To facilitate adoption, a
federal subsidy program was included that allows federal dollars to be used to
match state contributions made to give subsidies—which could not be larger
than the prior foster care payment—to families adopting children with special
needs. In 1997, Congress passed the Adoption and Safe Families Act (ASFA) to
strengthen these provisions. The time frame for making permanency decisions
was shortened to twelve months and the expectations that a child would be free
for adoption, even if there was not an immediately available adoptive family,
were added to the law, along with many other provisions.

The changes in the focus and completion of adoption has, subsequently,
been dramatic. In 1982, more than 50,000 children were legally free from their
parents and waiting to be placed (Maza, 1983). About 17,000 of these children
had the specific permanent plan of adoption and approximately 14,400 older
children were placed for adoption in the United States (Maximus, 1984). By
2004, more than 118,000 children were legally free for adoption and more than
52,000 children were adopted, almost all of whom were given adoption subsidies. The massive increase since 1975 in the placement of older foster children
and special-needs children for adoption has greatly changed the historic purpose
and scope of child welfare services.

The Adoption Assistance and Child Welfare Act encouraged states to develop
adoption subsidy programs for special-needs adoption and reimburses the state
for 50 percent of the subsidy costs. The intent was to ensure that families were
not penalized financially for adopting. Reforms to make subsidies available to
families that adopt special-needs children passed, over the objections that sentiment should be the only consideration in adoption. Instead, law acknowledged
subsidies as a means to facilitate the adoption of special-needs foster children
and promote new adoptions. Subsidies are meant to encourage families to adopt.
Families that adopt special-needs children are entitled to subsidies without a
means test, although their financial condition can be taken into account.

Adoption assistance payments are now provided in all states, and state adoption subsidy programs operate in virtually every state. Nationwide, adoption
assistance payments rose from $442,000 in 1981 to an estimated $100 million
in 1993 to more than $2 billion in 2007 (U.S. Senate, 1990; US DHHS, 2007).
In 2006, more money was expected to be spent by the federal government,

each day, on adoption subsidies than on foster care payments (Spar & Devere, 2001). Concerned about the growing number of children receiving adoption subsidies, some states have endeavored to cut adoption subsidies, despite the fact that they are already lower than foster care or group care payments and are much less expensive than paying for children who grow up in out-of-home care (Barth, Lee, Wildfire, & Guo, 2006). Court challenges to cuts in existing subsidies have successfully argued that they could not make such cuts to families that had accepted children into their families with the understanding of a higher subsidy payment (Eckholm, 2006).

Multiethnic Placement Act and Interethnic Adoption Provisions

The passage of the Howard M. Metzenbaum Multiethnic Placement Act of 1994 prohibits any agency or entity that receives federal assistance "to categorically deny to any person the opportunity to become an adoptive or a foster parent, solely on the basis of race, color, or national origin of the adoptive or foster parent, or the child, involved; or delay or deny the placement of a child for adoption or into foster care, or otherwise discriminate in making a placement decision, solely on the basis of race, color, or national origin of the adoptive or foster parent, or the child involved" (S. 553[a]I[A&B]). Initially identified as a "permissible consideration," agencies could consider the cultural ethnic or racial background of the child and the capacity of the prospective parents to meet the needs of the child as one of a number of factors in determining the best interests of the child. This was later stricken in the Interethnic Adoption Provisions, which amended the Multiethnic Placement Act and added penalties for failing to comply with this Act as a violation of the Civil Rights Act of 1964. The acts also require that states provide diligent recruitment of potential adoptive and foster families that reflect the ethnic and racial diversity of children in the state for whom foster and adoptive homes are needed.

The passage of this Act may have increased the likelihood of adoption for African American children; however, this is not a clear result of the law. The US DHHS has done little else to try to study the impact of the law. Shaw (2006) found no change in the proportion of multiethnic adoptions in California since the law. Several states have now been successfully sued by the Office of Civil Rights for failing to implement the law; Ohio received a $1.8m fine (US DHHS, Departmental Appeals Board, 2006) At the same time, the lengths of stay in foster care for African American children are declining because of more movement into guardianship and kinship adoptions (Wulczyn, 2003).

Other Acts

Tax cuts. In 1994 tax cuts were passed for all families who adopted and submitted their adoption expenses. This was the beginning of a steady series of actions that have endeavored to balance the national goal of placing children from foster care into adoption and the interests of adoptive parents (and private agencies and attorneys) who seek to defray the costs of independent, agency, and international adoptions. In more recent iterations, the tax cuts were changed to tax credits and made larger for families adopting from public agencies. Research then showed that these families were not using the credits because they did not have many expenses or much income. The *Economic Growth and Tax Relief Reconciliation Act* (P.L. 107-16) of 2002 includes provisions to extend permanently the adoption credit; increased the maximum credit to $10,000 per eligible child and created a flat tax credit for special needs adoptions so that parents do not need to document expenses for special needs adoptions.

As part of President's Adoption 2002 Initiative, which was an administrative program developed in 1996 by President William Clinton to double the number of adoptions in six years, an adoption incentive program was developed to give states a bonus for increasing the number of adoptions of foster children above their baseline. Although the effects of this program are unknown—as the bonuses are relatively small and the short-term cost of an adoption is high—this has now been established as federal policy, as part of the Adoption Promotion Act (P.L. 108-145) of 2003. This law provided additional incentives to states for increasing the number of children age nine and older who are adopted from foster care. PL 110-351 renews the Adoption Incentive GProgram for an additional five years. Somewhat perversely, the Act updates to FY 2007 the adoption baseline above which incentive payments are made (which usually raises the baseline) but then doubles the incentive payments for adoptions of children with special needs and older children adoptions above that baseline. The Act also permits states to receive an additional payment if the state's adoption rate exceeds its highest recorded foster care rate since 2002.

Most recently, the advances in support for college tuition and expenses for former foster youth has caught the idea of the adoption community. The College Cost Reduction and Access Act (P.L. 110-84) was passed to ensure that there would be no disincentives for adoption of older children from foster care and that they would continue to be eligible for any federal assistance given to emancipated foster youth. This legislation that makes it possible for adolescents in foster care to be adopted without losing access to college financial aid.

Current Adoption Practice

Recruitment of adoptive parents for foster children is arguably the most important element of adoption practice because once adoptive placements are made, adoptions generally require few ongoing services. Recruitment is especially critical for African American children because they remain strikingly overrepresented in foster care. Although adoption practices vary broadly, practitioners struggle to decide how to keep pace with emerging trends in a way that fits their agency and is in the best interests of children, families, and the community.

Adoption Planning for the Child

Permanency planning legislation provides grounds to free many children for adoption, but agencies have been slow to implement the specifics of the legislation, and many barriers to placement and permanence remain. Determining a child's eligibility for adoption continues to be a confused mixture of answers to three questions. Is the child (1) easily interested in adoption, (2) likely to be adopted, or (3) likely to remain adopted? Adjusting practice to the needs of these older children includes recognizing that some disruption is inevitable. As Cole (1986) conceptualized this, "The only failed adoption is the one you didn't try" (p. 4). Workers who recognize and accept the possibility of disruption in adoption find creative ways to facilitate adoptions for all waiting children and support the placement in accordance with the risk involved. Recent innovations in adoption practice are resulting in children getting adopted even though they are older than twenty-one (Barth & Chintapalli, 2009).

Not every child will be better off adopted than in long-term foster care or guardianship. Although many adoptive families struggle and may need post-adoption assistance, the general evidence of positive adoption outcomes is powerful (Barth, 2002; Triseliotis, 2002). The value of adoption and the relatively modest disruption rates of about 11 percent (Smith, Howard, Garnier, & Ryan, 2006) make adoption an excellent alternative over foster care. Experienced child welfare workers have lower adoption disruption rates for families that had been in their care. At the same time, children who are not adopted but who have had their parental rights terminated are likely to experience a variety of significant legal and personal disadvantages (Barth & Chintapalli, in press).

Speedy efforts to place children while they are young and better able to fit into an adoptive family's home represent the starting point for successful adoption. Adoption delayed is often adoption denied. Efforts to terminate parental rights more quickly when reunification is improbable and to move children into foster-adopt situations deserve full support and dissemination. At the same time, older children whose parent's rights have been terminated are too often unable to be adopted and are, therefore, suffering the legal consequences of having no legal family ties.

Recruitment of Adoptive Parents

Agencies continue to engage in a variety of methods to find adoptive families. Recent years have seen advances in search methods that involve information provided by the youth who will be adopted. In these procedures, social workers help youth to identify people who they have known and cared about and who might consider adopting them. In addition, there is a growing use of people-finder firms to seek relatives of children in foster care.

In addition to exchanges, parent recruitment also occurs through community education. Broad education in the community can reach groups of potential parents that may never have considered adoption. Beginning in 1979, Father George Clements, a priest in Chicago, challenged every African American church in Chicago through the One Church, One Child program to accept the responsibility and opportunity to have one member of each congregation adopt an African American child (Veronico, 1983). Federal and state governments subsequently provided years of support to One Church, One Child to encourage its replication. Many states now have a version of One Church, One Child and focus on recruitment of families from other ethnic groups. The program has continued to be used (Gibson, 2003) but has not yet been evaluated.

Another recruitment strategy that has shown promise involves using special features on television or in newspapers to present a particular child and a description of his or her strengths and needs. These media campaigns are modestly successful and inexpensive. Ethnic adoption fairs also bring interested parents and eligible children together in a picnic situation. Internet services are a growing tool for identifying children in need of adoption. More than seven thousand children listed on the Children's Bureau's Adoptuskids.org website have been adopted, as of April 2007.

Pre-placement Services

Home studies are a nearly 150-year-old tradition and continue to serve the primary function of screening adoptive families to protect children from harmful situations (Crea, Barth, & Chintapalli, 2007). A well-established but secondary function is to help adoptive families clarify their intentions and flexibility regarding the characteristics of children they seek to adopt. During the past decade, there has also been a greater use of the group process for training and support of pre-adoptive families so they are more able to parent special-needs children successfully. The group approach to pre-placement provides particular opportunities for ongoing support. Many of these groups prepare participants to become either adoptive or foster parents. Groups may last for as long as ten sessions and include guest presentations by current foster and adoptive parents. Prospective foster parents are told that they may change their minds and become adoptive parents instead. People who expressly want to adopt (and they usually outnumber those who want only to provide foster care) are oriented to the social services system and the legal and moral responsibility to facilitate the child's reunification with the birth family when that is the case goal. Adoptive families that begin the process in such multifamily groups often maintain contact with peers well beyond their time of contact with the social worker. Although group home studies have not been well evaluated, some evidence suggests that they strengthen high-risk placements (Barth & Berry, 1988) whereas other evidence suggests that they have little benefit (Puddy & Jackson, 2003).

Social workers try to provide adopting parents with all pertinent information about the child during pre-placement services. Because of the inevitable coordination problems and some confidentiality concerns, much valuable background information is not shared. This inefficiency could be redressed by rethinking the type of information that is collected and how it is summarized and transmitted to the families. However they accomplish it, social workers with more years of experience are more effective in supporting families so that they succeed in their adoptions—for each year of worker experience the adoption disruption rate decreases by 2 percent (Smith, et al., 2006).

The strong confirmation by researchers of the importance of information sharing calls for prompt action (Barth, 1988). Better information is associated with better outcomes. Also, the success of a few "wrongful adoption" cases is forcing agencies to change their information-sharing practices and states to change their laws to reduce liability. Nonetheless, some social workers continue to withhold information to increase the likelihood of adoption (Shulte, 2006).

Parents have argued that every social worker that knowingly denies available information to an adoptive applicant should be suspended from their job and reviewed for dismissal. We share their sentiment although not their policy recommendation. (We would allow agency review and employee discipline policies to govern the consequences.) Families are suing to show their outrage.

Agencies can prepare an information-sharing checklist for use by social workers and adoptive parents. The checklist could be included in every case record and would allow for each party to provide and initial receipt of information about a given child. Information that is not available can be duly noted. This should reduce the confusion about whether information was known but not shared or was not available. Use of a simple device like this may lead to better placements and lower family stress, perhaps averting disruptions. Some agencies are also videotaping the conference during which these issues were discussed in order to provide a record available to both parties, should it later be needed.

A few families have been so unhappy with the result of their adoptions that they have sued the agency that placed the child for adoption. These suits are (1) extremely unlikely events; (2) they can be prevented in almost all cases with additional attention to a few best practices; (3) they can be quite demoralizing to agencies and workers; and (4) they do not need to prevent any child from being adopted. In the past 15 years, more than 500,000 adoptions of former foster children have occurred. In Blair's (1992) review, only seventeen cases were known to be pending in five major states and six appellate cases were pending. (To this day, there is little legislation or case law that establishes wrongful adoption as a tort, thereby leaving most plaintiffs with a difficult case

Table 11.3
Steps to Avoid Liability

1. Convey the information that is known, fully, accurately, and with specific attention to the family that is hearing the information
2. Get good information from the biological parents including medical questionnaires, and interviews (which should be checked against each other)
3. Be forthright about information that is not known and the limitations of the process of collecting information (especially, that the birth mother may be the sole source of background information)
4. Children should receive medical examination prior to placement (or at least be given the opportunity to do so).

Source: Adapted from M. Freundlich and L. Peterson. (1998). Wrongful adoption: Law, policy, and practice. Washington, DC: Child Welfare League of America.

to make.) Assuming that the addition of cases from other states would double the number of cases, there were still about one wrongful adoption case for every ten thousand adoptions. If an adoption worker is involved in about ten adoptions per year, it will take one thousand years of adoption practice before a typical adoption worker would have a wrongful adoption case.

Most of the wrongful adoption cases were for children who were adopted when the standard was not to present full information to adoptive parents. Indeed, the thinking then was that adoption is so successful that the important thing was to get a child into an adoptive home and then the mood of adoption would take over and any sins committed in getting that child into the home would be absolved by the bliss of the adoptive relationship. We now know better. Adoption is very successful, but adopted children and the parents often struggle to overcome children's biogenetic and environmental disadvantages. A classic wrongful adoption suit can help clarify what can go wrong. In 1964 the Burrs applied to an Ohio county welfare department to adopt a male child younger than six months old. A few days later the caseworker called the Burrs and told them that a seventeen-month-old nice, healthy, baby boy, who had been born at a city hospital to an eighteen-year-old unwed mother living with her parents (who were mean to the boy), was being made available for adoption. It turned out that the child was born in a psychiatric hospital to a dually diagnosed schizophrenic and developmentally disabled mother!

Avoiding Wrongful Adoptions

It is important to provide all the information that is available (see Table 11.3). Provide it systematically. Develop a form that indicates what you do and do not have on the child. Offer the family the opportunity to tape record the information to be gathered from the child. The key issue is that families should not be deprived of information that they might need to make an informed decision about the adoption.

Although we do not have research on who files wrongful adoption suits, research has been gathered on this issue in the medical malpractice world. In many hospitals, insurers now require that every physician attend training every year on avoiding malpractice. The centerpiece of that discussion is developing and sustaining a good relationship with parents! The second piece of that is good record keeping. So maintaining a supportive relationship with excellent documentation is vitally important to avoiding wrongful adoptions.

Open Adoption

The practice of open adoption, or the continuance of contact or correspondence between the adopted child and birth parents, is increasingly common. An estimated 55 percent of adoptive families in California during 1988 to 1989 had contact with the birth family in the two years following placement (Berry, 1991). Henney, et al. (2003) examined the practices of 31 adoption agencies from 1987-1999 and showed that only 36 percent of agencies offered fully disclosed arrangements in 1987 but that, by 1999, 79 percent offered fully disclosed arrangements. At the end of that time, not one agency only offered confidential adoptions.

The benefits of open adoption are becoming more accepted, but remain controversial. On ideological grounds, because outcome data on open adoptions are scarce, Pannor and Baran (1984) called for "an end to all closed adoptions" (p. 245). They view the secrecy of conventional adoptions as an affront to the rights of adopted children. Kraft, Palombo, Woods, Mitchell, and Schmidt (1985a, 1985b) countered that open adoptions may interfere with the process of bonding between the adoptive parent and child. Other evidence suggests that the adoptive parents' control over their child's contact with birth parents is critical to the success of the placement (Barth & Berry; 1988) and the parents' comfort with the placement (Berry, 1991; Dunbar, 2006). Berge, Mendenhall, Wrobel, Grotevant, and McRoy (2006) examined adolescent's feelings on openness and found that "adolescents desired and benefited from having openness in their adoption arrangements"(p. 1036). Berge, et al. also found that adolescents desired more contact with birth moms, which demonstrated that the contact with the birth mothers was not harmful. Von Korff, Grotevant, and McRoy (2006) examined whether the degree of openness between adoptive and birth family members was associated with the behavioral and emotional adjustments of adolescents who had been adopted as babies. "The adoptive parents' reports indicate no significant association between openness and adolescent adjustment" (p. 531). "Adoptee reports suggested that externalizing behavior is higher in confidential as compared with ongoing fully disclosed arrangements," (p. 534) but the authors make no claims that openness causes better outcomes. They recommend that openness arrangements be voluntary and that openness decisions be made on a case-by-case basis.

Whereas most open adoptions continue to be voluntary on the adoptive parents' part, recent case law has added stipulations to adoption decrees that provide birth parents with visitation rights (Hollinger, 1993). A few countries (for instance, New Zealand) have made open adoptions the requirement for all adoptions on the grounds that it is in the child's best interest. These changes are in stark contrast to the historical notion of adoption as a parent-child relationship equivalent to the birth parent-child relationship and without condition. This change occurred despite the absence of noteworthy evidence that children in open adoptions have better outcomes than other children.

The potential benefit of open adoption is that provides a resource for coping with the typical transitions in the child's understanding about option as he or she moves toward adulthood. The danger for older children is that continued contact with birth parents may disrupt the development of the child's relationship with the new family. The older adoptive child and parent are trying to become a family and need a structure to do so. It may seem that the older a child, the less detrimental and more natural it is to retain ties to former caretakers. The danger in this logic is that older children have a more difficult time developing ties to their new family because they are also pushing toward independence, and this development may be preempted by contact with birth families. Open adoption can perhaps best be viewed as enrichment to a stable placement, not a necessity for all placements or a palliative for a troubled one.

Nontraditional Adoptions

The traditional requirement that adoptive parents be married couples who own a home with a full-time mother at home severely narrowed the field of possible adoptive parents. Although these requirements might have been helpful in reducing the field of applicants during the infant adoption boom, they were also erroneously promulgated to protect children from unsuitable parents. Instead, they limited the placement of special-needs children. The bigger pool of parents needed for these waiting children is not attainable without flexible requirements. Requirements for adoptive parents have typically been more flexible in public agencies than in private ones. Public agencies supervise adoptions with parents with lower incomes, lower education levels, older ages, and more children in the home than do private agencies (State of California Department of Social Services, 1987).

Agencies are beginning to recognize the potential of unconventional adoptive parents, especially single parents. An early study of single-parent adoptions (Branham, 1970) found that, in general, applicants were emotionally mature, tolerant, and independent and had a supportive network of relatives. Barth and Berry (1988) found that single parents adopted older and more difficult children with no more adoption disruptions than couples.

Modest changes in agency policy and practice has opened opportunities for adoption by gay and lesbian parents (Pace, 2005; Ryan, Pearlmutter, & Groza, 2004). In 2000, 29,000 adopted children lived with a female head of household and her unmarried partner and almost 29,000 adopted children lived with a male head of household and his unmarried partner (Krieder, 2003). These statistics do not indicate what percentage of these children live with same-sex partners or opposite-sex partners. Gay, lesbian, and bisexual foster parents face multiple challenges when beginning the adoption process, as it frequently begins by becoming foster parents (Downs & James, 2006). Despite being a valuable resource for our nation's foster children, Downs and James (2006) found that many gay, lesbian, and bisexual foster parents were met by lack of support, inappropriate social workers, and even legal resistance. Results of a study by Leung, Erich, and Kanenberg (2005) indicated that for children who were adopted by gay/lesbian headed families, there were no negative effects for their parenting. Additionally, higher levels of family functioning were found in gay/lesbian headed households with adopted children who were older, non-sibling grouped, and had more foster placements. These results indicate that gay/lesbian adoptions should be encouraged. Indeed, agency personnel have a clear understanding that gay and lesbian families are a vitally important resource for achieving social goals of ensuring that children have loving, legal, lifetime families (Brodzinsky, Patterson, & Vaziri, 2002). A new generation of work is clarifying important considerations in the assessment and support of gay and lesbian foster and adoptive parents (e.g., Mallon & Wornoff, 2006; Mallon, 2007).

Adoption of children by kin who cared for them as foster parents has increased in recent years. Kinship foster care has become the most common type of foster care in many urban areas (Barth, Courtney, Berrick, & Albert, 1994) and kinship adoptions have also grown in recent years. For children entering out-of-home care between 1990 and 2002, 26 percent of those who were placed into kinship care were adopted compared to 21 percent of children entering foster care (Wulczyn, Chen, & Hislop, 2006). This is partially responsible for their finding that African American children are now more likely than other children to be adopted even though their rate of adoption is slower than other children (Wulczyn, Chen, & Hislop, 2006). Although this is generally a more protective legal arrangement for children than foster care, kinship adoptions are more likely to be by older, less educated, poorer, single parents than other adoptions (Magruder, 1994).

Post-Placement Services

Agency support after placement may be needed for some children. Any placement will have challenges. The goal for the agency is to stay close enough to the family to be aware of these problems and guide the family to resources to aid in their resolution. However, many families are reluctant to seek services until it is too late because they are afraid they will lose their child.

Both the child and the parents have needs in post-placement services. Agencies typically maintain contact with the family during the first three to six months to reassure the child of continuity with his or her past and to enable the family to explore uncertainties without feeling lost (Fitzgerald, Murcer, & Murcer, 1982). The goal is to catch problems early in the placement before they escalate into unsalvageable disasters. The evidence is unequivocal that the needs of adoptive families for support and services last well beyond the first year (Festinger, 2006). Agencies must establish ways to provide services for high-risk placements throughout adolescence. Post-adoption services may be useful but they are specifically geared toward preserving placements on the verge of disruption. Rather, they tend to serve adoptees placed as infants, not older child adoptees, and help them reconcile their adoptions, make decisions about searching for birth parents, and deal with their concerns as they become adolescents and young adults.

Many agencies have introduced support groups of adoptive families for parents and children. It is often helpful for new adoptive parents and children to talk to fellow adopters and adoptees about what is normal in adoption and to share realistic expectations and feelings about the process. These groups also facilitate supportive relationships that parents and children can fall back on when they need to. Support groups probably operate best when started during the home study, but successful versions have been developed after placement to support high-risk placements.

There is a clamor for the development of post-placement and post-legalization services that meet the demands of supporting older-child adoptions. The call is for something far more than mandatory visits soon after the adoption and the availability of crisis intervention services. Although the principles underlying this demand are sound, a few concerns arise. First, post-adoption services should not be staffed at the expense of recruitment and home study efforts. Resources spent on conventional post-placement services are not as valuable to agencies and families as dollars spent on recruitment because most adoptions succeed with no significant agency effort after placement. Second, although referral to outside services is often useful, social workers or other adoptive families involved with the family should be available to assess the situation and coordinate post-placement services from other providers. Families are less likely to ask the agency for help when they lose contact with the worker who did their home study. The home study is a poignant process that builds strong bonds between the worker and family. The organization of services should facilitate a continuous relationship among the family, social worker, and other adoptive families who can assist in times of duress.

Adjusting to older-child adoptions is often difficult. At times, the future of the adoption may be in doubt. With so much riding on the outcome of such a crisis, it is unwise to rely on conventional social casework counseling or office-based psychotherapy. Adoption preservation services are needed. Although some early efforts to apply short-term and intensive methods of family preservation were not successful, derivative models have emerged and been reported by parents to be very valuable (Zosky, Howard, Smith, Howard, & Shelvin, 2005) and have been accompanied by changes in adoptive parents depression and children's behavior problems (Susan Smith, personal communication, November 16, 2007). Since permanency planning, family preservation services have emerged in most states. They have been used primarily for keeping children out of the child welfare or mental health systems and not to help preserve adoptive placements.

Relatively few adoptive families now have the benefit of intensive home-based, family preservation services to prevent adoption disruption, an observation that has not changed in the last twenty years. Yet, many states have developed at least some post-adoption services. For families in crisis, in-home interventions reduce the likelihood of alienation that can occur during out-of-home care. The specific presenting problems that precipitate adoption disruptions are those that signal the breakdown of other families, especially assault, running away, and noncompliance of latency and teenage children. Intensive services are costly, but if they are successful, their costs can be favorably weighed against the lifelong benefits that follow adoption. To date, there are no models of post adoption services that have been shown to be effective—admittedly a difficult evaluation challenge because these services tend to respond to families with a wide range of backgrounds and concerns. Despite the limitations in post-adoption services, there appears to be no greater risk of disruption in recent years than in the period when the adoption rate was only half as high (Smith, et al., 2006).

Conclusion

Current Status

Recent changes in adoption jeopardize its place in the child welfare services continuum. The child welfare service "system" is an amalgam of programs. The outcomes of efforts to prevent out-of-home placements, to reunify families, and to provide long-term care all depend on the quality of the programs that have previously worked with the children. Each program must work if the other programs are to do what they are intended to do. If older children receiving child welfare services are not adopted or able to stay adopted, then the rationale for moving quickly to terminate the rights of birth parents (after a determination that children cannot go home) is weakened. Indeed, even the pressure to leave children in, or return them to, unsafe birth families is intensified when permanent adoptive homes are unavailable, because social workers fear that children will experience more harm in a lifetime of foster care than at home. Many agencies will not free children from foster care until a stable home is all but guaranteed. Without confidence that terminating parental rights and freeing child for adoption will ultimately result in an adoption, judges lose their conviction to do so, time limits on foster care are rendered insignificant, and mandates for speedy permanency planning become moot. Successful older-child adoption services may not be the hub of effective child welfare services, but they are critical.

Not everyone believes that adoption is of great value to children and American society. Adoption foes are gaining greater attention as they argue that adoption is a cause of irreparable trauma to children and birth parents.. If adoption is to maintain a powerful role in child welfare services, the arguments for the resilience of children's capacity to make attachments (Eyer, 1992; Barth, et al., 2005), the benefits to the children of adoption (Rutter & Rutter, 1993), and the congruence between adoption and American values need better articulation and dissemination (Bartholet, 1993). Many social workers are not as sure as they once were of adoption's advantages over long-term foster care or guardianship and may fail to make a case about its value to foster families and children. Often, adoption is not viewed as a clear and desirable alternative to foster care.

Future Directions

Adoption is facing increasing scrutiny by all interested adult parties. Birth mothers and fathers, adopting parents, and adoption agencies and centers are developing new and more rigorous procedures for trying to ensure that their needs are met. These efforts may work against the interests of children who need adoptive homes. Despite the general success of adoption for all parties involved, a considerable tightening of adoption regulation and more procedural barriers to adoption may occur in the next decade. These procedures may result in diminished interest on the part of potential adoptive parents who will instead choose to pursue surrogacy arrangements or fertility treatments with lower success rates. Such strategies will not lead to the adoption of children in need of placement. Of the utmost importance is the public policy goal of increasing adoptive placements. In addition, a substantial challenge exists to find ways to make adoption a way to create and affirm family ethnic, and community relationships in all their manifestations. This involves supporting a range of adoptive arrangements that allow the child to recognize the significance of birth parents and siblings, racial and ethnic make-up, and cultural origins and give the child opportunities to acting on that recognition.

For Further Information

For useful adoption resources, visit the following web sites:

- http://www.adoptioninstitute.org/index.php
- http://www.childwelfare.gov/adoption/index.cfm
- http://www.nacac.org

12

Residential Group Care and Intensive Treatment Alternatives

Introduction[1]

Group care for children remains a service in flux. Concerns about effectiveness, child safety, and costs continue within the services research community (Burns & Hoagwood, 2002) as well as in discussions of best practices and policies for children and families (Whittaker, 2004; 2006). Recent evidence from Los Angeles suggests that child welfare involved youth who are served in group care are more likely to transition to juvenile services than those who are served in foster care—after adjusting, as well as possible, for differences that might have resulted in those placements (Ryan, Marshall, Herz, & Hernandez, in press). Other evidence indicates that the residential care intervention is, itself, not often a good fit for the need of the children served (Libby, et al., 2005).

Yet, for the first time in a good while, there is new research suggesting that the adverse outcomes of group care are not inevitable. For example, while long expressed concerns about "deviancy training" in group treatment conditions of all kinds including group care settings for antisocial youth continue to surface (Dishion, McCord, & Poulin, 1999; Dodge, Dishion, & Lansford, 2006), the field is gaining a better understanding of approaches that minimize the impact of these forces (Dodge, Dishion, & Lansford, 2006; Poulin, Dishion & Burraston, 2001). Recent work by Weiss, et al., (2005) suggests less significance for deviancy training within group treatment than the more extensive peer influences that occur outside of treatment. At the same time the research of Lee and Thompson (2008) finds that although a proportion of youth who entered group care did, indeed, worsen, equal sized groups did improve somewhat or markedly during teaching model family group treatment and that the overall outcomes for teaching family model treatment were as good or better than those of treatment foster care (Lee & Thompson, in press). So, the strong currents away from group care may now be slowed by evidence suggesting that some, well-managed, family-focused models create the kinds of positive powerful environments long envisioned (e.g., Wolins, 1974).

While it is difficult to summarize consensus within child welfare, the general trajectory continues to be markedly away from residential services and towards community and family-centered alternatives for those children and youth in need of intensive treatment services. Several national foundations (i.e., Casey Family Programs, Annie E. Casey Foundation, and the Dave Thomas Foundation) have initiatives to reduce the use of residential care because it involves placing children in non-family like settings and is viewed as pulling resources away from more preventive methods. Several states have new initiatives to reduce group care (e.g., California, Maryland)—some of it based on class action lawsuits and some of it based on a sense of best practice. In some class action settlements (e.g., Alabama) the consent decrees stipulate that children will not be in facilities with more than eight children. These initiatives tend to be somewhat indiscriminate in their decision to move away from residential care—including programs of all sizes and those that have a family focus for of care and those without—although there is a particular concern about not placing young children in group or shelter care (see. e.g., *Kenny A vs. Perdue* in GA, http://childwelfare.net/activities/kennya/kenny_a_case_overview_20060718.html, retrieved on December 13, 2007). Yet, these initiatives are not new and cap more than 140 years of debate about the value of group care and calls for its markedly reduced use and elimination (Wolins & Piliavin, 1964).

The thrust of the contemporary argument about group care is that it is expensive and restrictive and should be used only when there is clear and convincing evidence that the outcomes will be superior to those of foster care and other community-based services. "There is virtually no evidence to indicate that group care enhances the accomplishment of any of the goals of child welfare services: it is not more safe, or better at promoting development, it is not more stable, it does not achieve better long term outcomes, and it is not more efficient as the cost is far in excess of other forms of care" (Barth, 2002, p. 31 quoted in Whittaker, 2006). At the same time, the new evidence from Boys Town and the fact that group care continues to be used throughout the country argues that we should continue to look at the capacity of high-quality group care to complement other family interventions.

Indeed, group care may always be part of the children's services continuum and family-focused residential care has the best results among the various types of residential service (Barth, 2005). Such sentiments echo those expressed by others in the child mental health sector including the previously cited concerns about the dangers of "deviancy training," institutional abuse, and a lack of effectiveness data in the corpus of residential care outcome research (Barker, 1998; English, 2002; Kutash, Robbins, & Rivera, 1996). A research review prepared for the U.S. Surgeon General's Report on Mental Health observes:

Given the limitations of current research, it is risky to reach any strong conclusions about the effectiveness of residential treatment for adolescents. (Burns, Hoagwood, & Mrazek, 1999)

Nor are concerns about continued use of residential group care for children exclusively a U.S. preoccupation as the following observation by a leading U.K. children's services researcher suggests: "The context of the attack on residential homes is that many people no longer believe in them" (Sinclair, 2006, p. 207). Indeed, much international effort is expended to reduce the use of residential care in Eastern Europe and South American (Tobis, 2000; http://lnweb18.worldbank. org/eca/eca.nsf/0/5231989d8868de98852569640071dfa2?OpenDocument, retrieved on December 12, 2007).

Considering the weight of what could only be called an increasingly skeptical consensus about the continued reliance on residential care and treatment as a major child mental health service, or as an alternative to foster care—or, largely for reasons having to do with the potential for institutional abuse, social work researchers and practitioners need to direct serious attention including both theoretical and empirical analysis to the purposes, change theories, treatment protocols, expected outcomes, comparative advantages and organizational requisites for residential group child care if it is to retain its legitimacy as a viable service option for troubled children and their families.

This chapter will attempt to do four things:

1. Provide a brief summary of what might be taken as reasons for concern about residential group care for children.
2. Briefly explore demographics, service trends, and outcome research in residential group treatment.
3. Identify several community-centered intensive treatment alternatives to residential group treatment and the evidence supporting them and
4. Identify several key questions for improving intensive treatment services including residential group care practice and research.

Reasons for Concern about Residential Group Care

While virtually every sector of child welfare service explored in this book reveals unanswered questions awaiting further research and, in some cases, concerns about safety and child well-being, what factors explain the chorus of concerns about residential group care? As the following list suggests, the factors are likely to be multivariate, rather than stemming from a single source. To wit:

1. *The absence of a clear-cut diagnostic indicator for residential placement.* The identification of a scientifically based diagnostic criteria for favoring residential placement over family and community-centered alternatives continues to elude program planners and clinicians. Indeed, presumptions of severity of problems or intensity of services aside, many children who

previously would have made their way into residential treatment settings are now being served in a variety of family and community-centered alternatives. Libby, et al. (2005) showed that the children who do find their way into group care in Colorado are likely to receive the same schedule of treatments, regardless of what the original origins of their diagnosed problems. Barth and colleagues showed, using propensity score matching, that many children with basically the same levels of problems are placed into group care as are placed into intensive in-home services and that those who receive intensive in-home services do just as well, and possibly better, at one year post-discharge (Barth, et al., 2007).

2. *What is assumed to be a preference within some service systems for placement without first attempting some less radical community and family based interventions.* An observation strengthened by the fact that "intensity" of treatment, once thought the sine qua non of residential treatment may now be found in equal measure in less restrictive, community and family-centered alternatives such as "treatment foster care," "wraparound services," and "multi-systemic therapy" (Kutash & Robbins Rivera, 1996, p. 120; Swenson, Henggeler, Taylor, & Addison, 2005.)

3. *Concerns about young children's inability to form close relationships with a parent figure during their stay.* A set of concerns voiced, in particular, where very young children are involved and are in shift care (Berrick, Barth, Needell, & Jonson-Reid, 1997). Indeed, in one study of group care the group care workers had, on average, shorter lengths of stay on the job than the children had in the homes (Berrick, Courtney, & Barth, 1993).

4. *Fear of abuse and neglect within residential settings.* A story that will not go away, either in recently voiced concerns about past practices including some highly regarded treatment settings, or current exposes of institutional abuse in sectarian group care settings here and abroad. Recent reviews have raised again the highly variable quality of care across residential treatment settings (Pumariega, 2006) and the problems attendant to the growth of unlicensed settings, particular those involving wilderness programming (Friedman, et al., 2006)

5. *Questionable effectiveness of residential treatment.* Virtually every review of residential treatment research begins with a comment about the unevenness of the research corpus, with virtually none of the benefit of the doubt given as it is, say, to newer interventions which fit more closely with the value base of systems of care thinking and that have a family-focus (Curry, 1991; Pecora, Whittaker, Maluccio, & Barth, 2000; Ryan, et al., in press)

6. *A lack of consensus on critical intervention components.* A General Accounting Office (GAO) study (1994) conducted in the 1990s, established that while various lists of intervention components exist, there is little indication of which are *necessary* and which are *sufficient* ingredients in a quality residential treatment program: e.g., "therapeutic alliance" (Rauktis, et al., 2005).

7. *A lack of residential treatment theory development.* It is telling that recent reviews in child mental health (Burns & Hoagwood, 2002 and U.S. Depart-

ment of Health & Human Services, 1999) (*Surgeon General's Report on Mental Health*) must reach back to a model from the 1960s (Hobb's Project Re-ED) to muster even the most muted enthusiasm for any form of residential care and treatment. Ironically, at the same time, many of the same precepts of the Achievement Place model of group care that characterize the treatment framework at Boys Town are also characteristic of the most effective treatment foster care programs.

8. *Cost of care.* A first order argument for system reform is that 70 percent of service dollars continue to be spent on residential provision when lower cost, community-centered alternatives are available (Duchnowski, Kutash, & Friedman, 2002, p. 30)

9. *A continuing bias for family-based alternatives.* Since at the least the first decade of this century, there exists a presumption that residential care if used at all ought to be seen as a "last resort" (i.e., when all other options are exhausted). This is particularly so when child dependency is the primary issue. Preference should go to foster family care, adoption, guardianship, or other alternatives. In child mental health, this translates to viewing treatment foster care and intensive in-home services as a more desirable alternative to residential treatment.

For out-of-home placement as a whole, the single most stable trend line in child welfare for much of the twentieth century was the shifting ratio of children in foster family versus residential care as a proportion of the total number of children in out-of-home care. As Kadushin (1980) notes, from approximately the early 1930s to the mid 1970s, the percentage of children in residential care declined from 57 percent to 15 percent, while the percentage in family foster care increased from 43 percent to 85 percent for the total population of children served in out-of-home care. In the federal 2005 count of children involved with CWS who are in group care, 18 percent (94,000) are in group or residential care. The percentage of children in group settings is virtually unchanged since 1999, although the number of children did top 100,000 in 2001 and 2002 (http://www. acf.hhs.gov/programs/cb/stats_research/afcars/tar/report12.htm).

Recent estimates of the numbers of U.S. children in group care suggest a single night count approximating 200,000 of all types (i.e., mental health, child welfare, health, developmental disabilities, and juvenile justice), although the authors caution about the difficulties involved in obtaining valid and reliable information on the total number of children in residential care (Little, Kohm, and Thompson, 2005). Some child welfare involved youth are housed with youth from other programs (and, even, youth placed into residential care voluntarily by their parents) and others are kept apart. At this point, we have little evidence to guide us on whether youth in group care should be separately served by the source of payment for their placement.

The current use of residential care among child welfare recipients in the U.S. is significant—especially for very young children and for adolescents. That said, for some age groups of children, group and residential care account for more than half of all placements into out-of-home care. In some jurisdictions, the likelihood that a teenager will be placed in a group or residential setting goes as high as 80 percent. (The proportion is likely to be higher for youth involved with juvenile services.) This trend may be accelerating, as the number of families with the interest and capacity to provide foster care for adolescents may be declining.

Even among infants, placement in a group setting is surprisingly high. Recent research carried out at the University of Chicago suggests that group care utilization rates for infants receiving out-of-home care under CWS supervision ranges between 3 and 35 percent across American counties (Wulczyn, 2007). We expect that these numbers may be inflated when youth are served in other kinds of institutional facilities like crisis nurseries and in group homes that are providing extended care for children with severe and persistent cognitive and physical impairments.

Serious discussions of group care options for long-term care occur only at the margins of policy and practice debate: e.g., in the interest sparked by the Pew Memorial Trust, San Diego County, and others in "residential academies" and "residential education" (Whittaker, 2006). Recent evidence of the positive benefit of placement in boarding schools, for foster youth in the U.K., and an emerging literature on the San Pasqual School, in San Diego, may further the exploration of this form of out of home care for foster youth (Lee & Barth, under review).

Evidence of the Effectiveness of Group Residential Care and Treatment

While space limits what can be included here, Curry (1991); Pecora, Whittaker, Maluccio, and Barth, (2000); and, more recently, Barth (2002) offer a detailed analysis of residential care research in an American context. For European perspectives, please see Hellinckx, Broekaert, Vanden Berge, and Colton, (1991); the excellent U.K. review authored by Roger Bullock, Michael Little, and Spencer Millham for the Dartington Group (1993); and a recent meta-analysis of European residential research by Knorth, Harder, Zandberg, and Kendrick (2007). The thoughtful and previously cited review by Barth (2002) examines four key components of group care service outcomes: safety and well-being of children while in care, permanence, and reentry from care, long-term success of children in out-of-home care and costs of out-of-home care. Barth notes precious little evidence favoring group care settings over family-centered alternatives in any of these areas and concludes that, "placement in group care settings is not an essential component of child welfare services systems of care for the vast majority of children," and that "group care should only be considered for those children who have the most serious forms of mental illness and self-destructive behavior" (2002, p. iii, 31). While the author joins other children's services researchers in calling for the development of new and empirically tested models of residential care, he finds little in the existing corpus of residential care research to warrant service expansion. In large measure, this lack of confidence derives from the previously mentioned variability in quality control across group residential treatment settings (Pumariega, 2006), and the lack of specification of key intervention components- often accompanied by multiple weaknesses in prior research designs.

Needed are well-specified protocols for residential care and treatment, grounded in change theory, targeted to specific sub-groups of children and youth in need of intensive intervention and amenable to the rigorous randomized controlled trials that have become the *sine qua non* of intervention research. Given the concerns about residential care identified earlier in this chapter and the disinclination of federal and private funding bodies to invest in model development in this area, the prospects for such initiatives remain dim. In contrast, a number of promising model interventions advanced as alternatives to residential care and treatment presently command attention in the landscape of U.S. child mental health services and have been the recipients of significant developmental and research funding at the national level.

In the interim, there is growing evidence that group care that incorporates quality programming (Grietens & Hellinckx, 2004) and a family focus (Hooper, et al., 2000 have significant advantages in terms of achieved outcomes (Barth, 2005). A recent, rigorous study that compares family-based group care to treatment foster care offers renewed hope for the efficacy of quality and family-oriented group care. In this large study of children, six-month post-discharge outcomes were compared for youth who are on the campus of the legendary and Boys Town in Omaha, Nebraska and those who were served by Boys Town in treatment foster care in other communities. The youth on this campus live with a family who provides substantial continuity of care and also have the benefit of many after school activities and tailored educational offerings. This program is unique although there are many other smaller programs that also use cottages on a campus and employ the teaching family structure.

Statistical methods were used to risk adjust for the problems of children admitted to treatment foster care and group care and the result was that the outcomes were somewhat better on some indicators for group care and somewhat better on other indicators for treatment foster care. There was no hands-down winner in this treatment contest as group care outperformed treatment foster care on more outcome indicators (Lee & Thompson, in press).

In a related study, Lee followed 744 youth for 6 months after group care and showed that only a small percentage showed a higher rate of serious antisocial behavior incidents by the completion of their time at GBT (Lee and Thompson, under review). More than one-third made no progress—in part because they started with low baselines of antisocial behavior—and a substantial group improved. Although this is just one study, it does indicate that there is substantial importance in further understanding how quality programming and family-oriented social learning based programs can help to rehabilitate the reputation of group care and, perhaps, help to illuminate helpful elements that can be transferred to other forms of care.

Recent Intensive Service Alternatives within a Systems of Care Framework

Stimulated in part by funding from the National Institute of Mental Health (NIMH), a variety of initiatives have stimulated research and development on several specific interventions that offer alternatives to institutional care, as well as research on the fundamental organizational, community and policy infrastructure for effective child mental health services. A foundation for all child mental health intervention planning is the path-breaking Child and Adolescent Service System Program (CASSP) launched in 1984 by the National Institute for Mental Health to provide both a framework and technology for creating an integrated system of care for children with mental health needs. Central to the CASSP initiative and several successor programs emanating both from government and private foundation resources is the concept of a "system of care" defined as:

> A comprehensive spectrum of mental health and other necessary services which are organized into a coordinated network to meet the multiple and changing needs of children and adolescents with severe emotional disturbances and their families. (Stroul & Friedman, 1986, p. iv)

The system of care thus defined is based on three main elements:

1. The mental health service system efforts are driven by the needs and preferences of the child & family and are addressed by a strengths based approach.
2. The locus and management of services occur within a multi-agency collaborative environment and are grounded in a strong community base.
3. The services offered, the agencies participating and programs generated are responsive to cultural context and characteristics (Burns & Hoagwood, 2002, p. 19).

Initial optimism for systems of care thinking is tempered by the fact that while recent evaluations have documented better service access in communities that have implemented integrated systems of care coordination, no comparable advantages can as yet be detected with respect to child mental health outcomes (Bickman, 1999). Nonetheless, within this broad context of systems of care thinking, numerous specific intervention strategies have developed. Recent reviews identify a range of potentially promising interventions and the empirical evidence that supports them (Burns & Hoagwood, 2002, Epstein, Kutash, &

Duchnowski, 1998; Kutash, Robbins, & Rivera, 1996; Kazdin & Weisz, 2003). These include day treatment and school-based mental health programs, crisis and emergency services, intensive case management programs, mentoring programs, family support and education, and psychopharmacological interventions and interventions designed for specific at-risk populations such as homeless youth and youth with co-occurring substance abuse problems.

For purposes of illustration, we focus here on three interventions that have received considerable attention in children's mental health services in the U.S. and which have been the objects of numerous community replications and research study. These include:

- *Multisystemic Therapy* (MST) was developed principally by Dr. Scott Henggeler, a psychologist now at the Department of Psychiatry & Behavioral Sciences, Medical University of South Carolina (Henggeler & Lee, 2003 ; Henggeler, et al., 1998; Schoenwald & Rowland, 2002).
- *Treatment Foster Care (TFC)* developed in several clinical/research teams in the U.S. and represented here by the model (Multi-Dimensional Treatment Foster Care) principally developed by Dr. Patricia Chamberlain and colleagues at the Oregon Social Learning Center, a highly influential applied behavior analysis developmental research center one of whose founding members is Gerald Patterson (Chamberlain, 2002 & 2003; Chamberlain & Reid, 1998).
- *Wraparound Treatment* a novel, team oriented community centered intervention developed by a variety of individuals including Dr. John Burchard, now Professor of clinical psychology at the University of Vermont, John Van Den Berg ("The Alaska Youth Initiative"), Carl Dennis ("Kaleidoscope Project, Chicago), and others beginning in the early 1980s (Burchard, Bruns, & Burchard, 2002; Burns & Goldman, 1999).

What are the similarities and differences of these interventions and by what criteria should they be assessed? *"Multisystemic Therapy"* (MST) is described by its originators as:

an intensive, time-limited, home and family focused treatment approach….that targets directly for change those factors within the youth's family, peer group, school and neighborhood that are contributing his or her antisocial behavior. (Schoenwald, Borduin, & Henggeler, 1998: 486-487)

Consistent with many features of intensive family preservation services (low caseloads, delivery of services in home/school/community settings, time limits, twenty-four hour availability, comprehensive services), MST operates typically with master's level trained therapist/counselor teams with each counselor serving four to six families at a time for a duration of three to five months. The following core principles of MST inform all aspects of intervention and service delivery:

1. The primary purpose of assessment is to understand the fit between the identified problems and their broader systemic context.
2. Therapeutic contacts should emphasize the positive and should use systemic strengths as levers for change.
3. Interventions should be designed to promote responsible behavior and decrease irresponsible behavior among family members.
4. Interventions should be present-focused and action-oriented, targeting specific and well-defined problems.
5. Interventions should target sequences of behavior within and between multiple systems that maintain identified problems.
6. Interventions should be developmentally appropriate and fit the developmental needs of the youth.
7. Interventions should be designed to require daily or weekly effort by family members.
8. Intervention effectiveness is evaluated continuously from multiple perspectives, with providers assuming accountability for overcoming barriers to successful outcomes.
9. Interventions should be designed to promote treatment generalization and long-term maintenance of therapeutic change by empowering caregivers to address family members' needs across multiple systemic contexts (Schoenwald & Rowland, 2002, p. 99).

Whereas MST has been used extensively though not exclusively in work with anti-social youth within the juvenile justice system, recent efforts have extended the model as an alternative to psychiatric hospitalization for youth with serious mental health problems. MST's developers in fact see the principles and change strategies of the approach as a promising corrective to some of the disappointing results of early "systems of care" research noted earlier.

They note:

> ...given recent findings suggesting that systems of care initiatives may not, in and of themselves, succeed in improving clinical outcomes for youth...progress....will be enhanced by paying increased attention to the nature of treatment and treatment outcomes. *That is, the implementation of service changes (e.g., the introduction of wraparound services, home-based services, school-based mental health services, mentoring programs...) and service system changes (increased access, availability and array of services) are not likely to result in changes in clinical outcome unless services effectively alter those aspects of the youth's and family's natural ecology that are contributing to identified problems.* (Schoenwald, Borduin & Henggeler, 1998: 508, emphasis added)

A recent review of child mental health interventions by Burns & Hoagwood notes that "leading child treatment researchers (such as Kazdin & Weisz, 1998) concur that MST is a well validated treatment model" and reflects an impressive corpus of outcome research including several clinical trials (2002, p. 113). Studies show promising results for both juvenile justice and mental health clientele and studies in process are examining the infrastructure necessary to assure treatment fidelity, an "Achilles Heel" of much earlier family preservation demonstrations. At the moment, MST is enjoying considerable attention in states and local communities across North America and around the world as a model "evidence-based" ecologically oriented treatment program. In 2006 there were 347 approved MST teams around the world (http://mstconference.com/e-newsletter/spring06/, retrieved April 12, 2008). This interest continues despite a rigorous meta-analysis completed by Litell (2005) that raises key questions about the methodology of the many positive findings of MST (especially, that the studies are not independent and they did not account for all the children who started the study and dropped out).

Multi-systemic therapy has not completed any effectiveness trials with child welfare cases, at the time of this writing. The developer of MST (MST Services, affiliated with the Medical University of South Carolina) does not claim efficacy of this approach for abused and neglected children. A new analysis of data from an agency that has been supervised by MST for many years and has MST Clinical Services approved teams is also showing an impact on non-MST approved child welfare cases. The evaluation is based on services data—and not based on a randomized clinical trial—and indicates that MST may result in better outcomes for CWS involved youth than placement into a Re-Ed model residential program. This study, using propensity score matching to risk adjust the characteristics of youth served at home with MST or served in residential care, shows that the one-year outcomes were nearly significantly better (P < .06) for the youth who CWS involved youth received MST than those who were in residential care (Barth, et al., in press).

Treatment Foster Care (TFC)

TFC has been broadly defined as follows:

A service which provides treatment for troubled children within the private homes of trained families. The approach combines the normalizing influence of family-based care with specialized treatment interventions, thereby creating a therapeutic environment in the context of a nurturant family home. (Stroul, 1989, p.13 quoted in Kutash & Robbins Rivera, 1996, p. 69)

Treatment foster care has been developed in several agency sites throughout North America, such as the Pressley Ridge School in Pennsylvania and Girls and Boys Town in Nebraska. As noted earlier, one prominent model was developed at the Oregon Social Learning Center, an applied behavioral research site that has made extensive contributions to our understanding of behavioral intervention with aggressive, oppositional youth. This Oregon Social Learning Center Model of MTFC is described by Chamberlain as a "family-based alternative to residential, institutional and group care for children with significant behavioral, emotional and mental health problems" (2002: 117). Chamberlain identifies three key strategies underpinning MTFC practice:

1. A proactive approach is used for dealing with antisocial behavior and teaching pro-social behavior.
2. Program staff and MTFC parent's roles are stratified to create maximum flexibility and impact.
3. A consistent positive environment is created for program youth (For a detailed description of the "Multidimensional Treatment Foster Care Model," see Chamberlain, 2003)

These strategies are operationalized through a variety of program components including:

1. The child receives individual behavior therapy.
2. The child and family receive family therapy.
3. The foster families are supported with calls home on a daily basis (using the Parent Daily Report) and with support groups.
4. Individual, young coaches are assigned to foster youth so that they can be given life skill training in the community.
5. Placements are almost always limited to one child in a family.

A variety of support and clinical staff including case managers, therapists, foster parent recruiters, trainers, and lay telephone helpers assist and support the primary foster parents in their work with youth and provide as well outreach to the youth's biological parents.

At this point, the evidence base for treatment foster care, while still modest, includes a range of descriptive, quasi-experimental, and controlled clinical trials that report favorable outcomes in post-discharge adaptation and youth behavior, as well as treatment completion for youth who otherwise would be headed into residential treatment. Chamberlain notes a key limitation of the MTFC research base as follows:

> Results from preliminary studies on the efficacy of (M)TFC are promising but there are clear limitations….for example, it is not known what are the necessary and sufficient components of the (M)TFC model that lead to successful outcomes for the various populations of youngsters being served using this model. (Chamberlain, 2002: p. 137)

As with MST, there is considerable interest in many states and localities throughout the U.S. in replicating the MTFC model within the service sectors of juvenile justice, child mental health, and child welfare—in particular, as an alternative to the more expensive forms of residential placement such as residential treatment.

A recent innovation in CWS offers a glimpse of how MTFC might eventually have an impact on all of CWS. Project KEEP, in San Diego County, is a version of MTFC for foster families and kinship families who are already caring for children. The program is brought in to support existing families and has all of the components above (although they do not insist on one child per family and there is somewhat less emphasis on daily data collection). Preliminary results with six- to twelve-year-old children are very favorable; the foster parents are very positive about the intervention, the behavior problems of many children are dropping into the tolerable range, and significantly more children are exiting home or on to other positive exits (rather than having placement moves within the foster care program) (Chamberlain, et al., 2006; personal communication with Patricia Chamberlain, January 16, 2008). At the current time, Project KEEP is expanding and becoming institutionalized in San Diego County and Project KEEP-SAFE is under development and is directed at working with older youth.

Wraparound Treatment

This is described as an approach to treatment that has developed over the last fifteen years to help families with the most challenging children function more effectively in the community (Burchard, Bruns & Burchard, 2002: 69). Definitions of wraparound include "...a definable planning process that results in a unique set of community services that are individualized for a child and family to achieve a positive set of outcomes" (Burns & Goldman, 1999, as quoted in Burchard, et al. 2002). "[A]n approach to child mental health treatment that is child and family centered, focused on family strengths, community-based, culturally relevant, flexible and coordinated across agencies" (Vandenberg & Grealish, 1998; Burchard, Burchard, Sewell, & VanDenBerg, 1993 quoted in Burchard, et. al., 2002: p. 69).

Described by its originators as a "common sense" approach to child mental health treatment the core of which involves identifying the community services and supports that a family of a child with a serious mental health disorder needs and providing them as long as they are needed (Burchard, Bruns, & Burchard, 2002). Services and other forms of helping are strengths based and family-centered and highly individualized. Working in a collaborative team effort with families, the wraparound treatment team first identifies and then implements a coordinated set of interventions designed to address the child's primary mental health and behavioral concerns. From its origins in a few highly visible projects—Kaleidoscope in Chicago and the Alaska Youth Initiative in Alaska—Wraparound Treatment has been the object of demonstrations in a wide variety of community settings throughout North America and several national conferences have brought together practitioners, researchers, planners, and parents to share the latest knowledge on implementation. A leadership conference at Duke University yielded a set of "essential elements" and "requirements for practice" (for a detailed description of the wraparound approach, see Burchard, Bruns & Burchard, 2002: p. 72-73).

Wraparound is a very difficult intervention to evaluate because it is a broad-spectrum approach that overlaps with many other approaches. The evaluations do not have the rigor of MST or MTFC. The California Evidence Based Clearinghouse rates *Wraparound* as a "3" (promising practice) whereas it rates MTFC as a "1"; MST did not submit materials for review because they do not have a CWS program (http://www.cachildwelfareclearinghouse.org/program/68; retrieved April 18, 2008) Burchard, Bruns, and Burchard (2002) identify a research corpus on the Wraparound Treatment approach that consists of fifteen studies including two recently completed randomized clinical trials (RCTs). While results generally favor the children receiving Wraparound Treatment in terms of decline of behavioral symptoms and fewer placement changes post termination, study limitations include questions of treatment documentation and treatment integrity among others. The authors note a clear need to "operationally define and measure adherence to the essential elements" of the (Wraparound) process in order to ensure consistency.

Comparing Intervention Models

What, then, are their similarities and differences of these three promising interventions and by what criteria should they be assessed? Despite some apparent differences—MST, for example, relies most heavily on master's-level trained professionals for service delivery and does not have an explicit CWS program. A recent review by Burns & Hoagwood notes several shared characteristics:

- All three interventions function as components in a "system of care" and adhere to "systems of care" values.
- All are delivered in a community—home, school, neighborhood—context as opposed to an office.
- All three interventions have, in the main, operated in multiple service sectors: mental health, juvenile justice, child welfare. At the time of this writing, MST was not certified for work within CWS.
- All were developed and evaluated in "real world" community settings thus enhancing external validity.
- All lay claim to being less expensive to provide than institutional care (Burns & Hoagwood, 2002, p. 7).

As noted earlier, evaluations of virtually all of these interventions highlights the need for careful analysis and identification of the core intervention components themselves as a necessary requisite to the development of what truly may be described as "evidence based practices" in child mental health. As our earlier reported experiences with "intensive family preservation services" suggests, there are considerable difficulties that ensue when one moves forward with increasingly rigorous outcome studies absent a clear and precise understanding of what are thought to be critical and essential intervention components. Thorough documentation of these and other model interventions is a task of the highest priority in child mental health research. That said, each of these model innovations has already been the focus of multiple randomized control studies, nearly all of which favoring the experimental treatment over the control conditions. Yet, with the exception of the emerging work on Project KEEP, there is a noticeable void of randomized clinical trials with children under Child Welfare Services Supervision. The available studies tend to be of youth with conduct problems (MST) or in the juvenile justice system (MTFC). For the interested reader, Weisz (2004) and Kazdin and Weisz (2003), as well as Burns and Hoagwood (2002), Chamberlain (2003), and Swenson, Henggeler, Taylor, and Addison (2005) provide more detailed information on these studies.

As much interest has been generated in recent years through successful randomized control trials involving several of these and other promising non-residential alternatives, service agencies once wholly residential in their service now reflect a range of service options to meet differential needs of children in need of intensive services. One hopes that the increasing integration of these "evidence-based practice" models in residential care and treatment agencies will encourage cross-fertilization and the development of new and empirically tested intensive treatment services that include a group care component (Whittaker, Greene, Schubert, Blum, Cheng, Blum, Reed, Scott, Roy, & Savas, 2006).

A recent initiative championed by SAMSHA (2006) seeks to "build bridges" between residential provision and other services in "systems of care." A critical question for practice and practice research will be aligning and integrating what is known to be "culturally competent" practice with what is known to be "evidence-based practice" (Blasé and Fixsen, 2003; Miranda, et. al., 2005). This exploration should include a broad investigation of successful strategies for recruiting and engaging families of color in related service areas, such as adoption (McRoy, 2005; Leigh, 1998). At an even more fundamental level, the task of the child welfare worker will involve the leap from "efficacy" to "effectiveness," i.e., "bringing-to-scale" interventions that have produced meaningful outcomes in rigorously controlled research studies.

This will involve increased attention through research and development on creating a sustaining infrastructure—at the policy, organizational, agency, and individual practice levels—to make available "what works" to the vulnerable children and their families who need intensive services. Centers like the newly created National Implementation Research Network (Fixsen, et. al., 2005) will be valuable resources to child welfare practitioners, planners, and service agencies as they grapple with the multiple tasks and challenges of integrating evidence-based practices into mainstream services.

Some Key Questions for Residential Group Care and Its Alternatives

Looking to the future, residential group care for children as well as its community and family centered alternatives presents social work and sister disciplines with a series of interrelated questions.

Questions of Definition

- What precisely do we mean by the variety of forms of service that make up the spectrum of out of home care: group homes; intensive residential treatment; therapeutic foster care?
- What are the critical elements in and *defining* quality characteristics of each ?
- How do we balance and integrate *care* and *treatment* needs of children and what implications does each raise specific to group residential care settings (Whittaker, 2000)?

There is an acute need for more focused work on theoretical model development in residential care and treatment. There is some danger that as the field moves from "service" centered planning to "child/family" centered planning, we will lose a needed focus on residential care as a *total* milieu intervention. *Both* types of planning are needed if we are truly to understand the power of the residential milieu and then use it in creative ways to meet specific clinical and developmental needs of individual children and their families.

Questions of Intake

- For what types of child behavior problems is residential treatment or other forms of placement the "treatment of choice" as opposed to "the last resort"?
- What are the "offsets" to some of the presumed negatives associated with placement (e.g., separation from family/community/culture)? For example, the *intensity* of the treatment provided, the *physical safety* of the child, and the *protection* provided for both the community and the child?

Residential care and treatment is an expensive, complex, and radical intervention. It should be used judiciously and where it can achieve the most good. To achieve this will require some critical rethinking of conventional wisdom. For example, for an individual youth whose life trajectory is headed towards adult incarceration, maybe, as Mary Beth Curtis of Girls and Boys Town notes, the "least restrictive environment" is the one in which most growth (academic, social, physical) can occur for the immediate future and/or where "safe passage" may be provided.

Questions of Outcome

- What span of indicators signal "success" in residential group care and its alternatives?
- At what time points should they be measured and where?
- Should there be a "statute of limitations" on residential outcomes?

Discussion of "outcomes" is proceeding at a very past pace in the U.S. right now, largely as a result of fascination with "managed care" and "evidence-based treatment" closely linked to service contracting. In the residential arena, while there have been some benefits that derive solely from the outcomes discussion (a focus on realistic and well specified goal setting, for example), it is clear that *any* discussion of outcomes must be linked to a discussion of intake and program design issues as well. Otherwise, some residential establishments may find themselves being held accountable for child and family outcomes in areas where they are service-deficient, or for promising "results" in cases where they have inadequately assessed both risk and acuity.

Conclusions

Current Status

Child welfare services is endeavoring to develop a wider array of evidence supported interventions to address the needs of families and children in periods of high intensity needs. These programs are derivative of services with long histories but are developed with more research to guide their development and have stronger implementation models that helps to ensure that they can be replicated. At this time, though, the promise of these interventions from other fields for helping children involved with child welfare has not reached maturity—none of these approaches has convincingly shown its effectiveness with a child welfare supervised population.

Families with such intense and complex needs also need more options. Child welfare has been slow to develop a needed service continuum that softens the differences and blurs the boundaries between in-home and out of home options such as shared care, respite care, and partial placements. This is partly because the funding, in the U.S., for placements is much greater and more available than for in-home services and the rules by which funding can be claimed do not easily handle innovative approaches: for a more fulsome discussion of the "placement" issue (Whittaker & Maluccio, 2002). Kinship care and subsidized guardianship may be a step in that direction. So is the training of kinship caregivers to provide MTFC quality foster care. Moreover, it is critical that those who believe residential care and treatment has a niche to fill in the overall service spectrum make the case based on analysis buttressed by empirical outcome data. In particular, we need more tests of approaches in ways that allow us to see the relative contributions and best uses of wraparound, treatment foster care, multi-systemic treatment, along with residential treatment in an overall service system. So, for example, in Tennessee—which has a *managed care* (i.e., case capitation rather than per diem payment systems) approach to providing services—it is possible to receive payment for having a child in out of home care and, at the same time, starting to work with the family and provide MST, prior to the child's return home. This is very difficult to do in the majority of states even though it is often recognized that aftercare is necessary to achieve successful outcomes (Nelson & Nash, 2008).

Some other things that would be helpful include (Whittaker & Maluccio, 2002):

- Renewed commitment to the development of culturally competent group care practice models and joining this effort, inextricably, with efforts to integrate evidence-based practices" into group care settings;
- Redoubling our efforts at parent involvement (Jenson & Whittaker, 1987; Braziel, 1996);
- Expanding residential respite options for parents of high-resource needs children;
- Developing more creative short-term residential treatment;
- Focusing on child well being and family functioning as outcome measures, including studying honestly the limits as well as the potential of family centered service delivery. It would also include working to personalize residential care settings and reinforce primary caregivers (Trieschman, Whittaker & Brendtro, 1969);
- Developing models of whole family care, for example, by combining respite with holiday time and skill building for families;
- Examining the potential for the co-location of services, such as family support and residential care. This may include seeking partners to locate our residential programs in an overall service network;
- Conducting longitudinal research to study of developmental outcomes for youth in shared care and those temporarily placed. It would also include redesigning some group care settings for permanent living for special sub-groups of youth and re-examining communal alternatives (Levine, Brandt, & Whittaker, 1998).

Future Directions

Achieving even a few of these modest changes absent a more focused and thoughtful discussion on substitute care as a whole will not be easy. It is imperative that social work researchers and practitioners bring the worlds of policy, research, and practice in residential and foster care into much closer proximity so that we can assess what the challenges and strengths are in each domain and then chart a course of action for renewal. To do this, the field sorely needs fresh conceptual thinking on both the varieties of group care for children, as well as empirical research to test the efficacy of innovative group care designs. International perspectives on group care such as those cited earlier (Knorth, Harder, Zandberg, & Kendrick, 2007) will help to shed light on the issue of the proper place of group residential care and treatment in an overall service continuum and will be helpful as well in broadening and stimulating our limited and, typically, parochial discussions in the states. Social work has a clear stake-hold in addressing the issue of residential group care's future based on the profession's long-standing involvement in service delivery, research, and training and advocacy on behalf of children and youth in need of intensive treatment services.

Note

1. Portions of this chapter appeared earlier in Whittaker, J.K. (2008). "Children: Group Care" prepared for Mizrahi, T. and Davis, L. *Encylopedia of Social Work, 20th Edition.* New York & Oxford: Oxford University Press; and in Whittaker, (2000; 2004; and 2006).

For Further Information

For current issues, trends and directions in identifying the components of evidence-based intensive treatment services for troubled children and youth, see:

Chorpita, B.F., Becker, K.F. and Daleiden, E.L. (2007). Understanding the common elements of evidence-based practice: Misconceptions and clinical examples. *Journal of the American Academy of Child & Adolescent Psychiatry,* 45 (5): 647-652.

Weisz, J.R. and Gray, J.S. (2008) Evidence-based psychotherapy for children and adolescents: Data from the present and a model for the future. *Child and Adolescent Mental Health*, 13,(2): 54-65.

For a U.K. perspective on group residential care and treatment, see:

Sinclair, I. (2006). Residential care in the UK in McAuley, C., Pecora, P.J. and Rose, W. *Enhancing the Well-being of Children and Families through Effective Interventions: International Evidence for Practice.* London & Philadelphia: Jessica Kingsley Publishers: 203-217.

13

Organizational Requisites and Challenges to Effective Child Welfare Services

Introduction

The preceding chapters have outlined the major concepts and principles for providing effective child welfare services and clarified that CWS does not operate in isolation and is affected by local unemployment rates and community infrastructure such as housing, police and fire protection, public transportation, and other community risk, including protective and infrastructure factors. The availability and quality of other services is also critical, such as employment, health and mental health, education, vocational development, and juvenile justice. Community levels of racism, sexism, and other forms of discrimination also affect the ability of CWS to succeed in protecting children and strengthening families. Because agency capacity will be affected by these factors, these issues are mentioned as a cautionary note because supplemental agency supports may be needed if the community infrastructure is not adequate for supporting families.

Components of Organizational Excellence[1]

When we think about working for an excellent organization, what qualities spring to mind? What aspects of that organization differentiate it from others? Is excellence related to the presence of a clear focus on the service being delivered? Is it because staff members understand management's expectations and have a clear idea of what constitutes excellence? Are staff members acknowledged for increasing those identified elements of success? Are service recipients and staff valued by the organization?

To deliver effective services and be considered an excellent place to work, an organization must have a number of components in place. Workers and supervisors need to be supported in specific ways that complement the agency's mission and program objectives. Workforce, work place and the practice model all must be working well to have overall effectiveness. One cannot just address one without addressing the others (personal communication, Hal Lawson, February 5, 2008). Unfortunately, too many social workers and other human services practitioners work in "toxic organizational environments" characterized by unclear organizational missions, overcrowded office space, poor supervision, low salaries, large caseloads, and troubled working relations between co-workers or other program units (Cole, 1987; National Association of Social Workers, 2006; Ostroff, 2006; US General Accounting Office, 1995). These organizations may not adhere to many of the administrative or practice standards published by the Child Welfare League of America, Joint Commission on the Accreditation of Hospitals, Council on Accreditation, or other accrediting organizations (CWLA, 1984; JCAH, 2006; NASW, 2006). However, recent demands for system improvement have resulted in an increased number of state and county agencies seeking COA accreditation to enhance services and staffing. Furthermore, leaders of public and private agencies *are* paying attention to how the following organizational, managerial, and structural components support the effective delivery of human services.

1. *A clear organizational mission and program philosophy is widely disseminated throughout the organization.* A simple yet effective mission and philosophy statement that captures the organization's dedication to its services and those served signifies an understanding of the clients and communities being served. An effective agency organizes itself from the customer inward through the creation of customer-driven agency outcomes, services, and quality improvement processes ensuring that the most efficacious interventions are being provided (Patti, 2008).

2. *Leadership clearly understands what organizational excellence is in particular service areas.* This requires the specification of a "logic model" or theory of change for the program that outlines the key short-term, intermediate, and long-terms results to be achieved; what staff, equipment, and other resources will be necessary to achieve them; and the cost of achieving those outcomes.

3. *Organizational standards of quality and expected results.* Performance data should be brought to bear to establish benchmarks and track improvement or make corrections to stimulate improvement. When feasible, agencies should establish trend lines that repeatedly compare achieved standards of quality and key program expectations. Trend data help clarify patterns and counteract distraction that might otherwise result from an occasional tragic event, bad quarter, or extraordinary year.

4. *Workforce challenges are addressed.* Excellent service quality and outcomes can only be achieved with fundamental organizational commitment to hiring staff with the necessary prerequisite values, knowledge, and skills and providing staff with appropriate and adequate resources to accomplish their

jobs. Challenges such as maintaining realistic caseload sizes, workplace safety, salaries, and other components will be discussed.

5. *High quality ongoing coaching and monitoring of staff activities, and a strong system of supervisory capacity and supports.* Attention to human resource issues includes a positive organizational climate, treating staff with dignity, maximizing professional discretion to the extent possible, and development of staff through regular training opportunities.

6. *Wise use of effective intervention and other technologies.* Because technology can be an expensive distraction from the hard and non-glamorous work of day-to-day service delivery and supervision, it is important to balance the use of technology. In other words, a wise leader and supervisor carefully balances what kinds of technology staff really need versus the kinds of technology that staff want or that management thinks will improve productivity (e.g., teleconference facilities, network 2.0 functions, data-capturing white boards, voice activated computers, and dial-in web-based assessment measures).[2]

7. *Community-based services and careful interaction with the media builds political support and protection.* Many strong agency leaders have been brought down by a tragic event that was not well managed in the media—resulting in a loss of confidence in the upper reaches of the agency or community. Agencies need a carefully designed communications plan, including a crisis management plan for such predictable exigencies. Development of prior political and media support is also essential to buffer human services administrators and staff from the day-to-day controversies of this work?

The interrelationships between many of these factors are illustrated in Figure 13.1, Children's Defense Fund's Components of an effective child welfare workforce, and reinforced by the Baldrige Criteria for Performance Excellence Framework (U.S. Department of Commerce, 2006, p. 5) and the writings of Austin & Hopkins (2004). Note that while agency leaders and front-line supervisors may not be primarily responsible for all of these areas, they work within this larger context and that many readers of this book will soon be a supervisor or agency leader.

Establish a Clear Agency Mission, Philosophy, and Program Objectives

One of the most common characteristics of effective human service organizations is their use and commitment to a clear, well-defined, value-driven organizational mission (Peters & Waterman, 1983; Selznick, 1984). Growing numbers of child welfare agencies have been able to define and sustain their mission in ways that promote staff, client, and public understanding of what it is that they do. This image and clear sense of mission is bolstered by a supportive ideology: a particular set of values and beliefs about the organizational mission, service technology, and the clients served. Patti, et al. (1987) believes that organizational excellence is dependent upon:

Figure 13.1
Fourteen Components to Support an Effective Child Welfare Workforce
(CDF/CR Child Welfare Policy Workgroup)

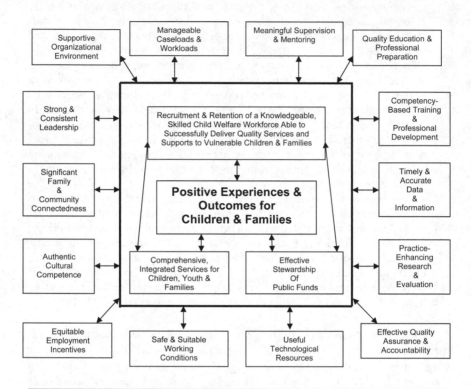

Source: Children's Defense Fund. (2006). *Components of an effective child welfare workforce to improve outcomes for children and families: What does the research tell us?* Retrieved May 21, 2008 from: http://www.childrensdefense.org/site/DocServer/CW_Workforce_Report_2.pdf?docID=3563. Reprinted with permission from the Children's Defense Fund.

...not only clear objectives, structured roles, competent personnel, and adequate resources to perform well, but more importantly, the organization needs values, symbols, and beliefs that attach a social significance to the organization's outcomes and processes, and that help to reconcile ever present ambiguity and uncertainty. (p. 378)

As with virtually all human service programs, CWS agencies function within a political and organizational context that heavily influences their organizational mission and philosophy. For example, a variety of family-centered child welfare services such as family support services, special-needs adoption, and post-adoption counseling have expanded during the past ten years. This occurred, in part, because it was recognized that permanency planning was a necessary but insufficient way to minimize the number of children being placed in substitute care. The extent to which a family-centered approach is documented as a cost-effective alternative to more traditional child welfare services will also increase its popularity because of fiscal austerity and the need to establish program accountability (Busch & Folaron, 2005).

An agency mission that places priority on a family-centered approach is also being promoted because of the "ideological fit" of such an agency mission with the standards of the Child and Family Services Review and of allied agencies involved with children's mental health. Many child welfare agencies are also reconsidering the agency mission in order to respond to the requirements of the CFSR to deepen their community partnerships so that they can show that they are working with education, juvenile justice, mental health, and the courts to achieve services to promote child well-being.

While this process often requires changes in state law, administrators and line staff feel it is worth the effort in terms of more effective targeting of services and lowering unreasonably high worker caseloads. These administrators may believe that child welfare staff should not act as public health enforcers, school attendance enforcement agents, or family therapists for local school systems for cases that do not very clearly involve child abuse or neglect. Other agencies are attempting to limit their child protection types of cases because of concern for abrogating parent rights and the need to try to allocate scarce resources to primary and secondary prevention programs rather than to the administrative costs of pursuing court-supervised interventions. A variety of innovative program designs have been proposed along those lines, along with a call for client-centered (Weissbourd, 1996) and outcome-oriented (Patti, 2008) services.

Leadership Has a Clear Understanding of Organizational Excellence

Organizational Outcomes Are Clear

As mentioned above and in Chapter 1, according to professional and federal standards, child welfare agencies need to achieve a critical set of outcomes in three broad outcome domains: *child safety*, *child permanence*, and *child and well-being* (US Department of Health and Human Services, 2003). Wulczyn and his colleagues suggest that the mandate for the child welfare system should be expressed as *achieving* safety and permanency outcomes and *ensuring* the child welfare system engages the education, health, and mental health systems. This will help the child welfare system rightfully take credit for working to create safe and stable families for children without creating an unrealistic expectation of improving a wide range of indicators of well-being. (Well being will be enhanced, naturally, with greater safety and permanency.)

Many child welfare agencies are building "logic models" that describe the interventions necessary to accomplish the desired service results. After outlining the philosophical principles, outcomes and performance measures of their child welfare programs, they determined what community and organizational capacity and funding is needed to achieve those results. These logic models are backed by concise practice protocols or guidelines where possible, within a management philosophy that "manages to outcomes rather than to process."

Note how organizational excellence is rooted in administrators being expert in the implementing interventions or services that will be most effective for meeting their customers' needs. This also involves paying attention to strategic planning, understanding the agency's market area, being focused on the well-being and skills of staff, and paying attention to program performance outcomes. Balancing service capacity and quality is a hallmark of a successful organization.

Interorganizational and Organizational Climate and Supports

A team approach of providing services to children and families requires that participating agencies demonstrate that they each have economic or other incentives to communicate, cooperate, and coordinate activities so that collaboration can occur. Integrating essential child welfare and ancillary services also can include integrating behavioral health services. Interorganizational coordination can have mixed results in improving service quality and outcomes if organizational climate and treatment of staff are not also considered (Glisson & Hemmelgarn, 1998; Glisson & James, 2002). It has been demonstrated that collaborative efforts are seldom successful based solely on participants' good will or intentions (Lindblom, 1990), a team approach of providing services to children and families requires that participating agencies have incentives to communicate, cooperate, and coordinate activities so that collaboration can occur.

Additional mechanisms for promoting collaboration include (1) funding and accountability criteria based on outcomes achieved; (2) setting program goals across disciplines; (3) encouraging the use of informal ties among managers to get things done across organizational lines; and (4) working together on outcomes with no single organization having control over all the processes involved. New state initiatives in Arizona and elsewhere are striving to achieve these breakthroughs to achieve new gains in program effectiveness (e.g., Arizona Department of Economic Security, 2006).

Factors within the organization are also important for effectiveness. Glisson and colleagues (2006) have shown that the application of these principles can have an impact on child welfare agency climate, culture, and on the turnover of child welfare workers. In this elegant study, the social work investigators designed an intervention at the agency level entitled ARC (Availability, Responsiveness, and Continuity) that involved consistent consultation with agency management about the way that they led their organization and responded to the needs of their staff. Using an experimental design, ten urban and sixteen rural case management teams were randomly assigned to either the ARC organizational intervention condition or to a control condition. The ARC organizational intervention reduced the probability of child welfare worker's quitting their jobs during the year by two-thirds and improved organizational climate in urban and rural case management teams. Glisson has also begun to demonstrate that reducing this high staff turnover and poor organizational climate has a direct impact on service quality and outcomes for children (Charles Glisson, personal communication, January 14, 2007) (see Figure 13.2).

Organizational Standards of Quality and Expected Results

Specify, Measure, and Use Agency Performance Data to Improve Services

Another organizational requisite for CWS that supports effective practice is the systematic collection and use of program evaluation data by program plan-

Figure 13.2
Key Organizational Factors Can Support Workers and Affect Service Outcomes

...this community-based study in Tennessee found that some of the factors associated with worker motivation outweighed system integration strategies. Glisson and his team set out to study if a services integration initiative, that also affected organizational structure, could improve outcomes of children. But they also measured other factors to see what else may be important such as organizational climate and culture. Organizational climate reflects the perceptions of the work environment, whereas organizational culture refers to the ways things are done in a work environment – the norms and expectations (Cooke & Szumal, 2000; James, 1982; Sorensen, 2002). What factors out-performed the services integration factors? What factors were associated with both a higher quality service delivery process and better child outcomes? The factors are noted below:

- Fairness in staff policies and practices
- Clarity in roles and responsibilities
- Less depersonalization—a positive work climate where workers felt personal support
- Less role overload
- Staff encouragement
- Supervisor identification with the organizational mission
- Low staff conflict regarding role
- Cooperation among staff
- Growth and advancement opportunities
- Emotional exhaustion was low
- Sense of personal accomplishment
- Job satisfaction

Source: Glisson & Hemmelgarn, 1998, p. 413.

ners, supervisors, and line staff. Any quality organization achieves success by delineating and meeting performance expectations. This is not done without a vibrant and practical *management information enterprise* that has the commitment of leadership, supervisors, and staff. This system enables regular collection and use of program performance data, including performance measurement, analysis, and knowledge management. Many organizations are drowning in data, but thirsty for usable information. Both service output and client outcomes data are important, as well as consumer perceptions about the quality of the service delivery process. But these data need to be organized and analyzed in ways that provides meaningful and timely information to affect decision making at multiple organizational levels.

Performance measurement ultimately should also be tied to a strong process management system, including on-going assessment of program fidelity, outputs, outcomes, and other aspects of quality. At a minimum, the evaluation data should at least be used to (1) ensure that care and services provided are in accordance with the purpose of the agency service; (2) assess the adequacy and efficiency of agency resources to carry out the objectives of the services; (3) ensure that each service carries out the intent of the agency in making it available; and (4) determine whether services are effective by using a valid research design to measure case outcomes for clients (CWLA, 1984, p. 20).

In setting or examining program performance levels, it is essential to monitor multiple criteria. For example, family reunification programs that are poorly designed (e.g., where reunifications occur too quickly or without sufficient after care) may result in shorter lengths of stay in foster care, but may also result in more children reentering foster care.

Now more than ever, child welfare agencies are being asked to increase the amount of evaluation effort in all program areas to refine prevention, treatment, and administrative efforts in this field. Many federal programs require "evaluation," which has typically meant clients served, but now federal programs—and many local ones—also ask for trend data on outcomes. Research efforts must, however, be realistic, empower communities, be carefully fitted to the program objectives, and incorporate a variety of approaches—quantitative and/or qualitative. Experts are urging that a more consumer-oriented management and service delivery system be adopted, where client outcome becomes more of the program focus rather than how much service was provided (Fetterman & Wandersman, 2007; Rapp & Poertner, 1988). Indeed, Blome and Steib (2007) have decried the "multiple watchers" involved in monitoring child welfare staff performance when what is urgently needed is a well trained and stable professional workforce with reasonable caseloads and adequate services to which to refer families.

The extent to which the agency management information system can support program evaluation depends on if they support turning data into information by supervisors and workers. Organizational integrity is increased when programs are validated through achievement of positive client outcomes. Cost-effectiveness data allow organizations to more clearly advocate for program funding. Standardized assessment instrument—such as the North Carolina Family Assessment Scales, the Achenbach Suite of Checklists, the Strengths and Difficulties Questionaire, and the Child Well-Being scales—are increasingly in use, although at least some of these instruments are not scored until much later and the information is not provided to the clients or workers (Barth, et al., 2007). Management information systems and required paperwork in many child welfare agencies are being redesigned to reduce duplication and provide more useful information regarding both client outcomes and worker performance—often with considerable initial disruption of office work. Yet, at least some results indicate that the additional time spent learning a new computer system was not time taken from interactions with clients (Weaver, Moses, Furman, & Lindsey, 2003).

Some Cautions about Performance Assessment: The Need to Focus on Quality and Understand What the Outcome and Quality Indicators Mean

Outcomes assessment should not pursued at the cost of ignoring the quality of the services that are provided. Use of better outcome measures can help determine and improve the quality of service. On the other hand, there is danger in overreliance on outcomes, given the present state of the field. For example, some state or local governments have transferred many child welfare services to a private provider, with minimal process guidelines or standards of quality but instead using a few outcome measures to guide agency practice and to govern their level of payment to the private agency. This may be especially likely to occur when there are capitated payments and few process requirements governing placement and service delivery. Using outcome measures as a wholesale substitute for requirements governing such things as staff qualifications, case planning, and review procedures and due process protections can be literally very dangerous to children.

Another danger in the wholesale substitution of outcome measures for quality standards or process requirements (such as licensure, qualifications, protocols for service selection, or required arrays of services) is that this prevents child welfare from becoming a mature field of practice. If there is no consistency in training or qualifications of staff, service selection, and available services, then we do not develop expertise in our field; for this reason the American Public Human Services Association has undertaken a massive effort to identify key indicators of quality public child welfare services delivery so that every state will have access to such information (Personal communication, Anita Light, December 11, 2007).

Finally, one of the challenges ahead is to link the daily activities and observable outcomes of child welfare services to their impact on the lives of children when they are no longer under the supervision of child welfare services. A focus on outcomes must never be allowed to become a focus on *child welfare services* outcomes—vulnerable children need our vigilance and assurances that we care about them as whole individuals, across all life domains.

Address Workforce Challenges

Overview

One of the most critical components of organizational excellence is attracting and maintaining a stable, motivated, and skilled work force. Child welfare agencies have much difficulty in the area. Privatization of human services in some jurisdictions has made it more difficult to support workers in the public sector. The current fiscal environment of resource scarcity or large fluctuations in funding from year to year has also hindered progress in addressing workforce issues. These factors, and strategies to change the situation, are discussed in this section. This section will describe workforce challenges and include some strategies for addressing them.

Low Minimal Qualifications for Child Welfare Positions

Qualifications remain low in many states. As late as the late 1990s, fewer than 15 percent of child welfare agencies require child welfare workers to hold either BSWs or MSWs (CWLA, 1999). The National Association of Social Workers (NASW), CWLA, and others recommend that child welfare administrators and supervisors have MSWs and previous child welfare experience, and that direct service workers have, at least, BSWs (US General Accountability Office, 2003). A study conducted in 1999 and 2000 found that about 40 percent of the approximately 50,000 American child welfare workers have BSWs or MSWs, still in approximately equal proportions (Barth, Lloyd, Christ, Chapman, & Dickinson, in press). This increase could be because of different methods used in the current study or could indicate a growth in the proportion of child welfare workers with social work training—perhaps a result of a decade of Title IVE programs that involve university and agency partnerships. In either case, the proportion continues to be low. Those workers with a BSW or MSW and working in non-urban settings were more satisfied in their work than those without. This relationship did not hold in urban settings. Even with low qualifications in many states, ninety (90) percent of states reported having difficulty in recruiting and retaining child welfare workers (GAO, 1995, 2003).[3]

More job-related or higher education boosts performance. Having a social work degree was associated with higher job satisfaction, greater perception of life-work balance, and greater supervisory support according to one study of twelve counties in a largely rural state (Smith, 2005). Furthermore, education, specifically holding an MSW, appears to be the best predictor of overall performance in social service work (Booz-Allen & Hamilton, 1987) and in one study was judged to provide the best preparation (Folaron & Hostetter, 2007). Child welfare staff with BSW and MSW degrees were found to be more effective in developing successful permanency plans for children who were in foster care for more than two years (Albers, Rittner, & Reilly, 1993). The Russell study also showed that turnover rates are higher in states that do not require baccalaureate degrees or MSWs for upper-level positions and do not engage in professionally oriented recruitment and retention activities (Russell, 1987, pp. 35-38) (for a review, please see Strolin, McCarthy, & Caringi, 2007). One recent study found that child welfare staff completing their MSW graduate degrees planned to stay within child welfare for between five to nine more years (Auerbach, McGowan, & LaPorte, 2007). Fox, Miller, and Barbee (2003) found that those BSW graduates who had participated in specialized child welfare training were rated better by their supervisors as better prepared and having higher job skills.

Despite the advantages of hiring professionally educated child welfare workers, many factors may account for the consistently low number of trained social work staff (Ellett & Leighninger, 2007)—not the least of which are poor working conditions in many child welfare agencies and the lack of sufficient child welfare focus in social work education. One of the first tasks involved in hiring capable staff members is the specification of the major job tasks to be performed in the position. Accurate position descriptions are essential for communicating to workers what is expected of them. The descriptions should accurately reflect the difficult job tasks that must be performed and the worker competencies—the major knowledge, skills, abilities, and attitudes—necessary for effective job performance. There is increased attention to promoting collaboration between child welfare agencies and human resource departments to enhance the connections between job descriptions, job requirements, and hiring practices (CSSP, http://www.cssp.org/uploadFiles/2431_CSSP_book1_FINAL.pdf).

Improving the Quality of Human Services through Results-Oriented Human Resource Management

Unfortunately, while some progress is being made in specifying the worker characteristics of successful child welfare staff, additional research needs to be conducted to specify more fully the competencies necessary for workers (and supervisors) to possess both at the time they are initially hired and later as full-fledged or "journeyman" staff members. Lack of these data has contributed in some state agencies to the weakening of educational standards for child welfare positions. In fact, given changes in state hiring standards for child welfare that weaken hiring requirements ("reclassification" or "declassification") poor working conditions, and high staff turnover, the number of child welfare staff with undergraduate and graduate degrees in social work remains low (IASWR, 2005; U.S. GAO, 2003). Furthermore, the hiring registers in many states lack BSW or MSW applicants, especially for rural areas. Thus, child welfare services are being provided by personnel with a wide variety of educational backgrounds;

some that are job related such as social work, psychology, or marriage and family counseling and many that are not.

This trend of underutilization of social work-trained staff is ironic in light of a small but growing number of studies that document the job relevance or superior job performance of workers with social work degrees or specialized child welfare training as part of a social work degree (Institute for the Advancement of Social Work Research, 2005). However, there still remains a need for more research that assesses the differential effectiveness of BSWs, MSWs, and other types of educated personnel in child welfare. And the continuing lack of professionally trained child welfare staff is to be expected, given high caseloads, de-emphasis in some states on worker provision of treatment-oriented services, fiscal pressures to keep salaries low, reduction in agency programs for tuition reimbursement and administrative leave, misinterpretation of Equal Employment Opportunity and Affirmative Action regulations, friction between unions and professional organizations, fewer social workers in policy and management positions, and other factors (e.g., IASWR, 2005; Reisch, 2006; U.S. GAO, 2003). These issues are discussed in the next section.

Lack of Worker Continuing Education and Training

There are two major federal funding sources for improving the child welfare workforce: the Title IV-B, Section 426 child welfare training program and Title IV-E training. Title IV-B provides discretionary grants to public and private non-profit institutions of higher education for full-time or part-time training programs (FY 2003 funding: $7 million). Title IV-E provides an enhanced federal match of 75 percent to fund training programs for both current and prospective child welfare staff. In FY 2001, 49 states received a total of $276 million in Title IV-E training reimbursements. The median state reimbursement was $3.1 million and ranged from $1,400 in Wyoming to $59 million in California (U.S. GAO, 2003; NASW, 2003). While that is the amount of IV-E training reimbursement, this is for all IV-E training, only part of which focuses on BSW and or MSW education of current or future workers.

University-Agency Child Welfare Training Partnerships, funded under Title IV-E, were found by GAO to have some positive impact on child welfare agencies' ability to recruit and retain child welfare staff. Today, partnerships exist in more than 40 states, and use more than $50 million annually to prepare workers for the challenges of child welfare service delivery (U.S. GAO, 2003).

High Worker Caseloads

A major reason why child welfare staff resign is their workload. Large caseloads and worker turnover delay the timeliness of investigations and limit the frequency of worker visits with children, hampering agencies' attainment of some key federal safety and permanency outcomes (US General Accounting Office, 2003). The average caseload for child welfare workers is between twenty-four and thirty-one children. Caseloads range from ten to one hundred children per worker (Alliance for Children and Families, American Public Human Services Association, & Child Welfare League of America, 2001). Although there is limited information about the relationship between workload and effectiveness in achieving child welfare goals, the CWLA recommends caseloads of between twelve and fifteen children per worker. The Council on Accreditation recommends that caseloads not exceed eighteen children per worker.

Caseloads are high, but *workloads* are even higher due to the growing complexity of each case and the increasingly legalized court processes that, especially, now involve more representatives for children. The unwillingness of the state and federal governments to invest in child welfare services results in a shortage of staff and high caseloads. A vicious cycle is created when poor working conditions cause staff members to leave. This turnover increases the caseloads for other staff that remain behind, requiring a longer period to recruit qualified staff because of heavy caseloads (Russell, 1987).

Many states and counties recognize the link between competent practice, adherence to policy standards, and reasonable workloads. In some states, like Illinois and Washington, the pursuit of accreditation of their child welfare programs helped establish reasonable caseload sizes that then can be funded and enforced. Other strategies include:

- Statewide adoption of CWLA caseload standards;
- Designing and implementing more sophisticated studies of workload standards;
- Passing state legislation to limit caseload sizes;
- Encouraging class action, civil rights, or other forms of lawsuits that argue for reduced caseloads; and
- Using more paraprofessional technicians to assist with casework tasks.

Low Salary Levels and Problems in Job Classification Hamper
Organizational Effectiveness

The Annie E. Casey Foundation (2004, p. 33), the National Association of Social Workers (2004), and others have documented that public child welfare worker salaries in many agencies are low, compared with other similar professions and positions. In addition, in October of 2003 NASW surveyed 716 members of a relatively new child welfare practice group among their membership.[4] They found that of those section members employed full-time, the median salary was $43,000. Only 13 percent of section members earn less than $30,000 for full-time work. Salaries increased with experience in the field, with those in the field twenty years or more earning a median salary nearly twice that of those in the field less than three years ($60,000 versus $32,300). Child welfare workers' salaries are significantly lower than salaries for employees in safer and supportive work environment, such as teachers, school counselors, nurses, and public-health social workers (GAO, 2003).

In one national study (Lindsay, 1988), salaries and promotion opportunities were two of the major factors identified by child welfare administrators that contribute to a positive or negative organizational climate. With the expansion of social work jobs in the private nonprofit and for-profit sectors, the competition for social workers puts the low-salaried child welfare positions at a distinct disadvantage. Social work licensing laws are now in all fifty states and may contribute to a situation where child welfare agencies become a training ground that enables new graduates to accrue the necessary clinical hours, but not stay with the agency beyond the point of clinical licensing. (At the same time, some states [e.g., Maryland] require child welfare workers to have a license so it helps keep the door open for additional training and professional development.)

Attracting qualified staff will require a multifaceted campaign involving public education, merit system refinements, administrator advocacy, and possible use of collective bargaining agreements. Other strategies include:

- supporting advocacy efforts by professional organizations to raise salaries and increase benefit packages;
- studying pay equity studies and bringing lawsuit; and
- requesting social services departments to reclassify position descriptions and other types of job analyses so that better descriptions of the social worker competencies required for effective service for child welfare positions are included.

Workplace Safety

Seventy percent of front-line caseworkers have been victims of violence or received threats of violence (AFSCME, 1998). One state found that 90 percent of its child protective services employees had experienced verbal threats; 30 percent experienced physical attacks; and 13 percent were threatened with weapons (GAO, 2003). When the group being surveyed had more voluntary agency staff participating, the number drops substantially. Nineteen percent of NASW child welfare section members report having been victims of violence, although 63 percent say they have been threatened at some point in their child welfare practice. One interesting note was how many social workers cited violent acts by *children*. However, 94 percent of section members say they generally feel safe making home visits. The overwhelming majority (98 percent) of these members make home visits alone. Ninety-two percent say they are "somewhat" or "very comfortable" making home visits alone (NASW, 2004). In 2007, in response to concerns about social worker safety, Congressman Dennis Moore introduced the Social Worker Safety Act (H.R. 2165).

Worker Turnover

Prevalence. Turnover of child welfare workers is estimated to be between 30 and 40 percent annually nationwide. The average tenure of child welfare workers is less than two years, although there is great variation by location. Rates range from a low of 0 percent to a high of 600 percent (U.S. GAO, 2003). These rates can be deceiving because many workers get promoted to supervisor early in their careers, and they are treated as "turnover." As a result, supervisors often have only three years of experience (U.S. GAO, 2003). Challenges to recruitment and retention include: low salaries; high caseloads/workloads; administrative burdens; risk of violence limited, non-supportive, or otherwise inadequate supervision; and insufficient training (DePanfilis & Zlotnik, in press; Jaquet, Clark, Morazes, & Withers, 2007; U.S. GAO, 2003).

Many states estimate that 60 percent of turnover is preventable (Alliance for Children and Families [ACF], American Public Human Services Association [APHSA], and The Child Welfare League of America [CWLA], 2001). There is some evidence that turnover is consistently higher in states that do not require any kind of degree for child welfare positions and consistently lower in states that require a master's degree in social work (MSW) (Russell, 1987). The National Council on Crime and Delinquency (2006) found a relationship between rates of child abuse and neglect and staff turnover looking at high and low functioning counties. Furthermore, other studies found that Title IV-E, Social work educated workers had higher retention rates than other BSW or MSWs (IASWR, 2005). For example, in Florida, staff without educational preparation for child welfare work are most likely to leave within one year of being hired (CWLA, 1990). More than 80 percent of child welfare workers who stay at their jobs beyond two years have completed at least one social work degree (Cicero-Reese & Black, 1998).

Why should we care about supporting and retaining staff members? Frontline workers represent one of the organization's most precious resources. Continued staff overload, burnout, and inadequate attention to the mental health stresses of workers is damaging, with fewer potential positive outcomes for children and families and greater potential cost to society of child abuse/neglect (AFCSME report at http://www.afscme.org/pol-leg/dj01.htm: National Council on Crime and Delinquency, 2006).

Not only are dollars drained from the organization, but knowledge is drained as well, especially since most business and human service organizations are not yet adept at storing and managing knowledge as a key form of information. If new worker orientation and on-the-job training is a form of investment, then maximizing employee retention is a way of maximizing a special return on investment (Ramiall, 2004). And if that knowledge is combined with a strong commitment to the organizational mission and strategies, then that investment is magnified: "competence magnified by commitment" (Ulrich, 1998, p. 125

as cited in Ramiall, 2004). What might not be obvious is the important connection between worker turnover, child stress, lack of foster parent support and resulting placement disruption.[5] In a recent foster care alumni study with the states of Oregon and Washington, Pecora, Kessler, Williams, O'Brien, et al. (2006) found a strong connection between placement change and a range of alumni outcomes. When they controlled for child behavioral difficulties, type of child maltreatment, and other intervening factors in statistical simulations, they found that minimizing placement change was one of the most powerful ways to increase the success of children in care by reducing negative mental health and other outcomes (Pecora, et al., 2010) (also, see Ryan & Testa, 2004).

Turnover of ongoing case managers does affect permanency for children. Dramatic findings were released from a study of private agencies in Milwaukee County that showcase how turnover of ongoing case managers does have an impact on permanency for children. The researchers examined what happened to that agency's ability to find permanent homes for children in foster care as staff turnover increased. They focused on 659 children who entered care in from January 1, 2003 through September of 2004 in Milwaukee County, and exited to permanency within the same time period. They found that increases in the number of worker changes lessened the chance of permanency achievement.

Figure 13.3
Fewer Changes in Caseworkers Increases the Chances of Permanency for Children[*]

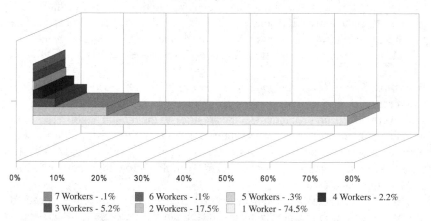

| 0% | 10% | 20% | 30% | 40% | 50% | 60% | 70% | 80% |

■ 7 Workers - .1%   ■ 6 Workers - .1%   ☐ 5 Workers - .3%   ■ 4 Workers - 2.2%
■ 3 Workers - 5.2%   ☐ 2 Workers - 17.5%   ☐ 1 Worker - 74.5%

[*]*Note:* Data reported represents 679 children who entered care in calendar year 2003 through September 2004 and exited within the same time period. Data reported to review staff by the Bureau of Milwaukee Child Welfare.
Source: Flower, C. McDonald, J. & Sumski, M. (2005). *Review of turnover in Milwaukee county private agency child welfare ongoing case management staff.* Milwaukee, WI: Milwaukee County Department of Social Services (Mimeograph), p. 27.

More specifically, children entering care during the time period who had only one worker achieved permanency in 74.5 percent of the cases. Furthermore, as the number of case managers for a child increased, the percentage of children achieving permanency dropped substantially, ranging from 17.5 percent for children who had two case managers to a low of 0.1 percent for those children who had 6 or 7 case managers (see Figure 13.3). So to the extent agencies can retain their best front line workers, they can maximize child placement stability because those workers know the children and are able to better support the foster parents.

Implement Purposeful Strategies to Boost Staff Retention Rates. The recent NASW child welfare specialty staff survey had three key findings related to worker motivation and retention: (1) Social workers in child welfare, at least those who are also members of NASW, are more satisfied with their jobs than the general population of child welfare workers; (2) Issues confronting children and families were the most challenging aspect of the job, *not* the workplace issues confronting the social workers; and (3) The single most satisfying aspect of the work of social workers in child welfare is "successes with children and families."

Competitive wages, valuable benefits, and job security are very important in attracting staff with MSW's and other job-relevant degrees to public child welfare. To retain them, however, states and counties need to take additional actions such as:

1. Review the job expectations of workers, and whether the caseloads and paperwork expectations indeed permit these workers to achieve the core objectives of the child welfare system.
2. Develop institutionalized mechanisms of support for the staff members, recognizing that child welfare work, by its very nature, is intense and emotionally draining. Establishing regular case conferences and promoting close collaboration between workers within the same program unit or across units would provide opportunities for sharing experiences and responsibilities. Fostering development of informal support networks among staff would also do much to enhance worker morale and prevent burnout. This includes promoting, to the extent possible, a reasonable approach to life-work balance.
3. Recognize the increased likelihood of worker burnout after about two years on the job and offer greater flexibility in movement from one program area to another.
4. Set up institutionalized mechanisms for regular two-way communication between workers and administration (beyond supervisors) for each group to hear first-hand about the realities of the other and to develop a collaborative, rather than adversarial, work environment.

5. Recognize the increased likelihood of worker burnout due to supervisory, organizational, and peer support contexts and create workplace, staffing, and support structures to decrease burnout (Curry, McCarragher, & Dellmann-Jenkins, 2005; Samantrai, 1990, p. 20, 1992; Smith, 2005).

Agency leaders and supervisors, to the extent that they are identified as aligned with the organization's mission and strategies, contribute to employee perceptions of positive organizational support, and ultimately to job retention (Eisenberger, Stinglhamber, Vandenberghe, Sucharski, & Rhoades, 2002).

Career ladders and succession planning through leadership development. This is becoming a key area as the baby boomers begin to retire from child welfare organizations. We must mentor, train, and develop younger staff for specialist and leadership positions (Austin & Hopkins, 2004), but there are few programs available to do so.

Improve Recruitment, Selection, and Training of Child Welfare Personnel

Besides striving to implement the factors for organizational effectiveness we reviewed at the beginning of this chapter, a number of focused strategies for improved deployment of professional staff have been identified. For example, we need to improve worker retention through some focused action, as discussed in the section below.

Improve Working Conditions to Establish a Positive Organizational Climate

There is no single answer to the question of how to address recruitment and retention problems. An agency that implements just one strategy (e.g., reducing direct-service worker caseload but not improving supervision and agency supports or having staff with the professional commitment to do the job) will probably not be very successful in the long run. It is a combination of organizational conditions and personal factors that current and prospective staff bring to their job that will result in improved retention, in some cases even when emotional exhaustion is high (Stalker, Mandell, Frensch, Harvey, & Wright, 2007).

Strategies for improving staffing requirements and results involves forming realistic career ladders with positions for technicians, midlevel practitioners, and family intervention and CPS specialists, as well as developing pay grades that do not require people to move to supervisory positions to obtain equitable salary increases. It also involves implementing and publicizing job validation or job effectiveness studies that document the knowledge and skills required for particular positions in child welfare. Policymakers need to be made aware of the increased costs involved in hiring and supervising undereducated or undertrained workers and the agency's increased vulnerability to and expenses incurred in defending charges of malpractice as well as high levels of turnover.

Agencies can encourage people with social work degrees to apply for child welfare positions by using special recruitment campaigns and job announcements that specify that social work degrees are preferred. But staff retention can also be enhanced by hiring staff with professional commitment and previous job-related experience, as well as the maturity to address the complex needs of the children and families served by the system. Last but not least, an organizational environment that values and supports staff will increase staff retention, as described in more detail in Figure 13.4.

If a family-centered approach to service delivery is to be implemented, part of that approach involves empowering clients. Workers also need to be empow-

Figure 13.4
Strategies for Increasing Worker Retention in Child Welfare

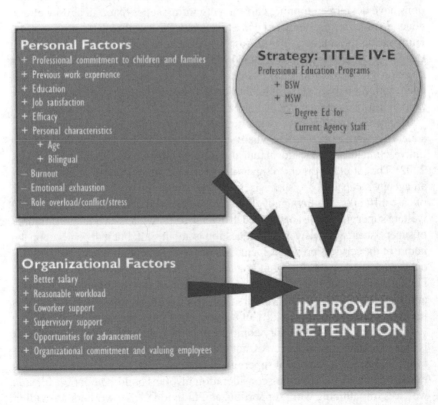

Source: Zlotnick, J.L., DePanfilis, D., Daining, D., & Lane, M.M. (2005). *Factors influencing retention of child welfare staff: A systematic review of research.* Washington, DC: IASWR. www.iaswr.org (p. 45).

ered, if they are expected to aid in the empowerment of others. Basic office and clerical supports are two important components of this support.

High-Quality Coaching, Performance Monitoring, and Supervision

Many child welfare cases involve families who are in crisis and have many needs. A high degree of worker autonomy is required as practitioners spend the vast majority of their time out of the office. Because a substantial number of the cases served by both public and private agencies involve child maltreatment, workers are required to make critical decisions regarding the risk of future child maltreatment. Workers in diverse program areas, such as child protective-services intake, youth services, foster care, and adoption, often need to develop strategies to maintain child safety at different points in the case process, including case closure.

Consequently, supervision of child welfare workers is one of the most demanding jobs in the human services—so much so that a number of organizations have developed training curricula regarding supervision in child welfare, generally, or for family-centered practice and CPS specifically (e.g., American Humane Association: see http://www.americanhumane.org/ Child Welfare League of America, Day & Cahn, 1988; Rykus & Hughes, 1998). Yet, even these programs cannot compensate for supervisors who lack practice experience, sound analytic skills (Gambrill, 1990), or a commitment to supporting (and empowering) their line workers.

Because of budget cuts, many human service agencies have increased the supervisory span of control to where supervisors are unable to fulfill the administrative, clinical, and educational functions of their position (Kadushin & Harkness, 2002). The ratio of workers to supervisors is one of many important indicators of an agency's capability to supervise their line staff adequately. Given the degree of case difficulty, the amount of clinical consultation required, and because child welfare supervisors must balance such diverse roles, what is an equitable number of supervisees? The answer to this question is about staff, but it depends upon the nature of the services provided, including the type of clients, clinical interventions employed, worker caseloads, and intensity of the service. This issue is also difficult to address because workloads vary by program area, amount of paperwork, and the capabilities of line workers. Yet, the extent of supervisory control is important along with the quality of supervision that is provided.

Another critical supervisory component is the degree to which a supervisor is able to balance the provision of staff "consideration" with "setting task structure." According to studies of supervisory effectiveness, both of these functions must be carried out. Providing consideration involves building relationships, as well as sympathizing with, supporting, and individualizing workers. Providing task structure is concerned with setting objectives, clarifying tasks, monitoring and evaluating performance, and providing task-specific feedback (Patti, et al., 1987). In other words, it is not sufficient for supervisors to be supportive alone, a set of structuring actions and expectations to fulfill the requirements of the role is essential as well (Day & Cahn, 1988; Robison, 2006).

Reform Staff Educational Programs

Schools of social work can play major roles in addressing the personnel crisis, as well as reforming service delivery in the public child welfare system. Although the federal government has recently been hesitant to increase support for child welfare traineeships for BSW and MSW students, social work education is the only academic program with a central mission to prepare students for child and family welfare. Increasingly, schools and programs of social work are being asked to address the personnel crisis through increasing child welfare course content and paid practicum placements. The promotion of public child welfare practice helps to familiarize students with and attract them to permanent jobs in public child welfare agencies. But child welfare agencies must try to designate a few of their high-performing staff as field instructors and decrease their workload so that they can provide high-quality training and supervision to the students. And the students need to be exposed to a healthy work environment, with reasonable caseloads, working hours, salaries, and benefits.

Not only are schools and programs of social work being encouraged to form new partnerships with public child welfare agencies, but in many cases in-service training programs as well as credential and degree acquisition initiatives are outgrowths of this sense of shared responsibility between the social work educational program and public child welfare agencies. In many states such as California, Illinois, and Washington, child welfare workers are drawing on state and federal dollars from Title IV-E of the Social Security Act to acquire MSWs. The challenges of child welfare staffing overwhelm individual responses by agencies or schools of social work. Newly developed protocols and agreements between education programs and public child welfare agencies regarding the various staffing, research, program development, educational, and administrative requirements are essential to meet the current staffing shortage.

Maximize Cultural Competence at an Organization Level

Child welfare agencies certainly differ in their staff composition and dedication to addressing issues of diversity—yet this is likely to be a critical factor in the provision of effective services (Gutiérrez & Nagda, 1996; Harper, et al., 2006). On a "Cultural Competence Continuum," how would the agency you know best rate on this scale (from worse to best)?

- *Destructiveness.* An agency that behaves in culturally destructive ways demonstrates evidence of blatant racism and genocide.
- *Incapacity.* An agency that avoids working with ethnic minorities and is inaccessible to people of color is culturally incapable.
- *Blindness.* An agency that believes that everyone is the same is culturally blind.

- *Pre-Competence.* An agency that tries to educate employees, but has no real knowledge about how to educate them, is culturally on the pre-competence level of the continuum.
- *Basic Competence.* An agency that is aware of and accepts differences, promotes cultural knowledge, has the ability to adapt practice skills to fit the cultural context of children and understands the dynamics of culturally destructive ways.

Selection of Effective Intervention and Other Technology

As child welfare agencies move to implement more fully a family-centered approach, there is a greater emphasis upon family empowerment and teaching families new skills for living (see Chapter 3). Service approaches that are based upon neighborhood offices, service delivery teams, community development specialists, and use of informal helping networks are being emphasized (Daro, Budde, Baker, Nesmith, & Harden, 2005; McCroskey, Furman, & Yoo, in preparation). In addition, administrators recognize that "maximizing productivity through people" is critical for the human services. This requires a concentration of effort, and the use of a well-formulated treatment technology. Despite limitations of our knowledge of human behavior there is a growing body of empirical research and practice wisdom that some agencies are aggressively tapping to provide their staff with the most powerful change technologies available (e.g., Kluger, Alexander, & Curtis, 2000; McCauley, Pecora, & Rose, 2006).

Child welfare administrators and workers, in designing their service approach, should be making careful decisions about the intervention technology to be used. The empirical evidence and practice wisdom supporting various approaches should be carefully examined before implementation. Indeed, many studies of policy and program implementation have emphasized how the need to choose the most effective service technology has been fatally overlooked (Fixsen, Naoom, Blase, Friedman, & Wallace, 2005). Unfortunately, determining which theoretical models should guide treatment interventions is complicated by the lack of evaluative research in the child welfare field. It is sobering to consider how relatively few evidence-based interventions are suitable for child welfare (Barth,2008). Fortunately, despite some limitations (e.g., Jensen, et al., 2005), there is growing use of EBP models such as Trauma-focused Cognitive Behavior Treatments, Functional Family Therapy, Parent Child Interaction Therapy, Multi-Dimensional Foster Family Treatment, and others (see Chapter 12 for a discussion of some of these).

Ancillary services essential for success must also be identified and provided. For example, what specific kinds of mental health, health care, education, vocational development, juvenile justice, and other services are needed? What kinds of integrated behavioral health services are essential?

Community-Based Services and Careful Interaction with the Media Builds Political Support and Protection

Community Partnerships

What kinds of political support are essential to buffer child welfare administrators and staff from the day-to-day controversies of this work? Despite the best efforts, children will occasionally be harmed during service delivery and agencies need to be supported to a point where staffs are not hesitant to make the right decisions about placement or reunification.

What can help staff feel supported and increase effectiveness are community partnerships. In Ft. Lauderdale, the Calvert Church took on the special role of supporting foster families in their community. In Spokane, a local car dealer provided used cars to a social service agency at a reduced cost to help needy families. In other cities, United Parcel Service and other employers have stepped up to hire youth in foster care to help provide them with employment experience. The point here is that workers need to feel that they are not alone in this work. Staffs need to feel that they are part of a *larger collaborative*.

Establish and Maintain a Positive Public Image as an Effective Agency

Media coverage about child welfare agencies often is controversial and unfair. For example, child welfare staffs are criticized for removing children from their homes and for leaving children at home who the public believes should have been placed in shelter or foster care. Child welfare agencies also have earned a poor public image in some areas because of poor services, overloaded telephone systems and receptionists, "inaccessible" workers, terrible office facilities, and other service delivery problems. Professionally trained caseworkers, like other professional groups, prefer to work in agencies with strong public support and a solid reputation for delivering effective services. Everyone wants to be part of an effective team. So we need to negotiate reasonable but high-reaching expectations for success with our funders. And then relentlessly drive towards achieving them—celebrating milestones of success along the way. This requires paying attention to how we design our organizational performance dashboards and what we do with the information on them.

So, to the extent possible, agencies are striving to have an organizational identity that is positive and pro-active around key practice issues, so staff feel like they are part of an effective team—even though the work is challenging and some of our most important child success indicators may not be immediately visible. Strategies for addressing this problem include improving child welfare agency use of the media through special public relations campaigns, publication of "success stories," newspaper columns authored by child welfare personnel, and talk show appearances. In addition, agency ombudsperson or constituent affairs representatives should listen and respond to client complaints or recommendations. Focused legislative efforts with state and local policymakers are essential to implementing and publicizing family preservation service and adoption programs to emphasize that public child welfare agencies preserve families and find permanent homes for children, rather than merely investigate reports of maltreatment and place children in foster care. Finally, it is helpful to promote attitudes among social work practitioners and faculty that emphasize child welfare as a vital and exciting area of practice, one that is often more challenging than private practice specialties.

Conclusion

Current Status

The challenges associated with recruiting, selecting, and retaining qualified child welfare staff are formidable but must be addressed, as effective child welfare services require personnel capable of providing skilled interventions. Low worker turnover is essential for providing a consistent level of service. Furthermore, the importance of adequate salaries (which require not only political advocacy, but also thorough documentation of the worker competencies necessary for effective job performance) has been highlighted by studies as an important factor not only for minimizing worker turnover, but for increasing job satisfaction as well (Jayaratne & Chess, 1985).

Future Directions

This chapter has highlighted some of the organizational requisites for child welfare services. Many challenges remain to be addressed, such as securing adequate program funding, using a universal intake process, designing supportive work environments, developing powerful intervention technologies, ensuring reasonable caseload sizes, and implementing supervision strategies that promote "best practice." If child welfare agencies effectively implement the service strategies described in the previous chapters, key organizational components must be in place. Family-centered approaches involve certain strategies for supporting parents and children. But in order to empower families, practitioners must first be empowered by the organizations within which they work.

Notes

1. Sections of this table are adapted from Pecora, Cherin, Bruce, & Arguello, 2009.
2. For examples of web-based, free instant-scoring assessment tools for human services see www.caseylifeskills.org.
3. For information regarding what worker competencies may be important for effective job performance in various child welfare program areas and research regarding the effectiveness of social work-trained staff, see the Institute of Social Work Research website.

4. A 2002 study conducted by NASW found that eight percent of the 90,000 regular members identified child welfare as their primary area of practice (NASW, 2002). In response to these members, NASW launched a new Child Welfare Specialty Practice Section that has grown to more than eight hundred members since its inception in July 2002. Section membership, while geared towards different social work practice areas, is open to all NASW members for an additional fee. In October 2003, NASW conducted a survey of all 716 members of the Child Welfare Specialty Practice Section and 534 responded (a 75 percent response rate), with 369 actually practicing in child welfare currently.

5. For more information about how staffing issues affects permanency planning and other performance issues see Albers, Reilly, and Rittner (1993); Ryan, Garnier, Zyphur, and Zhai (2006); and National Council on Crime and Delinquency, (2006). A 2003 GAO report (www.gao.gov/cgi-bin/getrpt?GAO-03-357) also tries to link outcomes for children to retention based on interviews with caseworkers, but no data are provided.

For Further Information

Austin, M. J., & Hopkins, K. M. (Eds.). (2004). *Supervision as collaboration in the human services: Building a learning culture.* Thousand Oaks, CA: Sage. A wide-ranging collection of chapters addressing the major functions of supervision.

Brohl, K. (2004). *The new miracle workers: overcoming contemporary challenges in child welfare work.* Washington, DC: CWLA Press. A strengths-oriented and solution-focused summary of child welfare work.

Edwards, R.L., & Yankey, J.A. (Eds.). (2006). *Effectively managing nonprofit organizations.* Washington, DC: National Association of Social Workers. Reviews major functions of managing nonprofit organizations, including planning, budgeting and human resources management.

Patti, R. J. (Ed) (2008). *Handbook of human services management.* Newbury Park, CA: Sage Press. This book describes the major phases of designing, implementing and managing human service programs.

Thomas, D. A. & Ely, R. J. (2002). Making differences matter: A new paradigm for managing diversity. In *Harvard Business Review on Managing Diversity*, (pp. 33-66). Boston, MA: Harvard Business School Press. A thoughtful perspective on managing diverse staff in organizations.

Wells, R. (2006). Managing child welfare agencies: What do we know about what works? *Children and Youth Services Review 28* (10) 1181-1194. Literature review of management and organizational factors associated with effective child welfare services.

Appendix

A Select List of Child Welfare-Related Federal Legislation[1]

Legislation	Purpose	References
National School Lunch Program	The National School Lunch Program (NSLP) [PL.101-147] was officially instituted as a United States federal policy with the passage of the National School Lunch Act in 1946. The program is intended to provide children in public and non-profit schools and residential child care institutions with a nutritionally balanced lunch each school day. The program also offers free and reduced priced lunches for eligible children from low-income families (United States Code, 1995). During fiscal year 1997, more than 26 million children —14.6 million of whom were from low-income families and received a free or reduced-priced lunch—consumed a lunch from the national program each day (FRAC, 1998). All children are eligible to eat a school lunch each day. Eligibility for free or reduced priced lunches is based on household income levels which must be reported on the National School Lunch Program Application form. Those children whose family's income is at or below 130 percent and 185 percent of the poverty line may eat lunch at a reduced price, which is not to exceed forty cents. Children from families with incomes over 185 percent of the poverty line pay a full price for lunch, although their meals are still subsidized to some extent (United States Code, 1995). The NSLP is administered by the Secretary of Agriculture. However, the program is still	United States Code (1995). See http://www. loc.gov/law/ guide/uscode.html

considered a Health and Human Services function, not an Agriculture function. The secretary receives money from the federal treasury to be allocated to the states. Based on the number of lunches served and the current value of food, the secretary distributes money and commodities to state educational agencies. The state educational agencies then allocate resources to the schools based on need and attendance. In addition, the secretary is responsible for providing technical assistance and training in food preparation to food service providers and schools (United States Code, 1995).

Supplemental Social Insurance (SSI)	SSI is a means-tested, monthly income program for the elderly and people with disabilities. The program is federally financed and generally federally administered, although some states supplement federal payments, and a few states administer their own programs directly. Children with disabilities have been able to receive SSI since the program's inception in 1972, and children's eligibility is based on functional limitations (Social Security Administration, 2000). Parents' income and assets relative to family size are used to determine whether or not a child can receive SSI.	
Child Abuse Prevention and Treatment Act of 1974 (P.L. 93-247)	Provides some financial assistance for demonstration programs for the prevention, identification, and treatment of child abuse and neglect; mandates that states must provide for the reporting of known or suspected instances of child abuse and neglect.	Light (1973), Stein (1984)
Juvenile Justice and Delinquency Prevention Act of 1974 (P.L. 93-415)	Provides funds to reduce the unnecessary and inappropriate detention of juveniles and to encourage state program initiatives in the prevention and treatment of juvenile delinquency and other status offenses.	Costin, Bell, & Downs (1991, p. 71-72)

Title XIX of the Social Security Act	Mainly provides health care to income-eligible persons and families. One of the sections of this act established the Early and Periodic Screening, Diagnosis, and Treatment program, which provides cost-effective health care to pregnant women and young children.	
The Education of all Handicapped Children Act of 1975 (P.L. 94-142)	Act requiring and supporting education and social services to handicapped children. The Act requires states to (1) offer programs for the full education of handicapped children between the ages of three to eighteen, (2) develop strategies for locating such children, (3) use intelligence testing that does not discriminate against the child racially or culturally, (4) develop an IEP for each child, and (5) offer learning opportunities in the least restrictive educational environment possible, with an emphasis on mainstreaming—integrating handicapped children into regular classrooms.	Costin, Bell, & Downs (1991, pp. 300-303), Singer & Butler (1987)
The Individuals with Disabilities Education Act (IDEA) (Began as the Education for All Handicapped Children Act of 1975— PL 94-142)	The Individuals with Disabilities Education Act (IDEA) began as the Education for All Handicapped Children Act of 1975 (PL 94-142) and gave all children with disabilities the right to a free and appropriate public education. This watershed civil rights law resulted from sustained advocacy by parents of children with disabilities.　　Special education has been shaped by the six core principles which formed the nucleus of the Education for All Handicapped Children Act: (1) zero reject, meaning schools could not opt to exclude any children with disabilities from instruction; (2) nondiscriminatory evaluation, by which every child receives an individualized, culturally- and linguistically-appropriate evaluation before being placed in special education; (3) individualized education plan (IEP)	Parish & Whisnant (2005).

a plan delineating current performance,
progress on past objectives, goals and
services for the school year and
evaluation of outcomes; (4) least
restrictive environment, which is the
goal that children with disabilities are
educated to the extent possible in
settings with non-disabled children;
(5) due process, which codifies the
legal steps to ensure school's fairness
and accountability in meeting the child's
needs and how parents can obtain relief
via a hearing or by second opinions; and
(6) parental participation, whereby parents
have the right to access their child's
education records, and participate in IEP
planning (Kirk, Gallagher, & Anastasiow,
1993, pp. 51-52).

The second part of IDEA that is important
for children served by child welfare
agencies is early intervention, which has
as its purpose the provision of prevention
and treatment services to improve cognitive,
social, and emotional development of the
youngest children (under the age of three).
Children receiving early intervention
services either are considered at-risk for
delayed development or have been identified
as having a developmental disability
(Ramey & Ramey, 1998).

P.L. 101-476   Act modifying services for special
education students.

Title XX of the   Through a block grant arrangement,   Mott (1976)
Social Security   provides states with federal funds for
Act (as amended   a variety of social service programs.
by the Omnibus
Reconciliation
Act of 1981)

The Indian Child Welfare Act of 1978 (P.L. 95-608)	Strengthens the standards governing removal of Native American children from their families. Provides for a variety of requirements and mechanisms for tribal government overseeing and services for children.	Miller, Hoffman & Turner (1980), Plantz, Hubbell, Barrett, & Dobrec (1989)
The Adoption Assistance and Child Welfare Act of 1980 (P.L. 96-272)	A child welfare reform legislation that uses funding incentives and procedural requirements to promote placement prevention and permanency planning.	Pine (1986)
Independent Living Initiative (P.L. 99-272)	Provides funding for services to prepare adolescents in foster care for living in the community on an independent basis.	Mech (1988), Foster Care Awareness Project (NFCAP). (2000).
P.L. 99-457	Mandates health, rehabilitation, education, and social services to children who have special needs from birth.	
Family Support Act of 1990	Establishes new initiatives for financial assistance for low-income families.	
1990 Farm Bill (P.L. 101-624)	The Food Stamp Program was re-authorized until 1995 as part of this bill.	http://thomas.loc. gov; http://www. connectforkids.org
Personal Responsibility and Work Opportunity Reconciliation Act (PRWORA). This funds the Temporary Assistance to Needy Families (TANF).	The largest income transfer program for poor families is Temporary Assistance to Needy Families (TANF). This is part of the nation's welfare system—administered by the states and funded jointly by state and federal governments. Low-income families of children with disabilities can also receive income transfers through TANF, which is the limited welfare program enacted in 1996 by the Personal Responsibility and Work Opportunity Reconciliation Act (PRWORA). TANF replaced Aid to Families with Dependent Children (AFDC), requires parents to work and limits receipt of cash benefits to a lifetime maximum of 60 months.	

TANF allows states to exempt up to 20% of their welfare caseload from work requirements but states have the discretion to establish more strict work participation rules.

See Plotnick, Chapter 4 in this volume.

Foster Care Independence Act of 1999 (P.L. 106-169) and the Educational Training Voucher Provisions

The Foster Care Independence Act of 1999 (P.L. 106-169) authorized the Education Training Voucher (ETV) program. Congress provided federal funding of $42 million for the first time in FY 2003 and increased funding to $45 million for FY 2004. In both years, the president requested $60 million in his budget.

National Foster Care Coalition (2000)

The voucher program is a component of the Chafee Independent Living Program, which helps older youth leaving foster care get the higher education, vocational training, and other education supports they need to move to self-sufficiency. Up to $5,000 per year is available to a young person for the cost of attending college or vocational school.

ETV funds are distributed to the states using the same formula as the Chafee Independent Living Program under the Foster Care Independence Act. If a state does not apply for funds for the ETV program, the funds are reallocated to other states based on their relative need. Although states are doing a good job generally of distributing these funds, more foster youth could take advantage of the vouchers if their availability were more widely known. An additional $60 million is needed for ETVs for youth leaving foster care at age 18 and those adopted from foster care at age 16 or older (CWLA, 2004a).

Keeping Children and Families Safe Act

Reauthorizes the Child Abuse Prevention and Treatment Act (CAPTA). Authorizes funds for grants to state child welfare agencies, competitive grants for research and demonstration programs, and grants to states for the establishment of community-based programs and activities designed to strengthen

and support families, all of which support
services to prevent and treat child abuse
and neglect. The Act amends the Adoption
Reform Act of 1978 (Adoption Opportunities),
focusing on the placement of older foster
children in adoptive homes with an emphasis
on child-specific recruitment strategies and
efforts to improve inter-jurisdictional adoptions.

This Act also includes amendments to the
Abandoned Infants Assistance Act, making
aid a priority to infants who are infected with
the HIV virus, have a life-threatening disease,
or have been perinatally exposed to a dangerous
drug. The Act also includes an amendment to
the Family Violence Prevention and Services Act,
extending for FY2004 through FY2008 authorization
of appropriations for specified family violence
prevention programs.

The Adoption Incentive Program (P.L. 108-145)

The Adoption Incentive Program was first
enacted as part of the Adoption and Safe
Families Act in 1997 to promote permanence
for children. In 2003, Congress passed the Adoption
Promotion Act of 2003 (P.L. 108-145) to reauthorize
the program with modifications.

The Adoption Incentive Program is designed
to encourage states to finalize adoptions of children
from foster care, with additional incentives for the
adoption of foster children with special needs.
States receive incentive payments for adoptions that
exceed an established baseline.

The Adoption Promotion Act revises the
incentive formula in current law, creating four
categories of payment. A state may receive:

- $4,000 for each foster child adopted above the
  established baseline of foster child adoptions;
- $6,000 for each foster child adopted whom the
  state classifies as having special needs, as long
  as the state also increases its overall adoptions;
- $8,000 for each older foster child adopted above
  the baseline of older foster child adoptions, as
  long as the state also increases its overall adoptions
  (an older child is defined as a child age 9 or older); and
- $4,000 for each older foster child adopted above

the baseline of older foster child adoptions when the number of older foster child adoptions increases, but the overall number of foster child adoptions does not increase.

The new law also resets the target number of adoptions a state must reach to receive a bonus payment. Because not all states qualified for the bonus in 2003, a new target was established for adoptions, based on the number of adoptions in 2002 rather than the old formula, which created a number based on fiscal years 1995-1997. Under the new law, to receive a payment in any of the categories (overall adoptions, special-needs adoptions, or older-child adoptions), a state must exceed the number of adoptions in these categories set in FY 2002. For any subsequent year, the baseline is the highest number of adoptions in 2002 or later. The new law allows Congress to approve $43 million annually for the payments. If states are not able to draw down all the funds, then the funds are returned to the U.S. Treasury and not reallocated for other adoption efforts. (CWLA, 2004a)[b]

Adoption Opportunities Program (Title II of the Child Abuse Prevention and Treatment Act, P.L. 108-36).

The Adoption Opportunities Program provides discretionary grants for demonstration projects that eliminate barriers to adoption and provide permanent, loving homes for children who would benefit from adoption— particularly children with special needs.

Several resources and supports exist under the Adoption Opportunities Program to assist in the adoption of children. For example, the Collaboration to AdoptUSKids recruits homes for children waiting to be adopted through its National Recruitment Campaign and has developed a network of adoptive parent groups. AdoptUSKids also maintains a national Internet photolisting of waiting children. In 2000, 52,000 families received information on how to proceed with adoption. The exchange currently lists 5,500 children waiting to be adopted.

The Adoption Opportunities Program has also funded the National Resource Center on Special Needs Adoption, which provides technical assistance and training on current issues in special-needs adoption—such as compliance with federal laws and regulations, permanency planning, and cultural competence—to state, tribal, and other child welfare organizations. Nearly 65,000 people in all 50 states, the District of Columbia, Guam, Puerto Rico, and the Virgin Islands have received special-needs adoption training through the center. Adoption Opportunities funds also support the National Adoption Assistance Training Resource and Information Network.

The network's services include a hotline that provides free information on adoption subsidies to parents interested in adopting children with special needs and a booklet on adoption assistance programs available in each state. Adoption Opportunities funding has also helped establish the National Adoption Information Clearinghouse (NAIC), a comprehensive information center on adoption.

Runaway, Homeless, and Missing Children Protection Act

Runaway, Homeless, and Missing Children Protection Act (which reauthorized the Runaway and Homeless Youth Act) authorizes $105 million for FY2004 for the establishment and operation of centers to provide shelter, protection from sexual and other abuse, counseling, and related services to runaway and homeless youth under 18 years of age. The Act authorized local groups to open "maternity group homes" for homeless pregnant teens or for those that have been abused.

These homes are required to educate runaway youth about parenting skills, child development, family budgeting, health and nutrition, and related skills to promote long-term independence and the health and well being of youth in their care. Children's advocates were generally pleased with the improvements in this re-authorization, however, groups noted that funding levels established in the Act are able to serve only a fraction of young people at risk of homelessness as they exit foster care or the juvenile justice system.

Legacy Provisions in the American Dream Downpayment Act

The LEGACY (Living Equitably: Grandparents Aiding Children and Youth) Act directs the Secretary of Housing and Urban Development to carry out: (1) a five-year pilot program in connection with the supportive housing program, known as Section 202 to provide assistance to private nonprofit organizations for expanding the supply of intergenerational dwelling units for intergenerational families (families headed by an elderly person); and (2) a five-year demonstration program for Section 8 rental assistance to families headed by a grandparent or relative who is raising a child.

The bill makes grandparent-headed and relative-headed families eligible for: (1) the Family Unification Program; (2) HOME program ECHO units; and (3) fair housing initiatives training, education, counseling, and outreach. It also directs the Secretary and the Director of the Bureau of the Census to conduct a joint study of such families' housing needs.

Extending Food Stamps to Eligible Immigrant Children

Once barred from participating in the Food Stamp program by the welfare reform act of 1996, immigrant children became eligible for Food Stamps as of October 1, 2003, as a result of a provision in the 2002 Farm Bill.

Protect Act (Amber Alert System)

The Amber Alert system, a national system to quickly alert the public about child abductions, was signed into law in April. Efforts are underway to get the system up and running in every state in the nation.

Fostering Connections to Success and Increasing Adoptions Act (P.L. 110-351)

The Fostering Connections to Success and Increasing Adoptions Act promotes permanent families for children through relative guardianship and adoption and improving education and health care. In addition, the bill provides, for the first time, many American Indian children access to important federal protections and support. The bill also provides additional supports to older youth who reach the age of majority without a permanent family by extending federal support for youth to age twenty-one. The main provisions of this new law are listed below:

1.   Connecting and Supporting Relative Caregivers – helping more vulnerable children who are in foster care or at risk of entering foster care stay connected with relatives through the following supports:

•   Federal subsidized guardianship program—offers federal support to children who leave foster care to live permanently with relative guardians. In order to be eligible, the child must be in the care of the relative caregiver who is a licensed foster parent for a period of at least six months, and the state must document why adoption or reunification is not appropriate for the child. Children fourteen and older must be consulted about the kinship guardianship arrangement and siblings may be placed in the same home and receive support even if some of them are not otherwise eligible. Kinship guardianship payments cannot exceed foster care maintenance payments. In addition, the state must provide post permanency supports including medical care for the child, and payment of nonrecurring expenses related to obtaining legal guardianship. Payments may continue, at state option, until age 21 (or age 19 or 20) if the guardianship agreement was entered into when the child was age 16 or older;

- Notice Requirement—states must provide relatives notice when children are removed from their parents' homes, giving them an early opportunity to be involved in caring for the children. States must "exercise due diligence" to identify and provide notice to all adult grandparents and other relatives within thirty days after the removal of a child from the parent's custody (subject to exceptions for family or domestic violence);

- Kinship Navigator programs—to help relatives connect the children with the services and supports they need. The law provides $15 million for each fiscal year (2009-2013) for a competitive grant program for "family connection grants" that can be used for any of four purposes including a kinship navigator program—of which $5 million is reserved for such purposes. The remaining $10 million can be used for navigators, intensive family finding, FGDM, or residential family treatment programs.

- Separate Licensing Standards—takes steps to address non-safety licensing requirements that create barriers to children living with relatives in foster care. The law codifies existing HHS guidance allowing states to waive certain non-safety related licensing standards on a case-by-case basis. These standards include things like square footage requirements and minimum numbers of bedrooms or bathrooms per person. It also requires the Department of Health and Human Services (HHS) to submit a report to Congress within two years that examines state licensing standards, states' use of case-by-case waivers, and the effect of the waivers on children in foster care, reviews the reasons relative foster family homes may not be able to be licensed, and recommends administrative or legislative actions to allow more children to be safely placed in foster care and be eligible for federal support.

2. Provides Additional Support to Older Youth and Increase Their Opportunities for Success by:

- Continuing federal support for children in foster care after age eighteen—The law allows states, at their option, to provide care and support to youth in foster care until the age of nineteen, twenty, or twenty-one, provided that the youth is (1) completing high school or an equivalency program; (2) enrolled in post-secondary or vocational school; (3) participating in a program or activity designed to promote,

or remove barriers to, employment; (4) employed for at
least 80 hours per month; or (5) incapable of doing any of
these activities due to a medical condition. The protections
and requirements currently in place for younger children in
foster care would continue to apply for youth ages eighteen
to twenty-one. These youth could be placed in a supervised
setting in which they are living independently, as well as in a
foster family home or group home. States could also extend
adoption assistance and/or guardianship payments on behalf
of youth ages nineteen, twenty, or twenty-one.

- Helping older youth successfully transition from foster care
  to independence—The Act requires child welfare agencies
  to help youth make this transition to adulthood by requiring,
  during the ninety-day period immediately before a youth exits
  from care at eighteen, nineteen, twenty, or twenty-one, the
  development of a personalized transition plan that identifies
  options for housing, health insurance, education, local
  opportunities for mentoring, continuing support services, work
  force supports, and employment services.

3. Grants Tribes Direct IV-E Access—The law ensures that
   Indian tribes have direct access to IV-E funded programs,
   including the foster care and adoption program as well as
   the newly proposed Child and Family Services Program,
   Subsidized Guardianship Program and Permanency Incentive
   Program. The bill also provides financial resources directly to
   Indian tribes to provide technical assistance and start up costs
   associated with implementation.

4. Improves Education Outcomes for Children Who Live in
   Out-Of-Home Care—by improving educational stability and
   ensuring seamless educational transitions for children and
   youth when school changes do occur through the following:

- Improves educational stability for children and youth in foster
  care by requiring states to ensure that placement of the child
  in foster care takes into account the appropriateness of the
  current educational setting and the proximity to the school in
  which the child is enrolled at the time of placement. The law
  also requires that the state child welfare agency coordinate
  with schools to ensure that child remains in the school in
  which the child is enrolled at the time of placement as long as
  it is in the child's best interest. In addition, the bill increases
  the amount of federal funding that may be used to cover
  education-related transportation costs for children in foster
  care.

- Promotes seamless educational transitions for children and
  youth when school changes do occur by requiring states to
  ensure that, in cases where remaining in the child's school is

not in his or her best interest, the child is immediately enrolled
in a new school and that the child's educational records are
provided to the new school.

- Provides for required educational attendance by requiring the
state to ensure that every school—age child in foster care, and
every school—age child receiving an adoption assistance or
subsidized guardianship payment, is enrolled as a full-time
elementary or secondary school student or has completed
secondary school.

5. Promotes Coordinated Health Care for Children in Out-of-
Home Care requires that states develop a plan for the oversight
and coordination of health, mental health, and dental services
for children in foster care. The plan must include an outline
of how the state will schedule and conduct health screenings,
how health needs identified through such screenings will
be treated, how medical information will be updated and
appropriately shared, ensure continuity of services, and
provide oversight of prescription medications.

6. Expands and Improves Adoption Assistance Programs

- De-links a child's eligibility for federal adoption assistance
payments from outdated AFDC income requirements. The
expansion of children eligible for federal adoption assistance
payments will be phased in over nine years, with older
children and those who have spent at least sixty consecutive
months in care, and their siblings, being eligible first. As
children are phased-in, those children with special needs who
are involuntarily or voluntarily placed with or relinquished
to the care of a licensed private child placement agency or
Indian tribal organization, as well as those in the care of
public state or local agencies, will also be eligible for adoption
assistance. Children who are eligible for SSI, based solely on
the medical and disability requirements, would automatically
be considered children with special needs and eligible
for adoption assistance without regard to the SSI income
requirements. Requires that savings resulting from these new
Title IV-E eligibility rules must be re-invested in services
(including post-adoption services) provided under Parts B and
E of Title IV of the Social Security Act.

- Expands the Adoption Incentives Program to promote the
adoption of children from foster care. It renews the Adoption
Incentive Grant Program for an additional five years, updates
to FY 2007 the adoption baseline above which incentive
payments are made, doubles the incentive payments for
adoptions of children with special needs and older children
adoptions, and gives states twenty-four months to use the
adoption incentive payments. The law also permits states

to receive an additional payment if the state's adoption rate exceeds its highest recorded foster child adoption rate since 2002.

- Makes older children adopted from foster care eligible for additional supports. Children sixteen and older adopted (or who leave to legal guardianship with a relative) from foster care eligible for independent living services and for education and training vouchers.

- Improves Outreach About the Adoption Tax Credit. The Act helps to ensure that children in foster care benefit from the adoption tax credit. Research shows that the majority of taxpayers taking advantage of the federal adoption tax credit had not adopted through public child welfare agencies but, rather, through private agencies or attorneys. The Act requires states to inform all people who are adopting or are known to be considering adopting a child in the custody of the state that they are potentially eligible for the adoption tax credit.

Improves the Child Welfare Workforce—The law allows states to be reimbursed for training provided to an expanded group of individuals and organizations including kinship caregivers, court personnel, CASA's, and non-agency workers providing child welfare services. States will be reimbursed for providing such training at 55% for FY09.

Sources:

- Children's Defense Fund and the Center for the Study of Law and Social Policy. (2008). Fostering Connections to Success and Increasing Adoptions Act (HR6893) Summary. Washington, D.C.: Author.
- Kids Count: A Project of the Annie E. Casey Foundation. Baltimore, MD 21202. www.kidscount.org.
- Pecora, P. J. (2006). Child welfare policies and programs. In J. Jenson and M. Fraser (Eds.) Social Policy for Children and Families: A Risk and Resilience Perspective. Newbury Park: Sage Press.
- Summaries prepared by the Public Policy Team of Casey Family Programs with the consultation of Children's Defense Fund, Child Welfare League of America, American Public Human Services Association, and the Alliance for Children

Note: A number of other pieces of legislation are important to child welfare services but are not summarized in this figure, including the Social Security Act of 1935, amendments to the Act passed in 1939, 1950, 1962, 1965, 1967, 1974, 1983, some of which are also known as the Title amendments of Title IV, IV-A, IV-B, IV-E, IV-F, and V. These title amendments established, terminated, or altered a wide range of income assistance, medical, social service, and other programs. For more information, see Costin et al. (1991), DiNitto & Dye (1989), Stein (1991).

References

Adams, P., & Nelson, K. (Eds.). (1995). *Reinventing human services: Community-and-family-centered practice*. New York: Aldine de Gruyter.

Ainsworth, F. (1996). Group care workers as parent educators. *Child & Youth Care Forum, 25*(1), 17-28.

Ainsworth, F., & Small, R. W. (1994). Family centered group care: Concept and implementation. *19*, 22-24.

Ainsworth, F., Maluccio, A. N., & Small, R. W. (1996). A framework for family centered group care practice: Guiding principles and practice implications. In D. Braziel (Ed.), *Family-focused practice in out-of-home care* (pp. 35-43). Washington, DC: Child Welfare League of America.

Ainsworth, F., Maluccio, A. N., & Thoburn, J. (2001). *Child Welfare Outcome Research in the United States, the United Kingdom and Australia*. Washington, DC: Child Welfare League of America.

Ainsworth, M. D. S. (1989). Attachments beyond infancy. *American Psychologist, 44*, 709-716.

Albers, E., Rittner, B., & Reilly, T. (1993). Children in foster care: Possible factors affecting permanency planning. *Child and Adolescent Social Work Journal, 10*(4), 329-341.

Aldgate, J. (1980). Identification of factors influencing children's length of stay in care. In J. Triseliotis (Ed.), *New developments in foster care and adoption* (pp. 22-40). London and Boston: Routledge and Kegan Paul.

Aldgate, J., & Hawley, D. (1986). *Recollections of disruptions: A study of foster care breakdowns*. London: National Foster Care Association.

Aldgate, J., Maluccio, A., & Reeves, C. (1989). *Adolescents in Foster Families*. London, Chicago: B. T. Batsford, Lyceum Books.

Alexander, G., & Huberty, T. J. (1993). *Caring for troubled children: The Villages follow-up study*. Bloomington, IN: The Villages of Indiana.

Allen, M. (1991). Crafting a federal legislative framework for child welfare reform. *American Journal of Orthopsychiatry, 61*(4), 610-623, 620.

Allen, M. L., & Knitzer, J. (1978). *Children without Homes*. Washington, DC: The Children's Defense Fund.

Allen, M., & Knitzer, J. (1983). Child welfare: Examining the policy framework. In B. McGowan, & Meezan, W. (Ed.), *Child welfare: Current dilemmas, future directions*. Itasca, IL: F.E. Peacock Publishers, Inc.

Allen, R. I., & Petr, C. G. (1998). Rethinking family-centered practice. *American Journal of Orthopsychiatry, 68*, 4-15.

Alliance for Children and Families, American Public Human Services Association, & Child Welfare League of America. (2001). *The Child Welfare Workforce Challenge: Result from a Preliminary Study*. Presented at the Finding Better Ways, Dallas, TX.

Altman, J. C. (2005). Engagement in children, youth, and family services: Current research and promising approaches. In G. Mallon & P. Hess (Eds.), *Child Welfare for the Twenty-First Century: A Handbook of Practices, Policies and Programs* (pp. 72-86). New York: Columbia University Press.

American Academy of Pediatrics Committee on Early Childhood Adoption and Dependent Care [AAP]. (2000). Developmental issues for young children in foster care. *Pediatrics, 106*, 1145-1150.

American Civil Liberties Union, Juvenile Rights Project (1977). ACLU Children's Rights Report. *1*(7).

American Federation of State, County, and Municipal Employees. (1998). *Double Jeopardy: Caseworkers at Risk Helping At-Risk Children: A Report on the Working Conditions Facing Child Welfare Workers*. Washington, DC: Author.

American Humane Association, & National Association of Public Child Welfare Administrators. (1996). *Matrices of Indicators prepared for the fourth annual roundtable on outcome measures in child welfare*. Presented at the Fourth National roundtable on outcome measures in child welfare.

American Humane Association, Children's Division, American Bar Association, Center on Children and the Law, Annie E. Casey Foundation, Casey Family Services, Institute for Human Services Management, & The Casey Family Program. (1998). *Assessing outcomes in child welfare services: Principles, concepts, and a framework of core indicators*. Englewood, CO: American Humane Association.

American Professional Society on the Abuse of Children. (1995). *Psychosocial evaluation of suspected psychological maltreatment in children and adolescents*. Chicago, IL: Author.

American Public Human Services Association. (2005). *Crossroads II: New Directions for Social Policy*. Washington, DC: Author.

America's Promise Alliance. (2006). *Every Child, Every Promise: Turning Failure into Action*. Alexandria, VA: Author.

America's Promise Alliance. (2007). *Under-equipped and unprepared: America's emerging workforce and the soft skills gap*. Alexandria, VA: America's Promise Alliance.

Anderson, G. R., Ryan, A. S., & Leashore, B. R. (Eds.). (1997). *The challenge of permanency planning in a multicultural society*. New York: The Haworth Press.

Anderson, G., Ryan, C., Taylor-Brown, S., & White-Gray, M. (1998). Introduction—HIV/AIDS and children, youths, and families: Lessons learned. *Child Welfare, 77*(2).

Anderson, P. G. (1989). The origin, emergence, and professional recognition of child protection. *Social Service Review, 63*(2), 222-244.

Andrews, A. B. (1997). Assessing neighborhood and community factors that influence children's well-being. In A. Ben-Arieh & H. Winterberger (Eds.), *Monitoring and measuring the state of children— Beyond survival*. (pp. 127-141). Vienna, Austria: European Centre.

Annie E. Casey Foundation. (2004). Who's Taking Care? Advocasey examines the staffing crisis in children and family services. *ADVOCASEY, 6*(1), 1-40.

Annie E. Casey Foundation. (2005). *Elders as resources: Basic Data: Kinship care*. Baltimore, MD: Annie E. Casey Foundation.

Appel, A. E., & Holden, G.W. (1998). The co-occurrence of spouse and physical abuse: A review and appraisal. *Journal of Family Psychology, 12*, 578-599.

Appleyard, K., Egeland, B., & Sroufe, A. (2007). Direct social support for young high risk children: relations with behavioral and emotional outcomes across time. *Journal of Abnormal Child Psychology, 35*(3), 443-457.

Ards, S. (1992). Understanding Patterns of Child Maltreatment. *Contemporary Policy Issues, 10*(4), 39-50.

Arguello, D. F. (1988). A comparative study of minority and nonminority executives in New Mexico human service organizations. Unpublished Doctoral Dissertation. University of Washington.

Argyris, C. (1993). *On Orginizational Learning*. Cambridge, MA: Blackwell Publishers.

Arizona Department of Economic Security. (2006). *Service integration: A partnership for safe and stable families in Arizona*. Phoenix, AZ: Arizona Department of Economic Security.

Arnold, L. S., Brecht, M. C., Hockett, A. B., Amspacher, K. A., & Grad, R. K. (1989). "Lessons from the Past." *American Journal of Maternal Child Nursing, 14*, 75-82.

Asop, R. (January 11, 2006). M.B.A. Recruiters' No. 1 Pet Peeve: Poor Writing and Speaking Skills. *Wall Street Journal*. Retrieved from http://www.careerjournal. com/myc/school/20060117-alsop.html

Assistant Secretary for Planning and Evaluation. (2001). *Assessing the context of permanency and reunification in the foster care system*. Washington, DC: US Department of Health and Human Services.

AuClaire, P., & Schwartz, I. M. (1986). *An evaluation of the effectiveness of intensive home-based services as an alternative to placement for adolescents and their families*. Minneapolis, MN: Hennepin County Community Services Department, and the University of Minnesota, Hubert H. Humphrey Institute of Public Affairs.

Auerbach, C., McGowan, B., & LaPorte, H. H. (2007). How does professional education impact the job outlook of public child welfare workers? *Journal of Public Child Welfare, 1*(3), 55-76.

Austin, M. J. (1981). *Supervisory management for the human services*. Englewood Cliffs, NJ: Prentice-Hall.

Austin, M. J., & Hopkins, K. M. (2004). *Supervision as collaboration in the human services: Building a learning culture*. Thousand Oaks, CA: Sage.

Austin, T., & Johnson, J. (1995). *The Effectiveness of Pennsylvania's Independent Living Initiative*. Shippensberg, PA: Center for Juvenile Justice Training and Research, Child Welfare Division.

Avery, R. (1998). Public agency adoption in New York State: Phase I report. In *Foster care histories of children freed for adoption in New York State: 1980-1993*. Ithaca: Cornell University.

Baird, C., Wagner, D., & Neuenfeldt, D. (1993). Actuarial risk assessment and case management in child protective services. In T. Tatara (Ed.), *Sixth National Roundtable on CPS Risk Assessment Summary of Highlights*. (pp. 152-168).

Baird, S. C. (1988). Development of risk assessment indices for the Alaska Department of Health and Social Services. In T. Tatara (Ed.), *Validation research in CPS risk assessment: Three recent studies*. (Occasional Monograph Series No. 2, pp. 84-142). Washington, DC: American Public Welfare Association.

Baker, A. J. L., Wulczyn, F., & Dale, N. (2005). Covariates of length of stay in residential treatment. *Child Welfare, 84*(3), 363-386.

Baldrige National Quality Program, & National Institute of Standards and Technology. (2004). *Criteria for Performance Excellence* (2005 ed.). Gaithersberg, MD.

Bamba, S., & Haight, W. L. (2007). Helping maltreated children find their Ibasho: Japanese perspectives on supporting the well-being of children in state care. *Children & Youth Services Review, 29*(4), 405-427.

Banach, M. (1998). The best interests of the child: Decision-making factors. *Families in Society—The Journal of Contemporary Human Services, 79*(3), 331-340.

Banks, L., Hicks Marlowe, J., Reid, J. B., Patterson, G. R., & Weinrott, M. R. (1991). A comparative evaluation of parent training interventions for families of chronic delinquents. *Journal of Abnormal Child Psychology, 19*, 15-33.

Barbell, K., & Freundlich, M. (2001). *An examination of foster car at the start of the 21st century*. Seattle, WA: Casey Family Programs.

Barber, J., & Delfabbro, P. (2003). *Children in foster care*. London: Allyn and Bacon.

Barnard, K. E. (1983). *Child health assessment: A literature review*. Seattle, WA: University of Washington, School of Nursing.

Barnard, K. E. (1998). Developing, implementing, and documenting interventions with parents and young children. *Zero to Three, 18*(4), 23-29.

Barnett, D., Manly, J.T., & Cicchetti, D. (1993). Defining child maltreatment: The interface between policy and research. In D. Cicchetti & S.L. Toth (Eds.). Child abuse, child development, and social policy (pp. 7-73). Norwood, NJ: Ablex Publishing Corporation.

Barth, R.P. (2005). Child welfare and race: Models of disproportionality. In D. Derezotes, J. Poertner & M. F. Testa (Eds.), *Race Matters in Child Welfare; The Overrepresentation of African American Children in the System*. Washington, DC: CWLA Press.

Barth, R. P. (2006). Group care and treatment foster care: An application of propensity score matching. In C. Canali, T. Vecchiato, & J. K. Whittaker (Eds.), *Assessing the "Evidence-base" of intervention for vulnerable children and their families* (p. 220-223). Padova, Italy: Fonzione Emanuela Zancan.

Barth, R. P. (1990). On their own: The experience of youth after foster care. *Child and Adolescent Social Work Journal, 7*(5), 419-446.

Barth, R. P. (1990). Theories guiding home-based intensive family preservation services. In J. K. Whittaker, J. M. Kinney, E. Tracy & C. Booth (Eds.), *Reaching high risk families: Intensive family preservation services* (pp. 91-114). Hawthorne: Aldine de Gruyter.

Barth, R. P. (1991). An experimental evaluation of in-home child abuse prevention services. *Child Abuse & Neglect, 15*, 363-375.

Barth, R. P. (1993). Long-term in-home services. In D. Besharov (Ed.), *When drug addicts have children: Reorienting child welfare's response. pp. 175-194*. Washington, DC: Child Welfare League of America.

Barth, R. P. (1994). Shared family care: Child protection and family preservation. *Social Work, 39*(5), 515-524.

Barth, R. P. (1997). Effects of age and race on the odds of adoption versus remaining in long-term out-of-home care. *Child Welfare, 76*(2), 285-308.

Barth, R. P. (1997). The costs and benefits of adoption. In R. Avery (Ed.), *Public Adoption Policy*. New York: Auburn House.

Barth, R. P. (2002). Outcomes of adoption and what they tell us about designing adoption services. *Adoption Quarterly, 6*, 45-60.

Barth, R. P. (2005). Residential care: From here to eternity. *International Journal of Social Welfare, 14*, 158-162.

Barth, R.P. (2008). The move to evidence-based practice: How well does it fit child welfare services? *Journal of Public Child Welfare*. 2, 145-172.

Barth, R. P., & Berry, M. (1987). Outcomes of child welfare services under permanency planning. *Social Service Review, 61*(1), 71-90.

Barth, R. P., & Berry, M. (1994). Implications of research on the welfare of children under permanency planning. In R. P. Barth, J. D. Berrick & N. Gilbert (Eds.), *Child welfare research review* (Vol. 1, pp. 323-368). New York: Columbia University Press.

Barth, R. P., & Blackwell, D. L. (1998). Death rates among California's foster care and former care populations. *Children & Youth Services Review, 20*(7), 577-604.

Barth, R. P., & Price, A. (1999). Shared family care: providing services to parents and children placed together in out-of-home care. *Child Welfare, 78*(1), 88-107.

Barth, R. P., Courtney, M. E., Berrick, J. D., & Albert, V. (1994). *From child abuse to permanency planning: Child welfare services pathways and placements*. New York: Aldine de Gruyter.

Barth, R. P., Crea, T. M., John, K., Thoburn, J., & Quinton, D. (2005). Beyond attachment theory and therapy: Towards sensitive and evidence-based interventions with foster and adoptive families in distress. *Child and Family Social Work, 10*, 257-268.

Barth, R. P., Gibbons, C., & Guo, S. (2006). Substance abuse treatment and the recurrence of maltreatment among caregivers with children living at home: A propensity score analysis. *Journal of Substance Abuse Treatment, 30*(2), 93-104.

Barth, R. P., Greeson, J. K. P., Guo, S. Y., Green, R. L., Hurley, S., & Sisson, J. (2007). Changes in family functioning and child behavior following intensive in-home therapy. *Children & Youth Services Review, 29*(8), 988-1009.

Barth, R. P., Greeson, J. K. P., Guo, S., Green, R. L., Hurley, S., & Sisson, J. (2007). Outcomes for youth receiving intensive in-home therapy or residential care: A comparison using propensity scores. *American Journal of Orthopsychiatry, 77*, 497-505.

Barth, R. P., Guo, G., Green, R. L., & McCrae, J. (2007). Kinship care and nonkinship foster care: Informing the new debate. In R. Haskins, F. Wulczyn & M. Webb (Eds.), *Child protection: Using research to improve policy and practice* (pp. 187-206). Washington, DC: Brookings.

Barth, R. P., Landsverk, J., Chamberlain, P., Reid, J. B., Rolls, J. A., Hurlburt, M. S., et al. (2005). Parent-Training Programs in Child Welfare Services: Planning for a More Evidence-Based Approach to Serving Biological Parents. *Research on Social Work Practice, 15*(5), 353-371.

Barth, R. P., Needell, B., Berrick, J. D., Albert, V., & Jonson-Reid, M. (1995). *Child welfare services to young children*. Presented at the Third Annual National Child Welfare Conference, Washington, DC.

Barth, R. P., Webster, D. II, & Lee, S. (2002). Adoption of American Indian children: Implications for implementing the Indian Child Welfare and Adoption and Safe Families Acts. *Children and Youth Services Review, 24*, 139-158.

Barth, R. P., Guo, S., Green, R. L., & McRae, J.S. (2007). Developmental outcomes for children in kinship and nonkinship care: Findings from the National Survey of Child and Adolescent Well-Being. In R. Haskins, F. Wulczyn, & M. B. Webb (Eds.). *Child protection: Using research to improve policy and practice*. (pp. 187-206) Washington, DC: Brookings.

Barth, R. P., Lee, C., Wildfire, J., & Guo, S. (2006). Estimating costs of foster care vs. adoption using propensity score matching. *Social Service Review, 80*, 127-158.

Barth, R.P., Lloyd, E.C., Christ, S., Chapman, M. & Dickinson, N.S. (2008). Child welfare worker characteristics and job satisfaction: A national study. *Social Work*, 53, 199-209.

Barth, R. P., Wildfire, J., & Green, R. (2006). Placement into foster care and the interplay of urbanicity, child behavior problems, and poverty. *American Journal of Orthopsychiatry, 76*(3), 358-366.

Barth, R. P., Wulczyn, F., & Crea, T. (2005). From anticipation to evidence: Research on the Adoption and Safe Families Act. *Journal of Law and Social Policy*, 371-399.

Barth, R.P. & Chintapallli, L. (2009). Permanence and impermanence for youth in out-of-home care. In B. Kerman, M. Freundlich & A.N. Maluccio (Eds.). Achieving permanency for older children and youth in foster care. (pp. 88-108) New York City: Oxford University Press.

Barth, R.P. (1988). Older children adoption and disruption. *Public Welfare, 46*(1), 23-29.

Barth, R.P. (2002). Institutions vs. foster homes: The empirical base for the second century of debate. Unpublished Paper. (Prepared for the Annie E. Casey Foundation), pp. 37.

Barth, R.P., & Berry, M. (1988). *Adoption and disruption: Risks, rates, and responses.* Hawthorne: Aldine de Gruyter.

Barth, R.P., Courtney, M., Berrick, J., & Albert, V. (1994). *From child abuse to permanency planning: Pathways through child welfare services.* New York: Aldine de Gruyter.

Bartholet, E. (1993). *Family bonds.* New York: Simon & Schuster.

Bartik, T.J. (2001). *Jobs for the poor: Can labor demand policies help?* New York: Russell Sage Foundation.

Bass, B. M. (1985). *Leadership and performance beyond expectations.* New York: The Free Press.

Bath, H. I., & Haapala, D. A. (1994). Family preservation services: What does the outcome research really tell us. *Social Service Review, 68*(3), 386-404.

Bath, H. I., Richey, C. A., & Haapala, D. A. (1992). Child age and outcome correlates in intensive family preservation services. *Children and Youth Services Review, 14*(5), 389-406.

Beem, C. (2007). Child welfare and the civic minimum. *Children and Youth Services Review, 29*(5), 618-636.

Beggs, M. (1996). *In a Day's Work: Four child welfare social workers in California.* San Francisco, CA: San Francisco Study Center.

Belsky, J. (1992). The etiology of child maltreatment: An ecological-contextual analysis. Paper commissioned by the National Academy of Science, Commission on Behavioral and Social Sciences and Education, Panel on Research on Child Abuse and Neglect.

Bending, R. L. (1997). Training child welfare workers to meet the requirements of the Indian Child Welfare Act. In G.R. Anderson, A.S. Ryan & B. R. Leashore (Eds.), *The challenge of permanency planning in a multicultural society.* (pp. 151-164.). New York: The Haworth Press.

Benedict, M. I., Zuravin, S., & Stallings, R. Y. (1996). Adult functioning of children who lived in kin versus nonrelative family foster homes. *Child Welfare, 75*(5), 529-549.

Benedict, M. I., Zuravin, S., Brandt, D., & Abbey, H. (1994). Types and frequency of child maltreatment by family foster care providers in an urban population. *Child Abuse & Neglect, 18*(7), 577-585.

Benson, P. L., Scales, P. C., Hawkins, J. D., Oesterle, S., & Hill, J. K. G. (2004). *Successful Young Adult Development.* Seattle, WA: The Bill and Melinda Gates Foundation.

Bent-Goodley, T. B., (Ed) (2003). *African-American Social Workers and Social Policy.* New York: The Haworth Press.

Berge, J.M., Mendenhall, T.J., Wrobel, G.M., Grotevant, H.D., & McRoy, R.G. (2006). Adolescents' feelings about openness in adoption: Implications for adoption agencies. *Child Welfare, 85*(6), 1011-1039.

Berger, L. (2004). Income, family structure, and child maltreatment risk. *Children and Youth Services Review 26,* 725–748.

Berger, L., Paxson, C., & Waldfogel, J. (2005). Income and child development, Center for Research on Child Wellbeing Working Paper. http://crcw.princeton.edu/working-papers/WP05-16-FF-Paxson.pdf

Bergman, A. B., Larsen, R. M., & Mueller, B. A. (1986). Changing spectrum of serious child abuse. *Pediatrics, 77,* 113-116.

Berliner, L. (1993). Is family preservation in the best interest of children? *Journal of Interpersonal Violence, 8,* 556-557.

Berliner, L. (2000). What is sexual abuse? In Dubowitz, H., & DePanfilis, D. (Eds.). Handbook for child protection practice (pp. 18-22). Thousand Oaks, CA: Sage.

Bernard, S. J., Paulozzi, L. J., & Wallace, L. J. D. (2007). *Fatal Injuries Among Children by Race and Ethnicity: United States—1999-2002.* Washington, DC: Center for

Disease Control: Division of Unintentional Injury Prevention, National Center for Injury Prevention and Control.

Bernstein, N. (2000). A rage to do better: Listening to young people from the foster care system. From www.pacificnews.org

Berrick, J. D. (1997). Assessing quality of care in kinship and foster family care. *Family Relations: Journal of Applied Family & Child Studies, 46*(3), 273-280.

Berrick, J. D., Barth, R. P., & Needell, B. (1994). A comparison of kinship foster homes and foster family homes: Implications for kinship foster care as family preservation. *Children and Youth Services Review, 16*(1-2), 33-63.

Berrick, J. D., Courtney, M. E., & Barth, R. P. (1993). Specialized foster care and group home care: Similarities and differences of children in care. *Children and Youth Services Review, 15*, 453-474

Berrick, J. D., Needell, B., Barth, R. P., & Jonson-Reid, M. (1998). *The tender years: Toward developmentally sensitive child welfare services for very young children.* New York: Oxford University Press.

Berrick, J.B., Barth, R.P., Needell, B., &Jonson-Reid, M. (1997). Group care and young children. *Social Service Review*, 71, 257-274.

Berridge, D., & Cleaver, D. (1987). *Foster home breakdown*. Oxford, England: Basil Blackwell.

Berry, M. (1988). A review of parent training programs in child welfare. *Social Service Review, 62*(3), 303-323.

Berry, M. (1991). Open adoption in a sample of 1296 families. *Children and Youth Services Review, 13,* 379-396.

Berry, M. (1997). *The family at risk—Issues and trends in family preservation services.* Columbia, SC: University of South Carolina Press.

Berry, M., & Cash, J. S. (1998). Creating community through psychoeducational groups in family preservation work. Families in Society. *The Journal of Contemporary Human Services, 79,* 15-23.

Berry, M., Barth, R. P., & Needell, B. (1996). Preparation, support, and satisfaction of adoptive families in agency and independent adoptions. *Child and Adolescent Social Work Journal, 13,* 157-183.

Berry, M., Propp, J., & Martens, P. (2007). The use of intensive family preservation services with adoptive families. *Child and Family Social Work, 12,* 43-53.

Besharov, D. J. (1984). Malpractice in child placement: civil liability for inadequate foster care services. *Child Welfare, 63*(3), 195-204.

Besharov, D. J. (1985). *The vulnerable social worker: Liability for serving children and families.* Silver Spring, MD: National Association of Social Workers.

Besharov, D. J. (1994). Looking beyond 30, 60, 90 days. *Children and Youth Services Review, 16,* 445-452.

Besharov, D. J., & Germanis, P. (1999). Is WIC as good as they say? *The Public Interest 134,* 21-36.

Besinger, B. A., Garland, A. F., Litrownik, A. J., & Landsverk, J. A. (1999). Caregiver substance abuse among maltreated children placed in out-of-home care. *Child Welfare, 78*(2), 221.

Besinger, B. A., Garland, A. F., Litrownik, A. J., & Landsverk, J. A. (1999). Caregiver substance abuse among maltreated children placed in out-of-home care. *Child Welfare, 78,* 221-239.

Bess, R., Andrews, C., Jantz, A., Russell, V., & Geen, R. (2002). *The Cost of Protecting Vulnerable Children III: What Factors Affect States' Fiscal Decisions?—Occasional Paper No. 61.* Washington, DC: Urban Institute, Assessing the New Federalism.

Biegel, D. E., Farkas, K. J., Abell, N., Goodin, J., & Friedman, B. (1988). *Social support networks and bibliography 1983-1987.* New York: Greenwood.

Biehal, N., & Wade, J. (1996). Looking back, looking forward: Care leavers, families and change. *Children & Youth Services Review, 18*(4-5), 425-445.

Biehal, N., Clayden, J., Stein, M., & Wade, J. (1995). *Moving on—Young people and leaving care schemes.* London: HMSO.

Billingsley, A., & Giovannoni, J. (1972). *Children of the Storm—Black children and American child welfare.* New York: John Wiley & Sons.

Bishop, D. M., & Frazier, C. (1997). The transfer of juveniles to criminal court: Does it make a difference. *Crime & Delinquency, 42,* 111-143.

Black, D. A., Heyman, R. E., & Slep, A. M. (2001). Risk factors for child abuse. *Aggression and Violent Behavior, 6,* 121-188.

Blanchard, E.L., & Barsh, R. L. (1980). What is best for tribal children: A response to Fischler. *Social Work, 25,* 350-357.

Blank, R. (2007). What we know, what we don't know, and what we need to know about welfare reform. Conference paper.

Blank, R. & Shierholz, H. (2006). Exploring gender differences in employment and wage trends among less-skilled workers. In *Working and poor: How economic and policy changes are affecting low-wage workers.* R. Blank, S. Danziger and R. Schoeni eds. New York: Russell Sage Foundation, pp. 23-58.

Blank, R. (2002). Evaluating welfare reform in the United States. *Journal of Economic Literature* 40 (December): 1105-1166.

Blau, D. (2003). Child care subsidy programs. In Moffitt (ed.). *Means-tested transfer programs in the United States*, Chicago, IL: National Bureau of Economic Research, pp. 443-516.

Blome, W. W. (1997). What happens to foster kids: Educational experiences of a random sample of foster care youth and a matched group of non-foster care youth. *Child & Adolescent Social Work Journal, 14*(1), 41-53.

Blome, W. W., & Steib, S. (2007). An examination of oversight and review in the child welfare system: The many watch the few serve the many. *Journal of Public Child Welfare, 1*(3), 3-26.

Bloom, M. (1985). *Life span development-Bases for preventive and interventive helping* (Second ed.). New York: Macmillan Publishing Co.

Blumenthal, K. (1983). Making foster family care responsive. In B. McGowan & W. Meezan (Eds.), *Child welfare: Current dilemmas—Future directions* (pp. 299-344). Itasca,, IL: F.E. Peacock.

Bonecutter, F. J., & Gleeson, J. P. (1997). *Achieving permanency for children in kinship foster care: A training manual.* Chicago: University of Illinois at Chicago, Jane Addams College of Social Work.

Booz-Allen, & Hamilton. (1987). *The Maryland social work services job analysis and personnel qualifications study.* Baltimore, MD: Maryland Department of Human Resources.

Boyd-Franklin, N. (1989). *Black families in therapy: A multisystems approach.* New York: Guilford Press.

Brace, C. L. (1872). *The dangerous classes of New York.* New York: Wyncoop & Hallenback.

Brace, C.L. (1859). *The best method of disposing of our pauper and vagrant children.* New York: Wynkoop, Hallenbeck & Thomas.

Brandford, C., & English, D. (2004). *Foster youth transition to independence study.* Seattle, WA: Office of Children's Administration Research, Washington Department of Social and Health Services.

Branham, E. (1970). One parent adoptions. *Children, 17*(3), 103-107.

Brassard, M. R., & Hart, S. (2000). What is psychological maltreatment? In Dubowitz, H., & DePanfilis, D. (Eds.). Handbook for child protection practice. (pp. 23-27). Thousand Oaks, CA: Sage.

Braziel, D. J. (Ed.). (1996). *Family-focused practice in out-of-home care*. Washington, DC: Child Welfare League of America.

Breakey, G., & Pratt, B. (1991). Healthy growth for Hawaii's *Healthy Start*: Toward a systematic statewide approach to the prevention of child abuse and neglect. *Zero to Three, 9*(4), 16-22.

Bremner, R. (Ed.). (1971). *Children and youth in America: A documentary history, 1865-1965* (Vol. 2). Cambridge, MA: Harvard University Press.

Bricker-Jenkins, M., Hooyman, N. R., & Gottlieb, N. (1991). *Feminist social work practice in clinical settings*. Beverly Hills, CA: Sage.

Brieland, D. (1987). History and evolution of social work practice. In *Encyclopedia of Social Work* (18th ed., Vol. 1, pp. 739-754). Silver Spring, MD: National Association of Social Workers.

Briere, J. (1992). *Child abuse trauma theory and treatment of the lasting effects*. Newbury Park, CA: Sage.

Briere, J., & Scott, C. (2006). *Principles of trauma therapy: A guide to symptoms, evaluation, and treatment*. Newbury Park, CA: Sage Publications.

Brissett-Chapman, S., & Issacs-Schockley, M. (1997). *Children in social peril: A community vision for preserving family care of African American children and youths (Report of the First African American Child Welfare Summit*. Washington, DC: CWLA Press.

Brittain, J. D., & Hunt, D. E. (2004). *Helping in child protective services: A competency-based casework handbook*. New York: Oxford University Press.

Brody, R. (2000). *Effectively managing human service organizations* (2nd ed.). Newbury Park, CA: Sage Press.

Brodzinsky, D., Patterson, C., & Vaziri, M. (2002). Adoption agency perspectives on lesbian and gay prospective parents: A national study. *Adoption Quarterly, 5*, 5-23.

Brohl, K. (2004). *The new miracle workers: overcoming contemporary challenges in child welfare work*. Washington, DC: CWLA Press.

Bronfenbrenner, U. (1979). *The Ecology of Human Development*. Cambridge, MA: Harvard University Press.

Bronfenbrenner, U. (1986). Ecology of the family as a context to human development: Research perspectives. *Developmental Psychology, 22*, 723-742.

Bronfenbrenner, U. (2004). *Making Human Being Human: Bioecological perspectives on human development*. Thousand Oaks, CA: Sage Publications.

Bronfenbrenner, U., & Morris, P. A. (1998). The ecology of developmental processes. In W. Damon (Ed.), *Handbook of child psychology* (Fifth ed., pp. 993-1028). New York: John Wiley & Sons, Inc.

Brooks, D., & Barth, R. P. (1998). Characteristics and outcomes of drug-exposed and non drug-exposed children in kinship and non-relative foster care. *Children & Youth Services Review, 20*(6), 475-501.

Brooks, D., & Barth, R. P. (1999). Adult transracial and inracial adoptees: Effects of race, gender, adoptive family structure, and placement history on adjustment outcomes. *American Journal of Orthopsychiatry, 69*, 87-99.

Brooks-Gunn, J., & Duncan, G. J. (1997). The effects of poverty on children. *The Future of Children, 7*(2), 55-71.

Brooks-Gunn, J., Klebanov, P. K., & Liaw, F. (1995). The learning, physical, and emotional environment of the home in the context of poverty: The Infant Health and Development program. *Children and Youth Services Review, 17*, 251-276.

Brown, J. D., & Bednar, L. M. (2006). Foster parent perceptions of placement breakdown. *Children and Youth Services Review, 28*(12), 1497-1511.

Brown, J. H., & Weil, M. (Eds.). (1992). *Family, practice: A curriculum plan for social service*. Washington, DC: Child Welfare League of America.

Browne, D., & Moloney, A. (2002). "Contact Irregular": a qualitative analysis of the impact of visiting patterns of natural parents on foster placements. *Child & Family Social Work, 7*(1), 35.

Bruce, E. J., & Austin, M. J. (2000). Social work supervision: Assessing the past and mapping the future. *The Clinical Supervisor, 19*(2), 85-107.

Bruner, C., & Scott, S. (1995). *Targeting family preservation services: Strategies and guidelines for the field.* Des Moines, IO: The Child and Family Policy Center.

Brunk, M., Henggeler, S. W., & Whelan, J. B. (1987). Comparison of multi-systemic therapy and parent training in the brief treatment of child abuse and neglect. *Journal of Consulting and Clinical Psychology, 55*, 171-178.

Bruns, E. J., & Burchard, J. D. (2000). Impact of respite care services for families with children experiencing emotional and behavioral problems. *Children's Services: Social Policy, Research, & Practice, 3*(1), 39-61.

Bryce, M. (1979). Home-based care: Development and rationale. In S. Maybanks & M. Bryce (Eds.), *Home-based services for children and families: Policy, practice, and research* (pp. 360). Springfield, IL: Charles C. Thomas.

Bryce, M., & Lloyd, J. C. (Eds.). (1981). *Treating families in the home: An alternative to placement.* Springfield, IL: Charles C. Thomas Publishers.

Buchard, J. D., Bruns, E. J., & Buchard, S. N. (2002). The Wraparound Approach. In B. J. Burns & K. Hoagwood (Eds.), *Community Treatment for Youth* (pp. 69-90). New York: Oxford University Press.

Bullock, R., Gooch, D., & Little, M. (1998). *Children Going Home—the re-unification of families.* Aldershot, England: Ashgate.

Bullock, R., Little, M., & Milham, S. (1993). *Residential care of children: A review of the research.* London: HMSO.

Burford, G., & Pennell, J. (1995). Family group decision-making: An innovation in child and family welfare. In B. Galaway & J. Hudson (Eds.), *Child welfare systems: Canadian research and policy implications* (pp. 140-153). Toronto: Thompson Educational Publications.

Burgess, G. J. (2006). *Legacy Living.* Provo, UT: Executive Excellence Publishing.

Burkhauser, R., & Sabia, J. (2007). The effectiveness of minimum-wage increases in reducing poverty: Past, present and future. *Contemporary Economic Policy* (April) 25: 262-281.

Burley, M., & Halpern, M. (2001). *Educational attainment of foster youth: Achievement and graduation outcomes for children in State care.* Olympia, WA: Washington State Institute for Public Policy.

Burnette, D. (1997). Grandmother caregivers in inner-city Latino families: A descriptive profile and informal social supports. In G.R. Anderson, A.S. Ryan & B. R. Leashore (Eds.), *The challenge of permanency planning in a multicultural society* (pp. 121-138). New York: The Haworth Press.

Burns, B.J. and Hoagwood, K. (2002). *Community Treatment for Youth: Evidence-Based Interventions for Severe Emotional and Behavioral Disorders.* New York: Oxford University Press.

Burns, B.J., Hoagwood, K. and Mrazek, P.J. (1999). Effective treatment for mental disorders in children and adolescents. *Clinical child and family psychology review*, 2, 199-254.

Burns, N. E. (1965). Supervision in Social Work. In H. L. Lurie (Ed.), *Encyclopedia of Social Work* (15th ed., Vol.). New York: National Association of Social Workers.

Burry, C. L., & Wright, L. (2006). Facilitating Visitation for Infants with Prenatal Substance Abuse. *Child Welfare, LXXXV*(6), 899-919.

Burt, M., & Pittman, K. (1985). *Testing the social safety net.* Washington, DC: Urban Institute.

Busch, M., & Folaron, G. (2005). Accessibility and clarity of state child welfare agency mission statements. *Child Welfare, 84*(3), 415-430.

Cadoret, R. J., Yates, W. R., Troughton, E., Woodworth, G., & Stewart, M. A. (1995). Genetic-environmental interaction in the genesis of agressivity and conduct disorders. *Archives of General Psychiatry, 52*(11), 916-924.

Cameron, G., & Vanderwoerd, J. (1997). *Protecting children and supporting families: Promising programs and organizational realities.* New York: Aldine de Gruyter.

Cancian, M. & Reed, D. (2001). Changes in family structure: Implications for poverty and related policy. In *Understanding poverty.* S. Danziger and R. Haveman eds. New York: Harvard University Press and Russell Sage Foundation, pp. 69-96.

Cantos, A. L., Gries, L. T., & Slis, V. (1997). Behavioral correlates of parental visiting during family foster care. *Child Welfare, 76*(2), 309-329.

Carbino, R. (1981). Developing a parent organization: new roles for parents of children in substitute care. In A.N. Maluccio & P. A. Sinanoglu (Eds.), *The challenge of partnership: Working with parents of children in foster care* (pp. 165-186). New York: Child Welfare League of America.

Carbino, R. (1991). Child abuse and neglect reports in foster care: The issue for foster families of "false" allegations. *Child & Youth Services, 15*(2), 233-247.

Card, D. & Krueger, A. (1995). *Myth and measurement: The new economics of the minimum wage.* Princeton, NJ: Princeton University Press.

Carlo, P. (1993). Family reunification practice in residential treatment for children. In B.A. Pine, R Warsh. & A. N. Maluccio (Eds.), *Together again: Family reunification in foster care* (pp. 93-117). Washington, DC: Child Welfare League of America.

Carlson, B. (1996). Children of battered women: Research, programs, and services. In A. Roberts (Ed.), *Helping battered women: New perspectives and remedies* (pp. 172-187). New York: Oxford University Press.

Carnegie Council on Adolescent Development. (1989). *Turning points: Preparing youth for the 21st century.* Washington, DC: CCAD.

Carrilio, T. E. (1998). *California safe and healthy families model program: A family support home visiting model.* The California Department of Social Services, Office of Child Abuse Prevention.

Carten, A. J. (1990). Building on the strengths of black foster families. In A. N. Maluccio, R. Krieger & B. A. Pine (Eds.), *Preparing adolescents for life after foster care-The central role of foster parents* (pp. 127-141). Washington, DC: Child Welfare League of America.

Carter, B., & McGoldrick, M. (Eds.). (1999). *The expanded family life cycle: Individual, family, and social perspectives.* (Third ed.). Boston: Allyn and Bacon.

Casey Family Programs. (1996). A supervision model for Casey Family Programs—Working paper (mimeograph). Seattle, WA: Author.

Casey Family Programs. (2000). *The Casey model of practice.* Seattle, WA: Casey Family Programs.

Casey Family Programs. (2001). *It's my life: A framework for youth transitioning from foster care to successful adulthood.* Seattle, WA: Casey Family Programs.

Casey Family Programs. (2003a). *Family, community, culture: Roots of permanency- A conceptual framework on permanency from Casey Family Programs.* Seattle, WA: Casey Family Programs.

Casey Family Programs. (2003b). *Higher education reform: Incorporating the needs of foster youth.* Seattle, WA: Casey Family Programs.

Casey Family Programs. (2004). *2005 Public Policy Agenda.* Seattle, WA: Author.

Casey Family Services. (1999). *The road to independence: Transitioning youth in foster care to independence.* Shelton, CT: Casey Family Services.

Casey National Resource Center for Family Support. (2003). *Siblings in Out-Of-Home Care: An overview*. Washington, DC: Casey National Resource Center for Family Support.

Catalano, R. F., & Hawkins, J. D. (1996). The social developmental model: A theory of antisocial behavior. In J. D. Hawkins (Ed.), *Delinquency and crime: Current theories*. New York: Cambridge University Press.

CDC (2008). Nonfatal maltreatment of infants—United States, October 2005—2006. *Morbidity and Mortality Weekly (MMWR), 57*(13), 336-339. Retrieved April 4, 2008 from http://www.cdc.gov/mmwr/preview/mmwrhtml/mm5713a2.htm.

Center for Child and Family Policy. (2004). *Multiple Response System Evaluation Report to the North Carolina Division of Social Services*. Durham, NC: Author.

Center for Disease Control and Prevention. (2005). *Preventing Child Maltreatment: Program Activities Guide*. Atlanta, GA: Author. Retrieved March 1, 2008 from http://www.cdc.gov/ncipc/dvp/preventing_CM—final.pdf.

Center for Family Life. (1997). *Center for Family Life annual progress report*. New York: Center for Family Life.

Center for the Study of Social Policy. (1994). *Results based decision making and budgeting*. Washington, DC: Fiscal Studies Policy Group, Center for the Study of Social Policy (mimeograph).

Center for the Study of Social Policy. (2006). *Places to Watch: Promising Practices to Address Racial Disproportionality in Child Welfare*. Washington, DC: Author.

Center on Budget and Policy Priorities (2007a). A $7.25 minimum wage would be a useful step in helping working families escape poverty. http://www.cbpp.org/1-5-07mw.htm. Accessed 6-1-07.

Center on Budget and Policy Priorities (2007b). Facts About tax credits for working families – the Earned Income Credit and Child Tax Credit http://www.cbpp.org/eic2007/EIC_Facts_Text.pdf. Accessed 26 July 2007.

Center on the Developing Child at Harvard University. (2007). *A Science-Based Framework for Early Childhood Policy: Using Evidence to Improve Outcomes in Learning, Behavior, and Health for Vulnerable Children*. Cambridge, MA: Harvard University, Center on the Developing Child.

Chadwick Center for Children and Families. (2004). *Closing the quality chasm in child abuse treatment: Identifying and disseminating best practices*. San Diego: Author.

Chaffin, M., Kelleher, K., & Hollenberg, J. (1996). Onset of physical abuse and neglect: Psychiatric, substance abuse and social risk factors from prospective community data. *Child Abuse and Neglect, 20*, 191-200.

Chaffin, M., Kelleher, K., & Hollenberg, J. (1996). Onset of physical abuse and neglect: Psychiatric, substance abuse, and social risk factors from prospective community data. *Child Abuse & Neglect, 20*, 191-203.

Chamberlain, P. (1994). *Family connections: Treatment foster care for adolescents with delinquency*. Eugene, OR: Castalia Press.

Chamberlain, P. (2003). *Treating chronic juvenile offenders: Advances made through the Oregon multidimensional treatment foster care model*. Washington, DC: American Psychological Association.

Chamberlain, P., Price, J. M., Reid, J. B., Landsverk, J., Fisher, P. A., & Stoolmiller, M. (2006). Who disrupts from placement in foster and kinship care? *Child Abuse & Neglect, 30*(4), 409-424.

Chambers, C. A. (1963). *Seedtime of reform: American social service and social action, 1918-1933*. Minneapolis, MN: University of Minnesota Press.

Chambless, D. L., & Hollon, S. D. (1998). Defining empirically supported therapies. *Journal of Consulting and Clinical Psychology, 66*, 7-18.

Chapman, M. V., Wall, A., & Barth, R. P. (2004). Children's Voices: The Perceptions of Children in Foster Care. *American Journal of Orthopsychiatry, 74*(3), 293.

Chasnoff, I. J. (1998). Silent violence: Is prevention a moral obligation? *Pediatrics, 102*(1), 145-148.

Chibnall, S., Dutch, N., Jones-Harden, B., Brown, A., Gourgine, R., Smith, J., et al. (2003). *Children of color in the child welfare system: Perspectives from the child welfare community*. Washington, DC: U.S. Department of Health and Human Services Administration for Children and Families Children's Bureau, Administration for Children and Families.

Chicago, IL: Annie E. Casey Foundation, Northwestern University School of Law: Institute for Policy Research.

Chicago, IL: The Chapin Hall Center for Children at University of Chicago. Chicago: Nelson-Hall Publishers.

Child Trends. (2002a). *Helping Teens develop healthy social skills and relationships: What the research shows about navigating adolescence*. Washington, DC: Child Trends (July).

Child Trends. (2002b). *Mentoring : A promising strategy for youth development*. Washington, DC: Child Trends (February).

Child Trends. (2008). *Federal Spending on child welfare report*. TBD.

Child Welfare Information Gateway (2005). Mandatory reporters of child abuse and neglect: Summary of state laws. Retrieved February 19, 2008 from http://www.childwelfare.gov/systemwide/laws_policies/statutes/manda.cfm#noteone

Child Welfare Information Gateway (undated). National and state statistics. Retrieved on February 18, 2008 from http://www.childwelfare.gov/can/prevalence/stats.cfm

Child Welfare Information Gateway. (2006). *Domestic Violence: Safety Planning*. Washington, DC: Author.

Child Welfare League of America, Public Policy Department. (1997). *Summary of the Adoption and Safe Families Act of 1997 (PL 105-89) (mimeograph)*. Washington, DC: Author. Reprinted with Permission.

Child Welfare League of America. (1984). *Standards for organization and administration for all child welfare services*. Washington, DC: Child Welfare League of America.

Child Welfare League of America. (1989). *Standards for Independent Living Service*. Washington, DC: Child Welfare League of America

Child Welfare League of America. (1990). *Florida Recruitment and Retention Study*. Washington, DC: Author.

Child Welfare League of America. (1991). *Serving the needs of gay and lesbian youths - Recommendations to a colloquium— Jan. 25-26 1991*. Washington. DC: Author.

Child Welfare League of America. (1994). *Kinship care: A natural bridge*. Washington, DC: Child Welfare League of America.

Child Welfare League of America. (1995). *Standards of Excellence for family foster care*. Washington, DC: Child Welfare League of America.

Child Welfare League of America. (1997). *Summary of the Adoption and Safe Families Act of 1997 (PL 105-89)*— Reprinted with Permission. Washington. DC: CWLA Public Policy Department.

Child Welfare League of America. (1999). *Minimum Education Required by State Child Welfare Agencies, Percent, By Degree Type, State Child Welfare Agency Survey*. Washington, DC: CWLA Press.

Child Welfare League of America. (2002). *Children of Color at a Glance: CWLA Fact Sheet and Relevant Research*: Retrieved online at http://ndas.cwla.org. Data Source: Length of Stay for Children in Care by Race/Ethnicity, 2002. Special Tabulation of 2002 Adoption and Foster Care Reporting System (AFCARS). Prepared by the Child Welfare League of America, National Data Analysis System.

Child Welfare League of America. (2003b). *Making children a national priority: A framework for community action*. Washington, DC: Child Welfare League of America.

Child Welfare League of America. (2004). *Adoption. A fact sheet in the CWLA 2004 Legislative agenda*. Washington. DC: Author.

Child Welfare League of America. (2004). *Children 2004: vision, action, results*. Washington. DC: Author.

Child Welfare League of America. (2007). *Best Practice Guidelines for Services to LGBT youth in out-of-home care*. Washington. DC: Author.

Child Welfare Watch. (2002). *No. 8, Fall (From Mayor's Management Reports) New York State Office of Children and Family Services Monitoring and Analysis Profiles*. New York: City Limits Community Information Service, New York University, Milano Graduate School.

Children and Youth Services Review, 27, 227-249.

Children's Bureau. Number of children listed on the website who have been adopted. Retrieved April 19, 2007 from http://adoptuskids.org

Children's Defense Fund. (2004). *How can I get involved? State fact sheets for grandparents and other relatives raising children*. Washington, DC: Author.

Chipungu, S. S., & Bent-Goodley, T. B. (2004). Meeting the challenges of contemporary foster care. *The Future of Children, 14*(1), 75-93.

Choi, S., & Ryan, J. P. (2007). Co-occurring problems for substance abusing mothers in child welfare: Matching services to improve family reunification. *Children and Youth Services Review, 29*(11), 1395-1410.

Christian, S., & National Conference of State Legislatures. (2006). *The changing landscape of Federal Child Welfare Financing*. Washington, DC: National Conference of State Legislators.

Cicchetti, D., & Lynch, M. (1993). Toward an ecological/transactional model of community violence and child maltreatment: Consequences for children's development. *Psychiatry, 56*, 96-118.

Cicero-Reese, B., & Black, P. (1998). Research Suggests Why Child Welfare Workers Stay on the Job. *Partnerships for Child Welfare, 5*(5).

Ciliberti, P. (1998). An Innovative Family Preservation Program in an African American Community: Longitudinal analysis. *Family Preservation Journal, 3*(2), 45-72.

Citro, C. & Michael, R. Eds. (1995). *Measuring poverty: A new approach*. Washington, DC: National Academy Press.

Clark, H. B. (2004). *Transition to Independence Process (TIP) System Development and Operations Manual*. Tampa, FL: Transition to Independence Process (TIP).

Clark, H. B., & Davis, M. (2000). *Transition to adulthood: A resource for assisting young people with emotional or behavioral difficulties*. Baltimore, MD: P. H. Brookes.

Clark, H. B., Prange, M. E., Lee, B., Boyd, L., et al. (1994). Improving adjustment outcomes for foster children with emotional and behavioral disorders: Early findings from a controlled study on individualized services. *Journal of Emotional & Behavioral Disorders, 2*(4), 207-218.

Clausen, J. M., Landsverk, J., Ganger, W., Chadwick, D., & Litrownik, A. (1998). Mental health problems of children in foster care. *Journal of Child & Family Studies, 7*(3), 283-296.

Clement, P.F. (1979). Families and foster care: Philadelphia in the late nineteenth century. *Social Service Review, 53*, 407-420.

Coakley, T. M. (2007). Examining African American fathers' involvement in permanency planning: An effort to reduce racial disproportionality in the child welfare system. *Children and Youth Services Review, In Press, Corrected Proof*.

Coates, R. B., Miller, A. D., & Ohlin, L. E. (1978). *Diversity in a youth correctional system*. Cambridge, MA: Ballinger.

Cohen, E., & Canan, L. (2006). Closer to Home: Parent mentors in child welfare. *Child Welfare, 85*(5), 867-884.

Cohen, J. A., & Mannarino, A. P. (2004). Treatment of childhood traumatic grief. *Journal of Clinical Child and Adolescent Psychology, 33*(4), 819-831.

Cohen, J. A., Mannarino, A. P., Zhitova, A. C., & Capone, M. E. (2003). Treating child-abuse related posttraumatic stress and comorbid substance abuse in adolescents. *Child Abuse & Neglect, 27*(12), 1345-1365.

Cohen, N. A. (Ed.). (1992). *Child welfare - A multicultural focus.* Boston, MA: Allyn and Bacon.

Coie, J. D., Lochman, J. E., Terry, R., & Hyman, C. (1992). Predicting early adolescent disorder from childhood aggression and peer rejection. *Journal of Consulting and Clinical Psychology, 60*, 783-792.

Cole, E. S. (1986). Post-legal adoption services: A time for decision. *Permanency Report, 4*(1), 1, 4.

Cole, E. S. (1987). *Keynote speech. Institute for Child Advocacy Conference, March 13-14, 1987.* (As reported in Update, Spring, 1987, pp.1-2). Paper presented, Cleveland, OH.

Cole, E. S. (1995). Becoming family-centered: Child welfare's challenge. *Families in Society: The Journal of Contemporary Human Services, 76*, 163-172.

Cole, E., & Duva, J. (1990). *Family preservation: An orientation for administrators & practitioners.* Washington, DC: Child Welfare League of America.

Coll, C. G., & Magnuson, K. (2000). Cultural differences as sources of developmental vulnerabilities and resources. In J. P. Shonkoff & S. J. Meisels (Eds.), *Handbook of early childhood intervention* (2nd ed., pp. 94-114). Cambridge: Cambridge University Press.

Collins, J. C., & Porras, J. I. (2002). *Built to Last: Successful Habits of Visionary Companies.* New York: Harper Business.

Collins, M. E. (2001). Transition to adulthood for vulnerable youths: A review of research and implications for policy. *Social Service Review, 75*, 271-291.

Comer, E. W., & Fraser, M. W. (1998). Evaluation of six family-support programs: Are they effective? *Families in Society: The Journal of Contemporary Human Services, 79*(2), 134-148.

Committee on Ways and Means, U.S. House of Representatives (2004). *2004 Green book: Background material and data on programs within the jurisdiction of the Committee on Ways and Means.* Washington, DC: U.S. Government Printing Office.

Conger, D., & Finkelstein, M. J. (2003). Foster Care and School Mobility. *Journal of Negro Education, 72*(1), 97.

Conger, D., & Rebeck, A. (2001). *How children's foster care experiences affect their education.* New York: New York City Administration for Children's Services.

Congressional Budget Office. (2007). The State Children's Health Insurance Program, May.

Conley, A. (2007). Differential Responses: A critical examination of a secondary prevention model. *Children & Youth Services Review, 29*(11), 1454-1468.

Connelly, C. D., Hazen, A. L., Coben, J. H., Kelleher, K. J., Barth, R. P., & Landsverk, J. A. (2006). **Persistence of intimate partner violence among families referred to child welfare.***Journal of Interpersonal Violence, 21*, 774-797.

Connelly, C. D., Hazen, A. L., Coben, J. H., Kelleher, K. J., Barth, R. P., & Landsverk, J. A. (2006). *Journal of Interpersonal Violence, 21*, 774-797.

Conners, N. A., Bradley, R. H., Mansell, L. W., Liu, J. Y., Roberts, T. J., Burgdorf, K., et al. (2004). Children of mothers with serious substance abuse problems: An accumulation of risks. *American Journal of Drug and Alcohol Abuse, 30*(1), 85-100.

Connolly, M., & McKenzie, M. (1999). *Effective participatory practice: Family group conferencing in child protection.* New York: Aldine de Gruyter.

Conway, T., & Hutson, R. S. (2007). *Is Kinship Care Good for Kids?* Washington. DC: Center for Law and Social Policy.

Cook, R. (1991). *A National Evaluation of Title IV-E Foster Care Independent Living Programs for Youth (Phase 2 Final Report, Volume 1.).* Rockville, MD: Westat Corporation.

Cook, R. (1997). Are we helping foster-care youth prepare for their future? In J. D. Berrick, R. Barth & N. Gilbert (Eds.), *Child Welfare Research Review* (Vol. 2, pp. 201-218). New York: Columbia University Press.

Cook, R. J. (1994). Are we helping foster care youth prepare for their future? *Children & Youth Services Review, 16*(3-4), 213-229.

Cook, R., Fleishman, E., & Grimes, V. (1989). *A National Evaluation of the Title IV-E Foster Care Independent Living Programs for Youth (contract No. 105-87-1608).* . Rockville: Westat, Inc.

Cook, R., Fleishman, E., & Grimes, V. (1991). *A National Evaluation of Title IV-E Foster Care Independent Living Programs for Youth. Phase 2 Final Report.* Rockville, MD: Westat Corporation.

Cooke, R. A., & Szumal, J. L. (2000). Using the Organizational Culture Inventory to understand the operating cultures of organizations. In N.M. Ashkanasy, C.P.M. Winderom & M. F. Peterson (Eds.), *Handbook of organizational culture and climate.* Thousand Oaks, CA: Sage Publications.

Costin, L. B., Bell, C. J., & Downs, S. W. (1991). *Child welfare: Policies and practices.* New York: Longman Publishing Group.

Coulton, C. I., & Pandey, S. (1992). Geographic Concentration of Poverty and Risk to Children in Urban Neighborhoods. *American Behavioral Scientist, 35,* 238-257.

Courtney, M. (1998). The politics and realities of transracial adoption. *Youth Law News, Jan-Feb,* 17-22.

Courtney, M. E., & Needell, B. (1997). Outcomes of kinship care: Lessons from California. In J. D. Berrick, R. P. Barth & N. Gilbert (Eds.), *Child welfare research review* (Vol. 2, pp. 130-149). New York: Columbia University Press.

Courtney, M. E., & Wong, Y.-L. I. (1996). Comparing the timing of exits from substitute care. *Children & Youth Services Review, 18*(4-5), 307-334.

Courtney, M. E., Barth, R. P., Berrick, J. D., Brooks, D., Needell, B., & Park, L. (1996). Race and child welfare services: Past research and future directions. *Child Welfare, 75,* 99-137.

Courtney, M. E., Piliavin, I., Grogan-Kaylor, A., & Nesmith, A. (2001). Foster youth transitions to adulthood: A longitudinal view of youth leaving care. *Child Welfare, 80*(6), 685-717.

Courtney, M. E., Piliavin, I., Grogan-Kaylor, A., & Nesmith, A. (2001). Foster youth transitions to adulthood: A longitudinal view of youth leaving care. *Child Welfare, 80*(6), 685-717.

Courtney, M., & Bost, N. (2002). *Review of literature on the effectiveness of independent living services.* Chicago: Chapin Hall.

Courtney, M., Dworsky, A., Cusick, G. R., Keller, T., Havlicek, J., Perez, A., et al. (2007). *Midwest evaluation of adult functioning of former foster youth: Outcomes at age 21.* Chicago, IL: University of Chicago, Chapin Hall Center for Children.

Courtney, M., Dworsky, A., Ruth, G., Keller, T., Havlicek, J., & Bost, N. (2005). *Midwest Evaluation of the Adult Functioning of Former Foster Youth: Outcomes at Age 19.* Chicago, IL: Chapin Hall Center for Children at the University of Chicago.

Courtney, M., Piliavin, I., & Grogan-Kaylor, A. (1995). *The Wisconsin study of youth aging out of out-of-home care; a portrait of children about to leave care.* Madison, WI: School of Social Work, University of Wisconsin-Madison.

Courtney, M., Piliavin, I., Grogan-Kaylor, A., & Nesmith, A. (1998). *Foster youth transitions to adulthood: Outcomes 12 to 18 months after leaving out-of-home care.* Madison, WI: School of Social Work and Institute for Research on Poverty, University of Wisconsin Madison.

Crampton, D. (2007). Research Review: Family group decision making: A promising practice in need of more programme theory and research. *Child and Family Social Work, 12*(2), 202-209.

Crea, T. M., Barth, R. P., & Chintapalli, L. K. (2007). Home study methods for evaluating prospective resource families: History, current challenges, and promising approaches. *Child Welfare, 86*, 141-159.

Crea, T. M., Barth, R.P., Chintapalli, L.K. & Buchanan, R.L. (2009). Structured home study evaluations: Perceived benefits of SAFE versus conventional home studies, *Adoption Quarterly.*

Cross, S.L. (2006). Indian family exception doctrine: Still losing children despite the Indian Child Welfare Act. *Child Welfare, 85*(4), 671-690.

Cross, T. L. (1989). Cultural competence continuum. *Focal Point, 3*(1), 1.

Crumbley, J., & Little, R. L. (Eds.). (1997). *Relatives raising children: An overview of kinship care.* Washington, DC: CWLA Press.

Curry, D., McCarragher, T., & Dellmann-Jenkins, M. (2005). Training, Transfer and Turnover: Exploring the relationship among transfer of learning factors and staff retention in child welfare. *Children & Youth Services Review, 27*(8), 931-948.

Curry, J. (1991). Outcome research on residential treatment: Implications and suggested directions. *American Journal of Orthopsychiatry, 61*, 348-358.

Curtis, C. M., & Alexander, R. A. (1996). The Multiethnic Placement Act: Implications for social work practice. *Child and Adolescent Social Work Journal, 13*, 401-410.

Curtis, P. A., Grady, D., Jr., & Kendall, J. C. (Eds.). (1999). *The foster care crisis: Translating research into policy and practice.* Lincoln, NE: University of Nebraska Press.

CWLA. (2003a). *CWLA Testimony Submitted to The House Subcommittee on Human Resources of the Committee on Ways and Means for the Hearing on the Implementation of the Adoption and Safe Families Act.* Washington, DC: Author.

Dalberth, B., Gibbs, D., & Berkman, N. (January, 2005). *Understanding adoption subsidies: An analysis of AFCARS data final report.* Research Triangle Park, NC: RTI International. Prepared for Office of the Assistant Secretary for Planning and Evaluation, U.S. Department of Health and Human Services.

D'Andrade, A., Frame, L., & Duerr-Berrick, J. (2006). Concurrent planning in public child welfare agencies: Oxymoron or work in progress? *Children and Youth Services Review, 28*(1), 78-95.

Danish, S. J., D'Angell, A. R., & Hauer, A. L. (1980). *Helping skills.* (Second ed.). New York: Human Sciences Press.

Danziger, S. & Gottschalk, P. (1995). *America unequal.* New York: Russell Sage Foundation.

Danzy, J., & Jackson, S. M. (1997). Family preservation and support services: A missed opportunity for kinship care. *Child Welfare, 76*, 31-44.

Daro, D. (1988). *Confronting child abuse: Research for effective program design.* New York: The Free Press.

Daro, D. (1993). Home visitation and preventing child abuse. *The APSAC Advisor, 6*(4), 1, 4.

Daro, D. (2005). *Home visitation: Assessing progress, managing expectations.* Chicago, IL: Chapin Hall Center for Children.

Daro, D., Budde, S., Baker, S., Nesmith, A., & Harden, A. (2005). *Creating community responsibility for child protection: Findings and implications from the evaluation of the community partnerships for protecting children initiative.* Chicago, IL: University of Chicago, Chapin Hall Center for Children.

Daro, D., Budde, S., Nesmith, A., & Harden, A. (2005). *Community Partnerships for Protecting Children: Phase II Outcome Evaluation.* Chicago, IL: Chapin Hall Center for Children.

Davis, I. P., Landsverk, J., Newton, R., & Ganger, W. (1996). Parental visiting and foster care reunification. *Children & Youth Services Review, 18*(4-5), 363-382.

Dawson, K., & Berry, M. (2002). Engaging Families in Child Welfare Services: An Evidence-Based Approach to Best Practice. *Child Welfare, 81*(2), 293-317.

Day, P., & Cahn, K. (1988). *Supervising family-centered practice: Using family systems tools to create a supporitve work environment.* Paper presented at the Second National Family-Based Services Conference. Boise, ID. October 17, 1988.

Delfabbro, P. H., Barber, J. G., & Cooper, L. (2002). The role of parental contact in substitute care. *Journal of Social Service Research, 28*(3), 19-39.

Denby, R. W., Curtis, C. M., & Alford, K. A. (1998). Family preservation services and special populations: The invisible target. *Families in Society: The Journal of Contemporary Human Services, 79,* 3-14.

DePanfilis, D. (2006). Child neglect: A guide for prevention, assessment, and intervention. Washington, DC: U.S. Department of Health and Human Services, Administration on Children and Families, Administration for Children, Youth, and Families, Children's Bureau, Office on Child Abuse and Neglect.

DePanfilis, D., & Dubowitz, H. (2005). Family connections: A program for preventing child neglect. *Child Maltreatment, 10*(2), 108-123.

DePanfilis, D., & Girvin, H. (2005). Investigating child maltreatment in out-of-home care: Barriers to good decision-making. *Children & Youth Services Review, 27,* 353-374.

DePanfilis, D., & Girvin, H. (2005). Investigating Child Maltreatment in out-of-home care: Barriers to effective decision-making. *Children and Youth Services Review, 27*(4), 353-374.

DePanfilis, D., & Hayward, R.A. (2006). *Ongoing child protective services (CPS) with methamphetamine using Families: Implementing promising practices.* Prepared for the National Resource Center for Child Protective Services, A program of the USDHHS, Children's Bureau. Retrieved February 26, 2007 from http://www.nrc-cps.org/PDF/Ongoing_CPS_with_Meth_Using_Families_Implementing_Promising_Practice10302006.pdf

DePanfilis, D., & Salus, M. K. (2003). *Child Protective Services: A guide for caseworkers* (Guide). Washington, DC: U.S. DHHS, Administration for Children and Families, Administration on Children, Youth and Families, Children's Bureau, Office on Child Abuse and Neglect.

DePanfilis, D., & Zlotnik, J. L. (2008). Retention of front-line staff in child welfare: A systematic review of research. *Children and Youth Services Review, 30*(9), 995-1008.

DePanfilis, D., Daining, C., Frick, K., Farber, J., & Levinthal, L. (2007). *Hitting the M.A.R.C. Establishing foster care minimum adequate rates for children, technical report.* New York: Children's Rights, Inc. (http://www.family.umaryland.edu/ryc_research_and_evaluation/child_welfare_research_files/fpr08-07.htm).

Derezotes, D., Poertner, J., & Testa, M. F. (2004). *Race Matters in Child Welfare: The Overrepresentation of African American Children in the System* Washington, DC: CWLA Press.

Derezotes, D., Poertner, J., & Testa, M. F. (2004). *Race Matters in Child Welfare: The Overrepresentation of African American Children in the System* Washington, DC: Child Welfare League of America.

Desetta, A. (Ed.). (1996). *The heart knows something different: Teenage voices from the foster care system.* New York: Persea Books.

Devore, W., & Schlesinger, E. G. (1996). *Ethnic-sensitive social work practice* (Fourth ed.). Boston: Allyn and Bacon.

Digre, P. (1996). Testimony before the US Senate Financing Committee (October 24). Washington, DC.

Dishion, T.J., McCord, J. & Poulin, F. (1999). When interventions harm. Peer groups and problem behavior. *American Psychologist*, 54, 755-765.

Dodge, K. A., Dishion, T. J., & Lansford, J. E. (2006). Findings and recommendations: A blueprint to minimize deviant peer influences in youth interventions and programs. In K. A. Dodge, T. J. Dishion & J. E. Lansford (Eds.), *Deviant Peer Influences in Programs for Youth* (pp. 366-395). New York: The Guilford Press.

Dore, M. M. (1999). Emotionally and behaviorally disturbed children in the child welfare system: Points of preventive intervention. *Children and Youth Services Review, 21*, 7-29.

Dore, M., Doris, J. M., & Wright, P. (1995). Identifying substance abuse in maltreating families: A child welfare challenge. *Child Abuse & Neglect, 19*, 531-548.

Downs , A. C., & Pecora, P. J. (2004). *Application of Erikson's Psychosical Development Theory to Foster Care Research (Working Paper No. 2)*. Seattle, WA: Casey Family Programs.

Downs, A.C., & James, S.E. (2006). Gay, lesbian, and bisexual foster parents: Strengths and challenges for the child welfare system. *Child Welfare, 85*(2), 281-298.

Doyle , J. J. (2007). Child Protection and Child Outcomes: Measuring the Effects of Foster Care. *American Economic Review*, 65.

Doyle, J. (2007). Child Protection and Child Outcomes: Measuring the Effects of Foster Care. *American Economic Review*.

Doyle, J. (2007). Child Protection and Child Outcomes: Measuring the Effects of Foster Care. *The American Economic Review, 97*, 1583-1610.

Drake, B., & Pandey, S. (1990). Understanding the relationship between neighborhood poverty and specific types of child maltreatment. *Child Abuse & Neglect, 20*, 1003-1018.

Dubowitz, H. (2000a). What is neglect? In Dubowitz, H., & DePanfilis, D. (Eds.). Handbook for child protection practice (pp. 10-14). Thousand Oaks, CA: Sage.

Dubowitz, H. (2000b). What is physical abuse? In Dubowitz, H., & DePanfilis, D. (Eds.). Handbook for child protection practice (pp. 15-17). Thousand Oaks, CA: Sage.

Duchnowski, A.J., Kutash, K. and Friedman, R.M. (2002). Community-based interventions in a system of care and outcomes framework. In Burns, B.J. and Hoagwood, K. *Community Treatment for Youth: Evidence-Based Interventions for Severe Emotional and Behavioral Disorders*. New York: Oxford University Press, 16-39.

Duggan, A. K., McFarlane, E. C., Windham, A. M., Rohde, C. A., Salkever, D. S., Fuddy, L., et al. (1999). Evaluation of Hawaii's healthy start program. *The Future of Children, 9*(1).

Dunbar, K. & Barth, R. P. (2007). Racial disproportionality, race disparity, and other race-related findings unpublished works derived from the Natural Survey of Child and Adolescent Well-Being. Seattle, WA: Casey Family Programs.

Dunbar, N., Van Dulmen, M.H., Ayers-Lopez, S., Berge, J.M., Christian, C., Grossman, G., et al. (2006). Processes linked to contact changes in adoptive kinship networks. *Family Process, 45*(4), 449-464.

Duncan, G., Yeung, W., Brooks-Gunn, J. & Smith, J. (1998). How much does childhood poverty affect the life chances of children? *American Sociological Review* (June) 63: 406-423.

Dunn, M.G., Tarter, R. E., Mezzich, A. C., Vanyukov, M., Kirsci, I., & Krillova, G. (2002). Origins and consequences of child neglect in substance abuse families. *Clinical Psychology Review, 22*, 1063-1090.

Dunst, C. J., Trivette, C. M., & Deal, A. G. (1988). *Enabling and empowering families: Principles and guidelines for practice.* Cambridge, MA: Brookline Books.

Dworsky, A., & Courtney, M. E. (2000). *Self-sufficiency of former foster youth in Wisconsin: Analysis of unemployment insurance wage data and public assistance data.* Washington, DC: Department of Health and Human Services, Office of the Assistant Secretary for Planning and Evaluation.

Dynarski, M. S., James-Burdumy, S. M., Moore, M., Rosenberg, L., Deke, J., & Mansfield, W. (2004). *When schools stay open late: The national evaluation of the 21st century community learning centers - New Findings.* Washington. DC: U.S. Department of Education, Institute of Education Sciences, National Center for Education Evaluation and Regional Assistance; and Mathematica Policy Research. Retrieved March 1, 2008 from http://ies.ed.gov/ncee/pdf/20043001.pdf.

Earle, R. (1995). Helping to Prevent Child Abuse-and Future Criminal Consequences: Hawaii's Healthy Start. *National Institute of Justice Program Focus Brief.*

Eckholm, D. (2006, May 2). Judge bars subsidy cuts in adopting foster children. *New York Times,* p.1.

Edelson, J. (2004). Should child exposure to adult domestic violence be defined as child maltreatment under the law? In P. G. Jaffe, L. Baker, & A. Cunningham (Eds.), *Ending domestic violence in the lives of children and parents: promising practices for safety, healing and prevention* (pp. 8-29). New York: Guilford.

Edelson, J. L. (1999). The overlap between child maltreatment and woman battering. *Violence Against Women, 5,* 134-154.

Edna McConnell Clark Foundation. (2004). *Theory of change behind the program for children.* New York: Author.

Edwards, R. l., & Yankey, J. A., (eds). (2006). *Effectively managing nonprofit organizations.* Washington. DC: National Association of Social Workers.

Egeland, B. (2007). Understanding Developmental Processes of Resiliance and Psychopathology: Implications for Policy and Practice. In A. S. Masten (Ed.), *Multilevel Dynamics in Developmental Psychopathology: Pathways to the Future* (pp. 83-118). New York: Routledge.

Eisenberger, R., Stinglhamber, F., Vandenberghe, C., Sucharski, I. L., & Rhoades, L. (2002). Perceived supervisor support: Contributions to perceived organizational support and employee retention. *Journal of Applied Psychology, 87*(3), 565-573.

Ellett, A. J., & Leighninger, L. (2007). What Happened? A Historical Analysis of the De-Professionalization of Child Welfare with Implications for Policy and Practice. *Journal of Public Child Welfare, 1*(1), 3-34.

Ellett, A. J., Ellis, J. I., Westbrook, T. M., & Dews, D. (2007). A qualitative study of 369 child welfare professionals' perspectives about factors contributing to employee retention and turnover. *Children and Youth Services Review, 29*(2), 264-281.

Ellwood, D. & Welty, E. (2000). Public service employment and mandatory work: A policy whose time has come and gone and come again? In R. Blank and D. Card (Eds.). *Finding jobs: Work and welfare reform.* New York: Russell Sage Foundation, pp. 299-372.

Ellwood, D. & Welty, E. (2000). Public service employment and mandatory work: A policy whose time has come and gone and come again? In R. Blank and D. Card (Eds). *Finding jobs: Work and welfare reform.* New York: Russell Sage Foundation, pp. 299-372.

Emery, J. (1993). The cases for agency adoption. *The Future of Children, 3*(1), 139-145.

English, D. J., Kouidou-Giles, S., & Plocke, M. (1994). Readiness for independence: A study of youth in foster care. *Children & Youth Services Review, 16*(3-4), 147-158.

Erera, P. (1997). Foster Parent's Attitudes toward Birth Parents and Caseworkers: Implications for Visitations. *Families in Society, 78*(5), 511-519.

Erikson, E. H. (1963). *Childhood and society* (2nd ed.). New York: W.W. Norton.

Erikson, E. H. (1985). *The life cycle completed*. New York: Norton.

Evans, M. E., & Armstrong, M. I. (1997). The development of a state's perspective on keeping children in the community: Strategies for change. In C. T. Nixon & D. A. Northrup (Eds.), *Evaluating mental health services: How do programs for children 'work' in the real world?* (Vol. 3, pp. 73-94).

Everett, J. E. (1995). Relative foster care: An emerging trend in foster care placement policy and practice. *Smith College Studies in Social Work, 65*(3), 239-254.

Everett, J. E., Chipungu, S. S., & Leashore, B. R. (Eds.). (1991). *Child welfare: An Africentric perspective*. New Brunswick, NJ: Rutgers University Press.

Eyer, D.E. (1992). *Mother-infant bonding: A scientific fiction*. New Haven: Yale University Press.

Fahlberg, V. (1991). *A Child's Journey Through Placement*. Indianapolis, IN: Perspectives Press.

Falicov, C. J. (Ed.). (1988). *Family transitions: Continuity and change over the life cycle*. New York: Guilford Press.

Family Resource Coalition. (1983). *Guidelines for family support practice*. Chicago, IL: Author.

Fanshel, D., & Shinn, E. B. (1978). Children in foster care: A longitudinal investigation. In. New York: Columbia University Press.

Fanshel, D., Finch, S. J., & Grundy, J. F. (1990). *Foster children in a life course perspective*. New York: Columbia University Press.

Fantuzzo, J., & Lindquist, C. (1989). The effect of observing conjugal violence on children: A review and analysis on research methodology. *Journal of Family Violence 4*(1), 77-94.

Farley, J. E. (1990). Family developmental task assessment: A prerequisite to family treatment. *Clinical Social Work Journal, 18*, 85-98.

Farmer, E. (1996). Family reunification with high risk children: Lessons from research. *Children & Youth Services Review, 18*(4-5), 403-424.

Farrington, D. P., Loeber, R., & Van Kammen, W. B. (1990). Long-term criminal outcomes of hyperactivity-impulsivity-attention deficit and conduct problems in childhood. In L. N. Robins & M. Rutter (Eds.), *Straight and devious pathways from childhood to adulthood* (pp. 62-81). New York: Cambridge University Press.

Farrington, D. P., Loeber, R., Elliott, D. S., Hawkins, J. D., Kandel, D. B., Klien, M. W., et al. (1993). Advancing knowledge about the onset of delinquency and crime. In B. B. Lahey & A. E. Kazdin (Eds.), *Advances in clinical child psychology* (Vol. 13, pp. 283-342). New York: Plenum Press.

Farrow, F. (1991). Services to families: The view from the states. *Families in Society: The Journal of Contemporary Human Services, 72*(5), 268-275.

Fay, M. (Ed.). (1989). *Speak out: An anthology of stories by youth in care*. Toronto: Pape Adolescent Resource Centre.

Feild, T. (1996). Managed care and child welfare: Will it work? *Public Welfare, 54*(3), 4-10.

Fein, E., & Maluccio, A. N. (1992). Permanency planning: Another remedy in jeopardy. *Social Service Review, 66*, 337-348.

Fein, E., & Staff, I. (1991). Implementing reunification services. *Families in Society: The Journal of Contemporary Human Services, 72*(6), 335-343.

Fein, E., Maluccio, A. N., Hamilton, V., & Ward, D. E. (1983). After foster care: Outcomes of permanency planning for children. *Child Welfare, 62*(6), 485-558.

Fein, E., Maluccio, A., & Kluger, M. (1990). *No more partings: An examination of long-term foster family care*. Washington, DC: Child Welfare League of America.

Feldman, L. H. (1991). Evaluating the impact of intensive family preservation services in New Jersey. In K. Wells & D. A. Biegel (Eds.), *Family preservation Services: Research and Evaluation* (pp. 47-71). Newbury Park, CA: Sage.

Ferguson, C. (2007). Wraparound: Definition, Context for Development, and Emergence in Child Welfare. *Journal of Public Child Welfare, 1*(2), 91-110.

Ferguson, R. (2001). Community revitalization, jobs and the well-being of the inner-city poor. In *Understanding poverty*. S. Danziger and R. Haveman eds. New York: Harvard University Press and Russell Sage Foundation, pp. 417-443.

Fernandez, E. (1996). *Significant harm: Unravelling child protection decisions and substitute care careers of children*. Aldershot, UK: Avebury-Ashgate Publishing.

Fernandez, E. (1999). Pathways in substitute care: Representation of placement careers of children using event history analysis. *Children & Youth Services Review, 21*(3), 177-216.

Fernandez, E. (2007). Supporting children and responding to their families: Capturing the evidence on family support. *Children & Youth Services Review, 29*(10), 1368-1394.

Fessler, A. (2006). *The girls who went away: The hidden history of women who surrendered children for adoption in the decades before Roe vs. Wade*. New York: Penguin Press.

Festinger, T. (1983). *No one ever asked us... A postscript to foster care*. New York: Columbia University Press.

Festinger, T. (1996). Going home and returning to foster care. *Children & Youth Services Review, 18*(4-5), 383-402.

Festinger, T. (2006). Adoption and after: Adoptive parents service needs. In M.M. Dore (Ed.). The postadoption experience: Adoptive families service needs and service outcomes. Washington, DC: Child Welfare League of America.

Fetterman, D., & Wandersman, A. (2007). Empowerment Evaluation: Yesterday, today, and tomorrow. *American Journal of Evaluation, 28*, 179-198.

Finegold, K., Wherry, L., & Schardin, S. (2004). *Block Grants: Details of the Bush Proposals*. Washington, DC: The Urban Institute, Program to Assess Changing Social Policies.

Finkelhor, D., Ormrod, R., Turner, H., & Hamby, S. L. (2005). The victimization of children and youth: A comprehensive, national survey. Child Maltreatment, 10, 5-25.

Finklelhor, D., & Jones, L. (2006). Why have child maltreatment and child victimization declined? Journal of Social Issues, 62, 685-716.

Fiscella, K., Kitzman H.J., Cole R.E., et al. (1998). Does child abuse predict adolescent pregnancy? *Pediatrics, 101*(4), 620-624.

Fischler, R.S. (1980). Protecting American Indian children. *Social Work, 25,* 341-349.

Fisher, A. (2002). *Finding Fish*. New York: Harper Collins Publishers.

Fisher, E. A. (2005). Facing the challenges of outcomes measurement: The role of transformational leadership. *Administration for Social Work, 29*(4), 35-49.

Fisher, P. A., Burraston, B., & Pears, K. (2005). The Early Intervention Foster Care Program: Permanent placement outcomes from a randomized trial. *Child Maltreatment, 10*(1), 61-71. Adoption Assistance and Child Welfare Act of 1980. P.L. 96-272, 94. Stat. 500.

Fisher, P. A., Gunnar, M. R., Chamberlain, P., & Reid, J. B. (2000). Preventive Intervention for Maltreated Preschool Children: Impact on Children's Behavior, Neuroendocrine Activity, and Foster Parent Functioning. *Journal of the American Academy of Child & Adolescent Psychiatry, 39*(11), 1356-1364.

Fitz-enz, J. (1997). It's costly to lose good employees. *Workforce, 50.*

Fitzgerald, J., Murcer, B., & Murcer, B. (1982). *Building new families through adoption and fostering*. Oxford, England: Basil Blackwell.

Fixsen, D. L., Naoom, S. F., Blase, K. A., Friedman, R. M. & Wallace, F. (2005). *Implementation Research: A Synthesis of the Literature*. Tampa, FL: University of South Florida, Louis de la Parte Florida Mental Health Institute, The National Implementation Research Network (FMHI Publication #231). Retrieved January 14, 2008 from http://nirn.fmhi.usf.edu.

Flango, V.E., & Caskey, M.M. (2005). Adoptions, 2000-2001. *Adoption Quarterly 8*(4), 23-43.

Flango, V.E., & Flango, C.R. (1993). Adoption statistics by state. *Child Welfare 72*, 311-319.

Flower, C., McDonald, J., & Sumski, M. (2005). *Review of turnover in Milwaukee County private agency child welfare ongoing case management staff*. Milwaukee, WI.: Milwaukee County Department of Social Services.

Folaron, G. (1993). Preparing children for reunification. In B.A. Pine, R. Warsh & A. N. Maluccio (Eds.), *Together again: Family reunification in foster care* (pp. 141-154). Washington, DC: Child Welfare League of America.

Folaron, G., & Hostetter, C. (2007). Is Social Work the Best Educational Degree for Child Welfare Practitioners? *Journal of Public Child Welfare, 1*(1), 65-84.

Folman, R. D. (1998). "I was tooken": How children experience removal from their parents preliminary to placement into foster care. *Adoption Quarterly, 2*(2), 7-35.

Fong, R. (1994). Family preservation: Making it work for Asians. *Child Welfare, 73*, 331-341.

Fong, R. (2001). Culturally Competent Social Work Practice: Past and Present. In R. Fong & S. Furuto (Eds.), *Culturally Competent Practice: Skill, Interventions, & Evaluations* (pp. 1-9). Boston: Allyn & Bacon.

Fontes, L. A. (2005). *Child Abuse and Culture: Working with Diverse Families*. New York: Guilford Press.

Fraiberg, S., Adelson, E., & Shapiro, V. (1975). Ghosts in the nursery: A psychoanalytic approach to the problems of impaired infant-mother relationships. *Journal of the American Academy of Child Psychiatry, 14*, 387-421.

Fraser, M. W. (Ed.). (2004). *Risk and resilience in childhood: An ecological perspective*. (2nd ed.). Washington, DC: NASW press.

Fraser, M. W., Kirby, L. D., & Smokowski, P. (2004). Risk and resilience in childhood. In M. W. Fraser (Ed.), *Risk and resilience in childhood: An ecological perspective* (pp. 13-66). Washington, DC: NASW Press.

Fraser, M. W., Pecora, P. J., & Haapala, D. A. (1991). *Families in Crisis: The Impact of Intensive Family Preservation Services*. Hawthorne, NY: Aldine de Gruyter.

Fraser, M. W., Walton, E., Lewis, R. E., & Pecora, P. J. (1996). An experiment in family reunification: Correlates of outcomes at one-year follow-up. *Children & Youth Services Review, 18*(4-5), 335-361.

Fraser, M., Nelson, K., & Rivard, J. (1997). Effectiveness of family preservation services. *Social Work Research, 21*(2), 138-153.

Freed, A. O. (1985). Linking developmental, family and life cycle theories. *Smith College Studies in Social Work, 65*, 169-182.

Freedman, M. W., & Boyer, N. C. (2000). The power to choose: Supports for families caring for individuals with developmental disabilities. *Health & Social Work, 25*(1), 59-68.

Freud, S. (1988). Cybernetic epistemology. In R. A. Dorfman (Ed.), *Paradigms of clinical social work* (pp. 356-387). New York: Brunner/Mazel.

Freundlich, M., & Avery, R. J. (2005). Planning for permanency for youth in congregate care. *Children & Youth Services Review, 27*(2), 115-134.

Freundlich, M., & Wright, L. (2003). *Post-Permanency Services*. Washington, DC: Casey Family Programs Center for Resource Family Support.

Freundlich, M., & Wright, L. (2003). *Post-permanency services.* Washington, DC: Casey Family Programs National Resource Center for Resource Family Support.

Friedman, M. (1997). *A guide to developing and using performance measures in results-based budgeting.* Washington, DC: The Finance Project.

Friedman, R. M.; Pinto, A.; Behar, L.; Bush, N.; Chirolla, A.; Epstein, M.; Green, A.; Hawkins, P.; Huff, B.; Huffine, C.; Mohr, W.; Seltzer, T.; Vaughn, C.; Whitehead, K.; Young, C. K. (2006). Unlicensed Residential Programs: The Next Challenge in Protecting Youth. *American Journal of Orthopsychiatry.* 76(3) 295-303.

Friend, C., Lambert, L., & Shlonsky, A. (Accepted 2008). From evolving discourses to new practice approaches in domestic violence and child protective services. *Children & Youth Services Review.*

Frost, S., & Jurich, A. P. (1983). *Follow-up study of children residing in The Villages* (Unpublished report). Topeka, KS: The Villages.

Gamble, D. N., & Weil, M. O. (1995). Citizen participation. In R. L. Edwards & J. G. Hopps (Eds.), *Encyclopedia of Social Work* (19th ed., Vol. 1, pp. 483-494). Washington, DC: NASW Press.

Gambrill, E. (1990). *Critical thinking in clinical practice.* San Francisco: Jossey-Bass.

Gambrill, E. (1997). *Social work practice: A critical thinker's guide.* New York: Oxford University Press.

Garbarino, J. (1992). *Children and families in the social environment* (Second ed.). New York: Aldine de Gruyter.

Garbarino, J. (1992). *Children and families in the social environment* (Second ed.). New York: Aldine de Gruyter.

Garbarino, J., & Ganzel, B. (2000). The Human Ecology of Early Risk. In S. J. Meisels & J. P. Shonkoff (Eds.), *Handbook of early childhood intervention* (2nd ed., pp. 76-93). Cambridge, MA: Cambridge University Press.

Garbarino, J., & Sherman, D. (1980). High-risk neighborhoods and high-risk families. *Child Development, 51,* 188-189.

Garbarino, J., Schellenbach, C. J., Sebes, J., & Associates. (1986). *Troubled youth, troubled families: Understanding families at risk for adolescent maltreatment.* New York: Aldine de Gruyter.

Garbarino, J., Stott, F. M., & Faculty of the Erikson Institute. (1989). *What children can tell us.* San Francisco: Jossey-Bass Publishers.

Garmezy, N. (1983). Stressors of Childhood. In N. Garmezy & M. Rutter (Eds.), *Stress, coping and development in children* (pp. 43-84). New York: McGraw Hill.

Garmezy, N. (1985). Stress resistant children: The search for protective factors. In J. E. Stevenson (Ed.), *Recent research in developmental psychopathology.* Oxford: Pergamon Press.

Geen, R. (2003). *Kinship foster care: Making the most of a valuble resource.* Washington, DC: Urban Institute Press.

Gelles, R., & Straus, M. (1988). *Intimate violence.* New York: Simon & Schuster.

Germain, C. G. (1991). *Human behavior in the social environment: An ecological view.* New York: Columbia University Press.

Germain, C. G., & Gitterman, A. (1996). *The life model of social work practice: Advances in theory & practice* (Second ed.). New York: Columbia University Press.

Gershoff, E., Aber, J.L., Raver, C.C. &, Lennon, M.C. (2007). Income is not enough: Incorporating material hardship Into models of income associations with parenting and child development, *Child Development* 78(1) pp. 70-95.

Gibbs, D., Berkman, N., Weitzenkamp, D., & Dalberth, B. (2007). Federal Support for Adoption Subsidies: State-Level Variations and the Impact for Adoptive Families. *Journal of Public Child Welfare, 1*(2), 71-90.

Gibson, T.J. (2003, October). One church one child: Targeting churches for adoption and foster care ministries in the Washington, DC area. *The Clergy Journal,* 10-14.

Gilligan, C. (1982). *In a different voice: Psychological theory and women's development.* Cambridge, MA: Harvard University Press.

Gilligan, R. (1997). Beyond permanence? The importance of resilience in child placement practice and planning. *Adoption & Fostering, 21,* 12-20.

Gitterman, A. (1996). Ecological perspective: Response to Professor Jerry Wakefield. *Social Service Review, 70,* 472-476.

Gitterman, A., & Shulman, L. (Eds.). (1994). *Mutual aid groups, vulnerable populations, and the life cycle* (Second ed.). New York: Columbia University Press.

Gleeson, J. P., & Craig, L. C. (1994). Kinship care in child welfare: An analysis of States' policies. *Children and Youth Services Review, 16,* 7-32.

Gleeson, J. P., O'Donnell, J., & Bonecutter, F. J. (1997). Understanding the complexity of practice in kinship foster care. *Child Welfare, 76*(6), 801-826.

Glisson, C. (2007). Assessing and Changing Organizational Culture and Climate for Effective Services. *Research on Social Work Practice, 17*(6), 736-747.

Glisson, C., & Durick, M. (1988). Predictors of job satisfaction and organizational commitment in human service organizations. *Administrative Science Quarterly, 33*(1), 61-81.

Glisson, C., & Hemmelgarn, A. (1998). The effects of organizational climate and interorganizational coordination on the quality and outcomes of children's service systems. *Child Abuse & Neglect, 22*(5), 401-421.

Glisson, C., & James, L. R. (2002). The cross-level effects of culture and climate in human service teams. *Journal of Organizational Behavior, 23,* 767-794.

Glisson, C., Dukes, D., & Green, P. (2006). The effects of the ARC organizational intervention on caseworker turnover, climate, and culture in children's service systems. *Child Abuse & Neglect, 30*(8), 855-880.

Goerge, R. M. (1990). The reunification process in substitute care. *Social Service Review, 64,* 422-457.

Goerge, R. M., Bilaver, L. A., Lee, B. J., Needell, B., Brookhart, A., & Jackman, W. (2002). *Employment outcomes for youth aging out of foster care.* Chicago, IL: University of Chicago, Chapin Hall Center for Children.

Goerge, R. M., Wulczyn, F. H., & Harden, A. W. (1994). *A report from the multistate data archive: Foster care dynamics 1983-1992.* Chicago, IL: Chapin Hall Center for Children, University of Chicago.

Goldberg-Glen, R., Sands, R. G., Cole, R. D., & Cristofalo, C. (1998). Multigenerational patterns and internal structures in families in which grandparents raise children. *Families in Society: The Journal of Contemporary Human Services, 79,* 477-489.

Goldman, J., & Salus, M. K. (2003). *A coordinated response to child abuse and neglect: The foundation for practice.* Washington, DC: U.S. Department of Health and Human Services, Administration on Children and Families, Administration for Children, Youth, and Families, Children's Bureau, Office on Child Abuse and Neglect.

Goldstein, J., Freud, A., & Solnit, A. (1973). *Beyond the Best Interests of the Child.* New York: The Free Press.

Goldstein, J., Solnit, A., Goldstein, S., & Freud, A. (1996). *The best interest of the child: The least detrimental alternative.* New York: Free Press.

Gomby, D. S., Culross, P. L., & Behrman, R. E. (1999). Home visiting recent program evaluations: Analysis and recommendations. *The Future of Children, 9*(1), 4-43.

Gomby, D. S., Culross, P. L., & Behrman, R. E. (1999). Home visiting recent program evaluations: Analysis and recommendations. *The Future of Children, 9*(1), 4-43.

Gomby, D., Larson, C. S., Lewit, E. M., & Behrman, R. E. (1993). Home visiting: Analysis and recommendations. *The Future of Children, 3,* 6-22.

Goodman, N., & et al. (2001). *It's my life: A framework for youth transitioning from foster care to successful adulthood*. Seattle, WA: Casey Family Programs.

Gordon, D. A., Arbuthnot, J., Gustafson, K. E., & McGreen, P. (1988). Home-based behavioral-systems family therapy with disadvantaged juvenile delinquents. *American Journal of Family Therapy, 16*(3), 243-255.

Gottlieb, B. (1988). *Marshaling social support*. Beverly Hills, CA: Sage Publications.

Graham, M., & Bryant, D. (1993). Characteristics of quality, effective service delivery systems for children with special needs. In D. Bryant & M. Graham (Eds.), *Implementing early intervention: From research to effective practice*. New York: Guilford Press.

Grazio, T. (1981). New perspectives on child abuse/neglect community education. *Child Welfare, 60*(5), 679-707.

Green, B. L., Rockhill, A., & Furrer, C. (2007). Does substance abuse treatment make a difference for child welfare case outcomes? A statewide longitudinal analysis. *Children and Youth Services Review, 29*(4), 460-473.

Greenberg, P. E., Sisitsky, T., Kessler, R. C., Finkelstein, S. N., Berndt, E. R., Davidson, J. R. T., et al. (1999). The economic burden of anxiety disorders in the 1990s. *Journal of Clinical Psychiatry, 60*, 427-435.

Greene, R. B., & Watkins, M. (Eds.). (1998). *Serving constituencies: Applying the ecological perspective*. New York: Aldine de Gruyter.

Grietens H, Hellinckx, W. (2004). Evaluating effects of residential treatment for juvenile offenders by statistical metaanalysis: a review. *Aggression and Violent Behavior* 9(4): 401–415.

Grimm, B. (Jan-March, 2007). Child deaths From abuse and neglect: Accurate data, public disclosure needed. *Youth Law News, 28*, 1–11. Retrieved April 4, 2008 from http://www.youthlaw.org/publications/yln/2007/january_march_2007/child_deaths_from_abuse_and_neglect/

Grogger, J. & Karoly, L. (2005). *Welfare reform: Effects of a decade of change*. Cambridge, MA: Harvard University Press.

Gross, E. (1989). *Contemporary federal policy towards American Indians*. New York: Greenwood Press.

Gunderson, S., Jones, R., & Scanland, K. (2005). *The Jobs Revolution: Changing how America works*. San Diego, CA: Copywriters Inc: A Division of the Greystone Group.

Gupta, A., & Blewett, J. (2007). Change for Children? The challenges and opportunities for the children's social work workforce. *Child and Family Social Work, 12*(2), 172-181.

Gutiérrez, L., & Nagda, B. A. (1996). The multicultural imperative in human services organizations: Issues for the Twenty-First Century. In P. Raffoul & C. A. McNeece (Eds.), *Future Issues for Social Work Practice* (pp. 203-213). Needham Heights, MA: Allyn & Bacon.

Haapala, D. A., & Kinney, J. (1979). Homebuilder's approach to the training of in-home therapists. In S. Maybanks & M. Bryce (Eds.), *Home-based services for children and families* (pp. 248-259). Springfield, IL: Charles C. Thomas.

Hackman, J. R., & Lawler, E. E., III. . (1971). Employee reactions to job characteristics. *Journal of Applied Psychology, 55*, 259-286.

Hacsi, T. (1995). From indenture to family foster care: A brief history of child placing. *Child Welfare, 74*, 162-180.

Haggerty, R. J., Sherrod, L. R., Garmezy, N., & Rutter, M. (1994). *Stress, risk, and resilience in children and adolescents: Processes, mechanisms, and interventions*. Cambridge, UK: Cambridge University Press.

Haight, W. L., Black, J. E., Mangelsdorf, S., Giorgio, G., Tata, L., Schoppe, S. J., et al. (2002). Making visits better: the perspectives of parents, foster parents, and child welfare workers. *Child Welfare, 81*(2), 173-202.

Haight, W. L., Kagle, J. D., & Black, J. E. (2003). Understanding and Supporting Parent-Child Relationships during Foster Care Visits: Attachment Theory and Research. *Social Work, 48*(2), 195-207.

Haight, W. L., Mangelsdorf, S., Black, J. E., Szewczyk, M., Schoppe, S. J., Giorgio, G., et al. (2005). Enhancing Parent-Child Interaction During Foster Care Visits: Experimental Assessment of an Intervention. *Child Welfare, LXXXIV*(4), 459-481.

Hair, E. C., Jager, J., & Garrett, S. B. (2002). *Helping teens develop healthy social skills and relationships: What the research shows about navigating adolescence.* Washington, DC: Child Trends.

Halpern, R. (1990). Fragile families, fragile solutions: An essay review. *Social Service Review, 64,* 637-648.

Hand, C. A. (2006). An Ojibwe perspective on the welfare of children: Lessons of the past and visions for the future. *Children and Youth Services Review, 28*(1), 20-46.

Harder, J. (2005). Prevention of Child Abuse and Neglect: An Evaluation of Home Visitation Parent Aide Program Using Recidivism Data. *Research on Social Work Practice, 15*(4), 246-256.

Hardin, M. (1992). *Establishing a core of services for families subject to state intervention.* Washington, DC: American Bar Association.

Hardin, M. (1996). *Family group conferences in child abuse and neglect cases: Learning from the experience of New Zealand.* Washington, DC: ABA Center on Children and the Law.

Hardina, D. (2005). Ten Characteristics of Empowerment-Oriented Organizations. *Administration in Social Work, 29*(3), 23-42.

Harper, M., Hernandez, M., Nesman, T., Mowery, D., Worthington, J., & Isaacs, M. (2006). Organizational Cultural Competence: A review of Assessment Protocols. Retrieved from http://rtckids.fmhi.usf.edu/publications.

Harrington, D., Zuravin, S. J., DePanfilis, D., Ting, L., & Dubowitz, H. (2002). The Neglect Scale: Confirmatory factor analysis in a low-income sample. *Child Maltreatment, 7,* 359-368.

Harris, J. R. (1995). Where is the Child's environment? A group socialization theory of development. *Psychological Review, 102*(3), 458-489.

Hartman, A., & Laird, J. (1983). *Family-centered social work practice.* New York: Free Press.

Haskins, R., Wulczyn, F., & Webb, M. B. (2007). *Child Protection REsearch from the National Survey of Child and Adolescent Well-Being.* Washington, DC: Brookings.

Hawaii State Department of Health. (1992). *MCHB Healthy Start Program.* Honolulu, HI: Author.

Hawkins, J. D. (2006). Science, social work, prevention: finding the intersections. *Social Work Research, 30*(3), 137-152.

Hayes, J. R., & Joseph, J. A. (1985). *Home based family centered project evaluation.* Columbus, OH: Metropolitan Human Services Commission.

Hebbeler, K. M., & Gerlach-Downie, S. G. (2002). Inside the Black Box of Home Visiting: A Qualitative Analysis of Why Intended Outcomes were not Achieved. *Early Childhood Research Quarterly, 17*(1), 28-51.

Heckman, J. J., & Masterov, D. V. (2007). *The Productivity Argument for Investing in Young Children.* presented at the T. W. Schultz Awards, Chicago, IL.

Heclo, H. (1994). Poverty politics. In *Confronting poverty: Prescriptions for change.* S. Danziger, G. Sandefur and D. Weinberg, eds. Cambridge, MA: Harvard University Press, pp. 396-437.

Hegar, R. L. (1989). Empowerment-based practice with children. *Social Service Review, 63*, 372-383.

Hegar, R. L., & Scannapieco, M. (Eds.). (1998). *Kinship foster care: Policy, practice, and research*. New York: Oxford University Press.

Heisterman, C.A. (1935). A summary of legislation on adoption. *Social Service Review, 9*, 269-293.

Hellinckx, W., Broekaert, E., Vanden Berge, A., & Colton, M. (Eds.). (1991). *Innovations in residential care*. Acco Leuven, Netherlands: Amersfoort.

Henggeler, S. W., & Sheidow, A. J. (2003). Conduct disorder and delinquency. *Journal of Marital and Family Therapy, 29*(4), 505-522.

Henggeler, S. W., Pickrel, S. G., & Brondino, M. J. (1999). Multisystemic Treatment of Substance-Abusing and -Dependent Delinquents: Outcomes, Treatment, Fidelity, and Transportability. *Mental Health Services Research, 1*(3), 171-184.

Henggeler, S. W., Rowland, M. D., Halliday Boynkins, C., Sheidow, A. J., Ward, D. M., Randell, J., et al. (2003). One-year follow-up of multisystemic therapy as an alternative to the hospitalization of youths in psychiatric crisis. *Journal of the American Academy of Child and Adolescent Psychiatry, 42*(5), 9.

Henggeler, S. W., Schoenwald, S. K., Borduin, C. M., Rowland, M., & Cunningham, P. B. (1998). *Multi-systemic treatment of antisocial behavior in children and adolescents*. New York: Guilford.

Henry, D. L. (2005). The 3-5-7 Model: Preparing children for permanency. *Children and Youth Services Review, 27*, 197-212.

Hernandez, M., Nesman, T., Isaacs, M., Callejas, L. M., & Mowery, D., (Eds.). (2006). *Examining the research base supporting culturally competent children's mental health services*. Retrieved from http://rtckids.fmhi.usf.edu/publications

Herrera, C., Grossman, J.B., Kauh, T.J., Feldman, A.F., McMaken, J. & Jucovy. L.Z. (2007). *Making a Difference in Schools: The Big Brothers Big Sisters School-Based Mentoring Impact Study*. Washington, DC: Public/Private Ventures. Retrieved May 30, 2008 from http://www.ppv.org/ppv/publications/assets/220_publication.pdf

Herrick, M. A., & Piccus, W. (2005). Sibling connections: The inmportance of nurturing sibling bonds in the foster care systerm. . *Children and Youth Services Review, 27*, 845-861.

Herrick, M. A., Williams, J., Pecora, P. J., Downs, A. C., & White, J. (in preparation). *Placement instability in child welfare and its implications for the functioning of foster care alumni*. Seattle, WA: Casey Family Programs.

Hershey, A. (1998). *Evaluation of Tribal Welfare-to-Work Programs*. Washington, DC: Mathematica Policy Research, Inc., The Urban Institute, and Support Services International, Inc.

Herskowitz, J., Seck, M., & Fogg C. (1989). *Substance abuse and family violence: I. Identification of drug and alcohol usage during child abuse investigations in Boston*. Boston: Massachusetts Department of Social Services. Office for Professional Services.

Hess, P. (1988). Case and context: Determinants of planned visit frequency in foster family care. *Child Welfare, 67*(4), 311-326.

Hess, P. M., & Proch, K. O. (1988). *Family visiting in out-of-home care: A guide to practice*. Washington, DC: Child Welfare League of America.

Hess, P. M., & Proch, K. O. (1993). Visiting: The heart of family reunification. In B. A. Pine, R. Warsh & A. N. Maluccio (Eds.), *Together again: Family reunification in foster care* (pp. 119-139). Washington, DC: Child Welfare League of America.

Hess, P., McGowan, B., & Botsko, M. (1997). *Final report of a study of the Center for Family Life in Sunset Park: Greater than the sum of its parts*. New York: Hess, P., McGowan, B., & Botsko, M.

Hess, P., McGowan, B., & Botsko, M. (2003). *Nurtoring the one, supporting the many: The Center for Family Life in Sunset Park*. New York: Columbia University Press.

Hill, M., & Aldgate, J. (Eds.). (1996). *Child welfare services: Developments in law, policy, practice, and research*. London, England: Jessica Kingsley.

Hill, R. B. (1972). *The strengths of black families*. New York: Emerson Hall.

Hill, R. B. (1997). *The strengths of African American families: Twenty-five years later*. Washington, DC: R & B Publishers.

Hill, R. B. (2001). *The role of race in foster care placement*. presented at the Race Matters Forum, University of Illinois at Urbana-Champaign.

Hill, R. B. (2005). The role of race in parental reunification. In D. Derezotes, M. F. Testa & J. Poertner (Eds.), *Race Matters in Child Welfare: The Overrepresentation of African American Children in the System*. Washington, DC: CWLA Press.

Hill, R. B. (2006). *Synthesis of Research on Disproportionality in Child Welfare: An Update*. Washington, DC: Casey Family Programs, Center for the Study of Social Policy Alliance for Racial Equality.

Hill, R. B. (2007). *Analysis of racial/ethnic disproportionality and disparity at the national, state and county levels*. Washington, DC: The Casey-CSSP Alliance for Racial Equity, Center for the Study of Social Policy.

Hines, A. M., Lemon, K., Wyatt, P., & Merdinger, J. (2004). Factors related to the disproportionate involvement of children of color in the child welfare system: A review and emerging themes. *Children and Youth Services Review, 26*, 507-527.

Hoagwood, K., Burns, B. J., Kiser, L., Ringeisen, H., & Schoenwald, S. K. (2001). Evidence-based practice in child and adolescent mental health services. *Psychiatric Services, 52*, 1179-1189.

Hodges, V. (1994). Assessing for strengths and protective factors in child abuse and neglect: Risk assessment with families of color. In P.J. Pecora & D. J. English (Eds.), *Multi-cultural guidelines for assessing family strengths and risk factors in child protective services*. Seattle, WA: School of Social Work, University of Washington and Washington State Department of Social Services.

Hodges, V. G., Guterman, N. B., Blythe, B. J., & Bronson, D. E. (1989). Intensive aftercare services for children. *Social Casework, 70*(7), 397-404.

Hogan, P. T., & Siu, S.-F. (1988). Minority children and the child welfare system: An historical perspective. *Social Work, 33*, 493-498.

Hoge, J., & Idalski, A. (2001). How Boysville of Michigan specifies and evaluates its Supervised Independent Living Program. In K. A. Nollan & A. C. Downs (Eds.), *Preparing youth for long-term success: Proceedings from the Casey Family Program National Independent Living Forum* (pp. 83-93). Washington, DC: Child Welfare League of America, Inc.

Holder, W., & Corey, M. (1987). *Child protective services risk management: A decision making handbook*. Charlotte, NC: ACTION for Child Protection.

Holder, W., & Hayes, K. (Eds.). (1984). *Malpractice and liability in child protective services*. Denver, CO: The American Humane Association.

Holland, S., Faulkner, A., & Perez-del-Aguila, R. (2005). Promoting stability and continuity of care for looked after children: a survey and critical review. *Child & Family Social Work, 10*(1), 29-41.

Holliday, M., & Cronin, R. (1990). Families first: a significant step toward family preservation. *Families in Society, 71*, 303-306.

Hollinger, J. (1993). Adoption law. *The Future of Children, 3*(1), 43-62. Immigration and Naturalization Service, Statistical Analysis Branch. (1991). *Statistical year books*.

Hollinger, J.H. (1989). Beyond the interests of the tribe: The Indian Child Welfare Act and the adoption of Indian Children. *University of Detroit Law Review, 66*, 452-491.

Holohan, C. J., Wilcox, B. L., Spearly, J. L., & Campbell, M. D. (1979). The ecological perspective in community mental health. *Community Mental Health Review, 4,* 1-9.

Holzer, H. (1994). Black employment problems: New evidence, old questions. *Journal of Policy Analysis and Management* (Fall) 13: 699-722.

Holzer, H., Schanzenbach, D., Duncan, G. & Ludwig, J. (2007). The economic costs of poverty in the United States: Subsequent effects of children growing up poor. National Poverty Center working paper 07-04, January.

Hormuth, P. (2001). *All grown up, nowhere to go: Texas teens in foster care transition.* Austin, TX: Center for Public Priorities.

Hornby, H., Zeller, D., & Karraker, D. (1996). Kinship care in America: What outcomes should policy seek? *Child Welfare, 75,* 397-418.

Horowitz, A.V., Widom, C.S., McLaughlin, J., & White, H.R. (2001). The impact of childhood abuse and neglect on adult mental health: A prospective study. *Journal of Health and Social Behavior, 42,* 184-201.

Hotz, V.J. & Scholz, K. (2003). The earned income tax credit. In R. Moffitt (ed.) *Means-tested transfer programs in the United States*, Chicago, IL: National Bureau of Economic Research, pp. 141-198.

Houlgate, L. D. (1988). *Family and state: The philosophy of family law.* Totowa, NJ: Rowman & Littlefield.

Howell, J. C., & Hawkins, J. D. (1998). *Prevention of Youth Violence* (No. 215).

Hoynes, H., Page, M. & Stevens, A. (2006). Poverty in America: Trends and explanations. *Journal of Economic Perspectives* (Winter) 20: 47-68.

Hudson, J., & Galaways, B., (Eds.). (1995). *Child Welfare in Canada - Research and policy implications.* Toronto: Thompson Educational Publishing.

Huebner, R. (2007). *Descriptors, predictors and outcomes of placement stability.* Paper presented at the Casey-CWLA Outcomes Benchmarking Roundtable, Washington, DC, March 1, 2007.

Huey, S. J., & Polo, A. J. (2008). Evidence-based psychosocial treatments for ethnic minority youth. *Journal of Clinical Child and Adolescent Psychology, 37*(1), 262-301.

Hughes, R. C., & Rykus, J. S. (1989). *Target: Competent staff: Competency-based in-service training for child welfare.* Washington, DC: Child Welfare League of America.

Humphrey, K. R., Trunbull, A. P., & Trunbull, H. R. (2006). Impact of the Adoption and Safe Families Act on youth and their families: Perspectives of foster care providers, youth with emotional disorders, service providers, and judges. *Children & Youth Services Review, 28*(1), 113-132.

Hussey, D. L., & Guo, S. (2005). Characteristics and Trajectories of Treatment Foster Care Youth. *Child Welfare, LXXXIV*(4), 485-506.

Hyde, C. A. (2004). Multicultural development in human services agencies: Challenges and solutions. *Social Work, 49*(1), 7-16.

Iida, E. E., Springer, F., Pecora, P. J., Bandstra, E. S., Edwards, M. C., Sale, E., et al. (2005). The SESS multi-site collaborative research initiative: Establishing common ground. *Child and Family Social Work, 10,* 217-228.

Illinois Department of Children and Family Services: Office of the Inspector General. (1997). *Recommendations for improving the State's child welfare response to families affected by parental substance abuse.* Springfield, IL: Illinois Department of Children and Family Services.

Indian Child Welfare Act of 1978. P.L. 95-608, 92 Stat. 3069.

Ingoldsby, B. B., & Smith, S. (Eds.). (1995). *Families in multicultural perspective.* New York: The Guilford Press.

Ingram, C. (1996). Kinship care: From last resort to first choice. *Child Welfare, 75,* 550-566.

Institute for Family Development. (2008). *Motivational interviewing in the Homebuilders® Model.* Federal Way, WA: Author. Retreived March 1, 2008 from http://www.institutefamily.org/pdf/MotivationalInterviewingHOMEBUILDERS.pdf.

Institute for the Advancement of Social Work Research (2005). Factors influencing retention of child welfare staff: A systematic review of research. Retrieved from www.iaswresarch.org

Institute for the Advancement of Social Work Research. (2002). *Annotate Bibliography with Commentary on Family-Center Practice.* Washington, DC: Author.

Interaction Associates (1997). Facilitative leadership workbook, Available from http://www.interactionassociates.com/pubwork_calendar.cfm

Isaacs, J. (2007). *Cost-effective investments in children.* The Brookings Institution, Budgeting for National Priorities Paper.

Jackson, S., Mathews, J., & Zuskin, R. (1998). *Supporting the kinship triad: A training curriculum.* Washington, DC: CWLA Press.

Jaffe, P., Wolfe, D., & Wilson, S. (1990). *Children of battered women.* Newbury Park, CA: Sage Publications.

Jaffe, P., Wolfe, D., Wilson, S., & Zak, L. (1986). Similarities in behavioral and social maladjustment among child victims and witnesses to family violence. *American Journal of Orthopsychiatry, 56*(1), 142-146.

Jaffe, S. R., Caspi, A., Moffitt, T.E., Polo-Tornas, M., & Taylor, A. (2007). Individual, family, and neighborhood factors distinguish resilient from non-resilient maltreated children: A cumulative stressors model. *Child Abuse & Neglect, 31,* 231-253.

James, B. (1989). *Treating traumatized children: New insights and creative interventions.* Lexington, MA: Lexington.

James, J., & Meirding, J. (1977). Early sexual experience and prostitution. *American Journal of Psychiatry, 134,* 1381-1385.

James, L. R. (1982). Aggression bias in estimates of perceptual agreement. *Journal of Applied Psychology, 67,* 219-229.

James, S. (2004). Why do foster care placements disrupt? An investigation of reasons for placement change in foster care. *Social Service Review, 78*(4), 601-627.

James, S. A., Hartnett, S. A., & Kalsbeek, W. D. (1983). John Henryism and blood pressure differences among black men. *Journal of Behavioral Medicine, 6*(3), 259-278.

James, S., & Meezan, W. (2002). Refining the evaluation of treatment foster care. *Families in Society, 83*(3), 233.

James, S., Landsverk, J., & Slymen, D. J. (2004). Placement movement in out-of-home care: Patterns and predictors. *Children and Youth Services Review, 26*(2), 185-206.

James, S., Landsverk, J., Slymen, D. J., & Leslie, L. K. (2004). Predictors of outpatient mental health service use: The role of foster care placement change. *Mental Health Services Research, 6*(3), 127-141.

James, S., Monn, A. R., Palinkas, L. A., & Leslie, L. K. (2008). Maintaining sibling relationships for children in foster and adoptive placements *Children & Youth Services Review, 30*(1), 90-106.

Jansson, B. S. (1994). *Social welfare policy: From theory to practice.* Pacific Grove, CA: Brooks/Cole.

Jaquet, S. E., Clark, S. J., Morazes, J. L., & Withers, R. (2007). The Role of Supervision in the Retention of Public Child Welfare Workers. *Journal of Public Child Welfare, 1*(3), 27-54.

Jaudes, P. K., Bilaver, L. A., Goerge, R. M., Masterson, J., & Catania, C. (2004). Improving Access to Health Care for Foster Children: The Illinois Model. *Child Welfare, 83*(3), 215.

Jayaratne, S., & Chess, W. A. (1985). Factors associated with job satisfaction and turnover among child welfare workers. In J. Laird & A. Hartman (Eds.), *A handbook of child welfare: Context, knowledge, and practice*. New York: Free Press.

Jekielek, S. M., Moore, K. A., Hair, E. C., & Scarupa, H. J. (2002). *Mentoring: A promising strategy for youth development*. Washington, DC: Child Trends.

Jensen, P. S., & Hoagwood, K. E., (Eds.). (2008). *Improving Children's Mental Health through Parent Empowerment: A Guide to Assisting Families*. New York: Oxford University Press.

Jensen, P. S., Weersing, R., Hoagwood, K. E., & Goldman, E. (2005). What is the evidence for evidence-based treatments? A hard look at the soft underbelly. *Mental Health Services Research, 7*(1), 53-74.

Jenson, J. M. (2007). Neighborhood and community effects on individual behavior and social functioning. *Social Work Research, 31*(4), 195-197.

Jenson, J. M., & Whittaker, J. K. (1987). Parental involvement in children's residential treatment: From preplacement to aftercare. *Children and Youth Services Review, 9*, 81-100.

Jenson, J., & Whittaker, J. K. (1987). Parental involvement in children's residential treatment: From pre-placement to aftercare. *Children and Youth Services Review, 9*(2), 81-100.

Johnson, K., Knitzer, J., & Kaufmann, R. (2003). *Making dollars follow sense: Financing early childhood mental health services to promote healthy social and emotional development in young children* (No. Policy Paper #4). New York: National Center for Children in Poverty, Columbia University, Mailman School of Public Health.

Johnson, P. R., Yoken, C., & Voss, R. (1995). Family foster care placement: The child's perspective. *Child Welfare, 74*(5), 959-974.

Joint Commission on the Accreditation of Hospitals. (2006). *Frequently Asked Questions about Behavioral Health Care Accreditation*.

Jones, L. (2001). *An evaluation of the Youth Empowerment Services Program (YES)*: Casey Family Programs.

Jones, L., & Landsverk, J. (2006). Residential Education: Examining a New Approach for Improving Outcomes for Foster Youth. *Children and Youth Services Review, 28*, 1152-1168.

Jones, M. A. (1985). *A second chance for families five years later: Follow-up of a program to prevent foster care*. New York: Child Welfare League of America.

Jones, M. A., & Moses, B. (1984). *West Virginia's former foster children: Their experiences in care and their lives as young adults*. New York: Child Welfare League of America.

Jones, M. A., Neuman, R., & Shyne, A. W. (1976). *A second chance for families: Evaluation of a program to reduce foster care*. New York: Child Welfare League of America.

Jones-Harden, B. (2004). Safety and stability for foster children: A developmental perspective. *Future Child, 14*(1), 30-47.

Jonson-Reid, M., & Barth, R. P. (2000). From Maltreatment Report To Juvenile Incarceration: The Role Of Child Welfare Services. *Child Abuse & Neglect, 24*(4), 505.

Kadushin, A. (1980). *Child welfare services* (3rd ed.). New York: Macmillan.

Kadushin, A. (1992). *Supervision in social work* (3rd ed.). New York: Columbia University Press.

Kadushin, A., & Harkness, D. (2002). *Supervision in social work* (4th ed.). New York: Columbia University Press.

Kadushin, A., & Martin, J. (1988). *Child Welfare Services* (Fourth ed.). New York: MacMillan.

Kagan, J. (1984). *The nature of the child*. New York: Basic Books.

Kagan, R., & Schlosberg, S. (1989). *Families in perpetual crisis*. New York: W.W. Norton.

Kagan, S. L., & Weissbourd, B. (Eds.). (1994). *Putting families first: America's family support movement and the challenge of change*. San Francisco: Jossey-Bass Publishers.

Kaiser Commission on Medicaid and the Uninsured. (2006). Understanding the recent changes in Medicaid spending and enrollment growth between 2000-2004, http://www.kff.org/medicaid/7499.cfm, accessed 18 July 2007.

Kamerman, S. B. (1999). Child welfare and the under-threes: An overview. *Zero To Three, 19*(3), 1-7.

Kamerman, S. B., & Kahn, A. J. (1990). Social services for children, youth and families in the United States. *Children & Youth Services Review, 12*(1-2), 184.

Kamerman, S., & Kahn, A. (1989). *Social services for children, youth and families in the U.S.* New York: Columbia University School of Social Work (The Annie E. Casey Foundation).

Kamerman, S. B., & Kahn, A. J. (1995). *Starting right: How America neglects its youngest children and what we can do about it*. New York: Oxford University Press.

Kaplan, L., & Girard, J. L. (1994). *Strengthening high-risk families: A handbook for practitioners*. New York: Lexington Books.

Karoly, L. A., Greenwood, P. W., Everingham, S. S., Houbé, J., Kilburn, M. R., Rydell, C. P., et al. (1998). *Investing In our children what we know and don't know about the costs and benefits of early childhood interventions*. Santa Monica, CA: RAND.

Katz, L. (1998). Wage subsidies for the disadvantaged. In R. Freeman and P. Gottschalk eds. *Generating jobs: How to increase demand for less-skilled workers*, New York: Russell Sage Foundation, pp. 21-53.

Katz, L. (1999). Concurrent planning: Benefits and pitfalls. *Child Welfare, 78*, 71-87.

Kazdin, A.E. and Weisz, J.R. (2003). *Evidence-Based Psychotherapies for Children and Adolescents*. New York: Guilford Press.

Kelleher, K., Chaffin, M., Hollenberg, J., & Fischer, E. (1994). Alcohol and drug disorders among physically abusive and neglectful parents in a community-based sample. *American Journal of Public Health, 84*, 1586-1590.

Keller, T. E., Wetherbee, K., LeProhn, N. S., Payne, V., Sim, K., & Lamont, E. R. (2001). Competencies and problem behaviors of children in family foster care: Variations by kinship placement status and race. *Children & Youth Services Review, 23*(12), 915-940.

Kelly, J. F., & Barnard, K. E. (1999). Parent Education Within a Relationship-Focused Model: Response. *Topics in Early Childhood Special Education*.

Kemp, S., & Marcenko, M. (2004). *Final Report—Evaluation of an intervention to connect birth and foster families*. San Francisco, CA: The Stuart Foundation.

Kemp, S., Marcenko, M., Vesneski, W., & Hoagwood, K. (2007). *Parent Empowerment and Engagement in Child Welfare: Promising Practices and Policy Opportunities*. presented at the Casey Foster Care Clinical R&D Project Consensus conference, Washington, DC.

Kemp, S., Whittaker, J. K., & Tracy, E. M. (1997). *Person-environment practice*. Hawthorne, NY: Aldine de Gruyter.

Kendall-Tackett, K., & Giacomoni, S. M. (Eds.). (2003). *Treating the lifetime health effects of childhood victimization*. Kingston, NJ: Civic Research Institute.

Kennell, J. H., Jerauld, R., Wolfe, H., Chesler, D., Kreger, N. D., McAlpine, W., et al. (1974). Maternal behavior one year after early and extended post-partum contact. *Developmental Medicine and Child Neurology, 16*, 172-179.

Kerbow, D. (1996). Patterns of urban student mobility and local school reform. *Journal of Education for Students Placed at Risk, 1*(2), 147-169.

Kerman, B., Maluccio, A. N., & Freundlich, M. (Eds.) (2009). *Achieving permanence for older children and youth in foster care.* New York: Columbia University Press.

Kerman, B., Wildfire, J., & Barth, R. P. (2002). Outcomes for young adults who experienced foster care. *Children & Youth Services Review, 24*(5), 319-344.

Kessler, R. C., & Magee, W. J. (1993). Childhood adversities and adult depression. *Psychological Medicine, 23*, 679-690.

Kessler, R., Pecora, P., Williams, J., Hiripi, E., O'Brien, K., English, D. J., et al. (2008). The effects of enhanced foster care on the long-term physical and mental health of foster care alumni. *Archives of General Psychiatry*, 65(6).

Kettner, P. M. (2002). *Achieving excellence in the management of human services organizations.* Boston, MA: Allyn & Bacon.

Kinney, J. M., Haapala, D. A., & Gast, J. E. (1981). Assessment of families in crisis. In M. Bryce & J. Lloyd (Eds.), *Treating families in the home: An alternative to placement* (pp. 50-67). Springfield, IL: Charles C. Thomas.

Kinney, J., & Haapala, D. A. (1984). *First year Homebuilder mental health project report.* . Federal Way, WA: Behavioral Sciences Institute.

Kinney, J., Haapala, D. A., Booth, C., & Leavitt, S. (1990). The Homebuilders model. In J. K. Whittaker, K. Kinney, E. M. Tracy & C. Booth (Eds.), *Reaching high-risk families-Intensive family preservation in human services* (pp. 31-64). New York: Aldine de Gruyter.

Kirby, L. D., & Fraser, M.W. (1997). Risk and resilience in childhood. In Fraser, M. W. (Ed). Risk and resilience in childhood (pp. 10-33). Washington, DC: NASW Press.

Kirk, R. S. (2000). *A Retrospective Evaluation Of North Carolina's Intensive Family Preservation Services Program.* Chapel Hill, NC: Jordan Institute for Families School of Social Work University of North Carolina at Chapel Hill.

Kirk, R. S., & Griffith, D. P. (2008). Impact of intensive family preservation services on disproportionality of out-of-home placement of children of color in one state's child welfare system. *Child Welfare, 87(5),*

Kirk, R. S., Griffith, D. P., & Gogan, H. (2004). Intensive Family Preservation Services: Demonstrating placement prevention using even history analysis. *Social Work Research, 28*(1), 5-15.

Kirk, R. S., Reed-Ashcraft, K. B., & Pecora, P. J. (2003). Implementing Family Preservation Services: A Case of Infidelity. *Family Preservation Journal, 6*(2), 59-81.

Kirk, S., Gallagher, J., & Asastasiow, N. (1993). *Educating Exceptional Children* (7th ed.). Boston: Houghton-Mifflin.

Kirsh, S., & Maidman, F. (1984). Child welfare problems and practice: An ecological approach. In F. Maidman (Ed.), *Child welfare: A source book of knowledge and practice* (pp. 1-14). New York: Child Welfare League of America.

Klaw, E. L., & Rhodes, J. E. (1995). Mentor relationships and the career development of pregnant and parenting African American teenagers. *Psychology of Women Quarterly, 19*(4), 551-563.

Kluger, M., Alexander, G., & Curtis, P. (Eds.). (2000). *What works in child welfare.* Washington, DC: Child Welfare League of America.

Knorth, E., Harder, E.T., Zandberg, T. & Kendrick, A.J. (2007). Children and young people under a roof: A selective meta-analysis on outcomes of residential care. Manuscript submitted for publication.

Knott, T., & Barber, J. (2004). *Do placement stability and parental visiting lead to better outcomes for children in foster care? Implications for the Australian Tracking Study (CECW Information Sheet #19).* Toronto, ON, Canada: Faculty of Social Work, University of Toronto.

Kohl, P. L. (2007). *Unsuccessful in-home child welfare service plans following a maltreat-ment investigation: Racial and Ethnic Differences.* Washington, DC: Casey-CSSP Alliance for Racial Equality in Child Welfare.

Kohl, P. L., Edleson, J. L., English, D. J., & Barth, R. P. (2005). Domestic violence and pathways into child welfare services: Findings from the National Survey of Child and Adolescent Well-Being. *Children & Youth Services Review, 27,* 1167-1182.

Kohl, P. L., Gibbons, C. B., & Green, R. L. (2005, January 16). *Findings from the National Survey of Child and Adolescent Well-Being (NSCAW): Applying innovative methods to understanding services and outcomes for maltreated children; Safety of children in child welfare services: Analysis of reported and undetected maltreatment over 18-months.* Paper presented at the Society for Social Work and Research, Miami, FL.

Kolko, D. J., & Swenson, C. C. (2005). Long-term Management of the Developmental Consequences in Child Physical Abuse. In R. M. Reece (Ed.), *Treatment of Child Abuse: Common Ground for Mental Health, Medical, and Legal Practitioners* (pp. 135-156). Baltimore, MD: The John Hopkins University Press.

Korbin, J., Coulton, C. I., Chard, S., Platt-Houston, C., & Su, M. (1998). Impoverishmnet and child maltreatment in African American and European American Neighborhoods. *Development & Psychopathology, 10*(2), 215-233.

Kosterman, R., Hawkins, D. J., Spath, R., Haggerty, K. P., & Zhu, K. (1997). Effects of a preventive parent-training intervention on observed family interactions: proximal outcomes from preparing for the drug free years. *Journal of Commuity Psychology, 25*(4), 338-352.

Kraft, A.D., Palombo, J., Woods, P.K., Mitchell, D., & Schmidt, A. W. (1985a). Some theoretical considerations on confidential adoptions: Part I. The birth mother. *Child and Adolescent Social Work, 2,* 13-21.

Kraft, A.D., Palombo, J., Woods, P.K., Mitchell, D., & Schmidt, A. W. (1985b). Some theoretical considerations on confidential adoptions: Part II. The adoptive mother. *Child and Adolescent Social Work, 2,* 69-82.

Kreider, R.M. (2003. October). *Adopted children and stepchildren: 2000* [Census 2000 Special Report]. Washington, DC: U.S. Department of Commerce, U.S. Census Bureau.

Kreilkamp, T. (1989). *Time-limited, intermittent therapy with children and families.* New York: Brunner/Mazel.

Krisberg, B., Schwartz, I. M., Litsky, P., & Austin, J. (1986). The watershed of juvenile justice reform. *Crime & Delinquency, 32,* 5-38.

Kroner, M. J. (1988). Living arrangement options for young people preparing for inde-pendent living. *Child Welfare, 67,* 547-562.

Krysik, J., LeCroy, C. W., & Ashford, J. B. (2008). Participant's perceptions of healthy families: A home visitation program to prevent child abuse and neglect. *Children & Youth Services Review, 30*(1), 45-61.

Ku, L., Lin, M. & Broaddus, M. (2007). Improving children's health: A chartbook about the roles of Medicaid and SCHIP, Center on Budget and Policy Priorities, January.

Kufeldt, K. (1994). Inclusive foster care: Implementation of the model. In B. McKenzie (Ed.), *Current perspectives on foster family care for children and youth* (pp. 84-111). Toronto: Wall & Emerson.

Kumpfer, K. L., Molgaard, V., & Spoth, R. (1996). The Strengthening Families Program for the prevention of delinquency and drug use. In R. D. Peters & R. J. McMahon (Eds.), *Preventing childhood disorders, substance abuse, and delinquency* (pp. 241-267). Thousand Oaks, CA: Sage Publications, Inc.

Kupsinel, M. M., & Dubsky, D. D. (1999). Behaviorally impaired children in out-of-home care. *Child Welfare, 78*(2), 297-310.

Kutash, K. and Robbins Rivera, V. (1996). *What Works in Children's Mental Health Services?*. Baltimore: Paul H. Brookes Publishing Company.

Lahti, J. (1982). A follow-up study of foster children in permanent placements. *Social Service Review, 56*, 556-571.

Laird, J. (1995). Family-centered practice in the postmodern era. *Families in Society: The Journal of Contemporary Human Services, 76*, 150-162.

Laird, J., & Hartman, A. (Eds.). (1985). *A handbook of child welfare*. New York: The Free Press.

LaLonde, R. (2003). Employment and training programs. In R. Moffitt (ed.) *Means-tested transfer programs in the United States*, Chicago, IL: National Bureau of Economic Research, pp. 517-588.

Landsverk, J., Burns, B. J., Stambaugh, L., & Rolls-Reutz, J. (2006). *Mental health care for children and adolescents*. Seattle, WA: Casey Family Programs.

Landsverk, J., Davis, I., Ganger, W., Newton, R., & Johnson, I. (1996). Impact of psychosocial functioning on reunification from out-of-home placement. *Children and Youth Services Review, 18*, 447-462.

Lansford, J.E., Dodge, K.A., Pettit, G. S., Bates, J.E., Crozier, J., & Kaplow, J. (2002). Long-term effects of early child physical maltreatment on psychological, behavioral, and academic problems in adolescence: A 12-year prospective study. *Archives of Pediatrics and Adolescent Medicine, 156*, 824-830.

Larner, M. B., Stevenson, C. S., & Behrman, R. E. (1998). Protecting children from abuse and neglect: Analysis and recommendations. *The Future of Children, 8*(1), 4-22.

Lasch, C. (1977). *Haven in a heartless world: The family besieged*. New York: Basic Books.

Lau, A.S. (2006) Making the case for selected and directed cultural adaptations of evidence-based treatments: examples from parent training. *Clinical Psychology: Science and Practice.* 13.4: 295-310.

Lauffer, A., & Carlson, B. E. (1979). *Resources for child placement and other human services: a Project CRAFT publication*. Newbury Park, CA: Sage Publications.

Leathers, S. J. (2002). Parental visiting and family reunification: could inclusive practice make a difference? *Child Welfare, 81*(4), 595-616.

Leathers, S. J. (2005). Separation from siblings: Associations with placement adaptation and outcomes among adolescents in long-term foster care. . *Children and Youth Services Review, 27*, 793-819.

Leathers, S. J., & Testa, M. F. (2006). Youth emancipating from care: caseworkers' reports on needs and services. *Child Welfare, 85*(3), 463-498.

LeCroy, C. W., & Krysik, J. (2007). Understanding and interpreting effect size measures. *Social Work Research, 31*(4), 243-248.

Lee, B. R. & Thompson, R. (2008a). Externalizing Behavior Trajectories for Youths in Group Care: A Study of Peer Contagion. Society for Social Work and Research. Washington, DC.

Lee, B. R., & Thompson, R. (2008b). Comparing outcomes for youth in treatment foster care and family-style group care. *Children and Youth Services Review, 30*(7), 746-757.Lee, B. R. (2007). Exploring peer contagion at Girls and Boys Town: Does it exist? *Data News You Can Use, 6* (4). Girls and Boys Town: National Research Institute.

Lee, B. R., & Barth, R.P. Residential education: An emerging resource for improving educational outcomes for youth in foster care. Unpublished manuscript available from the author at University of Maryland School of Social Work, Baltimore, MD.

Lehman, C., & O'Dell, K. (2002). *Powerhouse Evaluation Final Report*. Seattle, WA: Casey Family Programs.

Leibold, J., & Downs , A. C. (2002). *Rapid City Stepping Stones Life Skills Program Evaluation Report*. Seattle, WA: Casey Family Programs.

Leibold, J., & Downs, C. (2002). *San Antonio PAL Classes Evaluation Report*. Seattle, WA: The Casey Family Program.

Leichtman, M. (2006). Residential Treatment of Children and Adolescents: Past, Present, and Future. *American Journal of Orthopsychiatry*. 76(3) 285-294.

Leigh, J. W. (1998). *Communicating for cultural competence*. New York: Allyn & Bacon.

Leon, A. M. (1999). Family support model: Integrating service delivery in the twenty-first century. *Families in Society: The Journal of Contemporary Human Services, 80*, 14-24.

Leon, A. M., Mazur, R., Montalvo, E., & Rodrieguez, M. (1984). Self-help support groups for Hispanic mothers. *Child Welfare, 63*, 261-268.

Lerman, R. & Sorenson, E. (2003). Child support: Interactions between private and public transfers. Pp. 587-628 in R. Moffitt (ed.). *Means-tested transfer programs in the United States*, Chicago, IL: National Bureau of Economic Research.

Leung, P., Erich, S., & Kanenberg, H. (2005). A comparison of family functioning in gay/lesbian, heterosexual and special needs adoptions. *Children and Youth Services Review, 27*(9), 1031-1044.

Leventhal, J. M. (1996). Twenty years later: We do know how to prevent child abuse and neglect. *Child Abuse & Neglect, 20*(8), 647-653.

Leventhal, T., & Brooks-Gunn, J. (2004). A randomized study of neighborhood effects on low-income children's educational outcomes. *Developmental Psychology, 40*(4), 488-507.

Levine, C. I., Brandt, A., & Whittaker, J. K. (1998). *Staying together, living apart: New perspectives on youth group living from the AIDS epidemic* (from Planning and Placement Project). (Available from Carol Levine, The United Hospital Fund, 23rd Floor, 350 Fifth Avenue, New York, NY 10118, U.S.A.)

Lewin, K. (1935). *A dynamic theory of personality*. New York: McGraw-Hill.

Lewis, R. E. (1991). What are the characteristics of intensive family preservation services? In M.W. Fraser, P.J. Pecora & D. A. Haapala (Eds.), *Families in crisis: The impact of intensive family preservation services* (pp. 93-108). New York: Aldine de Gruyter.

Lewis, R. E., Walton, E., & Fraser, M. W. (1995). Examining family reunification services: A process analysis of a successful experiment. *Research on Social Work Practice, 5*(3), 259-282.

Libby, A. M., Coen, A. S., Price, D. A., Silverman, K., & Orton, H. D. (2005). Inside the Black Box: what constitutes a day in a residential treatment centre? *International Journal of Social Welfare, 14*(3), 176-183.

Library of Congress. (2005). *Statements on Introduced Bills and Joint Resolutions (Senate, July 28, 2005)*. Washington, DC: Author (Retrieved from http://thomas.loc. gov/cgi-bin/query/F?109:2:./yemp/~r109waKELi:e108822).

Lieberman, A. (1987). Separation in infancy and toddlerhood: Contributions of attachment theory and psychoanalysis. In J. Bloom-Fleschbach & S. Bloom-Fleschbach (Eds.), *The psychology of separation and loss: Perspectives on development, life transitions, and clinical practice* (pp. 109-135). San Francisco, CA: Jossey Bass Publishers.

Lieberman, A. A., Hornby, H., & Russell, M. (1988). Analyzing the educational backgrounds and work experiences of child welfare personnel: A national study. *Social Work, 33*(6), 485-489.

Light, R. (1973). Abused and neglected children in America: A study of alternative policies. *Harvard Educational Review 43*(4), 556-598.

Light, R. (1973). Abused and neglected children in America: A study of alternative policies. *Harvard Educational Review 43*(4), 556-598.

Linares, O., Montalto, D., Li, M., & Oza, V. S. (2006). A promising parent intervention in foster care. *Journal of Consulting and Clinical Psychology, 74*(1), 32-41.

Lindblad-Goldberg, M., Dore, M. M., & Stern, L. (1998). *Creating competence from chaos: A comprehensive guide to home-based services* (First ed.). New York: W.W. Norton & Company.

Lindsay, P. (1988). *National study of public child welfare salaries.* Portland, ME: University of Southern Maine, National Child Welfare Resource Center for Management and Administration.

Lindsey, D. (2004). *The welfare of children.* New York: Oxford University Press.

Lindsey, D., & Schwartz, I. M. (2004). Advances in child welfare: Innovations in child protection, adoptions and foster care. *Children & Youth Services Review, 26*(11), 999-1005.

Link, M. K. (1996). Permanency outcomes in kinship care: a study of children placed in kinship care in Erie County, New York. *Child Welfare, 75*(5), 509-528.

Lino, M. (2005). *Expenditures on Children by Families, 2004 (Misc. Publication No. 1528-2004).* Washington, DC: U.S. Department of Agriculture, Center for Nutrition Policy and Promotion. (Retrieved 12/7/06 from http://www.cnpp.usda.gov/Publications/CRC/crc2004.pdf).

Littell, J. H. (2005). Lessons from a systematic review of effects of multisystemic therapy. *Children and Youth Services Review, 27*(4), 445-463.

Littell, J. H., Schuerman, J. R., Rzepnicki, T. L., Howard, J., & Nagler, S. F. (1993). Shifting objectives in family preservation programs. In E. S. Morton & R. K. Grigsby (Eds.), *Advancing Family Preservation Practice* (pp. 99-118). Newbury Park, CA: Sage Publications.

Little, M., & Mount, K. (1999). *Prevention and early intervention with children in need.* Cambridge, England: Ashgate Publishing.

Little, M., Kohm, A. & Thompson, R. (2005). The impact of residential placement on child development: research and policy implications. *International Journal of Social Welfare*, 14: 200-209.

Littner, N. (1950). *Some traumatic effects of separation and placement.* New York: Child Welfare League of America.

Lloyd, J. C., Bryce, M. E., & Schultze, L. (1980). *Placement prevention and family reunification: A practitioner's handbook for the home-based family-centered program.* Iowa City: University of Iowa, School of Social Work, National Resource Center on Family-Based Services.

Loman, L. A., & Siegel, G. L. (2000). *A Review of Literature on Independent Living of Youths in Foster and Residential Care: A Report of the Institute of Applied Research.* St. Louis, MO: Institute of Applied Research.

Loman, L. A., & Siegel, G. L. (2005). Alternative Response in Minnesota: Findings of the Program Evaluation. *Protecting Children, 20*(2/3), 78-92.

Lovejoy, M., Graczyk, P., O'Hare, E., & Neuman, G. (2000). Maternal depression and parenting behavior: A meta-analytic review. *Clinical Psychology Review, 20*, 561-592.

Lupton, C. (1998). User empowerment or family self-reliance? The family group conference model. *British Journal of Social Work, 28*, 107-128.

Luther, S.S., Cicchetti, D., & Becker, B. (2000). The construct of resilience: A critical evaluation and guidelines for future work. *Child Development, 71*, 543-562.

Lynch, E. W., & Hanson, M. J. (1992). *Developing cross-cultural competence: A guide for working with young children and their families.* Baltimore: Paul H. Brookes Publishing Company.

Lynch, E. W., & Hanson, M. J. (Eds.). (1998). *Developing cross-cultural competence* (Second ed.). Baltimore, MD: Paul H. Brookes Publishing.

Maas, H. S., & Engler, R. E. (1959). *Children in need of parents.* New York: Columbia University Press.

MacLeod, J., & Nelson, G. (2000). Programs for the promotion of family wellness and prevention of child maltreatment: A meta-analytic review. *Child Abuse & Neglect, 24*(9), 1127-1149.

Magen, R. H., & Rose, S. D. (1994). Parents in groups: Problem solving versus behavioral skills training. *Research in Social Work, 4*(2), 172-191.

Magruder, J. (1994). Characteristics of relative and non-relative adoptions by California public adoption agencies. *Children and Youth Services Review, 16,* 123-131.

Magura, S., & Moses, B. S. (1984). Clients as evaluators in child protective services. *Child Welfare, 63*(2), 99-112.

Magura, S., & Moses, B.S. (1986). *Outcome measures for child welfare services.* Washington, DC: Child Welfare League of America.

Maier, H. W. (1978). *Three theories of child development* (Third ed.). New York City: Harper and Row.

Mallon, G. P. (1997). Toward a competent child welfare service delivery system for gay and lesbian adolescents and their families. In G.A. Anderson, A. S. Ryan & B. R. Leashore (Eds.), *The challenge of permanency planning in a multicultural society* (pp. 177-194). New York: The Haworth Press.

Mallon, G. (1998). *We don't exactly get the welcome wagon: The experiences of gay and lesbian adolescents in child welfare systems.* New York: Columbia University Press.

Mallon, G.P. (1999). *Let's get this straight: A gay- and lesbian-affirming approach to child welfare.* New York: Columbia University Press.

Mallon, G.P. (2007a). Assessing lesbian and gay prospective foster and adoptive families: A focus on the home study process. *Child Welfare, 86*(2), 67-86.

Mallon, G. P. (2007b). *Foundations of social work practice with lesbian, gay, bisexual, and transgender persons.* New York: Harrington Park Press.

Mallon, G. P. (2007c). *Lesbian and gay foster and adoptive parents: Recruiting, assessing, and supporting an untapped resource for children and youth in America's child welfare system.* Washington, DC: Child Welfare League of America.

Mallon, G.P., & Wornoff, R. (2006). Busting out of the child welfare closet: Lesbian, gay, bisexual, and transgender-affirming approaches to child welfare. *Child Welfare, 86*(2), 115-122.

Maluccio, A. (1981). An ecological perspective on practice with parents of children in foster care. In A.N. Maluccio. & P. A. Sinanoglu (Eds.), *The challenge of partnership: Working with parents of children in foster care.* New York: Child Welfare League of America.

Maluccio, A. N. (1991). Family preservation: An overview. In A. L. Sallee & J. C. Lloyd (Eds.), *Family preservation: Papers from the Institute for Social Work Editors 1990.* Riverdale, IL: National Association for Family-Based Services.

Maluccio, A. N. (1999). Action as a vehicle for promoting competence. In B. R. Compton & B. Galaway (Eds.), *Social work processes* (6th ed., pp. 354-365). Pacific Grove, CA: Brooks/Cole Publishing.

Maluccio, A. N., & Fein, E. (1987). Effects of permanency planning on foster children: A response. *Social Work, 32*(6), 546-548.

Maluccio, A. N., & Pecora, P. J. (in press). Foster family care: The United States perspective. In C. McCauley, P. J. Pecora & W. E. Rose (Eds.), *Enhancing the Well Being of Children and Families through Effective Interventions- UK and USA Evidence for Practice.* London and Philadelphia: Jessica Kingsley Publishers.

Maluccio, A. N., & Whittaker, J. K. (1988). Helping the biological families of children in out-of-home placement. In E. W. Nunnally & C. S. Chilman (Eds.), *Troubled relationships* (pp. 205-217).

Maluccio, A. N., Ainsworth, F., & Thoburn, J. (2001). *Child Welfare Outcome Research in the United States, the United Kingdom and Australia*. Washington, DC: Child Welfare League of America.

Maluccio, A. N., Fein, E., & Davis, I. (1994). Family reunification: Research findings, issues, and directions. *Child Welfare, 73*, 489-504.

Maluccio, A. N., Fein, E., & Olmstead, K. A. (1986). *Permanency planning for children: Concepts and methods*. London and New York: Routledge, Chapman and Hall.

Maluccio, A. N., Krieger, R., & Pine, B. A. (Eds.). (1990). *Preparing adolescents for life after foster care: The central role of foster parents*. Washington, DC: Child Welfare League of America.

Maluccio, A. N., Pine, B. A., & Tracy, E. M. (2002). *Social work practice with families and children*. New York: Columbia University Press.

Maluccio, A. N., Warsh, R., & Pine, B. A. (1993). Family reunification: An overview. In B. A. Pine, Warsh, R., & A. N. Maluccio (Eds.), *Together again: Family reunification in foster care* (pp. 3-19). Washington, DC: Child Welfare League of America.

Maluccio, A. N., Warsh, R., & Pine, B. A. (1993). Rethinking family reunification after foster care. *Community Alternatives: International Journal of Family Care, 5*(2), 1-17.

Maluccio, A., & Pecora, P. (2006). Family Foster Care in the USA. In C. McCauley, P. J. Pecora & W. E. Rose (Eds.), *Enhancing the Well Being of Children and Families through Effective Interventions-International Evidence for Practice* (pp. 187-202). London and Philadelphia: Jessica Kingsley Publishers.

Manalo, V., & Meezan, W. (2000). Toward building a typology of services for the evaluation of family support programs. *Child Welfare, 79*(4), 405-429.

Mankins, M. C., & Steele, R. (2005). Turning Great Strategy into Great Performance. *Harvard Business Review 83*(7), 64-72.

Mapp, S. C., & Steinberg, C. (2007). Birthfamilies as Permanency Resources for Children in Long-Term Foster Care. *Child Welfare, 86*(1), 29-51.

Marcenko, M. O., Spence, M., & Samost, L. (1996). Outcomes of a home visitation trial for pregnant and postpartum women at-risk for child placement. *Children & Youth Services Review, 18*(3), 243-259.

Marcenko, M., & Staerkel, F. (2006). Home visiting for parents of pre-school children in the US. In C. McCauley, P. J. Pecora & W. E. Rose (Eds.), *Enhancing the Well Being of Children and Families through Effective Interventions- UK and USA Evidence for Practice*. London & Philadelphia: Jessica Kingsley Publishers.

Marcia, J. E. (1980). Identity in adolescence. In J. Adelson (Ed.), *Handbook of adolescent psychology* (pp. 158-187). New York: Wiley.

Martin, F. E., & Palmer, T. (1997). Transitions to adulthood: A child welfare youth perspective. *Community Alternatives: International Journal of Community Care, 9*, 29-60.

Marts, E. J., Lee, R., McRoy, R., & McCroskey, J. (2008). Point of engagement: Reducing disproportionality and improving child and family outcomes. *Child Welfare, 87(2),*335-358.

Massinga, R., & Pecora, P. J. (2004). Providing better opportunities for older children in the child welfare system. *The Future of Children, 14*(1), 150-173.

Masten, A. S., & Wright, M. O. (1998). Cumulative risk and protection models of child maltreatment. In B. B. R. Rossman, & M.S. Rosenberg (Eds). *Multiple victimization of children* (pp. 7-30). New York: The Haworth Press, Inc.

Masten, A.S., & Coatsworth, J.D. (1995). Competence, resilience, and psychopathology. In D. Cicchetti & D. J. Cohen (Eds.), *Developmental psychopathology: Vol. 2. Risk, disorder, and adaptation* (pp. 715-752). New York: John Wiley and Sons.

Maximus, Inc. (1984). *Child welfare statistical fact book: 1984: Substitute care and adoption.* Washington, DC: Office of Human Development Series.

Maxwell, J. C. (1998). *21 irrefutable laws of leadership.* Nashville, TN: Thomas Nelson Publishers.

Maxwell, J. C. (2001). *The 17 indisputable laws of teamwork.* Nashville, TN: Thomas Nelson Publishers.

Maza, P. (unknown). The Role of the Single Mother in the Adoption of Children from the Child Welfare System. *Adoption News, 3*(4), 3.

Maza, P.L. (1983). Characteristics of children free for adoption. *Child Welfare* (Research Notes #2). Washington, DC: Children's Bureau, Administration for Children, Youth and Families.

McCartney, K., Dearing, B. A., Taylor, C., & Bub, K. L. (2007). Quality child care supports the achievement of low-income children: Direct and indirect pathways through caregiving and the home environment *Journal of Applied Developmental Psychology, 28*(5-6), 411-426.

McCauley, C., Pecora, P. J., & Rose, W. E. (Eds.). (2006). *Enhancing the Well Being of Children and Families through Effective Interventions - International Evidence for Practice.* London, England and Philadelphia, PA: Jessica Kingsley Publishers.

McCrory, J., Ayers-Lopez, S., & Green, D. (2006). Disproportionality in Child Welfare. *Protection Connection, 12*(4).

McCroskey, J., Furman, W., & Yoo, J. (in preparation). Finding common ground in community based child welfare: Qualitative data on Los Angeles County's point of engagement initiative..

McDermott, M. T. (2007). *Independent Adoption.* Retrieved January 21, 2007, from www.adoptivefamilies.com/articles.php?aid=1017

McDonald, J., Salyers, N., & Shaver, M. (2004). *The Foster Care Straitjacket. Innovation, Federal Financing & Accountability in State Foster Care Reform.* Urbana-Champaign, IL: Children and Family Research Center at the School of Social Work, University of Illinois at Urbana-Champaign.

McDonald, T. P., Allen, R. I., Westerfelt, A., & Piliavin, I. (1996). *Assessing the long-term effects of foster care: A research synthesis.* Washington, DC: CWLA Press.

McDonald, T., Bryson, S., & Poertner, J. (2006). Balancing reunification and reentry goals. *Children & Youth Services Review, 28*(1), pp. 47-58.

McFadden, J. E., & Downs, S. W. (1995). Family continuity: The new paradigm in permanence planning. *Community Alternatives: International Journal of Family Care, 7,* 39-59.

McGowan, B. (1990). Family-based services and public policy: Context and implications. In J. Whittaker, J.M. Kinney, E. Tracy & C. Booth (Eds.), *Reaching high-risk families.* New York: Aldine de Gruyter.

McKay, M. M., & Bannon, W. M. (2004). Engaging families in child mental health services. *Child and Adolescent Psychiatric Clinics of North America, 13*(4), 905-914.

McKenzie, B. (1998). *Rethinking orphanages for the 21st century.* Thousand Oaks, CA: Sage Press.

McKenzie, R. B. (1998). *Rethinking Orphanages for the 21st Century.* Thousand Oaks, CA: Sage Press.

McLanahan, S. (2004). Fragile families and the marriage agenda. in L. Kowaleski-Jones and N. Wolfinger. (Eds). *Fragile Families and the Marriage Agenda,* New York: Springer Science and Business Media, Inc., pp. 1-22.

McMillen, J. C., Rideout, G. B., Fisher, R. H., & Tucker, J. (1997). Independent living services: The views of former foster youth. *Families in Society: The Journal of Contemporary Human Services, 78,* 471-479.

McMillen, J., & Tucker, J. (1999). The status of older adolescents at exit from out-of-home care. *Child Welfare, 78*(3), 339-362.

McMurty, S. L., & Lie, G. W. (1992). Differential Exit Rate of Minority Children in Foster Care. *Social Work, Research and Abstracts, 28,* 42-48.

McRoy, R. (2004). The color of child welfare. In K. Davis & T. Bent-Goodley (Eds.), *The Color of Social Policy.* Alexandria, VA: Council on Social Work Education, pp. 37-64).

McRoy, R.G. (2005). African American Adoptions. In J. Everett, S. Chipungu & B. Leashore (Eds.), *Child Welfare Revisted—An Africentric Perspective* (pp.256-274). Rutgers University Press.

Meadowcroft, P., & Trout, B. A. (Eds.). (1990). *Troubled youth in treatment homes: A handbook of therapeutic foster care.* Washington, DC: Child Welfare League of America.

Meadowcroft, P., Thomlison, B., & Chamberlain, P. (1994). Treatment foster care services: a research agenda for child welfare. *Child Welfare, 73*(5), 565-581.

Mech, E. V. (1988). Independent-living services for at-risk adolescents. *Child Welfare, 67,* 483-634.

Mech, E. V., & Fung, C. C. (1999). Placement restrictiveness and educational achievement among emancipated foster youth. *Research on Social Work Practice, 9*(2), 213-228.

Mech, E. V., & Rycraft, J. R. (Eds.). (1995). *Preparing foster youths for adult living: Proceedings of an invitational research conference.* Washington, DC: Child Welfare League of America.

Mech, E. V., Pryde, J. A., & Rycraft, J. R. (1995). Mentors for adolescents in foster care. *Child & Adolescent Social Work Journal, 12*(4), 317-328.

Mederos, F., & Woldeguiorguis, I. (2003). Beyond cultural competence: What child protection managers need to know and do. *Child Welfare, 82*(2), 125-142.

Meezan, W., & McCroskey, J. (1996). Improving family functioning through intensive family preservation services: Results of the Los Angeles experiment. *Family Preservation Journal, 1*(Winter), 9-31.

Meezan, W., & McCroskey, J. (1997). *Family preservation and family functioning.* Washington, DC: CWLA Press.

Meezan, W., Katz, S., & Russo, E.M. (1978). *Adoptions without agencies: A study of independent adoptions.* New York: Child Welfare League of America.

Melaville, A. L., & Blank, M. J. (1993). *Together we can: A guide for crafting a profamily system of education and human services.* Washington, DC: U.S. Departments of Education and Health and Human Services.

Melton, G. B., & Barry, F. D. (Eds.). (1994). *Protecting children from abuse and neglect: Foundations for a new national strategy.* New York: The Guilford Press.

Merdinger, J. M., Hines, A. M., Osterling, K. L., & Wyatt, P. (2005). Pathways to college for former foster youth: Understanding factors that contribute to educational success. *Child Welfare, 84*(6), 867-896.

Merkel-Holguin, L. (1996). *Children who lose their parents to HIV/AIDS: Agency guidelines for adoptive and kinship placement.* Washington, DC: CWLA Press.

Merkel-Holguin, L., & Wilmot, L. (2004). *Family Group Conferencing: Responses to the most commonly asked questions.* Denver, CO: American Humane Association.

Merkel-Holguin, L., Nixon, P., & Burford, G. (2003). Learning with families: A synopsis of FGDM research and evaluation in child welfare. *Protecting Children, 18*(1&2), 2-11.

Messing, J. T. (2006). From the child's perspective: A qualitative analysis of kinship care placements. *Children and Youth Services Review, 28*(12), 1415-1434.

Michaud, L. (2000). Turn the tables on employee turnover: Five keys to maximum employee retention. Retrieved from http://www.frogpond.com/articles/docs/lmichaud02.doc

Miedema, B., & Nason-Clark, N. (1997). Foster care redesign: The dilemma contemporary foster families face. *Community Alternatives: The International Journal of Family Care, 9*, 15-28.

Miller, D. L., Hoffman, F., & Turner, D. (1980). A perspective on the Indian Child Welfare Act. *Social Casework, 61*, 468-471.

Miller, I. (1971). Supervision in Social Work. In *Encyclopedia of Social Work* (16th ed., Vol. 2, pp. 1544-1551). New York: National Association of Social Workers.

Miller, I. (1977). Supervision in Social Work. In *Encyclopedia of Social Work* (17th ed., Vol. 2, pp. 1494-1501). Washington, DC: National Association of Social Workers.

Miller, I. (1987). Supervision in Social Work. In *Encyclopedia of Social Work* (18th ed., Vol. 2, pp. 748-756). Silver Springs, MD: National Association of Social Workers.

Miller, K., Fein, E., Howe, G., Gaudio, C., & Bishop, G. (1984). Time-limited, goal-focused parent aide service. *Social Casework, 65*(8), 472-477.

Miller, W. R., & Rollnick, S. (2002). *Motivational Interviewing: Preparing People for Change*. New York: Guilford Press.

Milliken, B. (2007). *The Last Dropout: Stop the Epidemic!* Carlsbad, CA: Hay House Publishers.

Milner, J., Mitchell, L., & Hornsby, W. (2001). The child and family service review: A framework for changing practice. *Journal of Family Social Work, 6*(4), 5-18.

Mindel, C. H., Habenstein, R. W., & Wright, R. (1988). *Ethnic families in America: Patterns and variations*. New York: Elsevier.

Minty, B. (1999). Outcomes in long-term foster family care. *Journal of Child Psychology & Psychiatry & Allied Disciplines, 40*(7), 991-999.

Miranda, J., Guillermo, B., Lau, A., Kohn, L., Wei-Chin, H., & LaFromboise, T. (2005) State of the science on psychosocial interventions for ethnic minorities. *Annual Review of Clinical Psychology*, 1, 113-142.

Moen, P., Elder, G. H., & Luscher, K. (Eds.). (1995). *Examining lives in context: Perspectives on the ecology of human development*. Washington, DC: American Psychological Association.

Moffitt, R. (ed.). (2003). *Means-tested transfer programs in the United States*, Chicago, IL: National Bureau of Economic Research.

Mohrman, S. A., & Mohrman Jr., A. M. (1995). *Designing Team-Based Organizations*. San Francisco, CA: Jossey-Bass.

Montgomery, P., Donkoh, C., & Underhill, K. (2006). Independent living programs for young people leaving the care system: The state of the evidence. *Children and Youth Services Review, 28*(12), 1435-1448.

Moone, J. (1997). *States at a glance: Juveniles in public facilities, 1995*. Washington, DC: U.S. Dept. of Justice.

Mordock, J. B. (2002). *Managing for outcomes: A basic guide to the evaluation of best practices in the human services*. Washington, DC: Child Welfare League of America.

Morgan, L. J., Spears, L. S., & Kaplan, C. (2003). *A framework for community action: Making children a national priority*. Washington, DC: Child Welfare League of America.

Morton, T. (1999). The increasing colorization of America's child welfare system: The overrepresentation of African American Children. *Policy and Practice, 57*(4), 23-30.

Mott, P. E. (1976). *Meeting human needs: The social and political history of Title XX.* Columbus, OH: National Conference on Social Welfare.

Moye, J., & Rinker, R. (2002). It's a hard knock life: Does the Adoption and Safe Families Act of 1997 adequately address problems in the child welfare system? *Harvard Journal on Legislation, 38*(2), 375-394.

Mrazek, P. J., & Haggerty, R. J. (Eds.). (1994). *Reducing risks for mental disorders: Frontiers for preventive intervention research.* Washington, DC: National Academy Press.

Mumola, C. (2000). *Bureau of Justice Statistics Special Report: Incarcerated Parents and Their Children.* Washington, DC: U.S. Department of Justice, Office of Justice Programs.

Munson, C. E. (2001). *Handbook of Clinical Social Work Supervision* (3rd ed.). New York: Haworth Press.

Muskie School of Public Service. (1998). *Improving Economic Opportunities for Young People Served by the Foster Care System: Three Views on the Path to Independent Living (Phase One and Phase Two).* Portland, ME: University of Southern Maine.

Nair, P., Schuler, M. E., Black, M. M., Kettinger, L., & Harrington, D. (2003). Cumulative environmental risk in substance abusing women: Early intervention, parenting stress, child abuse potential and child development. *Child Abuse & Neglect, 27,* 997-1017.

Nancy J. Cohen, Muir, E., Lojkasek, M., Muir, R., Parker, C. J., Barwick, M., et al. (1999). Watch, wait, and wonder: Testing the effectiveness of a new approach to mother-infant psychotherapy. *Infant Mental Health Journal, 20*(4), 429-451.

Nash, J. K., & Fraser, M. W. (1998). After-school care for children: A resilience-based approach. *Families in Society: The Journal of Contemporary Human Services,* 370-383.

Nash, K. A. (1999). *Cultural Competence: A guide for human service agencies.* Washington, DC: Child Welfare League of America, Inc.

National Association of Public Child Welfare Administrators. (2006). *Disproportionate Representation in the Child Welfare System: Emerging Promising Practices Survey*: American Public Human Services Association,.

National Association of Social Workers. (2003). *If you're right for the job, it's the best job in the world.* Washington, DC: Author.

National Association of Social Workers. (2004). *If you're right for the job, it's the best job in the work: The National Association of Social Workers' child welfare specialty practice section members describe their experiences in child welfare.* Silver Spring, MD: Author. Retrieved November 17, 2007 from http://www.socialworkers.org/practice/children/NASWChildWelfareRpt062004.pdf.

National Association of Social Workers. (2006). *Assuring the Sufficiency of a Front-line Workforce: A National Study of Licensed Social Workers.* Washington, DC: Author.

National Center for Children in Poverty, Columbia University. (2005). *Who Are America's Poor Children?* New York: Author.

National Center for Youth Law (2007). *Improving the child welfare workforce: Lessons learned from class action litigation.* Retrieved from www.childrensrights.org

National Clearinghouse on Child Abuse and Neglect Information. (unknown). *Safety, Permanency, Well-being. Child Welfare Outcomes, 1999: Annual Report.* Washington, DC: Administration for Children and Families.

National Commission on Family Foster Care. (1991). *A blueprint for fostering infants, children and youth in the 1990's.* Washington, DC: Child Welfare League of America, in collaboration with the National Foster Parent Association.

National Committee for Adoption. (1989). *Adoption fact-book: United States data issues, regulations, and resources*. Washington, DC: Author.

National Conference of Juvenile and Family Court Judges. (2006). *Children's Exposure to Domestic Violence: A Guide to Research and Resources*. Reno, NV: Author.

National Conference of State Legislators. (2006). *The changing landscape of federal child welfare financing*. Washington, DC: National Conference of State Legislators.

National Council of Juvenile and Family Court Judges (1992). *Protocol for making reasonable efforts to preserve families in drug-related dependency cases*. Reno, NV: Author.

National Council of Juvenile and Family Court Judges, Child Welfare League of America, Youth Law Center, & National Center for Youth Law. (Not Dated). *Making reasonable efforts: Steps for keeping families together*. New York: Edna McConnell Clark Foundation.

National Council on Crime and Delinquency. (2006). *Relationship between staff turnover, child welfare system functioning and recurrent child abuse*. Houston, TX: Cornerstones for Kids.

National Foster Care Awareness Project. (2000). *Frequently Asked Questions II About the Foster Care Independence Act of 1999 and the John H. Chafee Foster Care Independence program*. Seattle, WA: Casey Family Programs and the Benton Foundation.

National Foster Care Awareness Project. (2005). *Frequently Asked Questions III: About the Chafee Foster Care Independence Program and the Chafee Educational and Training Voucher Program*. Washington, DC: Author.

National Institute on Drug Abuse. (2005b). Epidemiologic trends in drug abuse. *Advance Report and Highlights/Executive summary: Abuse of Stimulants and Other Drugs*. US Department of Health and Human Services, National Institutes of Health, Division of Epidemiologist Services and Prevention Research, National Institute on Drug Abuse (NIDA): Community Epidemiology Workgroup (CEWG). Retrieved February 26, 2008 from http://www.drugabuse.gov/PDF/CEWG/AdvReport106.pdf

National Research Council and the Institute of Medicine. (2009). *Preventing mental, emotional and behavioral disorders among young people: Progress and possibilities*. Washington, D.C.: National Research Council and the Institute of Medicine of the National Academies. http://www.nap.edu/catalog.php?record_id=12480

National Resource Center on Family-Centered Services and Permanency Planning at Hunter College School of Social Work. (2007). Family-Centered Practices. Retrieved from http:\\www.hunter.cuny.edu/socwork/nrcfcpp/info_services/family-centered-practice.html

National Survey of Child and Adolescent Well-Being, Research Group. (2005). *National survey of child and adolescent well-being: The characteristics of children and families entering child welfare services*. Washington, DC: Washington, DC: U.S. Department of Health and Human Services, Administration for Children and Families.

National Survey of Child and Adolescent Well-Being. (2005). *CPS Sample Component Wave 1 Data Analysis Report, April 2005*. Washington, DC: U.S. Department of Health & Human Services, Administration for Children & Families.

Needell, B., & Barth, R. P. (1998). Infants entering foster care compared to other infants using birth status indicators. *Child Abuse & Neglect, 22*(12), 1179-1187.

Needell, B., & Gilbert, N. (1997). Child welfare and the extended family. In J.D. Berrick, R. Barth & N. Gilbert (Eds.), *Child welfare research review* (Vol. 2, pp. 85-99). New York: Columbia University Press.

Needell, B., Webster, D., Barth, R. P., Armijo, M., & Fox, A. (1998). *Performance indicators for child welfare services in California, 1997*. Berkeley, CA: University of California, School of Social Welfare, Child Welfare Research Center.

Nelson, D. W. (2004). Moving youth from risk to opportunity. In *KIDS COUNT 2004 Data Book*. Baltimore, MD: Annie E. Casey Foundation.

Nelson, K. E., & Nash, J. K. (2008). The effectiveness of aftercare services for African American families in an intensive family preservation program. *Research on Social Work Practice, 18*(3), 189-197.

Nelson, K. M. (1992). Fostering homeless children and their parents too: the emergence of whole-family foster care. *Child Welfare, 71*(6), 575-584.

Nelson, K., Walters, B., Schweitzer, D., Blythe, B. J., & Pecora, P. J. (2009). *A 10 year review of family preservation research: Building the evidence base*. Seattle, WA: Casey Family Programs (www.casey.org).

New York City Administration for Children's Services. (2004). *New York City's child welfare system: Successful reform* New York City: New York City Administration for Children's Services.

Newman, B. M., & Newman, P. R. (1995). *Development through life: A psychosocial approach* (Sixth ed.). Pacific Grove, CA: Brooks/Cole.

Newton, R. R., Litrownik, A. J., & Landsverk, J. A. (2000). Children and youth in foster care: disentangling the relationship between problem behaviors and number of placements. *Child Abuse & Neglect, 24*(10), 1363-1374.

Nicoll, A., Holmes, K., Pecora, P. J., Roller-White, C., O'Brien, K., & Fain, A. (in preparation). In Their Own Words: Foster Care Alumni Talk About Transition Services to Prepare for Independent Living. In A.N. Maluccio & T. Vechiatto (Eds.), *Child welfare research: An international perspective*: (Book under review by publisher).

Nisivoccia, D. (1996). Working with kinship foster families: Principles for practice. *Community Alternatives: International Journal of Family Care, 8*(1), 1-21.

Nollan, K. A. (1996). *Self-Sufficiency Skills among Youth in Long-Term Foster Care - Doctoral Dissertation*. Seattle, WA: University of Washington.

Nollan, K. A. (2006). Support for young people leaving care in the USA. In C. McAuley, P. Pecora & W. Rose (Eds.), *Enhancing the well-being of children and families through effective interventions: Evidence for practice*. London: Jessica Kingsley Publishers.

Nollan, K. A., Wolf, M., Ansell, D., Burns, J., Barr, L., Copeland, W., et al. (2000). Ready or not: Assessing youths' preparedness for independent living. *Child Welfare, 79*(2), 159-176.

Nollan, K., Horn, M., Downs, A. C., & Pecora, P. J. (2003). *Ansell-Casey Life Skills Assessment (ACLSA) and Life Skills Guidebook and Manual*. Seattle, WA: Casey Family Programs.

Nollan, K., Pecora, P., Lewy, J., Bodonyi, J., Le Prohn, N., & Downs, A. C. (2000). *How are the children doing Part II? Assessing youth outcomes in family foster care*. Seattle, WA: Casey Family Programs.

Noonan, K., & Burke, K. (2005). Termination of parental rights: Which foster care children are affected? . *The Social Science Journal, 42*(2), 241-256.

Nunnally, E. W., Chilman, C. S., & Cox, F. M. (1988). Introduction to the Series. In E.W. Nunnally, C.S. Chilman & F.M. Cox (Eds.), *Troubled relationships: Families in Trouble series* (Vol. 3, pp. 7-14). Newbury Park, CA: Sage Publications.

O'Keefe, M. (1995). Predictors of child abuse in martially violent families. *Journal of Interpersonal Violence, 10*, 3-25.

O'Donnell, J. M., Johnson, W. E., Jr., D'Aunno, L. E., & Thornton, H. L. (2005). Fathers in child welfare: caseworkers' perspectives. *Child Welfare, 84*(3), 387-414.

Office of Early Childhood, Substance Abuse and Mental Health Administration,. (1998). *SAMHSA Handout*.

Office of Family Assistance. (2006). *Table 42, Temporary Assistance for Needy Families- Active Cases, TANF Families with no adult recipients receiving cash assistance October 2003 – September 2004*. Washington, DC: Administration for Children and Families, Office of Family Assistance.

Okun, B. F. (1996). *Understanding diverse families: What practitioners need to know*. New York: The Guilford Press.

Okwuje, I. & Johnson, N. (2006). A rising number of state earned income tax credits are helping working families escape poverty. http://www.cbpp.org/10-12-06sfp.pdf, accessed May 10, 2007.

Olds, D. (2006). The nurse-family partnership: An evidence-based preventive intervention. *Infant Mental Health Journal, 21*(1), 5-25.

Olds, D. L., & Henderson, C. R. (1989). The prevention of maltreatment. In D. Cicchetti & V. Carlson (Eds.), *Child maltreatment: Theory and research on the causes and consequences of child abuse and neglect*. New York: Cambridge University Press.

Olds, D. L., & Kitzman, H. (1995). Review of research on home visiting for pregnant women and parents of young children. *The Future of Children, 5*(3), 51-75.

Olds, D. L., Henderson, C. R., & Kitzman, H. (1994). Does prenatal and infancy nurse home visitation have enduring effects on qualities of parental caregiving and child health at 25 to 50 months of life? . *Pediatrics, 93*(1), 89-98.

Olds, D. L., Henderson, C. R., Chamberlin, R., & Tatelbaum, R. (1986). Preventing child abuse and neglect: A randomized trial of nurse home visitation. *Pediatrics, 78*, 65-78.

Olds, D., Henderson Jr., C., Eckenrode, J., Pettitt, L. M., Kitzman, H., Cole, B., et al. (1998). Reducing risks for antisocial behavior with a program of prenatal and early childhood home visitation. *Journal of Community Psychology, 26*(1), 65-83.

Olds, D., Henderson, C. R., Cole, R., Eckenrode, J., Kitzman, H., Luckey, D., et al. (1998). Long-term effects of nurse home visitation on children's criminal and antisocial behavior: 15-year follow-up of a randomized controlled trial. *Journal of the American Medical Association (JAMA), 280*(14), 1238-1244.

Olds, D., Henderson, C., Kitzman, H., Eckenrode, J., Cole, R., & Tatelbaum, R. (1998). The promise of home visitation: Results of two randomized trials. *Journal of Community Psychology, 26*(1), 5-21.

Olds, D., Henderson, C., Tatelbaum, R., & Chamberlin, R. (1988). Improving the life course development of socially disadvantaged mothers: A randomized trial of nurse home visitation. *American Journal of Public Health, 78*, 1436-1445.

Olsen, L. (1982). Services for minority children in out-of-home care. *Social Service Review, 56*, 572-585.

Ondersma, S. J. (2002). Predictors of neglect within low-SES families: The importance of substance abuse. *American Journal of Orthopsychiatry, 72*, 383-391.

Oosterman, M., Schuengal, C., Slot, N. W., Bullens, R. A. R., & Doreleijers, T. A. H. (2007). Disruptions in foster care: A review and meta-analysis. *Children and Youth Services Review, 29*(1), 53-76.

Open Home Foundation. (2007). *Presentation to the New Zealand Families Commission*. Wellington, NZ, September 5, 2007: (Mimeograph).

Osofsky, J. D., & Thompson, D. (2000). Adaptive and maladaptive parenting: Perspectives on risk and protective factors. In J. P. Shonkoff & S. J. Meisels (Eds.), *Handbook of early childhood intervention* (2nd ed., pp. 54-75). Cambridge: Cambridge University Press.

Ostroff, F. (2006). Change Management in Government. *Harvard Business Review, 84*(5), 141-147.

Ouellette, T., Burstein, N., Long, D. & Beecroft, E. (2004). *Measures of Material Hardship: Final Report*. Washington, DC: Office of the Assistant Secretary for Planning and Evaluation. U.S. Department of Health and Human Services.

Pace, P.R. (2005). Court upholds gay foster parents. *NASW News 2*(5).

Packard, T. (2004). The Supervisor as a Transformational Leader. In M. J. Austin & K. M. Hopkins (Eds.), *Supervision as collaboration in the human services: Building a learning culture*. Thousand Oaks, CA: Sage Press.

Palmer, S. E. (1995). *Maintaining family ties: Inclusive practice in foster care.* Washington, DC: Child Welfare League of America.

Pannor, R., & Baran, A. (1984). Open adoption as standard practice. *Child Welfare, 63,* 245-250.

Parish, S. L., & Whisnant, A. L. (2005). Policies and Programs for Children and Youth with Disabilities. In J. Jenson & M. Fraser (Eds.), *Policies and Programs for children, youth and families: An ecological perspective on integrated service delivery.* Newbury Park, CA: Sage Press.

Parish, S. L., & Whisnant, A. L. (2006). Policies and programs for children and youth with disabilities. In J. Jenson & J. Fraser (Eds.), *Policies and programs for children, youth and families: An ecological perspective on integrated service delivery.* Newbury Park, CA: Sage Press.

Park, J. M., Metraux, S., & Culhane, D. P. (2005). Childhood out-of-home placement and dynamics of public shelter utilization among young homeless adults. *Children & Youth Services Review, 27*(5), 533-546.

Pasztor, E. M., & McFadden, E. J. (2006). Foster parent associations: Advocacy, support and empowerment. *Families in Society - The Journal of Contemporary Human Services, 87,* 483-490.

Pasztor, E. M., & Wynne, S. F. (1995). *Foster parent retention and recruitment: The state of the art in practice and policy.* Washington, DC: Child Welfare League of America.

Patti, R. J. (2008). *Handbook of Human Services Management.* Newbury Park, CA: Sage Press.

Patti, R. J., (Ed). (2000). *The handbook of social welfare management.* Thousand Oaks CA: Sage.

Patti, R. J., Poertner, J., & Rapp, C. A. (1987). Managing for service effectiveness in social welfare organizations. *Social Work, 32*(5), 377-381

Paxson, C. & Waldfogel, J. (2002). Work, welfare, and child maltreatment, *Journal of Labor Economics*, 20(3), pp. 435-474.

Pecora, P. J. (1991). Investigating allegations of child maltreatment: The strengths and limitations of current risk assessment systems. *Child and Youth Services, 15*(2).

Pecora, P. J. (2006). Child Welfare Policies and Programs. In J. Jenson & M. Fraser (Eds.), *Social Policy for Children and Families: A Risk and Resilience Perspective.* Newbury Park: Sage Press.

Pecora, P. J. (2007, March 22). *Why Should the Child Welfare Field Focus on Minimizing Placement Change as Part of Permanency Planning for Children?* Paper presented at the California Permanency Conference, Davis, CA.

Pecora, P. J., & Austin, M. J. (1987). *Managing human services personnel.* Newbury Park, CA: Sage Press.

Pecora, P. J., & English, D. (1994). *Multi-cultural guidelines for assessing family strengths and risk factors in child protective services.* Seattle, WA: School of Social Work, University of Washington and Washington State Department of Social Services.

Pecora, P. J., & Wiggins, T. (2009). *Working Paper No. 1: A summary of foster care research data by outcome domain.* Seattle, WA: Casey Family Programs. www.casey.org/research.

Pecora, P. J., Cherin, D., Bruce, E. J., & Arguello, T. (2009). *Administrative supervision: A brief guide for managing social service and other non-profit organizations.* Newbury Park: Sage Publications.

Pecora, P. J., Delewski, C. H., Booth, C., Haapala, D. A., & Kinney, J. (1985). Home-based family-centered services: The impact of training on worker attitudes. *Child Welfare, 5,* 529-540.

Pecora, P. J., Fraser, M., Nelson, K., McCroskey, J., & Meezan, W. (1995). *Evaluating Family-Based Services*. New York: Aldine De Gruyter.

Pecora, P. J., Fraser, M.W., & Haapala, D.H. (1991). Intensive, home-based family preservation services: Client outcomes and issues for program design. In K. Wells & D. E. Biegel (Eds.), *Family preservation services: Research and evaluation*. Newbury Park, CA: Sage Press (pp. 3-32).

Pecora, P. J., Kessler, R. C., O'Brien, K., White, C. R., Williams, J., Hiripi, E., et al. (2006). Educational and employment outcomes of adults formerly placed in foster care: Results from the Northwest Foster Care Alumni Study. *Children and Youth Services Review, 28*, 1459-1481.

Pecora, P. J., Kessler, R. C., Williams, J., Downs, A. C., English, D., & White, J. (2010). *What works in family foster care?* New York and Oxford, England: Oxford University Press.

Pecora, P. J., Kessler, R. C., Williams, J., O'Brien, K., Downs, A. C., English, D., et al. (2005). *Improving Family Foster Care: Findings from the Northwest Foster Care Alumni Study*. Seattle, WA: Casey Family Programs.

Pecora, P., Kingery, K., Downs, A. C., Nollan, K., Touregenau, J., & Sim, K. (2003). Examining the effectiveness of family foster care: A select literature review of post-placement outcomes. (Working Paper No. 1).

Pecora, P., O'Brien, K., Plotnick, P. R., Kessler, R., Sepulveda, M., Williams, J., et al. (in preparation). Measuring the financial success of foster care alumni.

Pecora, P. J., Seelig, W. R., Zirps, F. A., & Davis, S. M. (1996). *Quality improvement and evaluation in child and family services: Managing into the next century*. Washington, DC: CWLA Press.

Pecora, P. J., Whittaker, J. K., & Maluccio, A. N. and Barth, R.P. (2000). *The child welfare challenge: Policy, practice, and research*. 2nd Edition. New York: Aldine de Gruyter.

Pecora, P. J., Williams, J., Kessler, R. C., Downs, A. C., O'Brien, K., Hiripi, E., et al. (2003). *Assessing the effects of foster care: Early results from the Casey*

Pecora, P., Williams, J., Downs , A. C., Kessler, R., O'Brien, K., Hiripi, E., et al. (2003). *What Casey Family Programs Intervention Components Provide the Most Leverage towards Achieving Key Program Outcomes?* (working Paper No. 8). Seattle, WA: Casey Family Programs.

Pelton, L. H. (1989). *For reasons of poverty: A critical analysis of the public child welfare system in the United States*: (1989).

Pelton, L. H. (1991). Beyond permanency planning: Restructuring the public child welfare system. *Social Work, 36*(4), 337-343.

Pelton, L. H. (1994). The role of material factors in child abuse and neglect. In G. B. Melton & F. D. Barry (Eds.), *Protecting children from abuse and neglect: Foundations for a new national strategy* (pp. 131-181). New York: The Guilford Press.

Pelzer, D. (2000). *A man named Dave: A story of triumph and forgiveness*. Deerfield Beach, FL: Health Communications.

Pennell, J. and Anderson, G.R. (2005). *Widening the circle: The practice and evaluation of family group conferencing with children, youths and their families*.Washington, DC: NASW Press.

Perry, R. E. (2006). Education and Child Welfare Supervisor Performance: Does a Social Work Degree Matter? *Research on Social Work Practice, 16*(6), 591-604.

Peters, T. J., & Waterman, R. H. (1983). *In search of excellence: Lessons from America's best run companies*. New York: Harper and Row.

Peterson, J. L., Kohrt, P. E., Shadoin, L. M., & Authier, K. J. (1995). *Building skills in high-risk families: Strategies for the home-based practitioner*. Boys Town, NB: The Boys Town Press.

Pew Commission on Children in Foster Care. (2004). *Fostering the future: Safety, permanence and well-being for children in foster care.* Philadelphia, PA: Pew Charitable Trusts.

Pew Foundation (2008a). *Life chances: The case for early investment in our kids.* Retrieved from www.pewtrusts.org/uploadedFiles/American_Prospect_1207_EarlyEdSpecialRep

Pew Foundation (2008b). *Time for reform: Investing in prevention: keeping children* Safe at Home. Retrieved from http:\\kidsarewaiting.org

Phillips, S. D., Burns, B. J., Wagner, H. R., & Barth, R. P. (2004). Parental arrest and children involved with child welfare services. *American Journal of Orthopsychiatry, 74*, 174-186.

Pierce, L., & Geremia, V. (1999). Family reunion services: An examination of a process used to successfully reunite families. *Family Preservation Journal 4*(1), 13-30.

Pike, V. (1976). Permanent families for foster children: The Oregon Project. *Children Today, 5,* 22-25.

Pike, V., Downs, S., Emlen, A., Downs, G., & Case, D. (1977). *Permanent planning for children in foster care: A handbook for social workers* (No. (OHDS) 78-30124). Washington, DC: US Department of Health, Education and Welfare.

Piliavin, I., Sosin, M., & Westerfelt, H. (1987). *Conditions contributing to long-term homelessness: An exploratory study* [IRP Discussion Paper No. 853-887]. Madison, WI: Institute for Research on Poverty, University of Wisconsin.

Pinderhughes, E. (1989). *Understanding race, ethnicity, and power: The key to efficacy in clinical practice.* New York: Free Press.

Pinderhughes, E. (1995). Empowering diverse populations: Family practice in the 21st century. *Families in Society: The Journal of Contemporary Human Services, 76,* 131-140.

Pinderhughes, E. (1997). Developing diversity competence in child welfare and permanency planning. In G.R. Anderson, A.S. Ryan & B. R. Leashore (Eds.), *The challenge of permanency planning in a multicultural society* (pp. 19-38). New York: The Haworth Press.

Pinderhughes, E. E. (1991). The delivery of child welfare services to African American clients. *American Journal of Orthopsychiatry, 61*(4), 599-605.

Pine, B. A. (1986). Child welfare reform and the political process. *Social Service Review, 60*(3), 339-359.

Pine, B. A., & Drachman, D. (2005). Effective Child Welfare Practice with Immigrant and Refugee Children and their Families. *Child Welfare, LXXXIV*(5), 537-562.

Pine, B. A., & Spath, R. (2007). *Final report of the evaluation of the Casey Family Services family reunification program: Executive Summary.* Shelton, CT: Casey Family Services.

Pine, B. A., Healy, L. M., & Maluccio, A. N. (2002). Developing measurable program objectives: A key to evaluation of family reunification programs. In T. Vecchiato, A.N. Maluccio & C. Canali (Eds.), *Evaluation in child and family services: Comparative client and program perspectives* (pp. 86-99). New York: Aldine de Gruyter.

Pine, B. A., Spath, R., & Gosteli, S. (2005). Defining and Achieving Family Reunification. In G. Mallon & P. M. Hess (Eds.), *Child Welfare for the 21st Century: A Handbook of Children, Youth, and Family Services: Practices, Policies, and Programs* (pp. 378-391). New York: Columbia University Press.

Pine, B. A., Spath, R., Maguda, A., Werrbach, G., & Jenson, C. (2007). *Final Report of the Evaluation of the Casey Family Services Family Reunification Program.* West Hartford, CT: University of Connecticut.

Pinkerton, J. (1994). *In Care at Home: Parenting, the State and Civil Society*. Aldershot, England: Avebury.

Pittman, K. (2002). Keeping our eyes on the prize. *Youth Today, 9*(2), 63.

Placek, P. J. (1999). National adoption data: Assembled for the National Council for Adoption. In W. Pierce & C. Marshner (Eds.), *Adoption Factbook III* (pp. 24-68). Washington, DC: National Committee on Adoption.

Plantz, M. C., Hubbell, R., Barrett, B. J., & Dobrec, A. (1989). Indian Child Welfare Act: A status report. *Children Today, 18*, 24-29.

Plantz, M.C., Hubbell, B.J., Barrett, B.J., & Dobrec, A. (1989). Indian child welfare: A status report. *Children Today, 18*(1), 24-29.

Poertner, J., Bussey, M., & Fluke, J. (1999). How safe are out-of-home placements? . *Children and Youth Services Review 21*(7), 549-563.

Polansky, N. A., Ammons, P. W., & Weathersby, B. L. (1983). Is there an American standard of child care? . *Social Work, 28*(5), 341-346.

Polansky, N. A., Gaudin, J. M., & Kilpatrick, A. C. (1992). Family radicals. *Children and Youth Services Review, 14*, 19-26.

Pope, S. M., Williams, J. R., Sirles, E. A., & Lally, E. M. (2005). *Family Preservation and Support Services: A Literature Review and Report on Outcome Measures*. Anchorage, AK: The University of Alaska, School of Social Work, Anchorage Child Welfare Evaluation Program.

Potter, C. C., & Klein-Rothchild, S. (2002). Getting home on time: Predicting timely permanence for young children. *Child Welfare, 2*, 123-150.

Poulin, F., Dishion, T.J. & Burraston, B. (2001). 3 year iatrogenic effects associated with aggregating high-risk adolescents in cognitive-behavioral preventive interventions. *Applied Developmental Science*, 5,4: 214-224

Prinz, R. (2008). *The Triple P System of Interventions: Background information - Handout accompanies to presentation*. Presented at the San Diego Conference on Child Maltreatment, San Diego, CA.

Proch, K., & Taber, M. A. (1985). Placement disruption: A review of research. *Children & Youth Services Review, 7*(4), 309-320.

Provence, S. (1989). Infants in institutions revisited. *Zero to Three, 9*(4), 1-4.

Puddy, R.W., & Jackson, Y. (2003). The development of parenting skills in foster parent training. *Children and Youth Services Review, 25*(12), 987-1013.

Pumariega, J. (2006)Residential Treatment for Youth: Introduction and a Cautionary Tale. *American Journal of Orthopsychiatry*. 76(3) 281-284.

Pumariega, J. (2006)Residential Treatment for Youth: Introduction and a Cautionary Tale. *American Journal of Orthopsychiatry*. 76(3) 281-284.

Rae-Grant, N., Thomas, B. H., Offord, D. R., & Boyle, M. H. (1989). Risk, protective factors, and the prevalence of behavioral and emotional disorders in children and adolescents. *Journal of American Academy Child and Adolescent Psychiatry, 28*(2), 262-268.

Rainwater, L. & Smeeding, T. (2003). *Poor kids in a rich country: America's children in comparative perspective*. New York: The Russell Sage Foundation.

Ramey, C. T., & Ramey, S. L. (1998). Early intervention and early experience. *American Psychologist, 53*, 109-120.

Ramey, C. T., Campbell, F. A., Burchinal, M., Skinner, M. L., Gardner, D. M., & Ramey, S. L. (2000). Persistent effects of early childhood education on high-risk children and their mothers. *Applied Developmental Science, 4*(1), 2-14.

Ramiall, S. (2004). A review of employee motivation theories and their implications for employee retention within organizations. *The Journal of American Academy of Business, 5*(1/2), 52-63.

Rapp, C. A. (1998). *The strengths model: Case management with people suffering from severe and persistent mental illness.* New York: Oxford University Press.

Rapp, C. A., & Poertner, J. (1988). Moving clients center stage through use of client outcomes. In R.J. Patti, J. Poertner & C.A. Rapp (Eds.), *Managing for service effectiveness insocial welfare organizations.* [A Special Issue of Administration in Social Work, *11*(3-4). New York: Haworth Press.

Rauktis, M.E, Vides de Andrade, A.R., Doucette, A., McDonough, L. & Reinhart, S. (2005). Treatment foster care and relationships: Understanding the role of therapeutic alliance between youth and treatment parent. *International Journal of Child & Family Welfare,* 8,4:146-15.

REACH Institute, Casey Family Programs, & Programs, A. E. C. (2007). *Parent engagement self-assessment manual.* New York: Authors.

Red Horse, J. G., Martinez, C., Day, P., Day, D., Poupart, J., & Sharnberg, D. (2000). *Family preservation: Concepts in American Indian communities.* Seattle, WA: Casey Family Programs,

Reilly, T. (2003). Transition from care: Status and outcomes of youth who age out of foster care. *Child Welfare, 82*(6), 727-746.

Reingold, D., Pirog, M., & Brady, D. (2007). Empirical Evidence on Faith-Based Organizations in an Era of Welfare Reform. *Social Service Review, 81*(2), 245-283.

Reisch, M. (2006). Guest Editorial: Workforce Study Falls Short. *Social Work, 51*(4), 291-293.

Rhodes, J. E. &. DuBois, D.L. (2006). *Understanding and Facilitating the Youth Mentoring Movement.* Washington, DC: Society for Research in Child Development. Retrieved May 30, 2008 from http://www.srcd.org/documents/publications/spr/spr20-3.pdf

Rice, D. L., & McFadden, E. J. (1988). A forum for foster children. *Child Welfare, 67*(3), 231-243.

Ricketts, W. (1991). *Lesbian and gay men as foster parents.* Portland, ME: University of Southern Maine, National Child Welfare Resource Center for Management and Administration.

Ricketts, W., & Achtenberg, R. (1989). Adoption and foster parenting for lesbians and gay men: Creating new traditions in family. *Marriage & Family Review, 14*(3-4), 83-118.

Rindfleisch, N., Bean, G., & Denby, R. (1998). Why foster parents continue and cease to foster. *Journal of Sociology & Social Welfare, 25*(1), 5-24.

Risley-Curtiss, C., & Stites, B. (2007). Improving healthcare for children entering foster care. *Child Welfare, 86*(4), 123-144.

Rivers, J. E., Maze, C. L., Hannah, S. A., & Lederman, C. S. (2007). Domestic Violence Screening and Service Acceptance Among Adult Victims in a Dependency Court Setting. *Child Welfare, 86*(1), 123-144.

Roberts, D. E. (2002). *Racial Disproportionality in the U.S. Child Welfare System: Documentation, Research on Causes, and Promising Practices (Working Paper #4).* Baltimore, MD

Roberts, D. E. (2002). *Shattered Bonds: The Color of Child Welfare.* New York: Civitas Books.

Robins, L. N. (1966). *Deviant children grown up: A sociological and psychiatric study of sociopathic personality.* Baltimore: Williams and Wilkins.

Robison, S. (2006). *Toward a high quality human services workforce: Six doable steps.* Houston, TX: Cornerstones for Kids.

Roditti, M. G. (1995). Child day care: A key building block of family support and family preservation programs. *Child Welfare, 74*(6), 1043-1068.

Roebuck, D. D. (2007). *Historical Overview of the Healthy Start Initiative and the NHSA.* presented at the National Healthy Start Association's Eighth Annual Spring Conference. Retrieved Oct. 24, 2007, from http:\\www.healthystartassoc.org\HS_Overview_2007.pdf

Roman, N. P., & Wolfe, P. B. (1997). The relationship between foster care and homelessness. *Public Welfare, 55*, 4-9.

Rosenberg, M. (1987). New directions for research on the psychological maltreatment of children. *American Psychologist, 42*(2), 166-171.

Rosenberg. (1983). The techniques of psychological assessment as applied to children in foster care and their families. In M. Hardin (Ed.), *Foster care children in the courts* (pp. 550-574).

Rossi, P. H. (1992). Assessing family preservation programs. *Children and Youth Services Review, 14*(1/2), 77-97.

Rothman, D. J. (1980). *Conscience and convenience: The asylum and its alternatives in progressive America*

Rowland, M. D., Halliday-Boykins, C. A., Henggeler, S. W., Cunningham, P. B., Lee, T. G., Kruesi, M. J. P., et al. (2005). A Randomized Trial of Multisystemic Therapy With Hawaii's Felix Class Youths. *Journal of Emotional & Behavioral Disorders, 13*(1), 13-23.

Rubin, D. M., Alessandrini, E. A., Feudtner, C., Mandell, D. S., Localio, A. R., & Hadley, T. (2004). Placement stability and mental health costs for children in foster care. *Pediatrics, 113*(5), 1336.

Rubin, D. M., O'Reilly, A. L. R., Luan, X. Q., & Localio, A. R. (2007). The impact of placement stability on behavioral well-being for children in foster care. *Pediatrics, 119*(2), 336-344.

Rubin, D., Halfon, N., Raghavan, R., & Rosenbaum, S. (2005). *Protecting Children in Foster Care: Why Proposed Medicaid Cuts Harm Our Nation's Most Vulnerable Youth* Seattle, WA: Casey Family Programs.

Rumberger, R. (2003). The causes and consequences of student mobility. *Journal of Negro Education, 72*, 6-21.

Rumberger, R., & Larson, K. (1998). Student mobility and the increased risk of high school dropout. . *American Journal of Education, 107*(1), 1-35.

Runyan, D. K., Curtis, P. A., Hunter, W. M., Black, M. M., Kotch, J. B., Bangdiwala, S., et al. (1998). Improving economic opportunities for young people served by the foster care system: Three views of the path to independent living. *Aggression & Violent Behavior, 3*(3), 275-285.

Russell, M. (1987). *1987 national study of public child welfare job requirements*. Portland, ME: University of Southern Maine, National Child Welfare Resource Center for Management and Administration.

Russo, R. J. (1999). Applying a strengths-based approach in working with people with developmental disabilities and their families. *Families in Society: The Journal of Contemporary Human Services, 80*, 25-33.

Rutter, M. (1979). Protective factors in children's responses to stress and disadvantage. In M. W. Kent & J. E. Rolf (Eds.), *Social competence in children* (Vol. 3). Hanover, NH: University Press of New England.

Rutter, M. (1981). *Maternal Deprivation Reassessed*. London, England: Penguin Books.

Rutter, M. (1981). Stress, coping and development: Some issues and some questions. *Journal of Child Psychology and Psychiatry, 22*(4), 323-356.

Rutter, M. (1985). Resilience in the face of adversity: Protective factors and resistance to psychiatric disorder. *British Journal of Psychiatry, 147*, 598-611.

Rutter, M. (1987). Psychosocial resilience and protective mechanisms. *American Journal of Orthopsychiatry, 57*, 316-331.

Rutter, M. (1989). Intergenerational continuities and discontinuities in serious parenting difficulties. In D. Cicchetti & V. Carlson (Eds.), *Child maltreatment: Theory and research on the causes and consequences of child abuse and neglect* (pp. 317-348). Cambridge, England: Cambridge University Press.

Rutter, M. (1990). Psychosocial resilience and protective mechanisms. In J. Rolf (Ed.), *Risk and protective factors in the development of psychopathology*. Cambridge, NY: Cambridge University Press.

Rutter, M., & Rutter, M. (1993). *Developing minds: Challenge and continuity across the life span.*   New York: Basic Books.

Rutter, M., & Sroufe, L. A. (2000). Developmental psychopathology: concepts and challenges. *Development and Psychopathology, 12*, 265-296.

Ryan, A. M. (2001). The peer group as a context for the development of young adolescent motivation and achievement. *Child Development, 72*, 1135-1150.

Ryan, A. S. (1997). Lessons learned from programs for unaccompanied refugee minors. In G.R. Anderson, A.S. Ryan & B. R. Leashore (Eds.), *The challenge of permanency planning in a multicultural society* (pp. 195-205). New York: The Haworth Press.

Ryan, J. A., & Testa, M. F. (2004). *Child maltreatment and juvenile delinquency: investigating the role of placement and placement instability.* Urbana-Champagn, IL: University of Illinois at Urbana-Champaign School of Social Work, Children and Family Research Center.

Ryan, J. P., Garnier, P., Zyphur, M., & Zhai, F. (2006). Investigating the effects of caseworker characteristics in child welfare. *Children and Youth Services Review, 28*(9), 993-1006.

Ryan, J. P., Marshall, J. M., Herz, D., & Hernandez, P. A. (2008). Juvenile delinquency in child welfare: Investigating group home effects. *Children and Youth Services Review, 30*(9), 1088-1099.Ryan, P., McFadden, E. J., & Warren, B. L. (1981). Foster families: A resource for helping parents. In A. N. Maluccio & P. A. Sinanoglu (Eds.), *The challenge of partnership: Working with parents of children in foster care* (pp. 189-199). New York: Child Welfare League of America.

Ryan, P., McFadden, E. J., Rice, D., & Warren, B. L. (1988). The role of foster parents in helping young people develop emancipation skills. *Child Welfare, 67*(6), 563-572.

Ryan, S.D., Pearlmutter, S., & Groza, V. (2004). Coming out of the closet: Opening agencies to gay and lesbian adoptive parents. *Social Work, 49*(1), 85-95.

Rykus, J. R., & Hughes, R. C. (1998). *Field guide to child welfare, Vol. I-IV.* Washington, DC: Child Welfare League of America Press.

Rykus, J. R., & Hughes, R. C. (1998). *Field guide to child welfare, Vol. IV: Placement and permanence.* Washington, DC: CWLA Press

Rzepnicki, T. L., Schuerman, J. R., & Johnson, P. R. (1997). Facing uncertainty: Reuniting high-risk families. In J.D. Berrick, R.P. Barth & N. Gilbert (Eds.), *Child Welfare Research Review* (Vol. II, pp. 229-251). New York: Columbia University Press.

Rzepnicki, T. L., Schuerman, J. R., Littell, J. H., Chak, A., & Lopez, M. (1994). An experimental study of family preservation services: Early findings from a parent survey. In R. P. Barth, J. D. Berrick & N. Gilbert (Eds.), *Child welfare research review* (pp. 60-82). New York: Columbia University Press.

Saint-Jacques, M., Cloutier, R., Pauze, R., Simard, M., Gagne, M., & Poulin, A. (2006). The Impact of serial transitions on behavioral and psychological problems among children in child protection services. *Child Welfare, 85*(6), 941-964.

Saleebey, D. (Ed.). (1997). *The strengths perspective in social work practice* (Second ed.). New York: Longman Publishers.

Samantrai, K. (1990). MSWs in Public Child Welfare: Why do they stay, and why do they leave, NASW *California News, Sept-Dec 1990.*

Samantrai, K. (1992). Factors in the decision to leave: Retaining social workers and MSWs in public child welfare. *Social Work, 37*(5), 454-458.

SAMSHA (2006). *Building bridges between residential and community based service delivery providers , families and youth.* Position statement available at www.systemsofcare.samsha.gov.

Sanchirico, A., Lau, W., Jablonka, K., & Russell, S. J. (1998). Foster parent involvement in service planning: Does it increase job satisfaction? *Children & Youth Services Review, 20*(4), 325-346.

Savin-Williams, R. C. (1995). Lesbian, gay male, and bisexual adolescents. In A. R. D'augelli & G. J. Patterson (Eds.), *Lesbian, gay and bisexual identities over the life span: Psychological perspectives* (pp. 165-189). New York: Oxford University Press.

Scannapieco, M. (1994). Home-based services program: Effectiveness with at risk families. *Children & Youth Services Review, 16*(5-6), 363-377.

Scannapieco, M., & Hegar, R. L. (Eds.). (1999). *Kinship Foster care--policy, practice, and research.* New York: Oxford University Press.

Scannapieco, M., Schagrin, J., & Scannapieco, T. (1995). Independent living programs: Do they make a difference? *Child & Adolescent Social Work Journal, 12*(5), 381-389.

Scarcella, C. A., Bess, R., Zielewski, E. H., Warner, L., & Geen, R. (2004). *The cost of protecting vulnerable children IV.* Washington, DC: The Urban Institute.

Schene, P. (2001). Meeting Each Family's Needs: Using Differential Response in the Reports of Child Abuse and Neglect. *Best Practice Next Practice*, (Spring 2001), 1-6.

Schiff, M. (2006). Leaving Care: Retrospective reports by alumni of Israeli group homes. *Social Work, 51*(4), 343-353.

Schiraldi, V., & Soler, M. (1998). The will of the people? The public's opinion of the Violent and Repeat Juvenile Offender Act of 1997. *Crime & Delinquency, 44*, 590-601.

Schmid, J., & Pollock, S. (2005). Family group conferencing: A mechanism for empowerment? *Canadian Review of Social Policy, Fall 2004*(54), 128-136.

Schochet, P. Z., Burghardt, J., & Glazerman, S. (2001). *National Job Corps Study: The Impacts of of Job Corps on Participants' Employment and Related Outcomes.* Washington, DC: Department of Labor, Employment and Training Administration.

Schoech, D., & Schkade, L. (1980). Computers helping caseworkers: Decisions support systems. *Child Welfare, 59*, 566-575.

Schoenwald, S. K., & Hoagwood, K. (2001). Effectiveness, transportability, and dissemination of interventions: What matters when? . *Psychiatric Services, 52*, 1190-1197.

Schoenwald, S.K., Borduin, C.K., & Henggeler, S.W. (1998). Multisystemic therapy: Changing the natural and service ecologies of adolescents and families. In Epstein, M. H., Kutash, K., & Duchnowski, A. (Eds.). (1998). *Outcomes for children and youth with emotional and behavioral disorders and their families: Programs and evaluation best practices* (pp.485-511). Austin, TX: Pro-Ed.

Schofield, G., Thoburn, J., Howell, D., & Dickens, J. (2005). The search for stability and permanence: Modeling the pathways of long-stay looked after children. *British Journal of Social Work*(Advance Access - Published Aug. 15, 2005), .

Schorr, E., & Marchand, V. (2007). *Pathways to Prevention of Child Abuse and Neglect*: California Department of Social Services, Children and Family Services Division Office of Child Abuse Prevention. The Pathways Mapping Initiative is also supported by the Annie E. Casey Foundation and the W.K. Kellogg Foundation.

Schorr, L. B. (1997). *Common purpose: Strengthening families and neighborhoods to rebuild America* (1st ed.). New York: Anchor Books.

Schorr, L., & Schorr, D. (1988). *Within our reach: Breaking the cycle of disadvantage.* New York: Anchor.

Schreiner, M. & Sherraden, M. (2007). *Can the poor save?* New Brunswick, NJ: Transaction Publishers.

Schriver, J. M. (1995). *Human behavior and the social environment: Shifting paradigms in essential knowledge for social work practice.* Boston: Allyn and Bacon.

Schuerman, J. R., Rzepnicki, T. L., & Littell, J. H. (1994). *Putting families first: An experiment in family preservation.* Hawthorne: Aldine de Gruyter.

Schuerman, J. R., Rzepnicki, T. L., Littell, J. H., & Chak, A. (1993). *Evaluation of the Illinois Family First placement prevention program: Final report.* Chicago, IL: Chapin Hall Center for Children, The University of Chicago.

Schulte, B. (2006, October 9). Virginia parents trying to unadopt trouble boy: Mother says caseworker failed to disclose child's stormy history. *The Washington Post,* pp. A01. Retrieved February 14, 2007 from http://www.washingtonpost.com/wpdyn/content/article/2006/10/08/AR2006100801

Schwartz, A. E. (2002). Societal Value and the Funding of Kinship Care. *Social Service Review, 76*(3), 430-459.

Schwartz, I. M. (1984). Getting tough with juveniles. *Public Welfare, 42,* 28-31.

Schwartz, I. M., & AuClaire, P. (1995). *Home-based services for troubled children.* Lincoln, NE: University of Nebraska Press.

Schweigert, F. J. (2006). The Meaning of Effectiveness in Assessing Community Initiatives. *American Journal of Evaluation, 27*(4), 416-436.

Scott, S., Bruner, C., Hastings, J., & Perlowski, K. (1995). *Family preservation services or placement: How to decide - The views of front-line workers and supervisors in Iowa.* Des Moines, IO: The Child and Family Policy Center.

Sedlak, A. J. (2001). A history of the National Incidence Study of Child Abuse and Neglect. Rockville, MD: Westat, Inc. Retrieved February 15, 2008 from https://www.nis4.org/NIS_History.pdf

Sedlak, A., & Schultz, D. (2001). Race Differences in Risk of Maltreatment in the General Child Population. In D. M. Derezotes, J. Poertner & M. F. Testa (Eds.), *Race Matters in Child Welfare; The Overrepresentation of African American Children in the System.* Washington, DC: CWLA Press.

See, L. A. (Ed.). (1998). *Human behavior in the social environment from an African American perspective.* Binghamton: The Haworth Press.

Selwyn, J., Sturgess, W., Quinton, D., & Baxter, C. (2006). *Costs and outcomes of non-infant adoptions.* London, England: British Association for Adoption and Fostering.

Selznick, P. (1984). *Leadership in administration.* Berkeley, CA: University of California Press.

Semidei, J., Radel, L. F., & Nolan, C. (2001). Substance abuse and child welfare: clear linkages and promising responses. *Child Welfare, 80*(2), 109-128.

Senge, P., Roberts, C., Ross, R., Smith, B., & Kleiner, A. (1994). *The fifth discipline fieldbook: Strategies and tools for building a learning organization.* New York: Doubleday.

Shapiro, T. & Wolff, E. (eds.). (2001). *Assets for the poor: The benefits of spreading asset ownership.* New York: The Russell Sage Foundation.

Shaw, T.V. (2006). *The Multi-ethnic Placement Act.* Unpublished paper, School of Social Welfare, University of California at Berkeley.

Sheehy, A. M., Oldham, E., Zanghi, M., Ansell, D., Correia, P., & Copeland, R. (2002). *Promising Practices: Supporting Transition of Youth Served by the Foster Care System*. Baltimore, Md: The Annie E. Casey Foundation.

Shonkoff, J. P. (2004). *Closing the gap between what we know, and what we do*. Chicago, IL: Ounce of Prevention Fund.

Shonkoff, J. P., & Phillips, D. A. (2000). *From neurons to neighborhoods: The science of early childhood development*. Washington, DC: National Academy Press.

Shulman, L. (1993). *Interactional supervision*. Washington, DC: National Association of Social Work Press.

Shulman, L. (1998). *Skills of helping individual families, groups, and communities* (4th ed.). Pacific Grove: Wadsworth Publishing.

Shustermann, G. R., Hollinshead, D., Fluke, J. D., & Tuan, Y. T. (2005). *Alternative responses to child maltreatment: Findings from NCANDS*. Washington, DC: Office of the Assistant Secretary for Planning and Evaluation, U.S. Department of Health and Human Services. Retrieved February 21, 2008 from http://aspe.hhs.gov/hsp/05/child-maltreat-resp/

Shyne, A., & Schroeder, A. W. (1978). *National study of social services to children and their families*. Rockville, MD: Westat.

Sia, C. C. J., & Breakey, G. F. (1985). The role of the medical home in child abuse prevention and positive child development. *Hawaii Medical Journal, 44*(7).

Siegel, L., & Lane, I. M. (1982). *Personnel and organizational psychology*. Homewood, IL: Richard D. Irwin.

Silver, J., DiLorenzo, P., Zukoski, M., Ross, P. E., Amster, B. J., & Schlegel, D. (1999). Starting young: Improving the health and developmental outcomes of infants and toddlers in the child welfare system. *Child Welfare, 78*(1), 148-165.

Simms, M. D., & Halfon, N. (1994). The health care needs of children in foster care: a research agenda. *Child Welfare, 73*(5), 505-524.

Sinclair, I. (2006). "Residential care in the UK. In C. McAuley, P.J. Pecora and W. Rose (Eds.) *Enhancing the well-being of children and families through effective interventions: international evidence for practice*, edited by. London: Jessica Kingsley Publishers, pp. 203-216.

Sinclair, R. (1998). Involving children in planning their care. *Child and Family Social Work, 3*, 137-142.

Singer, J. D., & Butler, J. A. (1987). The education for all handicapped children act: Schools as agents of social reform. *Harvard Educational Review, 57*(2), 125-152.

Singh, N. N., Lancioni, G. E., Singh Joy, S. D., Winton, A. S. W., Sabaawi, M., Wahler, R. G., et al. (2007). Adolescents with conduct disorder can be mindful of their aggressive behavior. *Journal of Emotional & Behavioral Disorders, 15*(1), 56-63.

Slingerland, W. H. (1919). *Child-placing in families*. New York: Russell Sage Foundation.

Smeeding, T. (2006). Government programs and social outcomes: The United States in comparative perspective. In A. Auerbach, D. Card and J. Quigley (eds.). *Public policy and the income distribution*. **New York: Russell Sage Foundation, pp. 149-218.**

Smith, B. (2005). Job retention in child welfare: Effects of perceived organizational support, supervisor support, and intrinsic job value. *Children & Youth Services Review, 28*(2), 153-169.

Smith, S. L., Howard, J. A., Garnier, P. C., & Ryan, S. D. (2006). Where are we now?: A post-ASFA examination of adoption disruption. *Adoption Quarterly: Innovations in community and clinical practice, theory, and research, 9*(4), 19-44.

Social Security Administration (2006). Annual Statistical Supplement, 2005. http://www.ssa.gov/policy/docs/statcomps/supplement/2005/5f.pdf, accessed May 9, 2007.

Social Security Administration (2007). Annual Statistical Supplement, 2006. http://www. ssa.gov/policy/docs/statcomps/supplement/2006/5f.pdf, accessed May 9, 2007.

Social Security Administration. (2000). Supplemental Security Income. Determining disability for a child under 18. Final rules. *Federal Register, September 11*(65), 54747-54790.

Solomon, B. (1976). *Black empowerment: Social work in oppressed communities*. New York: Columbia University Press.

Sorensen, J. B. (2002). The strength of corporate culture and the reliability of firm performance. *Administrative Science Quarterly, 47*, 70-91.

Sorenson, E. & Oliver, H. (2002). Policy reforms are needed to increase child support from poor fathers. Working paper, The Urban Institute, April.

Sotomayor, M. (Ed.). (1991). *Empowering Hispanic families: A critical issue for the '90s*. Milwaukee, WI: Family Service America.

Spaccarotelli, C. (2003). *Adoption and Safe Families Act: Has it made a difference?* . Washington, DC: Court Appointed Special Advocates Association.

Spaid, W. M., & Fraser, M. (1991). The correlates of success/failure in brief and intensive family treatment: Implications for family preservation services. *Children & Youth Services Review, 13*(1-2), 77-99.

Spar, K., & C. Devere (2001). Child Welfare Financing: Issues and Options. *Washington, DC: Congressional* Research Service.

Specht, H., & Courtney, M. E. (1994). *Unfaithful angels: How social work has abandoned its mission*. New York: Free Press.

Spielberger, J., Lyons, S., Gouvea, M., Haywood, T., & Winje, C. (2007). *The Palm Beach County Longitudinal Study Second Annual Report, Executive Summary*. Chicago, IL: Chapin Hall Center for Children.

Spoth, R. L., Kavanaugh, K. A., & Dishion, T. J. (2002). Family-centered preventive intervention science: Toward benefits to larger populations of children, youth and families. *Prevention Science, 3*, 145-152.

Stack, C. (1974). *All our kin: Strategies for survival in the Black Community*. New York: Harper and Row.

Staff, E., & Fein, E. (1994). Inside the black box: An exploration of service delivery in a family reunification program. *Child Welfare, 73*, 195-211.

Stalker, C. A., Mandell, D., Frensch, K. M., Harvey, C., & Wright, M. (2007). Child welfare workers who are exhausted yet satisfied with their jobs: How do they do it? *Child and Family Social Work, 12*(2), 182-191.

Stambaugh, L., Burns, B. J., Landsverk, J. A., & Reutz, J. R. (2007). Evidence-based treatment for children in child welfare. *Focal Point, 21*(1), 12-15.

Starfield, B. & Budetti, P. (1985). Child health status and risk factors. *Health Services Research*, 19:6 (February, part II): 817-886.

Starling, S. P., Holden, J. S., & Jenny, C. (1995). Abusive head trauma: The relationship of perpertrators to their victims. *Pediatrics, 95*, 259-262.

State of California Department of Social Services. (1987). *Characteristics of relinquishment adoptions in California, July, 1986: June, 1987*. Sacramento: Author.

Stehno, S. M. (1990). The elusive continuum of child welfare services: implications for minority children and youths. *Child Welfare, 69*(6), 551-562.

Stein, T. (1984). The Child Abuse Prevention and Treatment Act. *Social Service Review, 58*(2), 302-314.

Stein, T. (1998). *Child welfare and the law* (Revised ed.). Washington, DC: Child Welfare League of America.

Stein, T. J. (1985). Projects to prevent out-of-home placement. *Children & Youth Services Review, 7*(2-3), 109-121.

Stein, T. J. (1996). Child custody and visitation: The rights of lesbian and gay parents. *Social Service Review, 70*, 435-450.

Stein, T. J. (2003). The Adoption and Safe Families Act: How Congress overlooks available data and ignores systemic obstacles in pursuit of its political goals. *Children & Youth Services Review, 25*, 669-682.

Stein, T. J., & Rzepnicki, T. L. (1983). *Decision making at child welfare intake: A handbook for practitioners.* Washington, DC: Child Welfare League of America

Stein, T. J., Gambrill, E. D., & Wiltse, K. T. (1978). *Children in foster homes: Achieving continuity of care.* New York: Praeger.

Stevenson, K. M., Cheung, K.-F. M., & Leung, P. (1992). A new approach to training child protective services workers for ethnically sensitive practice. *Child Welfare, 71*(4), 291-305.

Stolley, K.S. (1993). Statistics on adoption in the United States. *The Future of Children. 3*(1), 26-42.

Stone, S. (2007). Child maltreatment, out-of-home placement and academic vulnerability: A fifteen-year review of evidence and future directions. *Children & Youth Services Review, 29*(2), 139-161.

Stovall, B. M., & Krieger, R. (1990). Preparing minority foster adolescents for adulthood: The need for ethnic competence. In A.N. Maluccio., R. Krieger & B.A. Pine (Eds.), *Preparing adolescents for life after foster care: The central role of foster parents* (pp. 147-161). Washington, DC: Child Welfare League of America.

Straus, M. A., Kinard, E. M., & Williams, L. J. (1995, July 23). The Neglect Scale. Paper presented at the Fourth International Conference on Family Violence Research, Durhan, NH.

Strolin, J. S., McCarthy, M., & Caringi, J. (2007). Causes and effects of child welfare workforce turnover: current state of knowledge and future directions. *Journal of Public Child Welfare, 1*(2), 29-52.

Stroul, B. A. (2002). *Systems of care: A framework for system reform in children's mental health (Issue brief).* Washington, DC: Georgetown University Child Development Center,

Stroul, B. A., & Friedman, R. M. (1996). The system of care concept and philosophy. In B. A. Stroul (Ed.), *Children's mental health: Creating systems of care in a changing society.* Baltimore: Paul H. Brookes Publishing.

Susser, E. S., Lin, S. P., Conover, S. A., & Struening, E. L. (1991). Childhood antecedents of homelessness in psychiatric patients. *Am J Psychiatry, 148*(8), 1026-1030.

Sweet, M., & Applebaum, M. (2004). Is home visting an effective strategy? A meta-analytic review of home visting programs for families with young children. *Child Development, 75*, 1435-1456.

Swenson, C.C., Henggeler, S.W., Taylor, I.S. and Addison, O.W. (2005). *Multisystemic therapy and neighborhood partnerships: Reducing adolescent violence and substance abus*e. New York & London: Guilford.

Taber, M. A., & Proch, K. (1987). Placement stability for adolescents in foster care: Findings from a program experiment. *Child Welfare, 66*(5), 433-445.

Takayama, J. I., Bergman, A. B., & Connell, F. A. (1994). Children in foster care in the state of Washington. Health care utilization and expenditures. *JAMA: Journal of the American Medical Association, 271*(23), 1850-1855.

Tatara, T. (1994). Some additional explanations for the recent rise in the U.S. child substitute care flow data and future research questions. In R.P. Barth, J.D. Berrick, & N. Gilbert (Eds.), *Child welfare research review* (pp. 126-145). New York: Columbia University Press.

Taussig, H. N., Clyman, R. B., & Landsverk, J. (2001). Children who return home from foster care: a 6-year prospective study of behavioral health outcomes in adolescence. *Pediatrics, 108*(1), E10.

Taylor, M. S. (1988). The effects of feedback on the behavior of organizational personnel. In R.J. Patti, J. Poertner & C. A. Rapp (Eds.), *Managing for service effectiveness in social welfare organizations* (pp. 191-204). New York: Haworth Press.

Testa, M. (1997). Kinship foster care in Illinois. In J.D. Berrick, R. Barth & N. Gilbert (Eds.), *Child Welfare Research Review* (Vol. 2, pp. 101-129). New York: Columbia University Press.

Testa, M. F. (2001). Kinship care and permanency. *Journal of Social Service Research, 28*(1), 25-43.

Testa, M. F. (2002). Subsidized guardianship: Testing an idea whose time has finally come. *Social Work Research, 26*(3), 145-158.

Testa, M. (in press). Kinship care policies for the next century. *The Future of Children.*

Testa, M. F., & Slack, K. S. (2002). The gift of kinship foster care. *Children & Youth Services Review, 24*(1-2), 79-108.

The Business Council and The Conference Board Partnership for 21st Century Skills, Corporate Voices for Working Families, and Society for Human Resource Management. (2006). *The business council survey of chief executives: CEO survey results, February 2006*: The Business Council and the Conference Board.

The Children and Family Research Center. (1999). *A child welfare research agenda for the State of Illinois*. Urbana, IL: The Children and Family Research Center, University of Illinois at Urbana-Champaign

The David and Lucille Packard Foundation. (1999). *The future of children home visiting: Recent program evaluations 9(1)*. Los Altos, CA: The David and Lucille Packard Foundation.

The National Academy of Sciences, Committee on Crossing the Quality Chasm: Adaptation to Mental Health and Addictive Disorders Board on Health Care Services. (2006). *Improving the Quality of Health Care for Mental and Substance-Abuse Conditions.* Washington, DC: Author.

The NSCAW Research Group. (2002). Methodological Lessons from the National Survey of Child and Adolescent Well-Being: The First Three Years of the USA's First National Probability Study of Children and Families Investigated for Abuse and Neglect. *Children and Youth Services Review, 24*(6-7), 513-541.

The Urban Institute, University of California Berkeley, & University of North Carolina at Chapel Hill. (2008). Coming of age: Employment outcomes for youth who age out of foster care through their middle twenties. Retrieved April 18, 2008, from http://aspe.hhs.gov/hsp/08/fosteremp/index.html

Theodore, A., Runyan, D., & Chang, J. J. (2007). Measuring the risk of physical neglect in a population-based sample. *Child Maltreatment, 12*, 96-105.

Thoburn, J., Murdoch, A., & O'Brien, A. (1986). *Permanence in child care*. Oxford, England: Basil Blackwell.

Thomas, D. A., & Ely, R. J. (2002). Making differences matter: A new paradigm for managing diversity. *Harvard Business Review on Managing Diversity*, 33-66.

Thomas, G. (1994). Travels in the trench between child welfare theory and practice: A case study of failed promises and prospects for renewal. *Children & Youth Services Review, 17*(1-2).

Thomlison, B. (2004). Child maltreatment: A risk and protective factor perspective in child maltreatment. In M.W. Fraser (Ed.), Risk *and resilience in childhood* (2nd ed.). (pp. 89-131). Washington, DC: NASW Press.

Thompson, R. A. (1995). *Preventing child maltreatment through social support: A critical analysis*. Thousand Oak, CA: Sage Publications.

Thompson, R. W., Huefner, J. C., Ringle, J. L., & Daly, D. L. (2004). *Adult outcomes of Girls and Boys Town youth: A follow-up report*. Paper presented at the 17th Annual Florida Mental Health Institute Conference. A system of care for children's mental health: Expanding the research base, Tampa: University of South Florida.

Timmer, S. G., Urquiza, A. J., Herschell, A. D., McGrath, J. M., Zebell, N. M., Porter, A. L., et al. (2006). Parent-Child Interaction Therapy: Application of an empirically supported treatment to maltreated children in foster care. *Child Welfare, 85*(6), 919-940.

Timmons-Mitchell, J., Bender, M. B., Kishna, M. A., & Mitchell, C. C. (2006). An independent effectiveness trial of multisystemic therapy with juvenile justice youth. *Journal of Clinical Child and Adolescent Psychology, 35*(2), 227-236.

Tjaden, P., & Thoennes, N. (2000). *Full report of the prevalence, incidence, and consequences of violence against women*. Washington, DC: U.S. Department of Justice, National Institute of Justice.

Tracy, E. (1994). Maternal substance abuse: Protecting the child, preserving the family. *Social Work, 39*, 534-540.

Tracy, E. M. (1990). Identifying social support resources of at-risk families. *Social Work, 35*(3), 252-258.

Tracy, E. M. (1995). Family preservation and home-based services. In R. L. Edwards & J. G. Hopps (Eds.), *Encyclopedia of Social Work* (19th ed., Vol. 2, pp. 973-983).

Trieschman, A. E., Whittaker, J. K., & Brendtro, L. K. (1969). *The other 23 hours: Child care work with emotional disturbed children in a therapeutic milieu*. New York: Aldine de Gruyter.

Triseliotis, J. (2002). Long-term foster care or adoption: The evidence examined. *Child and Family Social Work, 7*, 23-33.

Triseliotis, J., & Russell, J. (1984). *Hard to Place: The Outcome of Adoption and Residential Care*. London: Heinemann Educational Books.

Trocme, N. (1996). Development and preliminary evaluation of the Ontario Neglect Index. *Child Maltreatment, 1*, 145-155.

Tsui, M. S. (1997). Empirical research on social work supervision: The state of the art, 1970-1995. *Journal of Social Service Research, 23*(2), 39-51.

Tsui, M. S. (1997). The roots of social work supervision: An historical review. *Clinical Supervisor, 15*(2), 191-198.

Tsui, M. S. (2004). *Social work supervision: Contexts and concepts*. Thousand Oaks, CA: Sage Press.

U. S. Department of Health and Human Services (2005). *National Survey of Child and Adolescent Well-Being (NSCAW) CPS sample component wave 1 data analysis report*. Retrieved February 24, 2008 from http://www.acf.hhs.gov/programs/opre/abuse_neglect/nscaw/reports/cps_sample/cps_report_revised_090105.pdf

U. S. Department of Health and Human Services, Administration for Children and Families. (2003). Positive Youth Development. Retrieved August 7, 2003 from http://www.ncfy.com/ydfactsh.htm

U. S. Department of Health and Human Services, Administration for Children and Families,. (2005). *Alternative responses to child maltreatment: Findings from NCANDS*. Washington, DC: Author.

U. S. Department of Health and Human Services, Children's Bureau, Administration on Children, Youth and Families, National Clearinghouse on Child Abuse and Neglect Information. (2003). *Child maltreatment 2001*. Washington, DC: US government Printing Office.

U. S. Department of Health and Human Services, National Center on Child Abuse and Neglect. (1996). *Study findings: Study of national incidence and prevalence of child abuse and neglect (NIS-3)*. Washington, DC: Author.

U. S. Department of Health and Human Services. (2003). *The AFCARS report: Preliminary FY 2001 estimates as of March 2003*. Washington, DC

U. S. Department of Health and Human Services. (2003). *The AFCARS report: Preliminary FY 2001 estimates as of March 2003*. Washington, DC

U. S. General Accounting Office. (1994). *Residential care: Some high-risk youth benefit, but more study needed.* (Available from GAO, P.O. Box 6015, Gaithersburg, MD 20884-6015, U.S.A.)

U.S. Administration for Children and Families. (2003). *Children of Color in the Child Welfare System: Perspectives from the Child Welfare Community*. Washington, DC: US Department of Health and Human Services.

U.S. Advisory Board on Child Abuse and Neglect. (1991). *Creating caring communities*. Washington, DC: U.S. Department of Health and Human Services.

U.S. Bureau of the Census, American Community Profile. (2005). *Table 1. General Demographic Characteristics*.

U.S. Bureau of the Census, Current Population Survey, & Bureau(200b). *Special tabulations of the supplementary survey*. Washington, DC: Author.

U.S. Bureau of the Census, Population Estimates. (2005). *State Single Year of Age and Sex Population Estimates: April 1, 2000 to July 1, 2005*. Washington, DC: Author.

U.S. Bureau of the Census. (2004). *Facts for Features: Special Edition for national adoption month*. Washington, DC: Author.

U.S. Bureau of the Census. (2005). *Household Relationship and Living Arrangements of Children Under 18 Years, by Age, Sex, Race, Hispanic Origin: (Table C2)*. Washington, DC: Author.

U.S. Census Bureau (2006). Current Population Reports, P60-230, Custodial mothers and fathers and their child support: 2003. http://www.census.gov/hhes/www/childsupport/chldsu03.pdf accessed May 11, 2007.

U.S. Census Bureau (2007a).Poverty thresholds 2006. http://www.census.gov/hhes/www/poverty/threshld/thresh06.html, accessed May 10, 2007.

U.S. Census Bureau (2007b). *Statistical Abstract of the United States*. Washington, DC: Government Printing Office.

U.S. Census Bureau (2007c). Historical Poverty Tables. http://www.census.gov/hhes/www/poverty/histpov/hstpov4.html, accessed 18 July 2007.

U.S. Census Bureau. (2006a). *Americans Marrying Older, Living Alone More, See Households Shrinking, Census Bureau Reports*. Washington, DC: Author.

U.S. Department of Agriculture, Food and Nutrition Services, Office of Analysis,, Nutrition and Evaluation. (2007). *WIC Participant and Program Characteristics 2006 (WIC-06-PC)*. Alexandria, VA: Author. See http://www.fns.usda.gov/oane/MENU/Published/WIC/FILES/pc2006.pdf.

U.S. Department of Agriculture, Food, and Nutrition Services, Office of Analysis, Nutrition and Evaluation. (2001). *WIC Nutrition Education Demonstration Study: Child Intervention (CN-01-WICNECI)*. Alexandria, VA: Author.

U.S. Department of Commerce, National Institute of Standards and Technology [NIST] - Technology Administration. (2007). *2006 Baldridge National Quality Program: Criteria for Performance Excellence*. Gaithersburg, MD: Institute of Standards and Technology, Technology Administration. (Retrieved February 2, 2007 from http://www.quality.nist.gov).

U.S. Department of Health and Human Services (1999a). *Blending perspectives and building common ground. A report to Congress on substance abuse and child protection*. Washington, DC: U.S. Government Printing Office.

U.S. Department of Health and Human Services (undated-A). Welcome to the NIS-4. Retrieved February 15, 2008 from https://www.nis4.org/nishome.asp

U.S. Department of Health and Human Services (undated-B). *Table A: Data indicators for the Child and Family Services Review.* Retrieved April 3, 2008 from http://www.acf.hhs.gov/programs/cb/cwmonitoring/data_indicators.htm

U.S. Department of Health and Human Services, ACYF Children's Bureau. (2000). *The AFCARS Report: Current Estimates as of March, 31 1999.* Washington, DC: Author.

U.S. Department of Health and Human Services, Administration for Children and Families, Children's Bureau. (1998). *Child Maltreatment 1996: Reports from the states to the national child abuse and neglect data system.* Washington, DC: U.S. Government Printing Office.

U.S. Department of Health and Human Services, Administration for Children and Families,, Children's Bureau. (1999b). *Child maltreatment 1997: Reports from the states to the national child abuse and neglect data system.* Washington, DC: U.S. Government Printing Office.

U.S. Department of Health and Human Services, Administration for Children and Families, Children's Bureau. (1999c). *Title IV-E Independent Living Programs: A Decade in Review.* Washington, DC: Author.

U.S. Department of Health and Human Services, Administration for Children and Families. (2001). *Child maltreatment 1999 - Ten years of reporting.* Washington, DC: U.S. Government Printing Office.

U.S. Department of Health and Human Services, Administration for Children and Families,, Children's Bureau. (2004). *Adoption and Foster Care Analysis and Reporting System (AFCARS) Data as of May 2004.* Washington, DC: U.S. Department of Health and Human Services.

U.S. Department of Health and Human Services, Administration for Children and Families Administration on Children, Youth and Families, Children's Bureau. (2004a). *Adoption and Foster Care Analysis and Reporting System (AFCARS). Data as of May 2004.* Washington, DC: U.S. Government Printing Office.

U.S. Department of Health and Human Services, Administration for Children and Families,, Children's Bureau. (2004b). *Child maltreatment 2002.* Washington, DC: U.S. Government Printing Office.

U.S. Department of Health and Human Services, Administration for Children and Families, Children's Bureau. (2004c). *Child welfare outcomes 2003: Annual Report.* Washington, DC: Administration for Children and Families, Children's Bureau.

U.S. Department of Health and Human Services, Administration for Children and Families, Children's Bureau (2006c). The AFCARS report No. 13: Preliminary FY 2005 estimates as of September 2006. Washington, DC: US Department of Health and Human Services. Retrieved from http://www.acf.hhs.gov/programs/cb/stats_research/afcars/tar/report13.htm

U.S. Department of Health and Human Services, Administration for Children and Families (2007a). Caseload data. Retrieved December 6, 2007 from http://www.acf.hhs.gov/programs/ofa/caseload/caseloadindex.htm#2006

U.S. Department of Health and Human Services, Administration for Children and Families, Children's Bureau. (2007b). *Child Maltreatment 2005.* Washington, DC: National Child Abuse and Neglect Data System.

U.S. Department of Health and Human Services, Administration for Children and Families, Children's Bureau. (2007d). *Foster Care FY 1999-FY2004: Entries, exits, and numbers of children in care on the last day of each federal fiscal year.* Retrieved May 26, 2007, from http://www.acf.dhhs.gov/programs/cb/stats_research/afcars/statistics/entryexit2004.htm

U.S. Department of Health and Human Services, Administration for Children and Families, Children's Bureau (2008b). The AFCARS Report No. 14: Preliminary FY 2006 estimates as of January 2008. Washington, DC: US Department of Health and Human Services. Retrieved from http://www.acf.hhs.gov/programs/cb/stats_research/afcars

U.S. Department of Health and Human Services, Administration on Children, Youth and Families, National Center on Child Abuse and Neglect. (1993). A *report to Congress: Study of child maltreatment in alcohol abusing families.* Washington, DC: National Center on Child Abuse and Neglect.

U.S. Department of Health and Human Services, Administration on Children, Youth and Families, National Clearinghouse on Child Abuse and Neglect Information,. (2003a). *Child Maltreatment 2001.* Washington, DC: US Government Printing Office.

U.S. Department of Health and Human Services, Administration on Children, Youth and Families,, Children's Bureau,, Administration for Children and Families,, Office of Child Abuse and Neglect. (2003b). *Emerging practices in the prevention of child abuse and neglect.* Washington, DC: Author.

U.S. Department of Health and Human Services, Administration on Children, Youth and Families, Children's Bureau. (2003d). *Safety, Permanency and Well-Being: Child Welfare Outcomes 1998, 1999 & 2000* Washington, DC: Author.

U.S. Department of Health and Human Services, Administration on Children, Youth and Families, & National Clearinghouse on Child Abuse and Neglect Information. (2005). *Alternative responses to child maltreatment: Findings from NCANDS.* Washington, DC: Author.

U.S. Department of Health and Human Services, Administration on Children, Youth and Families. (2006b). *Child Maltreatment 2004* Washington, DC: U.S. Government Printing Office.

U.S. Department of Health and Human Services, Administration on Children, Youth and Families (2008a). *Child maltreatment 2006.* Washington, DC: U.S. Government Printing Office.

U.S. Department of Health and Human Services, Departmental Appeals Board. (2006a). *Case of Ohio Department of Job and Family Services.* Retrieved February 14, 2007, from http://www. hhs.gov/dab/decisions/dab2023.htm

U.S. Department of Health and Human Services, Office of the Assistant Secretary for Planning and Evaluation, (2003c). *National Study of Child Protective Services Systems and Reform Efforts: A Summary Report.* Washington, DC: US Department of Health and Human Services, Office of the Assistant Secretary for Planning and Evaluation.

U.S. Department of Health and Human Services, US Children's Bureau. (2002). *Trends in Foster Care and Adoption as of 11/01/02.* Washington, DC: US Department of Health and Human Services.

U.S. Department of Health and Human Services. (1999). *Blending perspectives and building common ground. A report to Congress on substance abuse and child protection.* Washington, DC: US Department of Health and Human Services

U.S. Department of Health and Human Services. (2004). How many children were adopted in 2000 and 2001? Washington, DC: Child Welfare Information Gateway. Retrieved February 8, 2007 from http://www.childwelfare.gov/pubs/s_adopted/s_adopted.pdf

U.S. Department of Health and Human Services. (2005). *Alternative Responses to Child Maltreatment: Findings from NCANDS.* Washington, DC: US Department of Health and Human Services, Office of the Assistant Secretary for Planning and Evaluation.

U.S. Department of Health and Human Services. (2005). *General findings from the federal Child and Family Services Review.* Washington, DC: Author.

U.S. Department of Health and Human Services. (2007c). *Fiscal Year 2007 Budget in Brief.* Retrieved on April 19, 2007 from http://www.hhs.gov/budget/parts.html

U.S. Department of State. (n.d.). *Immigrant visas issued to orphans coming to the U.S.* Retrieved April 22, 2007, from http://travel.state.gov/family/adoption/stats/stats_451.html#

U.S. General Accounting Office (1993). *Foster Care: Services to prevent out-of-home placements are limited by funding barriers.* Washington DC: Author (HRD 93-76).

U.S. General Accountability Office. (2005). *Better Data and Evaluation could Improve Processes and Program for Adopting Children with Special Needs.* Washington, DC: U.S. General Accountability Office.

U.S. General Accounting Office (1997). *Child protective services: Complex challenges require new strategies* (GAO/HEHS-97-115, July 21, 1997). Washington, DC: Author.

U.S. General Accounting Office. (1995). *Child Welfare complex Needs Strain Capacity to Provide Services. Report to Congressional Committees.* Washington, DC: Author.

U.S. General Accounting Office. (1998). *Foster Care: Implementation of the Multiethnic Placement Act Poses Difficult Challenges (GAO/HEHS-98-204).* Washington, DC: Author.

U.S. General Accounting Office. (2003). *HHS Could Play a Greater Role in Helping Child Welfare Agencies Recruit and Retain Staff.* Washington, DC: Author.

U.S. Government Accountability Office. (2007). *African American children in foster care: Additional HHS assistance needed to help states reduce the proportion in care. (GAO 07-816).* Washington, DC: Author.

U.S. Government Accounting Office. (2004). *Child and family services reviews better use of data and improved guidance could enhance HHS's oversight of state performance* (No. GAO-04-333). Washington, DC: US Government Printing Office.

U.S. House of Representatives, Ways and Means Committee. (2000). *2000 Green Book.* Washington, DC: Author.

U.S. Internal Revenue Service (2009). Table 4—Returns with Earned Income Credit, by Size of Adjusted Gross Income, Tax Year 2006. Retrieved March 15, 2009. From: http://www.irs.gov/pub/irs-soi/06in04ic.xls, accessed May 10, 2007.

U.S. Office of Child Support Enforcement (2005). Child support enforcement, FY 2004, Preliminary report. http://www.acf.dhhs.gov/programs/cse/pubs/2005/reports/preliminary_report/table_12.html, accessed May 11, 2007.

U.S. Senate, Committee on Finance. (1990). *Foster care, adoption assistance, and child welfare services.* Washington, DC: U.S. Government Printing Office.

Ulrich, D. (1998). A new mandate for human resources. *Harvard Business Review*(Reprint No. 98111).

Unger, S. (Ed.). (1978). *The destruction of American Indian families.* New York: Association on American Indian Affairs.

UNICEF (2007). Child poverty in perspective An overview of child well-being in rich countries, *Innocenti Report Card* 7, UNICEF Innocenti Research Centre, Florence, Italy.

United States Department of Justice. (2006). General information regarding the Combat Methamphetamine Epidemic Act of 2005. US Department of Justice, Drug Enforcement Administration, Office of Diversion Control. Retrieved February 26, 2008 from www.deadiversion.usdoj.gov/meth/cma2005.htm

United States General Accounting Office. (1995). *Foster Care: Health needs of many young children are unknown and unmet.* Washington, DC U/ S/ Government Printing Service.

United States General Accounting Office. (1999). *Effectiveness of Independent Living Services Unknown.* Retrieved. from.

United States General Accounting Office. (1999). *Foster Care: Effectiveness of Independent Living Services Unknown (GAO/HEHS-00-13).* Retrieved. from.

United States General Accounting Office. (2002). *Foster Care Recent Legislation Helps States Focus on Finding Permanent Homes for Children, but Long-Standing Barriers Remain - GAO Report -02-585.* Retrieved. from.

United States General Accounting Office. (2004). *Foster Youth: HHS Actions Could Improve Coordination of Services and Monitoring of States' Independent Living Programs.* Washington, DC: GAO.

Unknown. (2002). *The Impact of ASFA on Children and Families of Color, Proceedings of a Forum.* Washington, DC: Child Welfare League of America.

Unrau, Y. A. (2007). Research on Placement Moves: Seeking the perspectives of foster children. *Children & Youth Services Review, 29*(1), 122-137.

US Bureau of Labor Statistics. (2001-02). *Occupational Outlook Quarterly.* Washington, DC: Author.

Usher, C. L., Randolph, K. A., & Gogan, H. C. (1999). Placement patterns in foster care. *Social Service Review, 73*, 22-36.

Vanderploeg, J. J., Connell, C. M., Caron, C., Saunders, L., Katz, K. H., & Tebes, J. K. (2007). The impact of parental alcohol or drug removals on foster care placement experiences: A matched comparison group study. *Child Maltreatment, 12*, 125-136.

Veronico, A. (1983). One church, one child: Placing children with special needs. *Children Today, 12*, 6-10.

Von Korff, L., Grotevant, H.D., & McRoy, R.G. (2006). Openess arrangements and psychological   adjustment in adolescent adoptees. *Journal of Family Psychology, 20*(3), 531-534.

Wakefield, J. C. (1996). Does Social Work need the eco-system perspective? Part 1. Is the perspective useful? . *Social Service Review, 7*, 1-32.

Wald, J. S. (1976). State Intervention on Behalf of "neglected" children: Standards for removal of children from their homes, monitoring the status of children in foster care, and the termination of parental rights. *Stanford Law Review, 28*, 623-645.

Wald, J. S., & Bruns, E. J. (2006). The wraparound process: Individualized care planning and management for children and families. . In S. Rosenberg & J. Rosenberg (Eds.), *Community Mental Health Reader: Current Perspectives*: Routledge.

Wald, M. (1976). State intervention on behalf of "neglected" children: Standards for removal of children from their homes, monitoring the status of children in foster care, and termination of parental rights. *Stanford Law Review, 28*, 623, 645.

Wald, M. S. (1980). Thinking about public policy toward abuse and neglect of children: A review of "before the best interests of the child". . *Michigan Law Review, 78*, 645-693.

Waldfogel, J. (1998a). Rethinking the paradigm for child protection. *The Future of Children Protecting Children from Abuse and Neglect, 8*(1) 104-119.

Waldfogel, J. (1998b). *The future of child protection.* Cambridge, MA: Harvard University Press.

Walker, C. D., Zangrillo, P., & Smith, J. M. (1994). Parental drug abuse and African-American children in foster care. In R. P. Barth, J. D. Berrick & N. Gilbert (Eds.), *Child welfare research review* (pp. 109-122). New York: Columbia University Press.

Walker, J. S., & Bruns, E. J. (2006). The Wraparound Process: Indavidualized care planning and management for children and families. In S. Rosenberg & J. Rosenberg (Eds.), *Community Mental Health Reader*: Routledge.

Walker, P. J., & Tabbert, W. (Undated). *Culturally Sensitive Risk Assessment: An ethnographic approach*. Berkley, CA: University of California at Berkley, California Social Work Education Center, and Fresno State University.

Walsh, C., MacMillan, H., & Jamieson, E. (2002). The relationship between parental psychiatric disorder and child physical and sexual abuse: Findings from the Ontario Health Supplement. *Child Abuse & Neglect, 26*, 11-22.

Walton, E. (1998). In-home family-focused reunification: A six-year follow-up of a successful experiment. *Social Work Research, 22*(4), 205-214.

Walton, E., & Dodini, A. C. (1999). Intensive in-home family base services: Reactions from consumers and providers. *Family Preservation Journal, 4*, 31-51.

Walton, E., Fraser, M. W., Lewis, R. E., Pecora, P. J., & Walton, W. K. (1993). In-home family-focused reunification: An experimental study. *Child Welfare, 72*(5), 473-487.

Walton, E., Sandau-Beckler, P., & Mannes, M. (Eds.). (2001). *Balancing family-centered services and child well-being: Exploring issues in policy, practice, and research*. New York: Columbia University Press.

Wang, C. (1998). Current trends in child abuse reporting and fatalities: The results of the 1997 annual fifty state survey. Center for Child Abuse Prevention Research Working Paper 808. Chicago: Prevent Child Abuse America.

Wang, C. T., & Holton, J. (2008). *Total Estimated Cost of Child Abuse and Neglect in the United States*. Chicago, IL: Prevent Child Abuse America.

Wang, C., & Holton, J. (2007). Total estimated costs of child abuse and neglect in the United States. Chicago: Prevent Child Abuse America. Retrieved February 22, 2008 from http://www.preventchildabuse.org/about_us/media_releases/pcaa_pew_economic_impact_study_final.pdf

Warsh, R., Maluccio, A. N., & Pine, B. A. (1994). *Teaching family reunification: A sourcebook*. Washington, DC: Child Welfare League of America.

Warsh, R., Pine, B. A., & Maluccio, A. N. (1996). *Reconnecting families - A guide to strengthening family reunification services*. Washington, DC: CWLA Press. Washington, DC: U.S. Government Printing Office.

Watson, K. W. (1982). A bold, new model for foster family care. *Public Welfare, 40*, 14-21.

Weaver, D., Moses, T., Furman, W., & Lindsey, D. (2003). The effects of computerization on public child welfare practice. *Journal of Social Service Research, 29*(4), 67-80.

Webb, S., & Aldgate, J. (1991). Using respite care to prevent long-term family breakdown. *Adoption & Fostering, 15*, 6-13.

Webster, D., Barth, R. P., Needell, B., & Berrick, J. D. (1998, May, 1998). *Foster care, treatment foster family care and group care in California: An empirical analysis of lengths of stay and exits. .* Paper presented at the California Association for Services to Children, San Diego, CA.

Wedeven, T., Pecora, P. J., Hurwitz, M., Howell, R., & Newell, D. (1997). Examining the perceptions of alumni of long-term family foster care: A follow-up study. *Community Alternatives: International Journal of Family Care, 9*(1), 88-106.

Weeks, N.B. (1953). *Adoption for school-age children in institutions*. New York: Child Welfare League of America.

Weinfield, N. S., Ogawa, J. R., & Sroufe, L. A. (1997). Early attachment as a pathway to adolescent peer competence. *Journal of Research on Adolescence, 7*(3), *241-265*.

Weinstein, E. A. (1960). *The self-image of the foster child.*

Weiss, B., Caron, A., Ball, S., Tapp, J., Johnson, M. & Weisz, J.R. (2005). Iatrogenic effects of group treatment for antisocial youth, *Journal of Consulting & Clinical Psychology*, 73,6: 1036-1044.

Weiss, H. (1993). Home visits: Necessary but not sufficient. . *The Future of Children-Home Visiting, 3*(3), 113-128.

Weissbourd, R. (1996). *The vulnerable child*. Reading, MA: Addison-Wesley Publishing Co.

Weisz, J. R. (2004). *Psychotherapy for Children and Adolescents: Evidence-Based Treatments and Case Examples*. Cambridge and New York: Cambridge University Press.

Weisz, J. R., & Simpson-Gray, J. (2008). Evidence-based psychotherapy for children and adolescents: data from the present and a model for the future. *Child & Adolescent Mental Health, 13*(2), 54-56.

Weisz, J. R., Jensen-Doss, A., & Hawley, K. M. (2006). Evidence-based youth psychotherapies versus usual clinical care. *American Psychologist, 61*(7), 671-689.

Weisz, J. R., Weiss, H. B., & Donenberg, G. R. (1992). The lab versus the clinic: Effects of child and adolescent psychotherapy. . *American Psychologist, 47*(12), 1578-1585.

Wells, K., & Biegel, D. E. (1991). *Family preservation services: Research and evaluation*. . Newbury Park, CA: Sage.

Wells, K., & Tracy, E. M. (1996). Reorienting intensive family preservation services in relation to public child welfare practices. *Child Welfare, 75*(6), 662-692.

Wells, K., & Whittington, D. (1993). Child and family functioning after intensive family preservation services. *Social Service Review, 67*(1), 55-83.

Wells, S. J. (1994). Child protective services: Research for the future. *Child welfare: A research agenda for child welfare., LXXIII*(5), 431-447.

Wells, S., & Briggs, H., (Eds). (in press). Evidence-Based Practice in Child Welfare in the Context of Cultural Competency. *Children & Youth Services Review, Special journal issue*.

Werner, E. (1989). High-risk children in young adulthood: A longitudinal study from birth to 32 years. *American Journal of Orthopsychiatry,, 59*(1), 72-81.

Westermark, P. K., Hansson, K., & Vinnerljung, B. (2007). Foster parents in Multidimensional Treatment Foster Care: How do they deal with implementing standard treatment components? *Children & Youth Services Review, 29*(4), 442-459.

Wetzstein, C. (July 27, 2004). Overhaul of foster care eyed; GOP wants states to have funds flexibility. *The Washington Times*,

White, C. R., Havalchak, A., Jackson, L. J., O'Brien, K., & Pecora, P. J. (2007). *Casey Family Programs Young Adult Survey, 2006: Examining outcomes for young adults served in out-of-home care*. Seattle, WA: Casey Family Programs.

White, C. R., Havalchak, A., Jackson, L. J., O'Brien, K., & Pecora, P. J. (2007). *Mental health, ethnicity, sexuality, and spirituality among youth in foster care: Findings from the Casey Field Office Mental Health Study*. Seattle, WA: Casey Family Programs.

Whitley, D. M., White, K. R., Kelley, S. J., & Yorke, B. (1999). Strengths-based case management: the application to grandparents raising grandchildren. *Social Work, 80*, 110-119.

Whitmore, W.H. (1876). *The law of adoption in the United States*. Albany, NJ: J. Munsell.

Whittaker, J. K. (2000). What works in residential child care and treatment: Partnerships with families. In M. Kluger, G. Alexander, & P. Curtis (Eds.), *What works in child welfare?* Washington, DC: Child Welfare League of America, pp. 177-187.

Whittaker, J. K. (1979). *Caring for troubled children: Residential treatment in a community context*. . San Francisco

Whittaker, J. K. (1991). The leadership challenge in family-based practice: Implications for policy, practice, research, and education. In A. L. Sallee & J. C. Lloyd (Eds.), *Family preservation: Papers for the institute for social work educators 1990.* . Riverdale, IL: National Association for Family-Based Services.

Whittaker, J. K. (1997). Intensive Family Preservation Services with high-risk families in North America: Critical challenges for research, clinical intervention and policy. In W. Hellinckx & M. Colton (Eds.), *International Perspectives on Family.* UK: Ashgate.

Whittaker, J. K. (2006). "Residential Care in the U.S." in *Enhancing the Well-being of Children and Families through Effective Interventions: International Evidence for Practice.* In C. McAuley, P. J. Pecora and W. Rose (Eds.). London: Jessica Kingsley Publishers, pp. 217-228.

Whittaker, J. K., & Garbarino, J., & Associates. (1983). *Social support networks: Informal helping in the human services.* . New York: Aldine Publishing Company.

Whittaker, J. K., & Maluccio, A. N. (2002). Rethinking "child welfare": A reflective essay. *Social Service Review, 76,* 107-134.

Whittaker, J. K., & Tracy, E. M. (1989). *Social treatment: An introduction to interpersonal helping in social work practice* (2nd ed.). New York: Aldine de Gruyter.

Whittaker, J. K., Kinney, J. M., Tracy, E. M., & Booth, C. E. (1990). *Reaching high-risk families: Intensive family preservation in human services.* Hawthorne: Aldine de Gruyter.

Whittaker, J. K., Schinke, S. P., & Gilchrist, L. D. (1986). The ecological paradigm in child, youth, and family services: Implications for policy and practice. . *Social Service Review, 60,* 483-503.

Whittaker, J.K. & Maluccio, A.N. (2002). Re-thinking "Child Placement": A reflective essay. *Social Service Review,* 76, 108-134.

Whittaker, J.K. (2004)."The Re-invention of residential treatment: An agenda for research and practice" in B. Leventhal, M.D. (Ed) (2004). *Child & Adolescent Clinics of North America* (special issue), 267-278

Whittaker, J.K. (2008). "Children: Group Care" prepared for Mizrahi, T. and Davis, L. *Encyclopedia of Social Work, 20ᵗʰ Edition.* New York & Oxford: Oxford University Press.

Whittaker, J.K., Greene, K., Schubert, D., Blum, R., Cheng, K., Blum, K., Reed, N., Scott, K., Roy, R., Savas, S.A. (2006). Integrating evidence-based practice in the child mental health agency: A template for clinical and organizational change. *American Journal of Orthopsychiatry,* 76,2, 194-201.

Whittaker, K., Fine, D., Grasso, A., & Mooradian, J. (1990). *Differential patterns of family involvement in residential youth care and treatment: An empirical analysis. (unpublished manuscript).* Clinton, MI: Boysville of Michigan.

Widom, C. S., & Ames, M. A. (1994). Criminal consequences of childhood sexual victimization. *Child Abuse & Neglect, 18*(4), 303-318.

Widom, C.S. (1989). The cycle of violence. *Science, 244,* 160-166.

Widom, C.S., & Maxfield, M.G. (2001). *An update on the "cycle of violence"* (NCJ 184894). Washington, DC: National Institute of Justice.

Wilber, S., Ryan, C., & Marksamer, J. (2006). *Best practice guidelines: Serving LGBT youth in out-of-home care.* Washington, DC: Child Welfare League of America.

Wilhelm, M. O., & Creedy, J. (2002). Income mobility, inequality and social welfare. *Australian Economic Papers, 41*(2), 140-150.

Willems, D. N., & DeRubeis, R. (1981). *The effectiveness of intensive preventive services for families with abused, neglected, or disturbed children: Hudson county project final report.* . Trenton: Bureau of Research, New Jersey Division of Youth and Family Services.

Williams, B. K., ed. (1995). *Family centered services: A handbook for practitioners.* Iowa City, IA: The National Resource Center for Family Centered Practice.

Williams, J., Herrick, M., Pecora, P. J., & O'Brien, K. (2009). Working paper No. 4: Placement history and foster care experience. Retrieved May 6, 2009 from www. casey.org

Wilson, D. (2000). *Reducing multiple placements.* Olympia, WA: Division of Child and Family Services.

Wilson, D. B., & Chipungu, S. S. (1996). Introduction. Special issue on kinship care. *Child Welfare, 75,* 387-662.

Wilson, M. (1984). Mothers' and grandmothers' perceptions of parental behavior in three-generational Black families. *Child Development, 55*(4), 1333-1339.

Wiltse, K. T. (1980). Education and training for child welfare services. School of Social Welfare, University of California at Berkeley.

Wolf, M., Copeland, W., & Nollan, K. (1998). All in a day's work: Resources for teaching life skills. *Journal of Child and Youth Care, 12*(4), 1-10.

Wolfensberger, W. (1972). *The principle of normalization in the human services.* Toronto, Canada: National Institute of Mental Retardation.

Wolins, M. (1974). *Successful group care: Explorations in the powerful environment.* New York: Aldine De Gruyter.

Wolins, M., & Piliavin, I. (1964). *Institution and foster family: a century of debate.* New York: CWLA \

Wolins, M., & Piliavin, I. (1964). *Institution and foster family: a century of debate.* New York: CWLA

Wonacott, M. E. (2003). *Effectiveness of Short-Term Training For Self-Sufficiency. ERIC Digest.* Columbus, OH: ERIC Clearinghouse on Adult Career and Vocational Education.

Wooden, K. (1976). *Weeping in the playtime of others.* New York: McGraw-Hill.

Woolf, G. D. (1990). An outlook for foster care in the United States. *Child Welfare, 69*(1), 75-81.

Wornoff, R., & Mallon, G., (Eds.). (2006). *Lesbian, gay, bisexual and transgender issues in child welfare.* Washington, DC: Child Welfare League of America.

Wright, B. (1980). *An overview of the Indian Child Welfare Act of 1978.* State of Washington: Office of the Attorney General.

Wulczyn, F. (2003). Closing the gap: Are changing exit patterns reducing the time African American children spend in foster care relative to Caucasian children? *Children and Youth Services Review, 25*(5-6), 431-462.

Wulczyn, F. (2004). Family Reunification. *Future of Children, 14,* 95-113.

Wulczyn, F. (2007). Agent-Based Social Simulation in the Service of Child Welfare Issues: Defining the Demand for Residential and Group Care. Unpublished paper. Chicago, IL: University of Chicago, Chapin Hall Center for Children.

Wulczyn, F. H., & Hislop, K. (2001). *Children in Substitute Care at age 16.* Chicago: Chapin Hall.

Wulczyn, F. H., Chen, I., & Hislop, K. (2007). *Foster Care Dynamics 2000-2005: A Report from the Multistate Foster Care Data Archive.* Chicago, IL: University of Chicago, Chapin Hall Center for Children.

Wulczyn, F. H., Harden, A., & Goerge, R. M. (1997). *Foster care dynamics: 1983-1994: An update from the multistate foster care data archive.* Chicago: The University of Chicago, The Chapin Hall Center for Children.

Wulczyn, F., & Brunner-Hislop, K. (2001). *Teens in out-of-home care: Background data and implications. Findings from the Multistate Data Archive.* Unpublished Presentation. University of Chicago, Chapin Hall Center for Children.

Wulczyn, F., & Lery, B. (2007). *Racial Disparity in Foster Care Admissions.* Chicago, IL: University of Chicago, Chapin Hall Center for Children.

Wulczyn, F., Barth, R. P., Yuan, Y. T., Harden, B., & Landsverk, J. (2005). *Beyond common sense: Child welfare, child well-being, and the evidence for policy reform.* Somerset, NJ: Aldine Transaction.

Wulczyn, F., Kogan, J., & Harden, B. J. (2002). *Placement stability and movement trajectories.* Chicago: University of Chicago, Chapin Hall.

Wulczyn, F., Kogan, J., & Harden, B. J. (2003). Placement stability and movement Trajectories. *Social Service Review, 77*(2), 212-236.

Wulczyn, F., Zeidman, D., & Svirsky, A. (1997). HomeRebuilders: A family reunification demonstration program. In J. Duerr Berrick, R. P. Barth & N. Gilbert (Eds.), *Child welfare research review* (pp. 252-271). New York: Columbia University Press.

Wulczyn, F.H. (2007). Agent-Based Social Simulation in the Service of Child Welfare Issues: Defining the Demand for Residential and Group Care. Unpublished paper. Chapin Hall Center for Children.

Wulczyn, F.H., Chen, L.J., & Hislop, K.B. (2006). Adoption dynamics and the Adoption and Safe Families Act. *Social Service Review, 80*(4), 584-608.

Wynn, J. R., Merry, S. M., & Berg, P. G. (1995). *Children, families, and communities: Early Lessons from a new approach to social services.* Washington, DC: American Youth Policy Forum, et al.

Wynn, J., Costello, J., Halpern, R., & Richman, H. (1994). *Children, families, and communities: A new approach to social studies.*

Yinger, J. (2001). Housing discrimination and residential segregation as causes of poverty. In *Understanding poverty.* S. Danziger and R. Haveman (Eds.). New York: Harvard University Press and Russell Sage Foundation, pp. 359-391.

YMCA of the USA, Dartmouth Medical School, & Institute for American Values. (2003). *Hardwired to connect - The new scientific case for authoritative communities.* New York: Institute for American Values.

Yoo, J., Brooks, D., & Patti, R. J. (2007). Organizational Constructs as Predictors of Effectiveness in Child Welfare Interventions. *Child Welfare, 86*(1), 53-78.

Young, N. K., & Grella, C. E. (1998). Mental health and substance abuse treatment services for dually diagnosed clients: Results of a statewide survey of county administrators. *Journal of Behavioral Health Services & Research, 25,* 83-92.

Young, N., & Gardner, S. L. (2002). *Navigating the pathways: Lessons and promising practices in linking alcohol and drug services with child welfare.* Rockville, MD: Substance Abuse and Mental Health Services Administration, Center for Substance Abuse Treatment.

Young, N., Gardner, S., Coley, S., Schorr, L. B., & Bruner, C. (1994). *Making a difference: Moving to outcome-based accountability from comprehensive service reforms.* Des Moines, IA: National Center for Service Integration.

Yuan, Y. Y., McDonald, W. R., Alderson, J., & Struckman-Johnson, D. (1990). *Evaluation of AB 1562 in-home care demonstration projects: Final report.* . Sacramento, CA: Walter R. McDonald and Associates.

Zastrow, C., & Kirst-Ashman, K. (1987). *Understanding human behavior and the social environment*

Zielewski, E. H., Macomber, J., Bess, R., & Murray, J. (2006). *Families' connections to services in an alternative response system.* Washington, DC: Urban Institute.

Zerbe, J. R., Plotnick, R., Kessler, R. C., Pecora, P.J., Hiripi, E., O'Brien, K., Williams, J., English, D., & White, J. (In press.) Benefits and costs of intensive foster care services: The Casey Family Programs compared to state services. *Contemporary Economic Policy.* Published Online: Feb. 16, 2009: http://www3.interscience.wiley.com/journal/119880786/issue

Zigler, E., & Black, K. (1989). America's family support movement: Strengths and limitations. *American Journal of Orthopsychiatry, 59,* 6-20.

Zimmerman, R. B. (1982). *Foster care in retrospect. Studies in social welfare.* New Orleans: Tulane University Press, 1984.

Zlotnik, J. L., Rome, S. H., & DePanfilis, D. (1998). *Educating for child welfare practice - A compendium of exemplary syllabi.* Alexandria, VA: Council on Social Work Education.

Zosky, D. L., Howard, J.A., Smith, S. L., Howard, A. M., & Shelvini, K.H. (2005). *Adoption Quarterly, 8*(3), 1-24.

Zuravin, S. J., & DePanfilis, D. (1997). Factors affecting foster care placement of children receiving child protective services. *Social Work Research 21*, 34-42.

Zuravin, S., & al., E. (1997). Child Maltreatment in family foster care: Foster home correlates. In J. D. Berrick, R. P. Barth & N. Gilbert (Eds.), *Child Welfare Research Review* (pp. 189-200). New York: Columbia University Press.

Zuravin, S., & DePanfilis, D. (1996). Child maltreatment recurrences among families served by Child Protective Services. Final report to the National Center on Child Abuse and Neglect; Grant #90CA1497.

Zwiebel, C., & Strnad, C. (2002). *How states are helping foster care youth "age out": An assessment of state plans for use of Chafee funds.* St. Louis, MS: Jim Casey Youth Opportunities Initiative.

Subject Index

Author Index